# THE FOURTH GOSPEL

It was the Catechism, the Prayer Book, and, above all, reading portions of the Bible (more especially the 6th, 13th, 14th, 15th and 17th Chapters of St. John's Gospel, and St. John's Epistles) that formed my belief.

VISCOUNT HALIFAX

Ego in vita mea non legi librum simplicioribus verbis quam istum et tamen sunt inexpressibilia verba.

LUTHER

Where is the place of understanding?

JOB xxviii

*By the same authors*

★

THE RIDDLE OF THE NEW TESTAMENT

# THE
# FOURTH GOSPEL

*by the late*
EDWYN CLEMENT HOSKYNS
*Bart., D.D. (St. Andrews)*
*Fellow of Corpus Christi College, Cambridge*

*edited by*
FRANCIS NOEL DAVEY

FABER AND FABER LIMITED
24 Russell Square
London

The necessity of resetting the type for this Edition has given me the opportunity of making a number of minor corrections, nearly all of them concerned with faulty references or punctuation. Some of these blemishes were very generously brought to my notice by correspondents previously unknown to me—one of them, indeed, writing from an Australian manse. I have noted with gratitude criticisms and suggestions of a more far-reaching nature, but it does not seem to me to lie within my province as an editor even to consider acting upon them. My warm thanks are due to Miss Margaret Knowles and Mr. J. E. Padfield, both members of the staff of S.P.C.K., who have generously given much time and care in order to help me prepare this edition.

F.N.D.

6 May 1947

*First published in mcmxl*
*by Faber and Faber Limited*
*24 Russell Square London W.C.1*
*Second edition (revised) mcmxlvii*
*Reprinted mcmxlviii*
*Reprinted mcml*
*Reprinted mcmliv*
*Printed in Great Britain by*
*Latimer Trend & Co Ltd Plymouth*

# PREFACE

The theological eloquence of the Reformation was kindled by the theological eloquence of Saint Paul. Colet in Oxford and Luther in Wittenberg wrestled with the exposition of the Epistle to the Romans, and in so wrestling found the word that set the world on fire. This was no accident. The scandal of the mediæval church—the scandal that seemed to discredit the whole system of orthodox theology—could be removed only by the universal application of the principles that Saint Paul had been forced to apply to the churches committed to his charge. The necessity of re-defining all theology and ethics so that men might know that they stood under the grace of a God who would accept nothing more and nothing less than faith, caused every issue to be referred to the Apostle who had withstood both the Judaizing attempt to erect a barrier between God and man in the natural world, and the Hellenizing attempt to erect a barrier between God and man in the supernatural world. It was one of those classical moments of intense theological perception, when one Word, one Dogma, one cry of repentance, one assurance of reconciliation, appear to contain in themselves the whole truth of God and the whole duty of man. Men like Colet and Luther revered and exalted the Fourth Gospel, but for them the Epistle to the Romans remained—as Luther said towards the end of his life—'the door and key to Holy Scripture': and not for them only, but also for their countless followers who re-informed the stale dogmas of the Western church with the living theology of the Cross.

But whereas the theology of German Protestantism continued to be controlled primarily by the Pauline Epistles, the theology of the English Reformation soon sought a wider basis and a more positive idiom. Colet belonged to the Renaissance as much as to the Reformation. Erasmus, a somewhat fugitive figure on the Continent, found in England zealous Christians who could listen to other Fathers besides Saint Augustine, to other Apostles besides Saint Paul; men who could praise God in other measures besides those of the psalmist and learn of Him from other lips besides those of the prophets and wise men; men who refused to identify the culture of the ancient world with its blindness, and who rejoiced in their new knowledge of the Hellenic tradition without a sense of guilt. To such men the Fourth Gospel spoke in friendly terms. For this reason it has ever since exerted a powerful and creative influence upon the theology of the Church of England.

Yet, although the Fourth Gospel has commended itself to English

# PREFACE

Christianity partly because so many Englishmen have been nourished in the Hellenic tradition, its authority has never been construed as springing simply from what may be called its philosophical character. It demanded attention, not as the monument of a great Christian thinker or theologian, but as the historical reminiscences of an Apostle. Accordingly, when it became the practice to identify truth and historical fact, the Fourth Gospel came to be regarded as something alien and difficult. Even while its influence continued to be enormous, it had itself become a source of intellectual embarrassment to educated Christians. Hence, perhaps, the desperate attempt to commend it as an 'oriental' work, which would be unsealed with the conversion of the oriental mind; and the readiness—now that mysticism had come to be recognized as a respectable and reputable part of human experience —to reverence it as the fountain of Christian mysticism. To authorize it on such terms, however, only increased the difficulty of treating it scientifically. The English scholar whose faith had been nourished on a simple and unsophisticated use of the Fourth Gospel might, indeed, with some reluctance be persuaded to expose it to the questions made imperative by his own scholarly presuppositions: he was temperamentally incapable of subjecting it to the murky Persian and Alexandrian theories flung at him from the Continent. Consequently, although, as the INTRODUCTION will show, the last three generations of English scholars have contributed very materially to the scientific study of the Fourth Gospel, they have in effect appeared to be propounding about it not conclusions but hypotheses, and have never quite succeeded in reinstating it as an unquestionable, fundamental Christian source. So the Fourth Gospel, while being used as much as ever in the English pulpit and perhaps more than ever by the English bedside, has lain uneasily on the shelves of English theologians and the desks of English examiners.

In this situation it must be asked, not merely whether this embarrassed and ill-defined distrust of the Fourth Gospel is morally tolerable, but also whether what is tantamount to disuse of the Fourth Gospel altogether does not inevitably impoverish the whole field of modern Christian theology. It is this latter issue that Hoskyns wished to force upon the attention of the Church. Should these volumes help to do so, Hoskyns's uncompleted work will have been crowned with the success he would have desired.

In 1923, at the invitation of the Editor of the 'Westminster Commentaries', Hoskyns began to write a Commentary on the Fourth Gospel for that series. From then until the end of his life in 1937 he was constantly engaged upon it, laying it aside only in order to do certain pieces of work which he thought to some extent relevant to it: his Commentary on the Johannine Epistles in Gore's Commentary,

6

# PREFACE

*The Riddle of the New Testament* and its projected sequel, and his translation of Dr. Karl Barth's *Römerbrief*. So many years of work, fruitful though they were, were not sufficient. Like his greatest English predecessor, Westcott, Hoskyns died without having been able to give to the chief undertaking of his life final shape. It is probable that, had he completed it, the work would have had to be considerably compressed in order to conform to the scale of the 'Westminster Commentaries'. In any case, in its unfinished state it could not fulfil its original purpose. Accordingly, by the kindness of Messrs. Methuen, it is now presented as an independent work.

Since this work on the Fourth Gospel was never completed, and is composed of material left in various stages of preparation, it may be well to say something of Hoskyns's method, in so far as it can be reconstructed from his manuscripts. Like many others, he found writing irksome. Nevertheless, his procedure was governed, as he was fond of saying, by the precept: *solvitur scribendo*. First, he would attack a section, armed only with lexicons, grammars and concordance, and with his mind as far as possible evacuated of all that others had said about the section, and would write down what his study of the text suggested. Then the Fathers—not merely by means of the *Catenæ*—Philo, Josephus, the modern commentators, particularly Westcott, Holtzmann, Loisy, Bauer, Calmes, Lagrange and Bernard, and Strack-Billerbeck, were called in. The COMMENTARY now emerging was fashioned and refashioned; then written out in a 'fair copy'. Even so Hoskyns did not regard this as a final copy, but set it on one side till he should have written the main parts of the INTRODUCTION and come to see the wood as well as the trees. By 1930 he had covered the whole gospel in this way.

This reconstruction of Hoskyns's procedure has been given because large parts of the COMMENTARY have had to be supplied from the results of these early stages of his work. It is worth noticing that chapter ix, with which he started his study of the gospel, reached the form in which it is now printed in 1924. Moreover, the abundance of somewhat redundant scriptural references, and the slightly unselective array of quotations from other commentators, which mark the whole of this earlier material, were intended to provide a starting-point for a final revision, which would have been occupied more exclusively with the author's own judgements, and would have avoided unnecessary repetition.

The COMMENTARY provisionally completed, Hoskyns turned to the INTRODUCTION. By this time he had begun to formulate the fruits of his general New Testament work in *The Riddle of the New Testament*. A year later, although he had previously read little, if any, of Barth's work, and had paid less attention to him as a thinker, he spent six months

7

# PREFACE

translating the *Römerbrief*. Whatever its permanent value, this work undoubtedly imposed upon all who paid it serious attention the discipline of rethinking their theology and of refashioning their theological expression. Hoskyns not only paid it serious attention, but laboured to present it in clear and convincing English. While he did so, he wrestled with Barth's conclusions and busily jotted down notes for the theological sequel to the *Riddle*. He did not think Barth's exegesis the last word on Pauline theology, any more than Barth does himself. But just as Barth's dialectic quickened and intensified his theological activity, so did Barth's rugged eloquence evoke a vigorous and equally individual eloquence from him. Thus stimulated, he quickly laid out and completed the main chapters of the INTRODUCTION, leaving on one side those not so immediately relevant to the theological problem of the gospel. Then he returned to the COMMENTARY, and began it again, this time at the beginning of the gospel. Henceforth the form was to be different, modelled on the form which Hoskyns had thought so successful in the *Römerbrief*. The over-documented COMMENTARY was rid of many citations and references. Each section was prefaced by a summary of considerable extent. Several of the many projected DETACHED NOTES were written. Titles and sub-titles were determined. In this way nearly six chapters of the gospel were completed, the only considerable external influence being a copy of *Der Evangelist Johannes*, published by Adolf Schlatter in 1930, whose tattered cover and much-scored first six chapters show how sympathetic he found it. During the last year of his life Hoskyns hardly touched the work at all.

The various *strata* in this book may now be distinguished. Of the INTRODUCTION the first three chapters, about half the fourth chapter, and the fifth and sixth chapters, were completed and passed for the press by Hoskyns himself. The final chapter—'The Theological Tension of the Fourth Gospel'—must have been in his mind at the same time. It has been compiled mainly from two rough drafts, but that these were considered to be incomplete is shown from considerable notes in one of the most recent of Hoskyns's note-books, concerning the Historicity of the Fourth Gospel, notes upon which the Essay now printed as the seventh chapter has been based. As it now stands, this chapter is not as Hoskyns would have passed it for the press: the style is particularly restless and rough; it reads better aloud than silently; most of it, in fact, as the unity of nib and calligraphy shows, has been poured out at a single sitting. It would not have been left as it is, if only because Hoskyns could never rewrite without adding considerably to the matter in hand. But in essence it undoubtedly presents the major conclusions about the exegesis of the Fourth Gospel to which his long study had led him, and to those who were his pupils, or who listened to his lectures, the vivid, unpolished periods will perhaps hold a certain value that has been excluded from his more disciplined and self-critical final drafting.

Much the same may be said of the final paragraphs of the fourth chapter: 'The Historical Tension of the Fourth Gospel.' These paragraphs were probably written before the first half of the chapter—now in its final form—was revised. The fragmentariness of the second half is most regrettable: the revised manuscript ended with only two indications of how the argument was to be completed. 'Here add chapter vi' was the only basis for the paragraph beginning on page 76. The final bracketed paragraphs depend upon the tantalizing hint on page 77:

'There are two further illustrations of Marcan episodes moving into the centre of the whole theological structure of the Fourth Gospel. These are the Gethsemane narrative and the story of the Transfiguration. So fundamental, however, are the issues raised, that they are best deferred until other material relevant to the problem as a whole has been set out.'

For the rest, the INTRODUCTION palpably lacks a great deal which a reader rightly expects and which Hoskyns intended to provide. The actual evidence of the authorship would have been given and sifted; quotations from the Fourth Gospel in the Christian literature of the second century would have been listed and discussed; there would have been a full bibliography of Patristic commentaries and an examination of the relation between Philo and the Fourth Gospel; possibly there would have been a chapter upon the relation of Johannine to Pauline theology. It may be, however, that these omissions do not constitute so grave a lacuna as at first sight might seem probable. The fundamental questions that lie behind the problems of authorship and date are essentially dealt with in the chapters of the INTRODUCTION already written, and, while the known facts that bear upon the authorship, date, and use of the gospel are accessible to the English reader in more than one recent Commentary, what is the peculiar contribution of Hoskyns—to relate these questions to the fundamental theological issue of the gospel—is practically complete. It is therefore perhaps true that Hoskyns's eagerness to get to grips with the theological aspects of these problems, and his natural inclination to leave the cataloguing of evidence on one side, far from rendering his work fragmentary, have emphasized and clarified the essential unity and significance of what he has to say. As for the consideration of the relation between Johannine and Pauline thought: it is questionable whether this could have been examined with due gravity without overburdening an already extensive work, and it is probable that Hoskyns would himself have deferred the matter to that final work upon which he hoped one day to embark, a systematic *Theology and Ethics of the New Testament*.

The COMMENTARY was completed and passed for the press as far as p. 294. Thenceforward it has been left in the form in which Hoskyns had drafted it before 1931, with the addition of a few pages of commentary on xiii. 31–8, which had apparently never been completed, and a DETACHED NOTE summarizing the lexicographical background to παράκλητος. The chief cause for regret in this part of the COM-MENTARY is probably the absence of the introductions and summaries with which the first six chapters are interspersed, and of many pro-jected DETACHED NOTES. For, although the COMMENTARY would, no doubt, have been re-shaped, re-proportioned, and rid of many tentative suggestions, the material itself does indeed represent Hoskyns's con-sidered exegesis of the Fourth Gospel at the beginning of the most creative period of his life. It was, moreover, the preparation of this material more than any other one factor, with the possible exception of his University Lectures, that had made Hoskyns a creative theolo-gian. Therefore, while the INTRODUCTION and the first six chapters should alone be considered an authoritative expression of Hoskyns's understanding of the Fourth Gospel, the remainder deserves to be printed, not only for its informatory value, not only for the light it throws on the development of Hoskyns's theology, but also for its many typical examples of Hoskyns's authentic insight and judgement.

Final responsibility for any errors that may have crept into this book during its preparation for the press, or that may have remained unde-tected in the manuscript, which the author would undoubtedly have scrutinized and purged, must rest with the editor only. The editor wishes, moreover, to make it clear that, where he has felt bound to supplement the INTRODUCTION or the COMMENTARY, he offers no more than the briefest reconnaissance of the terrain and the barest suggestion of the author's probable plan of attack. He has not, as a rule, indicated those occasional passages which he has, for various reasons, rewritten, since he believes that his most revolutionary unacknowledged redaction is the reference to a book published since the author's death, where the author had referred to a private letter from the same writer.

The publication of this book has been expedited by the assistance of several of Hoskyns's former pupils, particularly the Rev. J. N. Sanders, Bye-Fellow of Peterhouse, who, besides investigating the notes on Tex-tual Criticism, has made many acute criticisms and suggestions, and Mr. F. V. A. Boyse, formerly Foundation Scholar of Corpus Christi College, who has prepared the Indexes.

The object of printing chapter and verse numbers in the headlines of the COMMENTARY is to enable the particular treatment of individual passages to be found as easily as possible. Plain numbers printed at the outside ends of the headlines show the scope of the commentary on the pages in question (e.g. pp. 174, 175). Should the reader open a volume in the middle of a DETACHED NOTE he will find the direction of the chapter and verse he desires indicated by an arrow (e.g. pp. 156, 157). Pages containing the text or an introductory summary have, on the *insides* of their headlines, the chapter and verse numbers of the complete

# PREFACE

section with which they are dealing, and usually *precede* the commentary on that section (e.g. pp. 168, 169); but the chapter and verse numbers of the shorter summaries frequent in the last part of the COMMENTARY are printed on the *outsides* of the headlines (e.g. pp. 298, 299).

The text is that of the Revised Version, by courtesy of the Delegates and Syndics of the Oxford and Cambridge University Presses.

FRANCIS NOEL DAVEY

*C.C.C. et B.M.V. Cantab.*
*In festo S. Ioan. Apost. ante Port. Lat. mcmxxxix.*

# TABLE OF CONTENTS

13

# TABLE OF CONTENTS

# TABLE OF CONTENTS

## INDEXES

# INTRODUCTION

## I. THE PROBLEM OF THE FOURTH GOSPEL

The Gospel according to Saint John is a strictly 'theological' work. Long ago Clement of Alexandria, fully aware of the broad distinction between the Fourth Gospel and the earlier gospels in which the bodily or 'sensible' facts concerning the life and death of Jesus had been set forth, defined it as the 'Spiritual' gospel; and the Church, surely with proper discernment, has consistently named its author 'The Theologian'. And yet it is not at once evident what in fact Clement meant by the word 'Spiritual', or what in fact the Church means when it honours Saint John not only as an Apostle but also as the 'Theologian'. The word 'Theologian' may be used to call attention to the work of a man who is moved, or even possessed, by certain ideas about God, ideas which he and his disciples are only too prone to identify with the Truth itself. Similarly the word 'Spiritual' may be used to suggest some peculiar religious intuition or emotion or experience which the 'spiritual' man or, at least, those who name him Master, may only too easily identify with the life that is not relative but eternal. Moreover, both words, if they do not actually convey a certain detachment or remoteness from the direct, accurate, and persistent observation of particular historical events, do at any rate tend to lay the emphasis elsewhere. It is, however, extremely doubtful whether, if the two words be thus defined, they are applicable to the Fourth Gospel or to its author. The two themes which form the ground-bass of the whole book—The Word of God and Eternal Life—refuse to be simply dissolved in the ideas of the author or merely identified with his peculiar spiritual experience. On the other hand, since it is concerned with the 'flesh' of Jesus, with His audible words and with His visible actions, the gospel is incurably and of set purpose realistic. The author of the Fourth Gospel bears witness. He insists with the whole power of his conviction that what he records is what actually and really occurred. His gospel, like the others, is a 'bodily' gospel. But, and this is the problem of the Fourth Gospel, the author has so presented the 'sensible' history of Jesus that his readers are confronted in that history, and precisely there, with what is beyond time and beyond visible occurrence, with the veritable Word of God and with the veritable life of eternity. If this be so, it is illegitimate for us to suppose that we are interpreting the gospel, if we for one moment think that we have solved the problem of the Fourth Gospel by maintaining either that the Evangelist has identified his ideas with the Truth of God or his spiritual experience with the eternal life of the Spirit of God, or that he has simply equated what any observer might have seen or heard of Jesus with that which eye hath not seen nor ear heard of the glory of God. This would be to make of the problem of the Fourth Gospel a problem, whereas it is in truth the Problem of all problems, for it is concerned with the relation between time and eternity, between what is finite and what is infinite, between phenomena and reality, in fact between men and God. But the surprising factor in the gospel is that the Problem of all problems is presented to us, forced upon us, with the urgency of an ultimate demand, not by transferring us into the realm of speculative philosophy or even of spiritual experience, not by passing from a moral Jesus to a metaphysical Son of God—whatever the word 'metaphysical' may mean in this context—but by confronting us with the precise and bodily history of Jesus, from whose 'belly' flowed rivers of living water, who came not by water only, but by water and blood, by whose blood men are saved and whose flesh men must eat. Only when we have seen the Problem there does the author of the gospel lead us on to see it also in those who believe on Him, in the 'We' of the gospel, and finally, moreover, to encounter it in all men, for in the perspective of the Fourth Gospel all men are God's creatures. This problem is, no doubt, the ultimate problem of the entire biblical literature; in the Fourth Gospel, however, it becomes so acute as to be unescapable and almost unbearable. We can, perhaps with some show of success, range the prophets of Israel wholly within the context of the events of their day. We can treat the synoptic gospels merely as records of what Jesus observably did and observably said in Palestine, or of what the primitive Christian communities thought that He had done and said. We can speak of Paul in terms of 'Paulinism' and explain him, with some degree of plausibility, on the background of a peculiar mystical experience. But when the same historical or psychological method is applied to the Fourth Gospel, the gospel becomes so uncomfortable that the method of treatment itself creaks and groans under our very fingers. Yet we have no other method. One thing is certain. The gospel was assuredly written down at a particular time and in a particular place by a man who had ideas, theological ideas, in his head and an experience, a religious experience, in his heart; moreover, he must have had a particular historical background. He must have been born somewhere and lived somewhere, and this cannot be irrelevant for our understanding of his book. There was a workshop in which the Fourth Gospel was fashioned, a workshop filled with particular ideas and particular experiences and containing, it seems, other Christian literature. It is to this workshop that we have of necessity to direct our attention. But the author has done his best, apparently with intention, to cover up his tracks. For his theme is not his own workshop but the workshop of God, and to this we have no direct access! Where are the author's personal ideas or reminiscences? Where is his personal experience? No doubt they are there; no doubt, indeed, there is nothing else there but what he thought and what he experienced. But he does not intend us to bury ourselves with him as though he were himself the goal of our inquiry. He has, in fact, so burnt himself out of his book that we cannot be certain that we have anywhere located him as a clear, intelligible figure in history. At the end of our inquiry he remains no more than a voice bearing witness to the glory of God. So anonymous is his book, so intentionally anonymous, that there is in it, apart from the shy little '*I suppose*' of the last verse, no 'ego' except the 'Ego' of Jesus, the Son of God. The author of the book has effaced himself, or, rather, has been decreased and sacrificed, in order that the Truth may be made known and in order that the Eternal Life which is in God may be declared.

In spite of much that may seem to point in an opposite direction, the Fourth Gospel is a rest-less book. Its theme is, it is true, the peace of God, but it is the peace—of God. And to this theme the crucifixion of Jesus is the proper theological rider. To it the narrative of the Fourth Gospel runs as inexorably as does the thought of Saint Paul. The hour of the death of Jesus is 'The Hour'. No doubt the gospel moves on to resurrection, but, like the thought of Saint Paul and the narrative of the earlier gospels, it moves to resurrection through death. And this movement is shown to be no peculiar movement concerning Jesus alone; with equal inevitability it marks His disciples also. *In the world ye shall have tribulation . . . He that eateth my flesh and drinketh my blood hath eternal life; and I will raise him up at the last day.* And yet, with a strange paradox, this restlessness is met by the peace of timelessness and of infinity both in Jesus and in His disciples, and this peace is encountered, not merely at the end of time and beyond the time series, but here and now. The glory of Jesus—is; so also is the glory of those who are His. He is what He was and what He will be, and they too are, at least, what they will be, and also, presumably, what they were (i. 11). It is as though resurrection and eternal life have veered round from both ends, from the End and from the Beginning, in order that they may be shown to constitute the reality which Jesus and His disciples—are, the reality that alone makes sense of the 'flesh'. By itself, *The flesh profiteth nothing.* The whole relative world of visible and audible things is in itself of no account, and this applies also to the 'flesh' of Jesus. It is without significance save in its relation to the Word and to the Spirit of God; *It is the Spirit that quickeneth.*

At this point the commentator almost falls into speculative philosophy, is almost persuaded that the Fourth Gospel moves in a realm accessible only to those who have mastered the intricacies of speculative theological thought. But to advance into that world would quite certainly be to proceed out of the world of the Fourth Gospel. Whatever

# INTRODUCTION

the Fourth Gospel may be, it is not a text-book of metaphysics. Primarily it is the text-book of the parish priest and the inspiration of the straight-forward layman. This is the testimony of the whole Church, wherever it has seriously preached the Gospel to the poor. No critical interpretation of the Fourth Gospel can therefore be adequate if it does not take full account of, and explain, this fact. The critic may range the gospel with Philo and the Alexandrian philosophers; but, and the question is important, did the poor and the ignorant, when they lay a-dying, ever ask their Rabbis to read to them out of the voluminous writings of Philo or of those like him? The problem to which the author of the Fourth Gospel addressed himself, the problem of the relation between what is finite and temporal and what is infinite and eternal, between 'flesh' and Spirit, and between 'flesh' and Word, is, no doubt, the ultimate problem of all philosophy; but there is something strange and unfamiliar in the road by which the Evangelist has been led to formulate the problem and to understand its meaning. It is to this strange factor and to this unfamiliar road that the critical commentator is bound to address himself. But he will not be true to the book he is studying if, at the end, the gospel does not still remain strange, restless, and unfamiliar.

The great weakness of much modern critical work on the Fourth Gospel is due to the continual assumption that the text would finally yield to historical or psychological investigation, that it would deliver up its secret in an almost tangible form. Criticism has proceeded on the supposition that somewhere or other in human experience—in Greek thought or in mysticism, in oriental mythology or in historical reminiscence, or, it may be, in the peace of Christian reflection and devotion, but, at any rate, somewhere in the observable life of the end of the first century or thereabouts—the Fourth Gospel could come to rest; that is to say, its obscurities would vanish before the progressive march of critical knowledge. The Fourth Gospel has, however, not come to rest; and this is not because, owing to some lack of knowledge which further patient study may, and surely will, rectify, the critic has just failed to reach an adequate solution of the problem, but because the theme of the book is beyond human knowledge, and because, if it did come to rest, it would have denied the theme which, in fact, it never denies.

# II. THE CONTROVERSY

THE CRITICAL ORTHODOXY—STRAUSS, BRUNO BAUER, FERDINAND
CHRISTIAN BAUR, SCHWEGLER, JÜLICHER, RÉVILLE, HEINRICH J.
HOLTZMANN, LOISY

To have comprehended the above-named critics under the one word 'orthodoxy' may perhaps seem strange and perverse. But, in their handling of the Fourth Gospel, not only do they display very remarkable general agreement but they are also convinced that the truth lies within their reach in a sense in which it does not lie within the reach of those who set themselves in opposition to them. Though it is not in the scope of this commentary to track out the course which critical investigation has taken during the past hundred years, it is nevertheless important that the reader should know something of this attitude to the Fourth Gospel as it was presented in almost classical form in the first edition of Loisy's vast commentary, which was published in 1903, and in the two competent works of Heinrich Holtzmann, his *Johanneisches Evangelium* (1893) and his *Lehrbuch der N.T. Theologie* (1897). These two commentators stood by birth and upbringing on opposite sides of the great abyss. The one was a Frenchman and a Roman Catholic, the other a Protestant and a German. Yet, in spite of this natural separation, both are in general agreement in their treatment of the Fourth Gospel and in their conclusions with regard to it. It will therefore be convenient if this agreement be set out in their own language and phraseology. In what follows the quotations are taken from Loisy, but the language is equally that of Holtzmann; indeed the terminology goes back through the works of the critics named above and has, moreover, wandered out into many present-day popular books on the New Testament.

The conclusions are as follows:[1] Controlled and permeated by its author's 'idea', 'notion', 'doctrine', 'teaching', 'conception', the Theology of the Fourth Gospel is 'Johannine Theology' and its Christ a 'Johannine Christ'. Upon the Evangelist's 'power of imagination' and 'energy of conviction' the whole movement and colour of his narrative depend. Setting out from his idea of Christ, his 'religious meditations' assume 'symbolic' form. In the unity of the symbol what is 'real' and what is the 'product' of his imagination are so fused together that it is impossible for him to distinguish the 'ideal from the real, the symbol

[1] See the Introduction to Loisy's Commentary, especially pp. 76–123, and *passim* in the Commentary itself. Compare also H. J. Holtzmann, *Lehrbuch der neutestamentlichen Theologie*, 2nd ed., vol. ii, pp. 390–584.

from its object, the theory from the history'. So powerful was his conviction, so vivid his imagination, that he was unable to differentiate between what came to him from tradition and what came to him 'from himself'. To take an example, in the story of the Healing of the Paralytic the history 'loses itself' in the discourse. No doubt the Evangelist did not intend to do more than disengage the 'spiritual truth' already contained in the earlier documents of Apostolic Christianity, but in the process of disengagement the 'real history' is 'lost sight of'. The 'veritable' parables, for example, have become 'something quite different' and the hardening of the Jews and the dullness of the disciples have been 'exploited' in the interests of Johannine theology and 'adapted' to his doctrine. Hence it comes about that the reality with which the Evangelist is concerned is not that of history but of 'mysticism'. He is concerned with 'supernatural life' and with 'mystical union'. Once recognize that, in reading the Fourth Gospel, we are in the presence of the first and greatest of Christian mystics, and his book is 'perfectly lucid'. Fail to appreciate this, and it becomes 'bizarre in its allusions, obscure in its language, and defective in its logic'. The gospel is 'allegoric' in the sense that it is written on the assumption that historical and terrestrial things have their supernatural and 'intelligible' counterparts which are accessible to the mind, or rather to the minds of those who have been 'initiated'. This allegorizing method is Alexandrian, not Palestinian. But we must be careful here, for the Evangelist does not develop his allegories in a philosophical direction, but according to the principles of 'mystical theology'. For this reason 'Matthew and Luke would be much more at home with the Fourth Gospel than would, for example, Philo'. The idea by which the whole gospel is controlled and which gives it its unity, is that of the 'Word Incarnate'; hence the divine Sonship is not, as in the synoptic gospels, 'religious and moral' but 'metaphysical'. The knowledge possessed by the 'Word—Son' is an ideal entity, a theological conception, not, as was the knowledge of Jesus, the 'simple expression of a psychological reality'. Moral instruction therefore yields to symbolic revelation, and the Johannine Christ has not come, as the friend of publicans and sinners, to call them to repentance; he has come, rather, to reunite the children of God. 'The apocalyptic prophecies of Jesus in the earlier gospels are far removed from this Christ, who speaks of heavenly things as an eyewitness, as one who knows them at their source and from all eternity'. In this context it is not surprising that there is nothing 'sad or terrible' in the death of the Johannine Christ. The manner in which the Evangelist handles the earlier eschatology is important here. The Johannine idea of immortality is not, it is true, altogether loosed from the tradition of Judaism, but nevertheless it is 'almost Hellenic'. Eschatology has undergone a 'psychological and mystical transformation'; it has been 'interiorized', 'individualized', in fact, 'spiritualized'. Consequently, eternal life is that which a Christian ought to 'realize in himself in the present', he ought to discover here and now all that the eschatology had 'promised'. The Christian Society should moreover become the Kingdom of Heaven upon earth and tend to realize it 'more and more'. It follows from this that there emerges in the Christianity of the Fourth Gospel a 'possibility of development', and for this reason it can be claimed that, more than any other New Testament document, the Fourth Gospel has contributed to 'plant Christianity in the Greek world and make of it the universal religion'. It contains the 'synthesis' between Greek mysticism and certain fundamental Semitic ideas. 'By a certain power of selection or superior instinct, by the inspiration of genius, he [the Evangelist] has extracted from the primitive Gospel—in which the historical figure of Christ was reflected without analysis—the essential notions of the Fatherhood of God, the law of love, and the universal role of Jesus, disengaged them from their framework, and provided them with the illumination and relief which were necessary if they were to impress the spirits of men who would have been too greatly repelled by the Jewish atmosphere in which they had their origin.' To sum up, the Evangelist composed a 'religious' book and, moreover, one which is 'profoundly Christian'. He did, it is true, make Jesus think and act as He had never either spoken or acted, but the Christ does not thereby 'cease to live in the discourses and actions which he has attributed to Him. The Spirit of Jesus has suggested to him that which was suitable to the interpretation of the Gospel without altering it.' The conception of love has enabled him to construct 'a moral theology and a moral mysticism'. His idea of the Christian community is therefore very catholic: 'He does not, it is true, conceive of the Church as an institution organized upon an hierarchical basis, but he does think of it as the permanent seat or organ of the Spirit who is the representative of the Christ in all those who are united by the law of love.' Composed by a mystic whose propagation of the Gospel was assuredly 'more restrained' than that of Paul, the Fourth Gospel was destined at first only for a small group of initiated persons. But its influence has been immense; and we have now to recognize in its author 'the true father of Christian theology, the founder of Christian dogma, and, in addition, the initiator of Christian mysticism'. With Loisy's lyrical conclusion may be compared the judgement of the Emperor Julian: 'It was this John who (by declaring that the Word was made flesh) wrought all the mischief' (Cyril *c. Julianum* x. 335, Migne ix. 1015).

### THE TRADITIONAL ORTHODOXY—BLEEK, DE WETTE, REUSS, LUTHARDT, GODET, ZAHN, SCHANZ, KNABENBAUER, LEPIN, GRANDMAISON, TILLMANN, LAGRANGE

The representatives of critical orthodoxy insist that, in composing his gospel, the fourth Evangelist had transferred the sphere of revelation from the realm of historical fact to the inner world of mystical thought and experience. Consequently, whether the revelation be regarded as genuine or not, there can be no adequate treatment of the gospel except it be recognized frankly that this transference had in fact taken place. Those critics who proceeded upon this assumption inevitably found themselves involved in an attack upon the traditional exegesis of the gospel. Indeed, Loisy's most bitter irony is directed against those who maintain that the Fourth Gospel is an authentic record. The representatives of traditional orthodoxy—particularly Schanz, Knabenbauer, and other modern Roman Catholic commentators, with whom are ranged Zahn 'and the majority of English-speaking scholars'—are so pilloried by Loisy that it appears that there is nothing more to be said. Much more, however, was said, and something was done; for Loisy was excommunicated and on the 29th of May, 1907, the Vatican Biblical Commission adopted the following formal conclusions with regard to the Gospel according to Saint John:

*The First Question—*

Is the constant, universal, and venerable tradition of the Church that the Apostle John and none other was the author of the Fourth Gospel—a tradition which reaches back to the second century and is known: (*a*) from direct and indirect statements in the writings of the Holy Fathers, of the Historians of the Church, and even of Heretics, statements which, since they must depend upon the followers of the Apostles or of their immediate successors, are necessarily related to the circumstances in which the Scriptures had their origin; (*b*) from the general and regular occurrence of the name of the author of the Fourth Gospel both in the Canon and in the lists of the Sacred Books; (*c*) from the earliest manuscripts and from translations of the Scriptures into other languages; (*d*) from the general and public Liturgy of the Church since very early days—to be accepted, quite apart from theological proof, as presenting evidence so strong that it can in no way be disturbed by arguments which critics have brought forward to prove the contrary? *Answer:* Yes.

*The Second Question—*

Do the text of the Fourth Gospel taken by itself, the testimony of the author, and the clear connection between the First Epistle of the Apostle John and the Gospel, furnish internal evidence bearing out the unswerving tradition according to which the Fourth Gospel is attributed to the Apostle John? And further, can the problems which emerge when the Fourth Gospel is compared with the other three be reasonably solved by paying due regard, as the Holy Fathers and Catholic commentators have always done, to the differences of time and plan, and to the different public for which or against which the author wrote? *Answer:* Yes to both questions.

*The Third Question—*

Is it legitimate—in spite of the constant practice of the whole Church from the earliest times of arguing from the Fourth Gospel, as from a document historical in the proper sense of the word (due regard being paid, of course, to the particular circumstances in which it was written and to the clear purpose of its author), and of bringing to light and establishing the divinity of Christ from the Actions and the Sayings of the Lord—to maintain that the events recorded in the Fourth Gospel serve, wholly or in part, an allegorical or a didactic symbolic purpose, and that the Lord's Sayings are not the veritable and proper speech of the Lord Himself, but are theological compositions of an author who placed them in his mouth? *Answer:* No.

Though the procedure of the Biblical Commission meant, of course, that the Vatican authorities intended in the future to exert a strict discipline over biblical work undertaken in the confines of the Roman Church, its actual findings do not constitute an intrusion of ecclesiastical administration into the field of technical scholarship. The ecclesiastical authorities did no more than ratify a number of conclusions which had been reached not only within the Roman obedience but elsewhere also. Many Anglican and Protestant theologians agree with their Roman colleagues in finding it impossible to interpret the Fourth Gospel in terms of mysticism of or mythology. Nor must it be supposed that the commentaries of Roman Catholic scholars which have appeared since the findings of the Biblical Commission have been written to order or without genuine scholarly conviction. The commentary, for example, of Lagrange, the venerable Dominican, which was published in 1924, manifestly refutes so ungenerous a suggestion. With the vast wealth of technical European scholarship at his back, Lagrange produced a commentary in which massive learning is controlled by mature judgement and set forth with extreme delicacy and reserve of expression. Consequently, it is plainly ridiculous to maintain that, while traditional orthodoxy can be supported only by uncritical reliance upon the weight of tradition or by accommodation to the requirements of ecclesiastical authority, critical orthodoxy alone is capable of presenting the results of modern scholarship. The general position of traditional orthodoxy as it is now justified by strictly critical methods cannot be disregarded. It will therefore be convenient to set out at this point the general conclusions reached by Lagrange, who was, perhaps,

25

the most impressive modern representative of traditional orthodoxy.

Throughout his commentary and especially in the introduction (pp. i–xii, cxliii–cli), Lagrange insists that those who regard the Fourth Gospel as the product of its author's imagination, or even of his mystical intuition, are fighting against the expressly declared purpose of the book, which has only to be read for the reader to perceive with what energy the author has 'affirmed the facts and emphasized the validity of his own witness'. For this reason those who treat the author as a man who was unable to distinguish between what had occurred and what he had himself imagined have 'failed to foist upon critics this dreamy personality, so persuaded that he had not dreamt'. The Fourth Gospel is what it claims to be—an historical book. Jesus did speak as the Evangelist said He did. The book is, indeed, 'didactic', but this is not because the author has become the teacher but because his book is a gospel in which Jesus is the Teacher. Similarly, Jesus acted as the Evangelist said He did. The book records concrete deeds, not because the mystical ideas of the author were bodied forth in his imagination, but because his book is the record of actions in which Jesus Himself bodied forth the meaning of His ministry. Lagrange's insistence upon the historicity of the teaching and action of Jesus as they have been set out in the Fourth Gospel does not, however, end in depressing its author to a mere chronicler. For Lagrange, John is the Theologian. It is he who has seen that the events of the Lord's life are supremely significant events. The significance lies, however, in the actual history. There John has seen it. It is therefore illegitimate to regard the history as myth or fable or allegory. Nevertheless, 'symbol' is a fit word to describe the author's manner of narrating the history. But even so, it must not be supposed to denote that which did not actually occur. A symbol is a picture or 'figure' made use of as the sign of an idea. An historical occurrence may itself suggest some further meaning. In this case history cannot be regarded as trivial or indifferent, or as a mere form by which a mystic is encouraged to think symbolically; still less can it be dismissed as the concretion of some theological or ritual myth, which first took historical form in its author's mind. In the Fourth Gospel the events of the Lord's life are shown to be signs; that is to say, they are shown to possess further significance. The Evangelist has been careful to select those historical facts which were 'most significant of what the Son of God had become for humanity'. But in spite of its author's acute sensitiveness to the further meaning, the meaning itself is left in a certain obscurity, whereas the actual teaching of the Lord and His actual deeds are recorded with luminous clarity and precision. Loisy's judgement that, whereas the symbolical meaning is thrown into clear relief, the historical background is rendered obscure and ulti-mately trivial, is subjected to careful examination and vigorously denied. Lagrange concludes that the Fourth Gospel, like the earlier narratives, must be treated primarily as a record of the events of the ministry of Jesus to which the Evangelist bears authentic witness.

In thus insisting upon the historicity of the Fourth Gospel and upon the genuineness of its author's witness, Lagrange does not for one moment deny that the gospel has a character of its own. He too speaks of the Evangelist's 'literary style'; he too draws attention to what is peculiarly 'Johannine', for example, the Prologue, the comments added in iii. 15b–21, the summary of the Lord's teaching in xii. 44–50. Nor is Lagrange here departing from normal Roman Catholic exegesis. Indeed, the Bishop of Strasbourg, Monsignor Ruch, in the course of an article contributed to the *Dictionnaire de théologie catholique* (1913), gives the conclusions of Catholic scholars upon this point in such a manner as to leave no doubt about it. He writes: 'Not only Protestant but also Catholic critics of all schools of thought (Calmet, Corluy, Fillion, Knabenbauer, Batiffol, Calmes, Mangenot, Fouard, Lagrange, Nouvelle, Chauvin, Fontaine, Jacquier, Lepin, Brassac, Lebreton, Venard) admit that, though the Evangelist preserves faithfully the teaching of the Saviour, yet, nevertheless, the discourses have been subjected to a certain labour of condensation and adaptation. The thoughts of the Incarnate Word have been clothed by the Evangelist in a characteristic literary form peculiar to himself. We ought not to be surprised when we come across abrupt transitions from one theme to another in a single discourse, for Saint John is capable of omitting transitions of thought, of summarizing developments or of passing them over, and of collecting together Sayings which originally came from different discourses and making of them one whole' (quoted by Lagrange on pp. cxlvii sq.). The peculiarity of the Fourth Gospel, however, is not due merely to its author's literary style and method. It is due also to the particular purpose for which it was originally written. But care is needed. The primary purpose of the gospel is the edification of its readers. It was written to recall to their minds the events of the Lord's life and to show that these provide a 'solid basis for their faith'. But this positive purpose of edification does not exclude a 'polemical' intention. There is in the gospel a polemic which must have its historical occasion. Whether the particular danger which threatened the Christians at the end of the first century and which was one of the causes that occasioned the writing of the gospel was 'Docetism', as Tillmann and others think, or whether it was, as Lagrange thinks, the more subtle separation of Christ from the historical Jesus which Irenæus associated with the name of Cerinthus, may be difficult to decide, but it can hardly be doubted that the arrangement of the gospel and its particular emphasis are to be explained by an especial purpose which goes beyond that of general edification. Against this false doctrine, whatever it may have been precisely, the author of the gospel steadily maintains that Jesus is the

Christ, the Son of God, and that to Jesus Christ as the Son of God worship is due.

Presented with the alternative that the Fourth Gospel is either a work of devout meditation or an historical document, traditional orthodoxy, after making due allowance for the author's literary style and for the particular polemic in which he has engaged himself, steadily and with great learning, and without hesitation, pronounces it to be the latter.

## THE CRITICAL *VIA MEDIA*—HISTORY *AND* INTERPRETATION—RENAN

Flanked by traditional orthodoxy on the one side and by critical orthodoxy on the other, the careful reader would seem to be encouraged to secure a balance between rigid historicity and mysticism or symbolism or metaphysical philosophy, and to search for the truth concerning the Fourth Gospel along some middle path. Ought it not to be possible to prove that the gospel contains a rigid core of historical tradition or reminiscence round which the author has assembled his mystical theology, or upon which he has built up his dogmatic, esoteric interpretation? Ought it not to be possible for the critic to recover from the gospel a new historical source for the life and teaching of Jesus, a source so primitive that it may well take its place side by side with the Marcan Gospel, side by side with the 'Q Material', with 'Special Matthew' and with 'Special Luke'? And may he not, after he has disentangled the interpretation which has been added to, or woven into, this primitive source, be able also to furnish the historian of the Sub-Apostolic Age with first-rate historical matter for a description of Greek Christianity at the beginning of the second century? Surely it must be along this middle road that the solution of the Fourth Gospel does, in fact, lie: a solution which, moreover, may not unreasonably be expected to do justice to the work both of radical and of conservative scholars.

And yet, though there are clear indications that this middle road ought to be the proper line of approach to the Fourth Gospel, it is disturbing to discover how completely blocked and barricaded that road seems to be. Wellhausen and Spitta and others have called attention to uncomfortable breaks in the narrative and to the glaring contradictions which are so marked a characteristic of the gospel. They have insisted that the analysis of the gospel must start with these breaks and contradictions, and that they must be treated, not as 'characteristic features of the author's physiognomy', but rather as signs of additions and alterations made by a redactor, signs that, in fact, the Fourth Gospel is not a literary unity. But, in spite of the skill and energy that Wellhausen and others have expended in attempts to handle the Fourth

Gospel as though it was composed after the manner of the books of the Pentateuch, it seems clear that it will not yield to such treatment. The Fourth Gospel will not be split up into different strata. In theory we ought, no doubt, to be able to say that this is history and that interpretation, that this belongs to the *Grundschrift* and that to the work of a redactor; but when the scholar comes actually to draw the line, to make the incision, he is forced into most precarious and arbitrary judgements, and is apt sooner or later to tumble over into the company of Holtzmann or of Lagrange, or else is compelled to admit defeat. Most liberal scholars would therefore agree with Harnack when, at the beginning of his famous lectures upon the Nature of Christianity, he cleared the ground for a description of the main features of the message delivered by Jesus Christ by stating that the Fourth Gospel cannot be treated as an historical source for His life and teaching: 'Only little of what its author says can be accepted, and that little with caution.' Nor indeed, in spite of his judgement that it is 'an authority of first rank for answering the question, What vivid views of Jesus' person, what kind of light and warmth, did the Gospel disengage?' did Harnack make serious use of it anywhere in the course of his lectures. The Fourth Gospel was allowed to disappear from the scene.

Nevertheless, when this has been said, proper justice must be done to Renan's heroic attempt to recover from the Fourth Gospel material for his romantic *Life of Jesus*, and to the skill with which he made these scattered, submerged fragments serve his general purpose. This is not the place to assess the whole value of Renan's work upon the gospels. It is, however, necessary to draw attention to the importance which he attached to the Fourth Gospel and, in particular, to the long appendix which he added to the thirteenth edition of the *Life* in order to defend the use that he had made of the gospel against the united protest of the radical critics of his day.

Renan wrote his *Life of Jesus* in Palestine. Surrounded by the beauty of the 'green, shady, smiling land of Galilee, where the animals are small and extremely gentle, where blackbirds rest on a blade of grass without bending it, where everything is delicate and harmonious', he found much of the Gospel story intelligible. It was borne in upon him that, sensitive to the delightful pastoral, to the poetic mysticism, of the Galilean countryside, Jesus—'founded the true Kingdom of God'. His early life was 'idyllic'; and as a 'delightful moralist', as a 'lovable character', he fascinated His hearers. This Galilean idyll was, however, disturbed; and in this disturbance lay, for Renan, the historical and moral problem of the life and teaching of Jesus. What was it that transformed the delightful and fascinating moralist, for whom heaven and earth were joined in one harmonious whole, into a 'transcendent revolutionary'? What was the disturbance that had penetrated so deeply into the soul of Jesus that He was compelled to a clear policy of death.

a policy in which the Jewish authorities were forced to play their part and rid themselves of one whose Jewish faith had been so completely lost that he was determined to abolish the Law, the Temple, and the Hierarchy? Renan was persuaded that this stern, revolutionary attitude to Judaism was an intrusion into the ministry of Jesus which urgently requires explanation; for, unlike many authors of modern 'Lives of Jesus', he could not regard his death merely as a murder or as the tragic conclusion of an otherwise idyllic life. To Renan the death of Jesus must have been the 'inevitable snapping of an intolerable tension in his ministry' in which the initiative lay with Jesus Himself. What then was the grim or 'gloomy' factor which deflected the course of the ministry?

Renan had no doubt about the answer to this question. The key to the problem of the life of Jesus is to be found in the geographical contrast between Galilee and the region of which Jerusalem is the centre. The region of Judæa is 'the saddest country in the world'. Everything that comes from Jerusalem is stamped with the harshness of Nature; grand it may be, but its grandeur is melancholy, sterile, and repellent. The grim southern part of Palestine constitutes the disturbing factor in the life of Jesus. There He encountered Johnthe Baptist; there He discovered the evil of the world; there Satan, the prince of this world, appeared to Him in terrible form; there He met with priests and doctors who did not do what they commanded others to do. It was Jerusalem that destroyed His faith in Judaism, compelled him to adopt as his policy the destruction of the Law and the Temple, and gave rise to His belief that He, as the Messiah, was appointed to be the agent of demolition. It was the strength of the evil in Jerusalem that forced upon Him the certainty that He would be the victim of His own audacity, that there must needs be crises and rending of hearts before the Kingdom of God could be established; in fact, that He must die, and that after His death He would come again in glory and those who had rejected Him would be confounded. It was the horror of Jerusalem that had thrust grim austerity upon a character nurtured and softened by the friendly and mystic air of Galilee, that introduced warfare into the teaching of Jesus and planted within Him a harsh disgust for the world. This severe self-abnegation did not proceed naturally from the subtle and cheerful moralist of other days; it proceeded rather from one who, engaged in ceaseless conflict with the official hypocrisy of the Pharisees, with the very nerve and sinew of Judaism, withdrew more and more from the pale of humanity. His controversy with the Pharisees was war to the death, and it was in the context of this essential opposition that death presented itself to his mind as a sacrifice destined to save mankind, and made him anxious to fulfil the proverb—that a prophet ought not to die outside Jerusalem. 'Socrates and Molière do but touch the skin, Jesus carries fire and rage to the very marrow.' It was therefore only just that 'this great master of irony should pay for His triumph with His life'.

At first sight it would appear that Renan had divided the ministry of Jesus into two irreconcilable parts and had so outlined His life that the earlier Galilean mysticism had been entirely superseded by the expectation of a great eschatological occurrence. Renan, however, held that this would be a grave misunderstanding. Jesus' conceptions of the Kingdom of God were not exhausted in apocalyptic visions. Besides the apocalyptic Kingdom, and behind the terrible picture of an eschatological judgement, there was for Jesus always the Kingdom of the soul, the feeling of sonship which the good man knows in his 'rest upon the bosom of the Father, a pure religion without forms, without temple, and without priest'. This latter Kingdom of the soul remains the essential teaching of Jesus, and it was this that was destined to survive, when the materialistic hope of an approaching end of the world wore itself out, and eschatology passed into the shallows of Christianity. The passing of the eschatology does not therefore mean that the Jesus of history had been suppressed, for He was 'more than the reformer of an obsolete religion; He was the creator of the eternal religion of humanity'.

Such was in outline the course of the history of Jesus of Nazareth as Renan reconstructed it from the Gospels. But he could never have pictured it as he did, had he not felt himself justified in making generous and critical use of the Fourth Gospel. Indeed, throughout his book he passes from the synoptic gospels to the Fourth Gospel, and from the Fourth Gospel back again to the synoptic gospels, with a surprisingly confident freedom. An essential part of the framework of his *Life* would have been lacking, had he not been able to draw upon the Fourth Gospel for an early Judæan and Jerusalem ministry and for a series of conflicts with the Pharisees in the heart of the Holy City. The frequent presence of Jesus in Jerusalem is the pivot upon which Renan's description of the movement of the ministry wholly depends. He could not have even begun to write as he did had he drawn his material from documents which left Jerusalem almost entirely outside the picture until the last few days of the ministry. Indeed, Renan regards the Galilean ministry itself as unintelligible apart from an early and concurrent ministry in Jerusalem. It is the Fourth Gospel that provides him with the key to the problem of the life of Jesus. Nor would he have been able to speak so confidently of the Kingdom of the soul, or of the sonship which the good man knows in his 'rest upon the bosom of the Father', or of the non-eschatological character of the essential teaching of Jesus, had he not constantly referred to the language of the Fourth Gospel in which, as he says, the true teaching of Jesus was 'brought to light at the end of the first century'.

It is therefore not surprising that Renan found himself compelled to justify the use he had made of the Fourth Gospel, since it was here that, as a liberal critic, he was most especially vulnerable. He therefore added to the thirteenth edition of the *Life* a long appendix in which he examined the Fourth Gospel paragraph by paragraph. Renan refused to acquiesce in the current opinion that a document written from a theological point of view was altogether suspect, and could contain no valuable historical material. On the contrary, in the case of the Fourth Gospel he claimed that he had been able by a careful critical analysis to disengage genuine historical traditions or reminiscences from their setting in midst of the theological notions which were, of course, far removed from the primitive Gospel.

In an appendix Renan called attention to the place-names scattered about in the Fourth Gospel, and pertinently asked what interest a pure theorist who was a member of some sect in Asia Minor could have had in Palestinian topography. Why should he have noted so carefully that John was *baptizing in Bethany* [*? Bethabara*] *beyond Jordan* and *in Ænon near to Salim*; or that Jesus encountered the woman of Samaria *at Sychar near to the parcel of ground that Jacob gave to his son*; or that there was a pool in Jerusalem *which is called in Hebrew Bethesda* [*? Bethzatha*], and another which was called *Siloam*; or that Jesus should have withdrawn *into the place where John was at the first baptizing*, and on another occasion *into the country near to the wilderness, into a city called Ephraim?* Equally pertinently he asked what allegorical meaning or mystical allusion can be attached to the fact that Nathanael was of *Cana in Galilee*, or that Philip and Andrew and Peter were *of Bethsaida*, or that Annas, and not Caiaphas, conducted the preliminary examination of Jesus, or that the brothers of Jesus, who did not believe in Him, urged Him to go into Judæa and make Himself known. Renan claimed that, if the Fourth Gospel be compared with the synoptic gospels, the former must again and again be pronounced more primitive. For example, the kiss of Judas is omitted in the Fourth Gospel, suggesting that, touching and beautiful as it is, it is legendary, though it finds a place in the synoptic gospels. Similarly, he found the parallel to the Gethsemane narrative in John xii. 27 sqq. less well arranged and 'manœuvred' than in the synoptic account, and therefore preferable, particularly since a tendency can be detected in the synoptic gospels to transfer to the last evening incidents which in fact took place earlier.

On the whole Renan agreed with the liberal critics that the discourses in the Fourth Gospel are artificial, that they reflect ideas current at the end of the first century, and that they do not preserve a genuine tradition of the teaching of Jesus. He thought, for example, that the discourse in ch. vi is of more importance for the history of eucharistic ideas than for the history of the ideas of Jesus, and that the theological disputes in ch. viii are valueless to the historian. But when this has been said, Renan would not allow the Pharisee Nicodemus, a resident in Jerusalem, to be dismissed as an altogether unhistorical personage. And more than this, he thought that certain threads of real historical importance could be detected even in the discourses. For example, in ch. vi the author has represented Jesus as making use of markedly sacramental language in the course of the ministry and not merely in the Upper Room. Is he not right in taking the origin of the Eucharist back behind the Last Supper, for did not Jesus assuredly bless and break and distribute the bread a hundred times, and did He not likewise often bless the cup? Moreover, does not this procedure mean that even the discourses, artificial as they are, do contain fragments of the veritable thought of Jesus, fragments which have been preserved in the midst of many 'lapses' due to the inability of the disciples to understand the Master's teaching? Renan is confident that in the discourse with the Woman of Samaria *vv*. 21 and 23—not *v*. 22—preserve a genuine Saying of Jesus, that the promise of the Spirit as the Advocate in the discourses in the Upper Room is a genuine recollection, and that xvi. 7 may not unreasonably be regarded as the germ out of which Luke produced his narrative of the Ascension. And so Renan concluded that, though for 'general historical colour' the Fourth Gospel is far inferior to the synoptic gospels, it nevertheless furnishes a better account of the 'material circumstances' of the life of Jesus. For when once the dogmatic interpretations have been removed, the reader has before him an historical tradition of primary importance, a tradition which may indeed be that of the apostle John. But throughout his analysis Renan is primarily concerned to force the question whether, in the face of the Judæan topographical details contained in the Fourth Gospel, and of incidents and personages that cannot be dislodged from the city of Jerusalem, it is possible to regard Galilee as having provided the 'theatre of the whole activity of Jesus'. Is not the historian bound to admit that an important part of the ministry must have taken place in Judæa?

Renan was, however, fully aware that his skill in disengaging the historical substratum in the Fourth Gospel from its dogmatic superstructure must remain suspect unless he could make historical sense of the narrative of the Raising of Lazarus. The miracle of the Raising of Lazarus is no mere dogmatic interlude in the drama of the Fourth Gospel. It is the turning-point of the whole historical movement, for it was the Raising of Lazarus that compelled the Jewish authorities to take immediate action. Renan could not allow the episode to disappear as a mere symbol or allegory, without throwing doubt upon his whole attitude to the Fourth Gospel. He therefore braced himself to recover the genuine history which lay embedded in the narrative. In order to do this, he fell back on that kind of pure rationalism which is ready to compromise the moral uprightness of Jesus Himself.

Having explained the eschatological element in the teaching of Jesus as an intrusion upon an earlier Galilean mysticism, forced upon Him by the heavy weight of evil that was Jerusalem, Renan regarded it as

**B**

inevitable that popular opinion would demand miracles from one who made such great claims for Himself. Nor was Jesus free to moderate the thirst of the multitude and of His disciples for the marvellous. He therefore became, in spite of Himself, a thaumaturgist. Miracles, which are 'usually the work of the public, not of him to whom they are attributed', were 'a violence done to Jesus by his age, a concession forced upon him by passing necessity'. For this reason Renan would not allow that the miraculous narratives contained in the four gospels ought to be dismissed as legendary additions by which Christians at a later time sought to magnify the grandeur of their Master. Belief in miracles, a belief which was accepted by Jesus, therefore belonged, according to Renan, to the original history, and for this reason he would not allow the occurrence of miraculous narratives to throw discredit upon the gospels as trustworthy historical documents. It would 'show lack of a good historical method to attach overmuch importance to our personal prejudices on this point'. With this presupposition Renan set to work to rationalize the narrative of the Raising of Lazarus, and to justify his use of the Fourth Gospel at the very point where he knew justification was most difficult.

The women, Martha and Mary—Lazarus—an ostentatious miracle directly related to the death of Jesus—this is the framework of the Johannine narrative. Renan had to prove that there is genuine history here. He therefore supposed the faithful Galilean disciples to have been disappointed at the absence of miracles in Jerusalem. There came a moment when they demanded an outstanding miracle that would impress the sceptics in the Holy City. Why not a resurrection from the dead? It was in this situation that the sisters Martha and Mary dared to broach the matter to Jesus. He answered their request, not with a miracle, but with the parable of Dives and Lazarus—the figure of Lazarus being evoked by the presence of Simon the Leper. Out of this conversation, however, the sisters 'imprudently and with excessive zeal' manufactured and spread abroad the story of a veritable miracle; and Jesus, 'whose conscience had lost something of its early purity', did not contradict it. The consequences were fatal; for the Sanhedrin were forced to act, and they decided immediately that one must die for the people.

It is not surprising that Renan's work exercised so little influence on serious criticism of the Fourth Gospel. Perhaps it has had too little influence. Liberal criticism dismissed him with scorn or, as Wellhausen did, in an aside, while conservative critics were not unnaturally angry. And yet Renan's attack on those who dismissed the Fourth Gospel as pure allegory had a great deal of substance in it. He failed, however, when he attempted to disentangle history from interpretation. His certainty of touch remains a pseudo-certainty, for the gospel stubbornly refuses to be dismembered, refuses to be divided into history *and* interpretation. The history invades the interpretation, and the interpretation pervades the history. Renan's line between the two was drawn arbitrarily. But what is even more significant than his personal failure is the failure of his method. No later critic has been able to draw the line between history and interpretation with any greater success than Renan. Many have, of course, attempted to do so, but they have failed because the gospel moves inexorably on as one great whole. Its author's major purpose was to maintain and to insist upon this unity. The commentator is therefore continually brought back to respect this deep-seated interlocking of history and interpretation. Separate the two, and the extremity of violence is done to the text. What Jesus *is* to the faith of the true Christian believer, He *was* in the flesh: this is the theme of the Fourth Gospel, and it is precisely this unity that constitutes the Problem of the Gospel.

ENGLISH WORK ON THE FOURTH GOSPEL—A SELECTION—WESTCOTT, LIGHTFOOT, SANDAY, EDWIN ABBOTT, STANTON, JAMES DRUMMOND, SCOTT HOLLAND, BURNEY, BERNARD, W. F. HOWARD;—BACON, E. F. SCOTT

The attitude of continental, 'progressive', New Testament scholars towards their English contemporaries was admirably illustrated by Loisy when, ranging them amongst the representatives of conservative erudition, he dismissed them with the scornful phrase—'et la plupart des savants de la langue anglaise'. This conservatism was supposed to be peculiarly characteristic of those scholars who were not only English, but also members of the Church of England. Indeed, it was a widely held opinion in liberal theological circles in Germany before the War that Sanday in Oxford and Stanton in Cambridge had been appointed by the Archbishop of Canterbury in order to defend orthodoxy; and to the majority of continental theologians English biblical work appeared learned, it is true, but nevertheless insular, provincial, traditional, Patristic, and apologetic. Nor is this judgement altogether surprising. Sanday, for example, talked quite frankly of 'defending' the Fourth Gospel against those who 'denied' it, and he did not hesitate to name his work 'apologetic'. The language of Lightfoot, when he came to deal with Saint John's Gospel, was even more explicit: he spoke of the 'attacks of the opponents of revealed religion', of 'assailants' and of the 'necessity of a thoroughness in the defence'. Accordingly it is not surprising that men who were convinced that they had been appointed to usher in a new era of free investigation, and to liberate the Christian religion from outworn dogmas, failed to see further than the word 'apologetic', failed to understand that in England defence is not incompatible with the spirit of free inquiry, and failed also to perceive that the critical method itself raised as many problems as it solved and that the right was not all on the side of those who named themselves 'progressive'.

Between the years 1890 and 1910 the Fourth Gospel provided the battleground upon which these larger issues were fought out, and the leading English theologians knew what they were doing when they entered the fray on a territory which they had not themselves chosen or adequately mapped out. And yet, they were none of them ill-equipped; for they were heirs to a broad culture and method of scholarship which was anything but insular or provincial. They were familiar, in a manner in which their opponents were not, with Patristic learning, and they moved, on the whole, more comfortably within the world of Christian orthodoxy; but, in spite of this, they neither sheltered themselves behind the massive protection of the former, nor rested upon the latter as though it provided an ultimate security. Indeed, it was precisely Sanday who, more than any other single Englishman of his day, noted carefully each new critical theory as it was propounded in Germany and made it known to those who were less sensitive than he was to new things. And yet it is strange how completely blind he seems to have been to the importance of the theological interpretation of the New Testament as it was expounded in the works, say, of Johann Christian Konrad von Hofmann, of Martin Kähler, or Karl Holl, or of Adolf Schlatter, who, throughout the long period of the domination of a merely critical historical method, unlike the conservatives Zahn and Bernhard Weiss, preserved within the historical discipline an apprehension that was strictly theological. And it is strange also that Sanday did so little to keep English scholarship during that period in touch with contemporary Roman Catholic commentators such as Schanz.

English works of the last generation must remain unintelligible unless it be recognized that the majority of educated Englishmen, whether they said so or not, felt that there was something wrong with the critical movement. This sense of dissatisfaction was wholly shared by leading English theologians. Nevertheless, they refused to regard the critical method as itself open to suspicion, for they were themselves working with its tools, and were themselves engaged in training Englishmen to use them. Nor was their dissatisfaction due to an inherent love of orthodoxy or of traditionalism. Rather, the general picture of the origins of the Christian religion that was emerging under the hands of well-known and respected leaders of the critical movement seemed to them to be wrong and unscientific, and ultimately propagandist. And it must now be owned that they had ample grounds for uneasiness and dissatisfaction. When Sanday delivered his lectures upon the 'Criticism of the Fourth Gospel', the commentaries of H. J. Holtsmann and Loisy had recently appeared, and also Wrede's book, *Das Messiasgeheimnis in den Evangelien*. Meanwhile Schmiedel's article 'John, the Son of Zebedee' had been made accessible to Englishmen in the *Encyclopædia Biblica*, and Harnack, at the zenith of his power, seemed to be carrying all before him with his popular lectures, 'What is Christianity?' and with his comprehensive *Chronologie der altchristl. Litteratur*. Now, however varied and distinct all this work may have been in detail, no intelligent English scholar could fail to perceive its general significance, and Sanday did not have to look far to find a quite clear and unmistakable statement of this. He found it in Wernle's *Beginnings of Christianity*, which had been translated into English in 1903. Wernle had written: 'John and Paul were not two theological factors, but one. Were we to accept that St. John formed his conception of Christianity either originally or directly from Jesus' teaching, we should have to refuse St. Paul all originality, for we should leave him scarcely a single independent thought. But it is St. Paul that is original; St. John is not. In St. Paul's letters we look, as through a window, into the factory where these great thoughts flash forth and are developed; in St. John we see the beginning of their transformation and decay' (vol. II, p. 275, cf. pp. 262, 264). Here every link between Jesus and Saint Paul and Saint John was being roughly sundered, and Saint John was declared to be but a decayed and transformed echo of Pauline originality. However roughly Wernle may have stated his opinion, Sanday knew that it was neither isolated nor peculiar, but that to it the dominant critical judgement was steadily moving. How widespread this opinion was may be illustrated from the introduction to the American Professor B. W. Bacon's book, *The Fourth Gospel in Research and Debate*. He was writing —and this is not the conclusion to his work, but its presupposition— about the dilemma with which readers of the synoptic gospels and of the Fourth Gospel are confronted: 'Either', he says, 'the former are right in their complete silence regarding pre-existence and incarnation, and their subordination of the doctrine of Jesus' person, in presenting his work and teaching as concerned with the Kingdom of God, with repentance and a filial disposition and life, as the requirement made by the common Father for that inheritance; or else John is right in making Jesus' work and message supremely a manifestation of his own glory as the incarnate Logos, effecting an atonement for the world, which has otherwise no access to God. Both views cannot be true, and to a very large extent it is the science of literary and historical criticism which must decide between them. . . . The criticism which has effected a transformation in our conception of Hebrew religious history by making the so-called Priestly Document the latest and historically speaking least reliable source of the Pentateuch, instead of the earliest and most fundamental, will accomplish a still more revolutionary change in our conception of New Testament Beginnings' (pp. 3, 4).

Bacon then goes on to state the precise nature of the revolution that the science of literary and historical criticism demands. Since the promulgation of the Creed of Nicæa every approach to an historical view of the origins of Christianity has been controlled by that 'metaphysical' conception of the person of Christ which had originally been introduced into Christianity by Saint Paul. In the story of the development of this Pauline 'speculation' the Fourth Gospel played a prominent part, for it provided the link between Pauline and Patristic speculation. This being so, it goes without saying that the Fourth Gospel is 'of little or no service to supplement historically the synoptic picture of the teaching and career of Jesus', since in it Christian theology was held in the grip of the 'Hellenistic conception of incarnation' and 'Jesus is formally and distinctly identified with the Logos principle of Heracleitus, the Ephesian philosopher of 500 B.C.' Bacon was, of course, aware that at certain points the gospel of Saint Mark overlapped with the theology of Saint Paul and Saint John, but this agreement caused no doubts to arise in his mind with regard to this neatly rounded-off reconstruction of the evolution of Christian theology, for 'even this narrative of Mark also comes to us as a Greek product, from the Pauline Church of Rome, framed in the interests of Pauline doctrine, saturated with Pauline phrases and ideas'. Having reached this point, however, Bacon saved himself abruptly from descending into the abyss of complete historical scepticism by bravely asserting that nevertheless, and in spite of the disturbance of the earlier tradition by Saint Paul, the older and simpler Christology *has* survived and can be critically disentangled, so that we are able to say that the real Jesus came forward 'taking up simply and loyally the prophetic and humanitarian reform of John the Baptist', and, when rid of the Pauline-Johannine speculations, all the factors, all the elements of his story 'fall within the known historical environment' (pp. 4–11).

This reference to American scholarship is relevant to the story of the more recent study of the Fourth Gospel in England, not only because it serves to explain the issues which faced English scholars at the beginning of the century, not only because it shows the position occupied by the Fourth Gospel in the general critical reconstruction and therefore explains why it stood in the centre of the controversy, but also because, writing in English, Bacon has exercised an influence in England as great as that which he exercised in his own country. Indeed, at the present time many English scholars feel themselves to be nearer to Bacon, at any rate in his negative attitude to the Fourth Gospel, than they do to the older and more strictly English theologians.

Be that as it may, the references to the work of Wernle and Bacon at any rate explain the uneasiness of the older English biblical scholars. To them it seemed as though the relation between Jesus and Saint Paul or Saint John had been rudely broken both theologically and historically, and that the critics were tumbling over the precipice into the abyss, chanting a hymn in praise of the nobility of free and unfettered debate and research and investigation. The nervous dissatisfaction of the leading English scholars was, no doubt, fundamentally theological, but they allowed themselves, perhaps inevitably, to be drawn into the minutiæ of critical investigation in which the larger theological issues tended to become more and more obscured. Lightfoot, Sanday, Stanton, then Alfred Plummer, and finally Archbishop Bernard followed the road which the liberal and radical critics had mapped out, and at each critical point they stood on the defensive, having apparently assumed that the Truth, the ultimate theological Truth, concerning Jesus of Nazareth, was an observable, analysable thing, which was capable of direct historical perception by believers and unbelievers alike, and that this observability of the Truth was indeed the meaning of the Church's doctrine of Incarnation since it meant that history and theology were in the end identical factors. This presupposition may nowhere have been clearly stated, but, nevertheless, it explains why they seemed unable to shake themselves free of a rigid historical conservatism and to lead the controversy into the realm of proper theological thought. And so it has come about that, when their defence was later felt to be inadequate, English theology tended to take refuge in that strangely elusive word 'mysticism', and to suppose that the difficult problems presented by the Pauline Epistles and the Johannine writings come to rest in a realm in which the distinction between history and inner spiritual experience is altogether blurred.

The older English scholars were, then, concerned with the Fourth Gospel, not, it is true, as a biography of Jesus, but still as an historical narrative, and they were persuaded, as scholars, that the historical evidence did not justify its dismissal as a product of Hellenistic speculation. With great care they once more sifted the well-worn external evidence to the early existence and influence of the book and to its apostolic authorship, and re-examined the evidence of the contents of the book itself in order to list its direct and indirect claims to be a genuine historical work. The result of this re-examination was, at any rate negatively, unanimous. They were convinced that the whole liberal edifice, with its nicely graded development from Jesus to the Council of Nicæa, had been erected upon the most slender foundations. At each point the arguments by which it was supported seemed to them at least unproved and in many cases definitely wrong. They therefore fell back upon the tradition of the Church as the most reasonable explanation of the riddle of the Fourth Gospel. It was the work of the Apostle John or at least of an eyewitness—Bernard, indeed, held that it contained the reminiscences of two eyewitnesses, the Apostle John and the Palestinian presbyter of the same name. To-day even writers who think that different strata can be detected in the composition of the Fourth Gospel still maintain that the greater part must be regarded as reminiscences and reflections of an eyewitness (for example Dr. A. E. Garvie, cf. W. F. Howard, p. 235). In the early period of the controversy English scholars received unexpected support from the cultured and quite independent work of the learned Unitarian divine, James Drummond, who from 1885 to 1906 was Principal of Manchester College.

But what is the situation now? The Fourth Gospel has to some extent passed out of the centre of New Testament work in England. That position is occupied by the synoptic gospels and by the epistles of Saint Paul. The problem of the Fourth Gospel is, however, only deferred, for when relegated to the periphery of New Testament work, it remains uncomfortable—and so do we! The older dissatisfaction still remains in England. Vigorous protests have recently been made by Nolloth, by Burney, by Mr. H. P. V. Nunn, by Lord Charnwood, and by the veteran scholar Armitage Robinson, against the growing tendency in England to acquiesce in the view that the Fourth Gospel is not to be treated as a genuine 'history' of the Life and Teaching of Jesus of Nazareth. But perhaps the most significant dissatisfaction is displayed by those who, though persuaded that the older English 'defence' of the gospel remains unsuccessful, are nevertheless unable to find a satisfactory niche for it in sub-apostolic Christianity. For them the historical and theological problem of the gospel is still unsolved. This attitude may be detected in a tendency to leave the gospel as a whole unexplained and to use it merely as a document from which something valuable may occasionally be extracted by a delicate use of the historical method. So, for example, the Johannine dating of the Crucifixion may be preferred, or the position of the episode of the Cleansing of the Temple accepted, or again the statement that the crowd wished to make Jesus a King (vi. 15) may be regarded as a genuine historical reminiscence. Such a procedure, however useful it may be, means that the possibility of interpreting the gospel has been surrendered. In any case, it is a procedure that the author of the gospel could not have contemplated. But it is still necessary to interpret the gospel as it stands, and many Englishmen therefore follow Miss Evelyn Underhill in treating the author as a 'mystic of the first rank'. They understand his work as mystical throughout, and so the tension of the historical—and even of the theological—problem is removed.

Although, no doubt, the more eminent older English commentators had striven bravely and with great learning for the historicity of the Fourth Gospel, it must not be forgotten that their conclusions had been severely challenged by their English contemporaries. Edwin Abbott's article on the 'Gospels' in the *Encyclopædia Biblica* and his patient work published in his two volumes *Johannine Vocabulary* and *Johannine Grammar* were available to all, whilst Estlin Carpenter and Professor Percy Gardner continued to keep English theology in close and sensitive touch with German liberalism. And behind all this there lay the haunting, cross-bench article on the Fourth Gospel in the *Encyclopædia Britannica* which had been contributed by the Baron von Hügel. More popular than any of these has been the work of E. F. Scott, now a Professor in America, but then a young Scotch theologian, and more influential still have been the seventh chapter of Professor Burkitt's book, *The Gospel History and its Transmission*, and the widely read last section of Dr. Streeter's *Four Gospels*. All these have contributed to the breaking down of the older conservative confidence, as even Sanday himself recognized, to judge from these words in his last book, *Divine Overruling* (p. 61, quoted by W. F. Howard, p. 21): 'I'm afraid there is one important point on which I was probably wrong—the Fourth Gospel. The problem is very complex and difficult; and I have such a love of simplicity that I expect my tendency was to simplify too much, and to try too much to reach a solution on the ground of common sense.'

And yet the Fourth Gospel still refuses to fit itself comfortably into the nook which critical or any other orthodoxy has so laboriously provided for it. It remains homeless.

No mention has so far been made of Westcott's commentary on Saint John's Gospel or of the fragments which remain of the teaching of Scott Holland. But Scott Holland was more than an elegant preacher and, when all is said and done, Westcott's commentary is still the classical English commentary. Both men were primarily theologians, and it was as theologians that they approached the Fourth Gospel. Westcott stood at the parting of the ways, for he belonged to a period in which the study of theology had not been altogether confounded with the study of history, and he lived before the time when the historians had driven the theologians almost completely out of the field. It was not possible, when Westcott was writing his commentary, for a leading English biblical scholar to comment on the Fourth Gospel as, for example, Alfred Plummer was later to comment, or to regard it as offering primarily an opportunity for competent philological and historical exegesis, or for engaging in critical conservative or radical historical speculation. When Westcott wrote his commentary the Fourth Gospel was still a great work of Christian Theology able to deliver up its secret only to those who were themselves sensitive to theological truth, prepared to assume that it is a 'good' book, and ready to listen to what it has to say without seeking to justify or defend it, or even to interpret and explain it, save on its own terms—in other words, to those who were not on edge in its presence. To recover this temper we have to go back to Westcott, and perhaps we shall have to go back behind him to such a writer as the Rev. R. M. Benson. The importance of Scott Holland and to some extent also of Du Bose lies in the fact that in more recent times they still preserved a theological approach to the study of the gospels.

As early as 1859, the three friends, Lightfoot, Westcott, and Hort, had planned a commentary on the whole of the New Testament. Westcott selected the Johannine writings: indeed, he was already working on the Fourth Gospel, which made upon him the impression of being a 'great Hebrew epic'. The plan of publishing a commentary on the Greek text of the gospel, a dream of his undergraduate days, was never far from his mind, and throughout his life he must have worked with it continually before him. The publication was, however, perpetually postponed, partly on account of the appearance of his commentary on the English text in the *Speaker's Commentary* (1880), and partly because of the pressure of other work. And so it came about that the original plan was never completed during his lifetime. It was left for his son to publish the commentary from the notes which he had added to the original *Speaker's Commentary*. The book therefore did not appear until 1908.

To the modern reader Westcott's commentary seems at first sight to be no more than an admirable illustration of conservative erudition. Westcott did not doubt that the gospel was written by the Apostle John, the son of Zebedee. The first sixty-six pages of the introduction are devoted to the now familiar argument from the indirect and direct evidence of the book itself and from the external evidence of its early use and apostolic authorship. The author was a Jew, a Palestinian Jew, an eyewitness, an apostle, was, in fact—Saint John. Moreover, throughout the commentary Westcott does not hesitate to proceed on the assumption that he is commenting upon a precise and accurate historical narrative. So far, then, there is nothing peculiar in Westcott's work, and, if this were all, it would be difficult to explain why it is that he exerted such deep-seated influence, or why it is that his commentary is unlikely to be superseded.

It is not until the reader arrives at the section of the introduction which is headed 'The Composition of the Gospel' that Westcott's work becomes really arresting. And at first even this section opens without any indication of what is to come, for he seems to be engaged merely in piecing together the scattered personal records of John, the son of Zebedee, from the synoptic gospels, the Johannine writings, the works of Irenæus, Eusebius, Jerome, and Augustine, judging these fragments to provide a 'consistent, if imperfect, conception of St. John'. But then follows a passage which is surely no piecing together of these scattered traits, but a mature judgement concerning the author of the gospel, based solely upon the gospel itself. Westcott writes: 'He regards everything on its divine side. For him the eternal is already; all is complete from the beginning, though wrought out step by step upon the stage of human action. All is absolute in itself, though marred by the weakness of believers. He sees the past and the future gathered up in the manifestation of the Son of God. This was the one fact in which the hope of the world lay. Of this he had been assured by the evidence of sense and thought. This he was constrained to proclaim: 'We have seen and do testify.' He had no laboured process to go through: he saw. He had no constructive proof to develop: he bore witness. His source of knowledge was direct, and his mode of bringing conviction was to affirm' (pp. lxxii, lxxiii). Further, proceeding as though his interest lay merely in defending the Church's tradition, Westcott asserts that the author of the gospel occupies a position 'remote from the events which he describes', and that he is therefore able to see the fulfilment of the original events in the 'condition of the Church about him', apprehending therein not merely that Jesus as the Christ fulfils the Jewish law, but that for that reason he is also the fulfilment of the Truth 'which is the heritage of humanity'. As Christ, Jesus 'establishes the organic union of Christianity with Judaism'; as the Son of God, He 'bears witness to the inherent universality of His mission and liberates Christianity from Jewish limitations'. Therefore between the synoptic narratives and the Fourth Gospel lies the 'experience of an organized Christian society', and, though Christ had already *made all things known* (xv. 15), yet there was 'need of the long teaching of time that His disciples might master the lessons which they had implicitly received'. And so, standing on the threshold of a new world, the Evangelist is able to 'feel the divine force of much that was before hard and mysterious. . . . Sayings became luminous which were riddles before their solution was given.' Westcott does not mean that the Evangelist was a philosopher who attached an interpretation, however adequate, to an original history, or that he was a mystic who depended upon independent and personal mystical experiences. Quite the contrary: 'His narrative is at once the most spiritual and the most concrete.' 'The revelation itself is complete, and yet the interpretation is set forth as the work of the Holy Spirit through all ages.' Having said this, Westcott is able to show that, at the supreme point where the two themes of Providence and Faith meet, Saint Paul and Saint John stand together. Human life is determined by the 'Hour' of the will of God, and the will or 'gift' of the Father is the 'spring of the believer's power'. Faith therefore assumes a new aspect. It is not, as so often in the synoptic narratives, merely the 'mediative energy in material deliverances, and the measure (so to speak) of material power; it is an energy of the whole nature, an active transference of the whole being into another life'. Since, however, the purpose of the Fourth Gospel was to show that this providence and this faith were preeminently true of the Lord's life, Saint John has provided an 'historical basis for the preaching of Saint Paul'.

It follows, then, that what distinguishes the Fourth Gospel is that it is 'shaped with a conscious design to illustrate and establish an assured conclusion'. The inspiring impulse was 'doctrinal' as Saint Luke's had been 'historical'. Having stated this abrupt distinction, Westcott pauses to warn the reader against misunderstanding and exaggeration at this point and to link again the Fourth Gospel to its predecessors. 'Christian doctrine', he writes, 'is history, and this is above all things the lesson of the Fourth Gospel. The synoptic narratives are implicit dogmas, no less truly than St. John's dogmas are concrete facts. The real difference is that the earliest Gospel contained the fundamental facts and words which experience afterwards interpreted, while the latest Gospel reviews the facts in the light of their interpretation.' Westcott then adds: 'But in both cases the exactness of historical truth is paramount', and concludes the paragraph by saying, 'The historic interest of St. John in the substance of his narrative is, in other words, purified and made more intense by the dogmatic significance with which he feels that each incident is charged.' The incidents recorded in the Fourth Gospel are therefore for Westcott precise history. But this does not mean that he supposed the discourses to have been spoken in the style or language in which they are there presented. 'It is', he writes on p. cxv (cf. also the following pages), 'quite conceivable that the meaning and effect of a long discourse, when reduced to a brief abstract, may be conveyed by the use of a different style, and even, to a certain extent, of different language from that actually employed.' Mere compression is not sufficient to explain the discourses in the Fourth Gospel, for 'compression involves the adaptation of phraseology'. The final question is, therefore, not whether the Evangelist has or has not employed his own style and language, but whether the words were fitted to convey to us the meaning of the Lord.

On the ground that the primary purpose of the fourth Evangelist was to set forth the 'meaning of the Lord', Westcott refuses to allow the Gospel to be understood either as a work of controversy, or as supplementary to the other gospels, or as an interpretation added to the original Gospel, or as a work of speculation, save in so far as right opinion leads to right action. The Evangelist 'makes no promise to compose a life of Christ, or to give a general view of his teaching, or to preserve a lively picture of the general effect He produced on average observers, or to compose a chapter on the general history of his own times, or to add his personal recollection to memoirs of the Lord already current'. His narrative is 'the mature expression of apostolic experience perfected by the teaching of the Holy Spirit. . . . He works out his own design, and it is our first business to consider how he works it out.' With these wise words Westcott recalls his readers to the actual text of the Fourth Gospel.

Scott Holland's work on the Fourth Gospel was far slighter than Westcott's; but it was undertaken in a more modern context, for the steady critical work upon the synoptic gospels lay behind and not in front of him. Scott Holland, however, like Westcott, was primarily a theologian, and it was as a theologian that he was puzzled by the synoptic gospels. In spite of the many critical reconstructions which had claimed to make sense of them, they seemed to him to remain incomplete and enigmatic.—'The primary effect of the Synoptic Gospels may be direct and simple; but, as soon as our attention has got to work on them, we see that, far from being self-sufficient and complete, they offer no explanation whatever of the presentation which they offer us. They give us no account of themselves. They raise problems for which they offer no solution. They provoke questions which they never attempt to answer. They leave off where it is impossible to stop. . . . The Synoptic record challenges us with a presentation of Jesus which it refuses to account for by the normal standards of humanity.' As he read the synoptic gospels, Scott Holland found himself standing before the 'enigma' of the man Jesus. He refused, however, to admit that the difficulties he saw were of his own making, or that they were due to the inadequacy of his perception or of his historical research. The enigma belonged to the radical structure of the synoptic gospels. Confronted, then, by the enigma of the synoptic gospels, he discovered that he was occupying a position which had long ago been occupied by the author of the Fourth Gospel; for it too assumes detailed and widespread knowledge of the earlier gospels, it too assumes their fragmentariness; it too assumes the possibility of their being misunderstood. But, whereas Scott Holland was puzzled, the author of the Fourth Gospel was not. Saint John was in possession of the solution of the enigma of Jesus, and he wrote his gospel in order to make it known to others. For his understanding of the synoptic gospels Scott Holland therefore found himself depending upon the Fourth Gospel, in which the inner enigma of Jesus was provided with its proper and satisfactory theological interpretation.

The importance, and to some extent the originality, of Scott Holland's work, lay in the manner in which he reformulated the problem of the gospels, and in his consequent insistence that the Fourth Gospel must remain unintelligible if it be removed from the synoptic gospels and treated as a separate and distinct problem. Scott Holland worked at the Fourth Gospel in the context provided by the synoptic gospels, not merely because the Church had set them together in the Canon, but because he was persuaded that it was the existence of the synoptic gospels that had evoked the Fourth Gospel and conditioned its form and matter.

Having brought the Fourth Gospel into this strict relationship with the earlier narratives, it is perhaps not surprising that Scott Holland and his collaborator, Mr. Wilfred Richmond, fell back upon a very 'conservative' estimate of it. Holding the Fourth Gospel to be the solution of the problem of the synoptic gospels, they seem to have become insensitive to the problem which the Fourth Gospel itself presents. Scott Holland held that the theological interpretation which Saint John offered to his readers consisted of his direct reminiscences. That is to say, the interpretation is itself history, a series of episodes in the observable life of Jesus, which the earlier evangelists had overlooked and omitted, but which were vital for the understanding of what they themselves had recorded. Scott Holland therefore took very seriously the tradition preserved by Eusebius (*H.E.* iii. 24) that Saint John wrote his gospel in order to supply an account of an early period of the Lord's life which had been omitted in the earlier gospels. Neither Scott Holland nor Mr. Wilfred Richmond meant, of course, that Saint John merely added a number of fresh episodes, but that he supplied precisely those which gave theological and historical coherence to the earlier narratives. An early Judæan ministry was, for example, of peculiar importance for Saint John's purpose, because, since it was addressed to the Jewish authorities in the very heart of Judaism, it was then and there that the Lord was compelled to set forth on behalf of Himself claims that during the later ministry in Galilee could only be suggested. The Fourth Gospel is therefore a work of interpretation; but the interpretation was not made up of allegory or of mysticism or of philosophical speculation. The interpretation consists of the historical reminiscences of a veritable eyewitness who, after long years of 'brooding meditation', had been enabled to see that what he remembered made sense of the synoptic gospels and provided them with a proper theological and historical background. What he had once seen as 'points' now became 'stars', and for this reason he wrote his gospel.

Whatever judgement may be pronounced upon the latter part of Scott Holland's work, it is difficult to resist the impression that he had seen the problem of the gospels more clearly than any other English New Testament scholar of his day. For this reason it may be claimed that the opening pages of his book form the best introduction in English to the study of the Fourth Gospel.

Attention has been drawn to the work of Westcott and Scott Holland because both were possessed of real theological concentration and because both brought this concentration to bear upon the study of the Fourth Gospel. Neither of them for one moment permitted the proper theological theme of the gospel, which provided them with the key not only to the synoptic gospels and to the Pauline epistles, but also to the whole biblical literature, to slip into an aside or into a somewhat romantic peroration. It is this theological concentration that distinguishes their work from the work of so many other much more competent historians. Neither of them could have wandered out into by-paths of erudition which, in the end, leave the Fourth Gospel almost unintelligible, after having formulated the theme of the gospel so precisely and so admirably as, for example, Bacon did almost in an aside. In the introductory chapter to his *Fourth Gospel in Research and Debate*, Bacon stated that the older, simpler Christology of the synoptic narratives 'demands the divine factor behind it just as all life does, just as the life of our own time does, because without this not even the simplest thing is intelligible' (p. 11). Yes, precisely, this is the theme of the Fourth Gospel, the theme which the Evangelist braced himself to set forth as the Very Truth, indeed as the veritable Gospel; as the meaning of the life of Jesus and of His disciples, indeed as the meaning of the whole created world or 'Cosmos'. But the Evangelist never supposed that this theme, this theological theme, was a straightforward, obvious truth which had only to be stated to be at once accepted. The Evangelist saw this truth as the ultimate and final Truth to which the majority of men are blind. His whole work therefore revolved round and round its exposition. Westcott and Scott Holland stood near the Evangelist because their critical and historical work also revolved round it, and was not permitted to be detached in its technical historical learning and erudition. For this reason their work deserves to be remembered at a time when we are struggling back with great difficulty to a theological interpretation of the gospels.

# III. THE EVANGELIST
## AND HIS READERS

THE Fourth Gospel must remain to a large extent enigmatic unless the purpose for which it was originally written can be defined in such a manner as to explain its author's vigour and concentration. He has forged his book into one whole, its unity being secured by a steady revolution round one central theme, indeed round one point where the author has seen the truth manifested in the darkness. To him the truth appears almost transparent; and it is this transparency that compels him to set forth the material he selects only in relation to the one truth. His work therefore contains no fragments, no isolated, scattered bits of information, no detached or detachable doctrines or dogmas, no independent rites or ceremonies. The man who wrote the Fourth Gospel was master of his material. His readers, however, though confronted by the same material, possessed no such victorious insight, no such vigorous and illuminated concentration. He sees them floundering in the midst of the truth; and he takes up his pen in order to save them from ignorant misunderstanding. He wrestles for their souls, and also for their bodies, for he is concerned not only with spirits, but with flesh and blood, with his readers' concrete thoughts and observable actions. The situation, as he sees it, is critical, and he throws himself into it, confident that he is able to disclose the truth.

But when this has been said, it is by no means clear what that situation really was, or why it seemed to him so precarious, so heavy with ultimate significance. Still less is it at once obvious why, in order to handle the situation adequately, he should have been compelled, not merely to write an epistle or a homily or a sermon, but to compose a gospel, to embark upon a new description of the Life and Teaching of Jesus, and, moreover, so to fashion this new description that the original context of Palestine might be shown to be the very context in which his readers were themselves actually encompassed some hundred years later. It is, however, clear that the modern commentator and the modern reader must, if they are to understand this new gospel, take up their position where the original readers once stood. They must even take up a position so precarious as to be identical with that which the Jews once occupied when they ranged themselves in opposition to Jesus. How otherwise is it possible to appreciate the confidence with which the author of the gospel takes his readers back to that scene, not as an historian merely, but as pastor, as theologian, and even as one who is able to speak with apostolic authority? But the situation demands a definition even more radical. The author did not require of his original readers that they should exercise skilful historical imagination or force themselves into a position not already theirs. He assumes that his readers stand where the Jews once stood. He assumes, indeed, that all men, because they are men, occupy this position. The Fourth Gospel is a universal, a catholic book. Though it was no doubt originally addressed to particular men and women, yet its author does not for one moment intend these especial readers to suppose that his work concerns them only. He claims to be setting forth the Truth, the veritable Gospel, not *a* truth or *a* gospel. He claims also to be setting forth the Truth in the midst of all-embracing falsehood. The truth, as he sees it is light in the midst of darkness, life in the midst of death. The modern reader will therefore not apprehend the Fourth Gospel as its author meant it to be apprehended, if he concludes that it was written against, say Gnosticism, or Docetism, or Ebionitism, or even against the Jews, and rests satisfied with that explanation, without at the same time recognizing that those ancient movements of religion are still deep-seated and destructive factors in our common life. If the gospel be relegated, dogmatically, to the past, it must remain, for all our historical imagination, a foreign, strange work, at times attractive, but also at times repellent; it must remain a buried work of early Christian apologetic, and not, as it claims to be, a book which in all its ramifications sets forth the very truth in the midst of what is altogether untrue. To set forth the truth was the author's purpose, and to attempt to interpret it otherwise than on its own terms is to destroy it, to make it irrelevant and therefore meaningless. He dared to write what was true for Jews, for Christians, and for all men. Unless this claim be steadily kept in mind the Fourth Gospel is bound sooner or later to be depressed into something that it constantly affirms that it is not. But, when this is said, the modern reader must by an effort of historical imagination first endeavour to place himself in the position of those for whom the gospel was originally written. Only he must not rest until this position is found to be charged with universal significance, until he stands here naturally because it is his inevitable position as a man. He must not rest until he stands where the Jews once stood and did not apprehend, and where Abraham and Isaiah once stood and did apprehend; until he stands confronted, not by the evolution of history, not even by the development of the Church, but by the Last Hour; until, that is to say, he stands confronted by the Truth, until the present time is confronted by eternity, and until the present place is met by the meaning of history —in fact, until he stands before God.

But where did the original readers of the Fourth Gospel once stand? What was in their minds? In what direction or directions were they moving? These are urgent, pressing questions. Yet the precise character and standing, not of the author only, but even of his readers, are obscure. Although he associates himself with the authoritative 'we' of those who *saw* the glory of the incarnate Word (i. 14), he nowhere specifies those whom he is addressing: *These things have been written that ye may believe that Jesus is the Son of God, and that believing ye may have life in his name* (xx. 31). It is therefore extremely difficult to gain from the gospel any direct information concerning its original readers, and for this reason it is hard to come by the key to its historical understanding.

In the First Epistle of John, which must be assumed to have come from the same hand as the gospel, a somewhat stronger light is thrown upon the readers of the epistle, and therefore, presumably, upon the original readers of the gospel also. Moreover, it seems at first sight that the author has himself emerged somewhat from the obscurity that envelops him in the gospel. Now he does address his readers in the first person, for the phrase *I write unto you* is recurrent (ii. 1, 7, 12, 13, 14, 21; v. 13). But even so he is strangely elusive, for he emerges only from the midst of the same authoritative 'we'—*These things we write unto you* (1 John i. 4)—which occurs also at the opening of the gospel (John i. 14); and at a crucial moment in the course of the Epistle he throws himself back again upon the first person plural—*And we have seen and do testify that the Father sent the Son to be the Saviour of the world* (iv. 14). The author occupies no independent, isolated position; he tells nothing about himself save the supreme fact that he speaks as one of those who heard the Word of life, and are therefore able to show forth and bear witness to the life which is eternal (i. 1–4). That he belongs to the apostolic company of those whose fellowship is with the Father and with His Son, Jesus Christ, is all that it is imperative for his readers to know about him. Similarly, little is said about the readers themselves, but that little is also important. We are told that their sins have been forgiven (ii. 12), that they are strong, that they have overcome the evil one, and that the Word of God dwelleth in them (ii. 13, 14). We are told also that, in spite of this security, they are in especial need of authoritative instruction in order that they may not sin (ii. 1), and, very particularly, that they need instruction concerning those who are seeking to lead them astray (ii. 26). And yet, though the situation is precarious, the author of the Epistle is careful to make it quite clear that he has no new information, no new teaching, to give his readers. He is imposing upon them no new commandment. He is but reminding them of the word that they have already heard and of the commandment that they have possessed from the beginning (ii. 7). His readers already know the truth, and require no man to teach them (ii. 27). They have been taught by Christ Himself, they have known the truth and have been taught by it (ii. 13, 20, 27, 29). If therefore they abide in His teaching, they will have confidence when He shall appear, and will not be ashamed before Him at His coming (ii. 28). *I am not writing*

*unto you beecause ye know not the truth but because ye know it* (ii. 21). The purpose of the author is not to introduce some new teaching, not to develop
and propound some new truth, but to show forth the meaning of what
his readers already know, and to do this at a moment when misunderstanding is actually leading to disaster.

But if it is clear that the Epistle was written for believing Christians,
it is also clear that the writer regards neither faith nor knowledge as
simple or obvious. Though he insists that the commandment is old,
that the teaching is what they already know; yet with equal insistence
he announces that the truth is nevertheless always new—*a new commandment write I unto you* (ii. 8). The commandment is new when the
light shines and the darkness disappears. The darkness in which all men,
even believers, stand, must again and again be dispersed by the true
light that is even now shining in the darkness (ii. 8). The writer is
therefore not concerned with reiterating old truths or with bringing
forward new information to be added to what his readers already know.
He is concerned with the apprehension of truth, and with that apprehension of it which is itself ethical action. The truth, he writes, must be
done (ii. 3, 6). And so, though the Christians to whom he addresses
the Epistle know the truth, they are nevertheless in a precious position. It is only too possible for them to fail to perceive the meaning of
the truth in which they stand, only too easy for them not to *abide* in
God or to *keep his commandments* (ii. 3–6, 24). It is at this point that a
concrete, particular situation emerges in the Epistle. The Christians
are actually being led astray by men who call themselves Christians,
but are not. It was the emergence of these pseudo-Christian leaders that
provoked the author to take up his pen; for he was persuaded that they
represented a dangerous and infectious misunderstanding of the truth.
In two passages (ii. 18–29; iv. 1–6) he describes them in some detail,
but their existence controls the whole Epistle. The Christians have been
placed in a situation so dangerous that the writer of the Epistle is convinced that the Last Hour has come (ii. 18). So great is the tension that
no historical understanding of the Epistle is possible unless the author
has provided his modern readers with sufficient material to disclose
the point at issue.

The apostasy with which the writer is confronted is no falling away
from religion. The leaders of the revolt did not even propose to return
to heathenism or to embrace Judaism. He is confronted by a persuasive
call to the Christians to separate themselves from the apostolic fellowship—*they went out from us* (ii. 19)—in order to serve God more spiritually
and with more profound and prophetic fervour. The author's descriptive language—*spirits, false prophets, anti-Christs* (iv. 1; ii. 18)—shows that
the revolt was possessed of the paraphernalia of progressive religion and
that it was setting forth under distinctively Christian flags. It claimed
to be spiritual, prophetic, and Christian. No wonder the simple be-

lievers were attracted by so great a show of religion. The writer of the Epistle is, however, quite certain that this is a movement of apostasy, whose leaders are neither spiritual men nor prophets nor Christian, and that in them the anti-Christ has veritably appeared, not, as was expected, in one person, but in a terrifying plurality—*as ye heard that antichrist cometh, even now have there arisen many antichrists; whereby we know that it is the last hour* (ii. 18). Their spirituality is the *spirit of antichrist* (iv. 3), and their prophecy is false prophecy (iv. 1). It is the time of the great testing of the Christians, who must now learn to distinguish the true prophets and the true spirits from false prophecy and false spirituality—*Beloved, believe not every spirit, but test the spirits* (iv. 1). And, moreover, the writer undertakes his task with confidence, because he knows that he can expose the cause of the revolt and can provide the faithful with a canon by which all prophecy, all spirituality, can be tested. Indeed, he welcomes the clarity of the issue, because an opportunity has thereby been provided of showing that not all who are moving within the Christian fellowship rightly belong within it (ii.19).

The author speaks with authority because he knows that in the very kernel of the apostolic gospel there is a scandal to sensitive souls, and that it is precisely this scandal that has caused the revolt. With admirable precision he shows that the issue touches the very heart of the truth. He is faced by no trivial irritation, by no humble doubt, and by no mere theological difficulty: he is faced by a real denial of Jesus Christ in the interest of a supposedly spiritual religion. The scandal of apostolic Christianity, the stumbling-block, is the concrete, historical figure of Jesus; and those ancient spiritual and prophetic men were in revolt against the apostolic claim that the Christ is or could have been —Jesus (ii. 22); they were in revolt against the possibility that *flesh*, concrete human and visible flesh, could be of any essential or permanent importance for a truly spiritual religion. The claim that the Christ has come *in flesh* (iv. 2) is therefore worse than meaningless to them: it is a veritable clogging of the free movement of the spirit of God. In such an attitude to the Spirit and to the flesh of Jesus the author of the Epistle detects not merely *a* revolt, but the ultimate and final eschatological Revolt against the very heart of apostolic Christianity. For the apostles, the concrete, visible, historical figure of Jesus provided the very ground of faith in God. To slide down into a purely spiritual religion is to plunge into an uncharted sea of pseudo-religion. To deny the incarnate Son of God is to deny the Father also and to usher in the Last Hour (ii. 22, 23; 18). Only those who continue to hear and abide in apostolic truth veritably know God (iv. 6). This does not, of course, mean that the word 'spiritual' has been surrendered. Indeed, it is precisely those who bear the apostolic witness to the mission of the Son that have received from Him the Spirit (iv. 13, 14); and it is precisely those who keep His commandments that know that they abide in Him, because they have indeed received the Spirit (iii. 24). So directly is the gift of the Spirit linked to the recognition of the mission of the Son, that the writer roundly asserts that no spirit that refuses to confess Jesus—the historic Jesus presented to men in flesh—can be of God (iv. 3, cf. 2 John 7). There can therefore be no advance from apostolic Christianity into the realm of the Spirit. All such advance is but a return to the world (iv. 1), however much it may be camouflaged by the strains of the song of the redeemed. Man cannot advance beyond the need of the flesh of Jesus, for His concrete and visible flesh is and remains the road to the Father. And, moreover, the goal to which that road leads is actually attained by those who are now steadfastly marching along it. Every one who believes that the Christ is Jesus has been born of God (v. 1) and is even now in possession of eternal life (v. 13).

The essential importance of the coming of Jesus in the flesh and of the commandments which He gave constitutes the theme of the Epistle. This theme is precisely and somewhat roughly summed up when the author comes to speak of the death of Jesus: *This is he who came by water and blood, Jesus Christ. Not by water only, but by water—and by blood* (v. 6; cf. i. 7, iii. 16). At times it appears to be almost an irrational dogma. But to the author of the Epistle it is neither irrational nor a mere dogma: it is rather the truth to which the Very Spirit of God bears unmistakable witness (v. 7). The theme is pregnant with moral significance. The writer sees the 'spiritual' unbelievers moving into manifest immorality. They are anti-Christs, not merely because they do not believe in the mission of the Son, but because, having disbelieved, they have thereby lost the control of His life and death over their behaviour, and have consequently fallen a prey to the evil of the world. The apostolic witness has moral implications which are genuinely visible in those who hold it fast, but which altogether escape those who have advanced beyond the Jesus of History. He who believes that Jesus is the Christ *overcometh the world* (v. 4, cf. ii. 13, 14). In removing themselves from the apostolic fellowship, the unbelievers, despite their spiritual claims, have in very truth *gone forth into the world* (iv. 1). They have become the children of the Devil; they are marked by unrighteousness and by that complete absence of charity towards their former brethren which amounts to murder, for *everyone who hateth his brother is a murderer* (iii. 10–17). And so it is clear that, to the author of the Epistle, faith and knowledge and righteousness are inextricably woven together. But—and this is the point—they are thus woven together because the concrete object of faith is Himself the point in history where righteousness and truth have met together and are displayed as indissolubly one. Thus it comes about that the phrase *to do the truth* alone is adequate to express the demand that has been laid upon the children of God.

At this point, however, the commentator is in grave danger of simplifying the subject-matter of the Epistle in two directions. He may define the righteousness that emerges from faith in such a manner as to make of it some concrete and visibly adequate obedience to the will of God, and he may therefore see in the death of Jesus no more than a supreme example of love. He may also, as an historian, lay so great an emphasis upon the peculiar spiritual anti-Christs whose existence evoked the Epistle, as to suggest that the author is concerned only with a very particular situation, say in Ephesus at the end of the first century. In both directions, however, the commentator would fail to do justice to the theme of the Epistle. Though the author can say quite boldly that he who has been born of God *doeth no sin*, nay more, that he *cannot sin* (iii. 9), and though he can speak of the death of Christ quite simply as the source of the knowledge of love and as the incitement to it (iii. 16); yet he means thereby neither that the Christian has passed beyond the sphere of sin nor that the death of Christ can be expressed altogether by the analogy of human moral action. At the beginning of his Epistle he lays it down that without exception no Christian can dare to claim to be without sin—*If we say that we have no sin, we deceive ourselves and the truth is not in us*. Confession of sins and the recognition of the necessity of forgiveness belong to the essence of apostolic Christianity (i. 8, 9); and they belong to its essence because both were assumed in the teaching of Jesus; indeed it was to sinners in need of forgiveness that He spake the Word of God. Therefore—*If we say that we have not sinned, we make him a liar, and his word is not in us* (i. 10). In this context the writer comes to speak most emphatically, and apparently most naturally, of the death of Christ. It is the blood of Jesus, the Son of God, that *cleanseth us from all sin* (i. 7). He is the propitiation—a manifestly sacrificial word which presupposes His death—for our sins, and as such is the Paraclete with the Father (ii. 1, 2). Nor is it merely at the beginning of the Epistle that the author so carefully emphasizes the fact of sin. He returns to the theme in the final exhortation where he is concerned to distinguish between sin that is unto *death* and sin that is *not unto death*, between sin that occurs beyond the realm of faith and is therefore unforgivable and the sin that occurs among believers and is therefore open to forgiveness (v. 16, 17). The passage is, no doubt, obscure; but in any case the writer recognizes the existence of sin, forgivable sin, among the believers, for whom intercessory prayer is urgently required. It follows from all this that love, which is the final achievement of righteousness, is no independent achievement attained by men on the basis of human faith and human knowledge. It is not we who have loved God, but God who loved us and sent His Son to be the propitiation for our sins (iv. 10). In order to preserve the primacy of the action of God, the author, who, like the Psalmist, *will make mention of thy righteousness only*, must go beyond the particular occasion that first moved him to write. He is impelled to see in the particular situation great general truths being brought to light, and to sum up the truth of apostolic Christianity as The Truth. Thus, in his concern with one particular group of Christians, he enunciates the ultimate truths of the relation between God and man, truths which he has apprehended in the concrete figure of Jesus Christ. Having apprehended them there, he moves on inexorably through the authoritative 'we', through the particular 'you', to the quite general statement that Jesus Christ is the propitiation not for our sins only—*but also for the sins of the whole world* (ii. 2). In another context he moves on and on in similar fashion until he comes to rest in the general and final statement that *God is love* (iv. 16). And so, confronted by the particular problems of particular Christians in a particular place, he steadily refuses to see them as isolated or peculiar. Rather, he recognizes them as weighted with general problems, with general truths and with general untruths. These condition human life as a whole, have been manifested in the concrete life and death of Jesus Christ, the Son of God, and can be apprehended as truth and as falsehood only by faith in Him and by knowledge of Him: *And we know that the Son of God is come, and hath given us an understanding, that we may know him that is true. . . . This is the true God, and eternal life* (v. 20).

The first Epistle of John is, then, a catholic Epistle. And it is catholic, not in spite of the fact that it was written for certain Greek-speaking Christians, not in spite of the fact that it was written for these Christians at a time when important prophetically minded brethren had gone forth out of their midst in order to explore proudly new regions of 'spirituality', but precisely for these very reasons. Particular occasions have universal implications and are fraught with ultimate, eschatological significance. To have seen these implications, to have apprehended this significance and to have set it forth with such luminous clarity, is the supreme achievement of the author. To speak in this connection of his 'achievement' would, however, be to misunderstand him altogether. The achievement by which the truth has been laid bare is the achievement of the Son of God. The author does no more than bear witness to the work of Jesus, with which he presumes his readers to be already familiar. His historical and theological labour consists quite simply in recalling his readers to the significance that adheres to and is latent in what they already know. For it is the significance of what they already know that they so easily misunderstand.

The pressing question now arises, What did his readers already know? What was it that was open to such facile and insidious misunderstanding? The Epistle provides us with very scanty material for answering this all-important question. We are made aware that the readers of the Epistle knew that Jesus had died, that He had summed up His teaching in one commandment, namely that His disciples should love one another. They knew, moreover, that He had come into the world as the Son of

God, that He was the Christ, that He came through water (whatever that may mean), that He overcame the world (whatever that may mean), that He would come again, and that men would stand before Him with boldness or in fear and trembling. But these are fragments, significant fragments of course, but, nevertheless, fragments of a larger whole. The readers must have known more than that to which definite reference is made in the Epistle. This further knowledge is indeed assumed in the author's use of the plural *commandments*. Jesus did not merely give one commandment; He was the teacher who gave *commandments* (ii. 27; iii. 23, 24). But the Epistle gives us no inkling of what these commandments were. It is assumed that the readers know them.

Did we possess only the Epistle the author's readers would still remain shadowy figures. We should know very little of what they had in their heads when they came to read the letter which was addressed to them with such passionate conviction. Fortunately, we have in our hands the Fourth Gospel also. The gospel is built up upon the very themes which hold the Epistle together. Indeed, the themes of gospel and Epistle are expressed in language so identical that it has been difficult in laying out the matter of the Epistle to avoid constant reference to the gospel in order to elucidate obscure points and to reinforce the general meaning. Therefore it must be assumed not only that the two works came from the same hand, but also that they were originally written for the same group of Christians. If this be so, it is not unreasonable to expect that the form and structure of the gospel will enable us to learn more about them, and, in particular, that it will enable us to discover what kind of knowledge they already possessed before the Fourth Gospel and the First Epistle were written. The expectation appears, moreover, the more likely to be fulfilled when it is recognized that, though at first sight the gospel seems to have been written for all Christians, yet in one important passage the same particular situation that underlies the Epistle appears also in the gospel.

In the sixth chapter the discourse moves on steadily to the point where the Jews are confronted in the crudest possible manner with the necessity of belief in Jesus: it is demanded of them that they should eat His flesh and drink His blood (vi. 51–9). The Jews are brought under judgement, and the place of judgement is the flesh of Jesus, His concrete historical figure. This test the Jews entirely fail to survive. To them it is quite naked blasphemy (vi. 52). But—and surely this is the remarkable turn in the narrative—the same test is rigorously applied to the disciples of Jesus also, and it is recorded that, like the Jews, many of His disciples failed at this supreme moment. They murmured and were offended at this hard saying, and *went back, and walked no more with him. Then said Jesus therefore unto the twelve, Would ye also go away? Simon Peter answered him, Lord, to whom shall we go? thou hast the words of eternal life* (vi. 66–9). The apostles alone remain, and even one of them was to betray Him

(vi. 70, 71). Here is quite clearly narrated the defection of disciples, a defection which is contrasted with the faith of the apostles, with the faith of the 'we' of the gospel. Defection and faith alike are conditioned by a stern, uncompromising reference to the flesh of Jesus. It is difficult to avoid the conclusion that the narrative is so phrased as to be pregnant with meaning for readers who, as is clearly stated in the First Epistle, were faced by a similar defection for an identical cause. The false prophets had *gone forth* from the apostolic community *into the world* as Judas had gone forth *into the night* (xiii, 30) and as the disciples *went back and walked no more with him* (vi. 66), because they did not believe in the *flesh* of Jesus and because they refused to see any significance in His *blood*. Like the Jews in the gospel, they supposed themselves to be in possession of superior spiritual insight, whereas in fact they were thereby making themselves known as children of the Devil, who was a murderer from the beginning (1 John iii. 10–12, cf. John viii. 44). The Jews murdered the Christ: the false prophets hate the brethren, and *every one that hateth his brother is a murderer* (1 John iii. 15). The very remarkable overlapping of the gospel with the Epistle at this point both in subject-matter and in phraseology suggests that the gospel will also provide information concerning the kind of knowledge of Jesus which the author presumes his readers to possess already.

# IV. THE HISTORICAL TENSION OF THE FOURTH GOSPEL

STANTON, V. H. *The Gospels as Historical Documents*, Part III, pp. 219 sqq.

ABBOT, E. A. *Johannine Vocabulary*, pp. 153 sqq.

GODET, F. *Commentary on the Gospel of St. John*, English Translation, vol. i., pp. 141 sqq.

WINDISCH, H. *Johannes und die Synoptiker*, pp. 41 sqq.

MODERN study of the Fourth Gospel has pressed upon the Church the problem of historicity: the author of the Fourth Gospel, however, with greater theological insight, presses upon his readers the far more important, far more disturbing, problem of history itself and of its meaning. Confronted by the flesh of Jesus, the son of man, he demands that men should remember what He had said (xiv. 26), nay more, that they should eat His flesh and drink His blood (vi. 52–6). Jesus—son of man—words—flesh—blood! It is difficult to imagine language that fixes attention more steadily upon the importance of history. But, with equal conviction, the Evangelist refuses to permit his readers to rest even upon this important and particular history. *It is the spirit that quickeneth, the flesh profiteth nothing.* Only in relation to Spirit and Truth are the words of Jesus significant (vi. 63); only in relation to His Word is His speech able to be understood (viii. 43). It therefore follows necessarily that His words, His actual words, require for their understanding the interpretation that the Spirit of Truth alone is able to provide (xiv. 26). In Himself, as a product of the evolution of history, the Son of Man is merely—a son of man (viii. 54); and His words and actions, if they be thought of merely as historical episodes, are trivial and meaningless (vii. 16–18). This is the witness of the author of the Fourth Gospel: a witness thrust like a dagger straight into the heart of the 'World', in so far as the world is regarded as existing of itself and in its own right; plunged like a dagger into the heart of history, if history contains within itself its own evident, analysable, and describable meaning. The very existence of Jesus is also threatened if, as the Jews suppose, He appeared upon the stage of history 'in all the certainty of his own self', and if their question, *Whom makest thou thyself?* (viii. 53), were anything less than what it is declared to be, the ultimate blasphemy (viii. 54, 55).

# THE HISTORICAL TENSION OF THE FOURTH GOSPEL

A man so acutely aware of the problem of history as the author of the Fourth Gospel, and one made aware of it, not because it formed an important chapter in a disciplined study of philosophy, but on account of the historical fact of the life and death of Jesus of Nazareth, must be presumed to have possessed a knowledge of His teaching and actions, and of the circumstances of His death, sufficient to have rendered the problem unescapable and to have enabled him to dare to compose, not a treatise upon the Christian religion, but a gospel. And more than this, the author's clear assumption that his readers were also confronted by the same problem, however vaguely or superficially they may have been conscious of it, is hardly intelligible unless they too possessed some similar knowledge of the life and death of Jesus of Nazareth. This common historical information may have reached the author and his readers through the oral tradition of the Church; it may have also reached them in the form of written documents; but it is possible, too, that in this locality, or in that, these sources of information may have been supplemented and corrected by direct personal reminiscence surviving at first or at second hand. In any case, the Fourth Gospel depends for its understanding upon the recognition that its author is moving within the orbit of historical tradition, a tradition with which he presumes his readers to be at least generally familiar. But when this is said, it must be borne in mind that our knowledge of the tradition of the Primitive Church and of the forms in which it was circulating at the end of the first century is somewhat tenuous. The substance and more particularly the emphasis of the general oral tradition as it was handed down by word of mouth are largely inaccessible to us. Even more inaccessible are those elusive reminiscences which may have survived into the second century, but which are now altogether lost, save in so far as echoes of them may have influenced this or that passage in the Fourth Gospel itself. For our knowledge of the oral tradition of the Church before the Fourth Gospel was written, we are altogether dependent upon the three small documents which we call the synoptic gospels. The letters of Saint Paul and a few other writings do, it is true, survive from the pre-Johannine period, and do, no doubt, add something to our historical knowledge of Jesus. But this additional material is not easy to handle, since Saint Paul and the author of the Epistle to the Hebrews are, like the author of the Fourth Gospel, more concerned with the problem of history than with the writing of it, and assume rather than collect the historical information that forced the problem upon their attention. The synoptic gospels provide the only available road to the form of the oral tradition of the Primitive Church. Any attempt to expose the background of the Fourth Gospel must therefore begin with a comparison between it and the synoptic gospels, and must be conducted in the hope that this comparison will reveal some strict relationship, if not between the Fourth Gospel and the synoptic gospels, at least between it and the tradition that has been preserved in them.

A comparison between the synoptic gospels and the Fourth Gospel is not, as is often supposed, a purely modern occupation. What is modern is the rigour with which this inquiry is conducted, and also the deductions that have been drawn from it. And it must be frankly owned that the result of this comparison is at first sight not at all encouraging; not encouraging, that is to say, if we hold, as we must, that the author of the Fourth Gospel has asked his readers to regard him as the custodian and protector of Apostolic Tradition and as an all-important witness to the historical foundations of Christian faith and knowledge; not encouraging, if we hold, as we must, that there is exposed in the synoptic gospels a very important cross-section of the oral tradition of the Church, by which we are enabled to gain some idea at least of the form and substance of the teaching of Jesus. To those familiar with the synoptic gospels the omissions in the Fourth Gospel constitute what seems to be its most unaccountable feature. Not merely have important single episodes—the Baptism and Transfiguration of Jesus, His Temptation, and the Agony in the Garden of Gethsemane, the memorable words spoken in the Upper Room, to say nothing of the story of His miraculous birth—no easily recognizable place in the Fourth Gospel, but impressive aspects of His teaching and whole classes of His actions are passed over in almost complete silence. Where are the sharp, crisp, isolated, aphoristic utterances, such as: *Wheresoever the carcase is, there will the vultures be gathered together?* Where are those terrifying imperatives, such as: *Let the dead bury their dead, but go thou and preach the kingdom of God?* No doubt, there are in the Fourth Gospel pregnant, quotable Sayings, but they are not aphoristic. Formulated in the midst of a discourse (e.g. xv. 13), or set at its beginning or ending (viii. 12, 58), they belong to the intimate literary and theological structure of the gospel as a whole, from which they cannot be detached without grave danger of misunderstanding. Where are the parables and parabolic sayings thrown out with such rich, prodigal wealth in order to press upon the crowds and upon the disciples the urgent claims of the Kingdom or Dominion of God? In the synoptic gospels the whole visible panorama of nature and the whole visible business of human behaviour burgeon with a mighty secret yearning to be made known; and in His parables Jesus does manifest this secret or *mystery* (Mark iv. 11), thereby conferring upon the smallest and most insignificant occurrences the supreme dignity of the revelation of God. The Fourth Gospel does, of course, contain what is known as the Parable of the Good Shepherd. But the word 'Parable' in this connection is misleading—indeed, the author of the Fourth Gospel has himself used a different word. The passage describing the Good Shepherd cannot be isolated from the discourse that is built upon it, a discourse that comes to rest, not in the peace of the Kingdom of God, but in the restlessness of the death of Jesus, in the commandment of mortality that has been laid upon Him by His Father. Only on the other side of obedience to this commandment does He speak of life and of love. *Therefore doth the Father love me because I lay down my life, that I may take it again* (x. 17). There are also in the Fourth Gospel, of course, references to the harvest, to the sowing of seed, to the fruits of the earth, to the vine and its branches. But they too are incidents in a broad discourse, incidents that appear for a moment and as quickly disappear (iv. 35–8, xii. 24, xv. 1 sqq.).

Not only, however, has the teaching of Jesus to the crowds and to the disciples taken on a new, unfamiliar form. Its very content seems to be altogether different. Where is the all-controlling, ever-recurring theme of the *Kingdom of God*? And where is the word *Gospel*? The latter occurs nowhere; the former has almost disappeared. The phrase *The Kingdom of God* appears only at the beginning of the discourse with Nicodemus (iii. 3, 5), though it is echoed in the conversation with Pilate: *My kingdom is not of this world* (xviii. 36). Its place is occupied by the *ego* of Jesus, the Son of God. Where too is the all-pervading tension provoked by the definition of the present time in terms of rough eschatology? And where is the insistent, precise call to repentance, urgent because it is uttered in the midst of this acute eschatological tension? Neither the verb *to repent* nor the noun *repentance* occurs in the Fourth Gospel. The rich eschatological language has almost completely disappeared from its author's vocabulary; so much so that it is something of a surprise to find it reappearing in the First Epistle: *Little children, it is the last hour* (1 John ii. 18). And yet, the removal of the <u>formal</u> eschatological tension does not mean that all tension has been removed from the teaching of Jesus. It is not that the author of the Fourth Gospel, unlike the more primitive Christians, stood confronted, not by the end, but by centuries of Christian and non-Christian history rolling out in a distant perspective before his eyes, so that the urgent divine imperative has been inevitably weakened. The tension in the Fourth Gospel is, if such a thing were possible, even more acute. The Fourth Gospel describes an <u>ultimate present tension</u>, the tension between flesh and Spirit, between life and Death and between death and Life, between darkness and Light, between Jesus and His disciples and the World, between those who believe and know and see and those who neither believe nor know, but are blind; in fact, the Fourth Gospel describes the tension between God and men. It vibrates and is set in motion at the point where trembling and arrogant human life is met by the Life that is eternal; at the point where men are confronted by Jesus, son of man and—Son of God. The Fourth Gospel is therefore wholly misunderstood when it is regarded as a haven of rest at which the Church arrived after the turmoil of the synoptic gospels, and in which delicate-minded Christians may now rejoice without embarking upon that other turbulent sea.

A comparison of the actions of Jesus described in the Fourth Gospel with those narrated in the synoptic gospels leads to the same embarrassing conclusion as the comparison of the record of His teaching. Where are the short compressed narratives of the healing of poor sick and distressed men and women? Where are the stories of the healing of men and women afflicted and possessed by evil spirits? Where is there any story of the healing of a leper or of a man with a withered hand? Where are the pictures of Jesus standing in the midst of the poor and the outcast, moving towards publicans and sinners and drawing to Himself the tiny children—irresistibly? The synoptic gospels are filled full of such stories, of such pictures, which in their cumulative effect show Him forth, not merely as a teacher, but pre-eminently as one who *went about doing good*, as one to whom the particular poor man, the particular diseased, helpless creature, offered an ever-present occasion for active human charity. So much is this the case that the contrast between poverty and wealth emerges as the major theme round which not only the teaching but also the actions of Jesus tend to revolve. In the Fourth Gospel there is no such precise concentration. The contrasted themes of poverty and wealth are markedly absent, at any rate in the form in which they occur in the earlier gospels. The word *poor* is mentioned only in relation to Judas's ostentatious—and hypocritical—concern about them (xii. 5–8, xiii. 29): the word *rich* is not used at all. There is no mention of publicans in the Fourth Gospel, nor is there any picture of Jesus in the midst of the children. Its author is concerned with grown men and women; and, save in the story of the nobleman's dying child (iv. 49), and in the passage emphasizing the theological significance of the pain of childbirth (xvi. 21), the word *child* is reserved for the description of men and women as *children of Abraham* (viii. 39), *children of God* (i. 12, xi. 52), and the diminutive *little children* for the disciples of Jesus (xxi. 5, cf. 1 John ii. 18; ii. 1, 12, v. 21). Miracles of healing are, of course, important in the Johannine narrative; indeed, supremely so. But how carefully are they chosen! How very carefully, too, are they woven into the comprehensive literary and theological structure of the gospel! The miracles that the Evangelist selects can no longer be understood merely as episodic, charitable, human actions; they are also, and indeed pre-eminently, *signs*, signs of the Truth, signs in concrete action of the Glory of the Word of God. They are opportunities for faith, not occasioned by it (ii. 11). They are, moreover, so fitted into the perspective of the gospel as to move in harmony with the development of its theological themes. The reader is led on and on until he reaches the story of the Raising of Lazarus. Beyond that there are no more miracles of healing—even Malchus's wound remains uncared for (xviii. 10, 11, cf. Mark xiv. 47, Matt. xxvi. 51, 52, but contrast Luke xxii. 50, 51).

The theme has been exhausted, has, in fact, reached its goal, when the gift of eternal life to men has been so vividly set forth. In somewhat similar fashion, the presence of Jesus in the midst of sinners, of rich and poor, and of children, so far from being disregarded and set aside, occupies the whole canvas. The theme is portrayed no longer in a series of episodes, but in one consistent picture, in which it is pressed to a final issue. The whole visible world of men and women—the Jews forming, as it were, a microcosm—is represented as blind (ix. 39–41) and deaf (viii. 47) and ignorant (viii. 19), so blind and helpless and crippled that 'poverty' seems a word too slight to describe men who are of their *father the devil* (viii. 44) and not merely 'possessed' by evil spirits. It is to such men and women that salvation, eternal life, is offered; and it is perhaps not surprising that the word 'wealth' is driven out of the author's vocabulary by the word *glory* (v. 44, xvii. 20–2). Moreover, Jesus Himself is the measure by which men may understand what genuine poverty is in this world (xii. 7, 8, xvi. 32, xix. 28), and what *glory* means in the invisible world from which He had come, in the world of the Father by whom He has been sent (xvii. 5, 18). In this vast context the whole conception of what children are moves from the periphery of an episode into the very centre of the one picture; and there the terrifying alternative arises: men are children of God or they are—of their father the devil (viii. 44). This alternative is not an episode in the Fourth Gospel or even in the history of Judaism: it is the tension of all history, its meaning; a tension that was, however, clearly manifested when the Jews were confronted by Jesus, the Son of God, and when they put Him to death. The distinction between children and grown men and women therefore becomes, in this context, either trivial or, what it assuredly is, a parable of quite ultimate significance: *Ye must be born again* (iii. 7)—*Verily I say unto you, Except ye turn* (A.V. *be converted), and become as little children, ye shall in no wise enter into the kingdom of heaven* (Matt. xviii. 3).

There is, however, a difference between the Fourth Gospel and the synoptic gospels even more surprising and embarrassing than that disclosed by the form of the teaching of Jesus, or by the manner in which His actions are narrated. In the perspective of the Fourth Gospel the scene of His ministry is altogether different. What has become of all the ramifications of the ministry in Galilee? Galilee has almost disappeared as the district where the greater part of His teaching was given and where most of His *mighty works* were done. The ministry in Galilee has been overlaid by the record of a ministry in Jerusalem. The topography of the Fourth Gospel is, in the main, Judæan; nay more, it is a Jerusalem topography. Moreover, Jesus speaks and acts not merely in Jerusalem, but in the Temple; and not merely in the Temple, but in the Temple on the occasion of a series of Jewish Feasts. This is, however, no mere topography, no mere attention to the Jewish Kalendar. The fourth Evangelist tells his story, his ears ringing with the words of the prophets of Israel, his mind conscious of their fulfilment: *The Lord will roar from Zion, and utter his voice from Jerusalem* (Amos i. 2, Joel iii. 16, cf. Jer. xxv. 30)—*Out of Zion shall go forth the law* (R.V. mg. *instruction*), *and the word of the Lord from Jerusalem* (Isa. ii. 3, Mic. iv. 2)—*The Redeemer shall come to Zion* (Isa. lix. 20, cf. Rom. xi. 26)—*The Lord hath filled Zion with judgement* (Isa. xxxiii. 5)—*The Lord shall comfort Zion* (Isa. li. 3)—*The Lord whom ye seek shall suddenly come to his temple* (Mal. iii. 1). Here is the background not only of the topography of the Fourth Gospel, but also of its disciplined vocabulary—*word, voice, judgement, seek, comforter.* In reading the witness of John we have not passed into the realm of timeless eternity or of measureless infinity; we have been brought rather to that time and to that place which above all others have no meaning apart from their relation to God. Galilee, of course, has not entirely disappeared, but the energy of the narrative is not directed towards it. Indeed, the vigour of the Evangelist is exercised in showing that mere information about the place from which Jesus came may come perilously near to complete misunderstanding. Pilate and the Jews knew whence Jesus came; they knew that He was *of Galilee, of Nazareth* (vii. 27, xix. 19). The question, Whence did Jesus come? admits, however, of no such facile, informatory answer (vii. 28, 29, xix. 9); and that it does not is a major theme of the Fourth Gospel. The question, Whence? is supremely relevant and concerns not Jesus only, but His disciples also (i. 13). *Salvation*, the author of the Fourth Gospel tells us, *is of the Jews* (iv. 22). He has taken this seriously. Accordingly he will not permit his readers to suppose that they can understand the ministry of Jesus theologically if they set it against the background of a half-Jewish, largely Gentile province of the Roman Empire. Judaism—Jewish faith and unbelief, Jewish worship, Jerusalem, the Temple, the Old Testament Scriptures—was the veritable background of the teaching of Jesus and of His actions, however much He may have said and done in Galilee. For this reason, when the Evangelist records Galilean incidents, or when he steps aside to record a ministry in Samaria, he is careful to emphasize that they are strictly related to the heart of Judaism. Thus, the water that is changed into wine in Cana of Galilee is not ordinary drinking-water, but water *set there after the Jews' manner of purifying* (ii. 6). The narrative in ch. vi. is a Galilean narrative, but it is told in the context of a Jewish Feast: *The Passover, the feast of the Jews was at hand.* The story of the nobleman at Cana of Galilee whose son was sick at Capernaum, which seems at first sight to be merely a detached episode, is introduced in order to contrast the reception of Jesus by the Galileans, who had *seen all the things that he did in Jerusalem at the feast: for they also went unto the feast,* with His lack of honour *in his own country*—Jerusalem! (iv. 44, 45, cf. vii. 1–9). The actual narrative is, moreover, bracketed by references to Jerusalem: *When he heard that Jesus was come out of Judæa into Galilee, he went unto him* (iv. 47)—*After this there was a feast of the Jews; and Jesus went up to Jerusalem* (v. 1). Similarly, the discourse with the woman of Samaria turns upon the adequacy and inadequacy of Jewish worship at Jerusalem, and it is to her that the words *Salvation is of the Jews* are addressed.

How completely different is the lay-out of the synoptic gospels! There the scene of the ministry of Jesus is quite firmly Galilee, until the final and unique journey to Jerusalem in order that there He may die, since *it cannot be that a prophet perish out of Jerusalem* (Luke xiii. 33). No doubt, it is possible to criticize the synoptic gospels precisely because of this arrangement, and to maintain that it is the result of editorial manipulation. There may have been journeys to Jerusalem which, for some reason or other, found no place in the earlier gospels. The existence of further tradition concerning events in Jerusalem may perhaps explain how it came about that the fourth Evangelist was able to do what he did. But mere additional information, even if it were the information of an eyewitness, does not explain what he has actually written. It does not, for example, explain the extraordinary situation revealed by a comparison between Mark vi. 2–4 (cf. Luke iv. 23) and John iv. 44, 45.

There is another difference, more subtle perhaps, but more fundamental and even more important, because it embraces all those differences to which attention has been drawn, and because the Fourth Gospel remains undiscovered, if it be not clearly recognized. The synoptic gospels consist of a large number of disconnected or semi-disconnected fragments, incidents, episodes, put together by the Evangelists within a broad, roomy framework, capable, without serious disturbance to the general plan of the books, of being expanded to hold additional material or contracted in order to render the material more manageable. In the midst of this rich, varied gallery the reader can wander about. He is magnificently free. He can pause and admire, where he will. He can select an incident, visualize it, meditate upon it, and then preach about it, allegorize it, interpret it, symbolize it, apply it to his own circumstances, use it to pillory his enemies or to encourage himself and his friends; he can, in fact, construe it according to his own will and satisfaction; and finally, he can interpret it so as to escape from the teaching of Saint Paul, say, in the Epistle to the Romans, or so as to thrust the Fourth Gospel well on to the periphery of the Christian Religion. And in doing all this he can pride himself that he is acting in obedience to the highest authority, that of the authentic teaching of Jesus of Nazareth, and that he is a true disciple of the 'Jesus of History' because he has heard Him speak and seen Him act. There are, no doubt, certain incidents that cause some difficulty—the Voice from Heaven at the Baptism and at the Transfiguration, the Crucifixion regarded as the fulfilment of Old Testament prophecy, the Stilling of the Storm, the Eschatological Discourse, and other episodes—but the psychology of religious experience, the creeping in of legendary material into the oral tradition, a certain capriciousness on the part of the primitive Christians in applying Old Testament passages to the career of Jesus, the influence of Saint Paul, are sufficient to explain these uncomfortable points! And in any case, there is much else in which the 'authentic history' is more adequately preserved. The synoptic gospels therefore, given a certain care in selection, are admirably adapted to provide short public or private lections in church or at home.

To the reader of the Fourth Gospel no such magnificent freedom is permitted. The selection of incidents has already been made, not at all as we should have made it. The interpretation has been given, and it is in form the interpretation of Jesus Himself, in substance the interpretation of the Holy Spirit of Truth (xiv. 26, xvi. 12–16). The Fourth Gospel records not primarily what the crowd of eyewitnesses saw and heard of the Jesus of History, but what the disciples saw of the *glory* of the Word of God (i. 14); what they apprehended, as believers, when Jesus *was risen from the dead* (ii. 22). The Fourth Gospel is less an apostolic witness to history than an Apostolic witness to that which is beyond history, but which is, nevertheless, the meaning of the 'Jesus of History', and therefore the meaning of all history. The reader of the Fourth Gospel has, therefore, to master a vocabulary. He has to apprehend a theme which is worked out in literary fashion. The Fourth Gospel, whatever may have been the original form of the material out of which it was made, is a literary unity, not an arrangement of incidents. The reader is required to move with the movement of the book. He has to bear carefully in mind what the author has already said. In reading the beginning, he must know the issue of the whole matter. Thus, the conclusion of the narrative of the Raising of Lazarus (xi. 43, 44) assumes that the reader has not forgotten the words already written in an earlier chapter: *The hour cometh in which all that are in the tombs shall hear his voice, and shall come forth* (v. 28, 29). Nor are the words in the earlier chapter entirely intelligible apart from some such narrative as the Raising of Lazarus, whilst both the words and the action are in the end meaningless apart from the Resurrection of Jesus Himself and apart from the avowed purpose for which the Fourth Gospel was written: *These are written, that ye may believe that Jesus is the Christ, the Son of God; and that believing ye may have life in his name* (xx. 31). Similarly, the apparently straightforward, matter-of-fact statement that *blood and water* came forth from the pierced side of the crucified Christ, receives a more than matter-of-fact significance when the incident is read in the context provided by the words spoken in vi. 53–7 and in vii. 37–9 (cf. 1 John i. 7, v. 8). Or again, the glaring and surely intentional paradox of the words, *I thirst* (xix. 28), altogether escapes the reader, if he has forgotten that He who spake that word is the same as He who said to the woman of Samaria: *Whosoever drinketh of the water that I shall give him shall never thirst* (iv. 10–15). Everywhere in the Fourth Gospel we are further confronted by this self-contained allusiveness (cf., for example, i. 30; iii. 26; 28; iv. 54; v. 33; vii. 21; 23; viii. 24; xi. 37; xii. 17; xiii. 15; 33; xviii. 9; 14; 32; xxi. 14). The book moves on spirally. Incidents and discourses are everywhere interlocked because they are adjusted to its disciplined theme. There is, therefore, in spite of its brevity, a certain leisureliness in the book; not because the author wastes time, but because he is determined that the reader shall be— shall we say?—overwhelmed by the singleness of the theme which is Jesus of Nazareth, son of man—Son of God, by the theme in which the tension of history is resolved only in God.

A comparison of the Fourth Gospel with the synoptic gospels and the laying bare of its literary character and of its self-contained allusiveness, have inevitably raised the problem of the gospel once again in an almost intolerably acute form. What has its author done? And why? What relation is there between his work and the earlier tradition? The preceding analysis almost compels us to detach the gospel from the position it holds in the Canon and to consider it an altogether independent literary achievement, written in order to supersede the whole body of primitive tradition, oral and written. Windisch has, in fact, so understood the gospel; for at the head of his book he boldly prints the text: *All that came before me are thieves and robbers* (x. 8), and by the side of this Johannine Saying the Pauline words: *Even though we have known Christ after the flesh, yet now we know him so no longer* (2 Cor. v. 16). Windisch presumably means that in the Fourth Gospel all touch with history has been surrendered, and surrendered purposely. Alternatively, we might, though this is more difficult, explain the uniqueness and independence of the Fourth Gospel by advancing to a stricter historical conservatism than that with which we are familiar, to a stricter historical orthodoxy than that of the early Fathers of the Church. We might utter a protest against the words 'omission' and 'transformation', and steer the Johannine ship altogether clear of the synoptic gospels and of the oral tradition. We might maintain that the author of the Fourth Gospel has not added a supplement to the historical knowledge of the primitive Church, but has completely superseded it by a far more correct account of the teaching and action of Jesus, and that he has done this not merely with the authority of an apostolic eyewitness, but with the even greater authority of that disciple whom Jesus loved, and to whom He confided the meaning of His life and death. In this case the Fourth Gospel would become the primary historical document, and the synoptic gospels documents of secondary historical importance. But neither of these incompatible possibilities is really open to us. Both are closed, if for no other reason than this, that each in its own way denies the tension of history, which is the major theme of the gospel. The latter solution would bury the gospel among the records of historical observation, precisely where it refuses to be buried: the former, even more destructively, would expose its author as a foremost leader in the ranks of those whom he so vigorously denounces as anti-Christs.

The questions now arise whether the author's allusiveness is exhausted in his allusions to what he has himself written and to the Old Testament Scriptures, and whether the gospel is so independent a Christian work as a first comparison with the synoptic gospels certainly suggests. The position which the book occupies in the traditional canon of Scripture sets it, however, not only in the context of the Old Testament, not only in the context of other Johannine writings, but also and most intimately in the context of the synoptic gospels. The Church clearly intends the book to be read in close connection with the earlier gospels, and not as an isolated, independent work. Has the Church, in thus binding the four gospels together, wellnigh destroyed the proper meaning of the last of them? Or has the Church thereby provided the clue for the unravelling of its even more important allusiveness? In other words, does the author of the Fourth Gospel presume his readers to be familiar with the current oral tradition of the primitive Church? And further, did he presume their familiarity with those actual written gospels which have survived for our knowledge and edification? Or, to put the problem more precisely, did the author of the Fourth Gospel assume his readers to be standing where we stand, when having read the gospels of Matthew and Mark and Luke, we suppose that we have understood them, and when, having understood them, as we suppose, we determine either to dismiss them as of very little value compared with our own direct spiritual experience or to treasure them as providing an entirely adequate and luminous picture of the 'Jesus of History' and of the meaning of His life and death? Whether the author of the Fourth Gospel and his readers knew the three synoptic gospels or whether they were dependent rather upon the oral tradition of the Church is a problem which we can handle only by the way of synoptic gospels, since we have no precise access to the oral tradition except in so far as it is set down in these earlier gospels. The important question is not whether the Fourth Gospel depends upon oral tradition, or upon written documents, or upon both, but whether it is or is not a work existing in its own right, and whether it is or is not to be interpreted independently and by itself.

The Fourth Gospel is, as it stands, a literary unity. Its subject-matter is altogether controlled and penetrated by a comprehensive theological theme set forth with so great an economy of language that very few words suffice to define it. *Father, Son, Life, Light, Love, Truth, Judgement, believing, knowing, seeing*—by means of these words the theme of the gospel is fully defined. The remaining vocabulary and the whole subject-matter moves towards, or away from, these final, satisfactory words. Yet, in spite of the simplicity of its form, the Fourth Gospel is not a simple book. One of the causes of this lack of simplicity is that it does not, in fact, exist in its own right and is not in itself adequate for its own understanding. The author of the gospel does not for one moment suppose that his readers will think that the miraculous actions of Jesus were limited to those which he has chosen to record (vi. 2, cf. xxi. 25). He has made a selection, a significant selection, no doubt, but a selection. Nor does he, in spite of the fact that his record consists of discourses rather than parables, suppose his readers to be ignorant that Jesus taught in parables: *These things have I spoken unto you in parables: the hour cometh, when I shall speak unto you no more in parables, but shall tell you plainly of the Father* (xvi. 25). When the disciples think that He taught in any other manner—*Lo, now speakest thou plainly, and speakest no parable* (xvi. 29)—they have altogether misunderstood the nature of His teaching, as the succeeding verses show. John the Baptist is an important witness at the beginning of the gospel, but what is said about him and what he himself says are almost unintelligible unless the reader knows already that his work, and very particularly his imprisonment, formed the starting-point of the ministry of Jesus, that he had baptized Him, that the story of the Baptism contained a reference to the Son of God and to a dove, that the Baptist disclaimed any pre-eminent position for himself and yet that, nevertheless, he had been brought into some connection with Elijah (i. 6, 21, 30-4, iii. 24). Knowledge of an extended ministry of Jesus in Galilee is less suppressed than assumed (iv. 43-5, vi. 1, 2, vii. 1). It is assumed that the readers of the gospel know that He came from Nazareth (i. 45, 46, xviii. 5, 7, xix. 19), that Capernaum was an important scene in the story of His ministry (ii. 12), that His leading disciples were Galileans (i. 43, 44), and that He had brethren who did not believe on Him but who formed a group of men distinct from the disciples (vii. 3-5). When fragments of eschatological language are introduced (iv. 21, vi. 39, 40, 54, cf. xxi. 22, 23), no explanation of them is added other than that required by the especial theme of the gospel. The Hour, the Last Day, Judgement, the Son of man, the imminent return of Jesus, are not introduced as though such words and phrases would be strange to the readers of the gospel. The strangeness seems to lie in the use the Evangelist makes of them rather than in the fact that he uses them. In the First Epistle this familiarity and strangeness are definitely mentioned: *Little children, it is the last hour: and as ye heard that antichrist cometh, even now have there arisen many antichrists; whereby we know that it is the last hour* (1 John ii. 18). The narrative of the Passion seems to assume its readers' knowledge of a trial before Caiaphas (xviii. 24, 28) and even of Simon of Cyrene, or at least of some one other than Jesus Himself, bearing the Cross on the road to Golgotha (xix. 17, Mark xv. 21).

It is perhaps not surprising that the original readers of the gospel should be expected to be able to fill in these gaps in the narrative and to catch its allusions. What is surprising is that, with the synoptic gospels before us, we too are able to fill in the gaps and recognize the allusions. We are not ignorant of Nazareth and Capernaum and Galilee, or of the Galilean provenance of the disciples. We know both the unbelief and the names of the brethren of the Lord (Mark iii. 31–5, cf. vi. 3). We know, not merely something about John's work and teaching, but precisely those things that make sense of the allusive narrative in the Fourth Gospel—the story of his baptism of Jesus, the dove, and the voice from heaven saying, *Thou art my Son*. We know too how closely John was associated with Elijah. We are very familiar with parables, with miracles of healing, and with the wide range of eschatological language. We even know of the expectation of the advent of the anti-Christ. We possess an account of the trial before Caiaphas, and we know that it was Simon of Cyrene, the father of Alexander and Rufus, who was compelled to bear the Cross. More important than all these things, the title Son of man is very well known to us, for round it the teaching of Jesus in all the strata from which the earlier gospels were composed tends to revolve in such a manner as to present the supreme enigma of the synoptic tradition. So enigmatic is this title that, so long as we are confined to the synoptic gospels, we seem unable to understand its meaning—an inability that we apparently share with the writers of those earlier gospels. What is true of the enigmatic character of the title Son of man is also true of those other titles—Christ, Son of God—that confront us in the older tradition.

But there is more to be detected in the Fourth Gospel than a general overlapping of our knowledge with that of its original readers, more even than a fleeting echo of familiar descriptive phrases, as, for example, when its author tells how Jesus said to the cripple at the pool of Bethesda, *Arise, take up thy bed and walk* (v. 8, 9, Mark ii. 11, 12), or how He healed a blind man with spittle (ix. 6, Mark viii. 23, cf. vii. 33). The Evangelist includes in his book particular incidents that occupy an important position in the synoptic gospels also; and in the course of narrating these incidents, he falls back on words, phrases and even whole sentences that are characteristic of the earlier tradition, and in particular of the tradition in its Marcan form. Nor is this verbal identity limited to significant words, phrases and sentences. In the narrative of the Feeding of the Five Thousand and the Walking on the Sea (vi. 1–21, Mark vi. 30–52), the command that the people should *sit down* on the *grass*, the proposal to spend 200 *pence*, the sufficiency of the *five loaves* and *two fishes*, the filling of *twelve baskets* with the *broken fragments; the mountain*, Jesus *alone* (Mark, John, not Matt.), **His words:**

*I am, be not afraid*, are verbally identical in the Greek. In addition, the demand for a sign (vi. 30) forms part of the Marcan account of the Feeding of the Four Thousand. The narratives of the Cleansing of the Temple (ii. 13–22, Mark xi. 15–18, 27, 28), in spite of very great differences in the treatment of the incident and of the occasion upon which it took place, contain verbal agreements: the description of the pandemonium that gave rise to the incident—*those that sold doves, tables, changers of money*—and display verbal affinities, both in the reference to Isa. lvi. 7 (Jer. vii. 11) and in the question of *the Jews* (Mark *chief priests and scribes and elders*), *What sign showest thou unto us, seing that thou doest these things* (Mark *By what authority doest thou these things?*). The words spoken by the crowd at the Entry into Jerusalem (xii. 13, Mark xi. 9) are verbally identical in the first clause; in the second, *The King of Israel* (cf. vi. 15, Luke xix. 38) characteristically takes the place of *The Kingdom of our father David*. When the fourth Evangelist comes to tell the story of the anointing of Jesus by a woman (xii. 1–8), he again, in spite of very great differences of context and of persons, weaves his narrative round phrases well known to us from the parallel Marcan narrative (Mark xiv. 3–9). Verbally identical are—*Bethany, ointment of pistic nard very costly, this ointment . . . sold for three hundred pence and given to the poor, let her alone . . . for ye have the poor always with you . . . but me ye have not always with you*: this sentence is, however, omitted from the Fourth Gospel in Codex Bezae, in the old Syriac Codex Sinaiticus, and in some manuscripts of the Armenian Version—a rather disturbing reminder of the possibilities of assimilation! Cf. the variant readings to John vi. 19. In the Johannine narrative of the Anointing at Bethany, Judas Iscariot plays an important part. In the Marcan account he is not mentioned, but he is nevertheless hovering in the background, for he steps forward into even greater prominence with the next incident that Mark records (Mark xiv. 10, 11). When we come to the five chapters in which the story of the Last Supper is described (chs. xiii–xvii), we seem to be altogether removed from the Marcan tradition. Yet, even here, the earlier tradition appears to lie subtly in the background. Three times we are verbally reminded of it. First, by the words, *Verily I say unto you that one of you shall betray me*, by the definition of the betrayer as he that *dippeth* with Jesus in the dish, by the description of the acute distress of the disciples, and by the haunting theme of Judas *going away* or *going forth* from the fellowship in order to *betray* or *deliver up* his master (xiii. 2, 21–30, Mark xiv. 10, 17–21): then, in the prophecy of Peter's denial, *Verily I say unto you*, before the *cock crow* twice, *thou shalt deny me thrice*, and in the strenuous protest of the Apostle when he declares his readiness to die with Jesus, appearing in Johannine form with he words, *I will lay down my life for thy sake* (xiii. 37, 38, Mark xiv. 29–31). And lastly, but most strangely, in the phrase, *Arise, let us be going*, used in the Fourth Gospel to break up the discourse into two parts, but in Mark belonging to the narrative of the arrest (xiv. 31, Mark xiv. 42). Formal verbal agreements in the narrative of the Passion itself are somewhat rare, though there is considerable overlapping even in matters of detail (e.g. xviii. 3, Mark xiv. 43). They do, however, occur. Peter draws his *sword, smiting the servant of the high priest,* and cutting off his *ear* (xviii. 10, Mark xiv. 47). In both gospels the narrative of the fulfilment of the prophecy of Peter's denial is separated into two parts (contrasted with Luke) by the record of the trial before a high priest (John Annas, Mark Caiaphas). Peter is *warming himself* in the company of the *servants* of the high priest; a question of one of them— a *maidservant*—being the immediate cause of his downfall, after which *immediately the cock crew* (xviii. 15–18, 25–7, Mark xiv. 53, 54, 66–72). The trial before Caiaphas is, as has already been noted (p. 69), presumed but not described (xviii. 24, 28). The Johannine narrative of the trial before Annas contains verbal echoes of what we know from the Marcan account of the trial before Caiaphas: Jesus was struck by a *servant* (Mark *servants*) with the *palm of the hand* (xviii. 22, Mark xiv. 65). The most characteristic feature in the Johannine account of the Trial of Jesus is the narrative of the conversations with Pilate. But their framework is already known to us from Mark. The Johannine account of the trial before Pilate begins, as Mark had begun it, with the question *Art thou the King of the Jews?* (xviii. 33, Mark xv. 2); it passes through the words, *Will ye that I release unto you the King of the Jews?* (xviii. 39, Mark xv. 9), through the twice-repeated, vehement *cry* of the *chief priests, Crucify him* (xix. 6, 15, Mark xv. 11–14), through the *scourging* by *Pilate* (xix. 1, Mark xv. 15) and the mocking by his *soldiers —plaiting* of the *crown of thorns,* clothing with the *purple* robe, the salutation, *Hail, King of the Jews* (xix. 2, 3; Mark xv. 16–20)—and it ends with the writing of the inscription to be set over the cross, *The King of the Jews* (xix. 19, Mark xv. 26), and with Joseph of Arimathæa's request to Pilate that he might be given leave to remove *the body of Jesus* since it was the Jewish *preparation* day (xix. 38–42, Mark xv. 42–5). Not only is the framework of the Johannine narrative here verbally identical with that of Mark, but, and this is even more significant, it is the Marcan account that contains the theme of Jesus the King, which is afterwards to form the subject-matter of the Johannine conversations between Jesus and Pilate. In the narrative of the scene of the Crucifixion itself the words *Golgotha, the place of a skull,* the description of the soldiers *parting the raiment* and *casting lots*—in the Fourth Gospel the allusion to Ps. xxii. 18 is emphasized—of the soldier filling a *sponge with vinegar* and *putting it upon* hyssop (Mark a *reed*) are Marcan-Johannine (xix. 17–30, Mark xv. 22–37). Finally, the Resurrection narrative opens with the account of *Mary Magdalene* arriving *early on the first day of the week* at *the tomb* and finding *the stone* removed from its proper place (xx. 1, Mark xvi. 1–4). Further detailed verbal comparison is, of course, impossible because of our ignorance of the original end of Saint Mark's Gospel. The readers of the Fourth Gospel, as it stands, are, however, presumed to know something about a command to Mary (? the women) to *tell the disciples* and to know also that there was an Appearance in Galilee; both of which are Marcan themes (xx. 2, 17, 18, xxi., Mark xvi. 7, 8, xiv. 28).

If it were merely a question of recovering the sources, literary or oral, which the author of the Fourth Gospel made use of in composing his book, it would be necessary, at this point, to step aside and consider whether these verbal agreements can be explained apart from the assumption that he was to a very considerable extent dependent upon a written document, and that that document was our Gospel according to Saint Mark. For the understanding of the Fourth Gospel, it is, however, more important that we should establish and expose the kind of knowledge of the life and death of Jesus which the original readers of the gospel were presumed to possess. The conclusion seems unescapable. They knew a great deal: and what they knew, they knew, roughly at least, in the form in which it lies before us in the Marcan Gospel. That is to say, their knowledge was episodic; they were familiar with a large number of particular incidents and Sayings; they knew about chief priests and pharisees and elders, about the disciples and the brethren of the Lord; they knew that Jesus had been tried before Caiaphas, that Mary Magdalene had found the tomb empty; and, presumably, they knew about resurrection appearances. But, and this is the crucial point, it is surely quite clear that the author of the Fourth Gospel is not content to leave this knowledge in the form in which it was already possessed by his readers. His book must have been a disturbing book. The urgent questions are, What has he done? and, Why did he do it? Upon the answers we give to these questions depends our understanding of his gospel.

Before an attempt is made to answer these questions, a further comparison must be drawn between the Fourth Gospel and Saint Mark's Gospel. Hitherto, we have been concerned mainly with narrative. But, after all, the Fourth Gospel largely consists of discourses. At first sight, these discourses seem to have no parallel in any of the other gospels, and very particularly no parallel in Saint Mark's Gospel. Further analysis, however, reveals a somewhat strange situation. Though, it is true, the discourses contain few verbal agreements such as are found in the purely narrative sections, yet from time to time the author of the Fourth Gospel seems to be revolving round Sayings of Jesus that are known to us in the Gospel of Mark; Sayings which, if they are known to us, we have very good ground for supposing to have been known also to those for whom the gospel was originally written. These familiar Sayings are not so much quoted, or embedded in a discourse; rather, they constitute its theme. It is as though they had been so welded into the author's theology that they had ceased to be detached or even detachable. They lie no longer on the periphery, as though they were just Sayings; rather they have moved into the centre and have taken control, not merely of single discourses, but of the whole presentation of what Jesus was and is.[1] For example, the Marcan Saying: *For whosoever will save his life shall lose it; but whosoever shall lose his life for my sake and the gospel's, the same shall save it* (Mark viii. 35) no doubt underlies the discourse spoken in answer to the Greeks who wished to *see Jesus* (xii. 20–30) and becomes almost audible in *v.* 25. But it is in the Fourth Gospel not a Saying among other Sayings; in it, rather, is voiced the imperative of God from which no man can escape, be he Jew or Greek: *He that hateth his life in this world, shall keep it unto life eternal.* This is, moreover, the imperative accepted by Jesus Himself. Here too a Marcan passage becomes fundamental. The words spoken in Gethsemane and recorded in Mark xiv. 34–6 are not wrung from Jesus merely under pressure of the horror of death, they are not an episode in His life; rather they voice its meaning, the meaning of the hour of death to which His life moved of divine necessity: *For this cause came I unto this hour* (xii. 27). The words spoken in Gethsemane are therefore relevant words, relevant to Greek and Jew, and for this reason they are echoed not only in the Johannine narrative of the Arrest (xviii. 11) but also in the course of an extended answer to the request of the Greeks. The Word did veritably become *flesh*, and it is in this context that the traditional account of the episode in Gethsemane becomes quite ultimately relevant. *My soul is exceedingly sorrowful unto death* (Mark xiv. 34)—*Now is my soul troubled* (xii. 27). At the moment, however, we are concerned, not with the meaning of what the fourth Evangelist wrote, but simply with its relation to Sayings of Jesus which we know from the Marcan narrative, and with which he simply presumes his readers to be familiar.

A further illustration of the movement of a Saying from what may be regarded as the periphery of the record of the teaching of Jesus into the very centre is provided by the Marcan Saying *I will destroy this temple that is made with hands, and in three days I will build another made without hands.* ((In the Marcan narrative it is no more than the rumour of a saying of Jesus made use of by false witnesses whose witness *agreed not together* (Mark xiv. 56–8), a rumour that furnishes the chief priests with a gibe as Jesus hangs on the cross (Mark xv. 29). In the Fourth Gospel Jesus, when asked for a sign of His authority to cleanse the temple, replies *Destroy this temple, and in three days I will raise it up.* The Jews take Him literally, but the readers of the gospel, and His disciples after His resurrection, know that He spoke of the temple of His body (ii. 18–22).

[1] The remaining part of this chapter has been supplied from material left by the author except the passages in brackets, which have been written by the editor to complete the argument indicated.

Far from merely providing an improbable and inadequate accusation, the Saying now utters a resounding challenge that confidently anticipates the supreme act by which Judaism will be superseded and the true worship of the Father inaugurated, namely the resurrection of Jesus from the dead. The Saying has become inseparable from the major themes of the gospel.))

In the five chapters that contain the teaching of Jesus given to His disciples and His prayer on behalf of those who shall believe on Him three themes are intertwined: the themes of obedience, of prayer, and of persecution. But these are themes which are formulated in the *logia* recorded by Mark. At the conclusion of the Beelzebub speech the true brethren of Jesus are defined in the presence of those who *sat round about him* and over against the scribes and his family or kinsmen or friends: *Whosoever shall do the will of God, the same is my brother, and sister, and mother* (Mark iii. 35). In the Fourth Gospel this obedience to the will of God becomes the central theme of the Gospel, for it is the meaning of the teaching and action of Jesus; not, however, as though He merely heralded a divine imperative, but that He Himself was the imperative, the point in history where the imperative of God is made known. As the Son of God His words constitute that imperative, and obedience to Jesus is obedience to the Father, the refusal to believe in Him the ultimate rejection of God. In the Fourth Gospel, it is not merely that the Marcan *logion* finds its echo in the words spoken to the disciples: *Ye are my friends, if ye do the things which I command you—for all things that I heard from my Father I have made known unto you—If ye keep my commandments, ye shall abide in my love; even as I have kept my Father's commandments, and abide in his love* (xv. 10–15). The theme of obedience, of love, is, however, no easy road: it is the road of persecution and death: *Greater love hath no man than this, that a man lay down his life for his friends* (xv. 13). Say obedience, we must say love; say love, we must say death; and say death, we must say life. And so the Marcan *logion* becomes no chance saying occurring at a certain point in the oral or written tradition. It embraces the whole meaning of Jesus and of His faithful disciples: it is moreover the judgement that falls on all who refuse to hear, and not merely on those who once were confronted by Jesus in Palestine.

The twin themes of obedience and life therefore raise the theme of persecution and embrace it. We know the theme of persecution in Mark, for it is formulated in the midst of the eschatological speech which forms chapter xiii: *And ye shall be hated of all men for my name's sake: but he that shall endure unto the end, the same shall be saved* (Mark xiii. 13). In the Fourth Gospel this theme is woven into the great discourses at the Last Supper, now less in the context of eschatology than in the context of the present opposition between Jesus and His disciples and the world; in the opposition between the Holy Spirit of God and the world;

in the opposition between the Truth and the world. It is in this equally ultimate context that the Saying reappears: *A servant is not greater than his lord. If they persecuted me, they will also persecute you; if they kept my word, they will keep yours also. But all these things will they do unto you for my name's sake, because they know not him that sent me.—I have given them thy word; and the world hated them, because they are not of the world, even as I am not of the world.—Sanctify them through thy truth: thy word is truth.—When he, the Spirit of truth, is come, he will guide you into all truth* (xv. 20–3, xvii. 14–18, xvi. 13). But here again, the theme of persecution is all-embracing; it penetrates the whole subject-matter; it is not expressed in an isolated *logion*; it is in no sense detachable, as though it could be passed over as occurring in some strange, outworn eschatological speech that may be dismissed as the intrusion into the gospel of an early Christian fly-sheet, that has no necessary connection with the meaning of the life of Jesus. The theme of persecution is, in the Fourth Gospel, worked out theologically, that is to say it is pushed to its ultimate issue as the inevitable conflict between truth and falsehood. *He was in the world . . . and the world knew him not. He came unto his own and his own received him not* (i. 10, 11). The persecution of the disciples of Jesus in the world is therefore the test of their discipleship. This ultimate theological issue cannot be understood if a reference to persecution be confined merely to a single Saying of Jesus that may be pushed on to the periphery of historical reminiscence.

((Precisely the same is true of such an episode as the Feeding of the Five Thousand. At first sight this might appear no more than the incorporation into the Fourth Gospel of a synoptic story. Certain verbal similarities, indeed, suggest that the author used the Feeding of the Five Thousand as his primary source, with some reference to the Feeding of the Four Thousand, both in their Marcan presentation. But, however detached these stories may have been in their synoptic setting, the story of the Feeding of the Five Thousand is not permitted to appear detached in the Fourth Gospel. On the next day a great discourse is delivered which, starting from a reference to the Feeding, goes on to consider the problems which it raised and which it answered. The essential meaning of eating and drinking is examined, and at once the hope which these human actions hold out and never realize, the hope of food that will satisfy eternally instead of merely satiating for a day, becomes the issue. Against the background of the manna in the wilderness—which, though certainly the gift of God, was not itself the bread from heaven—the Feeding of the Five Thousand is now seen to point to Jesus as the ultimate answer to man's hunger, while the cognate action of labouring for the means of life is seen to point to the true work of God, which is to believe on Jesus, through whom eternal life is given. So the discourse presses on to the death of Jesus, to the food and drink which are His body and His blood, and while, on the one hand, the

Christian Eucharist hovers in the background of all that is said, on the other hand the theme looks forward, through the great discourses of chapters xiii–xvii, to the death of Jesus on the Cross, apart from which the Feeding of the Five Thousand cannot be fully understood. It is when this consummation is anticipated (vi. 52 sqq.) that the final issues are laid bare, and *many of the disciples went back and walked no more with him*, while Simon Peter confesses, on behalf of the Twelve, that Jesus has *the words of eternal life*. The fact that the author of Mark had already seen that these episodes demand an elucidation which they do not contain, in a larger context than they themselves present, only bears out the conclusion that the fourth Evangelist is not just incorporating a synoptic episode into his material, but is developing his material under the pressure of the pregnant synoptic episodes.))

There are two further illustrations of Marcan episodes moving into the centre of the whole theological structure of the Fourth Gospel. These are the Gethsemane narrative and the story of the Transfiguration. So fundamental, however, are the issues raised, that they are best deferred until other material relevant to the problem as a whole has been set out.

Hitherto we have been concerned with overlapping Marcan-Johannine material; first with formal overlapping and then with the more subtle overlapping of subject-matter. But attractive as it would be to regard the fourth Evangelist as moving theologically round the Marcan Gospel only, that would be to simplify the problem. For there are occasions when the Fourth Gospel approximates more closely to the Lucan than to the Marcan form of the tradition and occasions when it approximates to the Matthæan form, though these are fewer and less striking. There are also occasions when the Evangelist seems to be drawing into the centre of the structure of his narrative Sayings that are Matthæan-Lucan, but not Marcan; Sayings, that is to say, which we know from the Q material that has found its way into the gospels of Matthew and Luke. The background lying behind the Fourth Gospel is larger and better stocked than we might at first have supposed, and upon it the fourth Evangelist moves, not as an isolated figure, but, presumably, in company with his Christian readers.

((Just as there are words and phrases and even sentences which are characteristic of the earlier tradition as it is preserved in Mark, so are there words and phrases and even sentences which seem to reflect the earlier tradition as it is preserved in Matthew and Luke. John the Baptist's denial that he is *the Christ* (i. 20) seems to answer the general speculation *whether haply he were the Christ* (Luke iii. 15): his witness that *this is the Son of God* (i. 34) approximates closely to the declaration made in the Matthæan version of the Baptism narrative (Matt. iii. 17). In the Fourth Gospel, as in the First, Peter is apostrophized by Jesus (i. 42, cf. Matt. xvi. 18). The setting of the scene for the Feeding of the Five

Thousand speaks of a great crowd following Jesus (vi. 2), as crowds are said to have done on this occasion by Matthew (Matt. xiv. 13) and by Luke (Luke ix. 11). Jesus goes up *into the mountain* (vi. 3) as He did when about to feed the Four Thousand, according to Matthew (xv. 29). His *lifting up His eyes* (vi. 5) is recorded in words identical with Luke's account of His behaviour when about to address those gathered on the plain (Luke vi. 20). Mary anoints the feet of Jesus (xii. 3), as did the woman with the alabaster cruse according to Luke (Luke vii. 38). At the entry into Jerusalem the multitudes hail Jesus as *King* (xii. 13), as they do in Luke (xix. 38), and the prophecy of Zechariah is explicitly quoted (xii. 15), as in Matthew (Matt. xxi. 5). As in Luke, so in the Fourth Gospel Satan enters into Judas as he prepares to betray Jesus (xiii. 27; Luke xxii. 3). The prophecy that Peter will deny Him is recounted in the Fourth Gospel in words more similar to those of Luke than to those of the other synoptists (xiii. 38); Luke xxii. 34). Both Third and Fourth Gospels specify that the *right* ear of the high priest's servant was cut off (xviii. 10; Luke xxii. 50), though the Fourth Gospel recalls Matthew in recording the words of Jesus to Peter *Put up the sword into the sheath* (xviii. 11, cf. Matt. xxvi. 52: the Greek is not verbally identical). In John (xviii. 12) as in Luke (xxii. 54) Jesus is *seized* and *led away*, Joseph of Arimathæa is said to have been a 'disciple' of Jesus (xix. 38), information supplied also by Matthew (xxvii. 57), and the *taking* of the *body* of Jesus is described in similar language in the First and Fourth Gospels (xix. 40; Matt. xxvii. 59). It is, however, Luke who, like John (xix. 41) records that *never man had yet lain* in the sepulchre (Luke xxiii. 53). Finally, the words of the risen Jesus to the woman in Matthew (Matt. xxviii. 10), like His words to Mary (xx. 17), include mention of *my brethren*.

This list of words and phrases does not exhaust the significant similarities between the Fourth Gospel and those of Matthew and Luke. There are certain parallel incidents which suggest that they must at any rate have had a common origin. The resurrection appearance by the side of the lake (xxi. 1–14) must in some way be related to the Lucan story of the miraculous draft of fishes (Luke v. 1–11). The second 'sign', the Healing of the Nobleman's Son in Capernaum (iv. 46–54), seems to have clear affinities with the Q story of the Healing of the Centurion's Servant (Matt. viii. 5–13; Luke vii. 1–10): while the detail that Jesus was *besought . . . that he would come down and heal his son; for he was at the point of death* (iv. 47) is conspicuously paralleled in Luke (Luke vii. 2), the detail that the healing was accomplished *at that hour*, (iv. 53), i.e. at the moment when Jesus says *Go thy way* is paralleled in Matthew (Matt. viii. 13).

Moreover, as in the case of Marcan material, a number of Sayings of Jesus found in Matthew or Luke, or in both these gospels, while presenting no noteworthy verbal coincidence, are yet immediately relevant to the discourses in the Fourth Gospel, and sometimes appear to lie behind their thematic development. Setting aside the curious coincidence of Luke xv. 31 and John xvi. 15, both Luke and John record Jesus triumphing at the discomfiture of the powers of darkness: *I beheld Satan fallen as lightning from heaven* (Luke x. 18): *Now shall the prince of this world be cast out* (xii. 31). The importunity of the Jews in Solomon's porch: *How long dost thou hold us in suspense? If thou art the Christ, tell us plainly* (John x. 24) is no casual echo of the chief priests and scribes in Luke: *If thou art the Christ, tell us* (Luke xxii. 67), for the answer of Jesus, *I told you, and ye believed not* (x. 25), not only recalls the Lucan *If I tell you, ye will not believe* (Luke xxii. 67), but introduces the further development of a theme already broached in the 'Parable' of the Good Shepherd. Again, the solemn commission of the apostles in the Fourth Gospel, *Whose soever sins ye forgive, they are forgiven unto them; and whose soever sins ye retain, they are retained* (xx. 23), recalls the Matthæan *Whatsoever thou shalt bind on earth shall be bound in heaven: and whatsoever thou shalt loose on earth shall be loosed in heaven* (Matt. xvi. 19, cf. Matt. xviii. 18).

But the correspondence is sometimes more subtle and far-reaching. In the Parable of the Sheep and the Goats, only found in Matthew, the King, presumably the Son of man come in glory, addresses first those to the right and then those to the left, in each case allotting to them the final position which their attitude to Him in this world has determined, and the parable is summed up with the words *And these shall go away into eternal punishment, but the righteous into eternal life* (Matt. xxv. 46). In the Fourth Gospel this is the particular theme of chapter v. 19–29, where the full import of hearing the word of Jesus and believing is worked out. This word is not His, but the Father's. It is therefore judgement, or eternal life. It applies to all men, who are all, apart from God's word, dead. *The hour is coming, and now is, when the dead shall hear the voice of the Son of God: and they that hear shall live* (v. 25). It reaches to the depths of the tomb: *The hour cometh, in which all that are in the tombs shall hear his voice, and shall come forth; they that have done good, unto the resurrection of life; and they that have done ill, unto the resurrection of judgement* (v. 28, 29). But the theme is not confined to this passage. It reverberates through the rest of the chapter. It lies behind the end of every great discourse, for each great word of Jesus is a judgement, in that it compels those who hear, or read it, to belief or unbelief. It underlies the controversy with the Jews, coming to the surface in such a sentence as *If a man keep my word, he shall never see death* (viii. 52). It reappears in the so-called Parable of the Good Shepherd (x. 3, 4) and in the discourse that follows: *Ye believe not, because ye are not of my sheep. My sheep hear my voice, and I know them, and they follow me: and I give unto them eternal life; and they shall never perish, and no one shall snatch them out of my hand* (x. 26, 27). Finally, it is dramatically illustrated in the story of Lazarus: *And when he had thus*

79

*spoken, he cried with a loud voice, Lazarus, come forth. He that was dead came
forth . . .* (xi. 43, 44).

This universal theme of judgement, however, calls to mind other
Sayings preserved in the synoptic gospels. Matthew refers the Q Saying
about the blind to the Pharisees, with the pointed addition. *Let them
alone; they are blind guides* (Matt. xv. 14). The story of the Man born
blind concludes: *And Jesus said, For judgement came I into this world, that
they which see not may see; and that they which see may become blind. Those of
the Pharisees which were with him heard these things, and said unto him, Are
we also blind? Jesus said unto them, If ye were blind, ye would have no sin: but
now ye say, We see; therefore your sin remaineth* (ix. 39–41). The point of
the Matthæan *logion* is pressed home and expanded as a fitting cul-
mination to a great sign; none the less, some such *logion* as that preserved by Matthew seems to lie behind the Evangelist's procedure.

The Q Saying *He that receiveth you receiveth me, and he that receiveth me
receiveth him that sent me* (Matt. x. 40, cf. Luke x. 16), although paralleled
in Mark (cf. Mark ix. 37 and parallels), is clearly in some way related
to John xiii. 20, but this is but one example of a constantly recurrent
and constantly reworded refrain (v. 23 sq., xii. 44) that culminates in
the sustained argument of chapter xvii (cf. especially xvii. 23).

But there is an even more conspicuous example of the penetration
of the whole subject-matter of the Fourth Gospel by a theme latent in
Q in an isolated *logion*. The famous Saying *All things have been delivered
unto me of my Father: and no one knoweth the Son, save the Father; neither doth
any know the Father, save the Son, and he to whomsoever the Son willeth to reveal
him* (Matt. xi. 27; Luke x. 22) has often provoked commentators to style
it Johannine before John. And in the Fourth Gospel, indeed, there is
more than one striking analogy to it. *The Father loveth the Son, and hath
given all things into his hand* (iii. 35). *I know him; because I am from him,
and he hath sent me* (vii. 29). *I know my own, and mine own know me, even as
the Father knoweth me, and I know the Father* (x. 14, 15). *Even as thou gavest
him authority over all flesh, that whatsoever thou hast given him, to them he should
give eternal life. And this is life eternal, that they should know thee, the only
true God, and him whom thou didst send, even Jesus Christ* (xvii. 2, 3). But
none of these passages is separable, either from its immediate context,
or from the fundamental thesis of the gospel as a whole. The revelation
of the Father, the consequent judgement of those who hear the Son's
words which are His Word, the corollary that those who come to Jesus
are given Him by God, because only those informed by God can know
the Son, the double, identical relation between Father and Son and
Son and believers, the reiterated insistence that knowledge of Jesus is
knowledge of God, and that knowledge of God is eternal life, cannot
be confined to particular sentences or even to particular discourses.
None of the analogies instanced above was taken from chapters xiii–xvi,
yet these chapters cannot be read without the Q *logion* coming con-

tinually to mind (cf. especially xiii. 3, 18, xiv. 6, 7, 9 sqq., 20–4, xv. 15, xvi. 15, 27, 28). Indeed, every discourse insists upon some corollary of this definition of the Son as the complete and unique God-given revelation of the Father. And it is as integral a part of the thesis of the Prologue as it is of the climactic conclusion of chapter xx.

The subtle relation between this isolated Q *logion* and a major theme of the Fourth Gospel is paralleled in the case of the Marcan stories of the Agony in Gethsemane and the Transfiguration, which may now be considered. In Mark these episodes are equally isolated. There is no episodic parallel to the revelation of Jesus in His unearthly, God-authenticated glory: neither is there any episodic parallel to His humiliated prayer, in sore amazement and trouble, that the Father may remove the cup of suffering if it be His will. The stark antithesis in the relation between Jesus and the Father is set forth in these two events, which should have been luminous to the disciples who failed to understand, or slept. It is, of course, true that this antithesis is implicit in other parts of the synoptic material, as is witnessed, for instance, in the tension between the kingdom come and the kingdom to come, between the straitening of the Son of man, and His glory on the clouds of heaven. But in the synoptic tradition the Christological and theological antithesis that illuminates this tension is explicitly presented only in these two episodes. In the Fourth Gospel, however, there are no such episodes: the Transfiguration, as an event, is ignored; so is the Agony in the Garden. And that this is deliberate is suggested by the fact that, instead, the heavenly glory of Jesus and His troubled humiliation are shown to condition every part of His life. What the disciples should have apprehended on the mountain—the ultimate context of God's glory in which Jesus must be set—is the apostolic presupposition upon which the gospel is based: *the Word became flesh, and dwelt among us, and we beheld his glory* (i. 14); and this glory is not insisted upon by any emphasizing of the gracious achievements of the early ministry, but increases, rather, as the hour of suffering draws near, and is consummated in the supreme humiliation of the Passion. *Father, the hour has come*—the hour which for so long was *not yet*, although it meant arrest and death (vii. 30, viii. 20): which is reached with the open declaration that His death is at hand (xii. 23) and the great matter of His departure from the world (xiii. 1): which has already been anticipated in the manifestation of His glory (ii. 11, xi. 40), but now—*Glorify thy Son, that thy Son also may glorify thee* (xvii. 1). Conversely, the travail of Gethsemane is removed back into the body of the gospel. From the beginning the utter dependence of the Son upon the Father is rigorously maintained (e.g. iv. 34, v. 30, vi. 38). The Son does not seek His own glory (viii. 50). This antithesis is consciously held together everywhere, and is set out most strikingly in the chapter that immediately precedes the last great discourses. *Now is my soul troubled; and what shall I say?*

*Father, save me from this hour. But for this cause came I unto this hour. Father, glorify thy name. There came therefore a voice out of heaven, I have both glorified it, and will glorify it again. . . . Jesus answered and said . . . I, if I be lifted up from the earth, will draw all men unto myself. This he said, signifying by what manner of death he should die* (xii. 27, 28, 30, 32, 33). The episodes of Transfiguration and Agony have not been omitted through ignorance or by an oversight. Rather, woven together in one consistent whole, they control the Christology of the Fourth Gospel. Yet, in the Gospel of Mark, their paradoxical statement of the double relation of the Son to the Father had already held most penetrating and unavoidable implications for the proper understanding of the isolated episodes of the synoptic tradition. The procedure of the fourth Evangelist may be said to have been demanded by the signal fact that the synoptic tradition contained stories of the Transfiguration and the Agony, side by side with episodic material whose latent theological implications became fully luminous in the light of these stories. To do justice to these stories, therefore—and to the episodic material—it was necessary that the material should be presented with its implications made fully and universally manifest, and that the stories themselves, whose significance would be misunderstood were they thought to be self-contained, should disappear.))

That the author of the Fourth Gospel had the three synoptic gospels before him when he composed his gospel is most improbable, for his relation to them is not that of an editor. But that he was familiar with the synoptic material, and even with its form, is certain. Yet it is perhaps even more important that he presumes this synoptic material to be less before the eyes of his readers than in their heads. He presumes, in fact, that it is in their hearts, so that he expects them to follow him when he moves round and round it, when he alludes to it, and when he writes it down, and most particularly when he refashions it. Yet the energy of the Fourth Gospel lies not in these synoptic passages, but in their refashioning in the context in which they are narrated, in what follows as a consequence of them, in what immediately precedes them, and finally in their clear theological setting. This allusiveness to what the readers already know is exceedingly difficult for us to disentangle, because we know no more of primitive Christian tradition than has found its place in the synoptic gospels. There must, however, have been a far wider circle of oral tradition, since otherwise it is difficult to explain much that stands in the Fourth Gospel. There must presumably have been incidents in the oral tradition centring round Cana of Galilee, and there must presumably have been more Samaritan material than has found a place in our first three gospels.

The Christians for whom the Fourth Gospel was written were in possession of a great deal of miscellaneous information concerning the

Lord's life, so miscellaneous that even when it had been arranged by Mark or Matthew or Luke, it still remained episodic, far more so if, in addition to these documents and perhaps others (Luke i. 1), there were also further edited episodes and traditions. Judging from all this material, Jesus must have seemed the Messiah indeed, but a very Jewish Messiah; a worker of miracles, but—yes, precisely—a worker of miracles; one who demanded faith, yes, but that they might be—healed, or in order that men possessed by demons might be restored to health; a herald of the Kingdom of God, yes, precisely, a prophet of the Kingdom which was to come, but which was continually deferred to a later date; a herald of the End which was to appear visibly—but which had not yet appeared; a Messiah who spoke in parables though interpreting everything openly to His disciples—but whose open teaching was no-where recorded; a teacher of an ethical demand, which men were required to fulfil—but which was either too hard (Mark x. 26) or too easy. This presentation of the life of Jesus in fragmentary episodes must have been a grave danger at the turn of the first century, for the scattered Christian communities had no generally accepted creed that would keep the evangelical episodes in a strict theological context, nor was their worship, whatever forms it may have taken, held to its final theme by an authoritative reading, say, of the opening verses of the Fourth Gospel. No doubt there were lurking, somewhere in the background, the Pauline epistles and perhaps writings such as the Epistle to the Hebrews, but to judge by 2 Peter the teaching of Paul must have seemed difficult and 'Pauline' (2 Pet. iii. 15, 16), and there is no evidence to show that writings like the Epistle to the Hebrews were widely known. The theologians who were to address themselves to this problem were to emerge later. There was as yet no Saint Ignatius to struggle for the meaning of the tradition. And so the ordinary Christian must have thrown himself loyally back on an oral tradition of the Lord's life, or on such ordered literary arrangements—'gospels'—of this tradition as were available to him.

No doubt most Christians were satisfied with this state of affairs: they repeated the stories that were the basis of their peculiarly Christian life. But there were others, and these seemingly the most intelligent, who desired more than this Jesus of oral and written tradition, who desired to be rid of this flesh and blood, and to move out into the direct realm of the Spirit. The choice seemed clear: either the Spirit or the flesh of the Jesus of history as portrayed in the tradition of the Church, in the tradition of the eyewitness. Spirit or History: this was the dilemma. Spirit or flesh: these were the alternatives. But the author of the Fourth Gospel saw the matter wholly otherwise. *Flesh*, history, aye, the flesh and blood of Jesus, *profiteth nothing*, if it be mere observable history, if it be that which was seen by the Pharisees, who also were eyewitnesses, if it be that which was seen by Pilate and by those others who neither believed nor knew. The flesh profiteth nothing if it was seen as flesh even by disciples who were apostles. Faith profiteth nothing, if it be faith which moves finally towards mere physical healing. Stories of miracles are profitless if they be mere stories of miracles. Moral exhortation is profitless if it be merely moral exhortation; if it be merely a series of commandments however impressively arranged in a sermon on a mountain or in a charge to disciples. Eschatology is profitless, if it be centred upon a 'day in a series of days', if, that is to say, it remains within the orbit of flesh. Parables are just stories if they do not revolve round a theme which must be believed in order to be known and seen. If the piety of the Christians, if the piety of the Church, turns upon, and is exhausted in, a series of historical episodes, however well they may be attested by eyewitnesses, it is a piety, a knowledge, *from below*, historical, and is the same kind as the knowledge of the Pharisees or the Jews. It is, in fact, darkness and misunderstanding. If the flesh of Jesus, if His appearance on the field of history, were exhausted in history and were to be understood as information to be collected together, then the Jews were right, and the claims He made for Himself were no more than self-made claims: Thou being a man, being flesh and blood, makest thyself equal with God. Likewise the gospel proclaimed by the Church is blasphemy. From so grave a misunderstanding of the Jesus of history, and of the tradition, oral and written, of His life, the author of the Fourth Gospel determines to rescue his readers. But he will not do this by throwing the Jesus of history to the winds—that is proving disastrous—but by insisting that the tradition itself has a meaning peering out of it at every point, a meaning which is 'beyond history', and which alone makes sense of history. To disclose this underlying meaning of the tradition he wrote his gospel. The freedom with which he did so is nothing less than staggering to us who have been brought up within the strait fetters of the 'Historical Method', who have almost completely lost the sense for the Problem of Theology, which is to set forth the non-historical truth that underlies all history and which is almost apparent in the life and death of Jesus. How can non-historical truth be set forth save in non-historical form? We continually demand that an evangelist should narrate nothing but observable history, which means that we are demanding of him that he should not be an evangelist. Nor is the fourth Evangelist here unique. The earlier gospels did not, in fact, narrate only what any eyes were able to observe, though they might seem to have done so. If they had, how could they have recorded the voice from Heaven at the Baptism, if they had not meant thereby that Jesus was the Son of God, even though no one had ever believed it, and that this is the Truth about Him? Or what do they intend to convey in the narrative of the Transfiguration, save that there was a relation between Jesus and the Father, visible to no human eye, a relation which conditioned His whole visible activity and which was partially apprehended, but altogether misunderstood, by the disciples? *He received from God the Father honour and glory when there came such a voice to him from the excellent glory saying, This is my beloved son in whom I am well pleased* (2 Pet. i. 17). No doubt these incidents could be dismissed as being themselves merely historical episodes, it being supposed that the voice at the Baptism was imagined by Jesus or by John the Baptist, and that the glory of the transfiguration was an experience subject to all manner of historical-psychological explanations. But the earlier evangelists did intend their readers to understand that Jesus was and is the Son of God, and that He was so because God had declared Him to be so. They were undoubtedly trying to convey absolute, not relative, truth, however inadequately. This is what the Fourth Evangelist makes so clear in order that all possible misunderstanding may be avoided. Jesus is the Son of God, not because He as a man claimed to be so, but because God sent Him into the world as His Son. Nor is the glory of this sonship something episodic or psychological; it cannot be observed by an historian or analysed by a psychologist. It is accessible only to those who believe, and only in this context can the author of the Fourth Gospel speak of knowing or seeing. But at this point we must be careful, for the precipice yawns. The visible, historical Jesus is the place in history where it is demanded that men should believe, and where they can so easily disbelieve, but where, if they disbelieve, the concrete history is found to be altogether meaningless, and where, if they believe, the fragmentary story of His life is woven into one whole, manifesting the glory of God and the glory of men who have been created by Him. There is no escape from history possible for the author of the Fourth Gospel, just as there can be no historical materialism in the presence of Jesus. He says, and He means, that men must eat His flesh and drink His blood, that they must be brought into full relationship with His stark historicity. But this relationship has no meaning and remains unprofitable unless the Spirit be veritably encountered there, unless that precise life is met by the Life that is eternal. *The Word became flesh*— dangerous language when divorced from its context in the Fourth Gospel, for the author does not mean that Spirit was turned into flesh and therefore became profitless, or that the Spirit or the Word of God became a thing visible to the historical eye. He does, however, mean that the flesh of Jesus was the place where men did, and still do, believe and disbelieve; where the division between those who believe and those who do not believe becomes an ultimate division between the children of God and the children of the Devil. Any relative distinction between faith and unbelief is unthinkable.

# V. THE AUTHORITY OF THE FOURTH GOSPEL

Adolf von Harnack. *Das 'Wir' in den Johanneischen Schriften.* Sitzungs-
berichte der Preussischen Akademie der Wissenschaften (Philo-
sophisch-historische Klasse), 1923, pp. 95–113.
K. H. Rengstorf. *Apostolat und Predigtamt.* Tübinger Studien zur
Systematischen Theologie, 1934.
*Theologisches Wörterbuch zum Neuen Testament:* edited by Gerhard
Kittel. Article: ἀπόστολος, ἀποστέλλειν.

The author of the Fourth Gospel does not emerge from his audience
in order to voice their opinions and to record them for the benefit of
posterity. He confronts his readers and speaks to them with authority.
Assuming their readiness to hear, he expects that they will understand
and accept what he has to say. It is therefore not only the modern reader
who is separated from the author of the Fourth Gospel by a wide gulf:
the original readers of the gospel also stood in the presence of one who
spoke to them with impersonal, almost hieratic, unapproachability.
And yet, this wide gulf can be, and has been, bridged. Those who have
attended and heard, who have believed and apprehended, who have
known and seen what he has seen, stand by his side in an unbroken
union and fellowship over against those who do not believe and do not
understand. The author of the Fourth Gospel is separated from his
readers only in order that *they all may be one*. And so it comes about, as
Harnack had noticed, that in his first Epistle he occupies a position
nearer to his readers than does the writer of any other New Testament
book. This separation and union is, no doubt, something of a paradox;
but it is a paradox that lies at the very heart of the Johannine writings.

Who, then, was the author of the Fourth Gospel? How did he come
to speak so authoritatively to his readers? And why, in spite of this
authority, did he determine to address them, not in the first person
singular but in the first person plural? Why, that is to say, though he
refused to be altogether buried in his work, did he so strictly preserve
his anonymity? These are troublesome questions; and it is tempting,
having formulated them, to pass on quickly to an interpretation of the
Gospel and leave its author to be known simply as 'The Author of the
Fourth Gospel'—especially tempting, since the problem of authorship
has occupied too large, and the steady work of interpretation too small,

a place in many recent Johannine studies, with the inevitable consequence that the theological world is 'on edge'. But, even if we do press
on quickly to interpretation, the question remains, since it is the interpretation of the book that itself raises the question of authorship. The
Fourth Gospel was not written merely because its author had something
to say, but because he possessed the necessary authority to demand a
hearing. It is this authority that underlies the Johannine Writings and
conditions their interpretation. But, when this is said, the problem of
the authorship of the Fourth Gospel is less the difficulty of attaching
a name to the man who wrote it—this may be beyond our capacity—
than of recovering a proper sense for what it really meant when Greek-
speaking Christians at the beginning of the second century were confronted by a man able to speak to them with commanding authority
and at the same time, at least in his writings, to submerge himself so
completely that he hardly appears above the horizon as a clearly
recognizable personality. Is this the authority of a mystic? Is it the
authority of a man possessed of important historical reminiscences of
the life of Jesus of Nazareth? Or does he speak with authority because
of some strange mingling of mysticism and historical memory received
at first or at second hand, and held together by a penetrating, unifying
power of meditation? These may be correct alternatives: but, if so, the
question why he does not appear as a clear, independent person still
remains unanswered. It still remains to be explained why he threw
himself back upon the first person plural, and why he should have
done so in such a manner as to convey the impression that in the 'we'
with whom he is in some way associated, lies the key both to his
authority and to his general avoidance of the pronoun 'ego'.

Both the gospel (i. 14) and the First Epistle (i. 1–4) open with an
impressive statement that the Truth which is to be set forth has been
veritably seen and veritably apprehended. Not merely seen, but seen
and—apprehended. The Truth is the Glory of the *Word of God*, of the
*Word of Life*, which was in the Beginning and from the Beginning *with
God*. That which has been seen and apprehended is the Truth apart
from which nothing has any existence at all. Strictly speaking, therefore, what has been seen is altogether invisible, or rather, is apprehended only by faith. Consequently, those who have seen and do testify
are those who have *known and believed* (1 John iv. 14–16). And yet, the
Truth is not apprehended merely by some unfettered exercise of faith,
and sight is not limited to an activity of the spiritual eye; nor is knowledge merely a matter of mystical perception. There was a place where
the glory of the Word of God became luminous, a time when the Word
of Life became almost transparent. There were men who saw *flesh*:
who with their ears heard words and with their eyes saw deeds done,
and who with their hands *handled* Him who spake the words and did the
deeds. These men, having heard and seen and felt, were finally led to

apprehend: they believed and knew and saw the glory of the Word of God, the glory of the *only begotten of the Father, full of grace and truth*. Forged into one fellowship or communion by their apprehension of what had been *manifested* to them, these men *bore witness*. They declared what they had seen and heard; and they dared to announce to the world that fellowship with them is—*fellowship with the Father and with his Son, Jesus Christ*. Nor was their witness merely by word of mouth. There were writings in which *these things* were set forth. This does not, of course, necessarily mean that the original disciples of Jesus wrote gospels; but it does mean that, when the Johannine Writings were written, the apostles had not been deprived of the capacity to write letters. *We declare that which we have seen and heard . . . and we write these things* (1 John i. 3, 4). Of one of these men it is, moreover, expressly stated that he not only bears permanent witness, but also *wrote these things*. But even he is not permitted to remain an isolated, independent individual. His witness is at once embraced and authenticated by a first person plural: *We know that his witness is true* (xxi. 24). With this solemn 'we', and with this majestic authorization, the Fourth Gospel ends as it had begun.

And so, behind the author of the Fourth Gospel there lies a witness by word and by pen which it is his purpose to preserve and to present to his readers as possessing supreme authority. But the use of the first person plural in the Johannine Writings is more complicated than is at first sight suggested in the opening verses of the gospel and of the first Epistle. The pronoun 'we' is capable of contraction to an 'ego' and of expansion far beyond the narrow circle of the original disciples: this double movement taking place without any diminution of authority. (The peculiar value of Harnack's paper lies in the care with which he has insisted both on this contraction and on this expansion.) Thus in the controversy with Diotrephes the writer of the third Epistle uses the first person plural to express the authority with which he himself speaks and writes: *Wherefore, if I come, I will remember his deeds . . . prating against us . . . and ye know that our record is true* (3 John 10, 12). Whereas, contrariwise, in the first Epistle, so far from thinking of his readers merely as a second party to be addressed, he sets them by his side and embraces them within the sacred circle denoted by the first person plural, so that the whole Christian community confronts the World and bears authoritative witness to it. So intimate is this unity that the first person plural, occurring as it does in 47 out of the 105 verses, very nearly—though not altogether (1 John ii. 13, 26)—drives out the epistolary distinction between 'I' or 'we' and 'you': *And this is his commandment, That we should believe on the name of his Son Jesus Christ, and love one another, as he gave us commandment. . . . Marvel not, my brethren, if the world hate you. We know that we have passed from death unto life, because we love the brethren. . . . If we receive the witness of men, the witness of God is greater: for this is the witness of*

God which he hath testified of his Son (1 John iii. 23, 13, 14, v. 9, cf. iii. ?, iv. 4–7).

It would, however, be altogether to misunderstand both the authoritative 'ego' that appears so confidently in the second and third Epistles and the equally authoritative but generalized 'we' that is characteristic of the First Epistle, if it were supposed that the author of the Johannine Writings was capable at difficult moments of falling back either upon some personal, individual authority of his own or upon a peculiar confidence in the organic, but equally independent, authority of the Church as a whole. And the misunderstanding would remain even if the word 'independent' were glossed and interpreted by the word 'spiritual'. The authority both of the 'ego' and of the generalized 'we' is a derived authority, properly intelligible only upon the basis of the particular first person plural of the original disciples of Jesus. It is their witness, rather than some esoteric or meditative authority of his own, that enables the author of the Johannine Writings to exercise authority; and it is this same apostolic witness, rather than any authority inherent in a growing organism, that is able to bind the whole believing Christian community into one fellowship, and to provide it with the capacity to make known to the world the meaning of the mission of Jesus and to declare the love of God. How important the creative witness of the original disciples was to the author of the Johannine Writings is surely obvious from the very simple fact, often neglected in this context, that the man who was apparently normally accustomed to speak and to write letters was compelled, in order to make his meaning clear, to compose a gospel. Yet, in the gospel which he composed, not only has he with great conviction dispossessed himself, but also—formally at least—removed right on to the periphery of his book those Greek-speaking Christians in whose midst he was living and working. In the Fourth Gospel attention is concentrated upon the mission of Jesus in Palestine and upon His communications to His original disciples; concentrated, moreover, in such a manner as to make it clear that those who have not seen and yet have believed are what they are because there once were men who believed because they did actually see (xx. 29). The writer of the gospel turned back to the record of Jesus and His disciples, not because he had only an historical interest in those earlier days, but in order that his own fellow-Christians *might believe that Jesus is the Christ, the Son of God*; and that believing they *might have life through his name* (xx. 31). Or rather, he turned back to that particular history, because there that which lies beyond historical observation was in fact made known and accepted and believed, and because this apprehension remained the authoritative basis of his own witness and of the general witness of the Church. Therefore it was only after he and the Greek-speaking Christians had been thrust on to the periphery that it was possible for them to return and occupy the position they hold in the Epistles. And they move into this position because, in the perspective of the gospel, there would be men who *shall believe* through the preaching of the original disciples—*through their word . . . that they may all be one* (xvii. 20, 21). This apostolic foundation of the Church conditions the movement and 'lay-out' of the gospel; its horizon narrowing until Jesus, after the final rejection by the Jewish authorities and by the crowds, is depicted alone with His disciples, entrusting to them His authoritative mission to the world in the power of the Holy Spirit of Truth (xiii–xvii, xx. 22, 23). Only after this severe concentration does the author of the Fourth Gospel permit his readers to occupy their proper position as fish caught by apostolic fishermen and as sheep under the care of an apostolic shepherd. Only, that is to say, at the end of the gospel does he let it be known—and even then in figurative language—that the *greater work* which the disciples of Jesus will do in His name (xiv. 12–14) and the *fruit* which they have been *chosen* and *ordained* to *go and bring forth* (xv. 16) are those Greek-speaking, gentile men and women for whom he has written his book and whose existence he had foreshadowed in the movement of the Samaritans to Jesus, the Saviour of the world (iv. 42, cf. vii. 35, xii. 20, 21).

The supposition that the author of the Johannine Writings provided the pronoun 'we' with two, if not three, distinct and independent meanings, and was consequently pulled in different directions by two, if not three, incompatible notions of authority, is difficult to maintain. Are we really to believe that there flits across his mind from time to time the thought of the authority of the original disciples, but that it is more generally submerged by the thought of the authority of the whole community of his contemporary fellow-Christians who now believe and know, and even now may be said to see the Truth; and who by virtue of their faith and knowledge authoritatively confront the world and speak over it both the condemnation and the love of God? And do we then finally reach the author's more settled conviction when at long last in the Third Epistle, in the controversy with Diotrephes, he stands forward himself with commanding authority and invests his own 'ego'—*when I come*—with the dignity of the first person plural—*our record* (meaning *my record*) is true? This tripartite analysis of the notions of authority lying at the back of the Johannine Writings breaks down, however, when the purpose of the gospel is borne steadily in mind. Neither the believing Christian community nor the author himself has been born out of the air. In spite of the notable, daring description of the Christians as *born of God*, as believing in Him, as knowing Him, as possessing Life and walking in Light, and even as *doing no sin*; in fact as men who are marked out and recognizable by the gift of the Holy Spirit of God: in spite of all this, the Christians are what they are and remain true to themselves only if they preserve the commandments of Jesus; only if they confess that He came in *flesh* (1 John iv. 2), that

He came *by water*, and not by water only, but *by blood* (1 John v. 6, 7); only if, confessing their sins, they acknowledge that they are cleansed and forgiven through *the blood of Jesus*, God's Son (1 John i. 7–10). The Christian is at once removed from the Truth and from the company of the Johannine 'we', is not born of God and does not overcome the world, but is rather overcome by it, the moment he ceases to believe that Jesus is the Son of God. With the mention of the name 'Jesus', a strict historical emphasis moves into the centre of the Johannine picture of the Church, an emphasis that inevitably carries with it the authority of the witness of the original disciples who saw and heard and touched. Once the name of Jesus has been spoken or written, their authority, so far from being submerged by the vigorous faith of later Christians, becomes central, precisely in order that exuberant independence in the Church may be subjected to proper direction and control. For this reason, the authoritative witness of the original disciples, of the strictly apostolic 'we', governs the whole edifice of the Christian community and alone is able to bring into being the authoritative first person plural of the general body of Christians. The Church that authoritatively confronts the world must first have been confronted and created by the witness and apprehension of the apostles; and it is this creative submission, rather than some supposed investing of himself with a majestic, wellnigh arrogant 'we', which explains the authority of the man who set himself to oppose Diotrephes, to encourage the *elect lady* (2 John) and to command *children* and *fathers* and *young men* alike (1 John ii. 13, 14). A properly Christian 'we' and a properly Christian 'ego' come into being only when those who believe have accepted, and been created by, the witness and apprehension of the original apostles. The Fourth Gospel was written in order that the Christians of a later generation might be confronted by the authority of this earlier witness and in order that, created by it, they also might be invested with apostolic authority. And so it comes about that the phrases in which the author of the Johannine Writings describes the Christians echo his description of the apostles: *And we have seen and do testify that the Father sent the Son to be the Saviour of the world. . . . And we have known and believed the love that God hath to us. . . . We are of God: he that knoweth God heareth us. . . . Hereby know we that we dwell in him, and he in us, because he hath given us of his Spirit* (1 John iv. 14, 16, 6, 13). *. . . . As the Father hath sent me, even so send I you. And when he had said this, he breathed on them, and saith unto them, Receive ye the Holy Ghost: whose soever sins ye forgive, they are forgiven unto them; whose soever sins ye retain, they are retained* (John xx. 21–3). So firmly is this perspective preserved that even the duty of Christians to love one another is set forth as no self-evident truth. They are to love one another *as he gave us commandment* (1 John iii. 23). That Jesus did give this commandment to His disciples is, of course, most carefully recorded in the gospel (xiii. 34, xv. 12). Whether these were, in fact, authentic words spoken by Jesus to His disciples, is not at the moment the point. The point is that, in the perspective of the Johannine Writings, the first person plural means primarily the original disciples of Jesus, and that it is precisely this plural that is capable of expansion to a general 'we' and of contraction to a particular 'ego'. This expansion and contraction is, however, possible only within the sphere of those who, though belonging to a later generation, have been so completely created by apostolic witness and formed by apostolic obedience that they are veritably carried across into the company of the original disciples of Jesus and invested with the authority of their mission. In this context the possibility has to be taken seriously into account that a man, not himself one of the original disciples of Jesus, may have been so completely absorbed by their testimony as to have been driven not only to bear witness to the world, but also to the Church, and to have done this with true, though derived, apostolic authority.

This pressing back to the original disciples of Jesus, as constituting the ground-bass underlying the authoritative melody of the Johannine Writings, may, however, be only too easily misunderstood. Important as their testimony is, it too is marked by submission. There is no free and independent apostolic position. In the Johannine Writings the apostles are neither great men, nor are they heroes. No single one of them—not even Peter, not even the Beloved Disciple—provides the author with a suitable theme for the exercise of any latent biographical skill he may have possessed. The original disciples form the link between Jesus and the believing Christians, they have no other importance, no other right to exist. They *followed* and *saw*. In these two verbs their significance is quite finally described. They followed *Jesus* (i. 37–42, xxi. 19–22); and they saw *his glory* (i. 14, 15). For this reason, in the gospel, the pronoun 'ego' belongs rightly only to Jesus. He alone speaks with proper authority, and only in dependence upon Him do the pronouns 'we' and, in the Epistle, 'I' possess any abiding significance. How strictly this dependence is maintained and how categorically it is demanded is seen in the final discourses of the gospel: *As the branch cannot bear fruit, except it abide in the vine; no more can ye, except ye abide in me.—If a man abide not in me, he is cast forth as a branch, and is withered; and men gather them, and cast them into the fire, and they are burned.—Apart from [severed from] me, ye can do nothing* (xv. 1–10, cf. xiv. 6, 21, 26, xv. 16, 17, 27, xvi. 33, xvii. 18). The use of the first person plural in iii. 11 and ix. 4 refers therefore primarily to the words and actions of Jesus: it embraces also the teaching and actions of the believing Christians in so far as they echo and reflect and reproduce what was once manifested by Jesus to His disciples (cf. iv. 22). Similarly the word 'Apostle' is never permitted to degenerate into a title. Indeed, the noun is only once used (xiii. 16), and seems to be avoided of set purpose in the passage where reference is made to the Twelve (vi. 60–71). This is surely not because the author disapproves of the word any more than he can be held to have disapproved of the words 'faith', 'knowledge', 'gospel' or 'repentance', but because he is concerned to carry it back to the point where its proper meaning can be understood. The 'disciples'—this is the normal Johannine word—were apostles only because they were 'sent' by Jesus and entrusted with His mission. The verb (ἀποστέλλειν) governs the whole gospel, just as the Hebrew verb (שׁלח: the noun שׁליח comes into prominence only with the later writings of the Rabbis) had governed the whole prophetic literature of the Old Testament. But it is the mission of Jesus upon which the whole emphasis is laid. He, the Apostle of God, is the point round which the whole language and reality of mission revolve. Jesus is *He whom God sent* (iii. 34, v. 36, vi. 29, 57, vii. 29, viii. 42, x. 36, xi. 42, xvii. 3). The mission of the disciples is therefore His mission, not their own. Their work is altogether dependent upon what has already been done: *I sent you to reap that whereon ye have not laboured* (iv. 38). Believing in the mission of Jesus, the disciples are sent into the world in order that the world may know that Jesus is God's Apostle. This is the theme of the seventeenth chapter: *As thou didst send me into the world, even so sent I them into the world.—That the world may believe that thou didst send me.—That the world may know that thou didst send me.—They* [the disciples] *believed that thou didst send me.—These knew that thou didst send me* (xvii. 18, 21, 23, 8, 25). The final commission and authorization of the disciples are consequently set quite firmly within this vast context of the mission of Jesus, the Son of God: *As the Father hath sent me, even so send I you. And when he had said this, he breathed on them* . . . (xx. 21). In spite of the *greater* works that they will do, they have to be reminded that *an apostle is not greater than he that sent him*. This generalization—and it is here, in this negation, that the noun most significantly occurs—covers not only the disciples, but also Jesus Himself. There is no free apostleship, for independence is the mark neither of a prophet nor of one who has received the gift of the Spirit (1 John iv. 1–3).

It might seem that with the name 'Jesus' we have reached the point at which the Johannine Writings come to rest; that we have arrived at the proper, final ground of their authority. But the author's theological perception is far too sensitive for him to allow his readers for one moment to suppose that he has avoided apostolic biographies only in order to write a supreme biography of the man Jesus, the Apostle of God, and that, with this in view, he has skilfully put together, in literary form, a series of reminiscences of the original disciples. It is not the extreme difficulty of defending the historicity of much that is recorded in the Fourth Gospel that forbids its being regarded as a serious biography. What forbids this explanation is the consistent and avowed theme of the book itself. The reader of the Fourth Gospel is not brought to rest with the visible, historical figure of Jesus. He does not end with His flesh, and certainly not with an independent, authoritative 'ego' of the man Jesus. That this is the goal to which or from which the Johannine Writings move is as categorically denied as is the independent authority of the apostles themselves. *The flesh profiteth nothing —The Son can do nothing of himself—I can of myself do nothing—If I bear witness of myself, my witness is not true* (vi. 63, v. 19, 30, 31). These are not casual, unimportant statements. They are the theological turning-points of the Johannine apprehension. Nor does the authoritative witness of the original disciples lie in what they actually saw, but in what they believed and knew as a consequence of what they had seen. Following Jesus, they heard what He said and saw what He did; but as Apostles, as the veritable 'we' of the Johannine Writings, they saw—the glory of the Word of God, of the Son of God. It was this faith and knowledge which alone gave them any apostolic authority at all, and which laid open the possibility of 'blessedness' for those who had not seen and yet had believed. Since the faith and knowledge of the original disciples succeeded to, but was not contemporary with, this following of Jesus from place to place, the author of the Fourth Gospel, like Saint Mark, shows no tendency to draw an idealistic picture of them in that early period. In spite of what is recorded in vi. 66–71, their faith remained tenuous and uncertain. They did not understand (xi. 12–16, xiii. 38, xiv. 8, 9); and at the end they left Jesus alone, and returned to their own homes (xvi. 29–33), even to their fishing (xxi. 1–3). Only the Beloved Disciple attains an anticipatory apostolic faith; and even he returned to Galilee to fish (xxi. 7). This picture of the disciples, who saw and did not see, is all the more striking, because the author of the Fourth Gospel—here contradicting the natural meaning of Saint Mark—roundly asserts that the disciples from the beginning recognized Jesus as the Messiah (i. 40–51). In the context of the gospel as a whole, this means, however, no more than that its author was fully aware how unsatisfactory the title 'Christ' was in the mouth of a Jew (cf. vii. 41)—or indeed of a Samaritan (iv. 25)—until it had been reformed and reinterpreted in the perspective of the Sonship of Jesus: *These things are written, that ye may believe that Jesus is the Christ —the Son of God* (xx. 31).

The disciples did, however, become confident witnesses. They did finally understand. They did apprehend the Truth which gave consistent, unified meaning to their scattered, isolated historical reminiscences. Only one of them was lost (xvii. 12). But this took place afterwards, through the gift of the Holy Spirit who recalled to their minds what had been said and done, and led them to apprehend its meaning and truth (xvi. 12–15, cf. xiv. 26, xv. 26, i. 31, ii. 22, xii. 16). Thus the ultimate authority underlying the Johannine Writings is strictly theological. The author refuses to permit his readers any rest until they have passed behind himself, behind the Church, to the Apostles, and behind them again to the flesh of Jesus, the son of man, and behind the visible, historical Jesus to the glory of the Son, of the Word, of God; until, that is to say, they come to rest in God, *whom no man hath seen at any time* (1 John iv. 12), but who manifested Himself in His Son, and through His Son to the world (xiv. 9).

# VI. THE FOURTH GOSPEL
# IN THE SECOND CENTURY

LIGHTFOOT, J. B. *The Apostolic Fathers.*
STANTON, V. H. *The Gospels as Historical Documents*, vol. i.
BAUER, W. *Rechtgläubigkeit und Ketzerei im ältesten Christentum.*
STREETER, B. H. *The Primitive Church.*

THE purpose of the Johannine Writings was to preserve in the midst of Greek-speaking Christianity at the beginning of the second century the authority of the faith and apprehension of the original disciples of Jesus; and consequently, to retain thereby the authority over the Church of the 'flesh' of Jesus the Apostle of God, in whose life and death the glory of God was manifested, not only to the original apostles, but also through them to the world. This would seem, at first sight, to be no unexpected or unreasonable aim; for, as Professor Lietzmann has said in his pamphlet 'Paulus'—reprinted from vol. i. of his *History of the Ancient Church*, but with the significant addition of this opening sentence: 'The Church has remembered and revered the Twelve Apostles, not only as the pillars upon which it rests, but also as exercising supreme authority over it. The Church is, moreover, fully aware that they occupy this position, not as isolated personalities, but as a corporate body.' The ancient Church did not, however, arrive at this settled conviction without acute, disruptive controversy. The controversies in the second century were so serious and of so fundamental a character that it must be asked whether they are at all intelligible if the Primitive Church did in fact possess any known tradition of apostolic solidarity. In the story of the advance of Christianity into the Greek world, were not the original disciples of Jesus of quite trivial importance? Peter may, indeed, have travelled about; and so perhaps may John. But what of the others? Was it not, after all, Paul who not only carried Christianity to the Gentiles, but was the real founder of Catholic Christianity? And is not therefore at least one great personality of far more importance than any unified and original and creative apostolic faith and apprehension? Are we not therefore bound to say with Dr. Streeter: 'The History of Catholic Christianity during the first five centuries is the history of a progressive standardization of a diversity which had its origin in the Apostolic age'; or at least, with Loisy, to limit the tradition which the Church felt itself bound to preserve to the 'continuity within the Christian communities of monotheistic faith, of Jewish-evangelical ethics, and of the worship of Jesus Christ (*La Naissance du Christianisme*, p. 416)? But it is exceedingly difficult to stop here. We are bound to go on and say that, if all these questions be answered in the affirmative, then it was the author of the Fourth Gospel who, in order to check the disruptive tendencies in the Church of his day, created the notion of apostolic solidarity and of a unified apostolic apprehension; and that therefore it was he who laid the foundations of the Church's teaching about the apostles, and indeed of its apostolic character. If this be the truth, it ought to be possible to isolate the Johannine Writings and to show that they exercised original and creative influence upon the Church of the second century, rather than that they voiced an already existing apostolic authority. This, it should be noted, is one aspect of an acute general problem that confronts the modern historian of Primitive Christianity up to the time of Irenæus. We have inherited the phrases 'Apostolic Christianity' and 'The Apostolic Fathers', but the point has been reached when these descriptive titles have become almost meaningless; since by 'Apostolic Christianity' we tend to mean 'Paulinism' or the vague, scintillating background of the churches which Saint Paul founded or visited or to which he addressed his letters; and by 'the Apostolic Fathers' we tend to mean the independent ideas and experiences of an Ignatius or a Polycarp. And as a by-product of all this, the Johannine Writings, and the Fourth Gospel in particular, become homeless and wellnigh unintelligible. A revolt against this whole picture of primitive Christianity is long overdue; and there are clear signs that it is being undertaken, owing partly to the present chaotic religious situation in Germany, and partly to a series of technical critical investigations carried on chiefly in the University of Tübingen, and associated with the names of Adolf Schlatter, Gerhard Kittel, and their pupil Heinrich Rengstorf. The issue at stake is whether it is or is not satisfactory to regard 'diversity' as the characteristic mark of primitive Christianity.

When, at the beginning of the fourth century, Eusebius undertook to write a history of the Church, he had proposed for himself no easy task. The Church in the second century had been undisciplined and chaotic. It was not until the writings of Irenæus had been circulated at the end of the second century that the teaching of the Church seemed to possess any coherence at all. The judgement of Apelles, the disciple and successor of Marcion, that 'doctrine should not be taken at all seriously, since each man ought to remain in his own belief', must have seemed a singularly reasonable deduction from the condition of the Church. It was with the licence of theological speculation that Irenæus had to deal. But Irenæus did not erect an orthodoxy and impose it upon the Church; or at least, that is not what he claimed to be doing. He claimed to possess a tradition of authoritative apostolic teaching, a tra-

D

dition supported by extant primitive Christian books. In this context he seized upon the Johannine Writings as of especial importance. In his letter to Florinus—a leading person in Rome, who propounded an attractive combination of Montanism and Gnosticism—Irenæus states that he is personally linked to the 'first succession from the apostles' through his old teacher Polycarp, at whose feet he had sat as a boy, and at whose feet Florinus might also have sat, since, like Irenæus himself, he too had been, as a young man, in Asia in Polycarp's company. The opportunity which Florinus missed, Irenæus had taken full advantage of: 'I distinctly recall the events of that time, better than those of recent years—for what we learn in childhood keeps pace with the growing mind and becomes part of it'. He remembered vividly how Polycarp sat, addressing the crowd, telling them of his 'intercourse with John and with others who had seen the Lord', and relating what they had said. Irenæus is horrified at the vast distinction between what he remembers Polycarp, 'the blessed and apostolic elder'—'apostolic' because of his dependence upon the 'eyewitnesses of the life of the Word' —to have taught, and what Florinus is now teaching. And he is sure that Polycarp would have been equally horrified; he would have 'cried aloud, and stopped his ears and said, as was his wont: "Good God! for what sort of time hast thou kept me, that I should endure these things!"' (Euseb. *H.E.* v. 20). What Irenæus remembered of the teaching of Polycarp was, however, no isolated, peculiar memory. His teaching was 'altogether in accordance with the Scriptures'; and the memory of Irenæus is corroborated also by the letters which Polycarp wrote 'whether to the neighbouring churches, confirming them, or to some of the brethren, admonishing and exhorting them' (Euseb. *H.E.* v. 20). To Irenæus the witness of Polycarp, of Scripture, and of the eyewitnesses, forms one consistent whole.

Behind Irenæus, then, stand Polycarp and the Church in Proconsular Asia at the beginning of the second century. Polycarp was bishop of Smyrna, where he was martyred at the age of eighty-six on the 23rd of February, A.D. 155. The pastoral letters of this 'apostolic and prophetic teacher'—as he is named in the circular letter written by the Church of Smyrna describing his martyrdom—have all disappeared, except the one answering a request of the elders of the Church at Philippi for a collection of the letters of Ignatius, which they thought would help them to confirm the faith of their people and to restore order in the Church. It is from this surviving letter alone that it is possible to gather, at first hand, the tone of Polycarp's teaching and the temper of his opponents. The Epistle begins: 'Polycarp and the elders that are with him to the Church of God which sojourneth at Philippi. . . . The stedfast root of your faith, famed from early days, still abides and bears fruit . . . unto our Lord Jesus Christ, who endured even death for our sins'. He then exhorts the Philippians to put aside vain and empty talking and the error 'of the majority'. If they remember the words of the Lord—here Polycarp quotes from the Sermon on the Mount—and pay attention to the wisdom of the 'blessed and glorious Paul, which he taught concerning the Word of Truth', they will be built up unto the faith which was given them. Christians must learn to walk in the commandment of the Lord and to serve Him, 'as He Himself gave commandment, and as the Apostles, who brought us the Gospel, and the Prophets, who proclaimed beforehand the coming of our Lord, did also command'. Of this obedient service, the deacons, as their name demands, must provide the example. It is their pre-eminent responsibility to act 'as servants of God and of Christ . . . walking according to the truth of the Lord who became the Servant of all'. This dependence upon the apostolic teaching is not merely of general religious importance, but of particular, urgent importance, in order that the Christians may abstain from 'false brethren and from those who bear the name of the Lord hypocritically and lead foolish men astray'. Polycarp is especially distressed about a certain Valens, a presbyter, who has shown himself to be 'ignorant of the office bestowed upon him', and about his wife, 'unto whom may the Lord grant true repentance'. Finally, he asks the Philippians to let him have any later information they may possess about Ignatius, and sends them a collection of his letters. The situation at Philippi, as in Asia Minor, is already acute, but it is not until towards the end of the letter that he betrays what is really at stake. At last, he compresses the issue into one poignant cry: 'Everyone who shall not confess that Jesus Christ has come in flesh is anti-Christ; and whosoever shall not confess the testimony of the Cross is of the devil.' Here, and here only, does the Epistle of Polycarp overlap formally with the Johannine Writings (John i. 14, vi. 53–6; 1 John iv. 2, 3; 2 John 7). There is, however, not the slightest suggestion in the Epistle that its author is here quoting from some authoritative Christian document. Rather, he is uttering a battle-cry, not a cry of his own invention, but the cry under which the Church, remaining true to the teaching of the apostles, assembles to fight for the very heart of its Gospel. Polycarp does, of course, appeal to authoritative scriptures. His letter is full of quotations, for 'whosoever shall pervert the oracles of the Lord to his own lusts and say that there is neither resurrection nor judgement, that man is the first-born of Satan'. He quotes seemingly from the Gospel of Matthew: he quotes from Pauline and sub-Pauline writings, from 1 Peter, from the letter of Clement to the Corinthians. He refers to the Epistles of Ignatius. He is, moreover, confident that the Philippians are 'well-trained in the sacred scriptures'. He reminds them of the righteousness and endurance of 'Paul and the other apostles', and of the example set before their very eyes by Ignatius and Zosimus and Rufus, and by others who 'came from themselves'. Polycarp stands created by Christian writings and by the witness of apostles. He stands, moreover, confronted by the same disturbance in the Church as that by which the author of the Johannine Writings had been confronted, and in the same locality. There is not, however, a single word to suggest that the appeal back to apostolic solidarity was, in fact, some new apologetic device, which had appeared first in a group of almost contemporary 'Johannine' writings, and which had been designed to meet a similar, if not identical, situation in Asia Minor a few years before. The appeal of Polycarp to the apostles manifestly does not depend upon the Johannine Writings.

If, as Lightfoot stated and as Irenæus certainly suggested, Asia Minor was the 'focus of activity in the Christian Church' during the first half of the second century, then, important as Polycarp is for our appreciation of the situation there, Ignatius is even more important. Ignatius of Antioch passed, like a meteor, through the Churches of Asia Minor, paying especial attention to Polycarp: 'Ask', he writes to him, 'for larger wisdom than thou hast.' Of the part played by Ignatius in the Church of Antioch and of the circumstances that led to his condemnation we know nothing. What we do know is his reaction to the state of Christianity in Proconsular Asia somewhere between A.D. 98 and 117; that is to say, he becomes a known person at the time when the Fourth Gospel was presumably being written, and in the same locality.

Ignatius had been condemned to martyrdom. His condemnation had been pronounced at Antioch, but he was to die as a public spectacle in Rome. As a Christian about to die, he passes through the cities of Asia Minor, receives the representatives of the various Churches, and, having received them, addresses their congregations in a series of letters. Seven letters of Ignatius have survived: three written from Smyrna to the Churches in Ephesus, Magnesia, and Tralles; two from Troas to the Churches in Philadelphia and Smyrna; and in addition to these, one to the Church in Rome written from Smyrna and one to Polycarp written from Troas. Now, what did Ignatius say? And why did he say what he did say? These are the relevant questions. The Ignatian letters are not explained when it is said that they were written to express the writer's gratitude for the kindness that had been shown to him, to strengthen respect for bishops, presbyters, and deacons, to protest against a particular form of heresy called Docetism, and lastly, in order to persuade the Churches in Asia Minor to help the Church in Antioch. None of these suggestions, in fact, explains the letters of Ignatius. Still less is he explained, when he is treated, or rather dismissed, as 'unhealthy', as possessed of the 'self-centredness of the neurotic temper', or as 'preoccupied with questions of ecclesiastical discipline and theological orthodoxy'. This is irritated language; and it is important that we should beware of irritation when we are dealing with a man who stands on the edge of the biblical literature and who has been created by it. No doubt, the Epistles of Ignatius are nervous; and no doubt,

Ignatius himself was not what we should call a 'balanced, well-poised personality'. But we have not done with him when this has been said. The judgement of Lightfoot here, as elsewhere, ought not to be forgotten: 'Impetuosity, fire, headstrongness (if it be not an injustice to apply this term to so noble an exhibition of fervid zeal and self-devotion), are impressed on every sentence in the Epistles of Ignatius.'

Ignatius was a Christian. As a Christian about to die, he wrote his letters. Because Paul lies behind him, because he knows himself called to be a disciple of Jesus Christ, he apprehends this movement to death to be fraught with theological significance, and with very particular theological significance for the Christians in Asia Minor. That he has been summoned to become a place where the especial character of the Church can be apprehended, is what gives him his authority. The possibility, however, that he may be unworthy to accept the call—'if I be but worthy'—is what disturbs his poise and balance. The combination of vocation with hesitation gives him the right to exhort the Christians, but it does not give him the right to issue commands as though he were 'already some great one'. With the assistance of the Church, however, he hopes to be 'enabled to be a disciple'. This uncertainty, this theological nervousness, ought not to cause modern theologians to adopt a superior attitude towards him, for it is out of this tension that theological perception is born, and from this same tension Prophets and Apostles once spoke. Ignatius stands within the orbit of biblical, historical theology, and—this is the point—he stands within this orbit, not in Palestine, but in Greek-speaking, Greek-thinking, Proconsular Asia. Standing where he does he is able to see his impending martyrdom as a dogmatic, theological, Christian event, as a visible occurrence, almost transparent with eternal significance; and which is therefore a parable of the faith of the Church. He understands his movement to death as a dogmatic witness to the truth of the Church, and as providing an opportunity which, if accepted by him and apprehended by others, will stand forth as a veritable 'Word of God'; but which, if regarded simply as an act of human heroism—'if', he writes to the Romans, 'you desire my flesh'—will degenerate into an opportunity for boasting; in which case, he will have become, not an intelligible word, but a 'mere cry'.

Nevertheless, the Epistles of Ignatius are held together by an urgent insistence upon the word 'flesh'. This is, of course, no mere playing with words or with some orthodoxy of language. Ignatius is going to be martyred; his flesh is about to be torn in pieces by wild beasts. He is therefore playing a part in a tangible, historical, visible occurrence. Not for one moment does he regard this event as trivial; not for one moment does he allow himself to take refuge in some other world of spiritual reality, unconnected with what is actually taking place. Rather, history, his own personal history, his 'flesh', is the place where the glory of God will be made known. The Epistles of Ignatius are saturated with the Christian answer to the problem of history. Ignatius is, moreover, confident that there is no other answer; confident, because the answer he is giving is the answer that Paul had already given to the same problem and that Apostles and Prophets had already given; confident, because that answer is the meaning of the 'flesh of Jesus'. The name of Jesus is both 'carnal and spiritual', and actions done 'after the flesh' in Jesus Christ are 'spiritual' actions. There is therefore a life of obedience 'arrayed from head to foot in the commandments of Jesus Christ'; and there are, there can be, there must be, men who are carried up, like stones, to the very summit of the building—'by the machinery of Jesus Christ'. All this language about 'flesh' is, however, capable of serious misunderstanding. There is here no exaltation of visible behaviour, as though it existed in its own right and by itself. To those who suppose this to be the case it is necessary to say quite roughly that 'Nothing visible is good'. Those who are in that sense 'fleshly' cannot do spiritual things; and it is impossible for those who are spiritual to do things that are in that sense 'fleshly'. Ignatius is not talking about flesh and spirit as though they were two independent, unrelated, or contrasted, things; he is talking about that bending of flesh to spirit in which truth is manifested. It is in this sense that the phrase 'in flesh and in spirit' rings like a clarion call, the call of the Church, through his Epistles, summoning men to quite straightforward moral action. Wives, for example, are to be true to their husbands 'in flesh and in spirit'; that is to say, their relation to their husbands is a proper relation of flesh, only if it be lived in the context of their love for the Lord and 'as the Lord loved the Church'. Similarly, celibacy may, no doubt, be demanded of the Christian; but if it be regarded as a thing in itself, it is a very dangerous condition of life: 'If anyone is able to abide in chastity to the honour of the flesh of the Lord, let him so abide—without boasting. If he boast, he is lost.' Ignatius therefore prays that there may be in the Churches that 'union of flesh and spirit which belongs to Jesus Christ'; but, lest he be misunderstood, adds at once that the reckoning of the Christian is, however, 'not with flesh, but with God who knoweth the secret things'.

What, then, does Ignatius mean, when he speaks of the 'union of flesh and spirit in Jesus Christ'? At this point he is not obscure, for it is the nerve-centre of his letters. He means first that Jesus Christ was a real, visible figure on the plane of history. He was 'truly of the race of David according to the flesh'—'truly born'—'truly baptized by John'—'truly nailed up in flesh under Pontius Pilate and Herod the Tetrarch'. These things were 'truly and certainly done' by Jesus Christ, and they took place 'in the time of the governorship of Pontius Pilate'. When, however, still insisting on this genuine historicity, Ignatius adds to the word 'flesh' the word 'spirit'—'in flesh and in spirit'—he does not leap irrelevantly into mysticism (though he does, of course, make use of mystical language) as though the world of the Spirit were some other world superimposed upon the flesh of Jesus. Jesus Christ is the 'Door of the Father'. In the concrete flesh of Jesus, in history, the Spirit is apprehended by faith; and when the Spirit is thus apprehended, there can be no deception, for the Spirit 'knoweth whence it cometh and whither it goeth'. The bending of the flesh to the spirit is the spiritual life according to the flesh in Christ Jesus, and its meaning is finally displayed on the Cross. The death of Christ is therefore the 'mystery whereby we attain unto faith'. Jesus Christ is the one Physician, 'of flesh and of Spirit'—'born and yet not born'—'Son of Mary and Son of God'—'first passible and then impassible'—'true life in death'—'God in man'. Because all this is most surely apprehended in the death of Jesus, Ignatius returns again and again to the scene of the crucifixion, and sees in the Cross the machinery by which the Christians who believe are carried upwards to the topmost story of the edifice of God. But it must be remembered that it is in the general context of flesh and spirit that Ignatius comes to speak of the death of Jesus as the supreme point in history where that which lies beyond historical observation and beyond sensible experience, but which makes sense of what can be and has been observed and experienced, is apprehended and obeyed. The death of Jesus is therefore the place where hope is born and obedience demanded. Ignatius knows, however, that he stands tremulously under this imperative of hope manifested in the death of Jesus; and he looks for assistance not merely to the Church, but far more confidently to Paul and to the other apostles, because the mark of an Apostle was that he was 'joined to His flesh and blood'. Ignatius does not mean by this merely that the apostles had seen Jesus and possessed reminiscences of His flesh. He means that they were Apostles because, through their historical relation to Jesus, they were found 'superior to death' and because their lives in the flesh had been bent to obedience to God. The Apostles apprehended and obeyed.

There is therefore to Ignatius no 'good action' that is independently or in itself sufficient or adequate, for the absence of independence is the meaning of the flesh of Jesus, the supreme meaning of His death. Jesus Christ did not act 'by Himself', nor did He act by Himself 'through His apostles'. His actions were good because they were done in dependence upon the Father, apart from whom 'He did nothing'. Christian 'good action' is therefore not a thing of 'present profession', not a thing that 'glitters in the eye'; it exists only when men are found in the power of faith unto the end'; for 'faith is the beginning and love the end'. This is the obedience to which Ignatius had been called: to perceive its meaning is to apprehend the vocation of the Church. 'I know', he says, 'who I am and to whom I am writing.' But—and this is the point upon which he insists—this knowledge and perception are impossible if the picture of the 'flesh' of Jesus, and supremely of His death, be not preserved in the heart of the Church and at the centre of its worship. And so he comes to speak of the Eucharist, since there the words 'flesh and blood' are unescapable, unescapable therefore the control of the Jesus of History over the life of the Church. To abstain from the Eucharist is to jeopardize the apprehension of the mission of the Church: 'Be ye therefore careful', he writes to the Philadelphians, 'to observe one Eucharist, for there is one flesh of our Lord Jesus Christ and one cup in communion with his blood'—and again to the Smyrnæans, referring to those who are acting contrary to the mind of God: 'They abstain from Eucharist and prayer, because they allow not that the Eucharist is the flesh of our Saviour Jesus Christ, which flesh suffered for our sins, and which the Father of his goodness raised up. . . . It is therefore meet that ye should abstain from such, and not speak of them either privately or in public; but should give heed to the Prophets, and especially to the Gospel, where the Passion is shown unto us and the Resurrection is accomplished.' How deeply the meaning of this has bitten into Ignatius's own life is seen from his words to the Ephesians: 'My spirit is devoted to the Cross, an offence to them that do not believe, but to us salvation and eternal life.'

It has been necessary to go back to the fundamental themes of the Ignatian Epistles in order to understand why he regarded bishops and presbyters as of so very great importance. The confidence of Ignatius in bishops especially requires some explanation. Ignatius is not concerned with ecclesiastical administration any more than he is concerned with some peculiar kind of developing ecclesiastical orthodoxy. He is concerned with the Church's apprehension of its mission, and consequently, with the preservation of the historical figure of Jesus. It is in this context, and only in this context, that the ministry of the Church gains any significance at all. Ignatius speaks of bishops, not as though they were persons exercising some strange kind of independent mystical authority (though here again at times he uses mystical language to express his meaning), but as men responsible for the preservation of the apostolic witness to Jesus. So confident is he that they do, in fact, preserve this witness, that he categorically demands obedience to them lest the Christians should lapse into theological and moral infidelity, lest, losing the control of the flesh of Jesus, they should 'have no care for love, none for the widow, none for the orphan, none for the afflicted, none for the prisoner, none for the hungry and thirsty'. Obedience to authority, no doubt, has in itself at all times theological and moral significance; but it is not for this reason that Ignatius demands obedience to bishops. He requires obedience to bishops and to the body of elders in order that the Churches may be confirmed in the 'ordinances of the Lord and of the Apostles'; in order that Christians may be subject to the 'Law of Jesus Christ and to the grace of God'. The presbyters represent to the local Church the 'Council of the Apostles': they are the 'College of Apostles'. Apart from this apostolic control there is not even the 'name of a Church'. When therefore Ignatius says that the Christians are 'wreathed with the spiritual circlet' of the presbytery, he is not using the word 'spiritual' loosely. The presbyters are spiritual only because of their relation to the apostles. The Ephesian Church is a properly Christian Church, because it has been 'ever of one mind with the apostles in the power of Jesus Christ', and because the Ephesian Christians are 'associated with Paul in the mysteries'. Similarly, the Church in Rome owed its peculiar distinction to the fact that it had been under the apostolic authority of 'Peter and Paul'. When Ignatius insists upon obedience to a bishop, he is not thinking of some independent, personal dictatorship, he is concerned only with obedience to God. Not to their youthful bishop are the Magnesian Christians to pay reverence, 'but to the Father of Jesus Christ, even to the Bishop of all'. Bauer names Ignatius 'The Man of organization', and seeks to explain his conception of the episcopate by a Hitlerite analogy. 'When', he writes, 'a man finds himself in a minority and his wishes disregarded by the powers that be, it is only too easy for him to demand dictatorship, in order to secure the supremacy of his own party. . . . This achieved, he can either bend to his will those who think differently from himself, or, if they resist, drive them out of the community altogether. . . . So, when once the congregation is placed under the authority of one bishop, the orthodox party, even though they be a minority, may hope to divide their opponents and "rule the roost" ' (pp. 65–7). But this administrative tyranny is precisely what Ignatius will not allow. He is concerned neither with administration nor with blind obedience to a bishop. He has to remind even Polycarp that he is made of 'flesh and spirit', and that therefore he must pray that 'invisible things may be revealed to him'; and he exhorts him to 'bring the more pestilent to submission by gentleness', because there can be no pride in a Christian bishop. Bishops are to be heard only because they speak 'concerning Jesus Christ in truth' and because there can be no 'bread of God' apart from the sanctuary of obedience. Ignatius does, it is true—and this is very remarkable—assume that the bishops do speak about Jesus Christ in truth; and he is therefore able to demand obedience to them. But this is because he is convinced that, quite apart from the apostolic witness which he is giving in his own flesh, the witness of the apostles is being preserved in Asia Minor by bishops and presbyters, although with very great difficulty and in the midst of very serious opposition. The situation is, in fact, so acute that he feels himself to be living in an eschatological tension—'These are the the last times'. The Church and the world stand over against one another as two separate 'coinages', each with its own peculiar stamp engraved upon it. But—and here lies the tension of the Ignatian Epistles—the coinage of the world is gaining currency in the Church. The Church must therefore be bent back to the obedience of the flesh to the Spirit; it must be joined to Jesus Christ in flesh and in spirit; united and elect in a true passion, and so attain its proper position as 'foreshadowed before the ages unto abiding and unchangeable glory'. To Ignatius this facing-about is possible only if the Church recovers and preserves the witness and example of the apostles. In this context, and in this context alone, he speaks about bishops and presbyters.[1]

If we pass quickly from the Ignatian Epistles to the Johannine Writings or from the Johannine Writings to the Ignatian Epistles, it is quite clear that both are evoked by a similar, if not identical, situation. Both writers gain strength and authority from their assurance that what they are saying depends, not merely upon apostolic reminiscence, but upon apostolic apprehension. The apostles saw the glory or spirit manifested in the 'flesh' of Jesus; and, having seen, they understood the meaning of His teaching and actions; but above all, they understood and accepted in their lives the meaning of His death. To both, the apostles are real people upon whose insight and example the mission of the Church depends. But—and surely this is very strange—though at rare moments Ignatius falls into language with which we are familiar from the Johannine Writings, at no point does he seem to be quoting from them. Not once, though he is moving round the same themes, does he seem aware of the existence of the Johannine Writings. Not once, moreover, though he is speaking about apostles and elders, and though he refers frequently by name to Christians in Asia Minor, does he ever mention the existence either of the Apostle, or of the Elder, John. Whatever explanation of the silence of Ignatius be given, one thing seems certain: it was not the author of the Johannine Writings who first brought into prominence the solidarity of the apostles or the authority of their witness.

[1] In the preceding summary, quotations have been made from the following passages in the Epistles of Ignatius: *Eph.* i–iii, vii, xi, xii, xviii; *Magn.* i, iii, vi, vii, ix, xiii; *Trall.* iii; *Rom.* ii–iv, viii; *Philad.* iv, vii, ix; *Smyrn.* ii, iii, vi, vii, xii; *Polyc.* ii, v.

# VII. THE FOURTH GOSPEL AND THE PROBLEM OF THE MEANING OF HISTORY

## by the Editor[1]

No doubt it was allowable for a schoolmaster—particularly as he had been privileged to teach Dr. Johnson English—to have 'published a spelling-book, and dedicated it to the Universe'; but it is exceedingly doubtful whether it is legitimate to concoct an idea or notion, or to produce an interpretation of history, and dedicate it to the world for its salvation, unless indeed there are good grounds for supposing that describable history is not only patient of this interpretation, not only seems to demand it, but has taken its course because it is governed by it, so that the notion or idea is no mere subsequent interpretation, but is itself the meaning of history.

The author of this book intended to consider the problem of history at the end of his INTRODUCTION, in order that the COMMENTARY itself might be undisturbed by inquisitions concerning the historicity of this or that detail or episode—inquisitions which he thought irrelevant on the grounds that the fourth Evangelist was well aware of the necessary relation between an Evangelist and the history which must be the medium of his Gospel, and that the primary function of the commentator is to lay bare, as fully as he can, the meaning attached by the Evangelist to what he wrote, and not to sit in judgement upon the Evangelist's success or failure in applying the methods of modern historians. There is no question but that the Evangelist himself believed his Gospel to have been revealed to men and forced upon himself in history and by history, and that this fact will have considerable importance for those who set out to collect evidence for the reconstruction of the historical details of the life of Jesus. But the eventual collection of historical details will be facilitated, not by a headlong percentage estimate of the number of incidents which may seem on grounds of intrinsic verisimilitude to be likely to have happened—such an estimate will at the best, by itself, remain subjective, and will, at the worst, obscure the primary meaning of the gospel—but by trying to understand the Evangelist's conscious object, and so learning what has controlled his choice. In the COM-

[1] See the note at the end of this chapter.

107

MENTARY, therefore, every detail must be considered first and foremost in relation to the Evangelist's purpose, and corroborative evidence from outside the gospel will be primarily useful if it helps more fully to display that purpose.

But how are the extent and nature of this corroborative evidence to be determined? Even though it is entirely possible that the Evangelist himself witnessed some of the events he narrates, or at any rate knew one or more eye-witnesses, it appears certain that he also depends upon a tradition, oral and written, substantially akin to that which lay behind the synoptic gospels. Very probably he knew one or more of these gospels in their extant form. In addition, his thought bears the marks of a wide knowledge of the Old Testament scriptures, while the Odes of Solomon as well as the Rabbinic writings seem to throw light upon his work. Nor can Greek thought be excluded from his formative background, not yet the religious manner of thought of Oriental mysticism. In fact the observable field behind the Fourth Gospel is highly complicated, and the Fourth Gospel is therefore misconstrued, not so much when its apparent and suggestive allusions to all these various environments are over-emphasized, as, rather, when the gospel is depressed into one particular environment and explained, far too simply, as a piece of oriental mysticism, or of the Jewish-hellenistic theology of Alexandria. No doubt an antidote to this danger is provided by the co-existence of traces of all these influences in the gospel. But the danger is entirely obviated when it is recognized that what chiefly conditions the apprehension of the fourth Evangelist is a truly Biblical realism. The fact of speech, the fact of paternity, the facts of light and darkness, water, bread, wine, the fact of life and death: these facts of created existence, and others like them, in the last analysis supply the fundamental material of the witness of the gospel. Beside this realistic apprehension of the theological meaning of things experienced by men in history, the imagery and symbolism and jargon of the ancient world seem dim and dead. For this realism displays the observable world as itself established by its own theological witness. It witnesses, indeed, 'beyond history', beyond itself, yet not away from itself to some second world running parallel with it but at no point touching it; not to some wholly other reality the discovery of which empties the observable world of final significance. The observable world witnesses in such a way that it *is* what it signifies; or, to speak more precisely, *is* what it signifies when seen by God and apprehended by men. Consequently, the language of faith, which is the language of the Fourth Gospel, treats the phenomenal world not as unreal and trivial except in so far as it furnishes symbols of theological speculation, but as possessing a dignity of reality which is for the first time made fully clear by the Christian revelation. Accordingly, the significance of the writings of Philo is not that they explain the theology of the gospel, for they do nothing of the kind. What they do is to introduce us into a world of thought in which the facts of daily life, or the history of the Old Testament, were being interpreted as symbols of the truths at which pagan theology was guessing; this world of thought was the common property of Judaism in so far as it was in contact with the Hellenistic world, and 'Philo' has preserved that extreme form of it which was current in the synagogues and schools of Alexandria. The fourth Evangelist deliberately adopts its symbols, but brings them out of the haze of Hellenistic Jewish theologizing into the concrete reality of the historical Christian tradition of the person of Jesus, as living in the daily experiences of the Church around him. [1]

To speak of history witnessing 'beyond itself'—whatever may be meant by that tortuous phrase—raises at once and most acutely the problem of history as it is presented in the Fourth Gospel. For however the gospel is approached and interpreted, it is clear that the Evangelist is recounting the history of Jesus of Nazareth, not merely for the sake of its describable actuality, but also for the sake of its significance. But if so, what authority does he attach to the actual history? How far is he disciplined by it? Is he in any degree submitted to it, or does he merely use it as a convenient symbolism, so that, when actual history that will serve his purpose is lacking, he feels able, with a good conscience, to invent history to express his needs? This problem necessarily haunts the whole gospel of the Word made flesh. It will, however, be convenient to broach it at the point at which it normally forces itself upon readers of the Fourth Gospel, namely in the Story of the Raising of Lazarus, in order that the ground may be cleared for an investigation, not of that story only, but of the meaning and authority of history in the Fourth Gospel as a whole.

Did Lazarus rise from the dead? This is almost always the first question that is asked of anyone who lectures or writes about the Fourth Gospel. It is, moreover, essentially a right question, not merely because so much seems to stand or fall with the answer to it, but because the conscious purpose of the fourth Evangelist seems to be to force his readers back upon the history—the flesh—of Jesus, in which, according to his account, the raising of Lazarus played so vital a part. But for this very reason the answer cannot be either a simple 'Yes' or a simple 'No'. The Evangelist is forcing his readers back upon the event of Jesus in

[1] I am indebted to the Rev. Canon W. L. Knox, D.D., for this judgement upon the significance of the writings of Philo. He adds this example of the fourth Evangelist's procedure: 'Thus the manna in the wilderness is no longer a symbol of the divine Logos, a concept which has no real place in Judaism but is introduced into it in order to find room for the Stoic concept of a divine Logos ordering the cosmos out of chaos, but in Jesus, apprehended in His historical life and in the daily life and worship of the Church as the true "Word" which explains the whole meaning of history.'

the flesh largely because he knows that that event—like any other event truly seen—cannot be adequately described as bare historical reminiscence. He is well acquainted with men who knew the facts of the life of Jesus but could not give a true description of what had happened, who had heard the speech of Jesus but not His Word, who reverenced His works but did not understand what they meant. To say either that Lazarus did unquestionably rise from the dead, without first considering what meaning the Evangelist attaches to history, and whether he is justified in his treatment of history, would equally obscure, not only what he meant when he recorded what took place at Bethany, but also what the synoptic tradition meant when it pictured Jesus quoting to the disciples of John, in exemplification of what they see and hear, the Isaianic hope: *the dead are raised.*

Nevertheless, three things must be said at once, all of which have a direct bearing upon the question of the raising of Lazarus. In the first place, to consider the possibility or the impossibility of raising a man from the dead lies altogether outside the scope of Biblical work. Biblical work can deal only with the facts comprised in and concerning the documents with which it is confronted. It has to try to establish exactly what an author wrote, what he meant his readers to understand by what he wrote, what sources he drew upon, what contexts—literary, cultural, intellectual—throw most light upon his idiom and thought, what independent evidence there is for the validity of his statements. To say, on the basis of the existing documentary evidence, that Lazarus, having died, was, or was not, restored to life, is a judgement that cannot be made by a Biblical theologian, and not even by a natural scientist, since the New Testament does not furnish any record of the event comparable to the minute analysis demanded by scientific observation.

But, in the second place, something must be said of the work of the fourth Evangelist upon the tradition of the Church. About the state of this earlier tradition there is very little information. It would seem[1] that the fourth Evangelist was trying to restate and draw out the meaning of the tradition known to his readers and to himself, and, further, that the material of the synoptic gospels furnishes the best indication of the form and content of this tradition. At many points the synoptic gospels show that the Evangelist was operating upon material at any rate closely parallel to synoptic incidents and sayings. At times—and this indeed will have to be considered more fully—he gives a particular emphasis to an incident, or shows the universal application of a saying, where its synoptic setting presents it in a more limited and even apparently radically different light. But there is no evidence that he is drawing his material from the empty air, or writing upon a clean slate. His general procedure, in fact, suggests most cogently that the tradition known to him con-

[1] Cf. the INTRODUCTION, Chapter iv, 'The Historical Tension of the Fourth Gospel'.

tained, not only stories such as the Feeding of the Five Thousand, but a story of the raising of a man from the dead, and even makes it appear probable that this story had more in common with the story of the Raising of Lazarus than has the story of the Widow's Son at Nain (Luke vii. 11–17).

In the third place it must be said that, whatever may have been the form in which such a story was told in the tradition known to the Evangelist, he himself thought it essential that Lazarus should be understood to be unmistakably physically dead—he allows no room for any explanation that he had been mistakenly buried in a trance—and that, in insisting upon this, he believed himself to be stating what was already implied in his source. It would therefore be difficult to conclude that the belief that Jesus raised a man from the dead originated with the author of the Fourth Gospel, even if the Lucan story of the Widow's Son at Nain, and the Marcan story of Jairus's daughter, were wanting. It must also be added—and this point cannot be emphasized too strongly—that the fourth Evangelist must not be credited with that nineteenth-century predisposition to differentiate between the stories of acts attributed to Jesus, with which we are still obsessed. Given that he was confronted in the tradition with the story of the Raising of Lazarus, he would have used it, or omitted to use it, just as he would have used, or omitted to use, the story of the healing of the woman with an issue of blood, not according to any criterion of the historical plausibility of either, but simply according to the suitability of either for his purpose as an evangelist.

It must still, however, be asked in what sense the story of the Raising of Lazarus, as set forth in the Fourth Gospel, can be said to be historical. For, whereas the synoptic gospels had represented the Cleansing of the Temple as the immediate cause of the death of Jesus, the Fourth Gospel sets the Cleansing of the Temple at the beginning of the ministry, and although it follows it up with a sustained controversy between Jesus and the Jews who more than once seek to kill Him, it is only when Lazarus has been raised from the dead that the chief priests and Pharisees take counsel that they may put Him to death. For the Evangelist, this is the supreme importance of the story. Is it to be supposed that he was guided, quite simply, by a tradition that was already in itself wholly divergent from the synoptic tradition: that he supplied, without hesitation or searching of heart, a chronological framework of the same kind as that of the synoptic gospels, although so different from it in detail? Or was his procedure governed by quite other considerations; considerations that necessitated the re-casting of his material in its own interests? Is it possible that there was no way of making the meaning of the tradition clear but by recasting it, since, beyond a certain point, the issues in the historical events were so far-reaching that the mere retailing of them in chronological sequence could not elucidate their true meaning? Can it be that, faced with the alternative of handling the material as a chronological historian or as a theologian, the fourth Evangelist chose, deliberately and under the pressure of his function as an evangelist, the latter course? It is at this point that it is necessary to pass from the immediate consideration of the Raising of Lazarus to the more fundamental and general problem of the relation between chronological history and the meaning of history as it is presented throughout the Fourth Gospel.

Brought up on the background of the last generation, we never escape from the problem of historicity. It haunts us always. Inevitably and axiomatically we expect from a historian, not only accuracy of observation and description, but also a moral judgement. When therefore we take a book like the Fourth Gospel into our hands, we set its author's work in our own perspective and judge him if he does not see with our eyes and record according to our standards. Some of us may indeed say that the 'Whig interpretation of history' has proved morally arrogant and its selection and description of events not above suspicion, yet even if we take sides against the Whig historians we do in fact accept their frame of reference. Our standards of historical research may have a more scrupulous technique, and our moral superiority may be less obvious, but we still assume that the meaning of history is described on the plane of history with reference to past and present and future.

If, therefore, the meaning of the Fourth Gospel is to be set forth, it is not simply a question of ranging the gospel and its author by the side of one or other of the modern answers to the problem of history. The modern historical controversy is indeed a proper one, and it is, no doubt, possible to place the New Testament within the varied setting of those philosophies of history with which we are familiar. But the New Testament in fact protests against the whole background of the controversy, namely, the assumption that the final word is with the historian. It is, precisely and specifically, the literature that denies this assumption; that denies it because it is throughout governed by eschatology, asserting that 'now' is the time, and accordingly ruling out not only the historical future, but also the past as a cause of the present. The New Testament cannot say, for instance, when it makes a judgement, that this or that behaviour is true 'at present', or 'under present circumstances', because these two phrases, in spite of claiming to speak for the present, do in fact call up the future in order to define the present and limit it. When Sir Samuel Hoare, on Thursday, 24 July 1935,[1] declared that the traffic in arms could not be permitted 'at present', he firmly fixed his hearers' attention on the future, when it might be permitted. This future was an untheological future. Equally untheological

[1] See *The Times*, Friday, 25 July, 1935.

is the defence of the study of history as the study of the past, on the grounds that, since the present is the product of the past, we study the past in order to understand the present. In such a case—to give an exaggerated illustration—the student either has his eye on himself, and the object of his study—let us say Pericles—ceases to be a dignified person, or, if we revolt from this treatment of Pericles, Pericles is made a person in himself, and so an object approved of, or disapproved of, by the student. Now contrast the historical perception of the Fourth Gospel. The dictum, *Salvation is of the Jews*, does not mean either that salvation is produced by the Jews, or that there will be a time when that will not be so: it does not enable us, either to be grateful to the Jews of the past for their services to us, or to be censorious of their behaviour because of their misuse of their opportunity. It speaks to the present *only*, because the present is seen only in relation to the mercy and judgement of God, and so is fraught with a dignity that is ultimate and wholly independent of chronological relationships, and that affects the Jews in their unbelief just as it affects the Christians who believe.

This ultimate, non-chronological, yet entirely crucial dignity of the present, is recognized by men, not as a general philosophical or speculative idea, but through the flesh of Jesus. It is not that the flesh of Jesus confronts them with timeless spirit, but rather that it *is* the point where time defined in relation to time means nothing. Jesus, according to these men, did not found a Church, if by that is meant that He was the first chapter of a growing society with a history, and that He did this, or did not do that: this is a fruitless and trivial controversy, which merely sets out to evaluate the acts of Jesus in relation to other events in time, and so obscures the theological dignity that alone made men His Apostles and gave them a Gospel. Therefore the evangelists do not occupy themselves with the writing of a history of the Church, but assert that men have been brought under, and stand under, either the love or the judgement of God, and that this fact secularizes neither side and deprives neither side of a quite ultimate dignity. It is a cruel exegesis that supposes the condemnation of the Jews to be merely their condemnation by an irritated evangelist, or merely a reminiscence of some moment when Jesus spoke hastily or in exasperation, or merely the product of a natural and easily explained tension betwen Jews and Christians at the beginning of the second century. The last is no doubt true, but neither is it what the Evangelist is writing about, nor does he give any indication that it was what had in fact moved him to write. That would make of the background of the Fourth Gospel a particular epoch in Church History, to be contrasted with other epochs, which is exactly what the Evangelist refuses to do, not because he is stupid, but because he is concerned with something else. Moreover, the Evangelist whose theme is the flesh of Jesus has to do with the ultimate significance, not of a limited number of particular, specifically 'theological' acts or sayings, but of episodes and incidents ranging over the whole gamut of human life and experience.

This relating of every episode to the final truth involves, if the episode is to be described, a re-description in a technically *non-historical* form; since, if the episode be described otherwise, description of it ceases to be *eschatological*, that is to say, related strictly in terms of final truth, and inevitably becomes a historical description, with all that that implies. Such a description in the end deprives Jesus, and then His disciples, and then men, and then the universe, of any final meaning. Similarly, to describe the blessings of Providence in technically historical language beggars and obscures the vital relation between men and God declared in Jesus. As a result of the tyranny of history, it is easy to conceive Providence as the manipulation by God of events within the time-sequence, for the immediate, temporal benefit of particular persons. It is also easy to identify God's will with a particular course of events, so that any-one who at any point fails to recognize and follow the path plotted out for Him by God may come to believe Himself less immediately under the Providence of God. But such conceptions are patently inimical to belief that God has revealed Himself in Jesus, not as bestowing temporal blessings upon temporal achievement—this He may, or may not, do—but as making eternal and absolute success out of apparent failure. Now the assurance of God's Providence is faith that He wills to extend this unprecedented, non-historical glorification to every part and moment of existence, however ephemeral and perverse. Man may resist and frustrate His will, and so stand not under grace but under judgement: he altogether misconstrues his situation with regard to God if he envisages his opportunities and responsibilities merely in terms of past, present and future, and so rids past, present and future alike of ultimate significance. This illustration from the danger of conceiving Providence historically is strictly relevant, since, in Christian thought, to see any part of creation eschatologically is to see it by faith in its final relation to God, under His judgement or under His mercy, and so as the potential object of His Providence. For the same reason the eschatological, that is to say, non-historical, description of events is necessary, immediately they have been seen to defy explanation in sole terms of their observable fact, and to demand explanation in terms of the final truth of God. There is, for instance, evolution in the Old Testament, and, as many recent writers have shown, it is perfectly possible to set forth Old Testament History, and Old Testament Religion, as a description of this evolution. The disadvantage of such an analysis lies, however, in the fact that the Old Testament is continually wrestling with the non-historical, ultimate problem of the relation of each and every point of history to God. The Old Testament writers, be they historians, prophets, psalmists, or wise men, see each situation confronted by the Word of God. They are driven to do so, of course, by history—

the history behind them which illuminates their own experience, and their own history which unveils to them the meaning of the experience behind them—but what is always of primary importance to them is the analysis of history, not in terms of itself, but in terms of the truth of God, to which, so they believe, it bears witness, and which dignifies it as the revelation of God. In spite of modern attempts to base a theology of gradual revelation upon an evolutionary description of Old Testament history, it still remains possible that the Old Testament analysis is the better theological analysis of history.

The necessity of describing history, in the interests of its own meaning, in non-historical language, may be paralleled from quite other fields than that of Biblical study. The science of biology provides a useful analogy. Biological description gives an account of transformations, but neither moral, nor eschatological, nor existential improvement. From the point of view of biological description, for instance, it is impossible to say that a man is more highly evolved than an ant. If criteria of comparison are sought in the adaptation of each, it would have to be admitted that the ant is better adapted to its mode of life than man is to his, and has survived for a longer period than that during which the human race has survived. Any other comparison, such as might be based upon the faculties or achievements of each, will redound in favour of man if its basis is anthropomorphic, but in favour of the ant, if its standards are hymenopterous. If any absolute comparison is to be made between the two, each must be related to something that is outside its own environments and mode of life, and even outside the observable field with which the science of biology is occupied. In other words, man and ant will have to be detached from their historical context and viewed in some quite different context—in some context, in fact, which biological description is, by its definition, incompetent to recognize.

Secular history in its technical sense, has to recognize similar limitations. It is quite possible to describe the history of western Europe during the last four centuries as a sequence in which cause and effect, relative success and relative failure, and evolution, are discernible. In such an analysis it will be quite possible to make comparisons between the burning of men at the stake in sixteenth-century England and the segregation of men in concentration camps in totalitarian states of the twentieth century. But whereas the confinement of a man in a concentration camp to-day results from a rigorous definition of the individual solely in terms of the State conceived as an entity whose fullest significance is observable since it lies within the field of history, the burning of a man at the stake in the sixteenth century depended upon a wholly different, non-historical analysis: namely that his body was to be burned in order that his soul might be preserved. There may be grounds upon which this analysis must be rejected, and even grounds upon which it can be compared absolutely with the totalitarian analysis. But whereas the totalitarian analysis can be described, vindicated or rejected by the historian, an analysis that involves the relation of man to God, and treats man as so related, falls outside the scope of the historian, who must note it and take account of it, but cannot sit in judgement upon it, unless he feels competent to include God and all that men have thought about Him within the field of observable history.

There is therefore no necessary, inevitable relation between observable evolution and the relation of any point or episode in it to the absolute; between the sequence of history and the meaning of history; between 'progress' and truth. When, for example, the Honourable Henry Hervey 'quited the army and took Orders' (—it was that Hervey of whom Dr. Johnson said: 'He was a vicious man, but very kind to me. If you call a dog Hervey I shall love him'), it did not mean that he exchanged a secular for a religious status; indeed, as an ecclesiastic, he acquired a new worldliness, for 'he married a sister of Sir Thomas Aston by whom he got the Aston estate, and assumed the name and arms of that family'; but it did mean that he took upon himself duties which are altogether meaningless apart from theological truth, meaningless, that is to say, in comparison with the important profession of a soldier.

These analogies show the necessary difference between describing history simply in relation to history—which is the procedure of the technical historian—and describing history in its theological significance. It would be far easier to make this distinction clear were there two words in English, as there are in German—*Geschichte* and *Historie*—one of which might be used for the bare relation of events, and the other reserved for the description of their meaning. Yet the point of the analogies would be misunderstood, were it merely concluded that there are two possible and equally satisfactory ways of describing events. Their point is, not only that events can rightly be described in a theological context as well as in their chronological sequence, but also that, if they are perceived as having theological significance, non-historical description of them alone does them justice: and not only that a subsequent apprehension of theological significance occasions this procedure, but also that the history itself, comparatively or entirely meaningless when analysed in terms of history, may almost demand this apprehension, quite apart from the goodness or badness, perception or blindness, of those with whom it is concerned. Moreover, even when history is being described non-historically, it must necessarily still be through the medium, or metaphor, of human experience. The Deuteronomic historian, nourished and illuminated by the history of his forefathers, has come, through the history of his own times and through his own immediate experience, to perceive the theological significance of the history lying behind him; yet he cannot transmit his apprehension to others in *unhistorical* language. His history, though non-historical, must still be written as history, because the events which he relates are not mere symbols. Unless he is entirely self-deceived, in so relating them he is demonstrating what they truly meant when they took place.

The way is now prepared for an examination of the fourth Evangelist's treatment of history. Yet it must once more be most emphatically stated that the argument by which this examination has been approached is in no sense intended to justify the invention of 'historical material' as a necessary means of expressing theological 'truths'. On the contrary, this argument has been intended to show that the description of history in simple terms of cause and effect, and of observable values, cannot do justice to events of which the significance was not limited to their observable fact, or to their observable relation to other observable facts. In spite of the almost unanimous convention of orthodox modern historians, such events *must* be described in non-historical language, and their detail, selection and arrangement *must* be controlled by their theological significance, unless their meaning as events in history is to be depressed into identity with their observable actuality. The fourth Evangelist is safeguarded from the charge of inventing history, or of using it merely as symbolism, by three considerations. In the first place his whole conscious intention is to force his readers back upon the life of Jesus in the flesh and upon His death in the flesh, as *the place of understanding*: he is therefore guilty of gross self-deception if he is inventing or distorting the visible likeness of Jesus to further his purpose. In the second place, what he is attempting to do, consciously, but as a theologian, is no more and no less than what is implied in the use made of the historical episodes and Sayings of Jesus by those who formulated the apostolic Gospel, so far as we can reconstruct their procedure from the synoptic gospels, and in the presentation of Jesus Christ as the sphere of God's revelation and salvation in the Epistles of Saint Paul and in the other New Testament scriptures. In the third place, his gospel, far from evacuating the observable world of anything but secondary importance, establishes it as the place where men, living in the flesh, are confronted by the last things of God: a strange procedure indeed if he regarded the history of Jesus in the real world as a pliable medium subject to his own theological insight. It may be that, at times, discrepancies between the Fourth and the synoptic gospels are due to differences in the detail and substance of their sources. It may also be, far more frequently, that the Fourth Gospel has been differently formulated because of the author's far deeper, and conscious, analysis of the history. In both cases his procedure has been forced upon him by the scandal and problem that complicates the whole New Testament: namely that the particular history of Jesus has been apprehended by the apostles and by the apostolic church as the essential and unique basis of the preaching and understanding of the Gospel of God.

That the Fourth Evangelist was well aware of the problem of attempting to express final truth in historical language is shown by his careful use of the future tense. Normally in the Fourth Gospel Jesus is represented as using the present tense, but it is a present completely unlimited by any past or any future: *I am the Resurrection, and the life* . . . (xi. 25) is as fully a non-chronological present as is *Before Abraham was, I am* (viii. 58). Conditioning this present is a past which, while necessitating at times the use of the aorist, has primarily not a chronological, but a non-historical, force: a past which safeguards the proper understanding of the Jesus who speaks in the present: *I came forth, and am come from God; for neither have I come of myself, but he sent me* (viii. 42). But in addition to this use of the present, Jesus uses the future; occasionally to express the repetition of the witness which He has given and which He is: *The Father loveth the Son, and sheweth him all things that himself doeth: and greater works than these will he shew him, that ye may marvel* (v. 20); but more often of the eschatological future which is, indeed, until *the hour* of the Passion, *not yet*, but which is equally misunderstood if it be construed as a future event or period rather than as the future revelation of the truth that already *is* because it is the truth of God. Thus *I am the resurrection and the life* continues *he that believeth on me, though he die, yet shall he live.* But this future, and the future in such a sentence as *And I, if I be lifted up from the earth, will draw all men unto myself* (xii. 32), do not look forward to a period when human life will be prolonged on earth as a result of belief in Jesus, or to a future when all men will flock to the risen Christ after He has been lifted up on the cross, but speak of the eternal life, and of the glory in His flesh, which already He truly brings and truly manifests, and which are the knowledge of the eternal glory of the Father. Although in the chronological sequence through which He moves as son of man there is still a future 'moment' of human apprehension (vii. 8, 30, viii. 59), yet once this 'moment' is reached (ii. 22, vii. 39, xii. 16, xiv. 26, xvi. 13: xii. 23, xiii. 1, 31, xvii. 1. sqq.) those whom He sends out as apostles have to speak of having *beheld his glory* (i. 14) at every moment in his life (cf. ii. 11, xi. 40). Thus in contradistinction to the Jews and to His own followers, who in their lack of apprehension use the future merely in a chronological sense (vii. 31, viii. 22, xi. 12, 48), Jesus uses the future either to show the consistency, in the past, present and future, of His own life, of His witness to the Father and of the Father's witness to Him (xii. 28, xiii. 31), or to express the final eschatological truth, or to emphasize the significant chronological movement of events towards the hour when His work shall be accomplished and the meaning of His whole life made manifest. There is on His lips no casual use of the future tense. Even the future in such a saying as *The cock shall not crow, till thou hast denied me thrice* (xiii. 38) is ultimately governed by the fact that the glory of God is being manifested in an event in history that is necessarily temporal.

In the Fourth Gospel, then, past, present and future all play a part, but not in order to trace out any sequence of chronological evolution of which the ultimate goal, still future, is the final realization of the Kingdom of God. All three are used, rather, to show that in Jesus men are immediately confronted by the last things; by Life and by Judgement, by the Love of God and by His condemnation. The chronological movement of history is indeed recognized, and has great theological importance, but it is in no sense a movement towards these last things. In Jesus the last things confront men as finally at the beginning of the gospel as they do at its end, and, by implication, wherever His Word is preached by the Apostles and those who believe through them; for at every point they confront men with the final work of God. (See the COMMENTARY, pp. 256-7.) The question must now be raised whether this is, or is not, the proper meaning of the synoptic eschatology.[1] It is true, of course, that not the thirteenth chapter of St. Mark's Gospel only, but each stratum of the synoptic gospels contains eschatological Sayings, references and parables; for the eschatology is in fact as ubiquitous in its distribution as it is awkward to the commentator. The most significant eschatology, however, is perhaps to be found in those Sayings and actions of Jesus which at first sight do not seem to be complicated by eschatology. The preaching of the *gospel* by Jesus, *saying, The time is fulfilled, and the kingdom of God is at hand: repent ye, and believe in the gospel* (Mark i. 14, 15): the presentation of Jesus as Lord of the Sabbath (Mark ii. 23-8), as proclaiming the forgiveness that belongs only to God (Mark ii. 1-12), as doing compassionate works (*passim*) while declaring the fulfilment in His coming of Old Testament prophecies of the messianic or final age of God (Mark iii. 20-30, cf. Matt. xii. 22-37, Luke xi. 14-23; Matt. xi. 4-6, Luke vii. 22, 23, cf. Luke iv. 18, 19; Matt. xii. 28, Luke xi. 20): the sermon which begins with Beatitudes declaring the coming of messianic blessings to men and women and above all to those who follow Jesus (Matt. v. 1-11, Luke vi. 20-2) and ends with the solemn warning that only those who hear the words of Jesus shall be secure in the time of tribulation (Matt. vii. 21-7, Luke vi. 46-9): the weeping over the city which does not recognize the meaning of His coming (Luke xix. 41-4): the Parables of the Wicked Husbandmen (Mark xii. 1-12) and of the Sheep and Goats (Matt. xxv. 31-46): alike pronounce the fulfilment of the Old Testament hope to be a present fact in Jesus, and the present response of men to His word and example to be weighty with final consequences

---

[1] It is beyond the scope of this essay to make anything like a full, or even adequate, examination of the synoptic eschatology. The arguments here suggested are to be found more fully worked out in such recent books as *The Riddle of the New Testament* (2nd ed. 1936); R. Bultmann, *Jesus and the Word*; C. H. Dodd, *The Parables of the Kingdom,* and *History and the Gospel*; and particularly in such articles of Kittel's *Wörterbuch* as εὐαγγελίζομαι, εὐαγγέλιον by Gerhard Friedrich.

beyond and outside the visible world order. Nor does the synoptic tradition lack affirmations of the absolute importance of the words of Jesus as the unique revelation of the Father (Mark ix. 2–8, iv. 1–12; Matt. xi. 25–30, Luke x. 21–4; Luke v. 1; Matt. xiii. 34, 35). Moreover, this firm recognition that the speech and acts of Jesus are misunderstood save as the revelation of the word of God active in His creation and already heavy with the final alternative of judgement or glory transcends even the apparently chronologically determined Sayings in Mark xiii: *Verily I say unto you, This generation shall not pass away, until all these things be accomplished. Heaven and earth shall pass away: but my words shall not pass away. But of that day or that hour knoweth no one, not even the angels in heaven, neither the Son, but the Father* (Mark xiii. 30–2). The knowledge which is being given to those who hear the word of Jesus, while it is wholly concerned with the last things of God that confront men in Jesus, is essentially not an historical knowledge at all, even in those parts of the synoptic gospels which seem most concerned with the forecasting of future events in the chronological order of this world. The Second Coming is not, in the synoptic gospels, the final act of God for which men wait and yearn, as they were used to do under the old dispensation. Their call as Christians, their understanding of the world as it is and of their purpose in the world as it is, their love for their fellows and their patient enduring of persecution within and without, are alike created and demanded by the knowledge which proceeds from the life, death and resurrection of Jesus, that the last things are now, already, fully upon them. There is still a future: there must be a term to this present tension in the flesh in which they are racked between the two orders, the two ages, to both of which they belong. Their Master knew the same tension, and also looked forward to its term (Luke xii. 50). But confidence in the future termination of the visible world, and in the consequent future revelation of the final position of men before God, never leads them to attach less than supreme importance to their present state before God and their present vocation in the world, but rather serves to increase their consciousness of it.

Since this is its consistent perspective, the synoptic material—the record of words and deeds, of the Passion and Death of Jesus—although composed of *historical* episodes and from first to last related in *historical* terms, must properly be called *theological*. It is, for instance, in the Gospel of Saint Mark, rightly prefixed by the phrase *The beginning of the gospel*, for all the history that follows is misconstrued if it be not recognized as declaring the final act of God. Now the eschatological language serves to point the theological significance of the history recorded, inasmuch as it presses home the warning that the history will be misunderstood apart from its present positing of the last things of God. But the eschatological language will become dangerously untheological if it be so detached and over-emphasized that it obscures the consistent theological bias with which the history is impressed. For history—a historical saying or episode—that is speaking simply of some future act of God is no longer theologically significant history, since it is no longer clearly defined as history in which God now finally confronts men. How easy it is to wrest the eschatology from its proper function, and so to evacuate its historical basis of its theological significance, may be seen from the many difficulties which have arisen when the Marcan Saying, *Verily I say unto you, There be some here of them that stand by, which shall in no wise taste of death, till they see the kingdom of God come with power* (Mark ix. 1), has been expounded without reference to the rest of the synoptic tradition. The focus of interest moves from the Saying itself, and from the theological illumination which it casts upon its setting in history, to speculation about some future fulfilment, and so the Saying is made a non-theological authority, either for deifying some future phenomenon in the experience of men—the Church, for instance—or for questioning the human foresight of Jesus. In either case the synoptic insistence that the history of Jesus bears the theological witness in itself, and is therefore the primary object of scrutiny and exegesis, is obscured. Thus divorced from the essential synoptic concentration upon history, eschatological theology may easily produce undisciplined legend, and become no more than an opportunity for creative imagination which loses the whole realism of accurate observation. But—and this is what the gospels themselves triumphantly maintain—there is no basis of theological knowledge except the real and observable world. *This is my beloved Son, hear him.—The Word was made flesh:* the whole activity of the evangelists proceeds from their confidence that in the final analysis the real and observable world, illuminated by the real and observable event of Jesus in the flesh, possesses in itself such immediate and direct witness to God that it is the witness of God to Himself. It is, perhaps, the conscious recognition of the danger of interpreting the eschatology with reference to a chronological future that has caused the Fourth Evangelist to lay aside—not entirely, but none the less significantly—eschatological theology, and to substitute for it the language of the Spirit. For the significance of the *Spirit* in the Fourth Gospel is precisely that of the eschatology as related to the history of Jesus in the synoptic tradition. It is the Spirit that is to bring home clearly to men that in Jesus they are confronted by the end. The Spirit in fact guards against any misconstruction of the words and signs of Jesus as 'penultimate'. It is this that lies behind the reminders that the followers of Jesus did not understand what He was saying and doing until the Spirit had come, just as it lies behind the rigorous relation of the Paraclete, the Spirit of Truth, to the historical flesh of Jesus. Because the historical Jesus is the place where men are confronted by the end, His word involves an ultimate judgement of the world and an ultimate manifestation of the love of God. In the unruly, still rebellious, tribulation of the visible world, when it is easy for believers to slip back out of the knowledge of the love of God, and for unbelievers to ignore the judgement that presses upon them, the Spirit consoles and convicts—not of future mercies and future retribution, but of present, though unseen, glory and of present, though unseen, rejection. It is not, however, that the moment when the last things have broken in upon history as an event is now past, and that the knowledge given by the Spirit brings assurance that those who have once been called can now rest in an easy security of contact with an unseen, spiritual world. On the contrary, the Spirit, in illuminating the words and works of Jesus, forces upon those who have heard and who hear them the continual present tension of acceptance or rejection to which they are exposed by the living Word of God. This is the grim moral of the apostasy in the church to which the Epistles of John are written, just as it is the grim lesson of the behaviour of the Jews, of Judas, and even of Peter, in the gospel. The work of the Spirit is to make it known that *now* the final things press upon those within the Church and upon those to whom the Word is preached, with the inevitable final implications that follow from this.

For such reasons it is not true to say that, although the eschatological language has not been altogether discarded in the Fourth Gospel, it has been essentially *transmuted*, as though originally eschatology meant the heralding of the end, but now is fulfilled in the coming of the Spirit. Rather, the language of the Spirit secures more explicitly the theological context of that urgent, final impact of God upon the world which the eschatology is concerned to proclaim. It *is* true to say that there has been an evolution of apostolic perception: that what has hitherto been expressed in traditional eschatological terms is now expressed as theology. But an evolution of perception involving the use of different categories implies neither that the truth perceived itself spoke of an evolution ushering in the last things, nor that there has taken place any evolution from the perception of one truth—which had erroneously been thought to be final—to the perception of another truth, now thought to be final. Moreover, this evolution of perception, which has replaced the synoptic use of traditional eschatological terms by a conscious theological language of the Spirit, appears to have been brought about, not by some individual partiality for theologizing on the part of the Fourth Evangelist, but by a necessity inherent in the synoptic material. Just as, a generation before, the author of Saint Mark's Gospel seems to have perceived that the isolated episodes and Sayings with which the apostolic missionaries edified their converts demanded, for their fuller understanding, to be set in the context of the Life, Death and Resurrection of Jesus as the Event of the Gospel of God, so the fourth Evangelist seems to have perceived that the theology inherent in these reminiscences—the theology which no doubt had all along secured their formulation and their survival in the tradition—must be made explicit and regulative in their own interests. Left to itself and detached from the evangelical context in which it had first occurred or from the apostolic context in which it had reinforced the Gospel, an episode or Saying, just because it bore the tantalizing marks of a reference outside itself, might easily become the basis of speculation or of secondary edification.[1] The only safeguard against this misuse of a tradition first formulated in the perception of Jesus and His apostles, that men are confronted by nothing less than the final things of God Himself, is a conscious theology. The doctrine of the Holy Spirit is the fourth ✓ Evangelist's protection against the imposition of an interpretation upon the history he records, just as it is also his protection against idealizing either himself or the original disciples. The events he records possessed their meaning before ever the disciples apprehended it. Later they saw, understood, and apprehended. The doctrine of the Holy Spirit has therefore primarily a negative importance. It is, of course, always possible to deny this by asserting that the doctrine is merely an outrageous attempt to dignify an idea by making it universal, but this can in fact be tested, ultimately by an analysis of the essential theological perception of the non-Johannine books of the New Testament, and primarily by a consideration of the Johannine theology as a whole.

The deviation from eschatology is observable not only in the fourth Evangelist's doctrine of the Spirit. It affects the whole underlying meaning of the Johannine theology, and brings into being a whole vocabulary designed to show the presently conceived relation of men to God declared in and effected by the history of Jesus. Such words and phrases as *to believe, to glorify, to abide in, to know, to rejoice, to be born of God, to love*, are redefined in the relation of Jesus to His Father manifest in His Life and Death, and through His Life and Death made accessible to those who apprehend the meaning of His Life and Death. The mainspring of Johannine Christology is not eschatology, but epiphany. Yet this is no sliding off into a Gnostic system of knowledge mediated apart from, and independently of, history. The Fourth Gospel begins by denying the possibility of any direct human knowledge of God: *No man hath seen God at any time. . . .* (i. 18): *No man hath ascended into heaven* (iii. 13): *Ye have neither heard his voice at any time, nor seen his form. . . .* (v. 37): *Not that any man hath seen the Father. . . .* (vi. 46): *Ye have not known him* (viii. 55). But these crushing negatives serve to introduce the one complete and scandalous exception, Jesus the Son of God: *The only begotten Son, which is in the bosom of the Father, he hath declared him* (i. 18): *The Son can do nothing of himself, but what he seeth the Father doing: for what things soever he doeth, these the Son also doeth in like manner* (v.

---

[1] e.g. Saint Luke's identification of *the abomination of desolation* (Mark xiii. 14, 15) as the armies round about Jerusalem (Luke xxi. 20, 21) and the same evangelist's use of a parable that turns upon an eschatologically perceived situation as an exhortation to daily prayer (Luke xviii. 1–8).

19): *I can of myself do nothing: as I hear, I judge: and my judgement is righteous; because I seek not mine own will, but the will of him that sent me* (v. 30, cf. iii. 13, vi. 46, viii. 55). The knowledge of God therefore, so far as men are concerned, depends upon their recognition of Jesus (v. 30–7, etc.), as He confronts them in human flesh, with audible words and visible acts.

Moreover, the knowledge of God through belief in the historical Jesus is never itself a knowledge separable from the history through which God confronts men. Mysticism is not Johannine, if by mysticism is meant an escape from the particular history, whether of Jesus, or of the believer; or a symbolizing of history; or an evaluation of history on the basis of personal and individual experience; or a free-moving, unfettered exercise of speculative religious imagination. It was the principal achievement of Irenæus in the battle with Gnosticism to have confronted the world of his day, not with a Christian Hellenistic mystical philosophy, but with the Church as a dogmatic, historical, Biblical way of salvation, in and through which men are confronted by the final revelation of God through Christ and by faith incorporated within it, so that Christians are at once confronted by the revelation of God and by the world that is ignorant of it. In this Irenæus was in no way departing from the model of the fourth Evangelist, who means by the knowledge of God, not knowledge of His existence or of His essence, but knowledge of His final salvation now confronting men in Jesus: His love, His Judgement, His gift of eternal life, His revelation of what is good or evil. Nothing else than this is implied when, in consecrating Himself and His disciples, Jesus prays: *And this is life eternal, that they should know thee the only true God, and him whom thou didst send, even Jesus Christ* (xvii. 3), and so points to the fulfilment, through and in His hour of glorification, of such Sayings as *This is the will of my Father, that every one that beholdeth the Son, and believeth on him, should have eternal life; and I will raise him up at the last day* (vi. 40).

This knowledge of God is an immediate apprehension, not of the Father, but of Jesus as an historic or actual phenomenon. It is only *he that believeth on the Son of God* that *hath the witness in himself* (1 John v. 10). There is, however, a necessary guiding of the perception through the Old Testament prophets, through John the Baptist, and through the miracles of Jesus, which are also *witnesses*; necessary, because otherwise knowledge would not fall within the range of vision. But all these witnesses may be misunderstood, even—and supremely—if they are thought to be signs that God is with Jesus (iii. 2, 3). They can be rightly understood as witnesses only by those who through the Death and Resurrection of Jesus have been given that insight into his flesh as the place where the glory of God is made known which can be described only parabolically, as, for instance, rebirth *of water and the Spirit*, because it is an insight that itself comes only from God. This God-given perception of the glory in the flesh of Jesus had been safeguarded in the synoptic tradition by such a refrain as *Who hath ears to hear, let him hear* (Mark iv. 9, etc.), or by the Saying *Flesh and blood hath not revealed it unto thee, but my Father which is in heaven* (Matt. xvi. 17). In the Fourth Gospel the visible witnesses, designed as they are to be means by which men may come to the knowledge of God in Jesus, themselves depend for their validity as witnesses upon the glorification of the Son by the Father, which is made known to men by faith alone, being beyond the range of present sight (xx. 29). All knowledge of God hangs, not only on the Life and Death of Jesus, but on His Resurrection.

This concentration of the knowledge of God upon Jesus might seem to involve a narrowing of the field of phenomena through which God reveals Himself, and an arbitrary limitation of their scope, and so bound to end in one-sidedness. But the contrary is the fact. As a result of the perception of the glory of God in Jesus, overwhelming as its particularity is, not only the visible witnesses of the Old Testament prophets, of John the Baptist and of the works of Jesus, but the whole *Cosmos* comes within the range of observation. Not only the Old Testament manna, but the universal phenomenon of bread, and behind bread, of the necessity of eating: not only the Baptism of John, but ceremonial washing, and behind it, the universal significance of water: not only Biblical themes like shepherds and sheep and vines, but the contexts of the human ordering of the means of life and the natural order of growth and fertility, now bear witness to the glory of God in Jesus, and are accordingly perceived to have theological significance. Even the compassionate acts of Jesus, the restoring of sight to the blind, of life to the dead, and the titles of Jesus, Word or Son, once they have been authenticated in His glorification, illuminate theologically the fact of human paternity, the fact of speech, the facts of life and death, of darkness and light.

So it is with the fourth Evangelist's treatment of the synoptic title *Son of man*. In the synoptic gospels, no doubt largely because of its frequent eschatological setting, a whole theology is embedded in the phrase. In the Fourth Gospel it has become detached from this setting, and is set side by side with *Son of God* and expresses the meaning of the history of Jesus of Nazareth. θεός-ἄνθρωπος becomes the theme—not a theme of speculative theology, though, when once the simplification has been made, it has, of necessity, speculative implications—but the theme of revelation. Jesus, the human Jesus, *Son of man*, is the place where the glory of God is revealed (iii. 13, vi. 27). Yet even so, the apprehension of the *Son of man* as the revelation of the Father depends, first upon His death (iii. 14, vi. 53, viii. 28, xii. 34 sqq.), and then upon His glorification and exaltation (i. 51, vi. 62, xii. 23, xiii. 31). The humanity of Jesus, thought of simply as humanity, is propounded as the focus of revelation, yet even so, men do not see God merely in observing His humanity, but only through that perception of His humanity which comes through His Death and is specifically God-given. Nevertheless, here too, when once the God-given perception of the observable phenomenon, in this case the *flesh* of Jesus, is bestowed; when, that is to say, His *flesh* is apprehended by the believer, not historically, but theologically; it holds in itself the promise which is God's will for all humanity (xvii. 22). This concentration upon the manhood of Jesus in contrast with His unobservable existence with God, for the sake of pointing the paradox of revelation and of declaring the theological hope which men have in Jesus, is not an innovation of the fourth Evangelist, but is a basic theme of the Pauline Epistles (cf. Gal. iv. 3–7) and of the Epistle to the Hebrews (ii. 5–18) and, in the end, of the synoptic tradition also, when the analysis of the subject-matter is pressed beyond a technical examination of the characteristic terminology with which the Evangelists are operating.

It is now possible to summarize the attitude of the fourth Evangelist to history. His gospel is consciously created by his recognition of the supreme importance of the history of Jesus, which not only mediates all that is to be known of God, but also, in so doing, confronts man with the last things of God *now*, in the history through which man is passing, and so relates the whole world in which he stands to God. But the truth made known in history is the truth *of God*: it is not, that is to say, the truth of observable history in relation to other points in observable history, but the truth of observable history in relation to Him whom *no man hath seen at any time*. The true understanding of the history of Jesus—and consequently of all observable history—therefore springs from that God-given perception of which the apostles who *beheld his glory*, and those who share their apprehension (xvii. 20), can confidently speak, and it cuts right across the chronological understanding of history. For this reason, in the interests of that history which has been seen to bear witness to God, it has to be detached from its chronological context and narrated non-historically, since only so can justice be done to its theological significance. Even the chronological movement of Jesus from His Baptism to the Cross, which in itself, as a chronological movement, is theologically significant, since it bears witness to the return of Jesus whence He came, and to the requisite movement of man to God, has to be rid of any semblance of evolution, lest God should be thought of as an historical end, or His action confined to a distant future. But this detachment from its chronological, technically historical setting, only serves to press home the supreme and unique significance of the history as the place where God has now, in Jesus, once and for all confronted men with those last things which have absolute importance for man's historical life in the flesh. This event of Jesus, wrested out of its chronological context, in which it might have appeared—as it *did* appear to the Jews—to be merely one event in a series of events, is shown to be *the* event which bestows upon all events their theological meaning, mediating the love of God and His judgement, eternal life and eternal condemnation.

The fourth Evangelist's procedure in regard to the history of Jesus must be justified or condemned by a full consideration of the synoptic gospels and of the attitude of the other New Testament theologians to the life of Jesus in the flesh. If here too the history is, from the earliest perceptible point, remembered and related, not because of its intrinsic chronological significance, but because it confronts men with the final act of God, His Kingdom, His Salvation; and if here too the understanding of this history is thought to be initiated, not by any analysable human experience, but by the act of God in bestowing belief in Jesus; then the fourth Evangelist's treatment of history must be regarded as forced upon him by the history which he has heard, by the gospel which he has received, by the apostolic Church to which he belongs, and not by some idiosyncrasy of his environment or of his temperament.

What then is to be said of such peculiarly Johannine episodes as the Raising of Lazarus? Has the author merely drawn into his gospel 'reminiscences of important but forgotten incidents' (Scott–Holland)? Dr. Johnson warns us that 'incidents which give excellence to a biography are of a volatile and evanescent kind, such as soon escape the memory and are rarely transmitted by tradition'. But these peculiar Johannine episodes are hardly volatile and evanescent; rather, they are very much the reverse. However positively we must maintain that there is no evidence that the fourth Evangelist invented episodes or Sayings of Jesus out of the air, it remains equally certain that his perception of the meaning of history forces him to set the history he narrates in the widest possible theological context, in the full light of His Christian perception of Jesus and with the fullest regard for the theological implications, not only of isolated episodes and fragmentary Sayings, but of the whole apostolic Gospel. Whatever was the actual chain of events by which the Crucifixion of Jesus was set in motion, His death was veritably brought about by His claim to hold out the eternal life of God to men and women, a claim which He made in declaring the advent of the Kingdom of God, and entry into the Kingdom of God through obedience to His call. Therefore, if this is the inevitable implication of the historical acts of Jesus vindicated and made perceptible to men by His Resurrection from the dead, it follows that the fourth Evangelist is doing no more than justice to the history behind him when he recounts the raising of a man from the dead with such circumstance and repercussions that it appears unmistakably to be the vital turning point of the gospel of *God* who *so loved the world, that he gave his only begotten Son, that whosoever believeth on him should not perish, but have eternal life.*

## NOTE

This essay is based upon fragments left by the author—fragments which seemed to demand inclusion, but which lacked sequence and were unaccompanied by any scheme or argument. The editor therefore tried to work them up into a connected essay, retaining as much as he could (including the quaint references to Dr. Johnson) but taking final responsibility for the conclusions reached. This does not mean that the essay is just as the editor would have planned, or concluded it, had he set out in the first instance to write it himself. But it will explain why, at the time of the first edition, he was anxious to distinguish it from the author's finished work by printing it out of its logical place. For this edition, however, it seems preferable to place it where it more naturally belongs.

# VIII. THE THEOLOGICAL TENSION
# OF THE FOURTH GOSPEL

IT is now possible to return to the consideration of the Problem propounded at the beginning of this Introduction. The survey of recent critical work upon the Fourth Gospel has shown how restless that work is, and has suggested that this restlessness is due less to some temporary inadequacy than to the theme of the Gospel itself. For the Gospel refuses to come to rest in any haven provided by historical or psychological (mystical) analysis. Say that the Gospel is the product of an author who has found rest in a state of mystical quietness and perfection, and its steady, consistent emphasis upon historicity, upon the flesh of Jesus the Son of man, renders the mystical commentator uneasy in its presence. Say that it is the work of an eyewitness whose reminiscences have been arranged, ordered and straightened out by himself or by some disciple familiar with his mind and manner of narrating his memories, and the book stirs angrily under our fingers, and declares that the flesh profiteth nothing; that mere historicity, mere reminiscences, would bury the truth irrecoverably in the earth; for the truth which Jesus *is* and *was* can be made known only by the Holy Spirit of God, who is the Spirit of Truth; and the Paraclete had not been given to the disciples while they were eyewitnesses of the life and passion of Jesus. Say that the Fourth Gospel is Hellenic, or that it emerges from the background of some mixture of Greek thought and Oriental mythology, and we are confounded by the Hebraic quality of the language in which it is written, by the author's rigid adherence to the Old Testament for his literary allusions, and by the frequent occurrence of Palestinian topographical details. Say that there is both historical reminiscence and spiritual interpretation in the book, and no doubt we are right; but go on and demand that the critic, or the spiritually minded interpreter, shall separate the history from the interpretation, and we force him to give up the attempt in despair, for the author of the book has set a barricade across that road, a barricade through which no one has yet passed or is likely to pass, since the Spiritual meaning of the life and death of Jesus belongs to the history and, indeed, made it what it was, for the Spirit gave reality to His observable words and to His observable actions—*it is the Spirit that quickeneth, the flesh profiteth nothing*. In other words, the theme of the Fourth Gospel is the non-historical that makes sense of history, the infinite that makes sense of time, God who makes sense of men and is therefore their Saviour. The specific technique of the author has been wrought out in order to grapple with this theme. For this reason, because the author has seen his theme so clearly and held to it so consistently, it is impossible for the critic to separate what is historical in the book from what is spiritual interpretation. To attempt to do so would be to misunderstand the theme altogether and to outrage the technique. At times, it is true, we are led to think that we can treat the work as a mere historical record —for instance, in chs. xviii and xix—but just when we suppose ourselves moving easily we find ourselves gyrating against a background that is foreign to us and beyond our observation. At other times the history seems to have completely disappeared, and we are tempted to speak freely of symbol or allegory or mysticism or metaphysics—we suppose ourselves in some serene world of the author's ideas or conceptions—only to be jerked roughly back to earth by a topographical fact, by a detail that refuses to be allegorized, by a reference to a feast of the Jews, or by an allusion that recalls us to the concrete, observable world of Palestine. Or again, we imagine that we can detect here and there— as, for example, in vi. 22–5—the line that divides history from interpretation. But the division cannot be maintained. There is no clear dividing line. The non-historical factor penetrates our supposed historical data and the historical factor is woven into what is manifestly non-historical. Moreover, the non-historical cannot be dismissed as Johannine interpretation. It is, rather, the veritable meaning of the history that has been set forth. The meaning of the life of Jesus is not a thing added by an interpreter, at a later date, to an already existing naked historical narrative or reminiscence: a thing which can be detached or removed by the critic in order that he may recover the naked events, and clothe them, maybe, with some other interpretation of his own. The meaning of the history of Jesus precedes and conditions its occurrence. This is what the author of the Fourth Gospel has seen. Faced by the life and death of Jesus, in its general or in its particular details, the fourth Evangelist knows that he is confronted by what is infinite and eternal. He finds himself standing at a point where all things become wellnigh transparent, where he is able to see what no eye hath seen. For in the flesh of Jesus he sees, not only His eternal sonship, but also the eternal sonship of His disciples; not only the eternal sonship of His disciples, but the light which lighteneth every man. And we dare not say that what he has seen is illusion, or merely an interpretation. For what he has seen does make sense of the fragments recorded in the synoptic gospels. Though it is no doubt hard for us to understand, the themes of the Fourth Gospel in a real sense go before the contents of the synoptic sources in such a way as to rescue them from dissolving into mere fragments, or, better perhaps, in such a way as to show the wholeness which is lying hidden in the various Marcan episodes or in the separate, detached sayings that make up what is called the Q material; a wholeness not secured by the skilled literary arrangements of the same material which we possess in the Gospels of Matthew and Luke.

The steady refusal of the Fourth Gospel to come to rest in any solution which conservative or radical scholars have propounded is the Problem of the Gospel. Explain the 'But' which the Gospel sets against our solutions and which pulls away the cup just when it is at our lips, and we shall have solved the riddle of the book. The 'But' which we here encounter is, however, no 'sneaking, evasive, half-bred sort of conjunction' which the honest interpreter is able to remove; it is, rather, the expression in a literary document of the restlessness of human life; it is the 'But' of an author vibrating under the tension of the relation between God and man, a tension which he has encountered in the figure of Jesus of Nazareth and of which he cannot be rid. For this strictly theological tension can be resolved only in the resurrection, in the resting places which Jesus has prepared in His Father's house, in the advent of the Holy Spirit of God, who is the teacher of the final and ultimate Truth. To this rest, to this solution of the Problem of his own book and of all human life, the author of the Fourth Gospel continually points and bears witness. But he is able to bear witness only because he has seen this theological tension in the flesh and blood of the Son of man and because he believes in the resurrection of the Son of God and in the present power of the Spirit of God, who enables men to apprehend the truth which is in Jesus: to perceive, that is to say, the meaning of those fragmentary records which for us are contained in the three synoptic gospels, and which for him and his readers were present in stories handed down orally as well as in some literary form. Whether the author was in possession of some reminiscences of an eyewitness which were contained neither in the oral tradition nor in the documents current amongst Christians at the end of the first century, we cannot say. All we can say is that, in whatever form and with whatever authority these scattered fragmentary stories of the life and death of Jesus came to him, he saw their meaning, apprehended them as proceeding from one source and pointing to one goal. He saw the glory of God making sense of the history, for it is the Spirit who giveth life—by itself the flesh is meaningless and unprofitable. This is not metaphysics, though it is what the true metaphysician is in the end talking about. Rather, this is Apostolic Christianity, the rough material from which a philosophy may perhaps spring. This is the truth as it was seen by the Apostles of the Lord, by those who had been called into the theological tension of human life at its most acute point, at the place where the Christ was crucified. How many who were called by Jesus to be His apostles apprehended the meaning of His call and became Apostles, we do not know. Whether the man who wrote the Fourth Gospel was both an apostle and an Apostle we do not know. But it is almost impossible to escape from the conviction that the reader of the Gospel is at the very heart of that Apostolic Christianity which must be radically distinguished from mysticism on the one hand and from mere historical reminiscences on the other.

What the tension of Apostolic Christianity was we must try to learn by returning once more to the exegesis of the relation between the Pauline Epistles, the Epistle to the Hebrews, the Johannine writings and—the synoptic gospels. For it is in the investigation of this relation that the true theological tension of Primitive Christianity appears, since it is this relation that points to the relation of historical occurrence to that which is beyond observation, to that which cometh without observation—to the Kingdom of God, to the Word of God, to Jesus as the Son of God, to the disciples of Jesus as men who have received the Spirit, and to all men as those who have received the Light of God, because they are His creatures.

The purpose of this commentary can now be defined. It must endeavour to hear and set forth the Meaning which the author of the Gospel has himself heard and seen in the concrete, historical life and death of Jesus of Nazareth, in His separate actions and in His audible words. The purpose of this commentary is to barricade the roads which seek to solve the problem either by regarding this Meaning as an idea of the author or as something which itself belongs to the mere hearing or sight of an eyewitness, regarded as historian, for in that case his faith would be not merely irrelevant, but actually suspect, since the eyewitness who believed could not be accepted as an impartial witness. The purpose of this commentary is also to barricade the roads which lead to a disentangling of history and interpretation. This triple barricading does not, however, originate in some perversity of the author of this commentary, but because these barricades have been erected by the original author of the book, and the meaning of his book must remain closed to those who tear down the barricades which he has so carefully erected. Did we say that he had 'erected' these barricades? No, we must not say this. He found the barricades there already, for he is persuaded that the meaning which he has heard does veritably lie in the history. Without it the history is meaningless. Take away the meaning and we should have merely the record of an eyewitness. Take away the history and we should be left only with a human notion or idea. Let the two stand as separable entities and both the unity of the figure of Jesus, indeed of all men and things, is roughly disrupted, and all becomes but sounding brass and a tinkling cymbal.

And so, if we are to interpret the Fourth Gospel, we must take our stand where the Evangelist stood and endeavour to follow him and to hear what he is saying. As his commentators we must assume that what he has heard, he did hear. And we must take him at his word when he says that the Spirit does bring to light the meaning that lies in the History of Jesus of Nazareth and that there was once a man who had veritably heard that meaning and set forth what he had heard.

This does not mean, however, that the commentator has lost all independence and become altogether a slave. His first responsibility, it is true, must be to surrender himself to his author: that is the necessary prolegomenon to exegesis. But the New Testament contains other books, which also claim to bear witness to the meaning of the life and death and resurrection of Jesus of Nazareth. The New Testament also contains other records of His words and actions, and these also presumably have some meaning. The relation between the Fourth Gospel and the Pauline epistles and the synoptic gospels, between the meaning of the Fourth Gospel and Paulinism and the meaning of the synoptic narratives, vitally concerns the commentator on the Fourth Gospel. This relationship must not, however, be dismissed superficially; we must not talk too glibly of the dependence of John upon Paul, nor be content with too easy a catalogue of the differences between the Fourth Gospel and the other three; nor must we too quickly set John and Paul on the one side of a line and the synoptic gospels on the other. The issue is too serious, the decision too momentous, for us to handle the problem presented by the various witnesses contained in the New Testament, save at the end of our work or at the end of a comment upon any particular passage. We have no right to assume from the beginning that Paul and John and Mark are moving in entirely different worlds and talking of entirely different things. Still less dare we assume from the beginning that the teaching of Jesus is moving round one theme, and that the energy of His apostles and evangelists is directed towards some wholly different theme or themes. And we dare not adopt this presupposition, not because it conflicts with ecclesiastical orthodoxy, but because it directly contradicts the claim of the authors whose works we are pledged to interpret. One and all claim to be talking about Jesus of Nazareth; they claim to have seen the meaning of what He said and did, to be, in fact, His apostles and evangelists, and to be concerned with what He propounded and with no other propositions. We must therefore assume that they mean what they say, until or unless we are driven and compelled to deny it. We must not set ourselves in array against them unless we have really busied ourselves with apprehending what it is that they are in fact saying.

The test that we must in the end apply to the Fourth Gospel, the test by which the Fourth Gospel stands or falls, is whether the Marcan narrative becomes more intelligible after reading the Fourth Gospel, whether the Pauline Epistles become more transparent, or whether the whole material presented to us in the New Testament is breaking up into unrelated fragments. If the latter be really and finally the case, we must then go back to speak of Johannine and Pauline theology. Once again we should be compelled to speak of the simplicity of the synoptic gospels, of the complexity of Pauline ideas, and of the unhistorical mysticism of the Fourth Gospel. If, for example, the synoptic narratives of miracles of healing are concerned merely with the cure of a paralytic, or of a blind man, or of some persons suffering from physical or mental disease; if their meaning is exhausted with such cures; if they have no other important meaning and relationship, then it is clear that the Fourth Gospel is talking about something quite different when it insists that the miracles of healing were signs of another, quite final healing. If, to take another example, the theme of the Lord's ministry in the synoptic gospels was the Kingdom of God of which Jesus was simply the herald and prophet, then it is clear that the reiterated '*I am*' of the Fourth Gospel has transferred the reader into some different realm. Or again, if the Fourth Gospel, with its emphasis upon the Spirit, really does open up what may rightly be called a process of evolution in history, and if, in order to secure this, it has discarded the more primitive eschatological language of the earlier tradition, then we should have to own that, at its very heart, it has moved into a world in which it is exceedingly difficult to recognize the authentic teaching of Jesus—that teaching which, according to the synoptic gospels, was proclaimed in the midst of an acute eschatological tension.

These, and many other like problems, are the final problems of New Testament exegesis, but they are *final* problems. They may, indeed they must, be formulated at the beginning of our work, but they can be handled adequately only when we have formulated them as theological problems, and when, as theologians, we have not only struggled with the meaning of the Fourth Gospel and of the Pauline Epistles, but have applied the same critical theological energy to the synoptic gospels, and to the meaning of the material which seems to underlie the synoptic gospels as they stand.

A commentary on the Fourth Gospel can therefore be no more than a preliminary work. It leads on to further study of the Pauline Epistles and of the synoptic gospels. For the Fourth Gospel should not be regarded merely as an appendix to other biblical work, as though it lay altogether on the periphery of the Bible. We must be prepared to find that the Fourth Gospel ought to be regarded as a necessary prolegomenon to the understanding, not only of the other books of the New Testament, but of the Old Testament as well. At any rate, we have no right to rule out this possibility *a priori*.

In introducing the reader to the study of the Fourth Gospel it has seemed supremely necessary to demand that he should take it seriously. It has not seemed so necessary to overwhelm him with information that will free him from the onus of reading what the Evangelist actually wrote, that will enable him to talk about the Gospel or sit for an examination upon it without having read it or sought to digest it. And so, without further delay, we advance to the book itself.

# COMMENTARY

## THE PROLOGUE

### I. 1–18

*1. 1. In the beginning was the Word, and the Word was with God, and the Word was God. 2. The same was in the beginning with God. 3. All things were made by him; and without him was not anything made that hath been made. 4. In him was life; and the life was the light of men. 5. And the light shineth in the darkness; and the darkness apprehended it not. 6. There came a man, sent from God, whose name was John. 7. The same came for witness, that he might bear witness of the light, that all might believe through him. 8. He was not the light, but came that he might bear witness of the light. 9. There was the true light, even the light which lighteth every man, coming into the world. 10. He was in the world, and the world was made by him, and the world knew him not. 11. He came unto his own, and they that were his own received him not. 12. But as many as received him, to them gave he the right to become children of God, even to them that believe on his name: 13. which were born, not of blood, nor of the will of the flesh, nor of the will of man, but of God. 14. And the Word became flesh, and dwelt among us (and we beheld his glory, glory as of the only begotten from the Father), full of grace and truth. 15. John beareth witness of him, and crieth, saying, This was he of whom I said, He that cometh after me is become before me: for he was before me. 16. For of his fulness we all received, and grace for grace. 17. For the law was given by Moses; grace and truth came by Jesus Christ. 18. No man hath seen God at any time; the only begotten Son, which is in the bosom of the Father, he hath declared him.*

'The business of the world is carried on by words'—so writes Sir Daniel Hall in the introduction to his *Digressions of a Man of Science*. The Evangelist is also confronted by the majestic power of words, for he is confronted by the words of Jesus. But the words of Jesus are not isolated maxims, detached aphorisms, or disjointed commands, powerful, but without connected meaning. Because of their essential unity the Evangelist is pressed from the plural to the singular, from 'words' to word, and from a series of words to The Word. The business of the world depends upon the Word of God both for its creation and for its salvation. In thus substituting the singular for the plural—Word for words, God for men —the Evangelist does not, however, lose himself in an abstraction. He too is concerned with words, for it is his purpose to portray a Jesus who spoke. He too is concerned with men of flesh and blood, for it is his purpose to confront his readers with Jesus and His apostles. But from the beginning, and throughout his work, he makes it clear that the words of Jesus are meaningless apart from their relation to the word of God, that the apostles are insignificant apart from their relation to the man Jesus, and that Jesus Himself profiteth nothing unless He be the incarnate Word of God. Word—words—the business of the world: these are the themes of the Fourth Gospel. Infinity—history, eternity—time, 'flesh' as the place where the Word of God is recognized, believed and known: these are the themes by which the Evangelist has been confronted in Jesus. The prologue to the Fourth Gospel does not move *to* Jesus but *from* Him. His coming is assumed in the very first verse and conditions the language throughout. The texture of the prologue is taken from the Old Testament Scriptures (e.g. Gen. i, Prov. viii); but it is altogether Christian. That Jesus once spoke is more fundamental for its understanding than is the history of Greek philosophy or the story of the westward progress of Oriental mysticism; more fundamental even than the first chapter of Genesis or the eighth chapter of the Proverbs. Accordingly, the prologue, like other literary introductions, is not so much a preface to the gospel as a summary of it. What the Evangelist meant by the Word, what indeed he meant by the architecture of his prologue, he has himself made known in the body of his work.

The Word which the Apostles had received from Jesus was no new thing. It had its origin neither in recent nor in ancient history, not even in the rhythm of the original act of creation. The Word which the Apostles received from Jesus is beyond time and beyond history: it belongs to eternity, and therefore to every epoch in time and to every race of men. The Word neither grows old and outworn, nor does it ever become some new thing. The Word of God is the Word *of* God. It is His meaning and will, and, for this reason, it is the meaning of the whole universe, which is the creation of God by His Word. The Word of God, is, however, no second entity, like Him, but less than He. Therefore, if it be said that the Word is with God, it must immediately, and in the same breath, be said that He *is* God. In Jesus, the Word came forth from God. This going forth carried with it, however, no diminution. The Word was not thereby separated or liberated from God. The Word is and remains the Life and Light and Glory of God. The particular, historical mission of the Word was therefore no isolated occurrence, no detached or detachable thing in itself: it took place in the midst of men upon whom the world, as the creation of the Word of God, powerfully presses its meaning and will. No man or thing stands beyond or outside this creation by the Word of God.

Jesus was rejected. But this rejection too is no mere single historical episode. The Word of God is the Life of men and of things. When this Life is recognized and accepted, it is Light; for Light is the manifestation of Life. But the proper sphere of light is darkness. Light does not avoid the darkness: it shines in it. The Light of the Word of God shines in the midst of black opposition; and this opposition is human history. In the context of this general opposition, Jesus was rejected. The darkness neither accepted nor comprehended the manifestation of Life. But, in spite of this opposition, the darkness neither did nor could overwhelm the Light of the Word of God.

The darkness surrounded Jesus—but not altogether. There was a prophetic witness; there was a man—and here the Evangelist falls into the straightforward narrative of prose—who pointed beyond himself. Sent and endowed by God, John exercised a universal prophetic witness to the Light. Faced by the prophet, men are confronted not merely by prophecy, but by Him to whom prophecy bears witness; they are confronted by the veritable Light that lightens all men, sets them in the truth, and makes known their proper and final position. Faced by John, men stand in the presence of Jesus.

To stand in the Light and to believe are not, however, identical positions. To believe is not merely to stand in the Light, but to possess it, to submit to it and to be led by it in thought and will, as the original disciples of Jesus were finally led and possessed by it and as the Evangelist had himself submitted to it. The history of John and Jesus reproduces a situation in which all men, present, past, and future, always stand; and the unbelief of the Jews does but reproduce general unbelief. All men stand in the truth. But when John uttered his witness, the Light of the creation had come near and, more than that, was in the world. And yet, the world that was His own knew Him not, and the race that had been brought most especially near the Light also knew Him not.

But, in spite of this vast history of the rejection by men of the Word of God, His coming was not in vain. There were men who accepted Him and believed on His name; that is to say, there were men who recognized the signs of His presence in their midst. On them He bestowed the power of Sonship. They became the sons of God. In this divine Sonship all human sonship receives its meaning; a meaning that can, however, only be expressed in a negative. Here is no known, natural sonship, the result of the mixing of bloods, of natural desire, and of an exercise of human will. Here is the ultimate and primal Sonship that has as its origin the creative gift of the will and power of God. But since men receive the Sonship from Jesus, and since only the Word of God can bring into being the children of God, Jesus was the Word made flesh. The Word of God had brought into being a man (the word 'flesh' means neither more nor less than this). This does not mean that the eternal Word of God was transformed into an observable, historical individual man. In that case faith would be disestablished; whereas in Jesus faith is altogether established. Indeed, apart from faith He is a meaningless figure in history and His flesh is unprofitable. That a man was created by the Word of God means that He became the place of revelation. The Word of God had been made known in the two tables of stone on which was engraved the law of God in commandments. The Word of God is now engraved, not in stone, but in human flesh. What the Temple had been, the man Jesus has now become more transparently—the tabernacle of God with men. As over the giving of the Law the grace and truth of God had appeared to Moses (Exod. xxxiv. 4-7) and as His glory had been manifest in Zion (Ps. xxiv. 7 sqq., cii. 16), so—but much more clearly—the glory and grace and truth of God were seen in the man Jesus, whose thought and words flowed from truth, and whose will and actions were governed by the grace of God.

There were men who saw what had been manifested in the flesh of Jesus. They saw the glory of God made known in His Son. This insight of faith gave them their office and marked them out as apostles. Since the Word of God is one and unique, there cannot be a plurality or a series of incarnations. Once, and once for all men, the revelation was made in the one and only begotten Son of God. The apostolic mission is, therefore, universal and unique. The apostolic office can never be submerged in general prophecy or in general mysticism. Prophecy, in the person of John, witnesses to Jesus and is both fulfilled and dissolved. The goal of prophecy has been attained, not in some new Jerusalem, not in a new heaven and a new earth, not in a rich number of new things, not in a company of men transformed into angels—the goal of prophecy is reached in the man Jesus and in those who have been created by Him. The Prophet yields to Jesus and to His apostles and Evangelists. John bears witness, not that some one will come, but that He has come. And so history, a particular history, moves into the centre of the picture; not, however, in such a manner that history now exists as a thing in itself. A particular history moves into the centre of the picture in its transparent relation to the Word and Glory and Truth and Grace of God. To this eternal relation John also bore witness. On the plane of mere historicity Jesus is younger than John. Seen, however, as John saw Him, in His relation to the eternal Word of God, Jesus is altogether pre-eminent. Such was the witness of John. The witness of the apostles is different. Unlike the prophets, unlike John, they did not precede Jesus on the plane of history. They succeeded Him, were created by Him, and owed to Him what they had become. What the apostles received from Jesus is summed up in the one word 'grace'. To Him they brought nothing of their own. Mercy and forgiveness had been poured out upon them in ever-renewed, ever-increasing measure —grace for grace. Thus by different roads the prophet and the apostles of Jesus converge upon the same point in history: they bear united witness to the Word incarnate and proclaim Him to the world.

Say 'prophet', and inevitably the figure of Moses is called up. The ministry of Jesus occurred, after all, in the context of a race owing allegiance not to John, but to Moses. The Evangelist sets forth the relation of Moses to Jesus in one pregnant sentence. Through Moses, the world, and Israel in particular, received the divine imperative—the Law. But the imperative of God does not give life: it kills. Through Jesus Christ, the world, and the Jews in particular, were confronted by grace and truth. And grace and truth do not kill: they give life. Moses and Jesus are not, however, two unrelated factors set side by side merely for purposes of comparison. The imperative of God is the necessary context in which alone the grace and truth of God can be heard and perceived. Salvation is, therefore, of the Jews. Historically, it was made known in the midst of those to whom had been entrusted the final imperative of God, and who, weighed down by the demand of God, had received promises which pointed beyond Judaism to the coming of the Christ. The Evangelist now asserts that the promise which is the fulfilment of Judaism, the fulfilment of the imperative of God, has taken place; and he adds to the word Christ the name Jesus: grace and truth came by Jesus Christ.

But here again, lest with the name Jesus observable history should occupy the final place and goal, and in order that grace and truth may be seen clearly to have their source and origin only in the invisible God, the preface to the Fourth Gospel ends as theologically it must end. It ends with a strong, unmistakable negation of mere historicity—*No man hath seen God at any time*. This negation is, however, at once shown to contain the paradox of faith and of history; for, nevertheless, Jesus, the Son of God, in His relation to the unseen God as Son to Father, has made God known. So the preface to the Fourth Gospel, with its movement from the Word to the Son of God, is both an introduction and a conclusion to the whole work. In it the themes of the gospel are set forth and summed up. The relation between creation and salvation, prophets and apostles, history and that which lies beyond history, time and eternity, law and grace, death and life, faith and unbelief—these are the themes of the Fourth Gospel, themes that meet and go apart, separate and meet, in the flesh, that is to say, in the human history of the man Jesus, in Jesus Christ, the Son of God, and Word of God.

# COMMENTARY

i. 1–5. Since the gospel is the record of the new creation, of the bringing into being of the sons of God, the opening verses of the prologue echo the style, vocabulary, syntax, and general sense of the opening verses of the Book of Genesis and of those passages in the Wisdom literature which depend upon the narrative of the Creation. *In the beginning, light, life, were made*, and the succession of co-ordinate sentences, are all reminiscent of Genesis i. *The Word*, too, recalls the successive utterances of God, by which order was originally brought out of chaos: *And God said, Let there be light, and there was light.* The allusive character of the language is not, however, thereby exhausted. The earlier evangelists had preserved the record of the preaching of John and his baptism of Jesus as the *beginning* of the Gospel or Word of God (Mark i. 1; Luke i. 2; Acts i. 22, cf. x. 37; Heb. ii. 3; John xv. 27; 2 John 5). Even the addition by Matthew and Luke of the narratives of the Virgin Birth of Jesus did not disturb the recognition that an account of the work of the Baptist formed the proper beginning of the story of the Life and Death of Jesus and of the utterance of the Word of God in their midst. The fourth Evangelist does not, of course, minimize the importance of John even in his prologue (*vv.* 6–8, 15); but in alluding to earlier records of Christian beginnings he is fully aware that the tradition is open to serious misunderstanding. The Word of God was not first audible when Jesus first spoke and acted. The Word made known then is the Word audible in the whole creation from its beginning: *In the beginning was the Word.*

*vv.* 1, 2. God is apprehended by men through His works. Attention is therefore first directed to the speech and action of God in the initial act of creation; but it is so directed as to prepare the way for what is announced in *v.* 14. The Word, who in the Beginning wrought the Creation, has now brought into being a man: He who was God became flesh; He who was with God tabernacled with men. What was manifested at the Beginning was not Law, as the Pharisees held, not reason or thought, as the Greek philosophers and later the Gnostics tended to suppose; but the creative power of the Word of God. *In the beginning*, here of the Creation (Cf. Gen. i, 1; Prov. viii. 22, 23; Ecclus. xxiv. 9; Matt. xix. 4, 8; Col. i. 15, 18; Rev. iii. 14). In the Johannine Writings the Beginning is, however, not confined to the Creation (1 John i. 1; ii. 13, 14). The period of the ministry of Jesus and especially its opening incidents (ii. 11, vi. 64, xv. 27, xvi. 4), and also the time of the first emergence of faith in Jesus, are all properly described as the Beginning (1 John ii. 24, iii. 11; 2 John 6).

*With God* (echoing Prov. viii. 30) . . . *was God*: literally, *with the God*, that is, with the invisible Father of all, contrasted with the anarthrous predicate *was God*. It is impossible to reproduce in English this contrast. The Coptic version alone has been able to reproduce the meaning of the original Greek. The Word is distinguished from the Father, without, however, thereby introducing any suggestion of lack of complete union between them. Since the anarthrous *Theos* is personal, more is stated than that the Word is divine. The Word of God is no neuter thing, no mere power: He acts with personal consciousness and will. The preposition *with* answers the question Where? or In whose company? (cf. 1 John i. 2; Mark vi. 3, ix. 19; 1 Thess. iii. 4). For Wisdom as the companion of God, cf. Prov. viii. 22, 27, 30; Wisd. ix. 4; Ecclus. i. 1. The emphasis upon the transcendent dependence of the Word upon the Father conditions the whole narrative which follows. As the incarnate Word or Son of God, the words and actions of Jesus are the manifestation to men of what He has seen with the Father (i. 18, vi. 46, viii. 38). Finally, the revelation completed, He prays that He may be glorified again with the glory that was His before the Creation (xvii. 5).

*vv. 3, 4.* The Hebraic antithetical parallelism of a positive and negative statement for the sake of emphasis is characteristic of the Johannine Writings (cf. iii. 16, 36; vi. 50; 1 John i . 5, ii. 4, 27, v. 12). Seen in its relation to the Word of God, the whole world of men and of things is one world; it is quite properly the universe. The recognition of the unity of creation is essential for the understanding of the Gospel. The mission of Jesus, the incarnate Word of God, concerns all humanity, since all men are the creation of God by the Word. Faith in Jesus is, therefore, laid upon all men as a necessity of this very life and being. For the creation of the universe through the agency of the Son of God and for a similar deduction of the necessity of faith, cf. 1 Cor. viii. 6; Col. i. 16; Heb. i. 2, 3. For creation by Wisdom and a like deduction see Prov. viii. 30; Wisd. vii. 12: Life belongs neither to nature nor to men independently. They live because of their relation to the Word of God.

[*That hath been made* may be taken either as the beginning of *v.* 4 or as the conclusion of *v.* 3; (*a*) *Without him was not anything made. That which came into being by him was* (*is*) *life* . . . (cf. R.V. mg.): (*b*) *Without him was not any thing made that hath been made. In him was life* . . . (A.V., R.V.). The rhythmical balance (Loisy), the grammatical structure of the sentences (Bauer), and the agreed rendering of the Gnostic writers and of the Fathers up till the middle of the fourth century, favour the punctuation of (*a*). Alexander of Alexandria in his letter to Alexander of Constantinople (Theodoret, *Hist. Eccl.*, i. 4) alone of the known Christian writers before A.D. 350 adopted the punctuation of (*b*). After A.D. 350, however, the Fathers in general abandoned the (*a*) rendering. Chrysostom, for example, exhorts his readers to 'relinquish' this reading and come to the recognized reading and explanation. And what is that? It is to make the sentence end at *was made*, and to begin the next sentence with *in* (*by*) *Him was Life* (*Hom.* 5). The explanation of the attitude of the later Fathers towards the (*a*) reading is simple enough. Its exploitation by heretics rendered it suspect. Support was found in it for Arian, Gnostic or otherwise heretical opinion, such as the creation of the Holy Spirit by the Word (see Chrysostom) or the production of the aeon Zoe (Life) as Emanation which preceded the creation of the material world. For a full discussion of the patristic evidence see Zahn, Excursus 1, pp. 697 sqq.; (cf. Westcott, additional note, vol. I, pp. 59 sqq.). It may, therefore, be concluded both that the exclusive adoption of the (*b*) reading was due primarily to a desire to defend orthodoxy, and that the (*a*) reading is in fact the more natural. (See, however, Schlatter, *D.E.J.*)]

*And the life was the light of men.* Light, already associated with life in the narrative of the Creation, is that by which men are enabled to recognize the operation of God in the world. Light presupposes life, just as death means darkness. In the later Jewish literature life and light emerge as the twin images adequate to describe the effects of obedience to the Wisdom of God revealed in the Mosaic Law (cf. 1 Bar. iv. 1; 2 Esdras xiv. 29, 30, Syriac Version, with Ps. cxix. 105; and 1 Bar. iv. 2, 3; 2 Bar. lix. 2, lxxvii. 16; 2 Esdras xiv. 20, 21, with Isa. ix. 2). In the New Testament both are transferred to describe, not obedience to the Law, but the grace of God that has been made known in Jesus Christ (Matt. iv. 16; Luke ii. 32; Acts iii. 15; 2 Tim. i. 10, etc.). In the Fourth Gospel the transference is complete, confident, and precise. As the Life of the World Jesus raises Lazarus from the dead (xi; cf. x. 10, xvii. 3): as the Light of the World, He heals the man born blind (ix; cf. iii. 19, viii. 12). These are not mere episodes, they are effective manifestations of the Word of God to all men.

*v.* 5. *And the light shineth in the darkness.* The world lieth in darkness (2 Esdras xiv. 20; 1 John v. 19). The Rabbis knew this because of the promise of a new heaven and a new earth, the Evangelist because Jesus had been rejected. Unlike the Gnostics, he advances no theory to explain the origin of this darkness. It is as much a fact as that human life is controlled by death. The two are indeed related, and he is satisfied with Gen. i–iii. Nevertheless, the light is shining in the darkness (xii. 35, 36; 1 John ii. 8, cf. Matt. v. 14–16; 2 Cor. iv. 6; Eph. v. 8; 1 Pet. ii. 9).

*And the darkness apprehended* (*overcame*, R.V. mg.) *it not.* The reference here is primarily not to the age-long opposition of men to God's revelation of Himself (1 Bar. iii. 12–14, cf. Ps. xxxvi), but to the opposition of the Jews to Jesus, which issued in the crucifixion. The double significance of the Greek verb—*to grasp with the mind* and so *to comprehend*, and *to grasp with the hand* and so *to overcome* or *destroy* (xii. 35; Mark ix. 18; 1 Thess. v. 4)—must be given full weight in the interpretation. (See, however, Burney, pp. 29, 30, and W. E. Barnes's criticism of Burney in *Theology*, July 1922.) The opposition of the Jews which effected the death of Jesus was rooted in their failure to apprehend Him or His teaching. The Light is, however, unconquerable. The victory of the Jews was, in fact, their defeat, for Jesus overcame the world (xvi. 33, cf. xii. 31, xiv. 30). The Evangelist sees vast implications in this victory of light over darkness. As Jesus, the Son of God, was not overcome by the Jews, the sons of their father, the Devil (viii. 44) so a similar victory is promised to those who believe in Jesus over their opponents who act in the power of the prince of this world (xvii. 14–16, cf. 1 John v. 4,

5, 18, 19), for He that is in them is greater than he that is in the world (1 John iv. 4).

*vv. 6–8. There was a man.* Literally, *there arose a man,* cf. Mark i. 4. The allusive rhythmical character of the prologue now vanishes and the Evangelist in straightforward prose requires his readers to stand in faith before a man sent and appointed to declare the will of God.

*Sent from God.* Jesus was also *sent* (iv. 34, v. 38, vii. 29, x. 36, xvii. 18, xx. 21, cf. Matt. xv. 24). Here, however, a contrast is implied. The mission of John was prophetic; the mission of Jesus that of the Word incarnate.

*Came for witness . . . of the light.* The work of John is carefully limited to one act of universal religious importance. All reference to John as the Baptist (see, however, v. 33, iii. 23) and as the preacher of repentance is omitted. He bore witness to the light. This was the purpose of his mission, and everything else is secondary. For further 'witnesses' in the Fourth Gospel see v. 31–7, 39; viii. 18; x. 25; xv. 27; xix. 35; and cf. 1 John v. 6–11.

*Believe through him.* That is, through John. Faith comes to rest not in John but in Him to whom he bore witness (cf. 1 Cor. iii. 5). The record of those who first believed on Jesus through the witness of John follows in *vv.* 35–42.

*He was not the light.* The relation between John and Jesus implies, however, a contrast (*vv.* 15, 19–36, iii. 22–36); a contrast which had already formed a recurring theme in the earlier Christian tradition (Mark. i. 7, 8, ii. 18, 19, ix. 12, 13; Matt. iii. 13–15, xi. 11, xvii. 13; Luke i. 17, 42–4). The Evangelist formulates this contrast in an emphatic negative, in order to show that John's humility, indeed, his repeated negations about himself (*vv.* 19–27), were essential to the performance of his mission. The important position that John may have occupied in contemporary Judaism is therefore irrelevant. There is no clear evidence that John had been exalted by Jews in opposition to Jesus. No doubt, he remained in Jewish memory as a great figure and his baptism was not forgotten. Josephus refers to him (*Ant.* xviii. 116 sqq.); there had been disciples of John in Ephesus (Acts xviii. 25, xix. 1–7); and there are obscure references to baptist-communities in the writings of Hegesippus and Epiphanius and in the Mishnah. The Evangelist is, however, concerned with John himself and his witness, not with what his followers or the Jews may have said about him.

[Professor Bultmann has recently elaborated a very remarkable theory to account for the references to John in the prologue and elsewhere in the gospel. He holds that, with the exception of *vv.* 6–8, 15, 17, the prologue was originally a Gnostic writing in which John was described as the incarnate Word; and that the author of the Fourth

Gospel made use of it, displaced John, substituted Jesus for him, and then reinserted John as the great witness (*Eucharisterion*, vol. II, pp. 23 sqq. *Z.N.T.W.* 1925, pp. 141 sqq.). For this theory the sacred books of the Mandæans provide the sole support. In 1915 Lidzbarski, the learned orientalist, published one of these books under the title *Das Johannesbuch der Mandäer* (cf. the same author's essay, 'Mandäische Liturgien', published in *Abh. d. Kön. Ges. d. Wiss. zu Göttingen*, Phil. Hist. Kl. N.F. xvii, 1, 1920). The original Mandæan book cannot have been written before the rise of Mohammedanism. Yet, in spite of the fact that the Mandæan Baptist community had been considerably influenced by Eastern Christianity—if indeed it was not a strange offshoot from the Church—Professor Bultmann assumes, first, that a Gnostic Baptist community existed at the beginning of the second century; secondly, that the surviving Mandæan literature rests upon tradition reaching back to that time or upon documents originating then; thirdly, that the founders of the Gnostic sect possessed a document containing the substance of the prologue to the Fourth Gospel, but applied to John; and lastly, that this document was sufficiently accessible for the author of the Fourth Gospel to have procured it and edited it for his own purposes.]

*vv.* 9–11. What John was not, Jesus was. John, therefore, bore witness neither to an abstraction, nor to a hope or promise to be realized in the future. The light *was, was in the world*. As the sun gives light to the whole world. the Word of God is the true—real as opposed to counterfeit—light that lightens all men. The coming of Jesus was fraught with ultimate all-embracing universalism, for in Him was manifested the light of the creative Word of God on whom all men depend for their very existence. The syntax of the phrase *coming into the world* is difficult. Since *every man coming into the world* is a common Rabbinic circumlocution for 'all men' (Schlatter, *D.E.J.*, Strack-Billerbeck), *v.* 9 may be translated quite simply, *there was the true light that lightens all men* (cf. R.V., A.V.), without any particular reference to the moment of birth. The particple *coming* may, however, be taken closely with the copulative *was* (periphrastic conjugation; cf. Moulton, *Grammar of NT Greek*, vol. I, p. 227, vol. II, p. 452). The translation is then: *the true light . . . was coming into the world* (R.V. mg.). This would, of course, be altogether Johannine (vi. 14, xi. 27, xviii. 37); and, indeed, is in the author's mind here, for he adds at once: *He was in the world*. Nevertheless, in view of the Rabbinic parallels, the former translation, with its emphasis on the universalism of the mission of Jesus, is perhaps preferable.

*The world knew him not* (Matt. xi. 27; 1 John iii. 1). The reference is still to the light (neuter in Greek); but since Jesus is the light of the world, the neuter is transformed into a masculine pronoun. The Evangelist does not write, *The world knew it not*. The mission of Jesus fulfils

Isa. liii. i (xii. 38). Even the disciples did not know Jesus of their own perception. This knowledge was given them of the Father (vi. 65, xvii).

*He came unto his own* (neuter plural, *his own property* or *home*), *and his own* (masculine plural, *his own servants* or *people*) *received him not*—that is, into His house (Matt. x 14). The House of Israel, the especial property of God, was the natural home of the true light. There, therefore, He took up His residence. The world failed to recognize Him; but the tenants of the Household of God openly rejected Him (ii. 13–22, with violence v. 18, cf. Mark xii 1–12). For Israel as God's possession see Exod. xix. 5; Deut. iv. 34, vii. 6: 'Five possessions did the Holy One, blessed is He, take to Himself in the world; and these are they: the Law is one possession, and the heaven and earth are one possession, Abraham is one possession, Israel is one possession, and the Temple is one possession' (*Aboth* vi. 10). There is, however, no final distinction between Israel and the world, between Jew and Greek. As the creation of God, all men are His property (Isa. lxvi. 1); and Jesus was in the world, not merely in Israel. This double reference to the whole earth and to Israel as God's possession has also its parallel in Exod. xix. 5.

*vv.* 12, 13. There is a new creation (Matt. iii 16). There are children of God who receive Jesus into their house. There are those who, believing in Jesus, have been reborn by the power of God. Rebirth is the operation of the grace of God, not a reward for obedience to the law. All who believe in Jesus, whether Jews or Greeks (x. 16), are empowered to become children of God. They are not of this world (xvii. 6, 16). Faith and rebirth are not two distinct stages in Christian enlightenment. The mysterious operation of the power of God, the spiritual new rebirth from above (iii. 1–11) is made known by the fact that men do receive Jesus by faith and do submit to visible baptism in His name. Those who believe are not potentially children of God: they are already His children, though it is not yet made clear what they will become (1 John iii. 2).

The process of the birth of a child according to the ordinary course of nature by the will of its parents, and especially of the father, is a parable of the birth of the children of God; but it is only a parable. In order to avoid confusion between the two, the divine generation must be expressed in a series of strong negatives.

*Not of blood*. Literally, *bloods*. Blood is the matter from which life is generated (Josephus, *Ant.* iv. 310). The plural, rather than the normal singular (Josephus, cf. Wisd. vii. 2), is used not merely to contrast the natural birth from the father who begets and the mother who bears the child with the bloodless birth of the children of God, nor merely in order to emphasize the distinction between birth which demands much outpouring of blood (bloods) and that which does not. A more subtle contrast is suggested. The Evangelist cannot write that the

Christians were not born of blood (singular), because their birth does in fact depend upon a death which later he describes as involving the outpouring of blood (xix. 34). For this reason the discourse with Nicodemus on regeneration leads up to the death of the Christ (iii. 16, cf. 1 John i. 7); for this reason too, perhaps, he chooses here the plural rather than the singular. For a discussion of the text see DETACHED NOTE 2, *The Birth of Jesus Christ in the Fourth Gospel*, pp. 163 sqq.

*Nor of the will of the flesh, nor of the will of man.* The birth of a child is not only the result of a natural process: it is the consequence of an act of the will of both human parents, and especially of the will of the man who desires a son to be like him. This is what the human father brings into being; not more, not less. But it is a parable of what lies beyond human fatherhood.

*But of God.* Beyond the whole process of nature, beyond every Jewish or other genealogy, beyond the action of the body, and beyond every act of human will, there are children who have been brought into being by the creative power and will of God.

*v.* 14. This new creation of the children of God, like the original creation of the world, is the consequence of the operation of the Word of God.

*And the Word became flesh.* Flesh means man, not body (Matt. xvi. 17). Though the birth of the children of God lies beyond history and beyond flesh, nevertheless it is apprehended, not merely on the plane of general history, regarded as a parable of that which lies beyond it, but in one particular historical occurrence, in one particular human life and death. There, by the operation of the Word of God, the divine Sonship has been manifested and recognized. The Evangelist does not make this statement in order to provide a starting point for philosophical or theological speculation, still less in order to move from history to some psychological mystical happening (1 John iv. 2; 2 John 7). He moves to history, to Jesus the Son of God. He moves also from the law delivered to Moses, from the Word of God inscribed on two tables of stone, to the Word of God written in the flesh of Jesus. What the law was powerless to effect, the incarnation of the Word of God has made known.

Jesus is the Son of God; and through His Sonship men who are otherwise no more than flesh, themselves attain Sonship, and become the children of God.

*And dwelt (tabernacled) among us (in our midst),* cf. xii. 35; Zech. ii. 11; Rev. vii. 15, xxi. 3. The allusion to nomadic life contained in the word *tabernacled* renders it a natural and effective symbol for the transitory character of human life lived in the body as in a tent (Wisd. ix. 15; 2 Cor. v. 1; 2 Pet. i. 14). The reference here, however, is rather to those passages in the Old Testament in which God is spoken of as dwelling in the midst of the Hebrew people in the Tabernacle containing the ark and the two tables of stone (Exod. xxxiii. 7 sqq., cf. 1 Kings viii. 10, 11), and in which the Wisdom is said to have tabernacled in Jacob (Ecclus. xxiv. 8). The more immediate reference is perhaps to the Palestinian use of the verb *shakan* (abide in, inhabit)—a word containing the same consonants as the Greek verb σκηνουν (*tabernacle*) —to denote the presence of God in the Temple and in the midst of the Jewish people (Schlatter, *D.E.J.* See also Burney, pp. 35 sqq., and Oesterley, *The Jewish Background of the Christian Liturgy*, pp. 224 sqq.). The Evangelist, writing after the destruction of the Temple, neither bemoans its loss, as Josephus did, nor substitutes the temple of nature for the Temple at Jerusalem, as did the Zealots (Schlatter, *D.E.J.*). The presence of God has not been withdrawn, for Jesus has taken the place of the Temple (ii. 21), and His Sonship is, as Matthew had recorded, greater than the Temple (Matt. xii. 6). Jesus gives men more than the Temple or the Jewish people ever had given, and His disciples take the place of the Jews. In the perspective of the gospel the abiding of the Word of God in flesh merges in the abiding of the Son of God in all those who believe in Him (xv. 5, xvii. 20 sqq., cf. 2 Cor. xii. 9; *Didache* x. 2). The translation *dwelt in us*, which lies on the periphery here, suggests therefore the final theme of the gospel. Cyril of Alexandria comments: 'For He who is by nature Son and God dwelt in us; wherefore in His Spirit do we cry *Abba, Father*'. In the Curetonian Syriac, in the Peshitto, and in the Diatessaron the phrase is translated, *He dwelt in our nature*.

*And we beheld his glory.* The phrase develops what is implied in the word *tabernacled* and demanded by the phrase *became flesh*. The Hebrew tabernacle was the centre of the manifestation of the glory of God to all the people (Exod. xl. 34 sqq.) and especially at the hour of sacrifice (Lev. ix. 6, 23). For the Psalmist the glory of God enters through the gates of the Temple (Ps. xxiv. 7 sqq.) or appears in Zion (Ps. cii. 16). The glory of God, the Hebrew *Kabod*, is His majestic splendour and power, revealed in the miracles in Egypt which were signs of His glory and greatness (Num. xiv. 22), at the giving of the Law (Exod. xxiv. 16, 17; Deut. v. 24), and at great moments when God appeared to His chosen servants, Moses (Exod. xxxiii. 18, 22), Ezekiel (Ezek. x. 4, 18, 19): cf. the Evangelist's comments on Isaiah's vision in xii. 41. This splendour was thought of as light or fire: *Behold, the Lord our God hath shewed us his glory and his greatness, and we have heard his voice out of the midst of the fire* (Deut. v. 24); the light is veiled with a cloud (Exod. xvi. 10). In the Targums the *Shekinah* is used as a circumlocution for God. For example, *I will walk among you* (Lev. xxvi. 12) becomes *I will make my Shekinah to dwell in your midst*. But the Shekinah is light (*The Jewish Encyclopædia* under 'Shekinah'). The manifestation of the glory of God is, however, in the Old Testament still incomplete. The hope for the future was that the glory of God would be exalted above all the earth, that all nations would see His glory (Is. lxvi. 18, cf. xxxv. 2) and that He would deliver His beloved by a great act of Judgement (Ps. lvii. 11, cviii. 5; Ezek. xxxix. 21 sqq.). In 2 Macc. ii. 5 sqq. a legend is preserved that Jeremiah hid the Tabernacle in a cavernous chamber, and that it would not be revealed *until . . . the glory of the Lord shall be seen*. If these passages be taken together it is clear that the Glory of God meant to a Jew the Majesty and Power of God as revealed in the history and worship of the Hebrew people, and in the personal and intimate experience of the great prophets of Israel: it also belonged to the Jewish eschatological terminology. To the author of the Fourth Gospel, however, Jewish hope has been fulfilled, not eschatologically, but in the incarnation of the Word, whose Body is the numinous Temple of God (ii. 21). *We beheld*. That is, not the community of the children of God (O. Holtzmann), but the original disciples of Jesus, in whose name the author writes. Nor can the word *beheld*, which is an aorist, mean 'see with immortal eyes' (Bauer), since elsewhere in the gospel the verb is used for ordinary sight (i. 38, iv. 35, vi. 5, xi. 45). No contrast is therefore intended between sensible and mystical vision. As in i. 32, a sensible vision forms the point of departure for faith (Lagrange). If a contrast is implied, it is between the original disciples, who believed in consequence of the actual vision of the Christ incarnate (cf. 1 John i. 1), and those *who have not seen, and yet have believed* (xx. 29), but who nevertheless, believe because of the witness of the original disciples.

*Glory as of the only begotten from the Father*. Since *only begotten* and *Father* are anarthrous in the Greek, the R.V. mg. translates *an only begotten from a father*. Both translations imply that *as of* introduces a comparison of the glory of the incarnate Word with the only begotten from the Father, or with an only begotten from a father; that is to say with an only son or with the Only Son of God. But it may be questioned whether this is the author's meaning. The Greek word translated *as [of]* may equally well introduce a precise definition (cf. Pss. Sol. xviii. 4). Saint Chrysostom says, 'The expression *as* does not in this place belong to similarity or comparison, but to confirmation and unquestionable definition' (cf. i. 32; see Lagrange against Bauer). The glory of Jesus corresponds with the uniqueness of His Sonship. The word *only begotten* is used of the Christ only in the Johannine Writings (i. 18, iii. 16, 18; 1 John iv. 9). This, however, does not justify commentators in suspecting the influence of non-Christian and non-Jewish divine titles, and still less of Gnostic or Mandæan mythology (see Bauer). *Only begotten* is here a synonym for the word *Beloved* in the synoptic narrative of the Baptism (Mark i. 11; Matt. iii. 17; Luke iii. 22, cf. Mark ix. 7). Both *beloved* and *only begotten* are used in the LXX to translate a single Hebrew word meaning *only* (Judges xi. 34; [cf. Tobit iii. 15, vi. 10]; Ps. xxxv. 17: Gen. xxii. 2, 12, 16; Jer. vi. 26; Amos viii. 10; cf. Luke vii. 12,

viii. 42, ix. 38, xx. 13; Heb. xi. 17; see *J.T.S.*, July 1919, pp. 339 sqq., Jan. 1926, pp. 113 sqq., and the detached note on 'the Beloved' as a Messianic title in Armitage Robinson, *St. Paul's Epistle to the Ephesians*, pp. 229 sqq.). The memory of Abraham's sacrifice of his *beloved* (*only begotten*) son Isaac may have contributed to the application of the word to the name Jesus (Schlatter, *D.E.J.*).

The Evangelist does not suggest that the Word became Son at the incarnation (Loisy), or that the incarnation took place at the Baptism (see note on i. 23). The Word is the Son of God both before and after the incarnation (iii. 16, vi. 46, vii. 29, xvii. 24; 1 John iv. 9). 'For not of prophet nor angel nor archangel, nor of the higher powers, nor of any other created nature—if other there be—but of the Master Himself, the only begotten Son Himself, of the very Lord of all, did we behold the glory' (Chrysostom).

*Full of grace and truth.* The glory of the Word of God is further defined, in accordance with Old Testament precedent, as *grace* (LXX *mercy*) and *truth* (Exod. xxxiii. 17–xxxiv. 7; Ps. xxv. 10, lvii. 10, 11, cviii. 4–6). The two words are parallel to life and light in the earlier verses of the prologue. The disobedience of the people of God and their oppression by the Gentiles constitute an appeal to God's mercy. The manifestation of the glory of God must, therefore, be an act of deliverance or mercy. Moreover, since God is trustworthy and steadfast, the revelation, in spite of the sin of the people, is also the manifestation of His truth. The Evangelist, however, does not adopt the traditional association of mercy and truth without considerable modification. Since he directs the attention of his readers to the gift of God rather than to the misery of men, the peculiarly Christian word *grace* is substituted for *mercy*; and truth comes to mean far more than steadfastness. The two words sum up the contents of the narrative that follows, and must be interpreted accordingly. The original disciples saw the glory of the Son of God manifested not merely in power but in grace (mercy) and truth. This does not mean that they stand in a mystical vision, but that they saw the miracles of Jesus and received His teaching. Grace—the word is not used outside the prologue—emerges as love, and is illustrated by the care with which the stories of the woman of Samaria, of the healing of the cripple at Bethesda and of the man born blind, and of the raising of Lazarus, are narrated. Truth emerges in the course of the narrative in the words and discourses of Jesus, which are the words of God (viii. 45 sqq., xvii. 17, xviii. 37, 38) and the means of sanctification (xv. 3, xvii. 17). In the Midrash on Ps. xxv. 10, quoted by Strack-Billerbeck, truth means the law. It is possible, therefore, that the contrast here is between the crushing imperative of the law of God and the mercy and love manifested in the truth of the words of Jesus (*v.* 17). The meaning of grace and truth is not, however, exhausted in the miracles and teaching of Jesus. The gospel moves on to the narrative of the crucifixion as the true and effective sacrifice for the sins of the world, and therefore as the perfect manifestation of love and truth. The note which concludes the narrative of the crucifixion—and *he that hath seen hath borne witness, and his witness is true* (xix. 35)—is significant because it links the crucifixion to the prologue: *and we beheld his glory . . . full of grace and truth*. The use of the word *grace* (mercy) in this passage and in *vv.* 16, 17 is sufficiently explained by its use in earlier Christian literature and in the Old Testament, without exploring its occurrence in the Hermetic literature and elsewhere (Bauer; G. P. Wetter, *Charis*).

*vv.* 15–17. The unique Sonship of Jesus is now depicted in the midst of those who directly or indirectly bear witness to Him: John and the original apostles directly, Moses indirectly and by a negation. Since, moreover, the witnesses are human witnesses, the Evangelist again falls into matter-of-fact prose.

*v.* 15. This verse does not break the development of the prologue; and its position is, therefore, the result neither of a dislocation in the text (Calmes) nor of a redaction (Bultmann). The relation between *only begotten* (*v.* 14) and *beloved* in the earlier narratives of the Baptism calls to mind the figure of John as the first direct human witness to the incarnate Son of God. The witness of John at the beginning of the gospel has its complementary parallel in the witness of the beloved disciple (? John) at its close (xix. 35, xxi. 24).

*Beareth witness . . . crieth saying. . . .* The witness of John is a permanent witness directing not only Jews but all men to Jesus. *Crieth* (perfect in form but present in meaning) is a technical Rabbinic term for the loud voice of a prophet who intends to be heard (vii. 28, 37, xii. 44; Rev. vii. 2; Rom. ix. 27; cf. the word *proclaim* in the synoptic gospels). *Saying* introduces the actual words of the prophet (Schlatter, *D.E.J.*). The Baptist does not here speak in general terms of the advent of the Messiah. He recognizes Jesus. *This was he of whom I spake.*

*After me . . . before me.* Matthew (iii. 11) thinks only of the superior authority of Jesus; the successor is greater than the forerunner. The Evangelist here uses the preposition *before* not only of place but also of time. The pre-existence of the Son of God is the ground of His superior authority: *For he was before me* (*v.* 18).

*v.* 16. The verse does not, as Heracleon supposed (Origen on vi. 3), continue the words of John, in which case *we all* would mean all the prophets. The Evangelist sets the apostles side by side with John. This witness corroborates his. The disciples did not only see the miracles and hear the teaching of the Son of God: they actually received of the fulness to which John had borne witness, for they received from Him the Spirit (xx. 21, 22, cf. vii. 38, 39, xix. 30; Col. i. 19, ii. 9). What the disciples once received now belongs to all who believe through their preaching. In the perspective of the gospel therefore *we all* is extended to embrace all true Christians. The habitation of the Word was not merely a habitation among the disciples; it was veritably a habitation *in* them (Col. ii. 10). Hence the Evangelist states that the coming of the Spirit is the coming of the Christ (xiv. 15–18).

*Grace for grace.* What the disciples received from Jesus, what bound them all together, was super-abounding grace. That is to say, grace was the ground upon which new grace was continuously superimposed. Grace was the foundation upon which the whole apostolic work rested, and for that reason is the irremovable basis of the life of the apostolic Church. The disciples of Jesus are continually purified in order that they may bear more fruit (xiii. 8, xv. 5, 8, 16, xvii. 17–19; 1 John i. 9).

*v.* 17. Though the incarnate Word has controlled the prologue throughout, the name Jesus is now spoken for the first time. It is called forth by the contrast between Moses the prophet of Israel and Jesus the Christ. Both are clear figures in history and both have performed their distinct, though related, work. Through Moses God gave Israel the law. The Jewish name Jesus links Christianity to Judaism, for both stand under the imperative given by God through Moses as a gift. But at this point Christianity and Judaism, the Church and the Synagogue, go apart, for to the name Jesus is added Christ. The imperative of God is the gift that kills. The law does not give life. But there has come into the world that which the law could not give (Rom. viii. 2). Through Jesus Christ came grace and truth. The law was a gift separable from the agent by whom it was given. Grace and truth, however, came not only *by* but *in* Jesus Christ, who is the truth embodied (xiv. 6). Throughout the gospel Jesus is therefore sharply contrasted both with Moses and with the law given through him (v. 46, vi. 32, viii. 32–6, ix. 28, 29), and for the same reason the baptism of John by water only is contrasted with Christian baptism of water and spirit (*v.* 26, iii. 5). But Moses is not thereby altogether dispossessed. He remains, as Saint Paul had seen, a negative witness to Jesus.

*v.* 18. *No man hath seen God at any time* (v. 37, vi. 46; 1 John iv. 12, 20, cf. Exod. xix. 21, xxxiii. 20, 23; Deut. iv. 12). In this sentence the whole historical relationship of men to God is set forth. God, as Josephus had said, is visible to no human eye. He sees, but is not seen. No theophany has vouchsafed the much desired (vi. 46, xiv. 8) vision of God. Nevertheless, He is not altogether isolated and removed. Men have heard His voice, for the Word is the means of His revelation to men. The 'madness' of the Jew consisted in his strict preference of the God whose word he alone had heard to the gods whom the surrounding nations had seen.

*The only begotten Son . . . hath declared him.* This is the answer of the Evangelist to the problem of faith. God is invisible; and there is no open vision of God vouchsafed to men. But the Word of God remains no longer in His prophetic obscurity. The Word of God has become transparent in Jesus, the only begotten Son of God; and He is therefore the adequate ground of faith. *Declared*. The technical term for the Rabbinic interpretation of the law (Schlatter, *D.E.J.*) and for the making known of divine secrets (Gen. xli. 8, Lev. xiv. 57). Jesus and the Rabbis are bound together as 'exegetes' of the mysteries of God. But whereas the Rabbis depend upon the law, Jesus, as the Son of God, depends upon what He has heard and seen with the Father (viii. 38). *Jesus is in the bosom of the Father*. The metaphor is not that of an infant in the arms of its father, but of the intimate companionship of a meal (xiii. 23, cf. Luke xvi. 22, 23). So complete is the union of Father and Son that in the end the language of sight can be recovered. *He that hath seen me hath seen the Father* (xii. 45, xiv. 9). Thus did Jesus veritably once and for all *declare* (aorist, not perfect) the Father. Sight comes to rest, not in a psychological, mystical experience, but in the historical relationship between the disciples and the man Jesus.

[This verse presents a difficult textual problem. The more important ancient manuscripts are divided between the readings *only begotten Son* (A.V., R.V.) and *(one who is) God only begotten* (R.V. mg.).[1] The latter is the reading in Codex Sinaiticus, Codex Vaticanus, the Paris Palimpsest, in two other important Greek manuscripts, in the Egyptian Versions, and in the Peshitto. It is supported by Valentinus the Gnostic (Iren., *Adv. Haer.* i. 8. 5), Clement of Alexandria, Origen (probably Heracleon also), and other Fathers. It looks, therefore, like an early authoritative Alexandrian reading. The former is the reading in all the known Latin manuscripts (with two exceptions), in the Curetonian Syriac, and in all the later Greek manuscripts (Codex Bezae is defective). It is supported by Eusebius, Athanasius, and most of the Greek Fathers after the fourth century, also by all the Latin Fathers, with the exception of the author of the treatise on Isa. vi. 1–7, attributed by Morin to Jerome. Irenæus knew both readings (*Adv. Haer.* iv. 20. 11, cf. 20. 6). The reading *only begotten* without any addition is found in two manuscripts of the Latin Vulgate. This reading, though perhaps supported by Ephraem and Aphraates, may be safely disregarded, in spite of the attractive theory that it was the original reading, expanded in Alexandria by the addition of *God* and in the West by the addition of *Son* (Resch, Blass). The evidence of the manuscripts taken by itself leads to no certain conclusion as to which of the two better readings is original. Nor does a general survey of the Fourth Gospel necessarily rule out either reading as non-Johannine, for *one who is God only begotten*

---

[1] The R.V. mg. translation *God only begotten* would be easier were a poorly attested reading, ὁ μονογενὴς θεός, accepted. The variant is, however, in the manuscripts cited above, μονογενὴς θεός, which is better rendered *one who is God only begotten* (the Egyptian Versions are not decisive one way or the other).

may be taken as complementary to i. 1, and *only begotten Son* as complementary to iii. 16, 18; 1 John iv. 9, etc. The immediate context seems, however, to be decisive; for *who is in the bosom of the Father* almost requires *only begotten Son*. See Westcott, additional notes to Chapter I; Lagrange; Zahn, Excursus III, pp. 712 sqq.]

DETACHED NOTE I

# THE WORD OF GOD

Apart from the first half of *v.* 14, *and the Word became flesh*, the very confident use of the Word rather than the Wisdom of God, and the clear ascription of personality rather than the mere literary personification of the Word (Wisdom)—apart from these things, the thought, phraseology, and even the rhythm of the prologue can be closely paralleled in the language of the Jewish Scriptures. The prologue to the Fourth Gospel would therefore have been, superficially at least, immediately intelligible to Jews. The terminology is that of ancient Jewish tradition and reflects a piety peculiarly Jewish. In the twenty-fourth chapter of the book of Ecclesiasticus, Jesus, the son of Sirach, bursts into the song of the glory of Wisdom. Created from the Beginning, she was the mist of the story of the Creation (Gen. ii. 6). She inhabited the Abyss, and was honoured by the host of Heaven. In every people and nation she had sought a resting place, but in Israel and in Jerusalem, the beloved city, she tabernacled, took root, and rested. The glorified people whom she honoured with her presence came to her; they ate and drank from her as from a vine; and those who submit to her guidance and serve her are removed from the degradation of sin. To live under the book of the covenant of the Most High God and to obey the Law of Moses is to live in the tabernacle of the Wisdom of God. This is no isolated passage, for the author of the Book of Baruch (iii. 9–iv. 4) in similar fashion sings the praise of the Wisdom of God revealed in the Law. There is none that knoweth her way, nor any that comprehendeth her path. The nations have not known the way of knowledge, and have perished because they did not possess Wisdom. But God, who knoweth all things, knoweth her, and gave Wisdom to Jacob. He presented her to Israel, His beloved. Then it was that Wisdom appeared upon earth and was conversant with men. All they who hold her fast are appointed to life, therefore, *Turn thee, O Jacob, and take hold of her: walk towards her shining in the presence of the Light thereof.* The Wisdom of God, hidden from the eyes of all living (Job xxviii, cf. 2 Esdras v. 9 (10), the clear effluence of the glory of the Almighty— but who, nevertheless, pervadeth and penetrateth all things, and against whom evil cannot prevail (Wisd. vii. 24–viii. 1)—had taken form and shape in the Law of Moses, which is the Word of God (Deut. xxx. 11–14). Brought forth from the Beginning or ever the earth was, Wisdom was with God, His first creation, the artificer and master-workman of the universe. She stretched out her hand and came to her own, but because of the wickedness of men she was regarded by none and found no resting place on earth; only Israel had she been received, and there she tabernacled with men (Prov. viii. 22–30, cf. iii. 19; Wisd. vii. 13, 22, viii. 3, 4, ix. 1–11, 2 Enoch xxx. 8, cf. xxxiii. 3, 4; Prov. i. 20–30, 1 Enoch xlii). Renewed by her, the faithful Israelites became the friends of God and His prophets and, since he alone loves God who lives with Wisdom, the Jews, living under the Law of God, became the children of Wisdom (Wisd. vii. 14, 27, 28; Ecclus. iv. 11, cf. Luke vii. 35, xi. 49). (See Rendel Harris, *The Origin of the Prologue to St. John's Gospel*; R. Bultmann, *Eucharisterion*, vol. II, pp. 3–13.) The teaching of the Old Testament Wisdom Literature concerning the Law was developed in the teaching of the early Jewish Rabbis.

Before the creation of the world the Law was with God. It lay on His knees whilst He sat on the throne of glory: 'Seven things existed 2000 years before the world—the Law, the throne of glory, the garden of Eden, penitence, the upper sanctuary, and the name of the Messiah. Upon what was the Law written? With black fire upon white fire, and it lay upon God's knee whilst he sat upon the throne of glory' (for this and the following Rabbinic citations see Strack-Billerbeck, *Kommentar zum N.T.*, vol. II, pp. 353–8, cf. Klein, 'The Mohammedan Theologians on the Koran', *The Religion of Islam*, p. 9). The Law was the light and life of the people of Israel: 'With five things is the Law compared; with water, with wine, with honey, with milk, and with oil. Oil which is poured out is Thy Name . . . as oil is life for the world, so are the words of the Law life for the world. As oil is light for the world, so are the words of the Law light for the world.' (Cf. Apoc. Bar. lix, 2, lxxvii. 16; 2 Esdras xiv. 20, 21.) The Law partook of the divine nature, for it was God's only begotten daughter—married to the people of Israel: 'My daughter, whom I have given thee, is my only daughter. From her I cannot be separated, nor can I say to thee, "Let her not company with thee", for she is thy wife. Yet grant me this favour. Everywhere whither thou goest prepare me an habitation that I may dwell with thee, so shall I not be bereft of my daughter. . . . Therefore is it written in the book of the Exodus xxv. 8, *Make me a sanctuary; that I may dwell in your midst*'.

In the later Old Testament Scriptures neither the Word of God nor His Holy Spirit attained so great an eminence as did His Wisdom. And yet the Word and the Spirit of God occupy a position in the Old Testament which renders them capable, if some pressure be exerted, of moving into the centre of the language of revelation. In the narrative of the creation the holy spirit hovered with creative power over the face of the waters, and each divine work evoked a new creature. Without doubt, the intrusion of the word of God and His spirit upon the domain of wisdom in certain passages in the book of Wisdom is due, in part, to the influence of the first chapter of the book of Genesis. *O God . . . who madest all things by thy word; and by thy wisdom formedst man . . .* (Wisd. ix. 1, 2); *Who ever gained knowledge of thy counsel, except thou gavest wisdom, and sentest thy holy spirit from on high?* (ib. ix. 17). In the earlier portions of the Old Testament the word of God has much the same significance as was attributed in the later writings to His wisdom; it expresses His creative power and omnipotence: *By the word of the Lord were the heavens made* (Ps. xxxiii. 6, cxlvii. 18, cf. Gen. i. 1–3). The call of the prophets and the mysterious advent of the message they were compelled to deliver was the result of the coming of the word of God (Jer. i. 4, 11; Ezek. iii. 16, 17). But chiefly the word of God denoted the divine Law given to Israel by Moses: *He sheweth His word unto Jacob, His statutes and His judgements unto Israel* (Ps. cxlvii. 19, cf. Isa. ii. 3, Deut. xxx. 11–14). Language controlled by the metaphor of the powerful speech of the Almighty was, therefore, fundamental in Judaism. But there is no clear evidence that the word of God was ever personified as was His wisdom. It is significant that in the Old Testament the Word, except when it refers to a definite saying (Dan. iv. 31), never stands by itself; it is followed always by a genitive or by some qualifying clause. *The Word of God* describes the action of God and the manifestation of His power and glory, and is used in the Targums as a reverent circumlocution for God. For example, the text of Gen. xx. 3, *God came to Abimelech* is rendered by Onkelos: *A word from before Yahwe came to Abimelech.* Neither in the Old Testament nor by the Rabbis was *The Word* used as it is in the prologue to the Fourth Gospel. But it was used in such a way that, were some influence brought to bear, a personification of the Word, quite apart from the semblance of personality which was attached to it as a circumlocution for God, might without great difficulty emerge. (For recent discussion of the significance of the Memra and its cognate words in Jewish Theology see Strack-Billerbeck, op. cit. vol. II, pp. 303–33; G. F. Moore, *Harvard Theological Review*, 1921, 'Christian Writers on Judaism'; 1922, 'Intermediaries in Jewish Theology'.)

It is now possible to state the problem presented by the prologue to the Fourth Gospel with considerable precision. How is it that the wealth of imagery descriptive of the glory of Wisdom has been transferred to honour the Word? And, what has brought about the reference to the Word as a clearly defined person rather than as a circumlocution for God, or as a poetic personification of an abstract idea?

Those familiar with the classical literature of Greece and Rome find the answer to this problem comparatively simple, and indeed Saint Augustine had already pointed the way to its apparently obvious solution. In his *Confessions* (vii. §13) he remarks that he had found in 'certain books of the Platonists . . . not indeed the very words [i.e. of the prologue to the Fourth Gospel], but to the very same purpose. . . . *But that he came unto his own, and his own received him not; but as many as received him, to them gave he power to become the sons of God, as many as believed in his name*; this I read not there. . . . But that *the Word* was made flesh, *and dwelt among us*, I read not there'. Saint Augustine, of course, is not dealing with the origin of the language of the prologue. He is drawing attention to the similarity between current Greek philosophical ideas and the language of the prologue, and also to the immense gulf which separates the two, since no Greek philosopher could have said *The Word became flesh*. When once, however, an historical explanation of the language of the prologue was required it seemed obvious that its author had consciously adopted the phraseology of Greek philosophy in order to interpret Christianity in terms of Greek thought and commend it to the Gentile world as a reputable philosophy. In some form or other this explanation is now widely accepted. 'The great example of the effect of the contact of Christianity with Greek thought is furnished by the Gospel of St. John and the Johannine Epistles. The Fourth Gospel was apparently written at Ephesus, probably between A.D. 100 and 110 by one who was well acquainted with the philosophy and mysticism of his time; he was also strongly influenced by Paul' (C. H. Moore, *The Religious Thought of the Greeks*, p. 318).

Religious and poetic tradition, itself the product of oracular, prophetic, mythological reflection, presented philosophers with a rich metaphorical language in which the powerful speech of the Gods, as the expression of their divine wisdom, played a large and important part. Religious usage rather than philosophical reflection gave the word *Logos* its double meaning of utterance or edict and reason or wisdom. In the fragments of Heraclitus the *Logos*, 'the omnipresent Wisdom by which all things are steered', is the divine Word received by the prophet, and becomes almost equivalent to God (see Adam, *The Religious Teachers of Greece*, pp. 216–34, against Burnet, *Early Greek Philosophy* (2nd edition) p. 146, n. 3).

But in spite of its somewhat occasional use in the long line of Greek philosophers from Heraclitus onwards, it was not until the philosophy of the Stoics appeared that the doctrine of the *Logos* was systematically elaborated so as to become the controlling philosophical idea by which the structure and unity of the Universe was explained. The Stoics held that each part of the Universe was permeated by one operative principle, the divine Reason (Logos), God. By this generative reason (*Logos spermatikos*) all things are begotten, and in every man this World-Reason is the directing power, in fact the soul under the guidance of which he is enabled to live in harmony with the Universe (Inge, art. 'Logos', §1, Hastings's *Encyclopædia of Religion and Ethics*; E. Bevan, *Stoics and Sceptics*). So convinced was Adam of the direct connection between the use of the word *Logos* in the prologue to the Fourth Gospel and in Greek philosophy that he selected *The Word* rather than *Reason* as the most adequate translation into English of the Stoic *Logos*, in order to make plain to the English reader 'the historical fact of the continuity of the *Logos* doctrine throughout its whole history on Grecian soil from Heraclitus down to Philo, Saint John and Justin Martyr' (op. cit., pp. 221, 222; Inge, *Christian Mysticism*, p. 47, note, and his article 'Logos', in Hastings's *Encyclopædia of Religion and Ethics*, cf. Hastings's *Dictionary of the Bible*, under 'Logos'). The introduction of Philo as the link between the philosophers of Greece and the Christian theologians suggests a modification of the direct relation between the prologue and Greek religious thought. The writings of Philo represent a synthesis between the Jewish Scriptures and Greek philosophy, in which the idea of the Logos plays an important part. Philo solves the problem of the relation between the supernatural, invisible, unknowable world and the material world by making use of the conception of the *Logos* as the active manifestation of God in the physical world. Under the influence of Greek thought, the idea of the Word of God, latent in the Jewish Scriptures, takes the place of His Wisdom in Philo's metaphysical mythology. Thus the *Logos* was the Beginning (*De Conf. Ling.* 146), the oldest of created beings (*De Migrat. Abrah.* 6), God's 'eldest Son' (*De Conf. Ling.* 63, *De Somn.* I. 229), in fact a 'second God' (*De Cherub.* 172), the origin of all light (*De Somn.* I. 75), 'full of graces' (*De Somn.* II. 183), and the prophet and interpreter of the divine will (*Quod Deus*, 138, *De Mut. Nom.* 18, *Leg. Alleg.* III. 207, cf. Bréhier, *Les idées philosophiques et religieuses de Philon d'Alexandrie*, pp. 83–111; Siegfried, *Philo von Alexandria*, pp. 219–29; Schürer, *The Jewish People in the time of Jesus Christ*, E.T. Div. II., vol. iii, pp. 374 sqq.; Hastings, *Encyclopædia of Religion and Ethics*, art. 'Alexandrian Theology' (Inge)). The theory that the prologue is directly dependent upon the writings of Philo, or upon the school of Alexandrian thought of which Philo was the most eminent representative, is undeniably attractive. But it rests upon a series of assumptions that can be justified only if it be held that parallel imagery demands a literary relationship. There is no evidence to suggest an Alexandrian provenance for the Fourth Gospel, nor can it be proved that Philonic terminology was generally familiar to Jews in the first century in Palestine, in Ephesus, or even in Alexandria itself. Philo was an isolated figure. In fact his writings were preserved by Christian, not by Jewish, theologians, because they came to appreciate the points of contact between Christian theology and the speculations of Philo. The theory that the prologue stands in a direct or indirect literary relationship to the Philonic writings, except in so far as both are dependent upon the Jewish Scriptures and upon Jewish tradition, raises more difficulties than it solves.

The whole theory of a direct connection between the prologue to the Fourth Gospel and Greek philosophy is open to very grave objections. The interpretation of the *Logos* in the prologue is intimately bound up with the interpretation of the gospel as a whole. The prologue is inseparable from the gospel. Jesus as the Word of God is therefore at once surrounded and embedded in other descriptions of Him. Jesus is also the Truth, the Light, the Life, the Way, the Resurrection, the Door. He is also the Bread which came down from heaven. No theory which explains the significance of the identification of Jesus with the Word, but which does not at the same time explain the further identifications which are of such importance to the author of the gospel, can be regarded as in the end satisfactory. Origen, indeed, used very strong language of those who distinguish the Word from the other titles of the Christ. It is, he says, 'nothing but stupidity' (*In Ioan.* i. 23). There is, moreover, nothing in the gospel, except the prologue interpreted from one point of view, to suggest that it was written to recommend Christianity in terms of Greek thought. The Greeks lie on the periphery of the Gospel, and are directly mentioned in one passage only (xii. 20 sqq.). The gospel was written pastorally for Christians and polemically against Jews. Nor are the recognizable allusions in the prologue allusions to Greek philosophy. They are Jewish throughout, and it is in the prologue itself that the author formulates his theme, and sets it in relation, not to Greek thought, but to the Jewish Law: *The law was given by Moses, grace and truth came by Jesus Christ.* This is the keystone upon which both the prologue and the whole work depend. Moreover the author did not write his gospel in order to prove that Jesus is the Word, but that He is the Christ, the Son of God. Nevertheless, he did begin his gospel by taking his readers back to the Word of God and set his record of the mission of Jesus in that context. If the simple explanation that he has done this in order to link what he has to say to the wisdom of the Greeks be regarded as unsatisfactory, some other explanation must be found.

It should not be forgotten that it is not in the Fourth Gospel that we first find mention of the Word of God in the New Testament. In the synoptic gospels and in the Acts of the Apostles the *Word*, with or without an explanatory genitive, is a synonym for the *Gospel*. It denotes the teaching of Jesus Christ, the Son of God, given publicly to the crowds by means of parables and miracles and privately to the disciples (Mark ii. 2, iv. 14, 33; Matt. xiii. 19, 21–3; Luke v. 1, ix. 28; Acts x. 36); it denotes also the substance of the missionary teaching of apostles and others concerning Jesus the Messiah (Mark xvi. 20; Acts iv. 4, 29, 31, vi. 2, 4, 7, viii. 4, 14, 25, x. 36, 44, xi. 1, 19, xiii. 5, 7, 49, xvi. 6, 32, xix. 20). Mark viii. 32 is an important passage. Here Jesus, for the first time in Saint Mark's Gospel, is said to have referred openly to His death and resurrection. The Evangelist checks his narrative at this point and adds the significant comment: *He spake the word openly*. That is to say, the final context of the Gospel or Word is defined in the death and resurrection of Jesus. Throughout the synoptic gospels and Acts *the Word of the Kingdom, the Word of God (of the Lord), the Mystery of the Kingdom, the Gospel*, are synonymous phrases expressing the fulfilment of Jewish messianic hope; and it is a major theme of the earlier evangelists that the hostility between the Jews and Jesus and His disciples became more and more pronounced as the contrast between the Law and the Gospel (the Word) of God became more and more clearly recognizable (Mark xii. 1–12, xiv. 55–65; Acts xiii. 44–52). The Evangelists told of the emergence in the midst of the Jews of the new covenant by which Judaism is at once fulfilled and superseded; and the new covenant is the Word of God, the Gospel of Jesus Christ, the Son of God. In this context the preface to Saint Luke's Gospel becomes peculiarly significant, for it contains the grammatically difficult description of the original disciples of Jesus as *those who from the beginning were eyewitnesses and ministers of the word*. Here, as in the prologue to the Fourth Gospel, *Beginning* and *Word* are closely associated in the preface to a narrative of the life and death and resurrection of Jesus. Moreover, Saint Mark's Gospel also open with the juxtaposition of *Beginning* and *Gospel*. For the earlier evangelists, the preaching of John, the baptism of Jesus, and His first teaching and miracles in Galilee were the beginning of the revelation of the Word or Gospel of God. Saint Luke clearly means by the Word more than the teaching of Jesus, for in the perspective of the Lucan writings *eyewitnesses and ministers of the word* means eyewitnesses and servants of Jesus, the Son of God. Nor, in Saint Mark's preface, can the *Gospel of Jesus Christ* mean merely the gospel which Jesus proclaimed, since in the course of the gospel Jesus as the Messiah becomes more and more the subject of His own teaching. Since, therefore, no evangelist could divorce the gospel or the word of God from Jesus Himself, both the gospel and the word of God are drawn into the orbit of His person. It is not that abstract ideas are being personified; it is rather that the revelation of the power of God is being brought into the closest possible relationship with the person of Jesus. In the opening verses of the first epistle of John the same juxtaposition of *beginning* and *word* occurs (1 John i. 1–4, 10). There too the word (of life) ceases to be merely a message proclaimed. The disciples have *seen, gazed upon, handled* . . . the Word of life and the Word is Jesus. So the neuter, *that which we have heard*, merges into a masculine, for the author is describing the relation of the disciples to Jesus and through Him to God. The whole passage is, in fact, leading up to the assertion of the fellowship of the disciples with the Father and with His Son, Jesus Christ (1 John i. 3), and recalls those passages in the gospel in which the Word of God, the

Word of Life, the Life, the Light, are pronounced to have been manifested in Jesus (i. 14, 34, 51, iii. 11-15, ix. 35-8, xiv. 9, xix. 35; xx. 17; vi. 40, xi. 25, xiv. 6, xvii. 3; iii. 16, 17, cf. 19-21, viii. 12, ix. 5, xii. 35, cf. vii. 33). It is therefore not surprising to find the saying *If ye abide in my word* (viii. 31) re-phrased in xv. 7 as *If ye abide in me, and my words abide in you* (cf. I John ii. 14, 24; Col. iii. 16 with I John ii. 6, iv. 12-15; Gal. ii. 5; and John xii. 48 with v. 22), nor to find it said that the Jews have not the Word of God abiding in them, because they do not *believe in him* whom God has sent (v. 38), whereas the disciples received the Word of God because they *knew of a truth that I came forth from thee, and they believed that thou didst send me.*

The procedure of Saint Paul is not fundamentally different from that of the author of the Fourth Gospel. In his Epistles the Gospel that is proclaimed is Jesus Christ (I Cor. i. 23; 2 Cor. iv. 1-6; Gal. iii. 1). The Christians are what they are only because of their relation to Him. For this reason, the rich vocabulary descriptive of the Christians is perpetually thrust back until the great words and phrases come to rest, not in the Christians, but in Jesus Christ Himself. He is the power and wisdom of God (I Cor. i. 24; Eph. iii. 10-12, cf. Ecclus. li. 23; Matt. xi. 28-30; Luke xi. 49; Matt. xxiii. 34). His work has propitiatory significance (Rom. iii. 25, 26; I John ii. 1). The Fulness of God dwelleth in Him bodily, in order that those who have apprehended the love of God there displayed may themselves be filled with the Fulness of God (Col. ii. 10; Eph. iii. 19; John i. 12-14, 16). He is the Mystery, hidden from all ages, but now made known through the Church (Eph. iii. 1-12). In the parallel passage (Col. i. 25-8), the Mystery is, however, the Word of God, hidden from all ages, but now manifested to His Saints— *which is Christ in you . . . whom we proclaim.* Similarly, the passage in Col. iii. 16 beginning with the words: *Let the word of Christ* (v.l. *God*) *dwell in you*, appears in Eph. iii. 17 as: *that Christ may dwell in your hearts* (cf. Col. iii. 15) *through faith.* Thus, though *the Gospel* (Rom. i. 16, x. 16), *the Gospel of Christ* (Rom. xv. 19; 2 Cor. ii. 12), *the Gospel of God* (Rom. xv. 16; 2 Cor. xi. 7), *the Word of God* (2 Cor. ii. 17, iv. 2), *the Word of Christ* (Col. iii. 16), *the Word* (Gal. vi. 6; Col. iv. 3) refer to the apostolic teaching, yet nevertheless, the apostolic proclamation of the Gospel or of the Word is quite simply and directly the preaching of Christ (Rom. i. 9, xv. 16; I Cor. iv. 15; 2 Cor. ii. 12, 17, iv. 1-6, cf. 2 Cor. v. 19, xi. 4-9; Col. iv. 3).

How deeply the phrase *the Word of God* was embedded in the primitive Christian vocabulary and how steadily and consistently it was pressed to describe the work of Christ is shown also by such passages as I Pet. i. 23, where the Christians, who were brought to God by Christ (I Pet. iii. 18), are said to have been reborn *by the resurrection* (I Pet. i. 3, cf. John xi. 25) and *through the word of God, which liveth and abideth* (I Pet. i. 23, cf. Jas. i. 18, 21); Titus ii. 5, where blasphemy against

F

the *Word of God* is hardly to be distinguished from blasphemy against Christ (cf. 1 Tim. vi. 3–5); Heb. ii. 2–4, where the Word which had been given through angels (the Mosaic Law of Gal. iii. 19) is contrasted with the salvation that had its *beginning in* the preaching of Jesus, the Son of God (Heb. i. 1–4), through whom the worlds were made and who sustains all things by the word ($\dot{\rho}\hat{\eta}\mu\alpha$) of His power—to have tasted the good word of God and then to fall away, is *to crucify the Son of God* (Heb. vi. 5, 6). But it is in the Book of Revelation that the closest parallel to the Fourth Gospel is found. The author (? editor) of the Christian Apocalypse, in agreement with other New Testament writers, normally uses *the Word* or *the Word of God* to denote the revelation of God attested by Jesus and by His disciples (Rev. i. 2, 9, iii. 8, 10, vi. 9, xii. 11, xx. 4). But in one passage the Word is formally identified with the Christ; it is His Name—*And he is arrayed in a garment sprinkled with blood: and his name is (has been) called The Word of God* (xix. 13, see Charles).

In all this there is no question of the influence of Greek philosophy. The workshop in which the Word of God was forged to take its natural place among the great theological descriptions of Jesus and His work is a Christian workshop: the tools are Christian tools. The apostolic theologians and evangelists of the primitive Church no doubt inherited this vocabulary from the Jews, but they transformed it in order to express what had been given them by Jesus. It seems difficult to avoid the conclusion that it was in this Christian workshop that the fourth Evangelist also worked. Allusions to the Wisdom Literature of the Jews underlie the prologue to his gospel, but its spirit has been transformed, so radically transformed, that Wisdom has been displaced from its central position. Wisdom has been dispossessed, not, however, under the pressure of Greek philosophy, but because the Evangelist stands under the creative power of the words of Jesus, words that so far from being haphazard and disjointed, proceed from one source. The Gospel is, as the earlier evangelists had declared, the Word of God. And Jesus is Himself the Gospel, *is* the Word of God. The fourth Evangelist does not personify the Word of God. The Word had created him, not he the Word; and the Word of God had confronted the apostles in the person of Jesus, the Son of God. The Word of God, petrified on Mount Sinai, written on two tables of stone, was incarnate in Jesus Christ. The Evangelist saw that this, with its negative and positive implications, was the very heart of the faith of the apostles. In the course of his Gospel, the Evangelist draws out what is involved in Jesus as the Word of God. He is the Light, the Life, the Truth, the Bread of Heaven, the Way, the Door, the Good Shepherd, and the Resurrection. There are in the Fourth Gospel no ragged, independent fragments, whirling about in their own right and of their own initiative. The figure of Jesus as the embodiment of the glory of the Word of God controls the whole matter of the Christian religion. Saint Luke says: *There arose no small stir con-*

*cerning the way* (Acts xix. 23, cf. 9, xxii. 4, xxiv. 14, 22). In the Fourth
Gospel, Jesus says: I am the Way (xiv. 6). Saint Luke writes that Saint
Paul *preached Jesus and the resurrection* (Acts xvii. 18). In the Fourth Gospel *and* has disappeared. Jesus says: *I am the resurrection.* This does not,
however, mean that the fourth Evangelist has introduced a new factor
into the teaching of Jesus and into the life of the Church. In the end,
no more is implied than when Saint Mark set down the Lord's command
that men should follow Him (Mark ii. 14, viii. 34, x. 21), or when Saint
Matthew, commenting upon the arrival of Jesus in Capernaum (Matt.
iv. 16), adds to his record the quotation from Isa. xlii. 7, or when Saint
Paul reminds the Galatian Christians of what had taken place when he
placarded Jesus Christ before their eyes crucified (Gal. iii. 1).

When all this has been said, the possibility remains that the Evangelist may have recognized that the Christian teaching concerning the
Word of God had further implications for Greeks familiar with the
Stoic conception of the divine Logos or Person. Of these, however, he
has given his readers no clear indication either in the prologue or in the
body of his gospel.

DETACHED NOTE 2

# THE BIRTH OF JESUS CHRIST IN THE FOURTH GOSPEL

The variant reading, *who was born* for *who were born,* in i. 13, involving
the reference of the whole verse to the birth of Jesus, is found in the
Verona Codex of the Old Latin Version, but in no other known manuscript of the Gospel. Tertullian, however, not only assumes a similar
reading, but denounces the reading *who were born* as a falsification by
the Valentinians of the true text in order to secure authoritative support
for their own conceptions of 'spirituality'. He writes (*De Carne Christi*,
xix, cf. xxiv): 'They (the Valentinians) maintain that it was written
thus, *who were born not of blood*. . . . But the sentence is in the singular
and refers to the Lord. He was born of God.' Tertullian then goes on to
argue that the whole verse must be taken to refer to the birth of Jesus
of the Virgin Mary, since each statement is a careful denial of human
paternal, but not of maternal, co-operation.

In spite, however, of the Verona Codex and of Tertullian's vigorous
attack, the evidence against the reading *who was born* is overwhelming.
Not only is the manuscript evidence in itself almost sufficient to rule
it out as the original reading, but the plural, picking up the plurals in
v. 12, *as many as received him—who believe in his name*, is grammatically

easier. The use of the analogy of birth to describe the new status of the Christians is, moreover, characteristically Johannine (1 John ii. 29, iii. 9, iv. 7, v. 1, 4, 18); and further, *v.* 13 in the plural form is especially appropriate as anticipating the theme of the discourse in iii. 1–21. For these reasons, the conclusion that the Evangelist wrote *who were born*, and that *v.* 13 is explanatory of *v.* 12 seems unavoidable. [If the variant reading arose on the basis of the Latin version—and the reading looks Western—it may owe its origin to the ambiguity of the relative *qui* which, like the English *who*, may be singular or plural and may therefore have been in this case referred to the immediately preceding *eius*.]

It is at this point, however, that the connection of thought between *v.* 13 and *v.* 14 emerges as a problem. The Evangelist did not write simply *The Word became flesh*, as though he were beginning a new topic. He wrote *And the Word became flesh*. That is to say, he links *v.* 14 closely to *v.* 13. The connection of thought is not difficult to follow. Indeed, Tertullian himself, commenting on iii. 6—*that which is born of Spirit is spirit*—wrote 'Now this description is even more applicable to Him (Jesus) than it is to those who believe on Him' (*De Carne Christi*, xviii), and, throughout the Johannine Writings, the whole organic life of the Christian community, and the regeneration of each single believer, is proclaimed to be dependent upon the advent of the Son of God in flesh (1 John iv. 2, 3; 2 John 7). The discourse in chapter iii begins with the assertion that no one is able to see or enter the Kingdom unless he be reborn from above of water and spirit. But the discourse does not end here. It moves on inexorably to define the nature of that faith upon which spiritual regeneration depends. The discourse moves to faith in the name of *the only begotten Son of God* (iii. 18) and to the witness of John the Baptist, *he that cometh from above is above all: he that is of the earth is of the earth, and of the earth he speaketh: he that cometh from heaven is above all* (iii. 31). The same connection of thought is expressed concisely in 1 John v. 18, *Whosoever is begotten of God sinneth not; but he that was begotten of God keepeth him* (cf. John xvii. 11–15, xviii. 37). To the Evangelist the thought of the regeneration of the believers at once suggests the thought of the Son of God who for their salvation became flesh and was born. Therefore in the perspective of the Johannine Writings, this would seem to be the connection between *v.* 13 and *v.* 14 in the prologue.

If then, the spiritual regeneration of the believers and the incarnation of the Word of God are closely related and mutually suggested in the connection between *vv.* 12 and 14, the question arises whether not only the fact of the incarnation, but also its mode does not determine the form in which the description of the spiritual birth of the Christians is described in *v.* 13. The question arises whether the language does not presuppose the Virgin Birth. In the opening paragraph of his letter to the Church in Smyrna, Saint Ignatius refers to the Virgin Birth in language that recalls the language of the prologue to the Fourth Gospel. He writes: 'The Lord Jesus Christ . . . is in truth of the family of David according to the flesh, God's Son by the will and power of God, truly born of a Virgin' (cf. Ign. *Eph.* xviii, *Trall.* ix). Justin Martyr (*Dial. c. Tryph.* lxiii) refers in similar language to the birth of the Son of God, 'Whose blood did not spring from the seed of man, but from the will of God'. Saint Irenæus, without apparently reading the singular in *v.* 13 of the prologue, quotes the passage, and then proceeds to apply it to the pure generation of the Word of God (*Adv. Haer.* iii. 16. 2; 19. 2, cf. Saint Augustine, *Confess.* vii. 9). The language of *v.* 13 was felt to be naturally applicable to the Virgin Birth, and Irenæus does so apply it. Similarly, the author of the *Epistola Apostolorum* had already, if the date assigned to it by Dr. Carl Schmidt be correct, understood *v.* 14 as referring directly to the Virgin Birth, 'I entered into her womb: I became flesh' (Coptic Version, vii. 10). In the light of the Epistles of Ignatius it would not seem unreasonable to assume that, at the beginning of the second century, phrases such as *not by the will of man, but by the will of God* were actually current or at least wholly natural with reference to the Virgin Birth of Jesus, and that the Evangelist and his readers were familiar with such language or that it would possess an obvious application to the birth of the Lord. If so, a background is provided for the sequence of *vv.* 12–14 in the prologue, and the Evangelist employs phraseology actually used of or obviously suggestive of the Virgin Birth, transferring or applying it to the desired spiritual miracle of Christian regeneration, but in such a way that the reference to the miraculous birth of Jesus is preserved and presumed; and then, developing the allusion, adds *And the Word was made flesh . . . and we beheld his glory, the glory as of the only begotten of the Father*. This connection of thought would be even more natural if Saint Luke's Gospel was known to the Evangelist and his readers. Whether this was so or not, the Evangelist in any case presumes that Jesus was of *Nazareth* (i. 45, 46, vii. 41, xviii. 5, 7), that the *son of Joseph* was an altogether inadequate description of His origin (see on i. 45), perhaps that He was born in Bethlehem (see on vii. 42). He seems also to be aware of current Jewish attacks upon the Virgin Birth, as, in fact, a birth of fornication (viii. 41). These references in the body of the gospel would all be easier to explain, if the Evangelist and his readers were familiar with the story of the Nativity roughly, at least, so we know it from St. Matthew's and St. Luke's gospels, if they knew from the oral or written traditions of the Church that Jesus was not the son of Joseph, that He was born in Bethlehem of the seed of David, that He came from Nazareth, and that He was born not of fornication, but of God.

Returning to *v.* 13 of the prologue—(*a*) In spite of all the difficulties, the singular *was born* has been accepted by some commentators as the original reading (Burney, pp. 34, 35, 43 sqq.). In this case the reference to the Virgin Birth is clear and unmistakable. [Harnack held that the whole of *v.* 14, without the relative and with the verb in the singular, was originally a gloss on *the Word became flesh*, a gloss which emanated from the Johannine circle and was added in order to introduce a definite reference to the Virgin Birth. Later, this gloss became part of the text of the gospel, and the relative was added. Finally, when the sentence was connected with *v.* 12 rather than with *v.* 14, the whole was transformed into the plural (*Zur Textkritik und Christologie der Schriften des Johannes*, 1915). Loisy agrees with Harnack in adopting the singular as the original reading, but thinks that it belongs to the original form of the prologue, and that, so far from referring to the Virgin Birth, it definitely excludes it, since the words *not of blood* exclude not only human paternity but human maternity also. Loisy's argument depends on his view that the Evangelist supposed the incarnation to have taken place at the Baptism (see note on i. 32)] (*b*) Others have adopted the plural as the original reading, and have drawn the deduction either that the Virgin Birth was unknown to the Evangelist, or that he disregarded it, or that he definitely discarded it. (*c*) The plural may still be accepted as the original reading, but the deduction drawn that the language contains an allusion to the Virgin Birth. In this case the singular *was born* is a corruption of the text, but a corruption that is neither unnatural nor unintelligent.

# THE WITNESS OF JOHN AND THE
# FIRST DISCIPLES OF JESUS

## i. 19–51

THE prologue is followed immediately by what seems to be the account of four straightforward, separate episodes. The Evangelist has, however, bound them so carefully together that no one of them can be detached without disturbing the movement of the gospel. The incidents are strictly consecutive, and the characters are closely related to one another—John, two of his disciples, the brother of one of them, Philip of the same city as Andrew and Peter, Nathanael already known to Philip. The narrative has, moreover, been so written that it forms a second, though subsidiary, introduction to the gospel as a whole.

### THE WITNESS OF JOHN TO ISRAEL

i. 19. *And this is the witness of John, when the Jews sent unto him from Jerusalem priests and Levites to ask him, Who art thou?* 20. *And he confessed, and denied not; and he confessed, I am not the Christ.* 21. *And they asked him, What then? Art thou Elijah? And he saith, I am not. Art thou the prophet? And he answered, No.* 22. *They said therefore unto him, Who art thou? that we may give an answer to them that sent us. What sayest thou of thyself?* 23. *He said, I am the voice of one crying in the wilderness, Make straight the way of the Lord, as said Isaiah the prophet.* 24. *And they had been sent from the Pharisees.* 25. *And they asked him, and said unto him, Why then baptizest thou, if thou art not the Christ, neither Elijah, neither the prophet?* 26. *John answered them, saying, I baptize with water: in the midst of you standeth one whom ye know not,* 27. *even he that cometh after me, the latchet of whose shoe I am not worthy to unloose.* 28. *These things were done in Bethany beyond Jordan, where John was baptizing.*

### THE WITNESS OF JOHN TO JESUS

29. *On the morrow he seeth Jesus coming unto him, and saith, Behold, the Lamb of God, which taketh away the sin of the world!* 30. *This is he of whom I said, After me cometh a man which is become before me: for he was before me.* 31. *And I knew him not; but that he should be made manifest to Israel, for this cause came I baptizing with water.* 32. *And John bare witness, saying, I have*

*beheld the Spirit descending as a dove out of heaven; and it abode upon him. 33. And I knew him not: but he that sent me to baptize with water, he said unto me, Upon whomsoever thou shalt see the Spirit descending, and abiding upon him, the same is he that baptizeth with the Holy Spirit. 34. And I have seen, and have borne witness that this is the Son of God.*

### THE FIRST DISCIPLES

*35. Again on the morrow John was standing, and two of his disciples; 36. and he looked upon Jesus as he walked, and saith, Behold, the Lamb of God! 37. And the two disciples heard him speak, and they followed Jesus. 38. And Jesus turned, and beheld them following, and saith unto them, What seek ye? And they said unto him, Rabbi (which is to say, being interpreted, Master), where abidest thou? 39. He saith unto them, Come, and ye shall see. They came therefore and saw where he abode; and they abode with him that day: it was about the tenth hour. 40. One of the two that heard John speak, and followed him, was Andrew, Simon Peter's brother. 41. He findeth first his own brother Simon, and saith unto him, We have found the Messiah (which is, being interpreted, Christ). 42. He brought him unto Jesus. Jesus looked upon him, and said, Thou art Simon the son of John: thou shalt be called Cephas (which is by interpretation, Peter).*

### PHILIP AND NATHANAEL

*43. On the morrow he was minded to go forth into Galilee, and he findeth Philip: and Jesus saith unto him, Follow me. 44. Now Philip was from Bethsaida, of the city of Andrew and Peter. 45. Philip findeth Nathanael, and saith unto him, We have found him, of whom Moses in the law, and the prophets, did write, Jesus of Nazareth, the son of Joseph. 46. And Nathanael said unto him, Can any good thing come out of Nazareth? Philip saith unto him, Come and see. 47. Jesus saw Nathanael coming to him, and saith of him, Behold, an Israelite indeed, in whom is no guile! 48. Nathanael saith unto him, Whence knowest thou me? Jesus answered and said unto him, Before Philip called thee, when thou wast under the fig tree, I saw thee. 49. Nathanael answered him, Rabbi, thou art the Son of God; thou art King of Israel. 50. Jesus answered and said unto him, Because I said unto thee, I saw thee underneath the fig tree, believest thou? thou shalt see greater things than these. 51. And he saith unto him, Verily, verily, I say unto you, Ye shall see the heaven opened, and the angels of God ascending and descending upon the Son of man.*

When the priestly and pharisaic deputation arrives to interrogate John concerning the authority of his mission to Israel, he speaks neither of sin nor of repentance, neither of the imminent advent of the Kingdom of God nor of the positive importance of himself and of his baptism. The Evangelist assumes that his readers know something of the events that preceded the arrival of the deputation; he assumes that they know the substance, at least, of what is recorded in the synoptic gospels (Mark i. 4–6; Matt. iii. 7–12). John now speaks only in negatives. In order that he may not be in any sense the object of his own preaching and action, he disowns every kind of movement towards himself. Not in him are the promises fulfilled. He can never be the leader of the people of God. His work is to direct men from himself to One who is already present in their midst. His theme, as the deputation rightly perceives, is the advent of the Christ. But it is not for him to occupy any positive role at His coming. Not only is he not the Messiah, but he must not even say 'I am . . .'. That right belongs only to Him that is come. It is not for him to say, 'I am the Elijah that is to come' (Mal. iv. 5, cf. Matt. xi. 14; Luke i. 17) or 'I am the Prophet like unto Moses' (Deut. xviii. 15). All that is required of him is to fulfil a prophecy that had been overlooked by both priests and Pharisees alike (Isa. xl. 3). He is no more than a voice, a voice crying in the desert, a voice that makes room for the coming of the Lord. Though he has no name, he does nevertheless baptize. But his baptism is itself an evacuation by which it is declared that all men, priests and Pharisees included, require to be purified. In itself it is no more than the washings of the Pharisees. It is a baptism with water only, which cannot purify the people of God. It can only make known the universal need of sanctification. The baptism of John can only direct men to Christ. Thus John deprives both himself of a name and his most characteristic work of all sufficiency in itself. And yet He to whom John bears witness already stands in the midst of Israel, has already come into the world. The Messiah has come and to Him in His immeasurable pre-eminence all men must turn for their salvation. But the priests and the Pharisees, in the pride of their own already existing righteousness, do not recognize Him. This also is the witness of John; and the deputation withdraws from the scene.

That the Christ would come, that He had indeed already come, was the witness of John to Israel, but that Jesus is the Messiah was not recognized by John until he had seen the descent of the dove, and even then his recognition was by revelation. When, therefore, on the next day Jesus came to John, the voice that had hitherto declared the general necessity of purification now directs men to Him that is able to remove the sin not only of Israel, not only of this or that individual, but of the whole world. Confronted by Jesus, John cannot be silent, he cannot any longer speak only in negatives, for he has seen the Christ and has, moreover, apprehended what it means for a man to be the Saviour of the world, what it means that Jesus is the Christ. Salvation presupposes sacrifice. Salvation from sin depends upon that sacrifice of which the lambs, consecrated morning and evening in the Temple to be the possession of God, provide the proper analogy. As the consecrated property of God, Jesus possesses the power of God unto forgiveness. The Evangelist and his readers perceive, of course, that the consecration of Jesus is a consecration unto death and that the death of Jesus is the fulfilment of the prophet's word. John himself, however, draws no such clear deduction. He declares merely that forgiveness, purification from sin, can be proclaimed only in the context of complete obedience to the will of God, only in the context of perfected love of the Father. Thus far, then, the prophet, standing in the presence of a man who is younger than he, has spoken only in terms of human love and obedience. But forgiveness, the removal of sin, is the forgiveness of God. Only His power can forgive sin. Confronted by Jesus, John is confronted by that which lies beyond human love and obedience however magnificent. In Jesus John is confronted by the eternity of the Word of God. And this is what the prophet also sees. He sees what no human eye can see or even conceive of without making of it a visible occurrence in the realm of observable history. John knew Him not. Even here therefore, the human witness of John remains a negative witness, the negative witness of a baptism with water only. But this is the sign that compels him to see beyond his own work and also beyond the visible obedience of Jesus. In this negative context, however, the positive witness must be declared, in order that men may be brought to stand where revelation alone can answer and explain the prophetic negations. At this point a dove has become the sign of that which no eye can see; and the Evangelist, in passing to the language of revelation —*He that sent me to baptize with water, he said unto me*—leaves the glaring contradiction, *I knew him not* (twice repeated)—*I have seen* (twice repeated) *the Spirit descending.* This context of the Spirit, which is the context of eternity, is in Jesus almost transparent, transparent because it is no temporary spiritual exaltation, but an eternal relationship. For this reason Jesus baptizes with the Holy Spirit, and in this context the word of forgiveness must be spoken, if John, if the Evangelist, is not, in speaking of the righteousness of Jesus, to fall back into Judaism or to anticipate the language of Pelagianism. The ignorance and the knowledge of John is no mere inconsistency in the evangelical tradition (for example, the contrast between Mark i. 9-11 and Matt. iii. 14, 15). John stands where the ultimate problem of human knowledge has become unescapable. John knows the obedience of the man Jesus and he sees this obedience set in the eternal context of the Holy Spirit of God. His sight is, however, no human deduction from his previous knowledge; it is sight in faith, in spirit, by revelation. But faith is no irrelevant leap in the dark, for it is that which makes sense of the man Jesus, it is the meaning of the dove in the story of His baptism—and John is here looking back on the historical circumstances of his baptism of Jesus: *it is the Spirit that quickeneth, the flesh profiteth nothing.* This does not mean that the flesh is without meaning, for *the Word became flesh,* and John saw and bore witness that this is the Son of God.

The witness of John to the obedience of Jesus the Lamb of God is accepted not by the crowd but by two of his own disciples. To them his words are almost a command, and they pass from the prophet to the Christ, from the negations of prophecy to the affirmation of its fulfilment. The first words of Jesus recorded in the Fourth Gospel are an interrogation. For what purpose are these two men following him? Even the disciples of Jesus cannot answer this question correctly, for they wish only to discover where He dwells in order that they may visit Him another day. But there is no escape, no possibility of a deferred visit. The two men have been given to Jesus; in the perspective of the gospel they have been given Him by God (vi. 65, xvii. 6), they are His property and henceforth it is demanded of them that they should be separated from Him only in order that they may bring others to Him. Persuaded that they have found the Christ, each disciple first brings his own brother: Andrew brings Simon, and James brings John, or John James (Mark i. 16–20). But the Evangelist has suppressed the name of the 'other disciple'. In Simon, Jesus saw, not a present bulwark, but a future firm foundation. He is, therefore, named by anticipation Cephas, Peter, Rock. What the other disciple is to be, the Evangelist does not say. There was, however, another pre-eminent disciple of Jesus. There was another, the Beloved Disciple, who lay on the bosom of Jesus, who stood under the Cross. There was a disciple whose name was John. What he saw, what he came to see, is set out in the Fourth Gospel as the true, ultimate faith of the Church, as the rational faith which makes sense of the active service of Peter and of the other apostles, and which makes sense also of the man Jesus. His personal relationship to Jesus forms, however, no mere episode in the life of the early Church; what he saw is no personal opinion or idea or experience of one isolated disciple. His relationship to Jesus and what he saw is the essential life of the whole community of Christians, however little they may apprehend it. What John was cannot, therefore, without grave danger of misunderstanding, be set forth as the experience of one individual, even of one of the apostles, since the purpose of the Fourth Gospel is not to record the opinions of one man or to write a biography of one of the apostles, but to make known the faith of the Church and the meaning of the history or 'flesh' of Jesus.

The gathering together of the disciples precedes the ministry in Galilee and is the first action of Jesus (cf. Mark i. 16–20). As it is narrated, it is, however, less an action of Jesus (but see vi. 70) than the record of the gift to Him of the disciples by the Father, as the name Nathanael—'given by God' suggests. The original disciples came to Him by no single road. Two came in obedience to the words of John, two because of a family tie, Philip as the result of a direct call given by Jesus Himself, Nathanael as the consequence of true Jewish scepticism, scepticism which is, however, broken down by the Lord's sympathy.

Can Nazareth be the home of the Christ? Can Joseph of Nazareth be His father? This is the scepticism of Nathanael, which proceeds from the pride of Israel, not from the insight of a true disciple of Jesus. On the basis of the pride of scepticism no faith can arise and no understanding of Nazareth or of Joseph be possible. Philip, with all his ignorant enthusiasm, is right, for he bids Nathanael come and see. Nathanael came and is declared to be a true Israelite, for in his scepticism he had seen the paradox of the Christ from Nazareth, and without guile, because, when the claim was made, he was honest enough not to hold himself aloof. And Jesus recognized him, knew him before Philip had spoken and before he had replied so coldly. This recognition by Jesus breaks down his pride . . . and he sees beyond Nazareth, beyond the son of Joseph, *Rabbi, thou art the Son of God; thou art the King of Israel*. This is indeed faith, but it is faith irrational and insecurely grounded. The glory of Jesus is greater, the humiliation also more profound. Nathanael is to see Him in the midst of the host of heaven, and he must see Him also as the Son—of man. Son of Joseph, Son of God, Son of man—Nazareth, Heaven—six disciples, the angels of God: thus the historical scene of Jesus and His six original disciples is set not in the context of a mission to the world (contrast Mark i. 17), but in the essential context of that which lies beyond observable history and experience. The apostolic mission beyond Israel to the world is secondary, for it has no meaning apart from what Jesus is and apart from what His disciples are in their relation to Him.

# COMMENTARY

### THE WITNESS OF JOHN TO ISRAEL

i. 19-28 (*cf. v.* 33). *And this is the witness of John*. The connective conjunction *and* introduces a new section (cf. ii. 13, ix. 1), but in such a manner that the transition from the prologue to straight historical narrative proceeds without interruption. It is no less required of a theologian that he should be an historian than it is of an historian that he should become a theologian. The question *Who art thou?* (*v.* 19, cf. viii. 25, xxi. 12) presumes the substance of what is recorded concerning John in the synoptic tradition (Mark i. 2-8 and parallels), since the problem of his authority would clearly not have arisen, had he not already spoken and acted roughly at least as is recorded in the synoptic gospels, and had his teaching not already raised expectations of the imminent advent of the Messiah (Luke iii. 15).

The prophet is confronted (*v.* 19) by *Jews, priests from Jerusalem Levites* (the Temple police, see Schürer Div. II, vol. II, pp. 264 sqq.)

and (v. 24) by *Pharisees*. The Evangelist is not here speaking of a race
marked by the peculiar purity of its physical descent or of a people
endowed with particular moral and intellectual qualities, especially
visible in its accredited leaders. To the Evangelist the Jews were Jews
because to them the law of God had been given, because to them the
prophets had spoken, and because to them the coming of the Messiah
had been promised (Rom. ii. 17–21). Salvation is therefore of the Jews
(iv. 22). They were a nation under the authority of God, this authority
being exercised through the priests who were responsible for the worship
in the Temple and through the Pharisees who were the guardians of the
Law. On the knowledge and understanding of priests and Pharisees,
and especially on their ability to recognize the Messiah when He came,
depended the destiny of the whole Jewish people. But the Jewish
authorities, with the approval of the populace in Jerusalem, had put
Jesus to death; and the Evangelist knows only too well that since that
time the Jews had consistently and with great bitterness everywhere
opposed and persecuted His disciples (Matt. xxviii. 15). Throughout
his gospel the Evangelist therefore uses the phrase *the Jews* to denote
the national rejection of the Christ and especially His rejection by the
Jewish authorities (ii. 18 sqq., v. 10, 15–18, vii. 13, 15, ix. 22, xviii. 12
&c.), by the Pharisees (iv. 1, ix. 13 &c.) and by the chief priests and
the Pharisees (vii. 32, 45, xi. 47, 57, xviii. 3). By their failure to recognize
the Messiah in whom the law and the prophets are fulfilled, the Jews
have shown that they have misunderstood their own worship (ii. 20),
their own practices of purification (ii. 6), the Sabbath (v. 18), the
Scriptures (v. 39, 40, 47), and the Passover (vi. 4); and so far from ac-
cepting the authority of God, they are actively engaged in the service
of their *father the devil* (viii. 44). (Cf. ii. 6, 13, v. 1, vi. 4, vii. 2, xi. 55;
viii. 17, x. 34, xv. 25, xviii. 31, xix. 7, see Bauer.) In the perspective of
the gospel, the Jews are therefore merged in the *World* (xv. 18), which,
though created by the Word of God, does not receive Him when He
comes into the world to His own. Indeed, it is in the open opposition
of the Jews that the general, though less self-conscious opposition of
the World is most clearly seen. The gulf which separates John from the
Jewish deputation, and which causes the Evangelist to speak of the Jews
as a distinct and separate people, is not due to the possibility that the
prophet had been born and exercised his whole ministry on the periphery of Palestinian Judaism and that the Evangelist was a Greek
writing for Greek Christians. The gulf is the ultimate gulf between
unbelief and faith, between blindness and sight, between death and life.
Therefore, though the use in the Fourth Gospel of the phrase *the Jews*
is most closely paralleled in the Gospel of Peter (i. 1, vi. 23, vii. 25,
xii. 50, 52) and in other sub-apostolic Christian writings, there is no
greater distinction between Jesus and His disciples and the Jews than
is set forth in the Parable of the Wicked Husbandmen (Mark xii. 1–12),

or is implied in the cursing and withering of the fig-tree (Judaism) when it failed to produce its fruit at the coming of the Messiah (Mark xi. 12–14, 20) and in the whole scene of the crucifixion as it is narrated in the synoptic gospels.

*vv.* 20–22. The Baptist not only denies that he is the Christ (cf. Acts xiii. 25) but disclaims all personal authority. The words *I am* are therefore in the Greek avoided altogether, even in *v.* 23, and although they constitute the blind man's admission of his identity (ix. 9), they seem to be reserved for Jesus as the Christ, the Son of God (xviii. 5, 8, &c.) just as elsewhere they refer to God (Rev. i. 8). In the gospel, Jesus alone is able to assign ultimate significance to men (i. 42, xvii. 20, 21; cf. Matt. xi. 14). It is clearly implied in the New Testament that the two prophets, Moses and Elijah, were associated in popular Jewish expectation with the advent of the Messiah (Rev. xi. 3, 6; Mark ix. 5 and parallels). The expectation was authorized by Deut. xviii. 15, 18; cf. 1 Macc. iv. 46, xiv. 41; John vi. 14, vii. 40; and by Mal. iv. 5; cf. Ecclus. xlviii. 10; Mark vi. 15, viii. 28, ix. 12. The reference to the coming of Elijah seems to be strangely absent from the Rabbinic Literature (Strack-Billerbeck 1, 954; see, however, Justin Martyr, *Dial. c. Tryph.* viii). In Acts iii. 22 and vii. 37, Jesus as the Christ is Himself *the prophet* who had been promised in Deut. xviii. 15. John's denial that he is Elijah superficially contradicts Mark ix. 12, 13; Matt. xi. 14, xvii. 11 sqq., where Jesus declares that John is the Elijah who was to come as the forerunner of the Messiah (the sayings are omitted by Luke, but see Luke i. 17). There is, however, no real contradiction, for it is one thing to be named Elijah by the Christ, but quite another for a man, even for a prophet, to assert it of himself; just as it was one thing for Simon to be named by Jesus Peter, whereas it would have been quite another had he said of himself 'I am the Rock'. It is therefore too subtle a refinement of exegesis to suppose that the Evangelist here rejects the identification of John with the Elijah of the Malachi passage, the prophet of the End, in order to assert that he more properly fulfils Isa. xl. 3. There is a similar superficial though unreal contradiction between *v.* 21b and Matt. xi. 9; Luke vii. 26.

In *v.* 22 the Evangelist for the first time makes characteristic use of the transitional, conjunctive particle, translated *then* (A.V.), *therefore* (R.V.). It 'carries along the narrative with no necessary thought of cause or result' (Robertson, *Grammar of the Greek New Testament*), and of the some two hundred occasions where it occurs in the Fourth Gospel only eight are in the discourses of Jesus. The particle is used in this conjunctive sense nowhere in the Book of Revelation and occurs only once in the Johannine Epistles (3 John 8).

*vv.* 23–7. The two sections of the Marcan narrative (Mark i. 2–4, 7–8) are here held apart by the insertion of the parenthesis in *v.* 24 and the question in *v.* 25. The authority of John depends neither upon personal inspiration nor upon deep personal conviction: it rests upon Scripture. In Mark i. 3 (cf. Matt. iii. 3; Luke iii. 4) the citation of Isa. xl. 3 is introduced as a comment by the Evangelist. Here it provides the prophet with his own authorization of his ministry. John is a voice by means of which men are summoned to faith (i. 7): Jesus is the Word of God in whom the apostles have believed (i. 12–14). The gulf between them cannot be bridged even by the humblest act of service (the action of doing up and undoing his master's sandals was the sign of a slave). The baptism of John by water only (cf. Acts i. 5, xix. 2–7) is therefore not the messianic baptism of water and Spirit (i. 33, iii. 5), nor is it merely a continuation of Jewish purification (iii. 25). John's baptism dissolves the latter, for it is the final call of God to repentance, and anticipates the former, for the Messiah has come and is even now standing in their midst. The deputation, however, withdraws without inquiring further of the prophet's meaning.

The embassy is stated in *v.* 24 to have been not merely priestly but also pharisaic. Whether it was sent by the Pharisees (R.V.) or was composed of Pharisees (A.V.) depends on which of two widely attested variant readings be adopted (see Bernard). The Evangelist makes no reference in his gospel to the scribes. He concentrates attention upon those who possessed real authority, and avoids allusions to wise men, just as in the prologue he had preferred Truth and Word to Wisdom. Nor does he mention the Sadducees, for they had disappeared as a party after the destruction of the Temple, and the name would therefore have been meaningless to his Greek readers. The servants of the Pharisees and of the high priests reappear at the arrest and at the trial before Annas (xviii. 3, 12, 18, 22; cf. vii. 32, 45, 46).

*v.* 28. *Bethany*: variant reading *Bethabara*. The connection between *Bethany* and *beyond Jordan* in x. 40, xi. 1 suggests that the Evangelist wrote *Bethany* here. Since later no village of that name was known in the vicinity of the Jordan and since in chapter xi Bethany is clearly distinguished from the place where John baptized and is, moreover, stated to be near Jerusalem (xi. 18), it may have been early corrected to *Bethabara*. Origen popularized the correction, if he did not himself make it (*In Ioan.* vi. 40).

## THE WITNESS OF JOHN TO JESUS

*v.* 29. The opening words echo the synoptic tradition (Mark i. 9 and parallels). The Evangelist does not, however, record that Jesus came from Nazareth nor that He came in order to be baptized (Matthew). His purpose is to emphasize the heavenly rather than the Galilean origin of Jesus (vii. 27 sqq., viii. 14, xix. 9) and to record the witness of John rather than the fact of the Baptism. This does not mean that either Galilee (ii. 1) or the Baptism (1 John v. 6) is unimportant: both are assumed.

Jesus is *The Lamb of God*. No new title or description is here introduced (1 Cor. v. 7; Acts viii. 32; 1 Pet. i. 19: Rev. v. 6, 8, 13, vi. 16, vii. 9 sqq., xii. 11, &c.). The faith of the apostles is authorized by the original and primary witness of John, who declares Jesus to be the property of God, by whose complete obedience the normal sacrifices in the Temple—a lamb without blemish was offered daily both morning and evening (Exod. xxix. 38–46) and even during the siege of Jerusalem these sacrifices were maintained in spite of very great difficulties (Schlatter, *D.E.J.*)—were fulfilled and superseded (ii. 18–22). The regal authority of Jesus is contrasted with the destructive tyranny of the enemies of God (Rev. xvii. 14). In the development of his narrative the Evangelist shows that the witness of John is applicable to the fulfilment both of the Passover (ii. 13, xix. 36 sqq.; Exod. xii. 7 sqq.; Heb. xi. 28) and of the prophecy in Isa. liii. 1 sqq. (xii. 38, cf. Luke xxii. 37; Acts viii. 32; Rom. x. 16; 1 Pet. ii. 22–5).

*Which taketh away the sin of the world*. The place of sacrifice is the place where the glory and grace of God is made known (Exod. xxix. 43). The obedience of the Son of man is therefore the place where the guilt of sin is taken away (1 John i. 7, iii. 5), and since His obedience is an ultimate obedience its consequences are universal (xvi. 33, cf. the *many* in Mark x. 45; Matt. xx. 28).

The uniqueness of the sacrifices in the Temple caused the Jews to regard them as possessing universal significance. Thus Josephus speaks of the priests in Jerusalem as men who 'preside over the universal worship' (*B.J.* iv. 324) and Philo of the efficacy of the high priest's prayer on the Day of Atonement for the peace and prosperity 'of all men' (*Leg. ad Gaium*, 306). The far greater uniqueness of the obedience of Jesus causes the Evangelist to speak of the sin of the world and of the necessity of forgiveness for all men. The guilt which the Christ removes is universal. Consequently, the Evangelist does not divide men into those who are sinners and those who are righteous, and in his gospel Nicodemus and the Woman of Samaria, when confronted by Jesus, occupy the same position (Schlatter).

*Taketh away* (R.V. mg. *beareth*). The Greek word is used frequently by the Evangelist, meaning to take up and remove out of the way (ii. 16, xi. 39, xix. 38, xx. 2, 13, 15), and so to destroy (x. 18, xi. 48, xv. 2, xix. 15, 31). Its use with *sins* as its object is Scriptural (LXX 1 Sam. xv. 25, xxv. 28; Exod. xxviii. 38, xxxiv. 7; Lev. x. 17; Mic. vii. 18, but not in Isa. liii. 4 sqq.). Jesus bears the consequence of human sin in order that its guilt may be removed. [The plural *sins*—normal in the Old Testament—occurs in 1 John iii. 5, in the Greek text of the *Gloria in excelsis*, in the early Western Service Books, and in the English Prayer Book.]

*vv*. 30–1. *And I knew him not* (*cf. v.* 33). John received the revelation in the context of his own personal ignorance (Mark i. 9–11) and in the context also of the inefficacy of his baptizing with water only. The light shone in the darkness: and in the darkness John becomes significant as pointing beyond himself to Him who in His ultimate and primal union with God is altogether superior and whose obedience is for this reason effective for the forgiveness of sin. The ignorance of John does not mean that he knew nothing of the man Jesus. What he did not know and what he could only know by revelation was that Jesus, the man from Nazareth (*v.* 45), is the Messiah, the Son of God from heaven (iii. 31–2, v. 31, vii. 27–9; cf. Mark i. 11; Matt. xvi. 17; 1 Cor. xii. 3; 2 Cor. v. 16). The prophetic witness to the Messiah (*vv.* 15, 27, 30) must, like the revelation of the Law, be declared to Israel, the people of God (Deut. i. 3), not in order that it may there be localized and confined, but because, being localized in Israel, it is universal, since 'what God performs in Israel is done for all mankind' (Schlatter, *D.E.J.*).

*vv.* 32–4. The Baptism of Jesus by John is here presumed to be familiar to the readers of the gospel (cf. Matt. iii. 16). The attention of the Evangelist is concentrated upon the dove, upon its descent, and upon its resting upon Jesus. This was the promised visible sign to John of the invisible abiding descent upon Jesus of the Holy Spirit of God. The visible occurrence and the invisible truth are set side by side, compared (for the comparative use of *as*, cf. xv. 6, Rev. iii. 3), and apprehended by John. Since, however, a sign is what it signifies, the prophet, seeing the dove, has seen the Spirit descending and knows not merely that his own ministry is fulfilled but by whom it is fulfilled: this is he that *baptizeth with the Holy Spirit*. The prophet alone is capable of hearing the voice from heaven, and he alone bears witness that Jesus, the man from Nazareth, is the Son of God from heaven (iii. 31, 32, vii. 27 sqq.). Jesus is the Son of God: this is not an idea about Him, but the absolute truth manifested by revelation and received only by faith (cf. the earlier narratives of the Baptism and Transfiguration). The witness of John, therefore, in spite of *vv.* 20, 25, comes to rest, not upon the messiahship of Jesus, but upon His messiahship defined in terms of Sonship; and from this point onwards the Sonship of Jesus—son of man, Son of God— becomes the consistent theme of the Fourth Gospel, the original and isolated testimony of John being echoed and substantiated by an ever-increasing number of believing witnesses (e.g. i. 49, 50, ix. 36–8, xi. 27, xx. 31).

[A few manuscripts (Codex Sinaiticus and two other Greek manuscripts, one manuscript of the Old Latin Version, the Old Syriac Version, the old Syriac Version and probably the London papyrus fragment 5), supported by Ambrose, substitute, perhaps under the influence of Luke ix. 35 (cf. Luke xxiii. 35; Isa. xlii. 1), the messianic title *the chosen of God* for the *Son of God* in *v.* 34. Both Loisy and Harnack adopt this variant reading. The two readings are conflated in three manuscripts of the Old Latin Version, in a few Greek manuscripts, and in the Egyptian Sahidic Version. For a discussion of the textual evidence, see Harnack, *Studien zur Gesch. des NTs und der alten Kirche*, 1931, pp. 127 sqq.]

The assertion that John did not merely proclaim the imminent advent of the Messiah, but also knew and spoke about Jesus, does not, of course, occur first in the Fourth Gospel (Matt. iii. 14, 15; the Q passage, Matt. xi. 2, 3, Luke vii. 19, 20; Luke i). On the other hand neither the Marcan Gospel, nor the references to the disciples of John in Acts xviii. 25–xix. 3, give any indication of any conscious recognition of Jesus by John. Both strands in the earlier tradition are, however, picked up by the fourth Evangelist and held apart. The man John *knew him not*: the prophet by revelation *saw and bare record*. Prophetic, like apostolic, apprehension is not the last step in the progress of human knowledge; it is not the result of speculation or of careful investigation; nor is it the consequence of some initial, intuitive perception of the divine significance of visible historical events. Prophetic apprehension rests upon revelation, apostolic apprehension upon the gift of the Holy Spirit of truth: *He that sent me to baptize with water, he said unto me* (v. 33)—*The Comforter, even the Holy Spirit, whom the Father will send in my name, he shall teach you all things* (xiv. 26. cf. xv. 26)—*The Spirit of truth: whom the world cannot receive; for it beholdeth him not, neither knoweth him: ye know him* (xiv. 17). The revelation about which the Evangelist speaks does not, however, take place in a vacuum: it takes place in the context of visible events, of audible words, in fact, in the context of the *flesh* of Jesus. In John's case, the baptism and the descent of the dove provide the opportunity of revelation. Later in his gospel the Evangelist insists that the audible teaching of Jesus, His words, provide the historical context in which revelation takes place: *He* [the Holy Spirit] *will bring to your remembrance all that I said unto you* (xiv. 26)—*He shall bear witness of me* (xv. 26, cf. xvi. 14). The witness of John, as recorded in the Fourth Gospel, introduces the theme of revelation that underlies the whole book (iii. 3, 6, 31, viii. 14, 15, 19). This very difficult theme does not, however, appear in primitive Christianity first in the Fourth Gospel; it is not peculiarly Johannine. When Saint Paul, confronted by the historical scene of the crucifixion, comes to say what apostolic apprehension is, he is compelled to speak of revelation (1 Cor. ii; cf. 1 Cor. xii. 3). Similarly, Jesus Himself, faced by the confession of Peter, makes the same assertion (Matt. xvi. 17). The disagreement in the earlier tradition with regard to the ignorance or knowledge of John concerning Jesus does not lead the fourth Evangelist to give his support to one side or the other; rather, it provides him with the opportunity of retaining and explaining both. John's ignorance was genuine human ignorance: *I knew him not*. His knowledge was by revelation: *He said unto me*.

[Loisy—and others have agreed with him—supposes that the descent of the Spirit is thought of by the fourth Evangelist as the moment or mode or symbol of the incarnation, that he has included the narrative in order to explain *v.* 14 of the prologue, *and the Word became flesh*, and that he has, therefore, depicted John as the eyewitness of the incarnation. There does not seem to be anything in the narrative to support this interpretation. John is the first of the long line of witnesses to the Sonship of Jesus, not the unique witness of the act of incarnation. Nor is there anything to suggest that the fourth Evangelist has substituted a doctrine of inspirational incarnation for the earlier record of the birth of Jesus, the Son of God.]

### THE FIRST DISCIPLES

*vv.* 35–9. Neither the crowd nor the Jewish authorities received the witness of John, and even his disciples (Mark ii. 18 sqq.; Matt. ix. 14 sqq.; Luke v. 33, 34; Acts xviii. 25–xix. 3) did not understand the meaning of his words (cf. iii. 11). When, however, on the next day he repeated his witness to the Lamb of God (see note on *v.* 29), two of his disciples left him and *followed Jesus* and abode with Him. They did not as yet understand the meaning of what they had done, for they address Jesus as *Rabbi*, a title which in the Fourth Gospel usually introduces an unintelligent or at least an inadequate question or action (i. 49, iii. 2, iv. 31, vi. 25, ix. 2, xi. 8, xx. 16), and there is nothing to suggest that they regarded what they had done as possessing any special significance. The two disciples simply went after Jesus in order to find out where He was living, and they passed the rest of the day with Him. The *tenth hour* means, according to the Jewish manner of reckoning adopted in the Fourth Gospel, that it was about 4.0 p.m. and evening was approaching. Their action is, however, by no means superficial, since in the perspective of the gospel the verbs *to follow* and *to abide* define the nature of true discipleship (viii. 12, x. 27, xii. 26, xiii. 36, 37, xxi. 19–22; cf. Mark i. 17, 18; Matt. iv. 20; Luke v. 10, 11; John vi. 56, x. 4–10, xiv. 2, 10, 23). The *abiding* of the disciples with Jesus anticipates the description of their abiding in Him even as He abides in the Father.

*vv.* 40–2. Since the Evangelist assumes his readers to be familiar with the earlier tradition (see INTRODUCTION, pp. 68 sqq.), these verses must be read on the background of the call of the two pairs of brothers— Simon and Andrew, James and John—recorded in Mark i. 16–20 and Matt. iv. 18–22 (cf. Luke v. 9–11). He states that there had been a relation between Jesus and the original disciples before the beginning of the ministry in Galilee (if Luke iv. 38 be compared with Luke v. 11, the third Evangelist also suggests some previous connection), that He had given Simon the name Cephas at their first meeting (contrast Matt. xvi. 18), that He had been recognized as the Messiah from the beginning (contrast Mark viii. 30), and that at least two of the original disciples had previously been disciples of John and had heard his witness to Jesus. In emphasizing this early recognition of Jesus as the Messiah, the Evangelist does not, as is often supposed, idealize the first disciples, since it is precisely the title Christ which requires interpretation. The disciples misunderstand Jesus no less in the Fourth Gospel (xvi. 29–32) than they do in Saint Mark's Gospel. One of the disciples who left John and abode with Jesus is here named. It was Andrew; and he at once brings his brother Simon, who receives the name Cephas, meaning *Rock* or *Stone* (R.V. mg.), by which he is to be known (cf. Mark iii. 16. For the significance of the name see 1 Pet. ii. 4–8). *Find* may imply previous search. The verb may, however, mean no more than *meet*, in which case it is suggested that what appeared to be by chance was, in fact, not so. *Find . . . and say* (repeated in *vv.* 43, 45) seems to reproduce a Hebrew idiom (Schlatter, *D.E.J.*). For the knowledge of Jesus, compare *v.* 48, ii. 25. *Messias—Christos*: the Hebrew word transliterated into Greek and then translated occurs also in iv. 25; elsewhere the Evangelist uses simply the word *Christ* (*v.* 20, vii. 26, 41, 42, xx. 31, &c.).

The other disciple of John remains unnamed. This would call for no comment, were it not that two pairs of brothers—already connected in the business of fishing (Luke v. 10)—constituted, according to the older tradition, the original and innermost disciples of Jesus, and were it not that the fourth Evangelist writes that Andrew was the *first* to bring *his own brother* to Jesus, thereby suggesting that the other of John's disciples also brought his brother. The Evangelist consistently uses the word *first*, not of the first of a series of persons, but of the first of two only (i. 15, 30, xix. 32, xx. 4, 8—v. 4 and viii. 7 do not belong to the original text of the gospel. Schlatter (*D.E.J.*) calls attention to the similar use of the word in Rev. xiii. 12, xx. 5, xxi. 1, and in Josephus). This seems to throw doubt upon the interpretation by which Andrew's *first* bringing of his brother is regarded as anticipating his later missionary activity (xii. 20–2) or by which Peter is regarded as the first of the other disciples named in the next paragraph (*vv.* 43–9, Lagrange). Godet's description of *v.* 41 as a 'delicate touch in the narrative which reveals the endeavour of the anonymous disciple to find his brother also' would seem to be not unjustified. The Evangelist has suppressed the names. If this be recognized, the passage properly belongs to the problem of the Beloved or Other Disciple who in the Evangelist's narrative of the Passion and Resurrection remains also unnamed, and who is, moreover, as here, closely associated with Peter (xiii. 23–5, xviii. 15, 16, xx. 2–10, xxi. 7, 20–3, cf. xix. 26, 27, 35. For the association of Peter and John in the Lucan writings see Acts iii. 1, 3, 4, 11, iv. 13, 19, viii. 14; Luke xxii. 8. In Luke viii. 51, ix. 28; Acts i. 13, the name John precedes that of James, and Peter and John are therefore brought together. The order James-John occurs in some manuscripts of the two passages in Luke, presumably as a consequence of scribal assimilation to what is normal elsewhere). In the Fourth Gospel neither John nor James nor their mother Salome is once named (cf. xix. 25 with Mark xv. 40 and Matt. xxvii. 56).

[Nevertheless, in spite of the above attempt to recover the author's delicate suggestions and allusions, the verse remains on other grounds obscure. The Greek word translated in the English Versions *his own* may be used in its unemphatic and 'exhausted' sense, and can therefore mean no more than *his* (Bauer; see, however, Moulton, *Grammar of NT Greek*, vol. I, p. 90, and Moulton-Milligan, *Vocabulary*, p. 298). Nor is the original of the Greek word translated *first* quite certain. Codex Sinaiticus and other Greek manuscripts read the masculine singular, which means most naturally that Andrew was *the first* to bring his brother. Other manuscripts, including Codex Vaticanus, have what might conceivably be the accusative masculine, but is more probably the neuter singular. *First* is then an adverb. In this case the meaning is presumably the same, but even less clearly expressed. The Sinaitic Syriac and two manuscripts of the Old Latin Version read *early in the morning* for *first*. This looks like a not very successful attempt to make sense of the undeniable obscurity of the original Greek (see, however, Bernard).]

### PHILIP AND NATHANAEL

*vv.* 43, 44. After receiving His first disciples, Jesus decided to depart from Judæa into Galilee. The Evangelist recalls and affirms the earlier tradition that His public ministry began in Galilee (Mark i. 14 and parallels). Since the journey into Galilee is neither mentioned nor described, it is not clear whether the locality of the call of Philip and of the word spoken to Nathanael is Galilee or Judæa. [The subject of the verbs in *v.* 43 must presumably be Jesus, for it is difficult to think that Andrew made the decision and that Jesus followed his lead. Wellhausen, however, supposes that it was Andrew who, after bringing his brother to Jesus, decided to return to Galilee, but who, before doing so, happened to meet Philip.]

Philip is mentioned in the synoptic gospels only in the lists of apostles (Mark iii. 18 and parallels). His name is purely Greek, and he occupies an important place both in the Fourth Gospel (vi. 5, 7, xii. 21, 22, xiv. 8, 9) and in the Church of Asia Minor (Euseb. *Hist. Eccl.* iii. 31, 39, v. 24). According to Polycrates, the two great apostolic luminaries who 'fell asleep' in Asia were Philip and John, the former having died in Hierapolis, the latter in Ephesus. There appears, however, to have been some confusion between Philip the apostle and Philip the evangelist, who is mentioned in Acts vi. 1 sqq. and xxi. 8). The Evangelist records that of the original disciples Philip alone followed Jesus in

obedience to that well-known imperative (Mark ii. 14, x. 21; Matt.
viii. 22, ix. 9; Luke v. 27, ix. 59) which was addressed to Peter after his
denial (xxi. 22). The parenthesis (*v.* 44, cf. xii. 21) calls attention to the
previous association of Philip with Andrew and Peter, and perhaps also
with James and John, who, according to Luke (*v.* 10), were partners
with Simon. For the importance of Bethsaida in the earlier tradition
see Mark vi. 45, viii. 22; Matt. xi. 21; Luke ix. 10, x. 13.

*vv.* 45–51. Nathanael (i.e. gift of God—Theodore—Dorotheos) is not
named in the synoptic gospels; but since Bartholomew is paired with
Philip in the lists of apostles, the two were early identified. Nathanael is
not mentioned again until xxi. 2, where he is said to have been *of Cana
of Galilee.*

*vv.* 45–51 are important not only because they record the first beginnings of the faith of a particular disciple, but also because they introduce the true interpretation of the words of the prologue *we saw his
glory* (*v.* 14) and of the twice repeated command *come and see* (*vv.* 39,
46). Philip is still satisfied with the assertion that Jesus, the son of
Joseph and the man from Nazareth, is the Christ who was foretold by
Moses and by the prophets of Israel, foretold, that is to say, in the two
complementary and authoritative parts of the Jewish scriptures. In the
development of the gospel this is shown to be altogether inadequate,
for the proper faith of the disciples must rest in their apprehension that
Jesus, the Son of Man from Nazareth, is the Son of God from heaven
(vi. 42, vii. 27 sqq., 41 sqq.). This is what Nathanael and the true
disciples of Jesus *will see* and this is His glory, which was first manifested
in the miracle of Cana (ii. 11).

Nathanael is at first wholly sceptical. Not only is it impossible for
the true messiah to come from Nazareth—indeed Galilean messiahs
had already caused disturbance enough (Josephus *Ant.* xx. 5; Acts v.
36, 37)—but it is impossible that any good thing should originate
thence. Nathanael uses intelligent human observation to set a firm
limit to the power of God. He does not, however, abide by his scepticism,
but comes to Jesus, who at once, echoing Ps. xxxii. 2 (cf. Rev. xiv. 5),
pronounces him to be not merely a typical Jew, but a proper Israelite,
one of the people of God. As the Good Shepherd, Jesus recognizes His
own sheep (x. 3). He knows the hearts of men (ii. 24, 25, cf. 1 Sam. ix.
19; 1 Cor. xiv. 24, 25) and, before Philip called Nathanael, had seen
and known him. *Under the fig-tree* would suggest to a Jew either domestic
comfort and peace (1 Kings iv. 25; Mic. iv. 4; Zech. iii. 10) or perhaps
the study of the law, since the Rabbis are said to have held their con-
ferences preferably under a tree and often under a fig-tree (Strack-
Billerbeck).

Nathanael rightly pronounces Jesus to be the Son of God, but, as
a true Jew, limits the sphere of His authority to Israel (cf. xii. 13). He
does not as yet understand that, as the Son of God, Jesus is the Saviour

of the world (iv. 42) or that His Kingdom is not *of this world* (xviii. 33–8). Nevertheless, personal experience of the knowledge of Jesus and faith which recognizes both His Sonship and His regal authority are the grounds upon which further perception is possible: *said I not unto thee, that, if thou believedst, thou shouldest see the glory of God* (xi. 40). To Nathanael and the other disciples the promise is therefore given that they will see *greater things*. The essential or heavenly glory of Jesus is more fundamental than an act of His prophetic knowledge.

The sight of the disciples is still to be directed towards the visible, historical figure of Jesus, towards His flesh, towards the Son of Man; but it is to be directed thither in order that they may see that which is beyond historical observation. Jesus is the place of revelation, the place over which the heaven has been opened (Matt. iii. 16; Rev. xix. 11). Jacob's vision and his perception that the place known normally as Luz is in fact Bethel, the House of God and the gate of heaven (Gen. xxviii. 10–17), provide the analogy by means of which the promised insight of the disciples is made known. The point of the comparison is not so much that 'What the patriarch saw but in a dream, the disciples will behold in reality' (Holtzmann), as that the place of the stone in the ancient story is now taken by the flesh and blood of Jesus the Son of man. He is the Door (x. 7, 9), the Way to the heavenly mansions of God (xiv. 1–7), the place where the vision of God is vouchsafed to men (xiv. 8–10). Through Him the will of God is made known, and on Him therefore, picking up the analogy, the angels of God ascend and descend. The importance in the architectonic structure of the Fourth Gospel of the words spoken to Nathanael is further emphasized by the reduplicated *Verily* with which they are introduced (iii. 3, 5, v. 19, 24, 25, vi. 53, viii. 58, x. 7, xiii. 21, xiv. 12, &c., cf. the *Verily, I say unto you* of the synoptic gospels, e.g. Mark iii. 28, Matt. v. 18, Luke xxiii. 43, &c.). Though the promise to the disciples is fulfilled finally by the gift of the Holy Spirit of truth (xiv. 26), yet the glory of Jesus is at once manifested in the miracle of Cana (ii. 11, cf. xi. 40) and will be made known paradoxically in the manner of His death (xii. 23, 32, 33, xiii. 31).

[The addition of the words translated *Hereafter* (cf. xiii. 19, xiv. 7) in Codex Alexandrinus and the majority of Greek manuscripts, in two manuscripts of the Old Latin Version, in the Syriac Peshitto and Harklean Versions, supported by Chrysostom and Augustine—they are, however, omitted in Codices Vaticanus and Sinaiticus, most manuscripts of the Old Latin, in the Vulgate and Egyptian Versions, supported by Origen, Epiphanius and Cyril—brings out the meaning of the Evangelist more clearly and has the effect of connecting the Saying more closely with the words spoken to the high priest, *Henceforth ye shall see the Son of man sitting at the right hand of power, and coming on the clouds of heaven* (Matt. xxvi. 64). The manifestation of the glory of Jesus not only belongs to the hope of the End, but is also a present reality made known in the actions of the Son of man and through the gift of the Spirit. Loisy, however, thinks that the open heaven and the ministering angels are reminiscent of the Marcan-Matthæan narrative of the baptism and temptation of Jesus rather than of the narrative of the passion. Some modern commentators (e.g. Bauer) have maintained that the Evangelist's use of the title 'Son of man' betrays the influence of some Gnostic or mythological speculation. Of this there is not the slightest trace. The Evangelist means by the title nothing mythological at all. He means by it the observable, historical, man Jesus, who possessed both flesh and blood; and he uses this phrase because it belongs unescapably to the earlier tradition of His teaching. Indeed, wherever the descriptive title occurs in the Fourth Gospel, it recalls particular sayings actually recorded in the synoptic gospels, and has, moreover, almost completely lost its eschatological significance (iii. 13, 14, vi. 62, viii. 28, ix. 35, xii. 23, 24, xiii. 31, cf. Mark viii. 31 and parallels, Matt. xvi. 13; John v. 27, cf. Mark xiii. 26, Matt. xxv. 31–46; John vi. 27, 53, cf. Mark xiv. 22–4; Luke xxii, 22).]

# TWO SIGNS

THE words of Christ are followed immediately by two acts in which His creative power is illustrated and set forth. Two festivals—the one domestic, the other national—offer the significant occasions of His first works. Throughout the gospel—including chapter vi (see vi. 4)—festivals of the Jews provide the scenes of His ministry. But, since there can be no rebirth apart from birth according to the natural order, a festival of marriage is the primary human celebration.

## JESUS CHANGES WATER INTO WINE

ii. 1. *And the third day there was a marriage in Cana of Galilee; and the mother of Jesus was there:* 2. *and Jesus also was bidden, and his disciples, to the marriage.* 3. *And when the wine failed, the mother of Jesus saith unto him, They have no wine.* 4. *And Jesus saith unto her, Woman, what have I to do with thee? mine hour is not yet come.* 5. *His mother saith unto the servants, Whatsoever he saith unto you, do it.* 6. *Now there were six waterpots of stone set there after the Jews' manner of purifying, containing two or three firkins apiece.* 7. *Jesus saith unto them, Fill the waterpots with water. And they filled them up to the brim.* 8. *And he saith unto them, Draw out now, and bear unto the ruler of the feast. And they bare it.* 9. *And when the ruler of the feast tasted the water now become wine, and knew not whence it was (but the servants which had drawn the water knew), the ruler of the feast calleth the bridegroom,* 10. *and saith unto him, Every man setteth on first the good wine; and when men have drunk freely, then that which is worse: thou hast kept the good wine until now.* 11. *This beginning of his signs did Jesus in Cana of Galilee, and manifested his glory; and his disciples believed on him.*

## JESUS CLEANSES THE TEMPLE

12. *After this he went down to Capernaum, he, and his mother, and his brethren, and his disciples: and there they abode not many days.*
13. *And the passover of the Jews was at hand, and Jesus went up to Jerusalem.*
14. *And he found in the temple those that sold oxen and sheep and doves, and the changers of money sitting:* 15. *and he made a scourge of cords, and cast all out of the temple, both the sheep and the oxen; and he poured out the changers' money, and overthrew their tables;* 16. *and to them that sold the doves he said, Take*

*these things hence; make not my Father's house a house of merchandise. 17. His
disciples remembered that it was written, The zeal of thine house shall eat me up.
18. The Jews therefore answered and said unto him, What sign shewest thou
unto us, seeing that thou doest these things? 19. Jesus answered and said unto
them, Destroy this temple, and in three days I will raise it up. 20. The Jews
therefore said, Forty and six years was this temple in building, and wilt thou raise
it up in three days? 21. But he spake of the temple of his body. 22. When therefore
he was raised from the dead, his disciples remembered that he spake this; and they
believed the scripture, and the word which Jesus had said.*

On the third day after the promise had been given to Nathanael,
Jesus and His disciples were invited to a wedding celebration in Cana
of Galilee, the city of Nathanael. The supply of wine was inadequate;
and the mother of Jesus, who was also one of the guests, turned to her
son, confident that He would be able to furnish what was lacking for
the proper conclusion of the feast. Jesus does not fail her; but, before
granting her request, He first makes it plain that He is no longer able
to act under her authority (contrast Luke ii. 51) or in response to her
wishes. The time of her authority is over: she must lose her son: this is
the destiny that has been laid upon her (Luke ii. 35). The time has
come for Him to await the hour of God, even though that hour is not
yet. Only as a sign of what will be when the hour is come does it lie
within His power to do what she asks. That He should fill up what is
lacking at a human festival of marriage is, after all, a proper parable
and sign of the Lamb of God that taketh away the sin of the world. To
do this sign, moreover, by using water set apart for Jewish purification
makes the sign even more relevant and effective, relevant, that is to
say, for His disciples and effective in directing their faith. What took
place was a creative act that is not and cannot be described. The great
waterpots stood there in the midst of the wedding scene, a reminder
that all is not well and that there is a need greater than that of a further
supply of wine. Purification was the theme of the mission of the Baptist
also, as it was of the law of Moses under which the whole wedding party
lived. Jesus therefore bade the servants fill the waterpots with water,
draw it out, and present it to the master of the feast.—The water was
made wine.—But neither the master nor the bridegroom knew whence
the wine had come. Only the servants, who had done what Jesus had
commanded them, knew that the gift was His.

This was the first public act in the ministry of Jesus. And it was not
trivial. For, though it was not the reality itself, it was a sign of the real
work of Jesus, and therefore a sign by which His glory was made known.
By this movement of words into action the disciples were bound more
closely to Christ. They believed on Him. But the Evangelist gives no
hint that they understood the meaning of what Jesus had done (cf. ii.
22–4).

Jesus did not remain in Cana. He went with His mother and brothers and His disciples to Capernaum. But He did not remain there for more than a few days. It was the passover season, and He must be about His Father's business in His Father's house at Jerusalem (cf. Luke ii. 49). The prophet Isaiah had called God's house *an house of prayer for all people* (Isa. lvi. 7). Jesus found it transformed into a market, made into a place of commerce. The altar of Mammon had been erected in the court of the temple of God. This was desecration—and Jesus acts at once with a whip in His hand and an allusion to the words of the prophet Jeremiah on His lips (Jer. vii. 11). What He did was itself a sign, a sign of the expected purification of the worship of God (Mal. iii. 3). At the time, the disciples saw no more than the relevance of the words of the Psalmist (Ps. lxix. 9). The Jews, however, recognizing at once the importance of the act, require a further sign to justify and authorize it. They received the sign they needed; but, since the truth lay beyond their comprehension, Jesus gave it them in veiled language. He will die at their hands, and in three days will build again what they have destroyed. The Jews, however, are unable even to imagine a temple erected otherwise than by vast expenditure of money and labour. Did not the temple in which they were standing take forty-six years to build? Neither did the disciples understand. But Jesus did not speak in vain, for afterwards, when He was raised from the dead, they understood both the deeper meaning of the Psalmist's words and the saying of Jesus concerning the temple and its rebuilding. Then, and then only, could they apprehend what it meant that God was present in the Body of His Son. And then, and then only, could they understand that, emptied of the presence of God, the temple in Jerusalem could not long remain intact.

# COMMENTARY

## JESUS CHANGES WATER INTO WINE

ii. 1–3. Cana (iv. 46, xxi. 2) is defined as *of Galilee* in order to distinguish it from other places of the same name (cf. Matt. ii. 1, xxi. 11). Josephus knew of a Cana in Cœle-Syria (*Ant.* xiii. 391, cf. *B.J.* i. 102, 334); another is mentioned in Joshua xix. 28 as situated in the land of Asher (cf. Eusebius. *Onomasticon, s.v.* Cana). Jerome told Marcella that he saw Cana from Nazareth (*Epist.* xlvi. 4). Modern geographers prefer *Khurbet Cana*, nine miles north of Nazareth (Sanday, *Sacred Sites of the Gospels*, p. 24). The inhabitants of Cana of Galilee took part in the Jewish War, its young men having sworn allegiance to the party of the Zealots; and Josephus resided there for some time (*Vita*, 86). Modern and ancient attempts to find a symbolical meaning in the name are wholly unconvincing: *possession* (i. 11, Matt. xxviii. 18, Origen); *zeal* (ii. 17, Abbott-Schmiedel, *Encycl. Bibl.*, p. 1800, n. 5); *a shaken reed* (Matt. xi. 7, Hönig).

The mother of Jesus, like the Beloved Disciple her spiritual son (xix. 25–7, cf. Rev. xii. 17), is unnamed, and she is not mentioned again until the narrative of the Passion. There is no indication, however, that the Evangelist has expanded or diminished her into a symbol of Judaism, the mother of the Messiah (Loisy, Heitmüller, and others). The sentence *They had no wine, for the wine of the marriage was exhausted* is added to *v.* 3 in Codex Sinaiticus, in some manuscripts of the Old Latin Version, in the margin of the Harklean Syriac Version, and in the Ethiopic Version.

*vv.* 4, 5. For the firm, almost rough, attitude of Jesus to His mother, cf. Mark iii. 32–5, and, in another connection, Matt. viii. 21, 22. The word *woman* does not, however, in the original Greek imply any disrespect (cf. iv. 21, xix. 26, xx. 13, 15; Matt. xv. 28; Bauer compares also Dio Cassius, li. 12. 5). But the phrase *what have I to do with thee?* translates a Hebrew idiom expressing a desire to be left in peace or an emphatic denial. (1 Kings xvii. 18; Mark i. 24; Matt. viii. 29; Luke viii. 28.) As an answer to a request it is equivalent to an emphatic refusal. The words therefore can hardly be paraphrased 'What does it concern us that they have no wine?' or 'What have I and thou to do with that?' (Nonnus, Luther, cf. Burkitt, *J.T.S.* vol. XIII, p. 594). The actions of Jesus are independent of every human attempt to influence Him (cf. ii. 18, iv. 48, vi. 26, 30, vii. 30, viii. 20). Irenæus comments, 'The action of the Son of God is dependent only on the will of the Father' (*Adv. Haer.* iii. 16. 7), and Quesnel sees here 'An example of that perfect disengagement from flesh and blood, and even from pious parents, with respect to divine matters and the Ecclesiastical ministry'. While declining to perform a prodigy, Jesus, nevertheless, gives His disciples a sign (cf. Matt. iv. 3; Luke iv. 3 with Matt. xiv. 19–21; Luke ix. 16, 17). For a similar refusal, followed in like manner by an action more significant than that originally desired, see iv. 47 sqq.

Josephus uses the word *hour* of the time of the ripening of fruits or of the marriageability of young people, the Evangelist (cf. Tosefta, *Sota* iv. 7) of the time appointed by God when Jewish purification and the worship at Jerusalem will be fulfilled (iv. 23). *The hour* is the hour of the death and glorification of Jesus, when He will by His blood cleanse those who believe in Him from sin and, by offering them His flesh to eat and His blood to drink, will bestow on them eternal life (vii. 30, viii. 20, xii. 23, 27, xiii. 1, xvi. 22, xvii. 1, xix. 34, vi. 54, 55; 1 John i. 7, v. 6). Until that time His actions are signs of what is to be and His words are parables (xvi. 25). 'This was the reason why, when Mary was urging Him to perform the wonderful miracle of the wine and was desirous before the time to partake of the cup of salvation, the Lord checked her untimely haste' (Irenæus. *Adv. Haer.* iii. 16. 7). His mother now leaves the initiative to her son.

*vv.* 6–11. *After the Jews' manner of purifying* (cf. Mark vii. 3, 4). There is no particular Galilean religion. *v.* 6 is no casual aside, since the distinction between Jewish purification and purification by Jesus forms a persistent theme in the early chapters of the Gospel. John baptized with water only, Christ with the Holy Spirit (i. 33); Nicodemus, the Pharisee, must be born again (from above) of water and spirit (iii. 1–21); the relation between baptism by John and Jewish purification on the one hand, and baptism by Christ on the other, forms a subject of controversy (iii. 22–30); after receiving the promise of the water of life (iv. 10–15), the woman of Samaria is told that both Jewish and Samaritan worship will be superseded (cf. Mark vii. 1–23; 1 Pet. iii. 18–22; Heb. ix. 13–14). The six waterpots were capable of holding 18 to 27 gallons each, that is, from 108 to 162 gallons in all. The Evangelist draws attention to the immense quantity of water not so much because he is thinking of the amount of purification required during the week of wedding ceremonies, but because he has in mind the fulness which all who believe in Jesus received from Him (i. 16). [Loisy supposes, however, that the number six, being an incomplete number, symbolizes the inadequacy of Judaism.] The verb *draw out* suggests, as Westcott noted, drawing from a well. In iv. 11–16, Jesus draws living water from the well of life. The obscurity caused by the use of the word here cannot be got rid of by supposing that the servants were ordered to draw the water from a well. More likely, the two metaphors are present in the Evangelist's mind. The official—*ruler of the feast* (R.V. mg. *steward*)—is not the toast master, who was chosen by lot from the guests to order the drinking, but the head waiter, whose duty it was to place in order the couches, arrange the courses and taste the food and wine before they were offered to the guests (Grimm-Thayer, *Lexicon*; see, however, Westcott). The steward, to whom the water of purification, now made wine, was presented in order that he might know its excellent quality and perhaps also as a sign (cf. Mark i. 44), *knew not whence it was—but the servants which had drawn the water knew.* In the perspective of the gospel, the steward's ignorance of origin anticipates the ignorance of Nicodemus (iii. 8), of the Samaritan woman (iv. 11), of the Jews in Jerusalem (vii. 25, 26, viii. 14, ix. 29, 30, and also of Pilate (xix. 9), just as the knowledge of the servants who obeyed the commands of Jesus anticipates the future knowledge of His obedient disciples. The last words of the steward are also significant. Correctly, but unconsciously (cf. xi. 50), he states the point at issue—the new wine is better than the old! (vii. 37, xv. 1; Mark ii. 22, cf. Mark xiv. 24, 25; Acts ii. 13). It is not, however, the man whose marriage is being celebrated **who** has withheld the good wine, but God, who has now sent His Son, the bridegroom (Mark ii. 19, 20), to give life to the world. *But when the fulness of the time* *came, God sent ... his Son, born of a woman, born under the law, that he might redeem them which were under the law* (Gal. iv. 4). 'God gave at first the old wine of the law, without strength, spirit or taste; and in the fulness of time He gave the new wine, of a strong and powerful taste, which enables us to fulfil the law, which inebriates the heart in a holy manner. . . .' (Quesnel).

The Evangelist does not draw out the meaning of his narrative, since he expects his readers to read his gospel to the end. But he does tell them that what Jesus did was a sign. In the Fourth Gospel the actions of Jesus are consistently named *signs* (ii. 23, iv. 54, vi. 2, 14, 26, vii. 31, ix. 16, x. 41, xi. 47, xii. 18, 37, xx. 30). In the Scriptures the word *sign* is applied to normal or abnormal occurrences which portend things that are about to take place (Isa. vii. 11, 14; Luke xxi. 11, 25; Matt. xxiv. 30; Acts ii. 19; Rev. xii. 1, xv. 1) and which authenticate those who have been entrusted with a divine mission (Exod. iv. 8, 17; Mark viii. 11, 12; Luke xi. 16, 29, 30, xxiii. 8; Matt. xii. 38, xvi. 1, 4). The signs of the Bible are characteristic in that they are usually of such a kind as to anticipate and show forth the nature both of what will take place and of the work of Him whom they authenticate. This is supremely so in the case of the actions of Jesus recorded in the Fourth Gospel. They are not narrated as prodigies, or wonders, nor do they merely authenticate Jesus. They are quite properly signs for parables of the nature of His work: they manifest His glory (i. 14, cf. vii. 4, xxi. 1). From very early days the Eastern Church has kept the 6th of January as the festival of the Epiphany of the incarnate Son of God, and has commemorated on that day the Nativity, the Manifestation of Christ to the wise men, His Baptism, and the first miracle that He wrought in Cana of Galilee (Bingham, *Antiquities*, pp. 1142 sqq.).

DETACHED NOTE 3

# CHRIST AS THE DISPENSER OF WINE

The Evangelist has recorded the miracle of Cana as a sign. There is therefore an obscurity in his narrative due to the presence in his mind, and also in the minds of his readers, of an analogous series of occurrences which provide the interpretation and meaning of the miracle. It has been the purpose of the preceding commentary to show that, though the Evangelist has not attached an interpretation to his account of the miracle, the gospel as a whole does set forth his meaning, a meaning which lies also in the earlier tradition of the ministry of Jesus. The Christ is the dispenser of the life of God, the author and giver of eternal life, which He offers to the world through His death and through the mission of His disciples. This is the fulfilment of Judaism, of which the miracle of Cana is a sign.

Recently, however, attempts have been made to set the narrative, neither on the background of Judaism, nor yet on the background of the earlier tradition of the ministry of Jesus, but on the background of popular Greek religion, and to discover in the description of Christ as the dispenser of wine a conscious or semi-conscious attempt to present the Lord of the Christians to the Greek world as the true and better Dionysos (Estlin Carpenter, pp. 379 sqq.). That Dionysos was regarded as the miraculous dispenser of wine is, of course, well known.

> One [of the Bacchantes] *dashed her thyrsus on the solid rock,*
> *Upstarted thence a gush of water; one*
> *Planted her reed upon the level earth,*
> *And the god poured from thence a stream of wine.*
>
> (Euripides, *Bacchae*, 704–707)

> *The plain flows with milk, flows with wine, flows with honey,*
> *The nectar of the bees, as the reek of the Syrian incense.*
>
> (ibid. 142, 143.)

The poets, Plato says, are inspired and possessed 'like Bacchic maidens who draw milk and honey from the rivers, when they are under the influence of Dionysos, but not when they are in their right mind' (*Ion*, 534). Pausanias, in his description of Elis, refers to a similar belief: 'Between the market-place and the Menius is an old theatre and a sanctuary of Dionysos: the image is by Praxiteles. No god is more revered by the Eleans than is Dionysos, and they say that he attends their festival of the Thyia. The place where they hold the festival called Thyia is about eight furlongs from the city. Three empty kettles are taken into the building and deposited there by the priests in the presence of the citizens and of any strangers who may happen to be staying in the country. On the doors of the building the priests, and all who choose to do so, put their seals. Next day they are free to examine the seals, and on entering the building they find the kettles full of wine. I was not there myself at the time of the festival, but the most respectable men of Elis, and strangers too, swore that the facts were as I have said' (*Description of Greece*, vi. 26. 1, translated with a commentary by Sir J. G. Frazer; cf. Pliny. *Nat. Hist.* ii. 231 (106), xxxi. 16). These and other similar passages form the basis of the theory that the fourth Evangelist transformed 'the miracles of Dionysos into an imaginative symbol of the glory of Christ' (Estlin Carpenter, p. 380). There is, however, neither in the actual narrative of the miracle of Cana nor anywhere in the rest of the gospel a hint of any such transformation. This does not, of course, mean that the episode may not later have been related to current beliefs about Dionysos, just as the description of Jesus as the

Good Shepherd was later related to Orpheus. For example, Epiphanius says that the town of Gerasa, one of the cities of the Decapolis, was the scene of an annual miracle. On the day of the Epiphany—also the day when the miracle of Cana was commemorated—the water of a fountain in the church was turned into wine. There is some reason to think that the church has been built on the site of an earlier temple dedicated to the infant Dionysos (see British School of Archæology in Jerusalem Supplementary Paper No. 3, *Churches at Jerash*, by J. W. Crowfoot, pp. 1, 2, 7).

Nor is there any reason to suppose that in writing his narrative the Evangelist was directly influenced by Alexandrian Jewish thought (Scott, pp. 56 sqq.). Philo had seen in the mysterious figure of Melchizedek a type of the Word who shall 'bring forth wine instead of water, and shall give your souls to drink, and shall cheer them with unmixed wine, in order that they may be wholly occupied with a divine intoxication, more sober than sobriety itself' (*Leg. alleg.* III. 82). In another passage he speaks of the Word as the 'wine-pourer of God, who will pour out sacred cups of true happiness' (*De Somn.* II. 249). But this is allegorizing of the Pentateuch and especially of Gen. xiv. 18. It has no analogy with what the fourth Evangelist wrote; and in any case, similarity of religious language, especially on so normal a theme as the gift of wine, does not imply literary dependence.

# COMMENTARY

## JESUS CLEANSES THE TEMPLE

ii. 12. There is a scriptural ring about the verse, cf. the repeated Deuteronomic phrase, *Thou, and thy son, and thy daughter, and thy manservant, and thy maidservant* (Deut. xii. 18, &c., Schlatter, *D.E.J.*). The brothers of Jesus are mentioned again in vii. 1–10, where it is said that they did not believe on Him (cf. Mark iii. 31; Matt. xii. 46; Luke viii. 19). According to the synoptic tradition, Capernaum was the centre of the early ministry. The descent—contrast the ascent in *v.* 13—from the hill-country to the sea of Tiberias, on the shore of which Capernaum lay, recalls Matt. iv. 13 (cf. Matt. ix. 1). The Evangelist is not ignorant of a longer ministry in Galilee (vii. 1); but now, owing to the proximity of the passover, Jesus did not remain there. The reading, *And there he* [not they] *abode not many days* (Codex Alexandrinus and some other manuscripts) perhaps gives the correct sense, His mother and brothers remaining presumably at Capernaum.

*vv.* 13–17. Jerusalem at the time of the passover was the **appropriate** place and occasion for Jesus to inaugurate His mission and explain its significance (cf. v. 1, vi. 4, xi. 55, xviii. 38, 39, xix. 14). In Jerusalem stood the temple of God; and the temple consecrated the city. It consecrated also the Jewish people, 'not because they offered their gifts there, but because it was the sign and guarantee of the presence of God in their midst' (Schlatter, *D.E.J.*). In the temple therefore priesthood and people are tested whether they seek the things of men, their own things, or the things of God. The Evangelist states that the passover was *of the Jews*, less in order to inform his gentile readers than to contrast Jewish sacrifice with that by which it is fulfilled (i. 29, 36, cf. 1 Cor. v. 7). Origen comments: 'The passover of the Jews consists of a sheep which is sacrificed, each man taking a sheep according to his father's house; and the passover is accompanied by the slaughter of thousands of rams and goats, in proportion to the number of the houses of the people. But our Passover is sacrificed for us, namely, Christ'. The contrast between the temple and that which is greater than the temple belongs also to the synoptic tradition (Matt. xii. 6–8).

The action of Jesus in the temple echoes Mal. iii. 1–3: *The Lord, whom ye seek, shall suddenly come to his temple; and the messenger of the covenant, whom ye delight in, behold, he cometh, saith the Lord of hosts. But who may abide the day of his coming? and who shall stand when he appeareth? . . . He shall purify the sons of Levi, and purge them as gold and silver; and they shall offer unto the Lord offerings in righteousness* (cf. Zech. xiv. 21 and vi. 12, 13).

The word translated *temple* in *vv.* 14, 15 denotes the whole compass of the sacred enclosure, including the entire aggregate of sacred buildings and courts. Another word, also translated *temple*, is used in *vv.* 19–21 to designate the *sanctuary* (R.V. mg.), which consisted of the Holy Place and the Holy of Holies. Oxen, sheep, and doves were necessary for the prescribed purification before the celebration of the passover ritual (xi. 55; 2 Chron. xxx. 18); the presence of money-changers was equally necessary if pilgrims were to be given an opportunity to receive the temple shekels and half-shekels in exchange for foreign currency which, though in ordinary use in the country, was forbidden in the temple (Edersheim, *Life and Times*, vol. I, pp. 367 sqq.). Two different words are used for *changers of money*. The one (*v.* 14) is found only in this passage and in literature dependent upon it. The other (*v.* 15, Mark xi. 15; Matt. xxi. 12) is found in the papyri, and must have been in fairly common use, since the Atticists condemned it as a vulgarism: the word —from which the Greeks got their Kollybos and Cicero his Collybus the money-lender—is of Semitic origin, formed from the same root as Caliph (deputy successor), and means properly one who changes coin of one country for that of another (Sayce, quoted by Burton, *Arabian Nights*, vol. IX, p. 3, n. 3). The scourge (cf. Mark xv. 15; Matt. xxvii. 26) was made of twisted rushes (*cords*, cf. Acts xxvii. 32). Neither the meaning of the words nor the general sense of the passage supports Westcott's judgement that the scourge was used as 'a symbol of authority and not as a weapon of offence'.

*He . . . cast all out of the temple, both the sheep and the oxen*—not all the merchants (A.V.) but all the animals. Dr. Eisler thinks that the sheep and oxen 'were being led up to the altar and the other slaughtering places for immediate sacrifice' (*The Quest*, January 1921). The authorized paraphernalia of Jewish sacrificial purification are either forcibly removed from the temple precincts or set in hopeless confusion. The action is not merely that of a Jewish reformer: it is a sign of the advent of the Messiah; it is not merely a protest against the irreverence and corruption of Jewish worship: it is a sign that the end of animal sacrifice is at hand (see *v.* 21). The Prophets of Israel had long ago attacked the whole system of animal sacrifice as a profanation of the worship of God (Isa. i. 11–17; Jer. vii. 22; Hos. v. 6, viii. 13; Amos iv. 4, 5, cf. Ps. l. 13).

*Make not my Father's house a house of merchandise.* The Jews made use even of the house of God as a means of making money. The purification of His Father's house (cf. Luke ii. 49) is required of the Son of God. The words that accompany the act of purification in the synoptic gospels (Mark xi, 17; Matt. xxi. 13; Luke xix. 46) are made up of quotations from Isa. lvi 7 and Jer. vii. 11: *My house shall be called a house of prayer* (*for all nations*, Mark), *but ye have made it a den of robbers*. The words of Jeremiah underlie also the parallel saying in the Fourth Gospel; only they are interpreted to mean that all profit—and not only dishonest profit—made out of the temple of God is irreconcilable with His true worship.

The perception of the disciples at the time—they see no more than that a consuming zeal for the purity of the temple has prophetic sanction (Ps. lxix. 9)—is contrasted with their later insight (*v.* 22) and with the irritated questioning of the Jews (*v.* 18). The word translated *eat up*, in addition to meaning that the mind is strongly moved, suggests also destruction (Rev. xi. 5, xx. 9). The disciples do not yet understand that the zeal of Jesus must be consummated in His own death or that the purification of which His action is a sign depends upon the sacrifice of His body (xix. 30, cf. xiii. 4–11, xvii. 19).

*vv.* 18–22. An authoritative and personal action of a prophet or of the Messiah, especially when accompanied by the claim that the temple is *his Father's house*, requires visible and audible attestation (cf. Matt. xxi. 23; Mark xi. 27). There have been false prophets and false Christs. The Jews, here the hierarchy as in i. 19 (*chief priests and elders*, Matt. xxi. 23), therefore demand a sign. [For the grammatical construction of *v.* 18 (cf. vii. 35, xii. 48, 49), see Abbott, *Johannine Grammar*, 2174 sqq.]

*Destroy this temple* [*sanctuary*], *and in three days I will raise it up*. The saying, which is implied in the synoptic tradition (Mark xiv. 58; Matt. xxvi. 61), is obscure because each of the important words is capable of two meanings. *Destroy* (literally *loose*) is used of the destruction of buildings (1 Esdras i. 55; Josephus *B.J.* vi. 32, cf. Mark xiii. 2), and also of the dissolution of human life (Euripides, *Iph. Taur.* 629): *raise* of building a city or house or temple or of setting up an image or altar (Deut. xvi. 22; 1 Esdras v. 43 LXX; Josephus *Ant.* iv. 123, viii. 95), and in Christian language of the resurrection of the dead and especially of the resurrection of Christ (Mark v. 41, xiv. 28; Acts iv. 10; 2 Cor. i. 9, &c.): *sanctuary* of the sacred edifice within a temple enclosure, containing the image of the god, or of the Holy of Holies, and also of the human body as the sanctuary of the soul or, in Christian language, of the Holy Spirit (1 Cor. vi. 19; 2 Cor. v. 1, vi. 16, cf. Col. ii. 9). The words can therefore be taken literally, *Destroy this temple, and in three days I will rebuild it*; or figuratively, *Kill this body, and in three days I will raise it from the dead;* or by a mixture of both, *Destroy this temple, and in three days I will raise this body from the dead,* i.e. to take its place. The real obscurity of the saying is due, however, not merely to the double meaning of the words, but to the interlocking of the events that underlie it. The rejection and putting to death of Jesus, His resurrection, the destruction of the temple and the end of animal sacrifice, the presence of God in the midst of the community of those who believe in Jesus, and the removal of sin—these are not isolated, separable occurrences. The sign that is given to the Jews is, therefore, the sign of the resurrection, and the answer of Jesus here is analogous to Matt. xii. 38–40 (Luke xi. 29, cf. Matt. xvi. 4), where the resurrection and its type, the rescue of Jonah from the belly of the whale, are the all-sufficient signs of the authority of Jesus. The resurrection is referred to as the work of Jesus (cf. x. 18). The normal passive *was raised* is, however, at once substituted in *v.* 22, just as in x. 18 the action of Jesus is at once stated to be in obedience to the commandment which He received from His Father.

The Jews, taking the words of Jesus literally, suppose Him to be claiming the possession of grotesque architectural capacity (for similar misunderstandings cf. iii. 4, iv. 11, 15, vi. 7, xi. 12, 24, xiv. 8). Proud of their achievement of piety, they remind Him that, nevertheless, the building of the temple took forty-six years. The reference is clearly to the temple of Herod. The number of years is inapplicable either to the temple of Solomon or, without strange calculations, to the temple of Zerubbabel (Abbott, *Classical Review*, 1894, pp. 89 sqq.). Herod began a radical reconstruction of Zerubbabel's temple in 20 B.C. It was not completed until about A.D. 63 (Josephus, *Ant.* xv. 380, xx. 219; see, however, *B.J.* i, 401. Schürer, *History of the Jewish People*, I, i. 437 sqq., and also p. 410). Forty-six years brings the date to about A.D. 26, which seems to suit very well the time of the ministry. It must then be assumed either that the rebuilding was discontinued somewhere between A.D. 26 and 30, which would make it possible to regard the temple as complete at that time (Westcott); or that some qualification should be supplied, such as, *and is still unfinished* (Bauer, Sanday)—but the aorist stands intractably in the text, and must, presumably, be translated *was built*, i.e. completed (see, however, Ezra v. 16); or that the reference is to the important part of the temple. Since none of these explanations is wholly satisfactory, Loisy has sought to explain the number symbolically. Origen asked his readers to consider whether forty does not mean the four elements of the world, and six the creation of the world on the sixth day. The author of the treatise *De Montibus Sina et Sion*—attributed to Cyprian—says that the number refers to Christ as the new Adam ($a = 1$, $\delta = 4$, $a = 1$, $\mu = 40$, the Greek letters spelling Adam). Since in viii. 57 the Jews said that Jesus was *not yet fifty years old*, it was thought in very early days that the number forty-six states His age at the time of the cleansing of the temple. Augustine refers to this interpretation in his *De Doct. Christ.* ii. 28, and discards it. Loisy, however, finds it satisfactory. The Evangelist considered the ministry to have covered four passovers (ii. 13, v. 1, vi. 4, xi. 55) and placed the crucifixion in the fiftieth year of the life of the incarnate Word. This gave him the number forty-six at the time of the first passover.

The narrative of the cleansing of the Temple concludes, as had the previous episode, with the record of the belief of the disciples, here contrasted with the unbelief of the Jews. The belief is, however, deferred belief. Not until after the resurrection did they understand the full implication of the words of the Psalmist, *The zeal of thine house shall eat me up*, or the meaning of the sign given to the Jews. The chief priests and Pharisees remembered what Jesus had said, and begged Pilate to guard the tomb lest the body of Jesus should be stolen (Matt. xxvii. 63, 64): the disciples remembered His words—and believed. *The scripture* (*v.* 22) may, however, refer not to Ps. lxix. 9 quoted in *v.* 17, but to the general or particular witness of the Old Testament to the Resurrection (xx. 9; Luke xxiv. 25-7, 44-6; Matt. xxvi. 54; Acts ii. 29-32; 1 Cor. xv. 4; Ps. xvi. 10 quoted in Acts ii. 27, cf. Mark xiv. 21).

Believing in the Resurrection of Jesus, the Evangelist now knows (cf. vii. 39, xii. 33) the meaning of the sign once given to the Jews in the temple at Jerusalem. *He spake of the temple of his body.* The truth of what the apostles had seen is summed up in the words *Corpus Christi*. The body of Jesus, His flesh, was the tabernacle of the Word (i. 14), the abiding place of the Spirit (i. 33, vii. 38, xix. 30), the shrine of the presence of God. *The Father is in me, and I in the Father* (x. 38, cf. xiv. 10, 11, 20, xvii. 21): offered as a sacrifice for the purification of the world. His body provides the food of the Christians upon which their life, their eternal life, depends (vi. 51 sqq.). In their faith and dependence upon Him, the whole body or community of believers are branches of the vine (xv. 1 sqq.); Saint Paul had already said that they are the body of Christ, the new Jerusalem, the new temple of God (Gal. iv. 26; Col. i. 18, 24; Eph. i. 23; 1 Cor. iii. 16, 17; 2 Cor. vi. 16; Eph. ii. 21, cf. 1 Pet. ii. 5, iv. 17). The Evangelist does not at once draw out the implications

of what he has said, any more than he did at the end of his narrative of
the miracle of Cana. Once again, he expects his readers to read his
book to the end. But he has formulated his theme, the theme of the true
and spiritual worship of God, by which the worship at Jerusalem has
been fulfilled and superseded (iv. 23, 24, cf. Rom. xii. 1; Matt. xii. 6).

The narrative of the Cleansing of the Temple raises in an acute form
the problem of the relation of the Fourth Gospel to the earlier tradition.
The problem does not concern merely the position of the incident—in
the synoptic gospels it belongs to the narrative of the Passion (Mark xi.
15–19; Matt. xxi. 12, 13; Luke xix. 45, 46), in the Fourth Gospel to the
opening of the ministry—but its meaning.

In form, all four accounts overlap (see INTRODUCTION, pp. 70 sq.):
even the additional material in the Fourth Gospel narrative is found
also in the earlier tradition, though in widely different contexts. The
saying concerning the destruction of the temple is implied by the
evidence of the false witnesses at the Trial (Mark xiv. 58; Matt. xxvi.
61) and by the crowds at the crucifixion (Mark xv. 29; Matt. xxvii. 39,
40); the demand for a sign, answered by a prophecy of the Resurrection,
is not peculiar to the Fourth Gospel (Matt. xii. 38–40, cf. Matt. xvi. 1–4,
xxi. 23; Luke xi. 29, 30; Mark viii. 11, 12), nor is the statement that the
disciples understood neither the scripture nor the words of Jesus until
after the Resurrection (Luke xxiv. 44, 45). Apart from the picture of
Jesus with a whip in His hand, the only apparently new factor lies in
the firm statement that Jesus spoke of His own body as the temple of
God. This, however, is not merely a somewhat irrelevant comment; it
is, according to the Evangelist, the true and original meaning of the
incident. Here, at first sight, lies the real difference, the real problem of
the Fourth Gospel. The earlier Evangelists seem to have seen in the
incident no more than an attempt of Jesus to purify the temple, the last
Evangelist brings it into relation with the advent of the new, spiritual
worship of God, and sees its whole meaning in that relationship. The
more acute problem, however, lies, as so often, less with the Fourth
Gospel than with its predecessors and with the actual meaning of acts
and words which the earlier Evangelists recorded, as distinct from
what they may have supposed their meaning to have been. If the incident were merely a cleansing of the temple, it stands in a very strange
setting. It is associated with the cursing and withering of the barren fig-
tree, clearly a parable of Judaism (Mark xi. 12–14, 20–2, cf. Luke xiii.
6–9); with the themes of the parable of the Wicked Husbandmen, the
destruction of the men who had murdered the son of the owner of the
vineyard, the transference of the property to others, and the miracle of
the new order raised upon the foundation of the stone that had been
rejected (Mark xii. 1–12); with teaching given to the disciples concerning the imminent destruction of the temple (Mark xiii. 2); and with

statements concerning the irrelevance of animal sacrifice altogether (Mark xii. 32–4, cf. Matt. ix. 13, xii. 7). All this, moreover, in the Marcan narrative leads on to the crucifixion of Jesus, not as the death of a man who appeared in Jerusalem as a reformer of Judaism, but as the death of One who claimed to be the Messiah, who pointed to the destruction of the temple and to the end of the old covenant, and who by His sacrificial and voluntary death inaugurated the new covenant in His blood (Mark xiv. 20–5). When, therefore, the fourth Evangelist sees in the Cleansing of the Temple a sign of the destruction of the sanctuary in Jerusalem and of the substitution for it of the temple of the body of Jesus, and consequently a sign of the new and spiritual worship of God, he is not necessarily imposing upon the incident a meaning foreign to the original action of Jesus. [Dr. Eisler has even supposed that the phrase *den of robbers*, quoted in the Marcan narrative from Jer. vii. 11, ought to be translated *den of slaughterers*. (Isa. i. 15; *The Quest*, January 1921; *J.T.S.* vol. XXIV, pp. 382 sqq., cf. O. Holtzmann, *Life of Jesus*, pp. 414 sqq.; but see Burkitt, *J.T.S.* vol. XXV, pp. 386 sqq.)]

It seems then that the synoptic gospels do, in fact, contain evidence that Jesus proclaimed the end of animal sacrifice. If this be so, the Saying quoted by Epiphanius from the Ebionite gospel (*Haereses* xxx. 16) may be in substance correct: 'I came to destroy the sacrifices, and if ye cease not from sacrifice, the Wrath will not cease from you.' It must, however, be remembered that there is, on the other hand, no evidence in the canonical gospels to suggest that Jesus attacked the worship in the temple in order to introduce a non-sacrificial worship after the manner of that recommended by 'Stoic philosophy or modern sentiment'. What made the temple sacrifices irrelevant was His own death. The Word of God was now written not on the bodies of animals, but on His own body, on His own flesh (i. 14, 29, 34). This is what the fourth Evangelist had clearly seen, apprehended, and believed.

If this be so, the important position of the Cleansing of the Temple at the beginning of the Fourth Gospel can be explained without assuming either that the temple was twice cleansed (Westcott, Schanz), or that the fourth Evangelist has preserved the proper position of the incident and that, consequently, its position in the Marcan narrative (followed by Matthew and Luke) is unhistorical (B. Weiss, Dr. Brooke). The fourth Evangelist is concerned more with the meaning of the words and actions of Jesus than with their original setting or relative order. Understood as he understood it, the cleansing of the Temple provided the key to a proper understanding both of the quite fundamental controversy of Jesus with the Jews and of the implications of discipleship. For this reason he placed it at the beginning of his gospel. He then moves onwards from it, determined that his readers shall in the end understand what it means, determined also that his readers shall finally understand what it means that the Word became flesh. And moreover, *Judgement must begin at the house of God* (1 Pet. iv. 17).

DETACHED NOTE 4

# THE RESURRECTION—IN THREE DAYS

The phrases *in three days*, *after three days*, and *on the third day*, occur in the prophecies of resurrection in the synoptic tradition (Mark xiv. 58, xv. 29; Matt. xxvi. 61, xxvii. 40, 63; Luke xiii. 32, cf. 1 Cor. xv. 4). That the words should occur also in the veiled reference to the Resurrection in the narrative of the Cleansing of the Temple in the Fourth Gospel is not surprising: *Destroy this temple and in three days I will raise it up* (ii. 19). They appear too in the addition to Mark xiii. 2 in Codex Bezae and in manuscripts of the Old Latin Version: *And in three days another (temple) shall be raised up without hands*. It is usually supposed that the phrase *in three days* and its variants refer to the precise day of the Resurrection (if so, the variations are troublesome), or that it means no more than 'after a short time' (Holtzmann).

In the East a clear distinction is made between the third and the fourth day. It is, for example, a widely observed rule in hospitality—it was the practice of Mohammed—for a guest to remain three days with his host (rest-day, drest-day, departure day). To remain longer, to remain on the fourth day, is a very serious matter. The custom is illustrated in the *Arabian Nights*: 'But whenever he (Wazir of King Shahryar) entered a realm whose ruler was subject to his suzerain, where he was greeted with magnificent gifts of gold and silver and all manner of presents fair and rare, he would tarry there three days, the term of the guest-rite; and, when he left on the fourth, he would be honourably escorted for a whole day's march' (*The Story of King Shahryar and his brother*). This 'instinct-made rule in hospitality' was adopted by Christians in the second (third?) century as a test of travelling prophets. If they continued their journey before the completion of the third day, they were true prophets; if they remained longer, they were to be treated as false prophets (*Didache*, xi). Three days may, therefore, be said to constitute a temporary habitation, the fourth day implies permanent residence.

A similar distinction between three days and the fourth day appears also in another connection. It seems to have been a widespread belief among the Jews, a belief of whose existence elsewhere there is evidence, that the soul of a dead man hovered near the corpse for three days hoping to return to the body, but that on the fourth day, when decomposition set in, the soul finally departed (Bousset, *Religion des Judentums*, second edition, p. 341, *n.*; Wetstein, note on John xi. 39; Frazer, *Folk*

*Lore in the Old Testament,* vol. I, pp. 71 sq.). With this belief may be compared the Zoroastrian doctrine that on the third night after death the soul finally abandons the body, and on the morning of the fourth day passes over the bridge Cinvat, where the good are separated from the bad (Nathan Söderblom, *La vie future d'après le Mazdeisme,* pp. 91–6).

Moreover, quite apart from any popular superstition, three days mark the period during which the ravages of death are not altogether visible. With the fourth day it is different. Martha supposes it impossible for Lazarus to be raised from the dead, because he had been four days in the grave (xi. 39). Again, the distinction between the third and the fourth day is the distinction between what may be temporary and what must be permanent. The prophet Hosea encouraged those who thought that the Lord had permanently humiliated them with the promise, *After two days will he revive us, on the third day he will raise us up, and we shall live before him* (Hos. vi. 2). They must not despair: before the fourth day God would act (cf. Jonah i. 17, quoted in Matt. xii, 40). When, therefore, it is said in the gospels that Jesus emphasized the importance of the third day after His death, what is meant is that He assured to His disciples that death could not permanently engulf Him, and that God would not suffer *His Holy One to see corruption* (Acts ii. 27; Ps. xvi. 10). He would be but a visitor to the dead, not a permanent resident in their midst.

# JESUS AND NICODEMUS
# THE RABBI

II. 23—III. 21

The reader of the gospel is now required to attend to the themes of a 'Johannine discourse'. If he is to understand the discourses, of which this is the first, he must understand them in their scriptural, biblical setting. Unless he is to do grave violence to the text, he is not free to put them in any other setting, ancient or modern. The Fourth Gospel is a biblical book, and the first discourse is spoken to a Jewish Rabbi. If these discourses seem to us to be so full of gaps that they appear to leap rather than move; or if, alternatively, they seem to us to be monotonous; or if they seem to be set quite out of their context by the introduction of the Evangelist's own comments; we must not be satisfied with these judgements of ours, since the Evangelist most assuredly did not think that what he wrote was fragmentary or monotonous or inconstant. We must not rest from exegesis until the apparent gaps have been filled up so completely that each discourse moves step by step as an ordered, a theologically ordered, whole: until, that is to say, what is said becomes intelligible and coherent speech, and until, moreover, it coheres with the biblical Palestinian background upon which the Evangelist has set it, even though he be writing in Greek, years after the temple was destroyed and when the Jews no longer congregated in Jerusalem. This is the energy of understanding which the Evangelist demanded of his original readers; and his book still makes the same demand upon us. Also, we shall be unlikely to persevere with such exegesis unless we assume that something important is being said. And above all, we must not rise from the first discourse with the feeling that though Nicodemus is a sensible person, the Evangelist is not.

ii. 23. *Now when he was in Jerusalem at the passover, during the feast, many believed on his name, beholding his signs which he did. 24. But Jesus did not trust himself unto them, for that he knew all men, 25. and because he needed not that any one should bear witness concerning man; for he himself knew what was in man.*
iii. 1. *Now there was a man of the Pharisees, named Nicodemus, a ruler of the Jews: 2. the same came unto him by night, and said to him, Rabbi, we know that thou art a teacher come from God: for no man can do these signs that thou doest, except God be with him. 3. Jesus answered and said unto him, Verily, verily, I say*

201

*unto thee, Except a man be born anew, he cannot see the kingdom of God. 4. Nico-*
*demus saith unto him, How can a man be born when he is old? can he enter a*
*second time into his mother's womb, and be born? 5. Jesus answered, Verily,*
*verily, I say unto thee, Except a man be born of water and the Spirit, he cannot*
*enter into the kingdom of God. 6. That which is born of the flesh is flesh; and that*
*which is born of the Spirit is spirit. 7. Marvel not that I said unto thee, Ye must*
*be born anew. 8. The wind bloweth where it listeth, and thou hearest the voice*
*thereof, but knowest not whence it cometh, and whither it goeth: so is every one that*
*is born of the Spirit. 9. Nicodemus answered and said unto him, How can these*
*things be? 10. Jesus answered and said unto him, Art thou the teacher of Israel,*
*and understandest not these things? 11. Verily, verily, I say unto thee, We speak*
*that we do know, and bear witness of that we have seen; and ye receive not our*
*witness. 12. If I told you earthly things, and ye believe not, how shall ye believe, if*
*I tell you heavenly things? 13. And no man hath ascended into heaven, but he that*
*descended out of heaven, even the Son of man, which is in heaven. 14. And as*
*Moses lifted up the serpent in the wilderness, even so must the Son of man be lifted*
*up: 15. that whosoever believeth may in him have eternal life.*

*16. For God so loved the world, that he gave his only begotten Son, that whoso-*
*ever believeth on him should not perish, but have eternal life. 17. For God sent not*
*the Son into the world to judge the world; but that the world should be saved*
*through him. 18. He that believeth on him is not judged: he that believeth not hath*
*been judged already, because he hath not believed on the name of the only begotten*
*Son of God. 19. And this is the judgement, that the light is come into the world,*
*and men loved the darkness rather than the light; for their works were evil.*
*20. For every one that doeth ill hateth the light, and cometh not to the light, lest*
*his works should be reproved. 21. But he that doeth the truth cometh to the light,*
*that his works may be made manifest, that they have been wrought in God.*

The passover festival had arrived; and Jesus was still in Jerusalem—
but not as a spectator. At the feast He did what He had already done
in Galilee: He healed the sick. The fourth Evangelist says He did *signs*,
actions which created such confidence among the crowds that *many
believed* in the power of His name. This confidence was, however, not
the faith that had compelled the Evangelist to write his book, nor was
it what Jesus had required of His disciples. Faith that moves from and
towards physical healing cannot be trusted; and Jesus, who, without
being informed, knew what was in man, knew its impurity. These
casual believers may be the stuff out of which disciples are made, but
they are not disciples, and may never become so. They stand outside
the truth, and the fourth Evangelist, unlike his predecessors, passes
quickly on.

Nevertheless, the action of Jesus and the reaction of the crowd raised
important theological issues; for physical healing is itself a parable,
and the confidence it evokes produces a situation eloquent of faith.
The arrival of Nicodemus, himself a theologian, therefore presented an

opportunity for relevant theological speech; and Jesus discourses openly and without reserve. He does not, however, discourse *with* Nicodemus, but *to* him; and *through* him to the readers of the gospel, for Nicodemus soon disappears in the darkness he had selected for his visit.

Though he occupied, as a teacher of Israel (*v.* 10), an important theological position among the Jews, Nicodemus was not a free man. Learned and pious, he and those associated with him—the *we* in *v.* 2 is important, cf. *v.* 11—were impressed by what Jesus said, and by His actions. Unlike some of their contemporaries (Mark iii. 22), they did not attribute His abnormal powers to some unhealthy, or even diabolical, influence. They recognized Him as a teacher sent from God. The evidence of His actions was for them undeniable. But Nicodemus dared not compromise himself in public, so he came under cover of night. Tied up by sensitiveness to the opinions of others, he was as far removed from Jesus as darkness from light. Jesus had much to forgive for this manner of approach. But since Nicodemus had come to the light Jesus tells him everything with complete freedom. He has nothing to hide; and He lays bare all the fundamental themes of His mission. The whole is in the part, and what follows is not a discourse, but The Discourse, the subject-matter of which is repeated in all subsequent discourses.

First, the theme of *Repentance*:—Knowledge, true theological knowledge and apprehension, capacity to see the dominion of God, is not secured by acquiring more and more information. Nicodemus already possessed quite sufficient information, both acquired and hereditary. The knowledge of God demands a re-orientation, a new creative beginning, so ultimate and fundamental that the initial fact of birth provides the only proper analogy; the only proper analogy, in the sense that all other analogies depend upon it. But Nicodemus does not understand this: nor does he understand what a sign or a parable is. By a strange paradox, the man who has come to converse about God and who is sure that he knows what a divine mission is, turns out to be, in spite of his delicate perceptions, a complete materialist. He can conceive of no birth other than that which has made him what he is. He has grown old in the service of God, and an old man cannot begin all over again. Indeed, is not the life he is now living as a Rabbi and a Pharisee the life demanded by God? Nicodemus is a materialist, not because he takes visible human life seriously, but because he does not see what it means: he does not see that human birth is itself speaking of that which lies beyond it and above it; it is speaking of the creative act of God, of birth from above. Jesus meets the expressed unbelief of Nicodemus by reasserting what He had said with even greater precision. It is not merely a question of knowledge, as though the Kingdom of God were a thing to be seen and known, as it were from outside. The dominion of God is that under which men must live; they must enter into it: for it is their proper life. But no one belongs to the Israel of God unless he has been purified and created by the Spirit of God. Of this birth and purification the rite of visible purification by water—here the figure of John the Baptist, who washed those who came to him, presses into the discourse—provides the second necessary analogy. Natural birth, baptism and purification, spiritual birth and spiritual purification, are all interlocking and analogous realities. It is not required of men that they should remove themselves or be removed into some esoteric and aloof spirituality. The practice of religion, like the fact of birth, belongs to the structure of human life: both are necessary signs of the dominion of God. But they must be recognized as signs. Flesh is flesh, whether it be the fact of birth or the initial act of religion. And what is produced from flesh is flesh. There is no evolution from flesh to Spirit. What a man is in his own eyes or in the eyes of his religious companions is at best a parable of what he is as the creation of God: at worst it is a darkness from which he must escape at all costs. Only *that which is born of the Spirit is spirit*. The man who is thus born—and here comes the third analogy—is like a gust of wind. Uncontrolled by our will, or desires, or capacity, we neither set the wind in motion nor guide it to its goal. And yet, how undeniable a thing wind is! We do not doubt either its power or its reality. So it is with the man who has been born of the Spirit. The man of the world, even though he be a Rabbi like Nicodemus, can locate neither the origin nor the destiny of those whom God has made His own by a creative act initiated by Himself. Beginning and ending belong to God, and men are what they are in relation to their origin and their destiny. The seriousness of Jesus when He speaks of the power of God, and His seriousness when He defines what human life is, are unintelligible to Nicodemus. It is a surprising experience to discover that a teacher of Israel, a theologian, can deny the reality of his subject: it is a terrifying experience to know that he can do so when actually in the presence of Jesus Himself.

And yet, what Jesus had said thus far is no new truth. Nicodemus has not been addressed by a man with peculiar ideas about the relation between God and men. As Nicodemus himself voiced the opinions of others (v. 2), so Jesus is no isolated person (v. 11). There are, and have been, men who speak because they know, and bear witness because they have seen. There have been prophets: there is a man named John baptizing in the desert: and there are men who have left all and followed Jesus. These all say the same thing; and it is with their testimony that Nicodemus and his like must first concern themselves, if they are to teach Israel and bear witness to the world. Instead, however, they establish themselves as Rabbis, and reject the truth which alone makes sense of their position.

Now comes the second theme; the theme *Jesus Himself*, the visible, historical man Jesus:—This second theme is strictly related to the first.

Nicodemus had passed quite rightly from signs to the mission of Jesus
(*v.* 2); and Jesus moves likewise from the one to the other. He has spoken
of earthly things common to all men, of birth and of water; and the
signs He had done in Galilee and Jerusalem, signs of new life and of
purification, were not essentially different from those signs which belong to the texture of quite normal human life. Now, however, He must
speak of His own mission. Though prophets have seen—darkly—what
was to come, and apostles will repeat what is about to be said, He alone
can say what His mission is.—Jesus speaks about heaven, about the
things of the Spirit of God, for only in that context is His mission intelligible at all. But Nicodemus is first reminded again that conversation about heavenly things must proceed from a serious attention to
visible, earthly things. This preliminary truth still holds when Jesus
speaks about Himself. The theme at its beginning and at its ending, and
also, indeed, in what lies betwixt and between—is heaven. But the place
of insight is earth, the son of man, the man Jesus, His flesh: He is the
place of revelation and the place of faith. Daniel the Prophet had
spoken of *one like unto a son of man coming with the clouds of heaven* (Dan.
vii. 13). His insight was, of course, true; but what he saw was seen *in the
night visions*, and is therefore a truth only too easily misunderstood.
Men, good men like Nicodemus, had thereby been led to indulge in
imaginings, to dream about, and hope for, mysterious happenings in
heaven, and to allow the things that took place on earth and before
their eyes to become purely matter of fact. Theologians were led to poise
themselves in mid-air, lose their balance, and forfeit their right to exist.
In fact, however, the quite concrete, firm earth is the place where God
wills to reveal Himself. No man has ascended into heaven; and, therefore, if true conversation be a sharing of human experience, heaven and
the Spirit of God are improper and impossible subjects of human conversation. Nicodemus had wished (*v.* 2) to converse with Jesus as one
Rabbi with another, but it soon becomes clear that he has nothing to
say, and can have nothing to say. This situation may seem to be hopeless; but it is precisely the situation in which the mission of Jesus
occurred and which therefore compels Him to speak of Himself. Though
no man has ascended into heaven, yet God has willed that there should
be a descent from heaven to earth; not an apparition or epiphany in the
sky, but a real descent into human flesh. This descent is the mission of
Jesus; and now at last the prophetic phrase *son of man* has received its
true historical meaning. Jesus, the man Jesus, can speak of heaven because He has left it, and because, though He has left it, it still remains
His home. It is possible that the Evangelist did not write the last words
of *v.* 13, *which is in heaven*. They are not, however, foreign to his meaning.
In the context of the discourse to Nicodemus they do not refer to the
return to the Father. Rather, they assert that though the son of man
belongs visibly to earth, He is—seen according to the Spirit—in heaven.

A man among men, yet heaven is His home, and though deprived of glory, He is not deprived of ultimate and essential union with the Father. It must not be forgotten that Saint Paul had said even of the Christians that they are by the blessing of God *in the heavenly places* (Eph. i. 3, ii. 6). How clear-cut this theme of descent is, and how far removed from theological speculation or religious dreaming, is shown by what comes next.

The third theme is *The Death of the Son of Man and the Love of God*:—The next step in the discourse is again strictly related to what has just been said. The descent of revelation is now defined as a descent not merely into human flesh, but into flesh that must die. The mission of the son of man is the mission of the Son of God dedicated to be *lifted up*. At first sight this would seem to mean glorification; and so, of course, in the final perspective it does. But the verb 'lift up' must first be rid of all glory, otherwise neither Nicodemus nor anyone else will understand what the prophetic phrase *son of man* really means. Here an anticipatory Old Testament incident, another prophetic analogy or parable or sign or whatever other term be used to denote that a thing does not exist by itself and in its own right, becomes important and relevant. The children of Israel sinned—in fact, they rejected Moses—and were punished by death in the desert. But Moses, in order to save them, fashioned a serpent—serpents had been the instruments of God for their destruction—and set it up, lifted it up, on a pole or stake like a condemned criminal for all to see. The people looked and—*lived* (Num. xxi. 4–9). The thing that Moses had made, a mere bit of brass, afterwards became a grave cause of superstition, so miserable and dangerous a thing it was in itself, and Hezekiah destroyed it (2 Kings xviii. 4). But the biblical story remained imperishable; it lay waiting till apt times and circumstances should give it an opportunity to discharge its office, and now it comes into its own. The son of man must so be lifted up. The Evangelist and his Christian readers know, of course, what this means. It means that the son of man, the visible historical Jesus, must be lifted up on a cross and die in public for all to see, as a dangerous disturber of the public peace. But for all those who have eyes to see, for those who believe, the place of death is the place of revelation. For this reason, the road to death, the death of the son of man, is the determined direction of the mission of the Son of God, determined, not by fate nor by mischance nor by the will of His enemies, but by the love of God for men. The death of the son of man is not, properly understood, a mere spectacle on the plane of history; it is the place of faith, the place where men are enabled to apprehend the eternal realm or kingdom of the Spirit of God, and where they are therefore enabled to enter into eternal life. They look—and live. This is the fulfilment of the mission of Jesus the only-begotten Son of God, because in it is made known the love of God to all men. *Only* begotten Son—all men (*whosoever*: the contrast is clearer in the original Greek than in the English versions): here the biblical insistence upon uniqueness, upon the word *one* or *only*, and the consequent insistence upon universality, upon the word *all*, presses to the forefront of the discourse (cf. Isa. xlv. 22–5). The juxtaposition of *only . . . all* carries with it a criticism of the judgement of Nicodemus that Jesus was just one in a series of those who have been and no doubt will be sent by God for the instruction of men, and a consequent criticism of the separation which Nicodemus imagines to exist between himself as a Rabbi and a Pharisee and other more ordinary men—he is not embraced by the word *all*—a separation which robs him of his freedom and of his capacity to repent and believe and apprehend. But it also carries with it a criticism of the various alternative roads of salvation suggested by that plurality of religions with which the Jews had long been surrounded. This plurality made the truth of uniqueness, and its necessary rider the truth of universality, exceedingly difficult to apprehend or to believe in. Jesus is the one gift of God for the salvation of the world— and yet unbelief persists. The discourse cannot therefore come to rest, it cannot end with the assertions that love and not justice is the final truth of God and that life and not death is the final destiny of man. The word *all* is qualified by the word 'faith'—*all who believe*—and the thought of the love of God is still crossed by the thought of His judgement. The discourse ends in a tension: it does not and cannot come to rest, for it is a human thing vibrating in the midst of a world that does not believe.

The fourth theme, *Judgement and Salvation, Works and Faith*:—The prophecy of Daniel and all the ramifications of Jewish theology dependent upon it and upon other such prophecies lie very near the surface of the discourse when Jesus speaks of the love of God for the world. Israel looked forward to the day when the dominion of the world would be destroyed. In his vision by night Daniel had actually seen the cruel tyranny of the beasts who had come up from the sea consumed, taken away and destroyed; and, moreover, it had been communicated to him that their overthrow was to be entrusted to *one like unto a son of man*, to *the saints of the Most High*, and that, the judgement completed, the dominion over the whole earth would be placed in his—their—hands for ever (Dan. vii. 2–9, 11–14, 18, 26–27). Daniel was troubled by this communication, his countenance was changed and he kept the matter in his heart (Dan. vii. 28). The Jews were, on the whole, not so easily disturbed; for it was the charter of their exemption from the judgement of God, the ground of their confidence in the future, and their consolation in distress. Most of them did not perceive how doubtful was the identification of the *one like unto a son of man* coming from heaven with the Messiah of their imaginings, and how exceedingly doubtful was the identification of the *saints of the Most High* with the Jewish folk living in Palestine or those of the Diaspora among the Gentiles. They therefore tended to overlook other prophecies in which Israel was to share, not in judging, but in being judged.

Jesus now overthrows the whole confidence of Jewish dominion. He overthrows it in the presence of Nicodemus, a Pharisee and a *ruler of the Jews*. He does this, not by idealizing the Greeks or any other nation or people, but by declaring the love of God for the world to be the meaning of His mission, the purpose of which is that the world might be saved—through Him. This does not, however, mean that the prophetic theme of judgement has been revoked, that it has been exhausted in past history or deferred until some future day. The very fact that the Son of God has come makes the present situation more, not less, acute. For though it means that the opportunity of salvation has been provided, it means also that to reject or to misunderstand the mission of the Son of God is to stand under the completed act of the judgement of God. And the generality of men do more easily reject than accept Him: they prefer darkness to light; and this is to stand condemned in their whole behaviour, in all their works. But what are these dark, evil works? And what is the doing of the truth with which they are contrasted? And why should the line of demarcation between be so clear-cut and fraught with such terrible consequences? And, above all, why should Jesus be the place where both judgement and salvation occur? The Evangelist seems to assume that his readers will understand; but his language is undeniably difficult.

Once again, the biblical background is important, for the reader is now confronted not by moralism but by that strictly theological imperative which embraces all human action and takes it to itself. He is confronted by the mission of the only begotten Son of God and by the love of God. The issue is, therefore, faith or unbelief. The Evangelist does not, however, use these nouns, just as he never uses the nouns 'knowledge' and 'ignorance': he uses the corresponding verbs—*He that believeth, he that believeth not*. Faith is not a separable fragment of human behaviour, nor is unbelief a detachable thing done in the midst of other things. Faith is not a wish that remains unfulfilled, nor is unbelief the refusal to stretch out towards some distant goal. To believe is to apprehend human action, all human action, in its relation to God: not to believe is not to recognize the only context in which human behaviour can be anything but trivial. The man who believes apprehends that every visible human act requires to be fulfilled by the invisible, corresponding and creative action of God. The man who believes recognizes that all human behaviour is by itself and in itself incomplete. The man who believes knows that God does fill up this incompleteness, and that, in filling it up, He makes of the human act a thing that has been wrought in God. This is the love of God. The Evangelist has already recalled such good works, this doing of the truth. The physical occurrence of birth when recognized as a sign of the creative power of the Spirit of

God is an action wrought in God. John, when he baptizes with water in the desert, does the truth, for he bears witness to purification by the Spirit of God. Moses, when he lifted up the serpent also in the desert, did a good work, for it required the exaltation and glorification of Jesus to make it true; otherwise it led men into superstition. These men do the truth because the truth is of God, and their actions bear witness to it. And Nicodemus in coming to Jesus has done a good work, if in so doing he apprehends that his whole religious behaviour requires to be made good and that it is not in itself the answer to the demand that has been made of Israel by God. But the generality of men hate this exposure of their behaviour. They will not face the pain of it. They do not think that their actions require to be fulfilled, for their affections are set upon themselves. Or, if they do recognize their own inadequacy, they do not believe in the possibility of their behaviour being made good. These men are atheists: they remain in the darkness, and their whole behaviour is evil. They stand under the majestic judgement of God. This is the issue raised by the historical figure of Jesus, by His words and actions, and finally by His death. The death of Jesus is the supremely good action, since it is that work which above all others makes room for the creative action of the love of God. The light which Jesus is (i. 5) penetrates every corner of human behaviour, and either lights it up or throws it into the darkness. There is no twilight in His presence, for he compels the final distinction between those who have everlasting life and those who have lost everything (*vv.* 15–16).

The Evangelist does not inform his readers whether Nicodemus believed or disbelieved, just as he gives them no information concerning the later history of the Samaritan woman, or of the man born blind, or of Lazarus, or even of the Beloved Disciple. This is not because they are to him no more than symbols, but because he is concerned with the meaning of the mission of Jesus for all men. The discourse therefore must not end otherwise than by leaving Nicodemus faced by the final issue of faith and unbelief, of salvation and judgement. To have satisfied the curiosity of his readers, even if he could have done so, would have disturbed the seriousness of the discourse and made of it a mere historical incident. Nevertheless, he does say later that Nicodemus made a public protest against the illegal manner in which the notables in Jerusalem were proposing to condemn Jesus without first hearing His own explanation of His actions (vii. 45–52), and also that at the end he performed the very charitable, human act of assisting Joseph of Arimathæa in caring for the body of Jesus according to the custom of the Jews and laying it to rest in a new tomb (xix. 39–42).

# COMMENTARY

ii. 23–5. The *passover* presumably covers the whole festival week which followed the act of sacrifice and the passover meal itself (vi. 4, vii. 2, see however Mark xiv. 1, 2). The untrustworthiness of the crowds during the feast suggests that the theological teaching given by the Pharisees to Israel was gravely inadequate; and these verses therefore provide a suitable introduction to the discourse to Nicodemus. Since the original readers of the gospel were familiar with stories of the acts of healing which Jesus had performed in Galilee, the Evangelist does not need to define the nature of the works—*signs*—which He did also in Jerusalem, and which occasioned the visit of Nicodemus by night (iii. 2). A section of the crowd 'believed', but did not believe: the same Greek word is used here and in *v.* 22 for confidence (A.V. *commit himself*, R.V. *trust himself*) and for belief (A.V. *believe on*, R.V. *believe in*): it calls attention to the relation and distinction between the confidence which the crowd has in Jesus and the confident understanding or belief which will be the characteristic mark of His true disciples; and in its negative form it denotes also the lack of trust which Jesus was compelled to exhibit in His relations with the generality of men, in that He could not trust Himself to them. The Evangelist's description of the knowledge of Jesus (cf. xxi. 17) echoes 1 Sam. xvi. 7, *The Lord seeth not as man seeth; for man looketh on the outward appearance, but the Lord looketh on the heart* (for the vanity which He finds there, see Ps. xciv. 11, Jer. xvii. 9–11).

iii. 1–2. Nicodemus—the name was a fairly common Greek name (Bauer), transliterated into Hebrew as *Naqdemon*—represents the governing authority of Judaism. Therefore he is not called a scribe, but a Pharisee and a *ruler of the Jews*, that is to say, a member of the Sanhedrin (vii. 26, 48, 50, xii. 42; Matt. ix. 18, 23; Luke xiv. 1, xviii. 18, xxiii. 13, 35, xxiv. 20; Acts iii. 17, &c.). He is, moreover, a responsible teacher, indeed *the teacher of Israel* (*v.* 10), for the whole people listened to what he had to say. It is probable that the Evangelist intends to suggest, at least to his Jewish readers, that he was a member of the wealthy, aristocratic, and distinguished family (see Strack-Billerbeck) which had furnished Aristobulus with his ambassador to Pompey in 63 B.C. (Josephus, *Ant.* xiv. 37); and which, if Palestinian tradition is right in agreeing with the Latin Version of Josephus that Gorion was the son not of Nicomedes but of Nicodemus (Schlatter, *D.E.J.*: see, however, Lagrange), nearly a century later provided a man competent to negotiate the terms of the surrender of the Roman garrison in Jerusalem (Josephus, *B.J.* ii. 451). It was the sister of this Gorion that gave the later Rabbis their classical example of the consequences of the destruction of Jerusalem; for, after enjoying vast wealth, she fell into abject poverty. That a man named Nicodemus should have played some part in the events which led up to the crucifixion is not surprising; and there seems no adequate ground for supposing him to have been a symbol invented by the Evangelist.

Nicodemus visited Jesus *by night* (cf. xix. 39). No doubt learned Jews were in the habit of discussing during the night, and no doubt they recommended it as especially suitable for the study of the law (Strack-Billerbeck). No doubt also it is not unreasonable to suggest that Nicodemus wished to secure solitude in order to converse with Jesus about the deep things of religion (Bornhäuser, quoted by Schlatter, *D.E.J.*). But darkness and night are in the Fourth Gospel sinister words (ix. 4, xi. 9–10, xiii. 30). Not only did Joseph of Arimathæa, who is associated with Nicodemus, act secretly *for fear of the Jews* (xix. 38–9), but the discourse to Nicodemus ends on a note of tension, the tension between those who come to the light and those who prefer the darkness (*vv.* 19–21). Nicodemus occupies a dangerous position betwixt and between; and this is suggested from the very beginning of the narrative. He addresses Jesus as *Rabbi . . . teacher*: the two words are synonymous in i. 39, xx. 16, Matt. xxiii. 8 (for the manner of address cf. i. 49, iii. 26, iv. 31, vi. 25, ix. 2, xi. 8). In the mouth of a Jewish Rabbis a teacher is a man who expounds the commandments of God (Matt. xxii. 16). Nicodemus does not say that Jesus is a prophet, but, because of His notable actions, he recognizes that His teaching is authorized by God, and that God is with Him (cf. Rev. xxi. 3). Nor is Nicodemus alone in this judgement (xii. 42, cf. Luke xviii. 18): the first person plural, *we know* (cf. *v.* 10), is, on account of the second person plural in *vv.* 7, 11, 12, a real plural and not a mere periphrasis for *I know*. There are other responsible Jews who are similarly impressed by what Jesus has done and who recognize that there stands in their midst a teacher sent from God. Of these men Nicodemus is the representative.

*vv.* 3–6. *Except a man be born again . . .* (A.V.). The Greek adverb translated *again* (R.V. *anew*, A.V., R.V. mg. *from above*) can mean either *from the beginning, completely, utterly* (Luke i. 3; Acts xxvi. 5; Oxyrhynchus Papyri IV, 745. 4 sq.); or *again, a second time* (Wisd. xix. 6; Gal. iv. 9; Bauer compares the *Oneirocritica* of Artemidorus, i. 13, where a father sees himself *born again* in the birth of his son, and Origen's commentary on Saint John's Gospel, where the answer to Peter's question *Domine, quo vadis?* is quoted from the Apocryphal Acts of Paul as 'I am going to be crucified *again*'); or the word may mean *from the upper country*, from Upper Egypt, for example, as opposed to the Delta (Papyri Hibeh 110. 66), *from above* (xix. 23; Matt. xxvii. 51) and so *from heaven* (cf. Gal. iv. 26; Col. iii. 1–2), that is to say, from God (iii. 31, viii. 23, xi. 41, xix. 11; Phil. iii. 14; Jas. i. 17; iii. 15, 17, cf. Job iii. 4). Its primary meaning, indeed, is *from above*, both in Classical and Hellenistic usage.

But owing to the various derivative meanings, which make it uncertain whether the word is used here as an adverb of place or of time, the exact meaning of the Saying was found difficult from very early days: Justin Martyr (*Apol.* i. 61) seems to have got rid of the obscurity by substituting a compound verb which can only mean *born again*; and Chrysostom, commenting on the passage, writes, 'Some understand the word *again* to mean *from heaven*, others *from the beginning*'. But as the discourse develops it becomes clear that the birth which is required is not merely a second birth—this is the misunderstanding of Nicodemus—but birth from above, birth of the Spirit (*v.* 5), birth from God (cf. i. 12, 13; 1 John ii. 29, iii. 9, iv. 7, v. 18). This is the fundamental meaning; but it necessarily carries with it an emphasis upon the newness, indeed the completeness, of the life which is given by God Himself (Schlatter, *D.E.J.*, cf. Büchsel in Kittel's *Theologisches Wörterbuch zum N.T.* I, pp. 376–8).

*See the kingdom of God* (Mark ix. 1; Luke ix. 27). The readers of the Gospel already know what this means, for they have heard the promise given to the disciples that they will *see the heaven opened, and the angels of God ascending and descending upon the Son of man* (cf. Col. i. 15–20, ii. 9). Only the sons of God (i. 12, 13) can, however, apprehend this; and Nicodemus, though confronted by the son of man, sees in Him no more than a teacher with whom it is possible to hold important conversation about the kingdom. The kingdom of God was a fundamental theme of Jewish theology, and for that reason it formed the controlling theme of the teaching of Jesus as it is recorded in the synoptic gospels (e.g. Mark i. 15; Matt. xii. 28). The phrase with its vast Jewish background haunted primitive Christianity down to the end of the New Testament period (Rev. xi. 15, xii. 10). In the Fourth Gospel, however, it is used only here and in *v.* 5. This does not mean that the Evangelist wished to drive it out of the Christian vocabulary. He has used it at this very important moment in his gospel, and he returns to it in the scene before Pilate when Jesus speaks of *My kingdom* which is not *of* [*from*] *this world* (xviii. 36). Confronted by a ruler of the Jews, Jesus speaks of the dominion of God; just as, when confronted by Pilate in the act of exercising the authority of Cæsar, He must speak of His own regal authority. Set in the context of human authority Jesus asserts both the kingship of God and His own regal authority (xviii. 37), an authority which is, moreover, blasphemously (xix. 2) and significantly (xix. 19–22) asserted of Him by others. But the Evangelist knows that all this language of Kingship is open to grave misunderstanding (vi. 15). Aware that a king requires service, if not of slaves at least of servants, Josephus seldom referred to God as King, and substituted 'Theocracy' for *the Kingdom of God* (Schlatter). The fourth Evangelist proceeds in somewhat similar fashion (xv. 15). The thought of the dominion of God and of the service due to Him lies behind what he has to say. But his proper theme is

Sonship: Jesus is the Son of God (i. 18) and His disciples are the children of God (i. 12). Nevertheless, it is required of children, as well as of slaves, that they should obey. As Jesus did, and can only do, the will of His Father (v. 19, 30) so His disciples must obey His commandments (xiv. 15, xv. 10). Sonship, so far from driving out obedience, makes of it the final meaning of human life: *He that hath my commandments, and keepeth them, he it is that loveth me: and he that loveth me shall be loved of my Father, and I will love him, and will manifest myself unto him* (xiv. 21).

[Though the theology of Judaism forms the immediate background of this discourse, it must be remembered that belief in the Kingdom of God often appears where there is little or no direct relationship with Judaism. The general fact of human authority itself tends to produce a longing for that sovereignty of which human sovereignty is a parable. Thus in the *Arabian Nights* 'The Kingdom' without further definition means the unseen dominion of God. *The tale of the King who kenned the quintessence of things* opens as follows: 'There came to a king of the kings, in his old age, a son, who grew up comely, quick-witted, clever: and, when he reached years of discretion and became a young man, his father said to him, "Take this realm and rule it in lieu of me, for I desire to flee from the sin of sovranty to Allah the Most High and don the woollen dress and devote all my time to devotion." Quoth the Prince, "And I am another who desireth to take refuge with the Almighty." So the king said, "Arise, let us flee forth and make for the mountains and there worship in shame before God the Most Great." ' (Burton, vol. IX, p. 137, cf. the conclusion of the story of *Hasan of Bassorah*, vol. VI, p. 296.)]

*Born of water and the Spirit—enter into the kingdom of God:*—Nicodemus did not regard a new beginning (*from their mother's womb* means from the beginning in Matt xix. 12) as unnecessary, but as impossible. Jesus therefore speaks more plainly. He solemnly repeats what He had said, but substitutes *of water and the Spirit* for the difficult adverb *anew* (*from above*), and *enter into* for *see* the kingdom of God. The new beginning required of Nicodemus and of all men is not a second beginning on the plane of visible history (i. 13); nor is it some dramatic, eschatological, miraculous historical occurrence (see Schlatter on *v.* 4). What is required is the new beginning from God, the birth *of the spirit* (the preposition translated *of* denotes both source and instrument). And this is a present possibility; but it is a possibility only from heaven, for the readers of the gospel already know that the Spirit of God descends from heaven (i. 33). Apart from this divine, heavenly renewal, all hope of entering the kingdom of God (Mark ix. 47, x. 25; Matt. v. 20, vii. 21, xviii. 3; Luke xviii. 24, 25; Acts xiv. 22) must be abandoned. There is therefore a human impossibility, as Nicodemus had rightly perceived but wrongly understood. But there is, nevertheless, a human action so near to the invisible truth as to be a necessary parable of it; there is indeed an action which can, by the grace of God, become what it signifies. The Spirit of God *moved upon the face of the waters* (Gen. i. 1, 2) and men are *sprinkled* with *clean water* (Ezek. xxxvi. 25–7). It is not, however, the juxtaposition of water and spirit in the first chapter of Genesis and in the prophecy of Ezekiel that provides the immediate background of the emphasis upon water in the discourse. The immediate background of the close association of spirit and water is provided by the relation between Jesus and John the Baptist (i. 26, 31–4) and by the relation also between Jesus and Jewish practices of purification by water (ii. 6, iii. 25). For the Evangelist and his readers the words are, however, even more directly applicable to Christian baptism (iv. 2). The Evangelist here and elsewhere (i. 13, 1 John ii. 29, iii. 9, iv. 7, v. 1) assumes that his readers are familiar with the description of baptism and conversion in terms of generation (1 Pet. i. 3, 22–3, ii. 2, iii. 18–22; Jas. i. 18; Titus iii. 5) or of creation (Rom. vi. 1–11; 1 Cor. iii. 1, 2; 2 Cor. v. 17; Gal. iv. 4–6, vi. 15, cf. Rom. xii. 2; Eph. iv. 22–4; Col. iii. 9, 10; Heb. v. 12–14). He assumes also that they are familiar with the purification which Jesus required of His disciples (Mark vii. 1–23), a purification so radical that only those who become as little children—Luke used the Greek word meaning *new-born babes* to introduce the Saying of Jesus (Luke xviii. 15)—can enter into the Kingdom of God (Mark x. 15; Matt. xviii. 3). The Evangelist is, therefore, not introducing the language of generation in order to accommodate Christianity to the soil of Hellenism, where immortality was supposed to be conferred by sacramental rengeration (Dieterich, *Mithrasliturgie*, pp. 11, 12, Reitzenstein, *Poimandres*, pp. 339 sqq., *Die Hellenistischen Mysterienreligionen*, pp. 33 sqq., referred to by Bauer, cf. Loisy, p. 158); he is rather confronting the visible Christian practice and experience of baptism with that invisible and spiritual baptism which is the miracle of God.

[Wellhausen—and he has been followed by others—proposed to delete the words *water and* from the original text of the gospel, supposing them to be an intrusion added in the interests of the Christian practice of baptism. For this not only is there no manuscript authority whatever, but the exclusion of the words deprives the discourse of its relation to i. 26, 33, iii. 22–7. (For the bearing of the citation in Justin Martyr, *Apol.* i. 61, on the text of the gospel, see Bernard.) The reference to water here is congruous with the steady emphasis upon water throughout the opening chapters of the gospel (ii. 1–10, iii. 23, iv. 7–15, 46, v. 2–9, cf. vii. 38, xiii. 5–11, xix. 34, 1 John v. 6–8), congruous also with the Evangelist's insistence on the importance of visible human action, in fact on the importance of the flesh (*v.* 6) in its relation to the Spirit. *v.* 8 is assimilated to *v.* 5 in Codex Sinaiticus and in the Old Latin and Old Syriac Versions and in 'Ambrosiaster'—*so is everyone that is born of water and the Spirit.*]

The embracing of water and spirit in one single phrase (in the Greek both words are anarthrous and governed by one preposition—*of water and Spirit*), and the linking together of two births by an adverb whose derivative meaning *a second time* can never become wholly dormant, are theologically possible only when the vast distinction between natural birth and birth from God and between cleansing by water and creative purification by the Spirit is clearly recognized and acknowledged. There are two orders of generation, *Flesh* and *Spirit*; and though the analogy between them is so close that the natural and visible process of generation is itself the means by which the second and spiritual order is apprehended and believed in, nevertheless, the one does not and cannot overflow into the other. Flesh is flesh, and Spirit is Spirit; and what is and has been begotten or born of each remains and must remain within the capacity of that which has begotten it or given it birth. Neither can take to itself the capacity of the other. This absolute theological principle in no way depreciates or befouls the flesh, as is clear from i. 14; from the Evangelist's whole-hearted affirmation of the natural order (i. 3), of religious rites (*passim*), of historical visible events (ii. 23); and above all by his affirmation of the death of the Son of man (*vv.* 14–15). What befouls the flesh is when it exalts itself arrogantly against the Spirit and makes itself equal with God (*v.* 18 and the discourse that follows, cf. Gal. iv. 29). Flesh has then become the 'World' (xv. 18–19), and has denied its proper function.

*vv.* 7–10. The biblical 'necessity'—*must, it is necessary* (*vv.* 14, 30, iv. 24, xx. 9; Mark viii. 31, xiii. 7; 1 Cor. xv. 53; Rev. iv. 1 sqq.)—denotes the absolute requirement of the will of God. The plural—*ye must*—is now used not only because, in the historical perspective of the discourse Nicodemus represents other Jews (*v.* 2), but also because the demand of God is universal. The effective, though invisible, operation of the Spirit ought not to cause men surprise, since the privy, imperceptible working of the wind testifies to the reality and power of what is beyond human sight (Eccles. xi. 5–6; Ecclus, xvi. 21, cf. Job ix. 11). The analogy (cf. xx. 22) is all the more remarkable because the same word (in Greek and Hebrew) means both wind and Spirit. The whole sentence about the wind is word for word directly applicable to the Spirit (cf. Acts ii. 2–4). [Bernard, following the Latin Versions and the early Fathers, actually preferred to translate the sentence as referring to the Spirit and not to the wind—*The Spirit breatheth* (R.V. mg.).] What those who have been born of the Spirit are, whence they come and whither they go, is incomprehensible to the world; as incomprehensible as Jesus Himself is to the Jews (viii. 14).

*vv.* 11–15. The Jews, who do not understand the inexorable demand of God, to which the natural, visible order bears unmistakable witness, are now confronted by those who speak because they know and bear witness because they have seen. The plural—*we know*—does not fall out of the historical perspective of the discourse. The discourse is coherent, and it coheres with what is said elsewhere in the gospel. The use of the plural here is not to be explained, as Bernard explained it, by supposing that the Evangelist, in order to bring his historical reminiscence into harmony with a later situation, turned the singular *I have seen* into the plural *we have seen* 'just as in *v.* 5 he has added *of water* to the original saying of the Lord about the need of spiritual birth' (Bernard on *v.* 11); nor is it any more satisfactorily explained by supposing, with Bauer, that the Evangelist has here betrayed that the whole discourse is really 'an address of the Christian community about Jesus, spoken through the Evangelist as through a megaphone'. The Evangelist has himself provided the explanation of the plurals, *we speak, we know, we bear witness, we have seen.* Jesus did not confront Judaism alone—this is the subject of the second part of the discourse in chapter v (*vv.* 30–47). The Baptist had already seen, had already spoken and borne witness to the power of the Spirit of God (i. 7, 32–4). Isaiah had spoken because he had seen (xii. 41), so too had Abraham (viii. 56) and Moses (v. 46) and all the people of Israel whose words provide the Jews with their proper and acknowledged subject of study (v. 39). Historically, this cloud of witnesses had preceded Jesus; and now, in addition to all these past, prophetic witnesses there stand beside Him His own disciples (ix. 4). They too have already seen enough and spoken sufficiently to provide an anticipation of what they will see and will speak (i. 38–51, ii. 11). No doubt, it is this last application of the plural *we* that controls the thought of the Evangelist, and of the readers of his gospel (i. 14; 1 John i. 1–4, see INTRODUCTION, pp. 86 sqq., and cf. Rev. i. 1–2). But the Jews did not, and, at the time when the Evangelist wrote his gospel, still did not, accept this combined and unified witness to the power of the Spirit of God.

*Earthly things . . . heavenly things* (cf. 1 Cor. xv. 40; 2 Cor. v. 1; Phil. ii. 2, iii. 19). The statement in *v.* 12 assumes that Nicodemus and those whom he represents desire to speak about heavenly things; and this is, indeed, the function of Israel and the peculiar responsibility of its accredited teachers. Orthodox Judaism seems to have been uneasy concerning those many poetic apocalyptic imaginings which were being offered to it in the form of legends describing the transportation of men to heaven in order that heavenly truth might be communicated to them and through them to the Jews (for example, *the Testament of Abraham, the Ascension of Isaiah, the book of Enoch*). Rabbi Jose (*c.* A.D. 150), echoing perhaps passages such as Wisd. ix. 16; Prov. xxx. 4 (cf. 2 Esdras iv. 21), said, 'Neither Moses nor Elijah ascended upwards, nor did the Glory (of God) descend downwards, for *The Heaven is the Lord's, and the earth hath he given to the sons of man*' (Ps. cxv. 16. Quoted from the Mekilta on Exod. xix. 20 by Schlatter, *D.E.J.* and by Strack-Billerbeck). Nevertheless, in spite of such protests, the hope of Israel was nowhere more forcibly expressed than in the language of apocalyptic eschatology.

Jesus, however, speaks not of hope but of faith, and of that faith which, so far from leaping out of the framework of the visible world altogether or preserving a very slender connection with it, is seriously concerned with the observable things of earth. The man who believes does speak of heavenly things, but he speaks of them only because the visible world, which is a 'beginning and a prophecy, and not a fulfilment' (Westcott) has first compelled him to faith. Jesus has spoken about earthly things—birth, water and wind—but Nicodemus has not thereby been moved to faith, and consequently, by a strange though common paradox, the man who desired to hear direct speech about heavenly things falls into a purely materialistic attitude to the things of earth and into dark fantasies concerning the things of heaven. For an accredited Jewish Rabbi to have thus misunderstood the nature of faith means that he has misunderstood the meaning of the Scriptures (e.g. Deut. xxx. 12, referred to in Rom. x, 6) and that further, more intimate conversation concerning heavenly things is impossible (1 Cor. iii. 1–2; Heb. vi. 1 sqq.).

*The Son of man:*—Jesus still speaks about the things that take place upon earth, for He speaks about the *Son of man*. He is, of course, speaking about Himself, as the readers of the gospel know from the earlier tradition, from what they have already read in i. 51 and from what they will read in v. 27, vi. 27, 53, 62, viii. 28, ix. 35, xii. 23, 34, xiii. 31. But He speaks in the third person (contrast vi. 41, but cf. Matt. x. 23). Though no one is competent to speak directly of the things that are in heaven, because no man has ascended thither; nevertheless, there has occurred (aorist, cf. i. 14) a descent from heaven (Eph. iv. 9). This occurrence though foreshadowed in the prophecy of Daniel (vii. 13), is altogether unique (iii. 31–2, vi. 41, 51, 62, viii. 23, cf. Matt. xi. 27), and it is, moreover, an invisible occurrence, lying beyond the capacity of direct, normal human sight (iii. 27). What men will see is the lifting up of the Son of man by the Jews (viii. 28). That is to say, they will see Him die (xii. 32, 33). The death of Jesus, however, so far from being, as the Jews suppose (xii. 34), the supreme sign of transitoriness, provides the supreme and unique opportunity for faith (for a discussion of the meaning of *lift up* in the Fourth Gospel, see E. A. Abbott, *The Son of Man*, pp. 443–475). The capacity of visible actions to awaken faith is illustrated by the restoration to life of the dying Israelites who looked at the brazen serpent which Moses had lifted up in the desert, and was recognized in the teaching of the Rabbis:—'It was not assuredly the uplifted hands of Moses that invigorated Israel and laid Amalek low. Israel looked at him, and, so long as he lifted up his hands, they believed on Him who had given Moses the command to act thus. God it was who did the signs and wonders on their behalf. Nor was it the serpent that killed and gave life. Israel looked, and, so long as Moses lifted up the serpent, they believed on Him who had commanded Moses to act thus. It was God who healed them' (Mekilta on Exod. xvii. 11, quoted by Schlatter, *D.E.J.*, cf. E. A. Abbott, *The Son of Man*, p. 462). Similarly, the purpose of the death of the Son of man is to awaken faith; but the gift which is given by God to all who believe is, ultimately, neither renewed physical energy nor the restoration to bodily health. The gift of God to those who believe in the mission of His Son is eternal life (vi. 32, 33, 40, xvii. 1–3). [It has frequently been suggested (e.g. Godet) that the Greek verb translated *lift up* was used by the Evangelist in order to reproduce the particular meaning *to be hung up on a cross, to be crucified*, which belonged to the Aramaic verb *Izdekef*, and that this explains both his comment in xii. 33 and the fact that he uses the corresponding Greek verb only in references to the death of Jesus (for criticisms of this explanation, see Bernard on iii. 14 and Burkitt, *J.T.S.*, vol. XX, pp. 336–8; for illustrations of the use of the Greek verb to suggest crucifixion, see Bauer).]

*Which is in heaven:*—If these words belonged to the original text of *v.* 13, they cannot have referred to the time after the Ascension, since the Evangelist is not accustomed to forget the historical context of his narrative altogether. They must, therefore, be understood to belong to the range of thought in which heaven means that invisible existence in or with God (i. 1 cf. xvii. 21–3) which is not incompatible with visible existence (i. 14, 18), and which makes possible the assertion that those who believe possess eternal life here and now. [The words are omitted in Codices Sinaiticus and Vaticanus and in some other manuscripts of the same textual family; in the Sahidic and in some manuscripts of the Bohairic Egyptian Versions; and in the text used by Cyril of Alexandria in making his Commentary. Westcott judged them to be a 'very early insertion'. (Additional Note to iii. 13, cf. Hort, *Select Readings*.) The words are, however, contained in the vast majority of Greek manuscripts —including the Koridethi Codex and the two groups of minuscule manuscripts known as family 1 and family 13, in all the existing Latin manuscripts and in most manuscripts of the Bohairic Egyptian Version; and, moreover, the variants *who was in heaven* (Sinaitic Syriac) and *who is from heaven* (Curetonian Syriac) are most easily explained as modifications to suit the context; in which case they presume the existence of the words in the Greek texts underlying the Old Syriac Versions. It is, therefore, still possible to hold, as Godet did, that, since addition is more difficult to explain than omission, the absence of the words in the group of exclusively Alexandrian manuscripts is due either to accidental omission, or to their rejection because of the difficulty of reconciling them with the historical context of the discourse.]

*vv.* 16–21. It follows from *vv.* 13–15 that the death of Jesus is in its final ground occasioned not by the will of man but by the love of God. He gave His only begotten Son (cf. i. 18, 1 John iv. 9), and delivered Him up to death (Rom. viii. 32, cf. Gen xxii. 2; Matt. xxvi. 2). Thus was the love of God manifested. This is the *heavenly* truth made known in the flesh of the Son of man (*v.* 12). The divine purpose of the mission

Jesus is, therefore, salvation and not judgement, eternal life and not destruction or corruption (Luke xix. 10). Since, however, the mission of Jesus—and pre-eminently the manner of His death—bring out into the open the radical distinction between those who believe and those who do not (1 John iv. 2, 3), the theme of judgement persists throughout the Fourth Gospel (v. 22–30, viii. 15–16, xii. 31, 47, 48, xvi. 11), and is used in ix. 39 to define the purpose of His coming into the world, *for judgement came I into this world*. The Greek verb *to judge* and the corresponding noun *judgement* mean first the act of separating or distinguishing and then the consequent act of pronouncing judgement upon what has been separated. The distinction between those who believe and those who do not believe involves, therefore, both salvation and condemnation (1 Cor. i. 18, 2 Cor. ii. 15, 16, iv. 3, 4, cf. Matt. vii. 13, 14); and the movement of eternal life from a future hope to a present ultimate reality (*v.* 15) carries with it also the corresponding movement of condemnation from the future to the present—*hath been judged already*.

*He that doeth evil . . . he that doeth the truth*. The Evangelist has spoken hitherto of justification or salvation by faith and of condemnation by unbelief, and of that ultimate separation between those who believe and those who do not believe which is disclosed by the mission of the Son of man. The rejection of Jesus—failure, that is to say, to apprehend the meaning of His mission—is the consequence, however, neither of mere ignorance nor mischance nor of the absence of some peculiar mystical capacity. The rejection of the light which is come into the world (i. 5, 9, 11, viii. 12) is the result of concrete evil behaviour. Men reject Jesus because their works are evil, and they believe in Him because they *do the truth*. The distinction between the two kinds of action is absolute (v. 29). The Greek words are so arranged in *vv.* 19–21 as to fix the attention of the readers of the gospel upon concrete, distinguishable, visible acts—*doeth . . . practiseth* (R.V. mg.); *evil works . . . foul things* (viii. 41, cf. Rev. xxi. 27, xxii. 15). The description of the contrasted behaviour as *doing the truth* (1 John i. 6) belongs to the biblical, prophetic language which in the Johannine vocabulary attracts to itself a series of almost synonymous phrases (see Schlatter): *do good* (v. 29), *do righteousness* (1 John ii. 29, iii. 7), *do the works* (*of Abraham*, viii. 39), *do judgement* (v. 27)—*do the works of the Father* (x. 37). The biblical, Johannine analysis of human behaviour is, however, not merely descriptive: it is a theological distinction between those actions which, regarded as complete in themselves, leave no room for the righteousness of God, and those actions—they may be visibly identical with actions judged to be evil—which make room for the righteousness of God. The latter demand faith, for they are in themselves incomplete, the former exclude it, for they are self-sufficient. The mission of Jesus—and pre-eminently His death—compel a final distinction between the two (ix. 39–41; Matt. vi. 23). Those who regard their behaviour as complete dare not come to the light lest their actions be *discovered* (A.V. mg. The Greek verb means first *expose* or *lay bare* then, as in Matt. xviii. 15, *reprove* and *convict*); those, on the other hand, whose actions have been wrought in God, that is to say, in such a manner as to require the action of God for their completion, apprehend the meaning of the mission of Jesus; and, in particular, they apprehend the meaning of His death, for beyond all other actions it is without meaning apart from the action of God by which it is fulfilled (vi. 28, ix. 3, 4).

# THE FINAL WITNESS OF
# JOHN THE BAPTIST

## III. 22–iv. 4

Wʜᴀᴛ had been said to Nicodemus is no intimate, meditative or mystical truth communicable only by Jesus to some solitary man. The truth must be announced everywhere and to all: it had, moreover, already been apprehended by John the Baptist and was proclaimed by him in public to his disciples (cf. *v.* 27 with vi. 65, xix. 11; *v.* 29 with xv. 11, xvi. 24, xvii. 13; 1 John i. 4; *v.* 31 with *vv.* 6, 13, viii. 23; 1 John iv. 5, 6; *v.* 32 with *vv.* 11–12, i. 5, 10, xv. 18, 19, xvii. 14; 1 John iii. 13; *v.* 33 with viii. 26, 1 John v. 10; *v.* 34 with vi. 63, xv. 26; *v.* 35 with v. 20, x. 17, xiii. 3, xvii. 2, 7, 22, 24; *v.* 36 with *vv.* 15, 18, v. 24–6, xx. 31, 1 John iv. 15). In the structure of the Fourth Gospel the final witness of John is, therefore, important: it is no mere bridge-passage, inserted by the Evangelist in order to link the discourse to Nicodemus with the discourse to the Woman of Samaria.

## THE CONTROVERSY CONCERNING BAPTISM

iii. 22. *After these things came Jesus and his disciples into the land of Judæa; and there he tarried with them, and baptized.* 23. *And John also was baptizing in Ænon near to Salim, because there was much water there: and they came, and were baptized.* 24. *For John was not yet cast into prison.* 25. *There arose therefore a questioning on the part of John's disciples with a Jew about purifying.* 26. *And they came unto John, and said to him, Rabbi, he that was with thee beyond Jordan, to whom thou has borne witness, behold, the same baptizeth, and all men come to him.*

## THE WORDS OF JOHN

27. *John answered and said, A man can receive nothing, except it have been given him from heaven.* 28. *Ye yourselves bear me witness, that I said, I am not the Christ, but, that I am sent before him.* 29. *He that hath the bride is the bridegroom: but the friend of the bridegroom, which standeth and heareth him, rejoiceth greatly because of the bridegroom's voice: this my joy therefore is fulfilled.* 30. *He must increase, but I must decrease.* 31. *He that cometh from above is above all: he that is of the earth is of the earth, and of the earth he speaketh:*

221

*he that cometh from heaven is above all. 32. What he hath seen and heard, of that he beareth witness; and no man receiveth his witness. 33. He that hath received his witness hath set his seal to this, that God is true. 34. For he whom God hath sent speaketh the words of God: for he giveth not the Spirit by measure. 35. The Father loveth the Son, and hath given all things into his hand. 36. He that believeth on the Son hath eternal life; but he that obeyeth not the Son shall not see life, but the wrath of God abideth on him.*

### JESUS DEPARTS TO GALILEE

*iv. 1. When therefore the Lord knew how that the Pharisees had heard that Jesus was making and baptizing more disciples than John 2. (although Jesus himself baptized not, but his disciples), 3. he left Judæa, and departed again into Galilee. 4. And he must needs pass through Samaria.*

John had removed himself northwards from the scene of his previous ministry (i. 28), and was baptizing in the neighbourhood of Bethshan, where there was much water. Jesus also was baptizing. He had withdrawn from Jerusalem, but He still remained in the land of Judæa with His disciples. And so, in the north and in the south—the geographical details are not unimportant—the daily Jewish ceremonies of purification by water were reinforced by a twofold, urgent, prophetic call to repentance. Since an unmistakable avowal of the need of purification is the necessary preliminary requirement for faith and knowledge (xiii. 8), and since the use of water, both for drinking and for purposes of cleansing, is a proper anticipatory analogy of the true work of Jesus (i. 26, 33, ii. 6–8, iii. 5, iv. 6–15, v. 7–9, vii. 37–9, xiii. 5–7, xix. 34, cf. 1 John v. 6–9 R.V.), the Evangelist is content, for a brief moment, to present his readers with the historical picture of an identical baptism performed both by John and by Jesus. Their action takes place at the same time and overlaps on the same plane; indeed, by deferring the imprisoning of John (contrast Mark i. 14, 15), he seems expressly to have made room for their common and contemporaneous work. This impression of identity is, however, not permitted to remain undisturbed. It is disturbed immediately, first by the words of John (iii. 31), then by the apparent contradiction of the opening sentences of the next incident (iv. 2), and then by the conversation with the Woman of Samaria (iv. 13–14, 23–7, cf. i. 33).

The call to repentance is the time of opportunity; but it is also provocative of controversy. The Jews were not unwilling to accept purification by water; and many displayed a significant preference for baptism by Jesus rather than by John. The disciples of John, no doubt, exaggerated this historical movement towards Jesus. But their exaggeration is not irrelevant, for the word *all—all men come to him*—belongs to the Johannine vocabulary of theological truth (i. 16, iii. 15, vi. 39,

40, xi. 48, xii. 32, xvii. 2, 21, xviii. 37). Responsible Jews were, however, made uneasy by the leakage of the people to strange prophets and unauthorized purifications, and the disciples of John were particularly disturbed by the general movement towards Jesus. In this irritated situation, controversy arose concerning the meaning of purification, and John was compelled to bear witness to the truth. But he speaks only of the movement to Jesus, only of his own relation to Him, for in this movement and in this relation every form of purification by water receives its final meaning and answer.

'Every man to his craft; the parson to the prayer-book, and the groom to his curry-comb.' All responsible human actions have their peculiar dignity—but only in relation to the order and benefaction of God (xix. 11). In themselves and of themselves and by themselves, they are nothing (v. 18, 19, 30). Not, however, in every human act is the relation of man to God at once recognizable. But there are—and here the proverb is wiser than it knows—actions, such as the act of prayer, the ministry of John, baptizing and being baptized with water, that are assuredly in themselves meaningless. Their meaning and importance depend entirely upon the near reality of a final, answering, corresponding, reverse motion from above, from heaven—from God. In making this assertion the Baptist begins where Jesus had begun in His discourse to Nicodemus (vv. 3–6). In so far as the movement of the crowds is governed by the expectation of purification by water only, it is a false movement; and alternatively, in so far as the critical attitude of the rulers to what the crowds are doing proceeds from mere scepticism (iv. 1), their criticism is false and blasphemous. The disciples of John know and can bear witness how strictly he had recognized and observed the severe limits imposed upon his expectant ministry (i. 23–7); a limitation that affects both the man who baptizes and those who have been baptized by him with water only (i. 37). The Baptist is not the Christ. He precedes Him, but only in order that he may bear witness to Him. This is the meaning of his work and the purpose for which he has been sent. An analogy will serve to make clear both the proximity of John to the Christ and the vast distinction between them: the same analogy will also explain the proper meaning of the movement of men from John to Jesus. A bride belongs only to her bridegroom. His friend stands, it is true, by his side and hears his speech; but, though he has procured the bride for the bridegroom and acted as his messenger, yet, when he hears the bridegroom's voice announcing his arrival, he knows that his work is done. Not for one moment does he suppose that he can take or share the bridegroom's place. He has seen the bride pass altogether under the protection of her husband. The joy of the friend of the bridegroom at the unapproachability of the bride is genuine and ungrudging, for his desire has been fulfilled. Saint John has seen the daughter of Israel pass to her proper husband, and he rejoices (Matt.

ix. 15) in his harsh negative mission. The Christ must increase, but he must decrease, and be withdrawn to prison and to death.

By means of the foregoing analogy, attention has been drawn to the distinction between the bridegroom and his friend. The analogy was, however, inadequate to explain the nature of the difference between Jesus and John. Of this difference more, therefore, must be said; but briefly, because it had already formed the major theme of the immediately preceding discourse to Nicodemus (*vv.* 6–17). Like all other men (*v.* 13), the Baptist is of the earth. Being his place of origin, earth provides him with the matter of his speech and action: his voice is a cry (i. 23), and his baptism is by water only. But—and here lies his unique distinction—the Baptist has recognized that his material ministry has been met and given form by the words and actions of Him who, being from heaven, is the master of all. The teaching and baptism of John must not, therefore, be set in competition with the teaching and baptism of Jesus, for the one is fulfilled and made good by the other. The meaning and answer and form which Jesus gives to the work of John is quite strictly *from above.* Jesus speaks of what He has seen and heard in heaven. It must, therefore, be stated categorically that no earth-born man receives His witness by an act of his own independent appreciation. Nevertheless, when this has been said, it must also be asserted categorically that there is a birth from above (*v.* 16), a proper capacity of receiving the witness of Jesus (Matt. xvi. 17; 1 Cor. xii. 3), an authentic human recognition, set like a seal to the power and truth of God. This human witness must not, however, be confounded with esoteric, nonhistorical mysticism, for it depends upon the visible historical mission of Jesus (*vv.* 13, 14): its peculiarity lies in its apostolicity. Nevertheless, in spite of, or rather because of, this historicity, it is the spiritual witness, for Jesus has been entrusted with the words of God, and on Him has been bestowed, not a fraction or portion or measure, but the whole fullness, of the Spirit (Col. ii. 9). To be baptized by Jesus is therefore to receive the gift of the Spirit. In Him is exercised and made known both the power and the love of God. Jesus is the Son of God (*v.* 17). The witness of John now moves to its inevitable conclusion. When Israel is confronted by Jesus—and, in the perspective of the Fourth Gospel, when the Greek-speaking world is confronted by Him through the teaching of His disciples (xvii. 20)—two roads meet and divide: the Way of Life and the Way of Death (*vv.* 16–19). To believe on the Son of God is to possess eternal life: to reject and disobey Him is to be removed from the life of the eternal realm or kingdom of God, to be incapable of beholding it (*v.* 3), and to stand therefore under His Wrath. The Evangelist records no further teaching of John. He describes neither his imprisonment nor the manner of his death (contrast Mark vi. 17–29; Matt. xiv. 3–12, but cf. the reserve of Luke iii. 19, 20). John has spoken, and that is sufficient.

The movement of the crowds first to John and then to Jesus necessarily involved a popular criticism of the normal Jewish manner of purifying and, consequently, of the righteousness of the Pharisees. Jesus knew, therefore, that, when the Pharisees had become aware of what was taking place, they were bound to regard the situation not merely as being provocative of controversy (iii. 25), but as requiring authoritative intervention (xi. 47–53, cf. Mark iii. 6). Since, however, the time had not yet come for Him to submit to their authority (ii. 4), He withdrew from Judæa (cf. vii. 1, xi. 54, xii. 36) and returned as quickly as possible to Galilee. He was, that is to say, compelled to pass through Samaria. In describing the situation that led to this speedy retirement, the Evangelist takes the opportunity of stating that, in fact, Jesus did not Himself baptize with water. The visible prophetic sign was entrusted to His disciples. They baptized with water: the meaning of their action lies hidden in the meaning of their discipleship. Nevertheless, the Pharisees were not wrong in supposing that Jesus was baptizing. The disciples baptized by His authority and in their action He acted. The Evangelist can therefore leave the contradiction *Jesus baptized* (iii. 22)—*Jesus baptized not*: it is explained by the words of John, by the whole theme of the gospel, and, in particular, by the words, *Except a man be born of water and of the Spirit, he cannot enter into the kingdom of God.*

# COMMENTARY

### THE CONTROVERSY CONCERNING BAPTISM

iii. 22–4. The purpose of the geographical note in *v.* 23 is to emphasize that John was not baptizing in the land of Judæa. The Greek tradition, represented by Eusebius (*Onomasticon, s.v.* Salim) and by the Madaba-mosaic (Cabrol, *Dict. d'Arch. Chrét.*, p. 827), places Salim eight miles south of Scythopolis (Bethshan); and this is supported by the Rabbinical references to Sholemi (Shelumi) (quoted by Schlatter, *D.E.J.*). The place was therefore situated in the Samaritan section of the Jordan valley and on the Galilean pilgrims' route to Jerusalem (Dalman, *Orte und Wege Jesu*, pp. 213–15; Lagrange, *Revue Biblique*, 1895, pp. 506 sqq.; for the abundant water of the district, see Adam Smith, *Hist. Geog. of the Holy Land*, p. 357). Epiphanius (*Haereses* lv. 2), on the other hand, locates Salim four miles east of Shechem, where there is still a village of that name. The juxtaposition of *Ænon* (*springs*; Joshua xv. 34, 61 LXX, Ezek. xlvii. 17) and *Salim* (*peace*) provides an opportunity for the allegorizing comment that the baptism of John was *near to*, but must not be identified with, peace (Bauer; Abbot, *Encycl. Bibl.*, 1796).

Many modern commentators (Godet, Plummer, Brooke, Bernard)

have judged the picture of a concurrent ministry of John and Jesus to be reminiscent of a time (overlooked or at least not recorded by the earlier evangelists) when Jesus, at the beginning of His ministry, associated Himself with John's call to repentance, and baptized as he did. 'At this point the work of Christ and of his forerunner met' (Westcott). There is no historical improbability in this. The question remains, however, whether the fourth Evangelist intended to describe both a concurrent and a co-ordinate ministry of John and Jesus; that is to say, whether he meant his readers to infer that for a short time Jesus ranged Himself with John and joined with him in preparing men for the advent of the Kingdom of God by baptizing them with water. The Evangelist has consistently asserted the quite final distinction between Jesus and all other men, including John (v. 13). Baptism by Jesus is baptism with the Spirit (vv. 5–8, i. 33); and that this is so is re-asserted in the final witness of John (vv. 31, 32, 34). The majority of commentators, from the Fathers (e.g. Augustine, Cyril of Alexandria) onwards, have therefore denied that the two baptisms can, without doing violence to the text, be regarded as co-ordinate. Thomas Aquinas held that, though baptism was not imposed as a necessity before the Passion, it was, nevertheless, instituted as a sacrament at the baptism of Christ (Summa, Pt. iii. Q. lxvii, A. 2); Maldonatus that Jesus 'from time to time baptized before His Passion, and baptized with the Holy Spirit'; Schanz that the baptism here recorded was a consecration to the messianic kingdom, more therefore than the baptism of John, but less than Christian baptism. These explanations were genuine attempts to comment on the scene without forgetting the precise statement in vii. 39 that the Spirit *was not yet* (given), or the future tenses in the references to the gift of the Spirit in xiv. 16, xv. 26, xvi. 7 (cf. xx. 22). Modern commentators, who are persuaded that the Fourth Gospel is not, in any ordinary sense of the word, an 'historical' document, have an easier task. They say that, in composing this scene, the Evangelist has in mind the distinction between material or legal ceremonies of purification by water and the new, spiritual Christian rite of Baptism; that, in order to provide the latter with the highest authority, he has created an imaginary historical scene and inserted it where the earlier evangelists had left a suitable gap, before John was put in prison and before Jesus had commenced his public ministry in Galilee; and that he is concerned not with Palestinian history but with the Church at the beginning of the second century; not with the historical Jesus, but with the glorified Christ; not with the original disciples, but with those who later initiated their converts into the mysteries of the Christian religion (e.g. Loisy, pp. 331–5, Heitmüller).

The dilemma of modern exegesis of the Fourth Gospel is perhaps nowhere more clearly illustrated than in the divergent and opposite handling of this passage. And yet, by paying strict attention to the actual theme of the gospel, it would seem possible, even here, to escape the dilemma. Here as elsewhere, the Evangelist is confronted by the problem of history. For him the problem is not solved either by depressing his gospel to an exact historical narrative of Palestinian events or by escaping from them into a veiled description of the ideas and experiences of Greek-speaking Christians a century later. The Jews, John, the original disciples—here the correction in iv. 2. is important—and their successors at the time when the gospel was written, baptized with water. The Jews were satisfied with the efficacy of their action, John was not; the original disciples of Jesus baptized in His visible presence, their successors in His invisible presence. Possessing the Spirit (i. 33, iii. 34) and as the Son of God (i. 34), Jesus is the answer to the inadequacy o. all visible historical baptism by water. To this John bore witness consciously, and the crowds, by moving from him to Jesus, unconsciously. At first the disciples of Jesus, though they baptized in His presence, did not understand the significance of what they were doing; but afterwards they believed and understood that their baptism with water was met and sanctified by the gift of the Holy Spirit. Thus it is that baptism with water is authorized by Jesus, and must be named His baptism, but is rightly so named only because, as the Son of God on whom and through whom the Holy Spirit is fully bestowed, His invisible and spiritual baptism gives baptism with water its proper meaning and answer: Jesus provides the matter of human cleansing by water with its proper form from above: *except a man be born of water and the Spirit, he cannot enter into the kingdom of God* (v. 5). Entrusted with the words of God (v. 34), He does not Himself baptize with water. But—and here He is followed by the Apostle Paul (1 Cor. i. 17)—He authorizes and makes sense of the material act of baptism which remains in the hands of His disciples: the action of Jesus is primary, that of His disciples secondary, 'for preaching is the prior thing, baptizing the posterior' (Tertullian, *De Bapt.* xiv).

The historical situation which has caught the attention of the Evangelist is the concurrent and co-ordinate baptizing with water by John and by the disciples of Jesus. This baptism grows out of the earth (v. 31) and out of the flesh (v. 6). 'If anyone should inquire' wrote Chrysostom, ' "In what was the baptism of the disciples better than that of John?" we will reply: "In nothing"; both were alike without the gift of the Spirit, both parties had one reason for baptizing, and that was to lead the baptized to Christ.' The earthy, human action is met and established —it is not superseded—by the corresponding baptism from above and of the Spirit. All this, as the Evangelist is fully aware, has further implications; for when he is writing his gospel, Greek-speaking Christians are likewise being baptized with water. The Evangelist co-ordinates and ranges together ancient Palestine and modern Greece, and then confronts both with the baptism of the Spirit. He does not falsify history;

he provides it with the answer to its problem: and this is his avowed purpose.

The answer to the problem of history, in this case to the problem of baptism with water, can, however, only be believed in and understood when visible human actions are seen to be in themselves inadequate. The Jews fall out of the context of faith, because they do not recognize the inadequacy of their own manner of purification by water. For this reason, the Evangelist records first that they engaged in controversy (v. 25), as though one form of baptism by water could be shown to be in itself better than another; then that the Pharisees were displeased at the growing number of the disciples of Jesus (iv. 1, xi. 47, 48, xii. 19, cf. Mark ii. 18) and then that, as a consequence, Jesus departed from them (iv. 3).

*vv.* 25, 26. The divergent and competing baptisms for purification gave rise to a corresponding verbal dispute. The disciples of John confidently (the preposition *on the part of* suggests that the initiative was theirs) engage in controversy with the Jews (R.V. *a Jew*) about purifying, but are themselves disturbed by the new and apparently more than geographical separation between John and Jesus: *He that was with thee . . . baptizeth, and all men come unto him* (*all* is weakened to *many* in the Sinaitic Syriac; but see xii. 19). Like Saint Paul (1 Cor. i. 20), the Evangelist does not interrupt his narrative in order to set out the points of the controversy. It was a disputation *of this world* (Josephus, *Ant.* xiii 293-8). His description of the baptism of John, *Ant.* xviii. 117, assumes that there had been controversy about it. The Pharisee in the Oxyrhynchus papyrus, V, 840. 24 sqq. says, in dispute with Jesus: 'I am clean; for I washed in the pool of David, and having descended by one staircase I ascended by another and I put on white and clean garments'; see Lagrange's article in the *Revue Biblique*, 1908, pp. 538-53. Nor does the Evangelist pause to analyse the irritated feelings of the disciples of John when they came to know that the crowds were now being baptized by Jesus. He hastens to tell how John stopped the dispute and justified the action of the people. What baptism is entirely depends upon what Jesus is and, apart from Him, conversations about purification must end in controversy.

[It is not 'certain' (Bauer) that the singular, *a Jew*, is the correct reading. The plural (A.V. and the Textus Receptus) is supported by the first hand of Codex Sinaiticus, by the Koridethi Codex, family 1 and the Ferrar group of manuscripts, by the Latin and Egyptian Versions, by the Curetonian Syriac, and by Origen. The singular is the reading in Codex Vaticanus and in the majority of Greek manuscripts, including Codex Alexandrinus and the Washington manuscript; it is introduced into Codex Sinaiticus by the third corrector. Since the singular is the easier reading, the plural may perhaps be preferred (Bernard —but Bultmann argues that the singular is the harder reading). If, however, the singular be adopted (Lagrange), the meaning is not thereby altered. The Jew would presumably, like Nicodemus (*v.* 2), be regarded by the Evangelist as representing other Jews. It has sometimes been claimed that both the plural and the singular are corruptions of a primitive reading that has nowhere survived in existing manuscripts of the gospel. Wellhausen emended the text to read: *A questioning between John's disciples and the disciples of Jesus.* (Cf. O. Holtzmann.) Baldensperger—and he received some support from Loisy—proposed: *A questioning between the disciples of John and Jesus.* And Westcott, though he did not venture to emend the text, drove out the representative of Judaism by discovering in the Jew a 'direct disciple' of Jesus.]

### THE WORDS OF JOHN

*vv.* 27–30. Men must receive as a gift the task that has been allotted them by God, whatever its consequences may be, for they are not competent to seize anything to themselves and for themselves (v. 18, 19, cf. Heb. v. 4; Phil. ii. 6). This generalized statement is applied by the Evangelist in two directions. John's work, like the work of Jesus (vi. 37, 38, 65, x. 29, xiv. 31, xvii. 4) and Pilate's judicial power (xix. 11), has been authorized and assigned to him by God (Mark xi. 30, cf. Matt. xiii. 11, 12). But also, a strict limit has been set to the scope of his mission, a limit which it would be blasphemy for him to overstep. In fact, however, he has not overstepped it (i. 20, 27, 30), as his disciples are themselves able to testify. He is not the Christ, but His forerunner: the words *sent before him* echo Mal. iii. 1 (cf. Matt. xi. 10).

The analogy of the bridegroom and the bride is biblical. Quite apart from the allegorical interpretation of the Song of Songs, which carried the book into the Old Testament canon and was certainly current in Palestine in the first century A.D. (Schlatter, *D.E.J.*), Israel had been described as God's bride in Exod. xxxiv. 15; Deut. xxxi. 16; Ps. lxxiii. 27; Isa. liv. 5; Ezek. xvi; Hos. ii. 19 sqq. In the Pauline Epistles and in the Book of Revelation, Christ is the bridegroom and the Church His bride (2 Cor. xi. 2; Eph. v. 22 sqq.; Rev. xix. 7 sqq., xxi. 2, 9, xxii. 17). And moreover, when the disciples of John unite with the disciples of the Pharisees to require of Jesus an explanation why His disciples do not fast, He answers by applying to Himself the analogy of the presence of the bridegroom, in order to explain their behaviour (Mark ii. 19, cf. Matt. ix. 15, xxii. 1 sqq., xxv. 1 sqq.). Here, however, the analogy is extended to include the friend of the bridegroom, whose duty it was to procure the bride for the bridegroom, to make the necessary preparations for the wedding, to preside at it and, finally, to stand before the bridal chamber until he heard the bridegroom's voice announcing his arrival (for a false friend see Judges xiv. 20). This is the office that, in relation to Christ, is claimed both by Saint Paul (2 Cor. xi. 2) and by

John. The joy of the forerunner is, in the perspective of the gospel, not weakened by the fact that the work of Jesus is to culminate in an act of sacrifice (i. 29, 36) and that He, like John, will be put to death violently; for the joy of the Baptist is fulfilled in the joy of Jesus Himself, which is completed only when the hour of His glorification has come (xv. 11, xvii. 1, 13, cf. xvi. 24, xxi. 19, 1 John i. 4).

*vv.* 31–6. The contrasted phrases *from above* or *from heaven* and *of the earth* were used by the Rabbis to express the distinction between the soul and the body. The phrase *above all*, which asserts the mastery of the former over the latter, belongs also to the same context, and provided both a theoretic basis for ethical behaviour and an opportunity for Gnostic doctrines of salvation. 'The soul of man is from heaven, his body is of the earth' (Sifre on Deuteronomy 306); 'The soul is from above' (Rabba on Lev. iv. 2); God says to the soul: 'I made thee above all' (Rabba on Lev. iv. 4; for these and other references see Schlatter, *D.E.J.*). The fourth Evangelist, like Saint Paul in 1 Cor. xv. 47, uses this technical psychological vocabulary, but rids it of all psychological meaning, or rather, makes of it a parable of the truth but not the truth itself. 'The Christ, not the soul, is from above' (Schlatter, cf. viii. 23): it is He, not the soul, that is master of all (Acts x. 36; Rom. ix. 5; Eph. i. 21, 22, cf. Luke x. 22; Matt. xi. 27, xxviii. 18). And those who believe in Him share His divine generation (i. 12, 13) and exercise His authority (xx. 21–3). The teaching of Jesus corresponds with His heavenly origin and is therefore unintelligible to men unless they have been born from above (i. 5, 10–13, cf. 1 John iv. 5). [The second *is above all* is omitted in Codex Sinaiticus (first hand) and Codex Bezae, in a number of Greek minuscules (including family 1), in several manuscripts of the Old Latin Version, in the Curetonian, but not in the Sinaitic, Syriac, and in the texts used by Tertullian, Origen, and Eusebius. The sentence therefore runs: *He that cometh from heaven beareth witness of what he hath seen and heard* (R.V. mg.).]

Sealing (*v.* 33) was used (Deissmann, *Bible Studies*, pp. 238, 239) for security (Matt. xxvii. 66, 2 Cor. i. 22; Eph. i. 13, iv. 30; Rev. vii. 3–8, xx. 3) for concealment (Rev. x. 4, xxii. 10), and for purposes of authentication (vi. 27, Esther viii. 8). The last furnishes the analogy here. The believer does not establish his own truth: he establishes the truth of God and of His promises (Mark xii. 14; Matt. xxii. 16; Rom. iii. 4; 2 Cor. vi. 8; 1 John v. 10). Such an attestation is given by Saint Paul in 2 Cor. i. 20. This attestation to the truth of God made known in the words of Jesus must be a spiritual (1 John v. 6) and believing (*v.* 36) attestation. The words of Jesus are not in themselves the words of God; they are His words because Jesus receives the Spirit from the Father, and because He receives the Spirit not 'by number, weight, and measure', that is to say not sporadically or in measured, fragmentary portions (Ezek. iv. 11, 16, cf. the Rabba on Lev. xv. 2, quoted by

Schlatter, 'The Holy Spirit that abideth upon the prophets abideth not save by measure'), but bountifully, continuously and without limitation (cf. the account of the Baptism of Jesus in the Gospel according to the Hebrews, 'The whole fount of the Holy Spirit descended and rested upon him'). To have apprehended this relation between the audible words of Jesus and the inaudible words of God is to seal and authenticate and attest the truth of God. This apprehension, however, belongs only to those who are born from above and of the Spirit (*vv.* 3, 5)—and here the words *He giveth not the Spirit by measure* receive their second and necessary application. Jesus is not only the receiver of the Spirit, but the giver also; and to be baptized by Him is to be baptized with the Spirit. Herein is the love of God (cf. iii. 16, v. 20, x. 17; Mark i. 11, ix. 7, xii. 6) and the authority of Jesus (xiii. 3, xvii. 2, 7, 22, 24). [The double reference of the words *He giveth not the Spirit by measure* was removed by the insertion—surely a gloss—of *God* as the subject of the verb (Codices Alexandrinus, Bezae, Koridethi, etc., and the Textus Receptus: it is omitted in Codices Vaticanus, Sinaiticus, Washington, and in the Paris palimpsest). Codex Vaticanus and the Sinaitic Syriac —perhaps to avoid an apparent contradiction of vii. 39—omit *the Spirit*, thus presuming *Christ* to be the subject.]

The distinction between those who believe on the Son and those who do not obey Him, with which the witness of John concludes, is not more sharp or severe than is the end of the discourse to Nicodemus (iii. 18–21, cf. ix. 41; 1 John iii. 4, v. 12). The eschatological future tense, *he shall not see life* (cf. iii. 3), remains in the context of the wrath of God (Rom. ii. 5; Eph. v. 5, 6), in spite of the preceding present tense, *He that believeth on the Son hath eternal life* (cf. iii. 15, vi. 47).

[Bernard (Introd., p. xxiii), judging *vv.* 31–6 to have been displaced from their original position, transposed them to follow iii. 21, Lewis (*Disarrangements*, pp. 25–31) to follow ii. 12. Lagrange treats them as reflections 'which the Evangelist added to his record of the witness of John'. But neither are they out of place where they are, nor does there seem to be any discernible break at *v.* 30.]

iv. 1–4. In Matt. iv. 12 the withdrawal to Galilee is stated to have been caused by the arrest of John. Some modern commentators (e.g. Bernard) treat the parenthesis in *v.* 2 as a gloss added by a later hand. There is, however, no support for this in the manuscripts, and it would seem more natural to regard it as a comment added by the Evangelist himself (cf. ii. 21). The earlier tradition gives no hint of baptism with water by Jesus or by His disciples during the ministry. The fact, however, that the disciples of Jesus did afterwards regard baptism as necessary (Acts ii. 41; Heb. vi. 1, 2) would be easier to explain had they before the crucifixion baptized under His authority. The necessity—*he must needs*—of passing through Samaria when time was a prime consideration is illustrated by Josephus: 'It was absolutely necessary for those that would go quickly to pass through that country [Samaria]; for by that road you may, in three days' time, go from Galilee to Jerusalem' (*Vita*, 269, cf. *Ant*. xx. 118, *B.J.* ii. 232). Normally in the Fourth Gospel the verb *it is necessary* denotes a divine requirement (iii. 7, 14, 30, iv. 20, 24, ix. 4, x. 16, xii. 34, xx. 9, cf. Mark viii. 31, ix. 11). [*Jesus*, not *the Lord*, is the reading in Codices Sinaiticus, Bezae, Koridethi, in a group of Greek minuscules (fam. 1) in six manuscripts of the Old Latin, and in the Curetonian as well as other Syriac Versions (Bernard). This may be the original reading; see, however, vi. 23, xi. 2, xx. 2, 18, 20, xxi. 12.]

# JESUS AND THE SAMARITANS

## IV. 5–42

But water is not used only for bathing and for purposes of religious purification: it is used also for drinking. Men, and animals too, perish for lack of water. And water is richly available; flowing and running and 'living' in streams and rivers, in which case it may be described as the gift of God; or reached by the digging of a well, in which case it may be thought of as the gift of some venerable patriarch who dug the well and gave it to his descendants. The whole range of physical and historical experience—water, life, running water, and wells, gift— offered a not unnatural vehicle of analogy or parable of truth. The *Oxford Dictionary* notes that the figurative use of water is 'chiefly biblical': *As the hart panteth after the water brooks, so panteth my soul after thee, O God. My soul is athirst for God, yea, even for the living God* (Ps. xlii. 1, 2). Jesus, seated, tired, and thirsty, by Jacob's well, provides the paradoxical situation that governs His conversation with a Samaritan woman who had come out from the neighbouring city with her waterpot to draw water.

Both John and Jesus had spoken hitherto only to Jews. But the scope of the Gospel was not, and could not be, thus limited. Jesus came into the world and to His own (i. 9, 10); He came to save the world (iii. 17) and to remove its sin (i. 29); He came to manifest the love of God for the world (iii. 16). When therefore He was compelled by the opposition of the Pharisees to escape into Galilee by the shortest and quickest route, that is to say, when he must needs pass through Samaria, the Evangelist seizes the opportunity of speaking of this wider mission. Though the Samaritans claimed that they were the true Israel and prided themselves upon the purity of their worship, they were in fact, as is stated in 2 Kings xvii. 24 sqq. (cf. Josephus *Ant.* ix. 288–91), Gentiles, the descendants of the heathen colonists transferred to Samaria by the King of Assyria from five Mesopotamian cities (Chrysostom on iv. 4). The narrative which begins with a compulsory flight of Jesus through Samaria ends with the Samaritans' recognition of Him as the Saviour of the World (*v.* 42); and the necessity of a fugitive itinerary becomes, in the perspective of the gospel, the divine and theological necessity of the mission of Jesus beyond the limits of Judaism (Acts xxviii. 28). The words *He must needs pass through Samaria* belong, therefore, both to the story of Jesus in Judæa and to the narrative of Jesus in the midst of the Samaritans.

### THE SAMARITAN WOMAN

iv. 5. *So he cometh to a city of Samaria, called Sychar, near to the parcel of ground that Jacob gave to his son Joseph:* 6. *and Jacob's well was there. Jesus therefore, being wearied with his journey, sat thus by the well. It was about the sixth hour.* 7. *There cometh a woman of Samaria to draw water: Jesus saith unto her, Give me to drink.*

### THE WATER OF LIFE

8. *For his disciples were gone away into the city to buy food.* 9. *The Samaritan woman therefore saith unto him, How is it that thou, being a Jew, askest drink of me, which am a Samaritan woman? (For Jews have no dealings with Samaritans.)* 10. *Jesus answered and said unto her, If thou knewest the gift of God, and who it is that saith to thee, Give me to drink; thou wouldest have asked of him, and he would have given thee living water.* 11. *The woman saith unto him, Sir, thou hast nothing to draw with, and the well is deep: from whence then hast thou that living water?* 12. *Art thou greater than our father Jacob, which gave us the well, and drank thereof himself, and his sons, and his cattle?* 13. *Jesus answered and said unto her, Every one that drinketh of this water shall thirst again:* 14. *but whosoever drinketh of the water that I shall give him shall never thirst; but the water that I shall give him shall become in him a well of water springing up unto eternal life.* 15. *The woman saith unto him, Sir, give me this water, that I thirst not, neither come all the way hither to draw.*

### THE TRUE WORSHIP OF GOD

16. *Jesus saith unto her, Go, call thy husband, and come hither.* 17. *The woman answered and said unto him, I have no husband. Jesus saith unto her, Thou saidst well, I have no husband:* 18. *for thou hast had five husbands; and he whom thou now hast is not thy husband: this hast thou said truly.* 19. *The woman saith unto him, Sir, I perceive that thou art a prophet.* 20. *Our fathers worshipped in this mountain; and ye say, that in Jerusalem is the place where men ought to worship.* 21. *Jesus saith unto her, Woman, believe me, the hour cometh, when neither in this mountain, nor in Jerusalem, shall ye worship the Father.* 22. *Ye worship that which ye know not: we worship that which we know: for salvation is from the Jews.* 23. *But the hour cometh, and now is, when the true worshippers shall worship the Father in spirit and truth: for such doth the Father seek to be his worshippers.* 24. *God is a Spirit: and they that worship him must worship in spirit and truth.* 25. *The woman saith unto him, I know that Messiah cometh (which is called Christ): when he is come, he will declare unto us all things.* 26. *Jesus saith unto her, I that speak unto thee am he.*

### THE HARVEST

27. *And upon this came his disciples; and they marvelled that he was speaking*

*with a woman; yet no man said, What seekest thou? or, Why speakest thou with her? 28. So the woman left her waterpot, and went away into the city, and saith to the men, 29. Come, see a man, which told me all things that ever I did: can this be the Christ? 30. They went out of the city, and were coming to him. 31. In the mean while the disciples prayed him, saying, Rabbi, eat. 32. But he said unto them, I have meat to eat that ye know not. 33. The disciples therefore said one to another, Hath any man brought him aught to eat? 34. Jesus saith unto them, My meat is to do the will of him that sent me, and to accomplish his work. 35. Say not ye, There are yet four months, and then cometh the harvest? behold, I say unto you, Lift up your eyes, and look on the fields, that they are white already unto harvest. 36. He that reapeth receiveth wages, and gathereth fruit unto life eternal; that he that soweth and he that reapeth may rejoice together. 37. For herein is the saying true, One soweth, and another reapeth. 38. I sent you to reap that whereon ye have not laboured: others have laboured, and ye are entered into their labour.*

### THE FAITH OF THE SAMARITANS

*39. And from that city many of the Samaritans believed on him because of the word of the woman, who testified, He told me all things that ever I did. 40. So when the Samaritans came unto him, they besought him to abide with them: and he abode there two days. 41. And many more believed because of his word; 42. and they said to the woman, Now we believe, not because of thy speaking: for we have heard for ourselves, and know that this is indeed the Saviour of the world.*

The district in which the discourse with the Woman of Samaria took place was rich in reminiscences of the patriarch Jacob. There was his terebinth (Schlatter), his well (v. 12), the property he had given to his son Joseph (v. 5), and there too was Joseph's grave (Acts vii. 16). And Jesus was sitting by the well in the heat of the midday sun, exhausted after His hurried journey from Judæa, and alone, because His disciples had gone to the city to buy food. But He did not remain long alone or without the opportunity of quenching His thirst. A woman came out of the city to draw water from the well. The details with which the story opens are important for the subsequent movement of the discourse.

Jesus' request to the woman to give Him water to drink might seem natural enough. But it was not so, for two reasons. First, as the woman says, Jews have no dealings with Samaritans; and secondly, as Jesus tells her, He who begs for water is Himself—the paradox is repeated even more poignantly in xix. 28—the giver of the flowing water of life. And moreover, she who is able to satisfy His thirst herself requires the water that He alone can give. The distinction which is here opened up is not the separation between a Jewish man and a Samaritan woman or between Jews and Samaritans, but the separation between God and man, between Jesus and a sinful daughter of men, between the Son of God and the whole people of Samaria. The wider gulf must first be bridged before arrogant human distinctions can be removed (Acts viii. 1–25).

The woman, seeing in Jesus no more than a casual, travelling Jew, hesitates to comply with His request. The seriousness of the situation lies, however, not in her hesitation, but in her failure to ask of Him the water of life, and in His consequent inability to give that for which she had not asked and for which she felt no need. The woman completely misunderstands the distinction that Jesus had made between well-water and 'living' water, between the gift of Jacob and the gift of God. She supposes Him to mean the running water of a stream contrasted with water that must be hoisted up from a well. Her Samaritan pride is at once outraged by the suggestion that a Jew could produce flowing water at the place where the patriarch Jacob had been compelled to sink a deep well in order to provide water for his children and for his beasts. The woman defends the sacred patriarchal well, just as previously (ii. 18–22) the Jews had defended the temple against the critical action of Jesus (Schlatter). There can be nothing better than what she already possesses. But the water of Jacob's well does not, even materially, justify the confidence of perfection that is placed in it. Like the sacrifices offered in the temple at Jerusalem (Heb. x. 1–18), it bears clear marks of its own inadequacy: it cannot satisfy; for, in spite of the labour of fetching and carrying, when men have drunk of it, they thirst again, and the whole labour must be repeated, as the woman knows only too well. The water that Jesus gives is altogether different, or rather, since the words are spoken at the well, is the reality of which the water given by Jacob is a sign or symbol. He that drinks of it is deprived of thirst: he will never thirst again, because, though a gift, it is a spring welling up permanently within him, and is his own possession, which makes of him a new creature. And so, the water that Jesus gives is not running water contrasted with water drawn from a well, but the eternal water of eternal life, of which both flowing water and well-water are true and proper analogies. Jesus is the giver of eternal life.

The situation is now reversed, and the woman makes her request. She asks Jesus to give her this water. But, as with Nicodemus (iii. 4, 9), her thoughts and needs are still confined within the framework of purely physical and visible occurrences. She asks in order that she may no longer be required to journey every day from the city to the well and to exert herself to fill her waterpot from its depths.—With one crisp command—*Go, call thy husband*—these narrow limits are broken through, and the disorders of her domestic life are laid bare. The woman is an adulteress. Her present man is no husband; and there were four, perhaps five, others. Like the land of Samaria itself, possessed by five different races, she belongs to no man, for she has become the property of five. When therefore she said that she had no husband, she had moved at last from superstitious folly to the cold truth. Her sin has been exposed (vii. 7, xvi. 8), and she has herself disclosed her need of salvation, her requirement of the water of life.

The woman now perceives that, though Jesus is a Jew and belongs therefore to another religious community, He is nevertheless a prophet, for He has laid bare her sin. Her question concerning the proper place of worship is not irrelevant: it is not that she desires merely to have a point of controversy settled by one whom she supposes capable of an authoritative judgement. A prophet exercises a purely negative ministry. He discloses sin and calls men to repentance. There is properly speaking no 'religion of the prophets'. They point to the place of forgiveness. In the realm of observable religion, it is the priest who exercises the ministry of forgiveness. The problem of the place of worship is therefore an entirely relevant problem for one whose sins have been made known. But at what altar is the Samaritan woman to make her sacrifice? At what sacred place is she to pray for forgiveness? Shall she go to Gerizim or to Jerusalem? No doubt she expects to be told that Jerusalem is the sanctuary of God. But it is not so. She is required neither to climb the near mountain of Gerizim nor to undertake a pilgrimage to Jerusalem. What is required of her is not that she should become a Jewess, but that she should believe, believe in the words of Jesus that the hour of the true worship of the Father is now come.— Here is woven into the discourse with a particular woman the general theme of the teaching of Jesus as it had been set out at the beginning of Saint Mark's Gospel: *The time is fulfilled, and the kingdom of God is at hand: repent ye, and believe the gospel.*—Before saying positively what the true worship of the Father is, Jesus steps aside in order to avoid a misunderstanding. It might seem from what has been said that no sacred place is of any especial importance, and that, therefore, all places of worship are equally near to the truth or equally distant from it. The controversy between Jews and Samaritans is, however, a proper one, and Jesus ranges Himself altogether on the side of the Jews. To the Samaritans, in spite of their claims, God is the unknown God (Acts xvii. 23). In Israel the dominion of God has been made known, and the true Israelites recognize His sovereignty. Israel therefore is the place from which salvation comes, and from the Jews proceeds the knowledge of God (Rom. iii. 2). This does not mean that the pride of Israel is exalted and the arrogance of Samaria condemned, for before the known majesty of God all human pride is silenced. The further distinction between the temple at Jerusalem and the observable human act of Christian worship which is directed towards the flesh and blood of Jesus the Son of man and which has already been hinted at in ii. 21, is not mentioned by the Evangelist here. The theme of Christian worship is reserved until the conclusion of the discourse on the Feeding of the Five Thousand (vi. 52-65).

The dispossession of both Gerizim and Jerusalem is now made good, not by a reference to Christian worship, but by that which makes sense of Christian (vi. 63) and of all other worship. He who had spoken to Nicodemus of the Spiritual birth from above which is God's answer to baptism by water (iii. 5-6) now speaks to the woman of Samaria of the true worship of the Father, which is spiritual because it makes room for the reverse and corresponding action of God from above. This reverse operation and power of God is defined as Spirit, just as elsewhere it is defined as love (1 John iv. 8) and as light (1 John i. 5). Without faith in the power of the Holy Spirit of God, all human worship is meaningless and must of necessity degenerate into ecclesiastical competition and sectarian controversy. But the Father awaits and seeks those who will worship Him in spirit and in truth. And now He seeks them confidently, knowing that they will be drawn to Him through the mission of His Son.

*The hour cometh and now is:*—This is messianic, not prophetic language; and, since the Samaritans shared in the hope of Israel, the woman of Samaria knows that Jesus is now speaking of that which lies beyond prophecy. He is speaking of the Messiah. The turning point of the discourse has now been reached, and Jesus offers her the water of life— *I am.* Jesus is more than either Jew or Samaritan had comprehended in the word 'Christ'. He is the answer of God to the sin of the world. And so the conversation with the adulteress moves to the same point as had the discourse to Nicodemus (iii. 16). The pride of the Samaritan woman is, however, less deep-seated than the pride of the Jewish theologian; and the road of recovery for the sin of dislocated human affection (Luke vii. 37, 38, 47, 48) is less rough and impassable than the way of return from the sin of dislocated human wisdom (1 Cor. i. 19, 20). Nevertheless, these two, the sin of false love and the sin of false wisdom, are the most destructive of all the enemies of mankind (Schlatter).

That Jesus had conversed with the woman could not be hid, and it has consequences both for His disciples and for the people of Samaria. The disciples return from the city, bringing the food they have purchased: the woman goes back to the city, without water and without her waterpot. The disciples, knowing that common custom required aloofness from women, are surprised that Jesus should have talked with a woman publicly; however, they say nothing and ask no questions: the woman, who had asked many questions, is now eloquent (*vv.* 39, 42) in persuading her countrymen to come and see the man who had penetrated her heart and laid bare her conduct, and in convincing them that He may indeed be the Messiah. The woman is successful and the men of Sychar set out for the well: meanwhile, the disciples, who have been for some time in the city, had done nothing but buy food;

and now they invite Jesus to share the meal they have prepared. But He is neither tired nor hungry, for He has partaken of that of which they have no knowledge. The disciples are as blind as the woman had been (*v.* 15). Jesus first explains, and then falls into a parable (cf. xii. 20, 21, 24). The will of God has been done, and of this food He has eaten. But there is more to be done, for the work of God must be completed and the unexpected harvest gathered. He bids His disciples lift up their eyes—the Samaritans are approaching the well—and look. The eschatological (cf. *v.* 23) parable of the harvest is now fulfilled; there are believers, if not in Judæa, at least in Samaria (Acts viii. 5, 6, 14). The harvest follows, moreover, close upon the sowing, and the analogy of the long period of inactivity between the two is disturbed by the truth. Jesus had taught the woman of Samaria and sowed the seed, and the disciples must at once gather the eternal fruit and receive the reapers' eternal reward that sower and reaper may rejoice together. They must even now undertake their apostolic work. The proverb, *one soweth and another reapeth*, is however even more generally true. The disciples not only gather where Jesus had sowed; they reap where John and the prophets, the ancient emissaries of God, had worked; and in the perspective of the gospel, Christians are what they are and do what they do, because the original disciples of Jesus exercised their apostolic ministry (xvii. 18–20): *others have laboured and ye are entered into their labour.*

The climax of the narrative is briefly recorded. Many of the Samaritans believe on Jesus through the testimony of the woman; and at their request He remains with them two days; not more, because His mission is to the Jews. The time is, however, sufficient for many more to believe through the word spoken by Jesus Himself and for their faith to penetrate further than it could have done through the talk of the woman: it is the Samaritans who recognize not only that Jesus is the Christ, but that He is the Saviour of the World.

# COMMENTARY

### THE SAMARITAN WOMAN

iv. 5–7. Apart from the Saying in which Jesus forbids His disciples to enter into any city of the Samaritans (Matt. x. 5), no mention is made either of Samaria or of Samaritans in the tradition of the ministry of Jesus as it is preserved in the first two gospels. In the Lucan writings, however, a peculiar significance is attached to Samaria, and the Samaritans emerge into considerable prominence. Luke edits the Marcan narrative of the journey to Jerusalem so as to secure the passage of Jesus through Samaria (Luke ix. 51, xvii. 11). His progress is opposed by the

Samaritans (Luke ix. 53–6), who are definitely stated to be of alien race (Luke xvii. 18, R.V. mg.). This opposition occasions the angry outburst of James and John (Luke ix. 53–6); but it is relieved by the signal act of faith of the Samaritan leper (Luke xvii. 15–19), and by the generous action of the good Samaritan in the parable (Luke x. 30–7). Luke emphasizes these Samaritan episodes because he sees in them not only an anticipation of the later apostolic mission in Samaria (Acts viii. 1 sqq.), but also a foreshadowing of the expansion of Christianity to the uttermost part of the earth (Acts i. 8). There is here an underlying correspondence between the Third and the Fourth Gospels: the faith of the Samaritan leper has its expanded counterpart in the faith of the Samaritans with which the Johannine record of the discourse with the woman of Samaria concludes; and John is as sensitive as Luke is to the implications of this faith. The existence of comparable but not identical material in the two gospels suggests that the fourth Evangelist has behind him a more extended cycle of tradition than is preserved in the synoptic gospels, and makes it extremely improbable that the Samaritan woman owes her existence to the Evangelist's 'creative imagination'.

The conversation takes place in the neighbourhood of Shechem (Neapolis, the modern Nablus). Shechem means *portion*; and it was sacred as the *parcel* of land bought by Jacob and given by him to Joseph, who was afterwards buried there (Gen. xxxiii. 19, xlviii. 22; Joshua xxiv. 32; Acts vii. 16, cf. Rabba Genesis 79. 7, quoted by Schlatter, *D.E.J.*). An ancient deep-dug well with a spring at its bottom still exists close to the ruins of Shechem, and is named *Bir Ya'kub*. The place by the well was known to the Rabbis and called by them 'The plane-trees' (Schlatter, *D.E.J.*). There is perhaps a reference to the well in Gen. xlix. 22; Deut. xxxiii. 28. And yet the Evangelist names the city not Shechem but Sychar. A village named *Askar* still exists close to Nablus, and it appears in the Madaba mosaic under the name *Sychora*; there are, moreover, references in the Talmud to a place named *Sokher*, which may also be located in the neighbourhood of Shechem (Schlatter, *D.E.J.*, see also Strack-Billerbeck). Both Schlatter and Lagrange suggest that the ancient site of Shechem was abandoned during the period of the Roman occupation; in which case Sychar-Askar may have been the place of the 'most important Samaritan community in the valley of Sichem' (Schlatter, *D.E.J.*). On the other hand, there is an opportunity here for an allegorical interpretation, which is, however, peremptorily dismissed by Dr. Adam Smith. Sychar means *drunken*; and Trench suggested that the Evangelist gave to Shechem this derogatory nickname (cf. Isa. xxviii. 1). This suggestion was afterwards developed by Abbott (Adam Smith, *Historical Geography*, chapter xviii; Trench, *Studies in the Gospels*, p. 86; E. A. Abbott, *Encycl. Bibl.*, 1801).

According to the Johannine reckoning the sixth hour is noon, and

Jesus was sitting exhausted—*thus* means *in these circumstances* or *in this condition* (xi. 48, xiii. 25; Rev. iii. 16), that is to say, tired by the journey (cf. Mark iv. 36). The scene recalls Exod. ii. 15 as expanded by Josephus: 'And when he [Moses] came to the city of Midian . . . he sat upon a certain well, and rested himself there, after his laborious journey and the affliction he had been in. It was not far from the city, and the time of day was noon' (*Ant.* ii. 257). Chrysostom comments '. . . not upon a throne, not upon a cushion, but simply and as He was, upon the ground'.

### THE WATER OF LIFE

*vv.* 8–15. The conversation with the woman is set in motion by the request of Jesus for water; its direction is, however, controlled by the paradox that He who asks is He who gives. Jesus asks for water from a well: He gives *living water*. The phrase *living water* may mean running as opposed to stagnant water, or the water of a flowing stream as opposed to well-water (Gen. xxvi. 19; Lev. xiv. 5; *Didache* vii. 1, 2), or it may denote the salvation of God of which the refreshing power of water is a sign and analogy. The recognition of the parabolic character of water is characteristically biblical: *I am Alpha and Omega, the beginning and the end. I will give unto him that is athirst of the fountain of the water of life freely* (Rev. xxi. 6). *The Lamb which is in the midst of the throne shall be their shepherd, and shall guide them unto fountains of waters of life* (Rev. vii. 17, cf. John vii. 38, 39; Rev. xxii. 1, 17; Isa. xii. 3, xliv. 3, lv. 1 sqq.; Jer. ii. 13; Ezek. xlvii. 1 sqq.; Zech. xiii. 1, xiv. 8; Ecclus. xv. 3). In the Targums references to water in the Old Testament are frequently interpreted as meaning the Holy Spirit of prophecy or the benefits of the Law: 'As water is life for the world, so are the words of the Torah life for the world' (Strack-Billerbeck on iv. 10). Philo compares wisdom, the divine Word, to a well bestowing life (*De Fuga*, 97). These Old Testament and Jewish references are quite sufficient to explain the background of the discourse; it does not seem necessary to add (as Bauer does in a detached note to *v.* 14 inserted in the second edition of his commentary) references to Mandæan and Hermetic texts. Such parallels belong to the study of comparative religion rather than to the exegesis of the Fourth Gospel.

The woman is first surprised that a Jew should ask anything of a Samaritan. She was well aware of the scorn with which the Samaritans were regarded by the Jews, who in the name of the law disturbed even the most natural human relations:—*With two nations is my soul vexed, and the third is no nation: They that sit upon the mountain of Samaria, and the Philistines, and that foolish people that dwelleth in Sichem* (Ecclus. l. 25–6). Josephus, like the Rabbis, named the Samaritans 'Chuthites' (*Ant.* ix. 288–90, x. 184), and Eliezer, the son of Hyrcanus, said, 'He that eateth the bread of the Chuthites is as one that eateth swine's flesh' (Schlatter

*D.E.J.*, on *v.* 9). [The words *For Jews have no dealings with the Samaritans* belong most naturally to the speech of the woman; they may, however, be taken as an explanatory comment of the Evangelist; or, since they are absent from Codex Bezae, Codex Sinaiticus, and from four manuscripts of the Old Latin Version, they may perhaps be a gloss added by a later hand.] The woman then supposes Jesus to be speaking of the distinction between well-water and running water, and regards His claim as both ridiculous and blasphemous (cf. vi. 52, vii. 35, viii. 22, 53). Jesus, however, glosses *living water* by *eternal life* and, retaining the analogy of a well, speaks of His gift as that which altogether deprives men of thirst (Isa. xlix. 10), since those who receive it will be in possession of a well of water springing up permanently within them (cf. 1 John iii. 9, v. 11). No one who has the water of eternal life bubbling up within him can be seized again with the horror or experience of thirst, or can imagine that there is no greater gift than the gift of the patriarch Jacob. The language of Ignatius shows certain affinities with this passage: 'My lust hath been crucified, and there is in me no fire of love for material things, but only water living and speaking in me, and saying to me from within "Come to the Father". I have no pleasure in the food of corruption or in the delights of this life. I desire the bread of God, which is the flesh of Jesus Christ, who was of the seed of David, and for drink I desire His blood which is love uncorruptible' (*Rom.* vii. 2, 3).

The woman, though still misunderstanding His meaning, finally makes her petition: she asks for water from Jesus. The Evangelist preserves (cf. *v.* 10, xiv. 13, 14, xvi. 23, 24) the strict relationship between giving and asking that is characteristic of the earlier tradition (Matt. vii. 7; Mark xi. 24). A proper request involves, however, a proper sense of need; and the woman's desires are still governed, as those of Nicodemus had been (iii. 4–9, cf. iv. 31–4, vi. 26, 27, 51, 52, x. 6), by the assumption that an abundant supply of the natural gifts of the material and visible world is all that it is necessary to ask. Gifts of another order are unnecessary, unintelligible, and unbelievable.

### THE TRUE WORSHIP OF GOD

*vv.* 16–26. Since the water of salvation is *for sin and for uncleanness* (Zech. xiii. 1), it was necessary that Jesus should lay bare the woman's sin (cf. vii. 7), just as it would be necessary for the Holy Spirit of truth to expose the sin of the world (xvi. 8). In spite of Bernard's vigorous, and of Schlatter's quiet, protests, it is difficult to avoid detecting in the mention of her five husbands an allusion to the five heathen peoples, who, with their different deities, had been introduced into Samaria (2 Kings xvii. 24, 28–30; Josephus, *Ant.* ix. 288–91); tempting also, with the medieval scribe who noted it in his copy of Josephus (*Z.N.T.W.* 1901, p. 166) to discover in her sixth and present husband, who is not her husband, an allusion to the superimposed worship of the God of Israel (2 Kings xvii. 28, 32-4. See Bauer's detached note on iv. 42 and Loisy). If so, the woman's private life corresponds with the history of her people; and in her sin, their sin—and also, in the perspective of the gospel, the sin of the world—is exposed.

The woman recognizes that the exposure of her sin means that she is confronted by a prophet (cf. ix. 17); and, since it is the work of a prophet to point also the place of forgiveness, she asks Him to make known to her the proper place of worship. The distinction between the true and the false worship of God had already formed the theme of the classical passage in the Old Testament concerning the Samaritans (2 Kings xvii. 28 sqq.); and it was also the subject of contemporary controversy between Samaritans and Jews. According to the Samaritans, Mt. Gerizim had been the scene of the sacrifice of Isaac and of Abraham's meeting with Melchizedek; and in their version of the Pentateuch it, and not Mt. Ebal, was the site of the first Hebrew sacrifice after the people had passed over Jordan into the Holy Land (Deut. xxvii. 4, cf. Deut. xi. 29, xxvii. 12). To the Jews, however, the sacred Samaritan mountain was no more than the seat of a sectarian worship founded by the renegade Manasseh, who had been expelled from Jerusalem for marrying the daughter of Sanballat (Neh. xiii. 28) and who had assisted his father-in-law to establish a separate sanctuary on Mt. Gerizim. Josephus described the Samaritans as perishing in their separate worship (*Ant.* xiii. 74-9, 256); Rabbi Eliezer (A.D. 90) held that they were men who from motives of fear had externally adopted Judaism whilst remaining heathen at heart, and who were consequently to be treated as non-Israelites; Rabbi Ishmael ben Jose (A.D. 180), commenting on Gen. xxxv. 4, supposed the images were still hidden under the mountain, and therefore pronounced Gerizim to be an idolatrous sanctuary (Strack-Billerbeck on Matt. x. 5, pp. 538, 549).

The woman has recognized in Jesus a prophet. It is therefore first required of her that she should understand what prophecy is, and believe it. Prophecy is criticism; criticism both of Gerizim and of Jerusalem. But it is prophetic criticism, because it is grounded upon the eschatological hope of Israel. *The time cometh, that I will gather all nations and tongues; and they shall come, and shall see my glory* (Isa. lxvi. 1, 18 sqq.). The privilege of Israel will then be dissolved for the benefit of all nations (Mal. i. 11). It is, however, the privilege of Israel that will be annulled. Herein is the proper distinction of Israel (Rom. ii. 17-20, iii. 1, 2, ix. 4, 5): the true Israelites know (cf. iii. 10, 11; contrast Ps. lxxvi. 1 with Isa. i. 3): the Samaritans—and behind them stand the Gentiles and their worship—do not know (Rom. i. 21-3), their worship is 'custom and the tradition of the fathers, not a movement of the will, based upon genuine apprehension' (Schlatter). For this reason, salvation is not of them, but *of the Jews*. Thus far the words of Jesus are wholly prophetic, wholly eschatological. [It is unnecessary to break the movement of the discourse by treating the first person plural in *v.* 22 as a comment of the Evangelist asserting that Christians know what they worship (Loisy, Bauer).]

But the woman is not confronted merely by a Jewish prophet whose words are reminiscent of what Isaiah had said, '*And it shall come to pass in the last days, that the mountain of the Lord's house shall be established . . . and all nations shall flow unto it . . . for out of Zion shall go forth the law, and the word of the Lord from Jerusalem*' (Isa. ii. 2, 3). An adversative particle follows, and the eschatological future tense is abruptly transformed into a present: *But the hour cometh—and now is*. Confronted by Jesus, the woman is met by the end and fulfilment of prophecy, that is to say, by the operation of the Spirit of God, and also by the consequent corresponding possibility of the advent of the true and spiritual worship of the Father, which is the fulfilment of both Jewish and Samaritan worship, and which is, in fact, the worship awaited by the Father. There can now be men, real men of flesh and blood, who, brought to the truth, must worship the Father in spirit. Neither the Evangelist nor the woman of Samaria understood this as it is understood, for example, by Bauer. They did not suppose it to mean that genuine worshippers of God are thereby 'freed from every chain that binds men to the realm of the flesh, to sacred times and places and ceremonies'; that the truly religious man 'obeys a purely inward spiritual worship of God'; and that the statement that *salvation is of the Jews* has been rendered meaningless because, according to the Evangelist, 'salvation does not proceed from them at all, but from the mission of the heavenly saviour of the world'; and that therefore the words *salvation is of the Jews* is an intrusion into the Fourth Gospel and belongs presumably to a non-Johannine earlier narrative in which Jesus discoursed with Samaritans 'from a Jewish point of view', and that the Evangelist by an oversight omitted to gloss it. On the contrary, the woman understands, surely rightly, that this is a messianic claim; the Evangelist knows that, precisely because the subject is the operation of the Spirit of God, he will have to speak so relentlessly about the flesh and blood of Jesus (vi. 51–9); and it is Jesus Himself who ends the discourse with the positive affirmation— *I am*. This may be simply the 'ordinary Greek affirmative', *I am He* (Plummer); but the words have a significant Old Testament background, *Therefore they shall know in that day that I am he that doth speak; behold, it is I* (Isa. lii. 6, R.V. mg. *here I am*).

Jesus—Jew, prophet, Christ—is the place in visible human history where the sacrifice (i. 29, ii. 21, iii. 14, vi. 51, xix. 28) that is met and made good by the life-giving power of the Spirit of God (vi. 63) is made; and men are brought by following Him to the place where by faith the active and creative love of God is known and acknowledged.

*God is spirit* (R.V. mg. The translation adopted in the text of the English versions is difficult to justify in view of the parallels in 1 John i. 5, iv. 8). This discipleship, and the worship which rests upon it, is the true and spiritual, or as Saint Paul says, *reasonable* (Rom. xii. 1) worship of the Father. The contrast between false and true worship does not, therefore, lie in a distinction between that worship which is directed towards some visible and material object and that which is abstracted from all contact with the visible world; nor does it lie in a distinction between sacrificial or outward and non-sacrificial or inward worship. False worship is worship directed towards a visible object regarded as in itself complete and final. Inadequate worship is worship that rests purely upon the hope of some future action of God. True worship is directed towards the flesh and blood of Jesus because there *ye shall see heaven open, and the angels of God ascending and descending upon the Son of man* (i. 51). In itself and by itself and of itself *the flesh*, even the flesh of Jesus —son of man, Jew, prophet, Christ—*profiteth nothing: it is the spirit that quickeneth* (vi. 63). This comment ought, of course, not to have been added here, since the Evangelist has reserved the explanation of these verses until the sixth chapter. So many modern commentators have, however, wrenched them out of their 'Johannine', and even out of their biblical context, that it has been difficult to retain the reserve of the Evangelist and the confidence which he has in the readers of his gospel.

[The literary evidence for Samaritan messianic expectations is later than the Fourth Gospel. But there is no reason to doubt that the Samaritans shared the hope of the Jews with relevant modifications. The messiah—*Ta'eb, He who returns* or, perhaps, *converts*—would renew the worship on Mt. Gerizim, gather together Jews and Gentiles, and rule in glory over them (Strack-Billerbeck on iv. 25, Merx, *Der Messias oder Ta'eb der Samaritaner*, quoted by Bauer). The woman makes no reference to these particular beliefs. To her the Christ is simply He who will *tell us all things*, that is to say, will declare the truth (cf. xvi. 13).]

### THE HARVEST

*vv.* 27–38. The conversation is ended abruptly by the arrival of the disciples; and an opportunity is provided for the woman to tell the Samaritans what had happened to her and for Jesus to explain to His disciples the importance of what was taking place before their eyes. They misunderstand the situation entirely, for they are surprised that Jesus should speak to a woman and imagine that He has been supplied with food without their knowledge. To converse in public with a woman was regarded by the Rabbis as at least suspicious: 'A man should say nothing in the street to a woman, not even to his own wife, still less to any other woman, because of the gossip of men' (Strack-Billerbeck). The Evangelist says that the woman left her waterpot behind her, partly in order to show how completely the purpose for which she had come to the well had been driven out of her mind, partly in order to contrast her behaviour with that of the disciples (*vv.* 31–3). She went as quickly as possible, unencumbered by having to carry a pot full of water on her head, and without difficulty persuaded the Samaritans to come and see the man whom she had good reason to suppose was the Christ.

The misunderstanding of the disciples is the same as that from which the woman had been delivered. The food of Jesus is not only to do God's will (Matt. vii. 21; Mark iii. 35, xiv. 36), but to complete, finish and accomplish His work. The word *finish* (R.V. *accomplish*) reappears in v. 36, xvii. 4, and in xix. 28, 30, where the death of Jesus is the act by which His work is completed and Scripture fulfilled.

It is the fact of completion that requires the analogy of the harvest to emphasize it and make it plain. The request of the Greeks to see Jesus (xii. 20–2) is met by similar parabolic language, with this difference, however, that the reference to the death of Jesus is explicit and the mission to the Gentiles follows the completion of His work: *Verily, verily, I say unto you, Except a grain of wheat fall into the earth and die, it abideth by itself alone; but if it die, it beareth much fruit* (xii. 24). In the perspective of the Fourth Gospel, therefore, the advancing Samaritans anticipate the movement of the Gentiles to Jesus which was the consequence of His death. The analogy of the harvest belongs to the synoptic tradition, where it has normally an eschatological meaning (Matt. xiii. 30, 39; Mark iv. 29, xiii. 28, 29; Matt. xxv. 26; Luke xix. 21, 22; Rev. xiv. 15). Here, however, as in the Q Saying, *The harvest truly is plenteous, but the labourers are few. Pray ye therefore the Lord of the harvest, that he send forth labourers into his harvest* (Matt. ix. 37, 38; Luke x. 2); there is no interval between sowing and reaping, no time of patient waiting (Mark xiii. 32–7). The period between the beginning of the rains and the month Kislev (December) was four months (Schlatter); but there is no clear evidence that *There are yet four months, and then cometh the harvest* was a 'rural saying' (Bernard; see, however, Strack-Billerbeck and cf. Jer. li. 33). It is better therefore taken as a further illustration of the misunderstanding of the disciples. They, looking at the fields, say rightly that the harvest is four months distant: Jesus, watching the advance of the Samaritans, pronounces the harvest to be now ready for the reapers. The disciples of Jesus are therefore bidden to see the Samaritans gather the fruit (xv. 16) and receive the wages of eternal life (Matt. x. 10, 41; Luke x. 7; Rev. xi. 18), in order that sower and reapers may rejoice together.

The proverbial distinction between the sower and the reaper (Deut. xx. 6, xxviii. 30; Job xxxi. 8; Mic. vi. 15, cf. Matt. xxv. 24; Luke xix. 21) here comes to rest in the distinction between Jesus and His disciples. To Him and not to them belongs the labour of salvation (*v.* 42). The plural *others have laboured* can, however, hardly be taken to be unreal, merely balancing the plural *ye are entered into their labour* and referring only to Jesus (Plummer). The parable of sower and reaper is so narrated as to cross various planes of interpretation. First, no doubt, the seed sown in the woman bears fruit in the harvest of the advancing Samaritans; then the work of the prophets, and especially of John the Baptist, is embraced by and completed in the work of Jesus; then the Samaritans disappear in the thought of the apostolic mission to the world based upon the mission of Jesus; and finally, the Evangelist addresses his contemporaries and exhorts them to reap the harvest, so that the *others* who have laboured become, as Bauer has noted, less Jesus and the prophets of Israel than Jesus and the apostolic generation. There may, indeed, be here a reference to the foundation of the Samaritan Church recorded in Acts viii (Schlatter, *D.E.J.*; O. Holtzmann, pp. 214, 215, cf. 58, 100; H. J. Holtzmann-Bauer, *Hand-Kommentar*, third edition). It should be noted that Luke associates John with the original mission in Samaria (Luke ix. 53–6; Acts viii. 14).

### THE FAITH OF THE SAMARITANS

*vv.* 39–42. The climax of the narrative is swiftly recorded. Many Samaritans had already believed on Jesus because they had accepted the witness of the woman to His penetrating knowledge. At their earnest request (imperfect tense) He consents to *abide* in their midst, but only for two days (contrast Luke ix. 53). Taught by the *word* of Jesus Himself, contrasted with the *speaking* (R.V.) of the woman, not only do many more believe, but, like Peter (vi. 69) they apprehend the meaning of His mission as the *Saviour of the world*. [*The Christ*, which is the reading of the majority of the manuscripts, seems to be a later addition. It is omitted in Codices Vaticanus, Sinaiticus, Washington, in the Paris palimpsest and in a few other Greek manuscripts, in some manuscripts of the Old Latin Version and in the Vulgate, in the Curetonian and Palestinian Syriac Versions, and in the Egyptian, Armenian, and Æthiopic Versions. The omission is also supported by the Latin translation of Irenæus, by Origen and Eusebius, and by Heracleon according to Origen. Compare similar variant readings in vi. 69.]

The pressing of faith to its proper resting place in the teaching of Jesus Himself and not merely in the teaching of His disciples conditions the form of the gospel throughout. Many modern commentators have judged *The Saviour of the world* to be a familiar Hellenistic title which has been transferred to Jesus by the Evangelist. Thus, in the second edition of his commentary (p. 191) Loisy writes: 'The fomula belongs neither to the Jewish nor to the evangelical tradition; its style and mysticism are pagan in origin' (cf. Bauer, Wellhausen). The title was applied to the Emperors from Nero to Hadrian, and the god Serapis was named by Aristides 'the Saviour of all men' (Lietzmann, *Der Weltheiland*). Philo too, commenting on Num. xx. 17–21, named God 'The Saviour of the universe', since He has opened sources, with which the waters of no cistern can be compared, for the sustenance of the heavenly soul (*Quod Deus*, 156). The theory that the fourth Evangelist has simply borrowed a phrase from Philo or transferred to Jesus a current Hellenistic title underestimates His capacity for crystallizing the meaning of Christian tradition into a short and pregnant phrase (cf. viii. 12, xii. 47, xiv. 6; 1 John iv. 8, &c.). The phrase *The Saviour of the world* is Johannine, but its meaning belongs essentially to the earlier Christian literature (Rom. i. 8, 16, xi. 11; 1 Cor. i. 23, 24; 2 Cor. v. 19; Phil. iii. 20; Eph. i. 20–3; 1 Tim. i. 15, ii. 3, 4, iv. 10; Heb. vii. 25; cf. Isa. xlix. 6; Luke ii. 32; Matt. xi. 28–30; Rev. xii. 10 sqq.). There is in the Fourth Gospel no easy transference of pagan titles carrying with them a pagan mysticism, nor are there literary allusions to non-biblical, non-Christian writers. The Evangelist formulates his generalizations out of the oral and literary material with which he is familiar as a Christian.

# THE MEANING OF THE
# EVANGELICAL ACTS OF HEALING

## IV. 43–V. 47

THE earlier synoptic tradition contains the record of many acts of healing. These actions had led to a tumultuous acceptance of Jesus by the crowds (Matt. iv. 23–5); but, since they were often done on the Sabbath and accompanied by a peculiar claim to authority, they led also to serious and deadly opposition on the part of the Jewish authorities (Mark ii. 6–10, iii. 1–6, 22). Hitherto, the fourth Evangelist had recorded no acts of healing. But now, aware that they are still being misunderstood, he includes two in his narrative, and sets out both their false and their true meaning. Miracles of healing are not the goal of faith nor are they the means by which Jesus sought to exalt Himself. The claim *I am*, first asserted in iv. 26, must be protected against the accusation of arrogance (v. 18).

The selection of two incidents in order to show how the action of Jesus may be misunderstood if it be not accompanied by important teaching, is characteristic of the Evangelist, at least in the first half of his gospel. He had already introduced the discourse to Nicodemus by recording the Miracle at Cana and the Cleansing of the Temple. Now the long speech to the Jews is prefaced and occasioned by the narrative of the Healing of the Nobleman's Son and of the Healing of the Cripple at the Pool of Bethesda. In both cases, the incidents are held together by similar movements of Jesus: He departs into Galilee (i. 43, iv. 43), arrives at Cana (ii. 1, iv. 46) and then almost immediately departs to Jerusalem in order to be present at the Feast of the Passover (ii. 13, v. 1, see note). In each case, moreover, the city of Capernaum falls into the background of the narrative (ii. 12, iv. 46). The discourse on the Bread of Life is likewise introduced by two closely connected incidents; and they too are carefully brought into relation with the Passover (vi. 4). Of these six selected episodes, four are recorded also in the synoptic gospels; it is therefore not unreasonable to suppose that the other two—the first miracle at Cana and the Healing of the Cripple at Bethesda—were familiar to the original readers of the gospel, though probably not in the form in which the Evangelist has recorded them.

### THE HEALING OF THE NOBLEMAN'S SON

iv. 43. *And after the two days he went forth from thence into Galilee.* 44. *For Jesus himself testified, that a prophet hath no honour in his own country.* 45. *So when he came into Galilee, the Galilæans received him, having seen all the things that he did in Jerusalem at the feast: for they also went unto the feast.*

46. *He came therefore again unto Cana of Galilee, where he made the water wine. And there was a certain nobleman, whose son was sick at Capernaum.* 47. *When he heard that Jesus was come out of Judæa into Galilee, he went unto him, and besought him that he would come down, and heal his son; for he was at the point of death.* 48. *Jesus therefore said unto him, Except ye see signs and wonders, ye will in no wise believe.* 49. *The nobleman saith unto him, Sir, come down ere my child die.* 50. *Jesus saith unto him, Go thy way; thy son liveth. The man believed the word that Jesus spake unto him, and he went his way.* 51. *And as he was now going down, his servants met him, saying, that his son lived.* 52. *So he inquired of them the hour when he began to amend. They said therefore unto him, Yesterday at the seventh hour the fever left him.* 53. *So the father knew that it was at that hour in which Jesus said unto him, Thy son liveth: and himself believed, and his whole house.* 54. *This is again the second sign that Jesus did, having come out of Judæa into Galilee.*

### THE HEALING OF A CRIPPLE IN JERUSALEM

v. 1. *After these things there was a feast of the Jews; and Jesus went up to Jerusalem.* 2. *Now there is in Jerusalem by the sheep gate a pool, which is called in Hebrew Bethesda, having five porches.* 3. *In these lay a multitude of them that were sick, blind, halt, withered.* 5. *And a certain man was there, which had been thirty and eight years in his infirmity.* 6. *When Jesus saw him lying, and knew that he had been now a long time in that case, he saith unto him, Wouldest thou be made whole?* 7. *The sick man answered him, Sir, I have no man, when the water is troubled, to put me into the pool: but while I am coming, another steppeth down before me.* 8. *Jesus saith unto him, Arise, take up thy bed, and walk.* 9. *And straightway the man was made whole, and took up his bed and walked. Now it was the sabbath on that day.* 10. *So the Jews said unto him that was cured, It is the sabbath, and it is not lawful for thee to take up thy bed.* 11. *But he answered them, He that made me whole, the same said unto me, Take up thy bed, and walk.* 12. *They asked him, Who is the man that said unto thee, Take up thy bed, and walk?* 13. *But he that was healed wist not who it was: for Jesus had conveyed himself away, a multitude being in the place.* 14. *Afterward Jesus findeth him in the temple, and said unto him, Behold, thou art made whole: sin no more, lest a worse thing befall thee.* 15. *The man went away, and told the Jews that it was Jesus which had made him whole.* 16. *And for this cause did the Jews persecute Jesus, because he did these things on the sabbath.* 17. *But Jesus answered them, My Father worketh even until*

*ow, and I work.* 18. *For this cause therefore the Jews sought the more to kill
*im, because he not only brake the sabbath, but also called God his own Father,
*naking himself equal with God.*

## THE DISCOURSE TO THE JEWS: I. THE AUTHORITY OF JESUS

19. *Jesus therefore answered and said unto them,*
*Verily, verily, I say unto you, The Son can do nothing of himself, but what he
*eeth the Father doing: for what things soever he doeth, these the Son also doeth
*n like manner.* 20. *For the Father loveth the Son, and sheweth him all things
*that himself doeth: and greater works than these will he shew him, that ye may
*narvel.* 21. *For as the Father raiseth the dead and quickeneth them, even so the
*Son also quickeneth whom he will.* 22. *For neither doth the Father judge any
*man, but he hath given all judgement unto the Son;* 23. *that all may honour the
*Son, even as they honour the Father. He that honoureth not the Son honoureth
*not the Father which sent him.* 24. *Verily, verily, I say unto you, He that heareth
*my word, and believeth him that sent me, hath eternal life, and cometh not into
*judgement, but hath passed out of death into life.* 25. *Verily, verily, I say unto
*you, The hour cometh, and now is, when the dead shall hear the voice of the Son
*of God; and they that hear shall live.* 26. *For as the Father hath life in himself,
*even so gave he to the Son also to have life in himself:* 27. *and he gave him au-
*thority to execute judgement, because he is the Son of man.* 28. *Marvel not at this:
*for the hour cometh, in which all that are in the tombs shall hear his voice,
*29. *and shall come forth; they that have done good, unto the resurrection of life;
*and they that have done ill, unto the resurrection of judgement.*

## II. THE ACCUSATION AGAINST THE JEWS

30. *I can of myself do nothing: as I hear, I judge: and my judgement is
*righteous; because I seek not mine own will, but the will of him that sent me.
*31. *If I bear witness of myself, my witness is not true.* 32. *It is another that
*beareth witness of me; and I know that the witness which he witnesseth of me is
*true.* 33. *Ye have sent unto John, and he hath borne witness unto the truth.
*34. *But the witness which I receive is not from man: howbeit I say these things,
*that ye may be saved.* 35. *He was the lamp that burneth and shineth: and ye
*were willing to rejoice for a season in his light.* 36. *But the witness which I have
*is greater than that of John: for the works which the Father hath given me to
*accomplish, the very works that I do, bear witness of me, that the Father hath
*sent me.* 37. *And the Father which sent me, he hath borne witness of me. Ye have
*neither heard his voice at any time, nor seen his form.* 38. *And ye have not his
*word abiding in you: for whom he sent, him ye believe not.* 39. *Ye search the
*scriptures, because ye think that in them ye have eternal life; and these are they
*which bear witness of me;* 40. *and ye will not come to me, that ye may have
*life.*

### III. THE CONDEMNATION OF THE JEWS

41. *I receive not glory from men.* 42. *But I know you, that ye have not the love of God in yourselves.* 43. *I am come in my Father's name, and ye receive me not: if another shall come in his own name, him ye will receive.* 44. *How can ye believe, which receive glory one of another, and the glory that cometh from the only God ye seek not?* 45. *Think not that I will accuse you to the Father: there is one that accuseth you, even Moses, on whom ye have set your hope.* 46. *For if ye believed Moses, ye would believe me; for he wrote of me.* 47. *But if ye believe not his writings, how shall ye believe my words?*

'To have believed without miracles was the excellency of the faith of the Samaritans; to believe, as the Galileans did, because of them is, at least, to yield to the authority of God and to advance further than did the generality of the Jews' (Quesnel). The Evangelist contrasts the men of Galilee who received Jesus with the men of His own native city who rejected Him; and he applies the proverb *A prophet hath no honour in his own country* not to Nazareth (Mark vi. 1, 4), but to Jerusalem. The Galilean pilgrims had seen what Jesus did in Jeruslaem at the feast; and on his arrival in Galilee they welcome Him. Now they are rewarded by another, second (ii. 1–11), miracle done in one of their own cities.

It happened that the son of an official of Herod Antipas, Tetrarch of Galilee—this is presumably the meaning of *courtier* (A.V. mg.), *king's officer* (R.V. mg.)—was at the point of death. The man, whose residence was at Capernaum, journeyed to Cana to beg Jesus to come down to Capernaum and heal his son. Without moving from where He was, Jesus healed the boy with a word. The whole episode, with its three times repeated phrase *Thy son liveth*, and ending, as it does, with the faith of the man and of his whole house, provides an illustration of the power of Jesus and of that faith which withers if it be not sustained by tangible, visible, and remarkable miracles (1 Cor. i. 22). This faith is criticized by Jesus, but nevertheless, He does what is required of Him because of the man's distress and because interlocking factors in the episode—faith, healing, death, life, the power of the word, father, son—are, when properly understood, signs, parables, or analogies of the truth. And so the Evangelist brackets the Healing of the Nobleman's Son with the Changing of the Water into Wine (ii. 11, iv. 54), since both are signs of the glory of Jesus, and are opportunities for faith as well as illustrations of it. In the Fourth Gospel, however, these Galilean events lie somewhat on the periphery of the ministry of Jesus. The home of the Messiah is Jerusalem; and the proper occasion for Him to make Himself known is a feast of the Jews, and so He returned at once from Galilee to Jerusalem, where the Jews were now assembled for the worship of God.

The Evangelist says that Jesus went first not to the Temple (see, however, *v.* 14) but to a sacred pool or spring, where, because of its intermittent, miraculous power, a congregation of sick and blind and halt and withered men was assembled, waiting and hoping to be restored to health. This scene of distress mingled with hope is no mere survival of ancient, primitive superstition. The visible capacity of water to heal as well as to cleanse and refresh is too widespread for Jesus or the Evangelist to dismiss its efficacy as trivial or unimportant: and the Jews too had been so far impressed by the healing capacity of this particular pool that they had—if *Bethesda* be the correct reading— named it the *House of Mercy*, and built five halls or porticoes or porches for the greater comfort of those who waited there.—There was, however, one friendless, isolated man, crippled, or perhaps paralysed, for thirty-eight years, who, like the rest, desired to be healed; but who, though possessing no other hope of salvation, had no expectation of reaching the pool when it was *troubled*, or as is explained in a gloss (*v.* 4) which may have formed no part of the original text of the gospel, of winning the unseemly race to the water. This was the man to whom Jesus spoke, whom He chose to heal, and to whom he gave the commandment to take up his bed and carry it through the crowd, as a sign that he had been wholly restored to health. He who had been hitherto a burden to others now carried his burden and walked. But it was the sabbath: and so, in bearing witness to an act of charity, he disobeyed the command of the prophet Jeremiah—*bear no burden on the sabbath day nor bring it in by the gates of Jerusalem* (Jer. xvii. 19–27)—and broke the law carefully guarded by the Jews against any careless or ostentatious infringement. He had therefore not gone far before he was stopped and questioned about the propriety of his conduct; but he confidently defended himself by appealing to the authority of the man who had healed him on the sabbath and commanded him to carry his bed. The cripple knew His power but not His name, for the man had spoken, mingled with the crowd, and gone. Later, Jesus met him in the Temple, and he was then able to give the Jews the information they required. Jesus had, in fact, spoken to him again; but, unlike the Woman of Samaria (iv. 39) he was silent about this further communication. There is a more serious disease than lameness or paralysis; there is a more serious possibility of judgement and there is a righteousness that sets men free. Jesus had spoken to him of his sin, and commanded him to be rid of it. At this point the cripple disappears from the story.

Thus far the narrative is simple and easily understood. The story is an episode; and the Evangelist turns it neither into an allegory, nor into a symbol, nor into a myth. But it is not merely an episode. Jesus was accustomed (the verbs in *v.* 16 are imperfects, not aorists) to heal the sick, and to do so on the sabbath; and, in telling the story, the Evangelist has carefully preserved the form and circumstances—a sick man healed, the word of Jesus, His authority, the sabbath, sin, controversy with Jewish authority—characteristic of Christian tradition, which we know from the synoptic gospels (e.g. Mark ii. 1–12) and with which no doubt his original readers were even more familiar. But it is not his intention to add another anecdote to the stock of Christian reminiscence; he is concerned with the meaning of these *Gesta Christi*, of all these acts of Jesus, with the possibility of the misunderstanding of Christian tradition by Christians (vi. 60, 66), and with the deep-seated, underlying cause of the rejection of Jesus by the Jews. Consequently the disappearance of the cripple does not end the story or cause a gap or break in the steady movement of the narrative. The analogy of father and son, indeed *only* son (i. 18), provides the framework of thought and experience in which the work of Jesus must be understood. *My Father worketh even until now, and I work:* this Saying covers the whole work of Jesus; and its very conciseness enables the Jews to formulate their charge against Him with equal precision. The words *and I work* may be taken to involve an arrogant *and* and an arrogant *I*. The Jews, who are neither trivial nor irrelevant, take them seriously and pronounce them to be be blasphemous. A man is exalting himself to equality with God. The issue between Jesus and the Jews is far more fundamental than a series of charitable infringements of the sabbath would suggest. They were aware that these actions cohered, and that they proceeded from and drew attention to a claim that seemed to them to invite men to that most subtle and dangerous form of idolatry by which men invest themselves and are invested with divine or semi-divine honours. To detect this, protest against it, stop it, and, if possible, to stop it by inflicting the penalty of death, was the purpose of the call of Israel, the meaning of prophecy, and the solemn responsibility of Judaism; and it was all the more necessary that they should be sensitive and strict in this matter, because oriental pseudo-religiosity was at that very time pressing upon European rulers this false opportunity of glorifying themselves. Now, in the behaviour and words of Jesus and in the stories that were circulating about Him, they detected the emergence of this very thing in the heart of Judaism itself. *Therefore they sought the more to kill him, because he not only brake the sabbath, but also called God his own Father— making himself equal with God.* Here is the real issue; and the Evangelist knows that it must not be obscured, if Christians are to understand the meaning of the words and actions of Jesus, and the meaning also of His death. The Saying, *My Father worketh even until now, and I work* therefore stands; but the meaning read into it by the Jews is so completely reversed that the charge of blasphemy is finally turned back upon them (*vv.* 42–4). *Making himself equal with God—The Son can do nothing of himself* (*v.* 19)—*I can of myself do nothing* (*v.* 30): what the reversing of *making himself* into *nothing of myself* means is the theme of the discourse that follows; upon this the understanding of the Fourth Gospel wholly depends. For this reason, the discourse precedes the series of *I am* sayings, since apart from it they are meaningless and blasphemous. In thus moving from an incident to an all-embracing saying, and then on to a discourse, the Evangelist does not for one moment lead his readers to suppose that he is imposing an interpretation upon the work of Jesus, as though there might be some other possible interpretation of it. The divine mission of the only begotten Son of God underlies the whole story of the life of Jesus and conditions each particular incident and episode. The purpose of the Evangelist is to lay bare the theological foundations of the observable history of Jesus, not to impose a 'Johannine' interpretation upon it. In the course of this exposure, he does not, as is often supposed, do violence to the earlier tradition. In so far as it is still accessible to us, the earlier tradition is likewise controlled, in its detached particulars as well as in its general form, by the fact of the unique, divine mission of the Son of God (e.g. Mark i. 11, ix. 7, xii. 6): a mission the characteristic feature of which is the obedience of the Son to the will of the Father (e.g. Mark xiv. 35, 36); which is authoritative precisely because of this obedience (Matt. xi. 25–30; Luke x. 21, 22; Matt. xii. 28; Luke xi. 20); and which is universal and final because of its eschatological framework and setting. The notion that the man Jesus raised himself to equality with God, or of his own initiative called God His Father, or that He *made himself* anything, or was *of himself* anything, would have been as serious an aberration of faith and of theology in the synoptic gospels as it is in the Fourth Gospel.

The Evangelist recognizes that the accusation of the Jews is a thrust at the very heart of the mission of the Church; for their accusation overthrows the work of Jesus by making of it a thing to be set beside, and compared with, the work of God. The work of Jesus must therefore be rejected as in the end grounded upon envy and egotism and rivalry and self-advertisement. This, however, is first misunderstanding, then denial that Jesus is the Son of God. The point of departure for the discourse is therefore not the healing of the cripple on the sabbath day (the miracle is not referred to again until vii. 22–4) but the accusation of the Jews that Jesus made *himself* equal with God. The discourse is prefaced by the solemn introduction *Jesus therefore answered and said* and by a reduplicated Amen, *Verily, verily, I say unto you*; and its first half opens with the words *The Son can do nothing of himself*, its second half (*v.* 30) with the words *I can of myself do nothing*. Sonship means obedience, not independence. That Jesus is the Son of God means that His works *are* the works of God. There is no independence in Jesus; there is in Him no mingling of service with the exercise of authority, no combination of obedience and freedom: 'He obeys the Father alone; and therefore the Father governs only through Him' (Schlatter).

The uniqueness of Jesus, His distinction, that is to say from all who preceded Him, including the prophets of Israel, lies in the fact that His obedience is complete because it depends not on faith but on sight. *No man hath seen God at any time* (i. 18) and no one *hath ascended into heaven* (iii. 13); but the Son doeth *what he seeth the Father doing*, indeed, there is no action of the Father that is hidden from the knowledge of the Son, *for the Father loveth the Son and sheweth him all things that himself doeth* (cf. iii. 35). Thus the initiative and authority of the mission of Jesus are carried back, as in iii. 16, to the love of God, and the readers of the gospel are already being prepared for the great assertions *He that hath seen me hath seen the Father* (xiv. 9) and *I and the Father are one* (x. 30). The Evangelist, however, does not even pause to ask how Jesus sees and knows. Jesus' knowledge is not a subject for psychological investigation. Nevertheless, the Evangelist knows that in Him men are confronted by the final things, by the things that belong to the End, by the raising of the dead and by the Judgement; he therefore knows that there is no road to God that can dispense men from the necessity of honouring Jesus. It is not possible to honour God and at the same time to pass by His Son or do Him dishonour. This is to dishonour God, for, though there may be many religions, there is but one road to the Father, but one place of certain theological apprehension and truth, and but one place where death has finally been overcome by life (xiv. 6).

The work of Jesus means that men are confronted by the last things and not merely by the things that lie betwixt and between beginning and ending. It follows that His miracles of healing must issue in the final work in which death itself is overcome. The healing of the sick and the blind and the deaf and the withered must reach on to that greater work by which the dead are raised to life. To raise up and quicken the dead is the final work of God; and it must also be the final work of the Son of God, in order that the Jews may marvel, and that the disciples whom Jesus has chosen may believe that He is the resurrection and the life, and believing may possess the life that is in Him (xv. 26, xx. 31); for those who bear His word and believe on the Father that sent Him escape condemnation and have passed out of death into life. So, in the architecture of the Fourth Gospel, the lesser works of healing lead on to the greater work of the raising of Lazarus from the dead. When this has been recorded the visible works of Jesus end, and indeed must end. But the raising of Lazarus is not an end in itself, for then the final work of Jesus would be some strange, half-superstitious and merely temporary return from the grave. The stories of the raising of the dead in the earlier tradition can only too easily be regarded merely as believable or unbelievable episodes in the life of Jesus; and against this misunderstanding the fourth Evangelist has carefully guarded his readers. The raising of Lazarus is narrated as a sign that the hour has come *when the dead shall hear the voice of the Son of God; and they that hear shall live*. Like all the other acts of Jesus, it is a parable of His victory over the world (xvi. 32, 33), of the judgement of the prince of this world (xvi. 11), and of the consequent passing from death to life of those who believe in Him. The fourth Evangelist here provides the theological framework in which it is possible for him to record, and for his readers to understand, the raising of Lazarus.

But there is a reverse side to this act of the love of God. Men marvel —and reject the mission of His Son (xii. 37–50, fulfilling Isa. vi. 10). Because the mission of the Son is the final act of the love of God, it must carry with it also the final judgement by which sin and unbelief are overthrown. Precisely because the Father has committed to the Son the work of salvation, He has also delegated to Him the whole work of condemnation and of executing judgement. Here as elsewhere (e.g. iii. 14, 15, vi. 27, 52–65) the Evangelist makes it clear that, in speaking of the relation between the Father and the Son and of the life that is in them, he is not speculating about some ultimate metaphysical relationship between God and the pre-existent Logos. Christians are under the authority of Jesus, the son of man, who gives life and exercises judgement because, standing in genuine historical opposition to the power of evil, He knows it, has been tempted by it, and has by it been brought to death. The death of Jesus is the rejection of the love of God (Mark xii. 6–9). The ancient eschatological phrase and title *Son of man* (Dan. vii. 13; 1 Enoch lxix. 27) has now come into its own and been fulfilled not in a detached and supernatural figure coming on the clouds of heaven, but in the man Jesus, in His flesh and blood. Jesus therefore executes the eschatological and final judgement of God *because he is the son of man* (the phrase is anarthrous). The Evangelist is now able to sum up the first section of the discourse by asserting that the purpose of the visible acts of Jesus is not that men should merely marvel—*marvel not* (cf. vii. 21)—but that they should perceive that they have been brought by them to the place where the final distinction is made between good and evil. The hour is come when the trumpet, which is the voice of the son of man, has sounded, and men shall hear and rise up and come forth out of their tombs to life or to judgement (Matt. xxv. 31–46). In the Fourth Gospel the history of Jesus possesses its proper, final, eschatological form—son of man, good and evil, death and life, judgement and salvation. But this form has not been imposed upon Jesus or upon the earlier tradition by the Evangelist: it is the meaning which the Father has impressed upon His Son and which Jesus, the son of man, understood, accepted, obeyed, and made known. His true disciples have apprehended this meaning, not by their own speculative ability or by the power of their own creative imagination, but by the gift of the Spirit of truth (xvi. 13).

The Evangelist now returns (*v.* 30) to the opening theme of the discourse and develops it not this time in general terms but with direct application to the Jews. They have asserted that Jesus *made himself equal with God*, and that therefore His Words are arrogant and blasphemous. This is once more denied categorically. As He does and can do nothing of Himself, but only what He seeth the Father doing (*v.* 19), so He speaks only what He hears. Therefore, in condemning the behaviour of men, He does but pronounce the judgement. He has heard spoken first by God, for He does not follow His own will or desire, but the will of Him that sent Him. Jesus knows that His witness is the true witness of God and that it requires no additional supplementary confirmation. He stands before Israel with this divine authorization (Mark i. 11) and those who truly believe in Him recognize and accept Him without requiring further evidence (1 John v. 9, 10). This does not mean, however, that Jesus appeared in the midst of Judaism as an isolated figure, possessing the witness of God in Himself and insisting, irrationally as it would seem, that men should believe in Him. In Israel, at least, He is accompanied and encircled by corroborative (cf. xii. 29, 30), external, visible and audible witnesses. The Jews have the witness of John ringing in their ears; they see the works of Jesus; and they have in their hands the scriptures which contain the witness of the prophets and the law of Moses. All these were given to the Jews in order that they might be saved: they did not provide the ground of the claim which Jesus made for Himself, that is to say, He did not deduce His authority from the words of men, prophets though they were, nor from His own actions, nor from some peculiar interpretation of the written words of scripture. This does not mean that these external witnesses are unimportant. The Jews have no direct access to God: they have neither heard His voice nor seen His form; and moreover, since they do not believe in Jesus, it is manifest that they have not the Word of God abiding in them. Possessing no direct apprehension of God, they are dependent upon external witnesses for their salvation. And these they misunderstand and reject. John was a burning, shining light in their midst; and they discovered in him no more than an 'interesting' figure. It was, no doubt, a delectable novelty to have among them a man who behaved and dressed in the manner and fashion of an ancient prophet, and to watch the crowds go after him into the desert (Matt. xi. 7–10). So they let him be for a time; but they allowed him to die without protest, having paid no serious attention to what he said or to the works of Him to whom he bore witness. Nor is it otherwise with their detailed exegesis of the scriptures. They engage themselves in the study of the Bible because they suppose that it ministers to their glory and gives them life. They think that the scriptures belong to the Jews, redound to their credit, and provide them with a life-giving religion. But the scriptures bear witness beyond themselves, beyond the Jews, to the Christ. They bear witness to Jesus, and it is He, not they, that gives life. The Jews, possessing the scriptures, reject Him whom the Father has sent; and this is because they twist them to their own praise and advantage, and make of the Bible an opportunity for satisfying their desire to use the opinions of others in order to exalt themselves. But the more they exalt themselves, the more completely God is dethroned (Matt. vi. 1-5), and the more completely is the theme of the scriptures inverted. The Jews are, in fact, guilty precisely of that blasphemy of which they accuse Jesus. Seeking their own glory, they betray that they have no love of God and no desire for the glory that He alone can give. This unbelief is grounded in the corruption of their affections. Every link between Jesus and the Jews is thereby shattered. He receives no glory from men: they live of the glory which they receive from one another. He has come in the name of the God whom they have rejected and whom they do not love: they receive only those who come in their own name, invested with their own authority. But it is not Jesus that will accuse them before God. The Jews are condemned by their own chosen advocate in whom they have placed their hope. The law of Moses is not a religion of salvation, it is the categorical imperative of God by which men are accused and exposed as sinners. It is this exposure of sin that makes of Moses the prophet of the Son of God. If, therefore, the Jews were properly to believe in Moses, if, that is to say, they were properly to long for the forgiveness of sin and for eternal life, they would now be believing in Jesus. To believe in Moses is to hope for the emissary of God and to receive Him when He comes, for Moses pointed to Jesus and wrote of Him. But if the Jews do not believe in the written scriptures, by which they are condemned, how can they be moved to faith by the life-saving spoken words of Jesus: *the law was given by Moses; grace and truth came by Jesus Christ* (i. 17).—And so the two parts of the discourse compose one whole which moves spirally and inexorably until the accusation of blasphemy made by the Jews against Jesus (v. 18) is turned back and riveted upon them (vv. 44-7).

# COMMENTARY

### THE HEALING OF THE NOBLEMAN'S SON

This is one of those passages in the Fourth Gospel which have a parallel in the tradition preserved in the synoptic gospels (Matt. viii. 5-13; Luke vii. 1-10). According to the earlier tradition the miracle took place at Capernaum at the conclusion of the Sermon on the Mount (Luke, Plain), and according to the modern analysis of the synoptic gospels the story belongs to the Q material, which is otherwise made up only of extracts from the teaching of Jesus. Here, though the nobleman's son and house are at Capernaum, the decisive words of healing are spoken at Cana. The outline of the story is the same in all three accounts: the appeal of the Gentile ruler, the miracle effected by a word spoken from a distance, the father's faith. The narrative in the Fourth Gospel is, however, simpler than in the other two, and as a consequence the emphasis falls on the three times repeated Word *thy son liveth*. And yet, in spite of this somewhat drastic simplification, certain phrases are retained which recall the earlier tradition, especially in its Lucan form: *He was at the point of death* (Luke vii. 2; John iv. 47); *at that hour* (Matt. viii. 13; John iv. 53); *when he heard concerning Jesus, he sent unto him . . . asking him that he would come and save his servant* (Luke vii. 3); *when he heard that Jesus . . . he went unto him, and besought him that he would come down and heal his son* (John iv. 47); the Greek word meaning *son* or *servant* is used once in John iv. 51 as it is in Luke vii. 7; the embassy of the friends of the centurion (Luke vii. 6 sqq.) bears some relation to the embassy of the servants (John iv. 51), though its purpose is entirely different. What is peculiar to the Johannine narrative is largely conse-quent upon the transference of the miracle from Capernaum to Cana. Both Origen and Chrysostom regarded the narrative in the Fourth Gospel as the record of a miracle not elsewhere recorded, and not as a version of the Lucan-Matthæan narrative, and with this judgement Westcott agreed.

*vv.* 44, 45. The proverb *A prophet is not without honour, save in his own country*—compare the protest of Apollonius of Tyana to his brother (*Epistle* 44, quoted by Bauer): 'How strange it is that whilst some regard me as equal to God, some even as God, hitherto my native city alone neglects me!'—is in the synoptic gospels (Mark vi. 1, 4; Matt. xiii. 54, 57; Luke iv. 23, 24) applied to the rejection of Jesus in Nazareth. A man's *own country* (*patris*) may mean his fatherland, as in classical Greek, or his native city as in Josephus *Ant*. xi. 165, where Nehemiah says, 'How can I fail to be troubled when I hear that the walls of my native city have been thrown down?' (cf. *B.J.* vi. 328), and in Philo, *Leg. ad Gaium*, 278, 'Jerusalem is my native city'. In the Fourth Gospel the home of Jesus, the Son of God, is heaven. Thence He came (vi. 38) and thither He goes (xiv. 2). But since the flesh of Jesus is the place where His primal origin is apprehended, He had, of necessity, like other men, a fatherland and a native city. The Evangelist (i. 46, ii. 1, vii. 3, 41, 52, xviii. 5, 7, xix. 19) presumes that his readers know that Jesus came from Galilee, and many commentators ancient and modern (Cyril of Alexandria, Chrysostom, Theophylact, Bauer, Heitmüller, Schlatter, etc.) have taken it that this is the assumption here, and that therefore the meaning is that Jesus retired to Galilee in order that He might be at peace and might not receive honour from men. This inter-pretation seems most unnatural. As Schlatter himself says (*D.E.J.*), Jerusalem is the home of every Jew; and this must be pre-eminently true of the Messiah (Luke ii. 41–50). Jerusalem is therefore the proper home of Jesus, and is here contrasted with Cana as Judæa is contrasted with Galilee. But Jerusalem rejected Him (i. 11, ii. 13–22, 24, iv. 1–3,

vii. 1) and *the Galileans received him, having seen all the things which he did in Jerusalem* (*v.* 45). Jesus was dishonoured in Jerusalem, His true native city, but was honoured in Samaria (iv. 39) and in Galilee the land of the Gentiles (Origen, Theodore of Mopsuestia, Schanz, Westcott, etc.). This means that a proverb which in the earlier tradition was applied to Nazareth is here applied to Jerusalem.

*vv.* 46–8. The Evangelist refers back to ii. 1. The Greek word translated *nobleman* (A.V. mg. *courtier* or *ruler*, R.V. *king's officer*) means either one born of royal blood or an official in the service of a king or emperor; 'This person was of royal race or possessed some dignity from his office to which the title noble was attached' (Chrysostom). Josephus uses the word to describe the relations and the servants, and even the troops of the Herodian rulers (*Ant.* xx. 214, xv. 289; *B.J.* ii. 431, 483, 596, v. 474). Since, in the parallel passages in the synoptic gospels, the story is told of a centurion, the word here is probably intended to refer to an officer in the service of Herod Antipas, tetrarch of Galilee, who is called a king in Mark vi. 14 and Matt. xiv. 9 (cf. Matt. ii. 22), but its significance lies in the fact that, whereas the rulers in Jerusalem rejected Jesus, the servant of a purely worldly prince[1] believed with his whole house (iv. 53). The man is driven to faith by the desire to be relieved in his distress. The faith produced by this and other such desires is not, however, the true faith (iv. 45, vi. 26, 29–33; Mark viii. 12; Matt. xii. 39, xvi. 4), but it is a parable of it, just as the particular distress is also a parable of the final distress that affects all men. The phrase *signs and wonders*, used in the Fourth Gospel here only, occurs frequently in the Old Testament (Deut. xxviii. 46, xxxiv. 11; Neh. ix. 10; Isa. viii. 18, xx. 3; Jer. xxxii. 20, 21) and in Acts (e.g. ii. 22, 43, xiv. 3). It is used four times in the Epistles (Rom. xv. 19; 2 Cor. xii. 12; 2 Thess. ii. 9; Heb. ii. 4), and twice in the synoptic gospels (Mark xiii. 22, cf. Matt. xxiv. 24) of the acts of false christs and false prophets. Its biblical usage tends to denote a certain failure of perception, 'They believed by hearing and not at the beholding of signs' (Rabba Exod. v. 16, quoted by Schlatter, *D.E.J.*).

*vv.* 49–50. The man, no more deterred by the rebuke than was the mother of Jesus in ii. 4, is dismissed authoritatively with words that recall the restoration to life of the widow's son by Elijah (1 Kings xvii. 23) and that point forward, since the miracle is a sign, to the theme of eternal life which is the subject of the discourse that follows (v. 25). As Lazarus was raised by the power of the word of Jesus (xi. 41–3) and as in the earlier tradition *only say the word and my servant shall be healed* (Matt. viii. 8, 13, cf. Luke vii. 7)—*He cast out the spirits with a word* (Matt. viii. 16), so here the word spoken in Cana is effective in Caper-

[1] This would be equally true if the variant reading *chieftain*, found in Codex Bezae and some manuscripts of the Old Latin and Egyptian Versions, were accepted.

naum and, since the officer believed the word, provides the form by which the final, eschatological truth is made known and apprehended, *He that heareth my word, and believeth him that sent me, hath eternal life, and cometh not into judgement, but hath passed out of death into life* (v. 24).

*vv.* 51–4. The boy's recovery was immediate and complete. Chrysostom's comment, 'He was all at once freed from the disease', does justice to the aorist *got better* as the English Versions (*began to amend*) do not. The Greek words translated *amend* are not found elsewhere in the biblical literature, nor in classical Greek in this sense; they are, however, so used in the papyri: 'With the assistance of the gods our sister has taken a turn for the better' (Oxyrhynchus Papyri VI, 937. 5, quoted in Moulton-Milligan, *Vocabulary of the Greek Testament*). The phrases *at that hour—the fever left him* overlap with a somewhat similar narrative recorded in the Babylonian and in the Jerusalem Talmud: 'The Fathers say: it happened that the son of Rabbi Gamaliel was sick, so he sent two scholars to Rabbi Chanina Ben Dosa to beg for mercy on him. Seeing them coming, he went up into the garret and prayed for mercy on him. When he came down, he said to them, "Go, the fever has left him". Then they asked him, "Art thou a prophet?" He said to them, "I am no prophet, neither am I a prophet's son, but it so happens that when my prayer is fluent in my mouth I know that it has been heard, but when it is not so, I know that it has been refused." Then they sat down and wrote and noted the time. When they came to Gamaliel he said to them, "By heaven! ye have done all that was necessary, for it happened that at that very hour the fever left him and he asked for water to drink" ' (Babylonian Talmud *Berakhoth* 34b, quoted by Strack-Billerbeck; the Jerusalem Talmud *Berakhoth* 9d is quoted in part by Schlatter *D.E.J.*). The officer and his whole house (cf. Acts x. 2, 44–8, xvi. 31–4), that is to say, his whole family and household (Matt. x. 6) are presented to the readers of the gospel as types of those who believe that Jesus came that men might have life and that they might have it more abundantly. In conclusion, the incident is brought into relation with the miracle of the changing of the water into wine (ii. 11), and both are defined not as wonders but as signs (for the repetition cf. xxi. 16; Matt. xxvi. 42; Acts x. 15). The emphasis is thereby laid upon the necessity of insight and not upon the capacity to make men marvel. The word *wonder* is never used by itself in the New Testament to describe the acts either of Jesus or of His disciples.

### THE HEALING OF A CRIPPLE IN JERUSALEM

The form of the narrative has its parallels in the earlier tradition. Luke tells (Luke xiii. 10–17) of a woman, crippled for eighteen years, who was healed on the sabbath and of the indignation of the ruler of the synagogue who protests against the *work* of Jesus. Mark records

(Mark ii. 1–12, cf. Matt. ix. 2–8; Luke v. 18–26) the healing of a paralytic with the words *Arise, take up thy bed and walk* as a sign of the avowed authority of Jesus to forgive sins which provoked the scribes (Luke, *scribes and Pharisees*) to accuse Jesus of blasphemy. So close is the parallel between the paralytic in Mark and the cripple in the Fourth Gospel that an early commentator, mentioned by Chrysostom (on John v. 8), supposed the two narratives to be variants of the same incident. Mark also records (Mark iii. 1–6) the healing of a man with a withered hand—Luke adds (Luke vi. 6) that it took place on a sabbath —as the direct cause of the decision of the Pharisees and Herodians to put Jesus to death. In the gospels and in Acts the healing of cripples is treated as significant, not because it is capable of being interpreted as a symbol of mystical and religious conversion, but because it is a sign of the End and of the advent of the Messiah. The miracles belong within the horizon of biblical eschatology as it had been formulated by the prophets of Israel, *Then shall the lame man leap as an hart* (Isa. xxxv. 6; Jer. xxxi. 8, 9, cf. Ps. cxlvi. 8; Job iv. 3, 4; Isa. xxix. 18, xxxii. 3, 4, lxi. 1; Matt. xi. 5; Luke vii. 22; Acts iii. 1–10, 24, xiv. 8–10). Nor does the fourth Evangelist pass over from eschatology into symbolism, as would seem to have taken place in the frescoes in the catacombs at Rome, where a lame man striding away with his bed on his shoulder is depicted as a symbol of the baptized Christian (Wilpert, *Die Malerei der Katakomben Roms*, pp. 264 sqq.). The lame man healed is a sign to the Jews that in Jesus they are confronted by the final judgement, by life or death, by the Son of man (v. 22, 27, 29). Even in the earlier tradition a Christological speech formed the proper conclusion to the narrative of a miracle of healing (Mark iii. 20–30; Acts iii. 11–26).

v. 1–4. The miracle took place in Jerusalem on a sabbath and during a Jewish feast. [The text varies in the most ancient manuscripts. Codices Vaticanus, Bezae, Alexandrinus, the Curetonian Syriac, and many others, supported by Origen, Chrysostom, and Epiphanius, read *a feast of the Jews*. Codex Sinaiticus and a few other Greek manuscripts, supported by Cyril of Alexandria and the Egyptian Versions, read *the feast of the Jews*. If the former be the original reading, and the substitution of the definite article be explained by assimilation to ii. 13, 23, iv. 45, vi. 4, xi. 56, xii. 1, 2, the Evangelist intended no more than to connect the miracle with a Jewish feast and explain the sudden journey to Jerusalem.] Jesus did not separate Himself from the Jews when they assembled to celebrate 'the saving acts of God and to delight in His grace' (Schlatter). But the Evangelist here lays no emphasis upon exact chronology. Ancient and modern commentators have, however, attempted to identify the feast. Chrysostom and Epiphanius suggested Pentecost; Tatian, Irenæus, Eusebius, and Origen (very tentatively), the Passover; some modern commentators, arguing that iv. 35 fixes the discourse with the Woman of Samaria in December, and that vi. 4 fixes the miracle of the feeding of the five thousand as having taken place in April, identify the unnamed feast with the feast of Purim, which was held in March (for the difficulties inherent in this view, see Loisy). Westcott suggested the feast of trumpets. If, however, *the feast of the Jews* is the original reading, the original reference was to the passover, and the definite article was later omitted in order to avoid allusions to one passover in ii. 13, 23 and iv. 45, to another in vi. 4 and to yet another here, which would make the chronology of the Fourth Gospel exceedingly difficult to follow. The tendency to avoid repeated references to the passover would seem to be supported by the apparent omission by Irenæus and Origen of the reference to the passover in vi. 4. But it may be that, in spite of chronological difficulties, repeated allusions to the passover were characteristic of the theology of the fourth Evangelist.

*There is in Jerusalem by the sheep gate a pool.* The use of the present indicative does not mean that the gospel was written before the destruction of Jerusalem (Josephus, *B.J.* vii. 3), any more than the imperfect in xi. 18 implies that Bethany had ceased to exist (Bauer). Josephus refers to the city as though it were still existing (Schlatter, *D.E.J.*). Since the word for gate is omitted in the Greek—a similar ellipsis is found as yet only in Pionius's *Life of Polycarp* (Bauer)—the text was early simplified: Chrysostom, supported by the original reading of Codex Sinaiticus and a few other manuscripts, read *a sheep pool*; and the Curetonian Syriac has merely a *pool*. The sheep gate is mentioned in Neh. iii. 1, 32, xii. 39 as the starting point for the building of the wall. A comment in Cramer's *Catena* says that the gate was so named because 'the sheep to be slaughtered at the feast were collected there'. The Hebrew (Aramaic) name of the pool appears in various forms in the manuscripts: *Bethesda* (House of Mercy), *Bethsaida* (cf. i. 44, xii. 21), *Belsetha* (Codex Bezae), *Bethzatha*. Josephus calls the northern suburb of the city *Bezetha* (*B.J.* ii. 328, 530, v. 151 (*bis*), 246); but here too the exact form of the name is uncertain. It has been suggested (see Holtzmann) that none of these names is correct, and that *Bethseta*, House of sheep, was the original reading (cf. the significance attaching to the place-names in ix. 7, xix. 17); and on the basis of this emendation Loisy permits himself to comment, 'The Good Shepherd comes to the pool of the sheep'. Jewish authorities mention no pool bearing any of these names. Augustine saw in the five porches a symbol of the five books of the Mosaic Law: 'These five porches signified the law which bears the sick but does not heal them, discovers them but does not cure them.' [Codex Bezae and some manuscripts of the Old Latin Version add *paralytics* to the list of sick folk. The conclusion of *v.* 3 and the whole of *v.* 4—*waiting for the moving of the water . . . with whatsoever disease he was holden*—are omitted in Codices Sinaiticus, Vaticanus, Bezae, Washington, and in four other Greek manuscripts, in some manuscripts of the Old Latin and in the Latin Vulgate, the Old Syriac, and early Egyptian Versions. The passage is also marked as doubtful in some other Greek manuscripts. It is, however, included in Codex Alexandrinus and the rest of the Greek manuscripts; the inclusion is supported by the majority of manuscripts of the Old Latin Version and by the Diatessaron; it was also accepted by Tertullian. The passage is either a gloss added to explain v. 7, or it belongs to the original text of the gospel, and was struck out in order to avoid giving support to popular pagan practices connected with sacred pools and streams (Robertson Smith, *Religion of the Semites*, pp. 159, 167, 182; Frazer, *Folk Lore in the Old Testament*, vol. ii, pp. 412–23).] Tertullian, on the other hand, and here he is supported by Chrysostom and by Patristic tradition (Cramer's *Catena*), saw in the action of the angel a prophetic intimation of the effectual sacrament of Baptism: 'This figure of corporeal healing sang of a spiritual healing according to the rule whereby things carnal are always antecedent as figurative of things spiritual' (Tertullian, *De Bapt.* v).

*vv.* 5–10. Since it is recorded in Deut. ii. 14 that, before they entered the promised land, the Hebrews had wandered thirty-eight years in the desert, the long period of the man's slavery to disease (cf. ix. 1) has been taken by ancient (Cramer's *Catena*) and modern (Loisy, Holtzmann) commentators as an allegory or symbol of Jewish unbelief. It is, however, doubtful whether the Evangelist intended so precise an allusion. He records the healing of the cripple as a sign to the Jews (vii. 23), and indeed to all men, rather than as a symbolical representation of the removal of the sin of Israel and of humanity (cf. *vv.* 8, 14 with viii. 32–6).

As in ii. 24, 25 (see Westcott, Additional Note), the Evangelist emphasizes the knowledge of Jesus (i. 42, 47, iv. 1, 17, 18, 29, v. 42, vi. 6, 15, 61, 64, vii. 29, viii. 14, 55, xi. 42, xii. 50, xiii. 1, 3, 11, 18, xvi. 19, xviii. 4, xix. 28, xxi. 17, cf. Mark xiv. 18–20, 27–30). In spite of the wider meaning which in the New Testament attaches to the adjective *whole* and to the verb *to make whole* (v. 14; Luke v. 31, 32, xv. 27; Titus i. 9, ii. 8; 3 John 2), the attention of the readers of the gospel is here, as in ix. 2, 3, directed first to the observable phenomenon of the removal of physical disease and to the observable behaviour of the cripple. The Evangelist records a signal act of charity towards a poor man. It is, therefore, illegitimate exegesis to press, as Bauer does, the suggestion of force which may belong to the phrase *put me* (literally, *cast me*, cf. ix. 34, x. 4, xiii. 2, xviii. 11, xx. 25, 27) *into the pool*, and then to regard the anxiety of the cripple to be plunged into the water as symbolical of the divine motion or pressure which leads men to baptism.

The word of Jesus is immediately effective (iv. 53, xi. 43, 44, cf. Jer. xvii. 14, 15. The precise obedience of the cripple to His command (cf. Mark ii. 4, 9–12) is important because his behaviour proclaimed the completeness of his cure and exposed the absence of charity among the Jews. What he did was a direct violation of the law (Jer. xvii. 19–27; Neh. xiii. 15–19, cf. Exod. xxi. 12–17; Num. xv. 32–6). According to the rules of the Mishnah, however, no accusation was valid unless a warning had first been given (Sifre Num. 113, referred to by Schlatter, *D.E.J.*). [The Evangelist retains the vulgar Greek word for *bed* which Mark had used (ii. 1–12, cf. Acts v. 15, ix. 33), and which Matthew and Luke had removed in their versions of the healing of the paralytic (see, Moulton-Milligan, *Vocabulary of the Greek Testament* under κράββατος).]

*vv.* 11–16. The narrative now moves to the conflict between the Jews and Jesus (cf. ix. 11–29) and to the more serious dislocation that is the consequence of sin (Mark ii. 5–10). In order to avoid a dangerous popular demonstration (vi. 15, cf. Acts xiv. 8–18), Jesus had *conveyed himself away* (viii. 59, cf. Luke iv. 30)—the Greek word (cf. Josephus *Ant.* vii. 83, ix. 120), which means *bend the head out of its true position*, and so *aside*; hence *to avoid* and so *to withdraw*, belongs to the LXX vocabulary, but is used only here in the New Testament. The cripple therefore did not know who it was that had made him whole (cf. ix. 12). Since, however, to have been healed by Jesus provides an opportunity for the recognition of the forgiveness and removal of sin (i. 29; 1 John iii. 8) and for faith (ix. 36), He makes Himself known to the cripple in the temple. 'The power of Jesus to give life and His authority to forgive sins are inseparable' (Schlatter); and so, the fact that the cripple was healed carried with it the necessity of the avoidance of sin, and his salvation involves the possibility of judgement (ix. 35; Matt. xii. 45; 1 Cor. xi. 30; Heb. vi. 6; 2 Pet. ii. 20–2; 1 John v. 16, 17). Unlike the blind man (ix. 38), the cripple uses his opportunity only to make Jesus known to the Jews. The imperfects in *v.* 16 show that the Evangelist regards the incident as typical of others. Jesus was accustomed to do such actions on the sabbath (Mark i. 21, 29, ii. 23–iii. 6; Luke xiii. 10–17, xiv. 1–6), and they were the cause of repeated attempts by the Jews to secure His person by force (Mark iii. 6). Miracles of healing led also to the examination and imprisonment of the apostles (Acts iv. 14–18, v. 16–18). The words *and sought to slay him* (Codex Alexandrinus, A.V.) in *v.* 16 are an interpolation from *v.* 18.

*vv.* 17–18. These verses provide the connecting link between the two miracles of healing which the Evangelist has chosen to record and the discourse which follows. The semi-philosophical reflections of Philo upon Gen. ii. 2 and the interpretations of the passage by the Rabbis provide no proper parallels to the saying of Jesus, *My Father worketh even until now, and I work*. Philo wrote, 'God never ceaseth from action. As it is the property of fire to burn and of snow to chill, so action belongs to God; and more than these, inasmuch as He is the source of action in all other beings'—'By rest I do not mean inaction, since that which is by nature energetic, that which is the cause of all things, can never desist from doing that which is most excellent' (Philo, *Leg. Alleg.* I. 5; *De Cherub.* 87). 'Rabbi Phinehas (*c.* 360), speaking in the name of Rabbi Hoshaiah (*c.* 225), said: "When thou sayest that God rested on this day from all His works, it means that He rested from work on His world; but He did not rest from work on the unrighteous and on the righteous." ' (Rabb. Genesis xi. For this and other similar citations from the Rabbis, see Strack-Billerbeck.) Here, however, the emphasis lies, not on the continuous and unbroken invisible work of God, but on the visible work of the Son of God. Jesus is the Son of God—*My Father*—and His work is the work of God. The significance of the words *even until now* does not therefore consist in the fact that His work cannot cease with the sabbath, but, as in ix. 4 (cf. 1 John ii. 9), that the hour of His death is not yet. In the work of Jesus the Jews are confronted by the work of God (iv. 34, xvii. 4, xix. 30). This work involves, not the violation of the law of the sabbath, but its complete overthrow and fulfilment; for its vacuum is filled with the creative, life-giving love of God. *The law was given by Moses; grace and truth came by Jesus Christ.* The continued work of Jesus *even until now* is therefore the time of the testing of Judaism and of its judgement (xv. 24).

The Jews recognize the vastness of the claim that lay behind the Saying of Jesus and consequently behind His actions on the sabbath; and they judge it to be that special form of blasphemy which it is their duty to punish by death. 'The mind that considers itself equal with God is self-loving and without God'—'Who could be a more determined enemy to the soul than the man that arrogantly appropriates to himself the especial attributes of deity? Now, creation is an especial attribute of God' (Philo, *Leg. Alleg.* I. 49; *De Cherub.* 77; cf. Josephus *Ant.* xix. 4, and Saint Paul's description of the Antichrist in 2 Thess. ii. 4).

### THE DISCOURSE TO THE JEWS: I. THE AUTHORITY OF JESUS

*vv.* 19, 20*a*. The divine mission of the Son of God is, of course, the ground theme of the whole gospel (iii. 35, vi. 38, 57, vii. 16 sqq., 28, viii. 26, 28, 38, 42, x. 18, 30, 37, 38, xii. 49, xiv. 9 sqq., 28, 31, xv. 5-10, xvi. 15, xvii. 9, 10). As Moses had been compelled by the revolt of Korah, Dathan and Abiram to assert (Num. xvi. 28, cf. xxiv. 13) the nature of his authority: *Hereby ye shall know that the Lord hath sent me to do all these works; for I have not done them of my own mind* (LXX *of myself*); so the Son of God, faced by the accusation of the Jews that He made Himself equal with God, deprives Himself of every claim to independence of action: *The Son can do nothing of himself.* The initiative of His mission is carried back to the place where alone it can properly rest, to His knowledge of the Father and to the love of the Father for the

Son. The knowledge of Jesus is the knowledge of the Son; that is to say, unlike the knowledge of the Jews (v. 37) or of the generality of men (i. 18): it is that direct apprehension or sight of the Father and of His actions which carries with it the capacity of doing whatever He sees the Father doing. Here the human analogy of the relation between father and son is provided with its final meaning. But the capacity of the Son to do the works of the Father and therefore to make Him known (i. 18, xiv. 9) depends in the end, not upon the knowledge of the Son, but upon the love of the Father for the Son. Here too the Evangelist builds upon the human analogy of the relation between father and son, for he substitutes the normal human verb *to love* for the rarer verb which he had used in the parallel passage in iii. 35. In Codex Bezae this pressure into the language of human affection has been avoided. The understanding of the opening verses of the discourse depends upon the recognition that the function of a son is to reproduce the thought and action of his father. This is indeed the fundamental doctrine of the relation between father and son in Hebrew biblical thought (Lofthouse, *The Father and the Son*, pp. 22–4). The modern sensitiveness to the folly of parents, assisted by the doctrine of progress, has obscured the biblical insight in this matter.

*vv.* 20*b*–23. The future tense—*will show* (contrast iii. 35) means that the Evangelist is not now speaking of the eternal relation between God and the Logos. He directs the attention of his readers to the historical mission of Jesus. There are greater works than have as yet been recorded, works that involve the final perception of the Son (Rev. i. 1) and constitute Him as the place in history where the final distinction is made between life and judgement. In Jesus the world is confronted by the End. This does not mean that the eschatology of the earlier tradition has been transmuted into an inner, present, spiritual mysticism: it means that the Evangelist judges the heart of Christian eschatology to lie less in the expectation of a second coming on the clouds of heaven than in the historical fact of Jesus, in His words and actions; there the final distinction is made between life and death. Because this is so, because, that is to say, ultimate truth is here made known, it is required of men that they should honour the Son as they honour the Father. The final authority has been delegated by the Father to the Son; and the Son is thereby invested with the freedom of the Father: all judgement is His, and He quickeneth *whom he will* (Ps. lxxii. 1–4) The absolute negative assertion must therefore be made: He that honoureth not the Son honoureth not the Father which sent Him (xv. 23; 1 John ii. 23, cf. Matt. x. 32, 33; Luke xii. 8, 9). And so the record of the public ministry of Jesus in the Fourth Gospel moves to life and to judgement: it moves through the lesser miracles to the raising of Lazarus, after which no miracle of Jesus is, or indeed can be, recorded; and it moves to the final judgement of the Jews (xii. 37–50) in which the prophecy of Isaiah (vi. 10) is fulfilled. This record of the public ministry of Jesus is, however, embraced by a far more fundamental setting forth of the themes of judgement and life; for it moves beyond the judgement of the Jews to the death of Jesus which is His victory over the world (xvi. 32, 33) and His judgement of the prince of this world (xvi. 11), and beyond the raising of Lazarus to the resurrection of Jesus from the dead. Here too the freedom of the Son is carefully preserved: *Therefore doth the Father love me, because I lay down my life, that I make take it again. No one taketh it away from me, but I lay it down of myself. I have power to lay it down, and I have power to take it again. This commandment received I from my Father* (x. 17, 18).

The power of Jesus to raise the dead is a delegated authority because it belongs to God only to give life. This is, of course, a fundamental biblical doctrine (Gen. i. ii; Deut. xxxii. 39; 1 Sam. ii. 6; 2 Kings v. 7; Ezek. xxxvii. 3–12; Hos. vi. 2; Wisd. xvi. 13; Mark xii. 26, 27; Rom. iv. 17, viii. 11). The Rabbis grounded their belief that God would raise the dead (*a*) upon utterances in the Scriptures, (*b*) upon actual narratives of the raising of the dead in the Old Testament, (*c*) upon rational argument. For example (*a*) The Sadducees questioned Rabbi Gamaliel (*c*. A.D. 90), 'Whence can you prove that God will raise the dead?' He answered, 'From the Torah (Deut. xxxi. 16), from the prophets (Isa. xxvi. 19), and from the Sacred Writings (Song of Songs vii. 10); (*b*) According to the traditional answer of God to those who denied His power, said to go back to Rabbi Judah (*c*. A.D. 150), God said: 'Why are ye amazed that I should raise the dead? Did I not long ago raise the dead in this world through Elijah, Elisha and Ezekiel? What shall be has been long ago in this world'; (*c*) 'The Emperor [Hadrian] said to Rabbi Gamaliel, "Ye say that those who are fallen asleep shall live again. They, however, have become dust. Can dust live again?" Then the daugher of Gamaliel said to her father, "Let him be, I will answer him." And he said, "There are in our city two potters. One fashions from water, the other from clay. Which of them is most deserving of praise?" The Emperor answered, "He that fashions from water." Then she said "If God creates a man from water [i.e. from the seed of man], how much more can he fashion a man from clay [i.e. from the dust of the grave]?" ' (Strack-Billerbeck on Matt. xxii. 32).

*vv*. 24–9. The preceding verses are, however, capable of serious misunderstanding. The readers of the gospel may be led to suppose that the authority of Jesus reaches its proper climax in the greater works of the raising of Lazarus and in similar miracles recorded in the earlier tradition (Mark v. 21–43; Luke vii. 11–17; cf. Matt. xi. 5; Luke vii. 22) or in His own resurrection from the dead. The discourse, however, now moves on through these illustrations of authority to the greatest work of Jesus, to His universal power to give life and raise the dead. The freedom of Jesus to quicken whom He will (*v*. 21) reaches beyond the children of Abraham, beyond the circumcised Jews, and even beyond His own resurrection. The importance of this moment in the movement of the discourse is emphasized by the twice-repeated *Verily, Verily* and by an even graver insistence upon an eschatological tension. It is The Hour; and the trumpet of the End (1 Thess. iv. 16) is merged in the voice of the Son of God which penetrates to the dead (xi. 43, 44, cf. Rev. iii. 20, 21): *He that heareth my word, and believeth him that sent me, hath eternal life, and cometh not into judgement, but hath passed out of death into life.* Here the eschatological, apostolic, and universal mission of the Church is defined as the gospel of life. But it is universal only in so far as the disciples of Jesus preserve His words in such a manner that the world may hear His voice and believe the Father that sent Him (xiv. 26, xvi. 4, xvii. 20, 21), and so pass from death to life. In the perspective of Christian thought the passage from death to life is the passing from sin to righteousness and the remission of sins, and from unbelief to faith (Eph. ii. 1, 15; Rom. vi. 13, xi. 15; Col. ii. 13; 1 Pet. i. 3, iv. 6; Matt. viii. 22; Luke ix. 60, xv. 24). In the discourse this passage is no mere stage in an evolutionary process: it is the eschatological occurrence. Those who hear the voice of Jesus stand even now within the final order of God (1 John iii. 13–15, v. 11, 12, cf. Heb. vi. 1). The emphasis upon hearing the voice of Jesus and upon faith deprives the words *The Son quickeneth whom he will*—in the Curetonian Syriac Version *those who believe in him* is substituted for *whom he will*—of any suggestion of capricious selection. Nevertheless, the act of faith is not a thing in itself, for it belongs within the sphere of the divine initiative (vi. 70, xvii. 6, cf. 1 Cor. xii. 3).

Once again, at the conclusion of the first half of the discourse, the Evangelist asserts the theme of his gospel, the purpose for which it was written. The place of life and of judgement, the place where the final eschatological decision is made, is no transcendental, mystical, supernatural activity of the Son or Word of God. The place of decision is the flesh of Jesus, His audible words and His visible death (xii. 31–4, xix. 30), in fact, the historical event of His mission. He gives life and executes judgement because He is *the Son of man* (the phrase is anarthrous in the Greek and is translated in the R.V. mg. *a son of man*). Here again, as in i. 51, iii. 15, vi. 27, 51–65, ix. 35 (see note), xii. 31–4, the man Jesus (Acts xvii. 31; Heb. ii. 14–18, iv. 15, 16) fulfils the half-mythical, eschatological notions of Dan. vii. 13 and 1 Enoch lxix. 27 and perhaps an even more widespread mythology revolving round the idea of the man from heaven (see Bultmann *passim*), and the phrase *The Son of man* is deprived of all mythical imaginings in the actual flesh and blood of the mission of the man Jesus. But, and this is the point, the eschatological significance of the phrase is retained. The man Jesus executes the judgement and gives life to the dead; and He does so because He possesses the authority of God and because He is the Son of man (Mark

ii. 10, 28). Thus the Evangelist holds his readers to the theme laid down in the prologue (i. 14), and also to the eschatology of the early Christian tradition.

There seems to be no adequate reason for supposing with Holtzmann, Grill, Bauer, Bultmann and Loisy (in the second edition of his commentary) that *vv.* 28, 29 have been added by a redactor; for, as Loisy had insisted in the first edition of his commentary (pp. 407, n. 1 and 410), the Evangelist has not, in emphasizing a present judgement, discarded altogether the expectation of a last day (vi. 39–44, xi. 24). He argues rather that those who know that there will be a day of resurrection unto life and unto judgement, and that there will be a final separation of those who have done good from those who have done evil, ought not to wonder and be surprised that the voice of the Son of God even now separates good from evil, exercises judgement and gives life.

## II. THE ACCUSATION AGAINST THE JEWS

The first half of the discourse reaches its conclusion with the assertion of the universality of the mission of the Son of God and of the Last Judgement. The Evangelist now returns to the accusation of the Jews that Jesus made Himself equal with God (*v.* 19) and addresses them directly in the first person: *I can of myself do nothing*, contrast *v.* 19b: *The Son can do nothing of himself.*

*vv.* 30–2. The witness of Jesus to Himself, is absolute and final (viii. 18), because His words, like His actions (*v.* 19), are the just judgements of the Father, spoken in accordance with His will. The works of Jesus are the works He has seen the Father do (*v.* 19): His words are the words He has heard the Father speak. The witness of Jesus to Himself is, therefore, not a witness *of himself*; it does not originate from Himself. If it did, it would be untrue. The law of evidence requires another witness. That Other is God; and His witness is true and sufficient both for Jesus Himself and for those who believe in Him (xii. 29, 30; 1 John v. 10a).

[Chrysostom took *another* (*v.* 32) as referring to John the Baptist. This interpretation may have given rise to the variant reading in Codices Sinaiticus, Bezae, and in some other manuscripts, *ye know* for *I know*. The external corroborative witnesses form the subject matter of the rest of the discourse but not of *v.* 32, which belongs to the introductory verses 30, 31 (Augustine, Cyril).]

Though, if rightly understood, the witness of Jesus to Himself is sufficient, it is manifestly inadequate for those who deny His authority and judge it to proceed from arrogance. The Jews require external evidence and ask Jesus to name His witnesses. This He now does. John bore witness to Him; His own works are visible witnesses to His divine authority; and the Old Testament Scriptures and Moses bear witness.

It is the agreement of separate witnesses that provides the criterion by which the truth may be distinguished from illusion.

*vv.* 33–5. The witness of John. The Evangelist assumes that his readers remember what has been stated in i. 19–32 (cf. i. 6, iii. 26–30). The Jews had sent to John and heard his witness (i. 19, 20, 26). On the two following days, he bore precise witness first to the crowd (i. 29) and then to two of his disciples (i. 35, 36). The witness of John was the witness *unto the truth* because it required to be made good by the action of God. Upon this human witness Jesus does not rely, but it is necessary for the salvation of the Jews, since, having no direct knowledge of the truth, they require an external witness in order that they may believe. John was the lamp which still burns and shines. The metaphor (2 Sam. xxi. 17; Ecclus. xlviii. 1; Matt. v. 14, 15; Luke xii. 35; 2 Pet. i. 19; Rev. xxi. 23, cf. Mekilta Exod. xviii. 27, quoted by Schlatter, *D.E.J.*) is strictly applied. Though a lamp gives light, it does not do so of itself. John was not the light (i. 7, 8). Nevertheless, his witness is a permanent witness to the light (note the perfect *he hath borne witness* in *v.* 33 and the present participles *burning* and *shining* in *v.* 35). The Jews, however, though they rightly rejoiced at his coming, regarded it merely as an episode in Jewish history that ended with his imprisonment (iii. 24). They rejoiced only *for a season* (Matt. xi. 7–11, 16–19, cf. xiii. 21); and this meant that they had paid no serious attention to him.

*v.* 36. The works of Jesus. The acts of Jesus Himself provide an even more important series of external witnesses to His divine mission than do the words of John. The Evangelist does not here draw out the importance of the miracles of Jesus, partly perhaps because it had already formed the theme of the first section of the discourse (*vv.* 19–23), partly because it is to be handled at even greater length in the next chapter and elsewhere (x. 25, 32, 38, xiv. 11, 12, xv. 24, cf. Matt. ix. 2–8, xi. 2–6, 20–4, xii. 28; Luke vii. 22). He does, however, state the two salient facts. The works of Jesus have been given Him by the Father to bear witness to the nature of His mission; and they are final, finished and complete acts. That is to say, so far from being experimental and tentative, they make known the final power of God to forgive sin and to give eternal life to His children. This completeness of the works of Jesus is most clearly manifested in His death (xix. 30, cf. iv. 34, xvii. 4). It is, therefore, in the light of that last work that the meaning of the others must be understood (vi. 51).

[Codices Vaticanus and Alexandrinus have the Greek word translated *greater* in what seems to be the nominative case and the masculine gender. This would require the translation, *I who am greater than John have the witness*, which is, however, impossible in the context, since the argument is not here concerned with the superiority of Jesus to John, but with the fact that the actions of Jesus are of greater efficacy for faith than are the words of John. The variant reading must, therefore, be due either to a scribal error or to the gratuitous addition of a final *n*, a phenomenon not unknown in Hellenistic Greek, which would in this case make the accusative appear to be the nominative (see Bauer, Lagrange, and Moulton, *Grammar of New Testament Greek*, vol. I, p. 49).]

*vv.* 37–40. The Old Testament Scriptures. To the witness of John the Baptist and of the works of Jesus is now added the witness of the Father in the Old Testament Scriptures. The permanent importance of this third witness is emphasized in the Greek by an emphatic *he* and by the perfect tense—*he hath borne witness*. The Jews to whom Jesus and His disciples speak have no direct knowledge or vision of God; they neither hear His voice (contrast xiv. 24) nor see His form (Deut. iv. 12, contrast i. 18, vi. 46, 47, xiv. 9), nor does His word abide in them (contrast xv. 7; 1 John ii. 14, 24). They do, however, possess the written Scriptures which are the witness of the Father to the Son; and these they persistently misunderstand, for they examine them on the false assumption—the Greek verb translated *ye think* (*v.* 39) is used several times elsewhere with this suggestion (*v.* 45, xi. 13, 31, xiii. 29, xvi. 2, xx. 15, cf. Matt. vi. 7)—that the written words of Scripture are themselves life-giving. They therefore 'exercise themselves in a great and profitable occupation in a manner not becoming its use' (Cyril). Being the witness of God to His Son, the Scriptures are prophetic, not life-giving. Those who properly read and understand the words of the prophets of Israel are thereby led to believe in Jesus (vi. 45). Not to believe in Him, not to come to Him and follow Him, is to abandon life and to misunderstand the Scriptures altogether (Matt. xi. 28, xxiii. 37; Mark x. 17, 21, 23, 28–31), for they provide in and by themselves no final vision of God and no truly spiritual religion. Judaism is fundamentally a negation (x. 8); and when it turns itself into a positive religion, it destroys itself. Thus the pride of the Jews in their indefatigable study of the Scriptures is undermined at its source.

*vv.* 37, 38 do not, therefore, as Chrysostom supposed, refer to the voice from heaven at the Baptism of Jesus (Mark i. 11 and parallels), but to the Old Testament Scriptures, and by implication to such passages as Ps. ii. 7, which forms the basis of the Evangelical narrative of the Baptism. The Greek verb in *v.* 39 translated *search* reproduces the Hebrew word *darash*: 'It is necessary to *examine* every passage containing the word "saying"' (Akiba, Sifre Num. 2), 'Thou knowest how to read, but not how to search' (Jerusalem Talmud *Berakhoth* 4d); it is frequently used by Philo for the investigation of the meaning of scripture (for illustrations see Schlatter, *D.E.J.*). The verb here may be an indicative, *Ye search the scriptures* (R.V.), or an imperative, *Search the scriptures* (A.V., R.V. mg.; see Field, *Notes on the Translation of the New Testament*, pp. 88 sqq.). Chrysostom and most of the Fathers took it as an imperative, but the argument, as Cyril saw, requires the indicative,

'We will then not read it as an imperative.' And yet, when this is said, an imperative lurks behind the indicative, for the Saying encourages the steady investigation of the Scriptures. What is discouraged, and indeed condemned, is every form of Old Testament study that proceeds on the assumption that there is such a thing as 'The Religion of the Old Testament' or 'The Religion of the Prophets of Israel'. For the Torah in the Rabbinic Literature as the source of salvation and life, indeed as itself the Tree of Life, see Strack-Billerbeck on Rom. iii. 1: 'This is the book of the commandments of God and the Law that endureth for ever. All they that hold it fast are appointed to life, but such as leave it shall die' (1 Baruch iv. 1, 2); 'If food, which is your life but for an hour, requires a blessing before and after it be eaten, how much more does the Torah, in which lies the world that is to be, require a blessing' (Rabbi Ishmael, c. 135, quoted by Strack-Billerbeck); 'He who has gained for himself words of the Law has gained for himself the life in the world to come (*Aboth* ii. 7).

### III. THE CONDEMNATION OF THE JEWS

The Jews have accused Jesus of egotism (*v.* 18). This accusation is now both rebutted and turned back upon them. He does, it is true, demand that men should come to Him (*v.* 40) and that all men should pay Him honour (*vv.* 22, 23); but this is not that His glory may be increased thereby, it is in order that they may receive eternal life. The glory of Jesus is enhanced, neither by the number of His disciples, nor by any external witness that is borne to Him by John the Baptist, nor by His own visible acts, nor by the words of Moses and the prophets of Israel. These are the means by which men are enabled to recognize His glory; they in no wise add to it. He is worthy to receive glory (Rev. iv. 11), because His authority is not from this world (xviii. 36). He has come *in the name* of the Father (*v.* 43, cf. iii. 18; Matt. xxi. 9). This alone constitutes His glory and authority (i. 14). His actions (ii. 11, ix. 4) and the very existence of His disciples (xv. 8, xvii. 10) do indeed show forth His glory, and His death makes it even more clearly manifest; but His veritable glorification is given Him by the Father and by the Father only (xvii. 1, 5). In no way does He glorify Himself (viii. 54). The rejection of Jesus by the Jews is therefore the rejection of God; and since His mission is the exposition of the love of God (iii. 16; 1 John iv. 9–11) His rejection by the Jews declares them to be void of the love of God—*I know you, that ye have not the love of God in yourselves*. This judgement means that the gulf between Jesus and the Jews is unbridgeable, for the division between them concerns the reality of God. They direct their eyes to God in order that their selfish desires may be strengthened —this is sin; He, in order that every trace of egotism and independent desire may be destroyed—this is righteousness (xvii. 25, 26).

The godlessness of which Jesus had been accused is now firmly riveted upon the Jews. They are altogether removed from the possibility of faith, because, seeking their own glory (vii. 18, xii. 43; Rom. x. 2, 3) and occupied in receiving glory from one another (Matt. xxiii. 6–8), they deprive themselves thereby of the glory that cometh from *the only God* (xvii. 3; Isa. xxxvii. 16). Some manuscripts, including Codex Vaticanus and the Washington Codex, read *the only one*, see Lagrange and R.V. mg. The mission of Jesus is, consequently, beyond their horizon, and they reject Him; not because He makes Himself, as they say, equal with God, for then they would have understood and accepted Him, since, were another to come in His own name, Him they would assuredly receive; but because, having come in His Father's name, He seeks His glory only, and that they cannot understand. Some modern commentators detect in the singular *another* (*v.* 43) a particular reference to the acceptance by the Jews of Bar Cochba how led the revolt of A.D. 135 (Wellhausen, see Bauer), or to the followers of Menahem, who, according to Josephus, adorned himself in royal garments and 'in a pompous manner' went up to worship in the Temple (*B.J.* ii. 442–4), or the applause with which Agrippa was received in Jerusalem as king (Schlatter, *D.E.J.*). The patristic writers tended to take it as a reference to the Anti-Christ (Irenæus, *Adv. Haer.* v. 25. 4, Eusebius, Cyril, Jerome). But it is doubtful whether, in view of the plural *one anohert* in the following verse, the singular should be pressed. The Evangelist is speaking of that general preference which men have of following those whose claims they can most easily appreciate, since they correspond so closely with their own desires (Mark xiii. 6, 21, 22; Luke xxi. 8; Acts v. 36, 37).

The ground of Jewish unbelief having been thus exposed, the discourse concludes by setting the Jews under the condemnation, not of Jesus, but of their own scriptures and of their own chosen advocate. Since Jesus has come to save men, not to judge them, to take away sin, not to punish it, the office of accuser is not His (Rev. xii. 10). Israel stands under the accusation of Moses (cf. Rabba Exod. 47, 14, where the Greek verb *to accuse* is translated into Hebrew). These variants are otherwise unknown. Since Moses bears witness to the mission of the Son (Luke xxiv. 44; Acts iii. 21 sqq.; 2 Cor. iii. 13–16), there is an essential unity between the work of the lawgiver and the work of the giver of life. This unity is broken by the unbelief of the Jews, and they are set under the inevitable accusation of Moses, for they remain in their sins under the condemnation of the law (viii. 24, ix. 41, xvi. 9). If they were now believers in Moses, they would now be believing in Jesus (the sentence is an unfulfilled condition in present time). When it is said that Moses *wrote* of Jesus (cf. *v.* 39), the Evangelist does not mean a merely superficial capacity of foretelling the future; he means that the condemnation of sin, which is the function of the law, has throughout been accompanied by the promise of the grace and forgiveness of God. Hope therefore ought to have been fixed not on Moses, but on Him of whom he spoke (i. 17, 45). With the coming of the Son of God, the hope of Israel is fulfilled, and the word *hope* is almost completely banished from the Johannine vocabulary: it occurs only in 1 John iii. 3. The reference here to what Moses wrote is therefore neither to any particular passage in the Pentateuch, such as, for example, Deut. xviii. 15 (Acts iii. 22, vii. 27) nor to some selection of so-called messianic passages; the reference is to the whole panorama of Old Testament Scriptures, grouped together under the name of Moses, because they revolve round the law of Moses and because his figure dominates all subsequent Jewish literature. The spoken words of Jesus must remain without meaning unless men have first been condemned as sinners. If therefore the Jews do not believe in the scriptures by which they are condemned, how can they believe in the words of Jesus by which they are restored to life?

The discourse ends because the healing of the ruler's son and of the cripple at Bethesda has now been provided with its proper theological meaning. The historical problem raised by the discourse, and indeed by the whole gospel, is not whether it reflects the tension between the Church and the Jews at the beginning of the second century A.D.; this it assuredly does. The problem is whether the Evangelist has been able to understand and define the controversy, because the same ultimate issue had already been presented and defined by Jesus in His conflict with the authorities of Judaism almost a century earlier, or whether he is simply speculating theologically and independently on the situation by which he is confronted, with perhaps some assistance from his predecessor Saint Paul.

# THE UNBELIEF OF THE GALILEANS

## VI. 1–VII. 1

THE Evangelist has described and explained the unbelief of the Jews in Jerusalem. He now proceeds, in spite of iv. 45–54, to expose the unbelief of the Galileans. The sections are parallel in structure: two miracles are first recorded in the language and form of primitive Christian tradition, but with just sufficient alteration to fit them into the framework of the Fourth Gospel; then one of them is taken as the basis of a discourse in which the gulf that separates Jesus from His hearers grows wider and wider until the distinction between them is shown to be an absolute distinction. In Jerusalem, the Jews defend the Law and the Scriptures in such a manner as to display their belief in themselves and their disbelief in God; in Capernaum, the Galileans combine materialism and superstition in such a manner as to display no greater capacity for faith. In order to expose the unbelief of the Galileans, the Evangelist selects the story of the Feeding of the Five Thousand. He tells it in its traditional form, in which it is accompanied by the story of the coming of Jesus to His disciples, walking on the sea (Mark vi. 31–52; Matt. xiv. 13–33; cf. Luke ix. 10–17; Mark viii. 1–9; Matt. xv. 32–9). The interpretation of this extract from the written and oral tradition of the Church belongs, no doubt, primarily to the exegesis of the synoptic gospels. But when this is said, it must not be forgotten that the Feeding of the Five Thousand has already been interpreted by the author of the Fourth Gospel. The Evangelist is, moreover, confident that he is setting forth its veritable meaning and not some speculation of his own about it. There is no break in his narrative. Jesus fed the multitude; and He provided His action with its proper meaning. He is the answer to the desire of men for food and for a King, just as He is the fulfilment of the Jewish Law and of the Jewish Scriptures. In their inability to apprehend this, the Galilean crowds of ordinary men and women were as far removed from the truth as their more instructed leaders in Jerusalem. Though the theme of judgement is less openly expressed in Capernaum than it had been in Jerusalem, nevertheless, it is the purpose of the Evangelist to set the whole people of Israel under the accusation of unbelief; and to record, on that background, the words of Peter in which he first formulated the apostolic faith of the Church and the apostolic apprehension of the meaning of the words and actions of Jesus: *Lord, to whom shall we go? thou hast the words of eternal life. And we have believed and know that thou art the Holy One of God* (vi. 68, 69).

The grouping of material into large sections, which, though complete in themselves, combine to form one theological whole, is so characteristic of the Evangelist that there seems to be no sufficient reason for suspecting that chapter vi is out of place in its present position. If it could be proved that the Evangelist was concerned to set before his readers a chronological and historical sequence of events and an easily recognizable itinerary of the ministry of Jesus; and if, in spite of the literary character of the gospel, the reference to the healing of the cripple in vii. 21–3 assumes the miracle to have just taken place; then, the present position of chapter vi is the consequence of an early disarrangement of the text of the gospel; and it would be attractive to attempt to restore the original order by transposing chapter v and vi. Theologically, however, the present order is neither meaningless nor untidy. The unbelief of the Galileans follows the unbelief of the Jews in Jerusalem; and the faith of the disciples of Jesus is contrasted with both.

### THE FEEDING OF THE FIVE THOUSAND

vi. 1. *After these things Jesus went away to the other side of the sea of Galilee, which is the sea of Tiberias. 2. And a great multitude followed him, because they beheld the signs which he did on them that were sick. 3. And Jesus went up into the mountain, and there he sat with his disciples. 4. Now the passover, the feast of the Jews, was at hand. 5. Jesus therefore lifting up his eyes, and seeing that a great multitude cometh unto him, saith unto Philip, Whence are we to buy bread, that these may eat? 6. And this he said to prove him: for he himself knew what he would do. 7. Philip answered him, Two hundred pennyworth of bread is not sufficient for them, that every one may take a little. 8. One of his disciples, Andrew, Simon Peter's brother, saith unto him, 9. There is a lad here, which hath five barley loaves, and two fishes: but what are these among so many? 10. Jesus said, Make the people sit down. Now there was much grass in the place. So the men sat down, in number about five thousand. 11. Jesus therefore took the loaves; and having given thanks, he distributed to them that were set down; likewise also of the fishes as much as they would. 12. And when they were filled, he saith unto his disciples, Gather up the broken pieces which remain over, that nothing be lost. 13. So they gathered them up, and filled twelve baskets with broken pieces from the five barley loaves, which remained over unto them that had eaten. 14. When therefore the people saw the sign which he did, they said, This is of a truth the prophet that cometh into the world. 15. Jesus therefore perceiving that they were about to come and take him by force, to make him king, withdrew again into the mountain himself alone.*

### THE WALKING ON THE SEA

16. *And when evening came, his disciples went down unto the sea; 17. and*

*they entered into a boat, and were going over the sea unto Capernaum. And it was now dark, and Jesus had not yet come to them. 18. And the sea was rising by reason of a great wind that blew. 19. When therefore they had rowed about five and twenty or thirty furlongs, they behold Jesus walking on the sea, and drawing nigh unto the boat: and they were afraid. 20. But he saith unto them, It is I; be not afraid. 21. They were willing therefore to receive him into the boat: and straightway the boat was at the land whither they were going.*

### THE DISCOURSE
#### THE MOVEMENT AND KNOWLEDGE OF THE CROWD

*22. On the morrow the multitude which stood on the other side of the sea saw that there was none other boat there, save one, and that Jesus entered not with his disciples into the boat, but that his disciples went away alone 23. (howbeit there came boats from Tiberias nigh unto the place where they ate the bread after the Lord had given thanks): 24. when the multitude therefore saw that Jesus was not there, neither his disciples, they themselves got into the boats, and came to Capernaum, seeking Jesus. 25. And when they found him on the other side of the sea, they said unto him, Rabbi, when camest thou hither?*

#### I. THE BREAD OF LIFE

*26. Jesus answered them and said, Verily, verily, I say unto you, Ye seek me, not because ye saw signs, but because ye ate of the loaves, and were filled. 27. Work not for the meat which perisheth, but for the meat which abideth unto eternal life, which the Son of man shall give unto you: for him the Father, even God, hath sealed. 28. They said therefore unto him, What must we do, that we may work the works of God? 29. Jesus answered and said unto them, This is the work of God, that ye believe on him whom he hath sent. 30. They said therefore unto him, What then doest thou for a sign, that we may see, and believe thee? what workest thou? 31. Our fathers ate the manna in the wilderness; as it is written, He gave them bread out of heaven to eat. 32. Jesus therefore said unto them, Verily, verily, I say unto you, It was not Moses that gave you the bread out of heaven; but my Father giveth you the true bread out of heaven. 33. For the bread of God is that which cometh down out of heaven, and giveth life unto the world. 34. They said therefore unto him, Lord, evermore give us this bread. 35. Jesus said unto them, I am the bread of life: he that cometh to me shall not hunger, and he that believeth on me shall never thirst. 36. But I said unto you, that ye have seen me, and yet believe not. 37. All that which the Father giveth me shall come unto me; and him that cometh to me I will in no wise cast out. 38. For I am come down from heaven, not to do mine own will, but the will of him that sent me. 39. And this is the will of him that sent me, that of all that which he hath given me I should lose nothing, but should raise it up at the last day. 40. For this is the will of my Father, that every one that beholdeth the Son, and believeth on him, should have eternal life; and I will raise him up at the last day.*

## II. THE BREAD OF LIFE IS THE FLESH OF THE SON OF GOD

41. *The Jews therefore murmured concerning him, because he said, I am the bread which came down out of heaven.* 42. *And they said, Is not this Jesus, the son of Joseph, whose father and mother we know? how doth he now say, I am come down out of heaven?* 43. *Jesus answered and said unto them, Murmur not among yourselves.* 44. *No man can come to me, except the Father which sent me draw him: and I will raise him up in the last day.* 45. *It is written in the prophets, And they shall all be taught of God. Every one that hath heard from the Father, and hath learned, cometh unto me.* 46. *Not that any man hath seen the Father, save he which is from God, he hath seen the Father.* 47. *Verily, verily, I say unto you, He that believeth hath eternal life.* 48. *I am the bread of life.* 49. *Your fathers did eat the manna in the wilderness, and they died.* 50. *This is the bread which cometh down out of heaven, that a man may eat thereof, and not die.* 51. *I am the living bread which came down out of heaven: if any man eat of this bread, he shall live for ever: yea and the bread which I will give is my flesh, for the life of the world.*

## III. THE FLESH AHD BLOOD OF THE SON OF MAN,
### THE TRUE FOOD OF THE FAITHFUL

52. *The Jews therefore strove one with another, saying, How can this man give us his flesh to eat?* 53. *Jesus therefore said unto them, Verily, verily, I say unto you, Except ye eat the flesh of the Son of man and drink his blood, ye have not life in yourselves.* 54. *He that eateth my flesh and drinketh my blood hath eternal life; and I will raise him up at the last day.* 55. *For my flesh is meat indeed, and my blood is drink indeed.* 56. *He that eateth my flesh and drinketh my blood abideth in me, and I in him.* 57. *As the living Father sent me, and I live because of the Father; so he that eateth me, he also shall live because of me.* 58. *This is the bread which came down out of heaven: not as the fathers did eat, and died: he that eateth this bread shall live for ever.* 59. *These things said he in the synagogue, as he taught in Capernaum.*

### THE UNBELIEF OF THE DISCIPLES OF JESUS
### AND THE FAITH OF THE ELEVEN

60. *Many therefore of his disciples, when they heard this, said, This is a hard saying; who can hear it?* 61. *But Jesus knowing in himself that his disciples murmured at this, said unto them, Doth this cause you to stumble?* 62. *What then if ye should behold the Son of man ascending where ne was before?* 63. *It is the spirit that quickeneth; the flesh profiteth nothing: the words that I have spoken unto you are spirit, and are life.* 64. *But there are some of you that believe not. For Jesus knew from the beginning who they were that believed not, and who it was that should betray him.* 65. *And he said, For this cause have I said unto*

*you, that no man can come unto me, except it be given unto him of the Father.*
*66. Upon this many of his disciples went back, and walked no more with him.*
*67. Jesus said therefore unto the twelve, Would ye also go away? 68. Simon Peter*
*answered him, Lord, to whom shall we go? thou hast the words of eternal life.*
*69. And we have believed and know that thou art the Holy One of God. 70. Jesus*
*answered them, Did not I choose you the twelve, and one of you is a devil?*
*71. Now he spake of Judas the son of Simon Iscariot, for he it was that should*
*betray him, being one of the twelve. vii. 1. And after these things Jesus walked*
*in Galilee: for he would not walk in Judæa, because the Jews sought to kill him.*

Excited by the power of Jesus to heal the sick, a large crowd of
Galileans followed Him into the deserted and mountainous district
east of the sea of Tiberias. What took place there was already familiar
to the readers of the gospel. But the Evangelist does not merely repeat
the story in its well-known form; he adds that, when Jesus fed the
multitude, *the passover was at hand.* And so, at that very time, the priests
were preparing to kill the lambs, and the Jews were assembling their
families to eat unleavened bread and the flesh of an unblemished lamb,
to commemorate their past deliverance from Egypt, to acknowledge
the power and the mercy of God, and to be reminded of their peculiarity as His chosen people. The passover was the most characteristic
*feast of the Jews,* because, though primarily the commemoration of a
past event, it also provided the ground of hope for a present deliverance
and for the arrival of a present deliverer. Men thought of the promised
prophet *like unto Moses* (Deut. xviii. 15) and of the messiah who would
be their king. It was therefore not irrelevant or, at least, it did not seem
to the Evangelist to be so, that Jesus should choose this occasion, when
the Jews were seeking to kill Him (v. 18), to gather His disciples about
Him and to feed the people with bread, or that afterwards, in the
synagogue at Capernaum (*v.* 59), He should proclaim Himself to be the
living bread and finally offer His flesh that men might live and not die.
The movement from the miracle to the discourse, from Moses to Jesus
(*vv.* 32–5, cf. i. 17), and, above all, from *bread* to *flesh,* is almost unintelligible unless the reference in *v.* 4 to the passover picks up i. 29, 36,
anticipates xix. 36 (Exod. xii. 46; Num. ix. 12), and governs the whole
narrative. In passing from the miracle to the discourse, the Evangelist
has not, as has recently been so often supposed, transferred himself and
his readers from a Jewish manner of thinking to one whose background
is pagen mythology and pagan rites and ceremonies, although, like
Saint Paul (1 Cor. x. 14–22), he may be aware what he has to say has
a counterpart in the vocabulary of pagan thought and pagan practice.
The words and the proposed action of the crowd, which he has also
added to the earlier tradition (*vv.* 14, 15), though proceeding from a
grave misunderstanding, point the way, nevertheless, to a true perception of the meaning of what Jesus had done. He is the fulfilment of the

hope of the Jews, and He is also their king (xviii. 37, xix. 19–22). Nor is the background in the end different from that of the Marcan and Matthæan narratives of the Last Supper, for there too the words—surely well known to the readers of the gospel—*This is my body . . . This is my blood* are set irrevocably on the background of the Jewish passover; and Luke, whatever may have been the original text of his account of the Last Supper and whatever interpretation be given to Luke xxii. 15, also sets the last gift to the disciples of food and drink (Luke xxiv. 30 is a post-resurrection episode) firmly in the context of the preparation for the passover of the Jews (Luke xxii. 12, 13). Since, however, references to the passover are, in the earlier tradition, confined to the narratives of the Passion, they may be taken as marking no more than the historical occasion of the death of Jesus, and their importance for the understanding of His words concerning His body or flesh and blood may easily be overlooked. It is the fourth Evangelist (cf. 1 Cor. v. 7, 8) that draws attention to the theological significance of the Jewish passover. The additions he has made to the earlier narratives of the feeding of the multitude may, of course, be direct or indirect historical reminiscences, but they are of more than historical importance.

But when this has been said, the crowd is a Galilean crowd, and the discourse moves on the broad basis of the general human need for food and of the satisfaction of that need. What Jesus, according to the earlier tradition, had said, and said abruptly, only to His disciples in the immediate context of His death, He says here openly to the men and women whom He had satisfied and *filled* (v. 12) with bread and fish. Though the final need of suffering humanity is satisfied no more by bread than it is by water (iv. 13), nevertheless the eating of food, like the quenching of thirst (v. 35, vii. 37), is a parable of the final satisfaction; it is, moreover, an effective parable when it is Jesus who gives and who speaks as He gives; and a transparently effective parable, analogy, and demonstration of eternal life, when bread is brought into relation with His flesh which He will give for the life of the world (v. 51); indeed, so transparently effective that the bread which He will give, which His original disciples afterwards received, and which the readers of the gospel were accustomed to eat, ceases to be a parable, an analogy, a symbol, an anticipation, or a demonstration, but—*is* His flesh (v. 51). Eternal life, apprehended through the words and actions of the Son of man and through the historical surrender of His life, and received through the eating of bread and drinking of wine that had been by His express words related to His flesh and blood—that is, to His visible, human life in its movement to death—does not thereby become itself a visible, tangible, observable and analysable, historical thing, any more than bread was to be transformed into material flesh or blood substituted for wine. To have assumed that the promise of the prophets is fulfilled, and the desire of the Jews and, indeed, of all men satisfied, by a rearrangement of human affairs undertaken by the force of human initiative, was the fundamental and persistent misunderstanding of the Galilean crowd; for, having experienced the power of Jesus to heal the sick and to provide food for the hungry, they proposed to *take him by force* and *make him king* (*v.* 14). This misunderstanding is unbelief (*vv.* 27–9, 36); and Jesus *withdrew into the mountain himself alone* (*v.* 15), and afterwards, in a long discourse, exposed the rejection of God (*vv.* 38–40) that is involved in such behaviour and in the ideas that make it possible (*vv.* 27–31). To have supposed, as the Jews did (*v.* 52), that the offering by Jesus of His flesh to eat was ridiculous, or that the offering of His flesh and blood was, if not ridiculous, at least so crude and *hard* (*vv.* 60, 61) a requirement that even those who had hitherto been His disciples were compelled to turn aside and walk no more with Him (*v.* 66), betrayed a similar deep-seated misunderstanding and unbelief (*v.* 64 contrasted with *v.* 69). By unbelief is not, of course, meant the natural and proper repugnance to believe that men, and even the man Jesus, can say and do anything, however ridiculous; nor does the word describe the behaviour of those whose credulity, though ready to accept almost anything, is checked at the last impossibility. The unbelief of the Jews and of a large number of the credulous disciples of Jesus lay in their inability to apprehend the nature of the gift by which God gives life to the world (*vv.* 32, 33) and in their consequent inability to perceive the revelation of that gift in the audible words and visible acts of Jesus (*vv.* 35, 36, 40, 45):—*It is the spirit that quickeneth; the flesh profiteth nothing: the words that I have spoken unto you are spirit, and are life* (*v.* 63).

To quicken or give life is the operation of the invisible spirit of God. Eternal life is the gift of God, the gift *from heaven* (*v.* 32b). Since God is invisible (*v.* 46), His gift is apprehended only by faith. Neither the Jews nor the Galilean crowds nor, in fact, the generality of men recognize this first step in the knowledge of God and of the world, this prolegomenon to theology and to life in the world; or, if they do recognize it, they do so only in theory; they do not take it so seriously that it governs all thought and experience and every human act. The Jews and the Galileans are religious, but they are religious in the sense that they make of the gift of God an observable and even edible thing, like the bread that Moses gave to their fathers; and so they expect the fulfilment of the purpose of God to be a future event, a repetition of what Moses did (*vv.* 30, 31, 58), more powerful perhaps and more universal, but nevertheless a thing that crystallizes into a king and a kingdom. This means in the end that what depends upon the energy of men is regarded as the realization of the goal and aim and purpose of God. With the theological vocabulary of Scripture on their lips and in their hearts, they labour and strive for that which—*perisheth* (*vv.* 26, 27). This is the *world* that does not believe, that in the pride of its 'fleshiness' cannot believe (*v.* 44), and that, by a strange paradox, misunderstands itself, its history, its 'flesh'; for when flesh has become the last word—*it profiteth nothing*. The crowds misunderstand the scriptural story of Moses and their fathers, they misunderstand the gift they have just received from Jesus of bread and fish, they misunderstand the political aspirations of Judaism, and finally they misunderstand of necessity the words of Jesus concerning His flesh and blood and the nature of His mission. To the Evangelist, the behaviour of the Jews and the Galileans is no mere isolated episode. The unbelief of the chosen people of God mirrors and reveals the unbelief of the world which does not recognize or apprehend that it owes its being to the Word of God (i. 3–5), and which overlooks the judgement that falls upon it when it thinks of itself as a thing-in-itself. So great is the sensitiveness of the Evangelist to the unbelief of the Jews and of the generality of men (i. 10, 11) that he cannot for one moment suppose that faith and knowledge can be secured by an appeal to philosophical or popular theology, even if it be formally correct philosophy or correct speculative or realistic theology. Jesus—His words and actions, and finally His offering of Himself—is the place, and here lies the stern seriousness and provocation of the sixth chapter of the Fourth Gospel, He is the only place (*vv.* 35, 40, 47, 48, 53) where human faith is secure from corruption: *Except ye eat the flesh of the Son of man and drink his blood, ye have not life in yourselves*. And moreover, this security of faith is itself the gift of God, even when men have been, like the Jews and the Galileans and the chosen disciples of Jesus, confronted by the deliverer and Saviour of the world (*vv.* 42–4, 64, 65).

The bald, dogmatic assertions that *it is the spirit that giveth life* and that *the flesh profiteth nothing* cannot therefore be taken to mean that the whole panorama of the natural world and the whole vista of human history are trivial and insignificant, but that, nevertheless, there is another supernatural, spiritual, heavenly world into which men and women must be transferred if they are to lay hold on eternity and escape from what is transitory. Nor can the third and last equally dogmatic statement in *v.* 63—*The words that I have spoken unto you are spirit, and are life*—be interpreted to mean that from the wreckage of the visible order of the flesh the audible words of Jesus alone survive as spiritual things that have, as it were, escaped, and been detached from, the general perishableness of human affairs. The importance assigned by the Evangelist in this very chapter to the work of Moses, to the history underlying the concrete existence of the Galilean crowd, to the bread and fish that had been given them, to the actions of Jesus as well as to His words, to His death, and to the flesh and blood, not of the Son of God, but of the Son of man (*v.* 53); his general insistence in the prologue to his gospel upon the creation of the world by the word of God

(i. 3), upon the relation to God which belongs to all men and women at the moment of their physical birth (i. 9), and upon the *flesh* of Jesus as the ground and occasion and place of Christian, apostolic apprehension of truth and of the glory of God (i. 14)—all this, and indeed much more, makes it quite impossible to suppose that at the conclusion of the discourse he should have denied everything he had said and fallen back upon an almost intolerable ultimate dualism and into a quite intolerable pessimism concerning the world in which men live and move and have their being. If, however, what had been said in the preceding discourse to the Jews is borne steadily in mind, and if the modern reader of the gospel permits himself no unauthorized rearrangement of the text and no excision of its 'uncomfortable points', what the Evangelist says is neither obscure nor inconsistent. The visible world, including the *flesh* of Jesus the Son of man, including also His audible words, is trivial and unimportant, if it is regarded as existing by and in itself and if its goal and purpose is attained by what it makes or shall make of itself (v. 18, 19, 30, 31). If history ends in *a* kingdom (v. 15, xix. 12, 15), if the meaning of the order of nature is exhausted in physical reproduction and generation (iii. 6), and if religion be content to assert that this behaviour and procedure is the meaning of the world, the goal of human affairs, and the final purpose of God; then, what can be seen and heard and investigated is meaningless and profitless. The vast, subtle, universal, and blasphemous philosophy of sin by which men are in various ways encircled and engulfed and by which they glorify themselves is destroyed by the words of Jesus. The actions of Jesus were not dumb deeds capable of a number of different interpretations, capable even of being interpreted so as to support this godless philosophy of life. His deeds were, all of them, like His death, accompanied by words that declared the glory of God and His kingdom. By His words Jesus gave to His actions the strictest theological setting and thereby gave to the world and to all human action their final meaning. For this reason—and here the present tense of the copulative verb *to be* is again unescapable—the words of Jesus *are* spirit and life, just as the Son of man *is* the Son of God, *is* the bread of life (vv. 35, 48), *is* the living bread which came down out of heaven (v. 51), *is* the truth, the resurrection and the life, and as the bread that has been related to His death, *is* His flesh. Since, however, this present tense is open to grave misunderstanding, and may indeed be used to justify that very rejection of God which it is the purpose of the Evangelist to exclude like all prophetic and apostolic scriptural writers, he guards it from misunderstanding by an unexpected use of the eschatological future—*I will raise him up at the last day* (vv. 39, 40, 44)—by the sudden introduction in v. 62 of a reference to the Ascension of Jesus (cf. iii. 13, xiv. 20) as that which authorizes and explains. His language about His flesh and blood, and by the two final assertions that *the flesh profiteth nothing* and that *it is the spirit that quickeneth.* A thing *is* what it signifies: finally, therefore, it is what it *is* to God. The visible world *is* God's creation, Jesus *is* His Son, the flesh and blood of the Son of man *are* the answer that God has given to the two questions of Job, *Whence then cometh wisdom? And where is the place of understanding?* (Job xxviii. 20), and His words *are* spirit and life. This does not mean that the spirit of God has been transformed into the flesh of Jesus, but it does mean that the Son of man is the accredited place of faith and of apprehension (i. 51).

It is the purpose of the Evangelist to declare that the knowledge of God and of the world is within the competence of men through faith in Jesus. Therefore, though in this section of the gospel he is concerned primarily with unbelief and especially with the unbelief of the Galileans, he never permits the faith and knowledge of the true disciples of Jesus to fall altogether out of sight. Faith and unbelief are closely related the one to the other. Unbelief can be understood only by those who believe, and the faith of the disciples did, in fact, spring out of unbelief. The original disciples of Jesus were Jews and Galileans. And so, in rewriting the story of the Feeding of the Five Thousand, he not only adds the reference to the passover and the words and intentions of the crowd, but also expands and makes more precise the conversation between Jesus and His disciples (cf. *vv.* 5–9 with Mark vi. 37, 38, viii. 4, 5). It was Philip who reckoned up the amount of money required to provide even a small meal for so large a crowd: it was Andrew, Peter's brother, who reckoned up the food that was actually available. Both disciples declare the resources at the disposal of Jesus to be wholly insufficient. In spite of their proximity to Jesus, and in spite of His employment of them to assist in the distribution of the food, their ideas do not differ radically from those of the crowd any more than they had differed from those of the woman of Samaria (iv. 33). Jesus therefore withdraws from them almost as completely as He withdraws from the crowd; and the words *it was now dark, and Jesus had not yet come to them* (*v.* 17b) are not without significance. At the conclusion of the discourse, the Evangelist returns to the disciples. He marks first the distinction between those who walked no more with Jesus and the twelve who remained, and then between the eleven headed by Peter, who believed and knew, and the one, Judas, who *is a devil* and was to betray Him. The traditional narrative of the confession of Peter underlies the conclusion of the discourse. Like Saint Luke, the Evangelist links the confession of Peter to the Feeding of the Five Thousand; but whereas Luke had deleted the reference to Satan, he transfers it from Simon Peter to Judas the son of Simon Iscariot (Mark viii. 27–33; Matt. xvi. 13–23; Luke ix. 10–22). What the faith of the disciples was and how their knowledge came to be what it was, the Evangelist does not now say; nor does he draw out the meaning of the story of the coming of Jesus to His disciples during the storm, or of the words spoken to them in their distress—*It is I: be not afraid* (*v.* 20). All this is for the present deferred, since it is to be the subject-matter of the last discourses of Jesus: *Let not your heart be troubled. . . . I come again, and will receive you unto myself* (xiv. 1–3). *. . . When he, the Spirit of truth, is come, he shall guide you into all the truth* (xvi. 13). He here records the Walking on the Sea, partly because it was so closely associated in the tradition with the Feeding of the Five Thousand, and partly because it was necessary in order to reunite Jesus and His disciples. But, though the crowd suspects a second miracle, *Rabbi, when camest thou hither?* (*v.* 25), no answer is given to this question and the story plays no part in the discourse, unless perhaps there be some connection between it and *v.* 62.

The sequence of thought that gives to the sixth chapter of Saint John's Gospel its steady movement and progress may at first sight seem to be peculiarly Johannine. But it forms the background of the synoptic tradition also. There too, in spite of the tumultuous acceptance of Jesus by the Galileans, His mission in their midst is pronounced to have been in the end unfruitful: *Then began he to upbraid the cities wherein most of his mighty works were done, because they repented not. Woe unto thee, Chorazin! woe unto thee, Bethsaida! . . . and thou, Capernaum. . . .* (Matt. xi. 20–4; Luke x. 12–15; a Q Saying). There too the story of the feeding of the crowds is narrated so as to anticipate and foreshadow the words and actions of Jesus at the Last Supper (cf. Mark vi. 41), viii. 6; Matt. xiv. 19, xv. 36; Luke ix. 16 with Mark xiv. 22–5; Matt. xxvi. 26–9; Luke xxii. 14–19, xxiv. 30–5; 1 Cor. xi. 23–6). There too the fact of satisfaction or fulness provided by a meal is *fulfilled* only in the Kingdom of God: *I will not eat it* [this passover], *until it be fulfilled in the kingdom of God. . . . I will not drink from henceforth of the fruit of the vine, until the kingdom of God shall come . . . I appoint unto you a kingdom, even as my Father appointed unto me, that ye may eat and drink at my table in my kingdom* (Luke xxii. 16, 18, 29, 30, cf. Mark xiv. 25; Matt. xxvi. 29). There too Jesus is the place in history where the kingdom or dominion or glory of God is accepted or rejected (e.g. Matt. x. 40, cf. xi. 27; Luke x. 16, cf. 22). There too the refusal to follow Him is the rejection of eternal life (Mark x. 13–31). There too the issue that is raised by the mission of Jesus, and most clearly by His teaching in parables, is the meaning of the whole visible world (e.g. Mark iv. 11, 12). There too this final meaning is no tangible, analysable, observable thing: it is apprehended only by faith (Mark iv. 40, xi. 22; Luke xvii. 19, 20). And the synoptic gospels, like the Fourth Gospel, move to the anticipation and demonstration of the faith of the disciples of Jesus and to the unbelief of the Jews: this is the meaning of the resurrection narratives and of the whole story of the Acts of the Apostles. The difference between the Fourth Gospel and the other three does not consist in a difference of theme, but in the clarity and consistence with which the later Evangelist has apprehended and set out for the benefit of the Greek-speaking Christians of the next generation the essential subject-matter of the earlier tradition.

If the above summary has at all caught and reproduced the run of the chapter taken as a whole, certain negative and positive conclusions follow. The discourse is not a 'Eucharistic Discourse', if by that title it is meant that the Evangelist has presented his readers with a reflection upon or a preachment about the Eucharistic practices, beliefs, and experiences of Christians at the beginning of the second century or earlier. Nor did he intend to set forth a prophetic and comprehensive direction by Jesus concerning the future eucharistic worship of the Church. Still less is the discourse 'anti-Eucharistic' or 'anti-Sacramental', if by the use of these ugly words it is to be understood that the Evangelist has purposely set the teaching of Jesus over against His actions, and digestion of His words over against participation in a mystical communal act. The sustained and primary purpose of the Evangelist is to declare the true meaning of an episode that stood importantly in the Christian tradition of the words and actions of Jesus. He was aware that the Feeding of the Five Thousand raised and solved more questions than could easily be detected in the form in which the story was normally told. In order that his readers may apprehend the episode, he places them midway between it and the occasion when, at the meal on the eve of His crucifixion, Jesus declared to His disciples alone the meaning of His life; that is to say, he set them midway between the apparent satisfaction provided by the partaking of food and drink, illustrated by the Feeding of the Five Thousand and the giving of the manna and the passover meal of the Jews, and the occasion when every kind of material and historical and psychological satisfaction is shown to be illusory, and when room is thereby made for the final satisfaction provided by the reverse and spiritual action of God which was the theme of the teaching of Jesus and the meaning of His life and death. In the context of this disillusionment and faith the Eucharist must, of course, be understood; but so must also the existence of the Church, and indeed of human life altogether. The theme of the discourse is, therefore, unbelief and faith. The theme is worked out in the history of Jesus and in the presence of the Galileans and of His original disciples. But it is so worked out that the world and the Church, confronted by the same final issue, may overlook and overhear.

# COMMENTARY

### THE FEEDING OF THE FIVE THOUSAND

vi. 1–4. *Went away—great multitude—followed* echo the form of the

288

narrative in the earlier tradition (Mark vi. 32–4; Luke ix. 11. See INTRODUCTION, pp. 70, 76, 77). The general reference to miracles of healing, the ascent of the mountain, the peculiar position occupied by the disciples recall Mark iii. 7–13; Matt. iv. 23–v. 2; Luke vi. 12–20, cf. Matt. xv. 29–32, and suggest that the miracle, as in Mark vi. 34; Luke ix. 11, was preceded by teaching. The sea of Galilee was called the sea of Tiberias (cf. xxi. 1) by the Rabbis (Strack-Billerbeck, Schlatter, *D.E.J.*), by Josephus (*B.J.* iii. 57, iv. 456), and by Pausanias (v. 7, 3); but it is not so named in the synoptic gospels. The city of Tiberias, on the western shore of the lake, was built by Herod Antipas in A.D. 26 in honour of the Emperor, to be the capital of Galilee. *v.* 4 is peculiar to the narrative of the Feeding of the Five Thousand in the Fourth Gospel. It was not introduced in order to assist the readers of the gospel to make out a chronology of the life of Jesus, but in order to provide them with the proper background of His acts and words. At the passover the Jews commemorated the freedom of Israel and were reminded of their own peculiar relation to God by a series of rites and ceremonies in which unleavened *bread* and the *flesh* and *blood* of an unblemished lamb were of especial significance (Exod. xii. 7, 8, 13, 46).

*vv.* 5–9. The conversation between Jesus and His disciples (Mark vi. 35–8) is here made more precise by the naming of Andrew and Philip (cf. i. 40–9, xii. 21, 22, xiv. 8, 9). The scepticism of Philip, the *lad*— there is no reason to suppose with Loisy that the Evangelist intends him to represent the deacon at the Eucharist—and the *barley bread* are reminiscent of the miracle of Elisha (2 Kings iv. 42). Barley was the food of cattle, barley bread of the very poor; the reference may, however, be to the bread commonly used during the passover season. The Greek word translated *fish* is a diminutive used in the papyri for fish suitable to be eaten 'as a tit-bit along with bread' (Moulton-Milligan, *Vocabulary of the Greek Testament*). The word is found neither in the LXX, except in one manuscript of Tobit (ii. 2, Codex Sinaiticus. See, however, Num. xi. 22), nor in the New Testament, except here and in xxi. 9–14.

*vv.* 10–13. The word 'Eucharist'—*when he had given thanks*—is repeated in the general reference to the miracle in *v.* 23 (see note). It belongs firmly to the synoptic tradition of the Feeding of the Four Thousand (Mark viii. 6; Matt. xv. 36) and of the Last Supper (Mark xiv. 23; Matt. xxvi. 27; Luke xxii. 19, cf. 1 Cor. xi. 24), and became almost a technical term in the letters of Ignatius (*Philad.* iv., *Smyrn.* vi. 2, viii. 1; cf. *Didache*, ix. 5, x. 1, 2, xiv. 1; Justin, *Apol.* i. 65, 66). In the synoptic narrative of the Feeding of the Five Thousand, however, Jesus *blessed* the bread. The reading in the A.V. *He distributed to the disciples, and the disciples to them that were set down* is weakly attested in the manuscripts, and is probably a gloss introduced from Matt. xiv. 19. The command that *nothing be lost* is explained in *v.* 39. That which has been given by God must not, and, indeed, cannot be lost. The care of the remains of the Eucharist was felt to be required by these words (Tert. *De Corona* 3, Orig. *Hom. in* Exod. xiii. 3; *Apost. Const.* viii. 13). This particular reference does not, however, seem to be intended by the Evangelist. The twelve baskets (Mark vi. 43) corresponds with the twelve apostles. The number of the apostles is assumed in the Fourth Gospel, but is directly mentioned only in vi. 67–71 and xx. 24.

*vv.* 14, 15. The consequences of the Feeding of the Five Thousand are recorded only in the Fourth Gospel. The crowd, judging that one who is able to feed them miraculously can also with miraculous power lead them against the Romans, decides to appoint as king the man whom God has manifestly appointed as His prophet. Movements of revolt were most frequent in Galilee, and they were led by men who were supposed to be prophets (Josephus, *Ant.* xvii. 271, 272, xx. 97, 98, 169; *B.J.* iii. 42, 43). Jesus, knowing what is involved in the excited applause of the crowd, flees—Codex Sinaiticus, some manuscripts of the Old Latin Version, the Vulgate, the Curetonian Syriac Version, Tertullian, and Augustine have the variant reading *flees* for *withdrew*—back into the mountain in order to be alone (Mark vi. 47) and, if the Evangelist assumes his readers to be familiar with the synoptic tradition (Mark vi. 46; Matt. xiv. 23), in order to pray. In spite of Loisy's comparison of ii. 3, 18 with Matt. iv. 3, 5, 6, there seems no reason to suppose that the Evangelist regarded the proposal of the Galileans as a temptation similar to that recorded in Matt. iv. 8, 9; Luke iv. 5–8. In the discourse that follows, the misunderstanding of the Galileans is set forth: treating the miracle merely as an act of feeding (*v.* 26), they misunderstand the nature of the salvation Jesus brings (*vv.* 33–5) and of His sovereignty over them (cf. xviii. 36, 37).

### THE WALKING ON THE SEA

*vv.* 16–21. The Walking on the Sea concludes the episode of the Feeding of the Five Thousand in the earlier tradition (Mark vi. 45–52; Matt. xiv. 22–33). Luke omitted the conclusion and, indeed, the whole of Mark vi. 45–viii. 25. As a consequence of this omission, the confession of Peter follows immediately after the Feeding of the Five Thousand in his gospel (Luke ix. 10–22, cf. John vi. 68, 69). The narrative of the Walking on the Sea in the Fourth Gospel is recognizably Johannine, but it assumes knowledge of the form of the earlier tradition. The disciples, apparently of their own initiative and not at the command of the Lord (Mark vi. 46), descend to the shore and embark for Capernaum (Bethsaida Mark vi. 45, omitted in Matthew, but cf. Luke ix. 10) in the only available boat (*v.* 22). Separated from Jesus, they are surrounded by darkness—Codices Sinaiticus and Bezae say that the darkness *overtook* (cf. i. 5) them—and caught by a great (Rev. vi. 12, 13, xi. 19, xvi. 9) wind and a rising sea. In the extremity of their danger, when

they are about three and a half miles from the shore, they are terrified
at the sight of Jesus walking on the sea. Their fear is, however, removed
by the words *I am; be not afraid* (prefaced in Mark vi. 50; Matt. xiv. 27,
by *Be of good cheer*). The mysterious statement *I am* (A.V., R.V. *It is I*)
is repeated in viii. 24, 58, xiii. 19, xviii. 5, 6 and is reminiscent of Exod.
iii. 14, cf. Deut. xxxii. 39; Isa. xli. 4, xliii. 10, 25, xlviii. 12; Rev. i. 8, 17.
The disciples wish to take Jesus up into the boat (Mark vi. 51; Matt.
xiv. 32); and (Bernard compares vii. 44, xvi. 19 for an unfulfilled wish,
but see i. 43, v. 35, viii. 44) they reach at once their safe destination.

The concluding words of the narrative are not an allusion to Philo's
description of the Logos as the pilot of the soul (*De Cherubim* 36; *De
Migrat. Abrah.* 6), but rather, as Bauer notes, to Ps. cvii. 28–30, *So he
bringeth them unto the haven where they would be*. The scribe of the comparatively unimportant Codex Nitriensis (R) recognized the allusion and
assimilated the text to the text of the Psalm. The Greek preposition
translated walking *on* the sea (Rev. x. 5, cf. Job ix. 8) can, of course,
be translated *by* or *along*, in which case it would mean 'by the sea shore',
as in xxi. 4 in some manuscripts; and the narrative would then be 'void
of miracle' (Bernard). In the context, however, this translation would
seem to be impossible. The boat was twenty-five to thirty furlongs
(about three and a half miles) from the shore, an accurate gloss on
Mark's *in the midst of the sea* (cf. the variant reading in Matt. xiv. 24,
Codices Vaticanus, Koridethi, *the boat was many furlongs distant from the
shore*). Josephus gives the width of the lake as forty furlongs (*B.J.* iii.
506); its greatest breadth is, however, about seven miles (Lagrange).
And moreover, the question in *v.* 25 presumes a second miracle. It is
therefore difficult to accept Bernard's statements that the supernatural
story in Mark and Matthew represents a 'transformation of the Johannine tradition' and that the fourth Evangelist has retold Mark's story
'in such a manner as to correct it, by omitting any suggestion of miracle'
(see Bernard's note on vi. 19 and Introduction, p. clxxvi).

THE DISCOURSE

THE MOVEMENT AND KNOWLEDGE OF THE CROWD

*vv.* 22–5. The discourse is delivered to the crowd that Jesus had
miraculously fed, and is built up on the basis of that feeding. The
conclusion of the narrative of the Walking on the Sea had, however,
left Jesus and His disciples at Capernaum, whilst the crowd remained
still on the other side of the Lake. The purpose of these verses is to show
why and how the five thousand or those of them who lived at Capernaum (Lagrange) or who were the most zealous (Westcott, Bernard)
crossed the lake and found Jesus. They had noticed that there had been
only one boat available for Jesus and His disciples and that the disciples alone had made use of it to cross the lake. In the morning Jesus

had disappeared and His disciples had not returned to fetch Him. Suspecting a second miracle, they draw the correct conclusion that He had rejoined His disciples at Capernaum. Fortunately, other boats arrive from Tiberias, and the crowd is transported in them to Capernaum, where they seek and find Jesus, and ask Him when and, presumably, how He has arrived there. Jesus directs their attention not to His own movements but to the significance of the fact that He has fed them.

[There are a number of variant readings in these verses. Most, if not all, of them are probably due to different attempts to smooth out the awkward grammatical construction of the original text (Bernard). The words *after that the Lord had given thanks* (v. 23) are omitted in Codex Bezae, in one important Greek minuscule, in the Sinaitic and Curetonian Syriac, and in two manuscripts of the Old Latin Version.]

### I. THE BREAD OF LIFE

The framework of the discourse had already been anticipated in iv. 7–15. Jesus is the Giver of Eternal Life. But now, the woman of Samaria yields to the crowd of Galileans, water to bread, the well of Jacob to the manna given by Moses; and in the last analysis, the water of Baptism is replaced by the bread of the Eucharist.

*vv.* 26–31. The crowd did not seek Jesus (v. 24): they sought the bread with which they had been filled. They did not recognize that, when they were filled with perishable bread, they did not receive the final satisfaction, but an effective sign of the imperishable bread which the Son of man will give them. The subject-matter of the discourse, stated concisely in the words *work . . . for the meat which abideth unto eternal life* (cf. iv. 14), is set in motion, not by the Feeding of the Five Thousand, but by the straightforward fact that the Galilean peasants work, and for that reason receive their sustenance from those for whom they work. This realistic situation is, however, not an end in itself. If, as Chrysostom says, men are 'nailed to the things of this life', their work has not been wrought in God nor are they men who do the truth (iii. 21, iv. 34). That they receive bread is a parable or sign of the gift of the abiding and eternal food which Jesus the Son of man will give them (contrast v. 27). And He will give this gift, not of His own initiative, but because He is sealed, authenticated and consecrated by God, because He is, in fact, His Son (*vv.* 32, 40, cf. i. 32). The act of sealing is the sign of ownership (Rev. vii. 3) and authenticity (iii. 33); it may also suggest the consecration or setting apart for sacrifice (Westcott, cf. x. 36, xvii. 14). The descriptive title *Son of man* echoes the earlier evangelical tradition, but is altogether removed from its eschatological setting. The gift of God is offered to men in and through the historical mission of His Son. The Evangelist, nevertheless, retains the future tense—*will give*—(contrast *v.* 32)—because the final gift of God is received and most clearly apprehended through the death of Jesus (*v.* 51, cf. iv. 14, vii. 39), which in the perspective of the narrative still lies in the future. [Codex Sinaiticus, Codex Bezae, two manuscripts of the Old Latin Version, Codex Fossatensis of the Vulgate, the Gothic Version, the Curetonian, but not the Sinaitic, Syriac, read *is giving*, presumably by assimilation to *v.* 32. The Savilian and Benedictine editions of Chrysostom's commentary have the present tense in the text of *v.* 27b set out for comment but the future tense in the body of the commentary.]

If the propriety of the analogy is not to be obscured, the primacy of the gift of food must not drive out the necessity of work, for the gift depends upon work done. The crowd therefore rightly asks the question, What then are the works required of men by God? The answer to this question is clear and unmistakably precise. There is but one work (contrast the singular in *v.* 29 with the plural in *v.* 28): it is required of men that they would believe in Him whom God has sent (1 John iii. 23). On this Act of faith everything depends. And yet, it would be to misunderstand what the Evangelist has here said, if it were supposed that the Act of faith were an act grounded in an independent, individual decision to believe. The Act of faith is itself the work of God (*v.* 44, cf. Rom. xii. 3). Neither the fourth Evangelist nor Saint Paul is driven finally to a Pelagian or even semi-Pelagian conception of faith. The crowd rightly perceives that what is being demanded of them is that they should believe in Jesus, *What then doest thou for a sign, that we may see, and believe thee?* Confronted by an absolute claim, for the authority to give eternal life is the final authority, the crowd requires a visible act that will correspond with and make evident the invisible sealing by God to which Jesus had referred as providing Him with His authority. Faith depends upon sight (Mark xv. 32) and sight requires something to see. The crowd therefore demands not only a strange occurrence like their feeding on the other side of the lake, which had led them to desire to make Him king, but a sign from heaven which would justify them in believing in Him as the giver of eternal life (Mark viii. 11; Matt. xvi. 1, cf. Luke xi. 16; 1 Cor. i. 22), and as entrusted with the final authority of God. What the crowd asked and demanded was that they should see food actually falling from heaven as their fathers had seen it falling in the desert (Exod. xvi. 4–36; Neh. ix. 15; Ps. lxxviii. 23–9, cv. 40; Wisd. xvi. 20, cf. Deut. viii. 3).

[The story of the miraculous provision of the manna in the desert provided the Rabbis with suitable language to describe the rich gifts of God in the messianic age (cf. Rev. ii. 17). 'Ye shall not find it [the manna] in this age, but ye shall find it in the age that is coming' (Mekilta Exod. xvi. 25): 'For whom has it now been prepared? For the righteous in the age that is coming. Everyone who believeth is worthy and eateth of it' (Tanchuma *Beshallach* xxi. 66): 'What did the first redeemer? He brought down the manna. And the last redeemer will bring down the manna' (Rabba Eccles. i. 9). For further references see Schlatter, *D.E.J.*, and Strack-Billerbeck, Charles on Rev. ii. 17. Philo found in the manna a type of the divine Logos, the heavenly sustenance of the soul (Westcott, Bauer). The reference by the fourth Evangelist to the manna need not therefore be due to his creative imagination. Indeed it may be that the Marcan account of the Feeding of the Five Thousand *in the desert* already contained the suggestion that the action of Jesus was the messianic counterpart of the miracle of Moses. Eisler (*Z.N.T.W.* 1925, vol. xxiv, pp. 190 sqq.) proposed to interpret the petition in the Lord's Prayer, *Give us to-day the bread for to-morrow* (Matt. vi. 11) as an allusion to the double gift of the manna on the day before the sabbath and therefore as an eschatological petition for the final messianic peace. The Rabbinic doctrine that the manna had been among the things created on the eve of the creation of the sabbath belongs within the same horizon of thought (Sifre Deut. 355, the Palestinian Targum on Exod. xvi. 15, see Schlatter, *D.E.J.*). The association by the fourth Evangelist of the manna both with the Feeding of the Five Thousand and with what is almost an echo of the petition in the Lord's Prayer (*vv.* 32, 34) may therefore be due to his sensitiveness to earlier Christian tradition (cf. 1 Cor. x. 3 sqq.).]

*vv.* 32–40. There is no simple answer to the question of the crowd. As Saint Paul knew (1 Cor. i. 18–26) there is no absolute and final visible miracle that can either authenticate Jesus or demonstrate the power of God. The whole of the rest of the discourse sets forth the answer of faith to the ignorant and, in the end, blasphemous question that had been asked. The fourth Evangelist, moreover, provides not *an* answer but *the* answer authorized by Jesus Himself. It is therefore prefaced by a reduplicated *Verily*.

[1]The truth is now stated clearly. He who descends from heaven is the Bread of God, given, not for the sustenance of a fugitive race, but for the life of the whole world. Those who follow Him and believe in Him will never hunger nor thirst. *I am the Bread of Life*. The crowd has seen, but, in spite of the words spoken in v. 30–47, does not believe; they possess, like the disciples in iv. 31–4, only material sight, and are able neither to perceive the sign in the miracle, nor to see in Jesus the Son of God. The permanent satisfaction of thirst as well as of hunger,

---

[1] From this point onwards the commentary was not given final form by the author, and is printed as it was written by him before 1931. The reader is referred to the editor's Preface for further information about the author's method, and the state of his work at the time of his death.

is added (cf. Matt. v. 6, vi. 31; Luke vi. 21, xii. 29; Rev. vii. 17), not in order to round off a literary phrase, but in anticipation of *vv.* 53–6, and suggests the wine of the Eucharist. The place of the fishes is taken by the Blood of the Christ, since at this point they provide no adequate symbol. No reference is therefore made to them in the discourse.

*vv.* 37–40. The problem of unbelief is resolved in the assertion that the whole activity of faith, and even the work of the Christ, depends upon the Father's will. The believers are the gift of God; they alone can come to the Son. Nor can the Son Himself outrun the Father's will (*v.* 30), that is, He cannot persuade to faith those whom the Father has not given Him. But of the true believers none will be refused and none will be lost (x. 28, xvii. 12). They possess eternal life because they see the Son and believe in Him. He will therefore raise them up at the last day. The phrase *I should lose nothing* refers back to *v.* 12. As the consecrated bread must not be wasted, so the believers who have been consecrated by God and presented to the Son cannot be lost. They will neither be refused when they come to the Saviour nor finally cast out into the outer darkness at the Judgement (cf. xii. 31; Matt. viii. 12, xxii. 13, xxv. 30). The unbelievers correspond with *the meat which perisheth*, the believers with *the meat which abideth unto eternal life* (*v.* 27). The whole action of the Christ as the Saviour is contrasted with the action of the Pharisees (ix. 34).

The permanence of belief when once attained is apparently contradicted by the apostasy of Judas (xvii. 12) who went out into the night (xiii. 30), and by the apostasy of his spiritual children, who separated themselves from the Christian fellowship and returned to the world because they ceased to believe that Jesus came *in flesh* (1 John iv. 1 sqq., cf. ii. 18 sqq.; 2 John 7, cf. xv. 6). The relation between Divine Grace or predestination and human freedom is not felt by the author of the Johannine writings to present a problem. He does not directly discuss it, and in this he agrees with the other New Testament writers. The unbelief of the Jews and the apostasy of those who had been Christians are clearly treated as a responsible action involving final destruction (v. 40). The Jews are exhorted to work for the true bread, and this work is defined as faith. But the whole problem of unbelief (cf. Rom. ix–xi) can also be treated as depending in the last instance upon the will of God. Even Judas goes *that the scripture might be fulfilled* (xvii. 12). The two truths are held together in no logical equilibrium.

### II. THE BREAD OF LIFE IS THE FLESH OF THE SON OF GOD

The murmuring of the Jews corresponds with the murmuring of their fathers in the desert. They preserve the genuine succession of unbelief. In the Son of God, who descended from heaven as the true manna, they can see only the son of Joseph and Mary. Such ignorance proves that they are unmoved by God and must therefore inevitably perish at the last day. There is only one means of salvation. The recognition of the Son is the acknowledgement of the Father. There is no other way to God. Only the Son has seen the Father, and has come direct from His Presence. Belief is life and unbelief is death. Against death the gift of Moses provided no security, but the gift of the Son is eternal life for those who eat the living Bread that descended from heaven. This Bread is the Flesh of the Son of God offered for the salvation of the world and consumed by the faithful.

*v.* 41. In accordance with the purpose of the discourse the crowd merges into the Jewish people and their rulers, which it represents (cf. v. 10, 15, 16, 18). For the murmuring cf. Exod. xvi. 2 sqq., xvii. 3; Num. xi. 1, xiv. 27; 1 Cor. x 10; Luke v. 30, xv. 2.

*v.* 42, cf. i. 46. The paternity of Jesus is as well known to the Jews in the synagogue at Capernaum as it is to the crowd in the synagogue at Nazareth (Luke iv. 22, cf. Mark vi. 3; Matt. xiii. 55). The author presumably has in mind the earlier tradition. The Codex Sinaiticus, one Old Latin manuscript and both the Old Syriac Versions omit *and mother* because Jesus was born of Mary. The paternity of Jesus was a point of controversy between Jews and Christians. In another passage, when the unknown paternity of Jesus is in question, the Jews acquiesce and the supposition of his illegitimate birth provides them with a suitable explanation (viii. 25–7, 41, see DETACHED NOTE 2, 'The Birth of Jesus in the Fourth Gospel', pp. 163 sqq.). The ignorance of the Jews is the result, not the cause, of their unbelief (Loisy).

*vv.* 43–5. The divine origin of Jesus is known only to those who are drawn (Hos. xi. 4) and taught of God (v. 37, xii. 40, cf. Mark iv. 11, 12; Matt. xiii. 10 sqq.; Luke viii. 18); and the prophecies in Isa. liv. 13; Jer. xxiv. 7, xxxi. 33, 34; Mic. iv. 2 are fulfilled by reference not to the Law but to the knowledge of the Son (cf. 1 John ii. 20–9; 1 Thess. iv. 9).

*v.* 46. The inability of the Jews to recognize the Son makes it impossible for them to know God, since He alone has seen the Father (i. 18, iii. 13, vii. 28, 29) and can bring the true and perfect revelation of God to men. In xiv. 9 the further consequence is drawn *He that hath seen Me, hath seen the Father*.

*vv.* 47–51a. The story of the manna (cf. *v.* 35) is now shown to contain its own refutation. Those who ate the manna died (Num. xiv. 23; Deut. i. 35), but the Son is the living Bread (cf. iv. 10, 14, vii. 38), and those who eat of the Bread that came down from heaven will live for ever. For the double meaning of *death*, cf. v. 58; Matt. x. 39. The resolution of *cometh down* into *came down* corresponds with the double truth which the author has to express. The Bread which the faithful receive (*cometh down*) depends for its efficacy upon the Incarnation of the Son of God (*came down*).

*v.* 51b. Cf. iii. 16, 17, xii. 32; 1 John ii. 1, 2, iv. 10.

The symbolism of the discourse, and of the Passover miracle which precedes it (*v.* 4), now demands a clear reference to the sacrifice of the Lamb and to the Eucharist as the feast upon the sacrifice. It is moreover peculiarly appropriate at this point because the death of the Christ most effectually moves men to faith (cf. *v.* 44 with xii. 32, 33). The saying contains a double reference. First, redemptive significance is assigned to the death of the Son of God, who is to offer His Flesh as a sacrifice for the life of the world; secondly sacrificial significance is assigned to the Eucharist, which is at once the concrete commemoration of the sacrifice once offered and the guarantee of its efficacy, and also communicates its benefits to those who partake with faith. Both these references are contained in the synoptic narrative of the Last Supper and in 1 Cor. xi. 23 sqq., of which the words here are reminiscent and explanatory. The substitution of *Flesh* for *Body* is the natural corollary to i. 14. *Flesh* not *Body* belongs to the Eucharistic terminology in Ignat. *Rom.* vii. 3; *Philad.* iv. 1, xi. 2; *Smyrn.* vi. 2, cf. Just. Mart. *Apol.* i. 66. The Eucharistic feast has its origin in the sacrificial death of the Son of God, and in the words of the Christ which formally invested that death with redemptive significance. In treating the discourse upon the Feeding of the Five Thousand as the occasion upon which the Christ did formally invest His death with such significance, the author of the Fourth Gospel anticipates the institution of the Eucharist, and for this reason perhaps it is presumed, but not recorded, in chapters xiii–xvii.

The variant readings *The bread which I will give for the life of the world is my flesh* and *The bread which I will give is my flesh, which I will give for the life of the world*, are explanatory glosses which clarify the sense of the passage, but do not alter its meaning.

### III. THE FLESH AND BLOOD OF THE SON OF MAN, THE TRUE FOOD OF THE FAITHFUL

The provocative utterance which concluded the last section of the discourse turns the murmuring of the Jews into articulate and violent wrangling. They understand the words of Jesus as an exhortation to anthropophagy. The Lord's answer is, first an even more explicit repetition of what He had said, adding that they must not only eat the Flesh of the Son of man, but also drink His Blood, and that only by so doing can they have life in themselves. To eat of His Flesh and to drink of His Blood is as necessary for salvation as to believe on Him who alone has seen the Father (*v.* 47). The former is the inevitable corollary of the latter. Then follows a further repetition of the provocative words, but substituting *munch* for *eat*. This rather vulgar word (see note on *v.* 54) makes the Saying more provocative still. No room is left for any 'spiritualizing' interpretation. The eating and drinking of the Flesh and Blood of the Son of man involve a real physical eating and drinking, although the Flesh and the Blood are altogether misconceived if they be thought of, as the Jews are determined to think of them, as the mere material of the human Body of Jesus, instead of being rigorously defined in terms of the significance wrought out and manifested in His sacrificial death. The apparent contradiction implied in the insistence that there must be a real physical eating and drinking of what is grievously misunderstood if it is interpreted purely physically is resolved and explained only if the conscious reference to the Eucharist is perceived. The Eucharistic food and drink are physically bread and wine, spiritually the Flesh and Blood of the Son of man; together they constitute the true food and drink of the faithful: the true food and drink because they effect the sacred union of the Son of God with those who believe on Him, and thus communicate eternal life and guarantee immortality. The union of the Father and the Son is thereby extended to embrace the believers also. As the Father communicates life to the Son, so the Son communicates life to those who feed on Him, and will bestow on them immortality. It is now abundantly clear that the incarnate Son of God, the Son of man, is the Bread who came down from heaven, and that the manna is the type of the Son and of the Eucharistic Feast: but only the type. They who ate the manna died; they who feed upon the Son will live for ever. Such was the discourse delivered by the Lord in the Synagogue at Capernaum.

*v.* 52. Cf. the misunderstanding of Nicodemus, iii. 4. Lagrange follows Zahn in suggesting that the Jews quarrelled because some understood the words literally, some figuratively of receiving teaching, cf. the Rabbinic exegesis of Isa. lv. 1; Prov. ix. 5, quoted in Strack-Billerbeck on *v.* 35. But by *strove together* the author probably merely intends to express an intensification of the murmuring of *v.* 41. The opposition of the Jews grows with the development of the teaching.

*v.* 53. The words are rendered even more objectionable by the addition of *Son of man* and of *drinking His Blood*. The drinking of blood was expressly forbidden in Lev. xvii. 10–14, cf. Acts xv. 29. Nor does the declaration that there is no other means of salvation (cf. *vv.* 46, 47) make the words more acceptable.

The absolute character of the utterance provided the Greek Fathers with an authorization of the Eastern custom of admitting infants to Communion. The Western Fathers defended the practice of the Western Church by noting that, whereas faith is demanded in *vv.* 35, 45, 47, it is not mentioned in iii. 3 sqq., and therefore concluded that infants could be admitted to Baptism but not to the Eucharist (see Lagrange). Faith is, however, presumed in iii. 15, 16, 36.

*v.* 54. The Greek word substituted for *eat* means literally *munch*, i.e. eat so as to be heard (Bauer)—it was originally used to describe animals eating. The word is used of eating corn or cereals, not usually of eating meat. In *v.* 58 and xiii. 18 its object is 'bread'. The choice of the word here therefore serves a double purpose. It emphasizes a real physical eating (cf. Matt. xxiv. 38), and appropriately points the unmistakable reference to the Eucharist.

*v.* 56. The union of Jesus with His faithful disciples is a participation in the divine life which the Son receives from the Father, cf. xiv. 20, 23, xv. 4–7, xvii. 11, 23; 1 John ii. 24, iii. 6, 24, iv. 15, 16. 'We abide in Him, because we are His members; but He abides in us, because we are His temple' (Saint Augustine). Codex Bezae, both Greek and Latin, adds *As the Father is in Me and I am in the Father, Verily, verily, I say unto you, Unless ye receive the Body of the Son of man as the Bread of Life, ye have not life in Him.* Two manuscripts of the Old Latin Version have the latter half in its positive form. The addition has the appearance of a gloss, *Body* not *Flesh* is suspicious, and the first half may be an interpolation from x. 38 (see, however, Loisy).

*v.* 57. Since the Greek preposition translated *because of* in the R.V., *by* in the A.V., is capable of two meanings, Lagrange follows Saint Thomas Aquinas and Saint Augustine in suggesting that a second nuance is intended by the author. The Son both owes His life to the Father and lives for His sake; so also the believer both receives life from the Son and consecrates his life to His service.

*v.* 59. *In the synagogue*, better, perhaps, *in synagogue* (cf. the English phrase 'in church' and xviii. 20), emphasizes the public and solemn character of the discourse. It is suitable that the nature of the true worship of God should be disclosed to the Jews in the framework of that worship of which it is the fulfilment. Westcott notes that the 'history of the manna is appointed to be read in the synagogues at Morning Service'. Codex Bezae, two manuscripts of the Old Latin Version, and Saint Augustine add that the discourse was delivered *on the sabbath day*.

### THE UNBELIEF OF THE DISCIPLES OF JESUS
### AND THE FAITH OF THE ELEVEN

The revelation of the ultimate verities of Christian faith and worship leads to an outburst of unbelief among the disciples of Jesus. The author refuses to abandon the apparent materialism of Christian language, even though it causes the unbelief of the Jews to invade the Christian Community. Christianity cannot otherwise express itself, since the Eucharist depends for its efficacy upon the concretion of the Word in flesh, the descent of the Son of God, and upon His death as a sacrifice. This whole Spiritual activity of vivifying the flesh reaches its climax in the Resurrection and Ascension of the Son of man. There is therefore present to the author's mind no contrast between flesh and spirit, or between matter and spirit. The contrast is between dead flesh or matter and living flesh or matter. In itself flesh is flesh and it profiteth nothing for life or salvation, but, if penetrated by the Spirit of God, it becomes both vivified and vivifying. This is the Gospel, and this is the Christian religion. As the incarnate Word is living flesh in the power of the Spirit, so the words of the Son of God give life to what is otherwise dead and profitless. They are therefore Spirit, and they are Life. Thus Lazarus is brought to life by the word of Jesus, and by the word of the Lord the sheep are summoned from their old and profitless pasturage to a new life. The Incarnation, the Death and Resurrection of Jesus, the raising of Lazarus, the regeneration of the believers, is the expression of the creative Spiritual activity of God, the vivification of the flesh. Into this perspective the water of Baptism and the bread and wine of the Eucharist are drawn. In an earlier passage the writer had called attention to the words of the Lord by which water was consecrated for the purpose of regeneration; so here he records words which not only assign to His death redemptive significance, but also consecrate bread and wine to be His flesh and Blood, the means by which the benefits of His sacrifice can be appropriated, and by which immortality is given to mortal men. In this special sense the general efficacy of the words of Jesus is applied. *The words that I have spoken unto you are spirit, and are life.* Saint Peter voices the faith and knowledge of the true believers, and in contrast to the Jews and to the unbelieving Christians, avoids crude materialism on the one hand and false spirituality on the other. Jesus is the Holy One of God, who has the words of eternal life, and there is no other Saviour. Contrasted with Saint Peter the author introduces Judas, the Betrayer, one of the twelve. He is personified Apostasy, the spiritual father of all apostates. The ultimate distinction between Saint Peter and Judas, and between true and false Christians, is that whereas the former have been given to the Christ by the Father Himself, the latter have not.

*vv.* 60, 61. The saying is hard, not so much because the words are difficult to understand but because they are difficult to believe. Its crude materialism and rough expression render it a cause of stumbling even to the disciples. The language is 'offensive, not unintelligible' (Westcott).

*v.* 62. The return to the Father (vii. 33, xiii. 3, xvi. 5, 7, 28), which is the ascent into heaven (iii. 13, xx. 17), corresponds with the descent of the Son of man and forms the climax of the miraculous revelation of the Son of God. The Incarnation, Death, and Resurrection of the Christ are the necessary prolegomena, not only to eating His Flesh and drinking His Blood, but also to understanding what this means. To the unbelievers the whole is an accumulation of material and incredible miracles, but to those who possess the true supernatural faith because they have been drawn by the Father, the whole is seen to move on a different plane, since neither the Christ nor the Eucharistic food are *of this world*. The eating of the Flesh of the glorified Son of man cannot be a merely physical process (Bauer). Therefore, rightly understood, the Resurrection and the Ascension provide the solution to the riddle of the Eucharistic terminology (2 Cor. v. 16).

*v.* 63. For the combination of *Spirit* and *Life*, cf. 2 Macc. xiv. 46; 2 Cor. iii. 3, and of *Words* and *Spirit*, cf. iii. 34. Jesus is both the teacher and the dispenser of miraculous food in the Marcan and Lucan narratives of the Feeding of the Five Thousand (Mark vi. 34; Luke ix. 11, omitted by Matthew). Only flesh which has been vivified by the words of the Son of God is living flesh; apart from the Spirit flesh is dead and powerless to give life. This general principle applies to the flesh of the Son of God, who is the Word, and to the consecrated bread and wine of the Eucharist. Hence *the words which I have spoken unto you* refer in the first instance to the discourse upon the Feeding of the Five Thousand and upon the Walking on the Sea, in which He declared Himself to be the Living Bread (*v.* 35), His death to be the effective sacrifice for the life of the World, and bread (and wine) to be His Flesh and Blood, of which if a man eat, he shall live for ever. Since, however, the whole teaching of Jesus is life-giving, the reference passes beyond the particular discourse to the whole, and to this Saint Peter bears witness in *v.* 68. To the author of the Fourth Gospel the words of Jesus are not primarily teaching about God and Truth and immortality, but rather, effective, creative, life-giving utterances (iv. 50, 53, v. 24, ix. 7, 11, x. 3, xi. 43, 44, xv. 3), which effect the transformation from death to life and from dead to living flesh, or preserve such transformation when it has once been effected. The Word incarnate is living flesh and as such is not subject to corruption; consequently, His words are creative acts, by which the regenerate believers who have the Word of God, or the Spirit of God, abiding in them (iii. 5–8, v. 38, viii. 31–7, 51, 52, xii. 48–50, xiv. 17, xv. 7, xvii. 16, 17), and the material of Christian worship (water, bread, wine) have become living flesh or matter. The conception is in its origin magical, but the writer is convinced that Christianity is the spiritual religion, and that its organic activity is the activity of God, who is Himself Spirit (iv. 24), and is the reproduction and completion of His action in the creation of the Universe, when God said and it was done and the Spirit of God moved upon the face of the waters (Gen. i). Eisler has noted that a play upon words may underlie the saying in *v.* 63, since the single Aramaic word *bisra* means both *flesh* and *good news*, Gospel (*Z.N.T.W.* 1925, XXIV, pp. 185 sqq.).

*vv.* 64–6. Unbelief, not the unavoidable crudity of the Christian terminology, is the true cause of widespread apostasy. False disciples as well as the unbelieving Jews are the concern of the author. In his epistles the nature of their unbelief is more clearly specified. They desired a more purely spiritual religion, and refused to acknowledge that the Son of God had come *in flesh*, or that Jesus is the Christ, thus denying both the Father and the Son (1 John ii. 22 sqq., iv. 3; 2 John 7).

For this reason they had left the Christian fellowship and gone out into the world (1 John ii. 19, iv. 1; 2 John 7). In the Ignatian Epistles it is further stated that they refused to partake of the Eucharist because it was a partaking of the Flesh and Blood of the Lord (*Smyrn.* v–vii). Their action was logical and consistent. With such action as this the author is here dealing. He declares it to be apostasy grounded upon unbelief, and a repetition of the betrayal of Judas. He guards Christianity from the accusation that such defection involves weakness by asserting that the apostles are known to the Lord from the beginning (xv. 27, xvi. 4), as Judas was. They were called (*v.* 70), but they were not given by the Father, and moreover, they serve a mysterious divine purpose. Judas was the 'instrument of a necessary crime' (Loisy), and his betrayal was according to prophecy (xiii. 18), and the apostates are set for the proof of the true believers (cf. 1 John iv. 1–6).

*vv.* 67–71. The Twelve (the eleven) are implied in *v.* 13, but directly mentioned only here and in xx. 24. Their call is not recorded (Mark iii. 14 and parallels), but is presumed (cf. xiii. 18, xv. 16, 19). This passage is the Johannine counterpart to the confession of Peter at Cæsarea Philippi (Mark viii. 27–33; Matt. xvi. 13–23; Luke ix. 18–22). The Lucan narrative is in two particulars closely parallel to the Johannine, since in the gospel of Luke the earlier material is manipulated so that the confession of Peter follows immediately upon the Feeding of the Five Thousand, and because he omits the identification of Peter with Satan. [The tendency to assimilate the Johannine version of the confession to the synoptic version has caused the intrusion into the text of variant readings to *the Holy One of God*, the reading of Codices Sinaiticus, Vaticanus, Ephraemi Rescriptus, Bezae and one other Greek manuscript, supported by Nonnus and Cosmas Alexandrinus. Many Greek manuscripts, two manuscripts of the Old Latin Version, the Syriac Peshitto and the Harklean, Basil, Chrysostom, and Victorinus, substitute the Matthæan confession, *the Christ, the Son of the living God.* Tertullian has simply *the Christ* (Mark viii. 29). Some manuscripts of both Egyptian Versions frequently have the combination *the Christ, the Holy One of God.* One manuscript of the Old Latin Version and the Curetonian Syriac read *the Son of God.* Some Greek minuscules (family 1, 33, 565), the Vulgate, two manuscripts of the Old Latin Version, the Sinaitic Syriac, some manuscripts of the Egyptian Bohairic Version and Cyril of Alexandria read *the Christ, the Son of God.* It can hardly be doubted that *the Holy One of God* is the original reading, and that assimilation partial or complete is the cause of the intrusion of the variants.]

Peter, echoing *v.* 63, voices the true belief and knowledge. Jesus is the only Saviour. His are the words which give eternal life because He is *the Holy One of God.* The title belongs to the synoptic tradition (Mark i. 24; Luke iv. 34), where it is equivalent to *the Christ.* In the Fourth Gospel it expresses the consecration of the Son to be the Saviour of the

World (x. 36, xvii. 17 sqq., cf. Rev. iii. 7). The misunderstanding of Peter, which causes the Lord to identify him with Satan immediately after his confession (Mark viii. 33; Matt. xvi. 23), is omitted, as in Luke. Subsequent history proved that Judas, not Peter, was the veritable demon. Judas is therefore presented to the readers as a devil (cf. xiii. 2, 27; Luke xxii. 3). Similarly, in the First Epistle the apostates are children of the Devil (1 John iii. 10), anti-Christs and false prophets inspired by the Spirit of deceit (1 John iv. 1–6).

Simon, the father of Judas, is mentioned only in the Fourth Gospel (xiii. 26). In xii. 4 and xiv. 22 Judas is called simply *Iscariot*, as in the synoptic gospels (Mark iii. 19, &c.).

The introduction of Judas, the betrayer, closes a section of the gospel. Henceforth it becomes the narrative of the Via Crucis.

*We have believed and know.* Knowledge is intensified, and permanent belief, which has not yet passed into sight (1 John iii. 2, see, however, xx. 28, 29). For the association of knowledge and belief, cf. viii. 30–2, x. 38, xvii. 8; 1 John iv. 16, and of knowledge and sight, cf. xiv. 7 (see Bauer detached note, pp. 99 sqq., Scott, pp. 271 sqq.). The emphasis on the knowledge of the disciples, contrasted with their belief, preserves the climax of Peter's confession in the synoptic gospels. This belief, which in i. 35–45, 49 was inadequate, now becomes knowledge. It should be noted in this connection that whereas in the Fourth Gospel Jesus both knows and sees God (vii. 29, viii. 55, x. 15), it is never stated that He believed in Him.

vii. 1. The essential unbelief of the Galileans now having been exposed, the detailed messianic teaching and action recorded, in the earlier tradition, to have taken place in Galilee are quickly passed over with the words *and Jesus walked* (i.e. *was coming and going*, cf. xxi. 18; Mark xi. 27) *in Galilee*. Although the Evangelist has shown the unbelief of the Galileans to be as fundamental as that of the Jews in Jerusalem, he represents the Galilean ministry as a retirement (cf. iv. 3) occasioned by the intention of the Jews to put Jesus to death. The particular reference is to the miracle of the cure of the cripple in Jerusalem on the Sabbath day, which provoked the accusation of blasphemy and the murderous hostility of the Jews (*v.* 18). The author now passes definitely to the record of the final public conflict with the Jews (cf. Mark x. 1; Matt. xix. 1; Luke ix. 51). Galilee is left behind and is introduced again only as the scene of an appearance of the risen Lord (ch. xxi).

DETACHED NOTE 5

# THE INTERPRETATION OF
# THE SIXTH CHAPTER

Modern commentators have noted that the problem of exegesis is to resolve the apparent contradiction between the Eucharistic language in *vv.* 51–8 and the saying in *v.* 63, echoed in *v.* 69: *It is the Spirit that quickeneth; the flesh profiteth nothing: the words that I have spoken unto you are spirit, and are life.* Various solutions have been proposed. (*a*) The Language of the discourse is metaphorical, and *v.* 63 gives the author's precise meaning. The teaching of the Lord is the meat and drink of the faithful. This interpretation is further developed by asserting that the author has made use of the Eucharistic language of Primitive Christianity, and preserved it by giving it a 'spiritual' interpretation. (Kreyenbühl, *Das Evang. der Wahrheit*, I. 458, II. 58 sqq.; Wernle, *Z.N.T.W.* 1900, p. 59; Schmiedel, *Religionsgeschichtliche Volksbücher*, I, 12, p. 68, cf. Scott, pp. 122 sqq.). The Reformers tended to interpret the passage of assimilating by faith the benefits of Christ's atoning sacrifice (Calvin, cf. Cajetan 'Clare igitur apparet quod non est ad literam sermo de manducare et bibere sacramentum Eucharistiae, sed de manducare et bibere mortem Jesu.' (*b*) *vv.* 51–8 are sacramental, but it is impossible to harmonize them with the discourse as a whole, or with *v.* 63. Therefore they are an interpolation by a later hand (Wellhausen, cf. Spitta, and also Andersen, *Z.N.T.W.*, 1908, pp. 163, 164). (*c*) The discourse is homogeneous, and is sacrificial and sacramental. It is to be explained on the background of non-Jewish sacrificial cults to which the author assimilates the Christian religion, by borrowing language familiar to his Greek or Oriental readers. Bauer therefore interprets *v.* 63 of the consecration of the Eucharistic elements to be the sacrificial food of immortality (Bauer, Loisy, *Le Sacrifice*, pp. 403–18). In the preceding commentary an attempt has been made to show that no one of these theories provides a satisfactory solution of the problem. There is no evidence that the author of the Fourth Gospel has in mind a contrast between a spiritual religion of the Word and a material sacramental religion. Everything points in an opposite direction. Christianity is the spiritual religion not because it is divorced from the physical world, but because the Flesh has been submitted to the Spirit, and thereby vivified. The Body of the Christ and the bodies of those who believe in Him are Living Flesh; and water, bread, and wine have been vivified as the means by which this transformation may be effected. The author is making it clear that Christianity is neither crude materialism nor the 'pure religion of the Spirit' in its anti-sacramental sense. The Jews falsely imagine it to be the former, and the anti-Christs, who discard both the incarnation and the Eucharist, desire to transform it into the latter. The dislocation of the discourse on the assumption that it is possible to separate an original stratum from later interpolations is only a learned method of saying that a scholar is unable to penetrate the author's meaning, and prefers to substitute two or more disjointed fragments for one homogeneous whole. The disclosure of the correspondence between Græco-Oriental mythology and cultus and the ideas and ceremonies which underlie the Sixth Chapter provides an interesting study in comparative religion, but is of very little value in tracing the genesis of the Johannine phraseology or for the interpretation of its meaning. The writer is giving a Christian explanation of an earlier Christian tradition and of a common Christian practice. The tradition of the Last Supper and the practice of the Eucharist is given him, and it involves a supernatural Christology and the sacrificial interpretation of the Lord's death. This complex interweaving of ideas into one sacrificial whole is not the result of an assimilation to pagan ideas taking place in the mind of the author; it is rather his Christian heritage which he is defending against a charge of materialism and against a movement within Christianity itself, which was critical of language that seemed crude and unspiritual. The saying in *v.* 63 must therefore not be applied merely to the consecration of the Eucharistic elements. A wider application is demanded both by the discourse as a whole and by Saint Peter's confession in *v.* 69.

*The living Bread* or *Flesh* is to the author of the gospel a comprehensive symbolical phrase containing a whole series of suggestions. It is to him what *Corpus Christi* is to a Catholic Christian. Fundamentally it suggests the Christ incarnate, offered as a sacrifice, and finally glorified. It is then extended to embrace the regenerate believers who have been saved by the Christ. They are the true and living Bread which must not and indeed cannot be lost. These suggestions are all focused in the Eucharist, which is not considered as a rite isolated or detached from Christian faith as a whole, but as the concretion of the Christ incarnate, sacrificed and glorified for the nourishment of the faithful. The whole process by which the flesh mediates life is the action of the Word of God and of the words of the Son. The Christ expressly and formally consecrated His Body and Blood to be the perfect sacrifice for the salvation of the world; He spoke the creative words which called men from death to life; He made bread and wine to be His flesh and Blood. He is, in fact, the Word incarnate. *v.* 63 is the expression of all this, and must be applied to the discourse as a whole, not merely to one section of it, and also to the whole of the Lord's teaching. It can hardly be doubted that this interpenetration of Word and Sacrament is to be explained not only by the author's use of specific Eucharistic imagery and phraseology, but by the current practice of Eucharistic worship with which he was familiar. There is no reason to suppose that the primitive Christian Eucharist consisted merely of partaking of the bread and wine consecrated to be the Body and Blood of the Lord. It was also the occasion of formally recognizing the redemptive significance of the death of the Lord, and of prophetic and didactic discourse, combining the memory both of the words of the Lord spoken at the Last Supper and of the discourse which in the Marcan-Lucan account preceded the Feeding of the Five Thousand. Thus when the author comes to record the ideal Eucharist in chapters xiii–xvii, he portrays the Lord Himself as purifying His guests, delivering the Eucharistic discourse and offering the prayer of thanksgiving. There is therefore in his mind no conceivable contrast between discourse and Eucharist, any more than there should be to those who to-day at a rite that is at once liturgical and sacrificial hear the reading of the Gospel, await the words of consecration, and feed sacramentally upon the Body and Blood of the Lord.

The patristic exegesis of the Sixth Chapter or references to its teaching are often far more satisfactory than the explanatory notes of modern commentators, because they do not refer it exclusively *either* to teaching *or* to sacrament. They choose to emphasize now one aspect of the symbolism, now another, as it is convenient to them at the moment. The apparent contradictions which emerge are the contradictions of the Fourth Gospel, contradictions which are, however, capable of synthesis in a wider view of the Eucharistic rite. Thus Clement of Alexandria speaks of the teaching of the Lord as meat, flesh, bread, wine, which are in an allegory assimilated by faith (*Paed.* I, vi. 46, 47, cf. Euseb. *De eccl. Theol.* iii. 12). In his *Excerpta ex Theodoto* (ch. xiii), however, the partaking of the *Flesh* of the Christ in the Eucharist is mentioned with the addition that the *Flesh* is *His Body—which is the Church* (cf. Saint Augustine *in Ioan. Ev. Tractatus* xxvi. 15, 18, 19, xxvii. 6). Saint Augustine, while applying the *Flesh* of the Lord to the Church, adds at once that the sacrament of the unity of the Body and Blood of Christ 'is prepared on the Lord's table in some places daily . . .'; and in another passage speaks of the command to '*eat the Flesh of the Son of man* as a figure enjoining that we should share in the sufferings of our Lord, and that we should retain a sweet and profitable memory of the fact that His flesh was wounded and crucified for us' (*De Doct. Christ.* iii. 16). Normally, of course, the references of the Fathers are to the Eucharist (see Cramer's *Catena*, Chrys., Isho'dad, etc.). The apparent contradictions in the patristic interpretations of the Sixth Chapter were frankly recognized at the Council of Trent (Session xxi, ch. 1). For the controversy which preceded the decision see F. Cavallera, *Revue d'Hist. Eccl.* 1909, pp. 687–709, cited by Lagrange, p. 194. The Western Church in the sixteenth century was in some difficulty over the Eucharistic application of the Sixth Chapter, since it involved Communion in both kinds. Hence the desire vigorously expressed at the Council of Trent to apply it solely to the Lord's teaching. Cajetan's distinction between eating and drinking the sacrament of the Eucharist and eating and drinking the death of Jesus is designed to protect the custom of the Western Church. (For the various interpretations of the chapter cf. Lagrange, pp. 192 sqq., Bauer, pp. 95 sqq., Holtzmann, pp. 140–53, De la Taille, *Mysterium Fidei*, pp. 79 sqq.)

# THE MESSIAH
# AT THE FEAST OF TABERNACLES

## VII. 2–52

### JESUS AND HIS UNBELIEVING BRETHREN

vii. 2. *Now the feast of the Jews, the feast of tabernacles, was at hand.
3. His brethren therefore said unto him, Depart hence, and go into Judæa, that
thy disciples also may behold thy works which thou doest. 4. For no man doeth
anything in secret, and himself seeketh to be known openly. If thou doest these
things, manifest thyself to the world. 5. For even his brethren did not believe
on him. 6. Jesus therefore saith unto them, My time is not yet come; but your
time is alway ready. 7. The world cannot hate you; but me it hateth, because
I testify of it, that its works are evil. 8. Go ye up unto the feast: I go not up
yet unto this feast; because my time is not yet fulfilled. 9. And having said these
things unto them, he abode still in Galilee.*

### JESUS GOES UP TO THE FEAST OF TABERNACLES

*10. But when his brethren were gone up unto the feast, then went he also up,
not publicly, but as it were in secret. 11. The Jews therefore sought him at the
feast, and said, Where is he? 12. And there was much murmuring among the
multitudes concerning him: some said, He is a good man; others said, Not so,
but he leadeth the multitude astray. 13. Howbeit no man spake openly of him
for fear of the Jews.*

### THE FULFILMENT OF THE MOSAIC LAW CONCERNING
### THE SABBATH AND CONCERNING CIRCUMCISION

*14. But when it was now the midst of the feast Jesus went up into the temple,
and taught. 15. The Jews therefore marvelled, saying, How knoweth this ma[n]
letters, having never learned? 16. Jesus therefore answered them, and said, M[y]
teaching is not mine, but his that sent me. 17. If any man willeth to do his will
he shall know of the teaching, whether it be of God, or whether I speak fro[m]
myself. 18. He that speaketh from himself seeketh his own glory: but he tha[t]
seeketh the glory of him that sent me, the same is true, and no unrighteousness i[s]
in him. 19. Did not Moses give you the law, and yet none of you doeth the law.
Why seek ye to kill me? 20. The multitude answered, Thou hast a devil: wh[o]
seeketh to kill thee? 21. Jesus answered and said unto them, I did one work, an[d]*

*ye all marvel. 22. For this cause hath Moses given you circumcision (not that it is of Moses, but of the fathers); and on the sabbath ye circumcise a man. 23. If a man receiveth circumcision on the sabbath, that the law of Moses may not be broken; are ye wroth with me, because I made a man every whit whole on the sabbath? 24. Judge not according to appearance, but judge righteous judgement.*

### THE ADVENT OF THE MESSIAH

*25. Some therefore of them of Jerusalem said, Is not this he whom they seek to kill? 26. And lo, he speaketh openly, and they say nothing unto him. Can it be that the rulers indeed know that this is the Christ? 27. Howbeit we know this man whence he is: but when the Christ cometh, no one knoweth whence he is. 28. Jesus therefore cried in the temple, teaching and saying, Ye both know me, and know whence I am; and I am not come of myself, but he that sent me is true, whom ye know not. 29. I know him; because I am from him, and he sent me. 30. They sought therefore to take him: and no man laid his hand on him, because his hour was not yet come.*

### THE DEPARTURE OF THE MESSIAH AND THE JUDGEMENT
### PRONOUNCED UPON THE UNBELIEVING JEWS

*31. But of the multitude many believed on him; and they said, When the Christ shall come, will he do more signs than those which this man hath done? 32. The Pharisees heard the multitude murmuring these things concerning him; and the chief priests and the Pharisees sent officers to take him. 33. Jesus therefore said, Yet a little while am I with you, and I go unto him that sent me. 34. Ye shall seek me, and shall not find me: and where I am, ye cannot come. 35. The Jews therefore said among themselves, Whither will this man go that we shall not find him? will he go unto the Dispersion among the Greeks, and teach the Greeks? 36. What is this word that he said, Ye shall seek me, and shall not find me: and where I am, ye cannot come?*

### THE PROMISE TO THE BELIEVERS AND
### THE ADVENT OF THE SPIRIT

*37. Now on the last day, the great day of the feast, Jesus stood and cried, saying, If any man thirst, let him come unto me, and drink. 38. He that believeth on me, as the scripture hath said, out of his belly shall flow rivers of living water. 39. But this spake he of the Spirit, which they that believed on him were to receive: for the Spirit was not yet given; because Jesus was not yet glorified.*

### THE EFFECT OF THE WORDS OF JESUS UPON THE CROWD
### AND THE FAILURE OF THE SANHEDRIN TO
### SECURE HIS ARREST

*40. Some of the multitude therefore, when they heard these words, said, This*

*is of a truth the prophet. 41. Others said, This is the Christ. But some said,
What, doth the Christ come out of Galilee? 42. Hath not the scripture said that
the Christ cometh of the seed of David, and from Bethlehem, the village where
David was? 43. So there arose a division in the multitude because of him.
44. And some of them would have taken him; but no man laid hands on him.
45. The officers therefore came to the chief priests and Pharisees; and they said
unto them, Why did ye not bring him? 46. The officers answered, Never man so
spake. 47. The Pharisees therefore answered them, Are ye also led astray?
48. Hath any of the rulers believed on him, or of the Pharisees? 49. But this
multitude which knoweth not the law are accursed. 50. Nicodemus saith unto
them (he that came to him before, being one of them), 51. Doth our law judge
a man, except it first hear from himself and know what he doeth? 52. They
answered and said unto him, Art thou also of Galilee? Search, and see that out
of Galilee ariseth no prophet.*

### JESUS AND HIS UNBELIEVING BRETHREN

vii. 2–9. The most popular of the Jewish national festivals, the Feast
of Tabernacles, provides the occasion for the return of Jesus to Jerusalem. The author names this autumn (September–October) festival *The
feast of the construction of tabernacles* (booths), making use of its Deuteronomic title (LXX, Deut. xvi. 16, xxxi. 10, cf. Zech. xiv. 16 sqq.).
Thanksgiving for the ingathering of the harvest (Exod. xxiii. 16) was
combined with the thankful commemoration of the miracles of God
during the period of the wandering in the Arabian desert (Lev. xxiii.
43); and the erection of tents on the roof, or in the courts of the houses
and in the streets, was the characteristic feature from which it took its
name (Neh. viii. 15, 16; Lev. xxiii. 42). Josephus describes it as 'the
most sacred and most important feast of the Hebrews' (*Ant.* viii. 100,
cf. xv. 50). For an exhaustive treatment of the customs of the feast see
Strack-Billerbeck, vol. II, pp. 774–812). Perhaps to the writer of the
gospel the significance of the busy erection of tabernacles is first fully
seen in the arrival, in the midst of the feast, of Jesus in whom the Word
of God veritably *tabernacled* in the midst of His people (i. 14).

The narrative of the arrival of Jesus and of the discourse He delivered
in the Temple is prefaced by a rather enigmatic conversation between
Him and His natural or physical brethren. The brothers are sharply
distinguished from the disciples, and the distinction reappears in ii. 12
and in Mark iii. 21, 31–5, where the mother of Jesus is associated with
His brethren. The physical brothers of Jesus are pronounced by the
Evangelist to have been unbelievers, and the words which Jesus
addresses to them reinforce and explain this judgement. The disciples
with whom they are contrasted are therefore the men whose faith formed
the climax of the immediately preceding episode (vi. 69). Some modern
commentators obliterate this distinction by interpreting the words of

the brethren *that thy disciples also may behold thy works which thou doest* as referring to disciples in Jerusalem (Bernard). But in the Fourth Gospel the phrase 'the disciples' is a fixed term for the disciples who followed Jesus and were His constant companions throughout the ministry (ii. 2, 12, iii. 22, iv. 2, vi. 22 and *passim*). The only exception is xix. 38, where Joseph of Arimathæa is called *a disciple of Jesus, but secretly for fear of the Jews*. This, however, does not justify the existence in the mind of the author of a group of disciples in Jerusalem. The nature of the unbelief of the brethren of Jesus, rather than the imposition of an unnatural meaning to the phrase *thy disciples*, provides the key to the interpretation of this introductory passage.

The action of the brethren is parallel to that of the mother of Jesus in ii. 1-11. She knew the miraculous power of her Son, and desired Him to display it in public for the material benefit of the guests at a marriage feast, and she is sternly rebuked. His brethren, like their mother, are fully aware of the miraculous powers of their Brother. The words *If thou doest these things*, far from implying unbelief in His power (Bernard), state the ground upon which their advice rests (Westcott, Bauer, cf. Matt. iv. 3; Rom. v. 17; 1 Pet. i. 17). Since He has miraculous power, He should use it in a wider sphere, in order that the wavering faith of the disciples may reach the level of their own vigorous belief. At their initiative He is therefore urged to abandon the narrow sphere of His miraculous activity and boldly and openly perform His wonders in Jerusalem and manifest Himself there to the world, since no one who conceals himself can expect public recognition. The action of the brethren of Jesus is similar to the action of those who would make Him a king (vi. 15), similar also to that of the Devil in the earlier narrative of the Temptation (Matt. iv. 1 sqq.; Luke iv. 1 sqq.). Chrysostom comments well: 'What unbelief is here? They exhort Him to work miracles.' The author of the gospel roundly declares this incitement to display unbelief. The words of Jesus reveal that His brethren belong wholly to the world. Their supreme misunderstanding lies in their distinction between secret and public, which covers a false distinction between glorious and inglorious (v. 41-4), bold and cowardly. There will be a public ministry of Jesus in Jerusalem (vii. 26, x. 24, 25, xi. 54, xviii. 20): but it consists in the public exposition of the sin of the world and the provocation of its hatred (iii. 19, xiv. 17, xv. 18, 19, xvi. 20, 33, xvii. 9, 14, 25). There is also a glorious display of power, but it consists in secret obedience to the will of the Father and in the transmission of the truth to the disciples in private (xvi. 25, 29, cf. Mark viii. 15), and is displayed completely in the death of the Christ (xii. 32). The Greek words for *secret* and *public* cover an Aramaic and Rabbinic distinction, as Schlatter noted in his commentary (*Die Sprache und Heimat des vierten Evangeliums*, p. 81), and Strack-Billerbeck shows that *to walk secretly* is equivalent to walking humbly before God (cf. Matt. vi. 4, 6).

*The time* (Mark i. 15, xiii. 33; Matt. xxvi. 18), or, as the Evangelist usually writes, *the hour* (xii. 23, 27, xiii. 1, xvi. 32, xvii. 1, xix. 27), for the display of the glory of God in the humiliation of the Christ is, however, *not yet* (ii. 4, vii. 30, 39, viii. 20), and Jesus refuses to go up to the Feast. Since, however, His brethren belong to the world, they can journey to Jerusalem openly, whenever they please, and attend its feasts in complete security. The world is their affectionate friend and can show them no enmity (xv. 19, xvii. 14). For Jesus there is no such freedom. The time of His Jerusalem is the Passover of His death, the Time laid upon Him by the Father. And so, whilst His brethren make their secure and public pilgrimage to Jerusalem, He remains in Galilee. For the variant readings *I go not up yet unto this feast* (R.V.), *I go not up unto this feast* (R.V. mg.), see note on vii. 10 sqq.

### JESUS GOES UP TO THE FEAST OF TABERNACLES

*vv.* 10-13. If the reading *I go not up yet unto this feast* (*v.* 8), which is supported by the majority of the Greek uncials, including Codex Vaticanus and the Koridethi and Washington manuscripts, is the original reading, there is no contradiction. Jesus merely delays His journey and allows His brethren to precede Him. But, since the reading *I go not up to this feast* is strikingly supported by Codices Sinaiticus and Bezae, by both manuscripts of the Old Syriac Version, by the majority of Old Latin manuscripts and the Vulgate, and by Tatian and other Fathers, the original text seems to have contained the glaring contradiction *I go not up unto this feast—Then went he also up*, which caused Porphyry to accuse Jesus of inconsistency (Jerome *contra Pelag.* ii. 17) and Schopenhauer to deduce that 'Jesus Christ did of set purpose utter a falsehood' (*Grundprobleme der Ethik*, second edition, p. 225, cited by Holtzmann on vii. 10). The commentator has therefore to interpret the contradiction (cf. ii. 4, 7-9, iii. 22, iv. 1, 2, xi. 6) and to suppose *not yet* to have been introduced into the text in order to gloze over the contradiction. It may be that the addition *not publicly but as it were in secret* sufficiently explains the distinction between going and not going. Jesus refuses to go to Jerusalem in solemn and open festival pilgrimage (Lagrange). He does, however, go secretly to fulfil His mission, but not to take part in the feast. Loisy imagines the distinction to be a journey undertaken at the invitation of unbelievers and a journey in obedience to the will of the Father. He writes, 'As it is not fitting for the incarnate Word to do his first miracle and inaugurate his Galilean-Judæan ministry at the invitation of his mother according to the flesh, so also it is not fitting for him to inaugurate the purely Judæan ministry which was to crown the work of salvation at the instigation of his brothers' (first edition, p. 491). But it may be doubted whether either of these explanations satisfactorily accounts for a contradiction that suggests a more subtle resolution. In

the Fourth Gospel the verb *to go up* is important and significant. It is
used naturally to describe the journeying of Jesus or others to Jerusalem
(ii. 13, v. 1, xi. 55, xii. 20, cf. vii. 14); but it is used also for the ascent
of Jesus to the Father (iii. 13, vi. 62, xx. 17) and its use is closely related
to the equally significant verb *to lift up* (iii. 14, viii. 28, xii. 32, 34). In
the Evangelist's thought the death and resurrection form one act of
ascension or lifting up to the Father. If this latter meaning of the word
*go up* is present to the mind of the author, the contradiction is resolved
in a subtle play upon words. Jesus does go up to Jerusalem to the Feast
of Tabernacles, but His ascent for the salvation of the world is deferred
by the will of the Father until the Time of the more significant feast of
the Passover. The phrase *unto this feast* may even grammatically have
the meaning *at this feast* (cf. 1. 18), and Ephraem in referring the words
to the ascent on the cross seems actually to have appealed to the reading
*at this feast* (*Commentary on the Diatessaron*, ed. Auch-Moes, p. 167).
Epiphanius comments 'He speaks to His brothers spiritually and in a
mystery and they did not understand what He said. For he told them
that He would not ascend at that feast neither into heaven nor on the
cross to fulfil the plan of His suffering and the mystery of salvation'
(*Haereses* li. 25). Westcott seems to have this interpretation in mind:
'Perhaps, however, it is best to give a fuller force to the "going up",
and to suppose that the thought of the next Paschal journey, when "the
time was fulfilled", already shapes the words' (compare also Bauer,
second edition, pp. 103, 104).

Jesus then goes up to the Feast of Tabernacles *as it were in secret*.
There is no docetic mystery about His journey, as Loisy supposes. It
is no mysterious journey, for Jesus did nothing in secret (cf. xviii. 20);
but it is not a public pilgrimage. In Jerusalem the situation is one of
acute tension. The rulers were seeking Him whom they dared not even
name (cf. ix. 12, xix. 21), presumably in order to put Him to death
(v. 18, vii. 1, 19, 25, viii. 37, &c., cf. vii. 30, x. 39). The crowd wavers
in its ignorant opinion concerning Him; but dares no open expression.
There is simply a restless muttering (not grumbling against Him as in
vi. 61). Some hold Him for a good man (cf. Matt. xxv. 21, 23; Luke
xix. 17), others regard Him as a public deceiver; but all are frightened
lest their opinion may bring them into collision with the authorities.

### THE FULFILMENT OF THE MOSAIC LAW CONCERNING
### THE SABBATH AND CONCERNING CIRCUMCISION

*vv.* 14–24. Once again (ii. 13) the Lord whom they sought (*v.* 11)
came suddenly to His temple (Mal. iii. 1); this time in order to declare
the significance of that one great act of complete restoration to health
wrought upon the cripple on the Sabbath day (v. 2–18), which had
caused the Jews earnestly to plot His death. The discourse picks up

and develops the theme of v. 19–47, and both discourses are solemn interpretations of the same miracle. For a discussion of theories of re-arrangement of the text so as to bring the two discourses together cf. p. 278.

Jesus appeared in the Temple in the *midst of the feast*. Since an eighth day had been added to the original seven days of the feast (Lev. xxiii. 34–6), He arrived on the fourth day when the feast was at its height, and at once began His teaching, reserving however, its final conclusion for the last great day (vii. 37). The readers of the gospel well know that the teaching of the Lord to the Jews rested upon a creative interpreta-tion of their sacred Scriptures, and its purpose was to declare their fulfil-ment in Him: *If ye believed Moses, ye would believe me; for he wrote of me. But if he believe not his writings, how shall ye believe my words* (v. 46, 47)? The precise form of the opening section of the discourse is conditioned by the expressed wonder of the Jews that one who is so untaught should be so confident in exposition (Mark i. 22, vi. 2) and by their unexpressed deduction that He is His own authority and that His teaching proceeds from His own instruction: *How knoweth this man letters* (writings) *having never learned?* If these words stood by themselves, they would mean simply that Jesus was illiterate, unable to read or write, since the Greek adjective *without letters* meant precisely this (see Moulton-Milligan, *Vocabulary of the Greek Testament* under γράμματα, and Bauer). But in its context, and especially in reference to v. 46, *letters* means the writings of Moses. To the Jewish authorities Jesus is one of the ignorant crowd which is accursed and *knoweth not the law* (vii. 49), and His claim to interpret it in public is a blasphemous impertinence. The interpreta-tion of the scriptures is safely entrusted to those who are disciples of the Jewish doctors and to them only (see Strack-Billerbeck). In Acts iv. 13 a similar ignorance of the disciples of Jesus is probably intended by the author (cf. Acts xxvi. 24, and perhaps Isa. xxix. 12, though the word *unlearned* may there mean simply *unable to read*). The discourse then pro-ceeds to throw the ignorance back upon His accusers, and to show that He whom they name 'autodidact' is in fact 'theodidact' (Holtzmann) and that His action is the fulfilment of the law.

The teaching of Jesus is the teaching of God: *I spake not of myself; but the Father which sent me, he hath given me a commandment, what I should say, and what I should speak . . . the things therefore which I speak, even as the Father hath said unto me, so I speak* (xii. 49, 50, cf. viii. 26 sqq., xiv. 10, 24, xvi. 13; Num. xvi. 28). Philo, commenting on Deut. xviii. 15, wrote 'The Prophet will act simply as the organ of divine revelation (*De special Leg.* I. 65). Only those, however, who do the will of God (vi. 45, xviii. 37, cf. iii. 20, 21, v. 30) can perceive the source of the teaching of Jesus; yet the Jews ought to be able to distinguish between pride and humility. Jesus does not vaunt His power of invention, but boasts the glory of God in His humility (v. 41, 44, viii. 50, xii. 43). In this humility righteousness and truth are exposed, and the Jews manifest their apostasy by judging Him to be unrighteous and by desiring His death (v. 18, viii. 48 sqq., x. 20). The phrase *doing the will of God* is now made explicit. To *do His will* is to *do His Law* which Moses gave them. For a similar parallelism compare Ps. xl. 8, *I delight to do thy will, O my God; yea, thy law is within my heart.* And yet, though in the particular perspective of the discourse it is the violation of the Law of Moses that prevents the Jews from perceiving that the teaching of Jesus is the teaching of God, in the wider perspective those who do the will of God and therefore recognize the teaching of Jesus are the gentile believers (iv. 46, x. 16, xi. 52).

Jesus has exposed the desire of the Jews to kill Him, and has characterized their intention as the violation of the Law of Moses. Whereupon the crowd, denying the intention of putting Him to death, judges Him to be possessed (viii. 48, 49, x. 20; Mark iii. 21 sqq.; Matt. xi. 18; Luke vii. 33. It should be noted that in the Marcan narrative the accusation of possession (iii. 21 sqq.) follows closely upon the miracle of the healing of the Paralytic (ii. 1–12), the controversy concerning the sabbath (ii. 23–iii. 5) and the definite decision of the Pharisees and the Herodians to put Jesus to death). It may be that the author intends a distinction between *the crowd*, which is genuinely ignorant, and the authorities—*the Jews*—who alone are responsible for planning His death and who alone have knowledge of the plan (*vv.* 12, 13, 31, 32). But the distinction is not maintained (*v.* 25), and the phrase *the Jews* seems often to be simply equivalent to *the crowd* (viii. 31 sqq., xii. 9, &c.). In this case their ignorance is simply a lie, and Jesus, disregarding it, continues to expound the significance of His healing of the cripple on the sabbath day. The exegesis of *vv.* 21–3 depends upon full weight being given to the words *For this cause hath Moses given you circumcision.* Some commentators (Bernard) take *for this cause* with the preceding sentence and translate *and ye all marvel because of it* (R.V. mg.), a procedure that has some authority in the Old Latin and Bohairic versions (see Lagrange). The next sentence then begins *Moses hath given. . . .* But, though this is a possible translation (cf. Mark vi. 6), it has no analogy in the Johannine writings, and vi. 65, viii. 47, xiii. 11, xvi. 15 seem decisively against it (Westcott). *For this cause* must therefore introduce an explanation of the gift of circumcision by Moses to the Jews. Most modern commentators (Bauer, Holtzmann, and many others) take the sentence as elliptical and reconstruct its meaning: Moses, knowing that it would conflict with the sabbath, gave the Jews circumcision in order to teach them that the Sabbath Law is not inviolable. But this is very clumsy, since in the context it is not merely the breaking of the sabbath that is explained and justified, but the healing of the cripple on the sabbath. If v. 46 be kept firmly in mind—*Moses wrote of me*—(cf. v. 39, 40) the meaning is not really difficult. Moses gave the Jews circumcision

and the right to break the sabbath for the purpose of performing circumcision, *for this cause*, namely that it should be a type and anticipation
of that greater and entire healing by the Christ, which also of necessity
displaces the sabbath. The action of Jesus in making the cripple every
whit *whole* (v. 6, 9) on the sabbath day is therefore the divine fulfilment both of the original gift of circumcision and of the continuous
Jewish practice of circumcising on the sabbath (cf. the argument in
Matt. xii. 11; Luke xiii. 15). The old order is fulfilled and abrogated
in that complete purgation from sin (v. 14) which is effected by faith
in Jesus as the Christ (cf. ii. 6 note, xiii. 8, 10), and Moses gave the Jews
circumcision in order that they might understand the full significance
of the miracle which Jesus did to the cripple on the sabbath day. In
seeking His death they deny their learning in the Scriptures and oppose
the will of God. Their whole blasphemous behaviour rests upon a false
judgement which discerns only the outward form (xi. 44, cf. Deut. i.
16, 17) of what Jesus had done. They judge according to the flesh
(viii. 15), and perceive only a violation of the sabbath punishable by
death. The true judgement according to the Spirit is that Jesus is the
Messiah, the Saviour of the world, and that His action is the messianic
salvation promised in the Scriptures and fulfilled in their midst.

The command that a child was to be circumcised on the eighth day
(Lev. xii. 3) necessarily involved circumcision on the sabbath if the
eighth day was a sabbath. That the Jews did practise circumcision on
the sabbath is abundantly proved by the sayings of the Rabbis. 'Rabbi
Jose (A.D. 150) said: "See, how beloved [with God] is the Law of circumcision; it displaces the sabbath."' 'It is permissible to perform on the
Sabbath everything necessary for circumcision' (*Shab.* 18. 3. For these
and other citations see Strack-Billerbeck.) The distinction between the
partial healing of circumcision and some whole healing has its striking
parallel: 'Rabbi Eliezer answered and said: "If circumcision, which
concerns one of a man's 248 limbs, displaces the Sabbath, how much
more must a man's whole body (i.e. if his life be in danger) displace
the Sabbath"' (*Yoma* 85b, cited by Strack-Billerbeck on vii. 23). The
parenthesis (cf. iv. 2, vi. 46) *not that it is of Moses, but of the fathers* need
not be taken as a correction added by the Evangelist or by some scribe.
The purpose of the author is to emphasize the dignity and importance
of circumcision. The Law concerning it was given by Moses (Lev. xii.
3), but its origin reaches back to the Patriarchs, in fact, according to the
Book of Genesis, to Abraham (Gen. xvii. 10, xxi. 4, cf. Acts vii. 8;
Rom. iv. 11).

### THE ADVENT OF THE MESSIAH

*vv.* 25–30. The interpretation of the miracle at Bethesda summarized
in the preceding verses is justified only if Jesus be the Messiah. The ques-

tion of the messiahship and of the criteria by which the Messiah can be recognized now logically emerges as the central theme of the narrative which follows. The theme is introduced by that section of the crowd permanently resident in Jerusalem, who were well aware of the official attitude to Jesus (the word *Jerusalemite* is used in the New Testament only here and in Mark i. 5). They are surprised at the liberty afforded Jesus to teach in public, and suppose—wrongly, as the readers of the gospel know—that it must have been granted Him by the authorities, and that it indicates a change of policy. Perhaps the rulers have evidence which proves that after all He is in very truth the Christ. The messiahship is therefore introduced, not as the only true deduction from the nature of the teaching of Jesus, but as a possible explanation of the liberty supposed to have been officially permitted Him. The explanation is then summarily dismissed, not as the result of careful attention to His teaching, but by the application of a simple test of true messiahship. The coming of the true Messiah is veiled in mystery, the coming of Jesus is surrounded by no messianic obscurity: He is a man of Nazareth and has come from Galilee (i. 45, 46, xviii. 5, 7, xix. 19; ii. 11–13, iv. 54, v. 1, vii. 9, 10). It is therefore impossible to consider Him seriously as the Messiah. Many commentators (e.g. Holtzmann) suppose that the criterion is the paternity of Jesus (i. 45, vi. 42, cf. Isa. liii. 8), but there is nothing in the context to suggest this. The contrast is not Son of Joseph—Son of God or Son of David, but a known man coming from Galilee contrasted with the sudden appearance of a hitherto unknown Messiah. No doubt the question of the paternity of Jesus does lie in the background; later it emerges as a clear issue (viii. 19, 36 sqq., cf. vii. 42), and, in spite of i. 45 and vi. 42, it is precisely the unknown paternity of Jesus that gives the Jews a ground of accusation against Him. The accusation is summed up in words which stand in obvious contradiction to the argument here: *as for this man, we know not whence he is* (ix. 29).

The Jewish belief in the unexpected appearance of the Messiah, *no one knoweth whence he is*, rests ultimately upon the teaching of the prophets (e.g. Isa. vii. 14–17; Mal. iii. 1; Dan. vii. 13). It was developed in the books of Enoch and 2 Esdras (1 Enoch xlvi, xlviii; 2 Esdras vii. 28, xiii. 32, cf. 2 Baruch xxiv. 2; Stanton, *The Jewish and the Christian Messiah*, pp. 44–74, Charles, *Eschatology*, pp. 260–6, 339–45, Bousset, *Religion des Judentums*, second edition, pp. 255 sqq.). Justin Martyr refers to the belief in the *Dialogue against Trypho*: 'although the Messiah be already born and exists somewhere, yet he is unknown and is himself ignorant of his messiahship, nor has he any power, until Elijah come and anoint him and make him known' (ch. viii. cf. ch. cx). Westcott cites a Rabbinic saying, 'Three things come wholly unexpected, Messiah, a godsend, and a scorpion', and Strack-Billerbeck remarks that in the Rabbinic writings the Messiah is said to 'appear'. It should be noted that the author of the Fourth Gospel also describes the coming of Jesus to the temple as a sudden appearance, and says definitely that He came up from Galilee *not publicly, but as it were in secret* (vii. 10, cf. ii. 13).

The summary dismissal of the messiahship of Jesus by the Jerusalemites cannot be disregarded, and Jesus Himself solemnly intervenes. The note of solemnity is marked by the emphatic word *cried* (vii. 37, xi. 43, xii. 44, cf. i. 15; Matt. xxvii. 50) and by the repetition of the scene of the teaching *in the temple*. Jesus picks out the important judgement of the crowd *we know this man whence he is* and accepts it as true. He has taught previously in public and has come from Galilee, and He is no stranger to them. But their deduction from this knowledge is shown to be wholly false, since precisely in this open happening lies the supreme messianic act of God. This is the paradox of the Christian Messiah. As He previously declared His teaching to be from God (vii. 16 sqq.) so now He declares His public movements to be conditioned by the divine mission. He has neither moved in Galilee nor removed from Galilee to Jerusalem, nor, in fact, entered the world at His own instigation. These were not spontaneous acts. They are sure missionary marks, which declare Him to have been sent by Him who alone fulfils His promises and who alone can authorize and direct the genuine (i. 9) mission of the Messiah (v. 19, 30, viii. 28, 42, xiv. 10). The complete failure of the men of Jerusalem to recognize in Him the Messiah therefore involves their complete ignorance of God (viii. 19, 54, 55), and their ignorance is contrasted with the knowledge of Jesus who is from God and was sent by Him (cf. Matt. xi. 27; Luke x. 22) and, by implication, with the knowledge of the Christian believers (iv. 22, xvii. 25, 26). Once again the Jews' knowledge that Jesus came from Galilee is denounced as mere knowledge according to the flesh, with which is contrasted the spiritual knowledge that perceives in the man from Nazareth of Galilee the Messiah of God and the Saviour of the world. The Jerusalemites, fully aware of the gravity of the denunciation pronounced against them, sought to procure His arrest (v. 44, viii. 20, x. 39), but they were powerless even to touch Him, because the appointed hour of His arrest had not yet come (ii. 4, vii. 6, 8, viii. 20, xiii. 1).

In the preceding comment, the word *Jerusalemites* has been taken to mean the men of Jerusalem as distinguished from *the crowds* and *the Jews*, but it may be doubted whether this distinction can be strictly maintained.

## THE DEPARTURE OF THE MESSIAH AND THE JUDGEMENT
### PRONOUNCED UPON THE UNBELIEVING JEWS

*vv.* 31–6. The controversy concerning the Advent of the Messiah is now balanced by the record of the misunderstanding of the Jewish authorities concerning the departure of Jesus (viii. 14). The discourse moves in a series of striking utterances of Jesus set in the framework of the tentative and inadequate belief of the crowd and of the consistent unbelief of the Chief Priests and the Pharisees. There emerges among the crowd a serious movement of faith in Jesus as the Messiah grounded upon the number of the miracles of Jesus (Matt. xii. 22-4). This represents an extension of the unbelief of the brethren of Jesus (vii. 3), which was exposed by the declaration of Jesus that a correct understanding of one miracle provides a wholly sufficient ground of true faith (vii. 21-4). The appeal to the number of the miracles of Jesus therefore betrays a misunderstanding of the messiahship of Jesus which is equivalent to unbelief. The Chief Priests and the Pharisees (i.e. the Sanhedrin, see Bernard, cf. i. 24, vii. 45, xi. 47, 57; Matt. xxi. 45, xxvii. 62), however, taking a serious view of this movement of popular faith, decide on His immediate arrest, and dispatch their police to seize Him (vii. 45, xviii. 3, 12, 18, xix. 6). Jesus meets this tense situation with an utterance sufficiently enigmatic to disturb His enemies, but transparently clear, and pregnant with consolation to the readers of the gospel (xiv. 1 sqq.). The form of the saying echoes the prophetic demand for the search for the Lord God and the conviction of the imminence of His salvation and judgement (Deut. iv. 29; Hos. v. 6; Isa. lv. 6). The Time is near at hand (xii. 35, xiii. 33, xiv. 19, xvi. 16, cf. Isa. liv. 7). The departure of Jesus, which is deferred only for *a little while*, is a departure to arrest and death; but the arrest and death of the Christ is in fact the migration of Jesus to Him who sent Him (xvi. 5), the return to the bosom of the Father (i. 18), and the perfection of the work of salvation (viii. 14, 21, xiii. 3, 33, 36, xiv. 4, 5, 28, xvi. 5, 10, 17, xix. 30, cf. Mark xiv. 21). The opportunity for the search for the Messiah *while he may be found* (Isa. lv. 6) is therefore severely limited. When it is passed the desire of the Jews to find the Messiah must remain unsatisfied, for He has gone into heaven, whither they cannot follow him. The Jews therefore stand condemned and must die in their sin (viii. 21), for they have sought the Messiah only to put Him to death. In direct contrast to this utter condemnation is set the promise to the true disciples of Jesus. They alone can follow Jesus to the Father (xii. 26, xiii. 36, xiv. 1, xvii. 24).

The Jews, wholly misunderstanding the words of Jesus, yet become prophetic in their ignorance (cf. viii. 22, xi. 50, xix. 19-22). They suggest His intention to find security in the Gentile world and to discover a further activity in the inauguration of a mission to the Greeks; just as later (viii. 22) they suggest that only His self-inflicted death can remove Him from their power. So they caricature but yet express the truth. The Christian mission to the Gentiles is not grounded upon the flight of Jesus from the violence of the Jews. It depends upon His complete and voluntary submission to their hatred and is conditioned by

His death (xii. 20 sqq.), but is directed by the risen Lord (xxi. 1–14) and is secure in His ascended security.

The phrase *The Dispersion of the Greeks* (R.V. mg.), *Dispersion among the Greeks* (R.V.), is awkward. The word *Diaspora* is the normal Jewish technical term for the Jews scattered among the Gentiles (Deut. xxviii. 25; Ps. cxlvii. 2; 2 Macc. i. 27). If this be the sense here, as most modern commentators take it to be (Bauer, Bernard, Strack-Billerbeck), the meaning of the whole sentence is that Jesus will go to the Jews in the Diaspora and will proceed also to teach even the Greeks. But the word *Diaspora* is capable of a deflected meaning. In 1 Pet. i. 1 it seems to refer to the Christians. The author of the Fourth Gospel in xi. 52 describes the Gentile mission as the gathering together of the *scattered children of God* (cf. x. 16). It may therefore be that this description causes a deflection in the meaning of the word *Diaspora* here. If so, the phrase should be translated *The Dispersion of the Greeks*, and the meaning is that the Jews in their prophetic ignorance point to the fulfilment of Isa. xlix. 1: *Listen, O isles, unto me; and hearken, ye peoples, from far.*

### THE PROMISE TO THE BELIEVERS AND THE ADVENT OF THE SPIRIT

*vv.* 37–9. The judgement pronounced by Jesus upon the unbelieving Jews is now balanced by the promise of eternal life to those who believe in Him. The living water flows from the Christ to His faithful disciples, and from them to the world. The importance of this promise is heightened by the manner of its introduction. It was the great and last day of the Feast, and Jesus *stood and cried* (see note on *v.* 28). The last day of the feast was probably the eighth day, named *great* because it was kept with the dignity and ritual of a Sabbath (Lev. xxiii. 36; Num. xxix. 35; Josephus, *Ant.* iii. 247). Strack-Billerbeck, however, argue for the seventh day, because the ceremonies of the eighth day were distinct from those characteristic of the feasts of Tabernacles, and because, whereas there is Rabbinic evidence for the practice of the ceremony of the Drawing of the Water accompanied by the reading of Isa. xii. 3 during the seven days of the feast, there is no evidence for its continuance on the eighth day (Strack-Billerbeck, vol. II, pp. 799–805, 808, 809, and their note ad loc.). The argument presupposes that the words of Jesus were occasioned by the ceremony. But it should be noted, first that the evidence for the ceremony is wholly Rabbinic, there being no allusion to it in the Old Testament or in the writings of Josephus; secondly that, if there was such a ceremony, it was concerned with the drawing of water, not with the drinking of it; and thirdly that the theme reappears constantly in the gospel in passages where there is no connection with the feast of Tabernacles (iv. 14 sqq., vi. 35, xix. 34; 1 John v. 6–8). It would therefore seem better not to press the relation of the

Saying to the ceremony (Bernard, Wellhausen), and consequently to understand by the last and great day of the feast the eighth day, which is sufficiently supported both in the Old Testament and in Josephus (see above. For the ceremonies of the eighth day see Strack-Billerbeck, vol. II, pp. 808–12).

The general meaning of the saying is clear enough. Jesus proclaims Himself the donor of the water of life to all who believe, thus justifying the faith of the Samaritans in Him as the Saviour of the World (iv. 42) and giving the true answer to His brethren who desired Him to manifest Himself to the world (v. 4). Great difficulty is, however, caused by the punctuation of the Saying and by the form and application of the Old Testament citation. If the sentence is punctuated with a full stop after *he that believeth on me*, the two parts of the Saying are parallel:

> *If any man thirst let him come unto me;*
> *And let him drink that believeth on me.*

Accordingly the citation is applied to the water which flows from Jesus (cf. xix. 34). This punctuation and meaning is supported by the colometry of the Old Latin manuscripts *d* and *e*, and by the manner in which the passage is interpreted by Cyprian: 'The Lord cries that he who thirsts should come and drink from the rivers of living water which flowed from His belly' (*Ep.* lxxiii. 11). The anonymous tracts *de Rebaptismate* (ch. xiv) and *de Montibus Sina et Sion* (ch. ix), falsely attributed to Cyprian, and other Latin Fathers support the same punctuation (*J.T.S.* xxiv, pp. 66–70, cf. also Eusebius *Hist. Eccl.* v. 1. 22). On the other hand, the Greek Fathers Origen, Cyril of Jerusalem, Basil, and Athanasius (for references see Bernard), unanimously presuppose the punctuation adopted by A.V. and R.V. That is to say, the stop is placed after *let him drink*, with the result that *He that believeth on me* is a suspended nominative as in i. 12, vi. 39, viii. 45, xv. 2, xvii. 2, cf. Acts vii. 40, and the citation is applied to the believer. Thus a subsidiary meaning is introduced; not only is Jesus the donor of the water of life, but also those who believe on Him give life to the world, since the grammatical construction demands the application to the believer of the words *out of his belly shall flow rivers of living water*.

In this controversy of exegesis the commentators range themselves tentatively in more or less equal numbers on one side or the other. All that they ask of their readers is that they should make their choice. It is precisely at this point that a criticism of the commentators is required. Here, as elsewhere in the gospel (see note on i. 13), both meanings are wholly Johannine. Jesus is portrayed as the donor of the water of life in the discourse with the woman of Samaria (iv. 10 sqq., cf. ii. 1–11, vi. 35), and the picture of the water flowing from the side of the crucified Saviour of the World (xix. 34, cf. 1 John v. 6–8) almost demands the primary application of the citation here to Jesus. But the subsidiary allusion is also Johannine, and appears elsewhere in close connection with the primary meaning. In the discourse with the woman of Samaria not only is Jesus presented as the well of Life, but whoever drinks from that well becomes himself *a well of water springing up unto eternal life* (iv. 14, cf. xvii. 8 with xvii. 20 and xix. 34 with xx. 22, 23). It may also be noted that 1 John v. 6–8 is closely followed by the words *He that believeth on the Son of God hath the witness in him* (1 John v. 10). The explanation of the possibility of a double punctuation and of the consequent obscurity both of the grammer and of the application of the citation is that the subsidiary meaning presses upon the primary meaning in the author's mind and this jostling causes a disturbance in the construction of the Saying. Jesus is the Saviour of the World, but the mission is entrusted to His faithful disciples (xxi. 1–17, cf. xiv. 12, xv. 18); consequently, words which apply primarily to Jesus may also be applied to His disciples. For example, the ignorance of the Jews concerning the origin and destiny of Jesus, *ye know not whence I come or whither I go* (viii. 14), reappears in the ignorance concerning the nature of all who are born of the Spirit (iii. 8). Similarly, the metaphor of the seed dying in order that it may bring forth fruit is applied first to the death of the Christ and then to the necessity of the suffering of the believers (xii. 23–6).

The form of the Old Testament citation *Out of his belly shall flow rivers of living water* presents very great difficulty, and especially the word *belly*. The Old Testament does not contain these words; and, though it does contain passages of similar meaning (Exod. xvii. 6; Num. xx. 8–11; Isa. xli. 18, xliii. 20, lv. 1, lviii. 11; Ezek. xlvii. 1–12; Joel iii. 18; Zech. xiii. 1, xiv. 8), in none of them, nor in the LXX version of them, does the Hebrew or Greek word for *belly* occur. It is therefore commonly supposed either that the saying represents the general scriptural tenor of these Old Testament passages and is not strictly a quotation (Westcott) or that the author is referring to some apocryphal saying (Bauer). But the singular *the Scripture* rather than the plural *the Scriptures* suggests that the author has a particular passage in mind (ii. 22, x. 35, xiii. 18, xvii. 12, xix. 24, 28, 36, 37, contrasted with *v.* 36; see, however, xx. 9), and Strack-Billerbeck are able to quote no Midrash to assist the commentator. In Deut. viii. 15, 16, the two miracles of the gift of manna and the gift of *water out of the rock of flint* are singled out and associated (cf. Ps. lxxviii. 20, cv. 40, 41) as signs of the power of God and of the establishment of His covenant (Deut. viii. 18). The author of the gospel has already declared the fulfilment of the original gift of manna (vi. 31–5), and it is not unreasonable to suppose that he now proceeds to declare the fulfilment of the other great miracle of Moses. Jesus is the Rock from which the true water flows forth for the salvation of the world (cf. 1 Cor. x. 4) as He is the Bread which came down from heaven and *giveth life unto the world* (vi. 33).

The exact words are not a quotation. They are a Christian Midrash, which summarizes the prophetic significance of the mosaic miracle. Why then the word *belly*? Holtzmann suggests that the author was thinking of a fountain whose water flows from the belly of a sculptured figure. This is, however, very un-Johannine, and a suggestion of despair. More probably the thought of the author is conditioned by the picture of the water flowing from the *side* of the crucified Lord (xix. 34), *belly* being a synonym for *side*, but having also in contemporary usage, like *heart* or *reins*, a conventional significance as the seat of the emotions. Strack-Billerbeck are able to show that the Hebrew word for *belly* was used in the Rabbinic literature simply to mean *person*: 'Rabbi Judah has said: "Every command which contains a duty binding upon a person",' where the word for 'person' is 'belly'. Codex Alexandrinus reads *heart* for *belly* in the text of Rev. x. 9 and both words are used in the LXX, though in the case of *heart* rarely, to translate the Hebrew בֶּטֶן. The comment of Chrysostom is therefore admirably correct: 'By *belly* he here meaneth the heart, as in another place it saith, *And thy Law in the midst of my belly*' (Ps. xl. 10, in the Greek version of the Theodotion and in the LXX of Codices Sinaiticus and Alexandrinus). Chrysostom, followed by Isho'dad, evades the problem of identifying or explaining the quotation by placing a stop after *as the scripture hath said*, so that the quotation is simply *He that believeth on me* (perhaps Chrysostom is thinking of Isa. xxviii. 16), and *out of his belly*, &c., become the words of Jesus and not a quotation: 'But where hath the Scripture said that *rivers of living water shall flow from his belly*? Nowhere. What then meaneth *He that believeth on me, as the scriptures did say*? A stop must be placed here in order that *the rivers shall flow from his belly* may be His assertion (i.e. of Christ and not of the Scripture)'.

The Saying of Jesus is then interpreted of the Advent of the Spirit, whose mission is deferred until Jesus be glorified (cf. ii. 21, 22). As yet the Spirit is confined to Jesus Himself (i. 33, iii. 34, vi. 62, 63), only when the work of salvation is accomplished can the Spirit be given to the believers. The necessary delaying of the gift of the Spirit is one of the themes of the discourse in the Upper Room (xiv. 26, xvi. 7, cf. Luke xxiv. 49; Acts i. 5, 8, 13). The word *glorify* denotes the death, the resurrection and the return of Jesus to the Father, and in the gospel each stage of this glorification is marked by the gift of the Spirit to one or more of the disciples, the death (xix. 30, see note), the resurrection (xx. 22), the return to the Father (xiv. 26, xvi. 7, cf. vi. 62, 63). For the varied application of the word *glorify* see xii. 16, 23, 28, xiii. 31 sqq., xvi. 14, xvii. 1, 5, 10 and compare the use of the word *lift up* (iii. 14, viii. 28, xii. 32–4). For illustrations of Rabbinic allegorical interpretations of Old Testament passages containing the word *waters* with reference to the Holy Spirit see Strack-Billerbeck on iv. 10.

[It can hardly be doubted that the harsh reading *Spirit was not yet* is original. It is preserved in Codex Sinaiticus, six other Greek manuscripts, a few manuscripts of the Latin Vulgate, and the Bohairic and Armenian Versions, and is supported by Origen and Cyril of Alexandria. The variant readings avoid the possible but unintelligent interpretation that the Spirit as yet had no existence by adding *given* (Codex Vaticanus and two manuscripts of the Old Latin Version) or *upon them* (Codex Bezae and one manuscript of the Old Latin Version), or by a paraphrase *they had not yet received Spirit* (Egyptian Sahidic Version), whilst in many manuscripts, headed by Codex Vaticanus, the words are dignified by the addition of *Holy* to *Spirit* (R.V. mg.).]

### THE EFFECT OF THE WORDS OF JESUS UPON THE CROWD
### AND THE FAILURE OF THE SANHEDRIN TO
### SECURE HIS ARREST

*vv.* 40–52. The words of Jesus exceed the intelligence of the crowd and effect a division among His hearers (cf. Mark viii. 28, 29). Some are vaguely conscious of a messianic importance attaching to His person. He is the Prophet who should precede the Messiah (Mal. iv. 5, cf. i. 21, and Bauer, detached note), or He is the Prophet foretold by Moses (Deut. xviii. 15): in any case He is the supreme Prophet, whose teaching and action are unique (vi. 14). Others formally proclaim Him to be the Christ. Others declare that the prophecy of the origin of the Messiah rules out the messiahship of Jesus. Some, associating themselves with the known policy of the Sanhedrin, desire to lay hands on Him, but are unable to do so. Thus the people of God were rent into quarrelling parties by the advent of the Messiah (ix. 16, x. 19). The author of the gospel pauses to note the precise scriptural ground of the Jewish denial of the messiahship of Jesus. The Old Testament passage is Mic. v. 2, where it is said that the Ruler, whose goings forth are from of old, from everlasting, shall come forth out of Behtlehem Ephrathah; the significance of Bethlehem being that it was David's village (1 Sam. xvii. 15), and that therefore the Messiah would be of David's seed (2 Sam. vii. 12 sqq.; Ps. cxxxii. 11; Isa. xi. 1; Jer. xxiii. 5). But Jesus came forth from Galilee (iv. 44, vii. 9, 10), and was of Nazareth (i. 45). The objection is answered in the first and third gospels (Matt. ii. 1–6; Luke ii. 4), but the author of the Fourth Gospel leaves it mysteriously unanswered. He supposes his readers to know the answer, and if he presumes a knowledge of the Virgin Birth, he knows also that it is open to an even graver objection (viii. 41), and in any case the supreme task of the Evangelist is to declare Jesus to be the Christ, the Son of God, and to this purpose he has devoted his literary energy (xx. 31).

The author now returns to the emissaries who had been sent to arrest Jesus (*v.* 32). They had been dispatched in the middle of the Feast, but it has concluded (*v.* 37) without their being able to fulfil their task. The power of His teaching makes it impossible for them to interfere. The Pharisees, seeing at once that their police have been infected by the teaching of Jesus and share in the deception of the crowd (*v.* 12), remind them that their opinion must be regulated by those of their superiors. Proudly secure in their knowledge of the Law they assert that no single member of the Sanhedrin has been disturbed by the teaching of this Galilean. The wavering faith of the crowd does but betray their ignorance of the Law and the curse under which they are set because of their ignorance (Deut. xxvii. 26, xxviii. 15 sqq.; Ps. cxix. 21). The rulers, however, are shown to be neither solid in their loyalty (cf. xii. 42) nor secure in their knowledge of the Law, for Nicodemus, one of their number, had already visited Jesus, as the readers of the gospel well know (iii. 1 sqq., xix. 39); and it is he who now reminds them that this procedure against Jesus is in flagrant violation of the Law. The Law demands that the judges in Israel should *hear the causes* (Deut. i. 16 sqq., cf. Exod. xxiii. 1 sqq.; Deut. xvii. 4; Jos. *Ant.* xiv. 167; *B.J.* i. 209); the Sanhedrin has, however, hurried to arrest Jesus without first hearing Him or taking pains to discover what, in fact, it is that He is doing. The Pharisees make no attempt to answer the accusation, since the issue is not really the legality of their action, but the claim of Jesus to be the Christ. They therefore rudely and scornfully silence Nicodemus by stating that only a Galilean, ignorant of the Scriptures, could suppose that even a prophet could emerge from Galilee. Thus they deny the power of God, and betray their ignorance of the Scriptures, for Jonah, the Prophet, was of Gath-Hepher, a village in Galilee. Rabbi Eliezer boasted with greater truth, 'Thou hast no single tribe in Israel from which prophets have not arisen' (compare the parallel saying cited by Strack-Billerbeck: 'Thou hast no city in the land of Israel in which there have not been prophets').

The judgement pronounced by the Pharisees upon the multitude, that they are ignorant of the Law and accursed, is sufficiently supported in the Rabbinic literature (see the exhaustive note in Strack-Billerbeck). In the Old Testament the phrase 'The people of the land' is used to denote (*a*) the whole people of Israel, (*b*) the people as opposed to the rulers, (*c*) the heathen resident in the land. It is the second meaning that is developed in the Rabbinic literature. There the phrase is a technical term for the laymen who are not instructed in the Law. Since piety rested upon the study of the Law it followed that, as Hillel said, 'The people of the land are impious' (*Aboth* ii. 5)—'The people of the land cannot be trusted in matters of Mine and Thine' (*Aboth* v. 10). The attitude is summed up in a Midrash (Strack-Billerbeck, vol. II, p. 495), 'Jephtha could have gone to the High Priest Phinehas and have been freed from his oath; but he said "I am the king, and should I go to Phinehas?" And Phinehas said "I am High Priest and the son of a

High Priest, should I go to one of the people of the land" (i.e. to one ignorant of the Law)?'—For the clear distinction between the Pharisaic *Chaberim* and the people of the land see Strack-Billerbeck, vol. II, pp. 500–17.

In the comment on *v.* 52 the words *Search, and see that out of Galilee ariseth no prophet* have been taken to mean *search* in the Scriptures. This is supported by the meaning of the word *search* in v. 39, by the variant reading *has been raised for* ariseth, and by the context in which the words stand, since knowledge or ignorance of the Law is the subject of the controversy. Some commentators, however, desire to avoid attributing to the Pharisees ignorance of the origin of Jonah, press the present *ariseth* and give a general meaning to the word *search*, so that the sentence means simply 'From your knowledge of Galilee, Do you consider it the kind of district to produce a prophet!'

For the commentary upon *The Woman taken in Adultery* (vii. 53–viii. 11), see APPENDIX, pp. 563–72.

# THE SECOND GREAT DISCOURSE
# CONCERNING
# THE UNBELIEF OF THE JEWS

## VIII. 12-59

THE second of the two great discourses against the Jews (v. 19–47, viii. 12–59) is in extent the most considerable. With these two extended discourses, the undeveloped discourses in xiii. 31–6 and xii. 44–50 and the short pregnant utterances contained in ch. vii are closely associated, and their adequate interpretation depends upon this material being taken as one whole in which the words of the Prologue *He came unto his own, and his own received him not* are expanded and explained. As in the discourses to the disciples (chs. xiv–xvi) the themes remain constant throughout—the origin and destiny of Jesus, the nature of His witness to Himself, and the judgement pronounced upon the Jews—and characteristic phrases or key words tend to recur; but at each repetition of theme or phrase or key word its significance is extended by some modification in its application, so that the meaning of any single passage depends upon delicacy of allusion rather than upon directness of statement (compare v. 30–7, vii. 16, 28, 29, viii. 13–18, 28, 42, xii. 32, 49; v. 22, 30, vii. 24, viii. 15, 16, xii. 48; vii. 34–6, viii. 21, 22; vii. 20, viii. 48, 52; v. 39, 40, 45–7, vii. 19, viii. 39; v. 35, viii. 12, xii. 35, 36, 45; see also vii. 37, 38).

The removal of vii. 53–viii. 11 from the text of the gospel brings the discourse in ch. viii. into close connection with ch. vii. The scene is the same. Jesus is teaching in the Temple (vii. 14, 37, viii. 20, 59), His exact position in or near the Treasury being carefully noted (viii. 20). The impression left upon the readers of the gospel is that the Feast of Tabernacles is still in progress, and that the themes promulgated in the utterances of Jesus recorded in ch. vii are again picked up and developed in a continuous discourse. The relation between chs. vii and viii is not unlike the relation between ch. xiv. and chs. xv–xvi, the break at vii. 52 corresponding with the break at xiv. 31.

The discourse is divided into three sections introduced by the words *again therefore He spake* (vv. 12, 21, cf. x. 7) or *Jesus therefore said* (v. 31), and is broken by hostile interruptions of the Pharisees (v. 13), the Jews (vv. 22, 25), and the Jews who believed in Him (vv. 33, 39, 48, 52,

53, 57), by which the progress of the discourse is conditioned and directed.

## THE WITNESS OF JESUS AND THE WITNESS OF THE FATHER

viii. 12. *Again therefore Jesus spake unto them, saying, I am the light of the world: he that followeth me shall not walk in the darkness, but shall have the light of life.* 13. *The Pharisees therefore said unto him, Thou bearest witness of thyself; thy witness is not true.* 14. *Jesus answered and said unto them, Even if I bear witness of myself, my witness is true; for I know whence I came, and whither I go; but ye know not whence I come, or whither I go.* 15. *Ye judge after the flesh; I judge no man.* 16. *Yea and if I judge, my judgement is true; for I am not alone, but I and the Father that sent me.* 17. *Yea and in your law it is written, that the witness of two men is true.* 18. *I am he that beareth witness of myself, and the Father that sent me beareth witness of me.* 19. *They said therefore unto him, Where is thy Father? Jesus answered, Ye know neither me, nor my Father: if ye knew me, ye would know my Father also.* 20. *These words spake he in the treasury, as he taught in the temple: and no man took him; because his hour was not yet come.*

## THE DESTINY OF UNBELIEF

21. *He said therefore again unto them, I go away, and ye shall seek me, and shall die in your sin: whither I go, ye cannot come.* 22. *The Jews therefore said, Will he kill himself, that he saith, Whither I go, ye cannot come?* 23. *And he said unto them, Ye are from beneath; I am from above: ye are of this world; I am not of this world.* 24. *I said therefore unto you, that ye shall die in your sins: for except ye believe that I am he, ye shall die in your sins.* 25. *They said therefore unto him, Who art thou? Jesus said unto them, Even that which I have also spoken unto you from the beginning.* 26. *I have many things to speak and to judge concerning you: howbeit he that sent me is true; and the things which I heard from him, these speak I unto the world.* 27. *They perceived not that he spake to them of the Father.* 28. *Jesus therefore said, When ye have lifted up the Son of man, then shall ye know that I am he, and that I do nothing of myself, but as the Father taught me, I speak these things.* 29. *And he that sent me is with me; he hath not left me alone; for I do always the things that are pleasing to him.* 30. *As he spake these things, many believed on him.*

## JESUS, THE SON OF GOD, LIBERATES MEN
## FROM THE SLAVERY OF SIN

31. *Jesus therefore said to those Jews which had believed him, If ye abide in my word, then are ye truly my disciples;* 32. *and ye shall know the truth, and the truth shall make you free.* 33. *They answered unto him, We be Abraham's seed, and have never yet been in bondage to any man: how sayest thou, Ye shall*

*be made free? 34. Jesus answered them, Verily, verily, I say unto you, Every one that committeth sin is the bondservant of sin. 35. And the bondservant abideth not in the house for ever: the son abideth for ever. 36. If therefore the Son shall make you free, ye shall be free indeed.*

## JESUS PRONOUNCES THE UNBELIEVING JEWS TO BE THE SONS OF THE DEVIL, WHO IS THE ANTI-CHRIST

*37. I know that ye are Abraham's seed; yet ye seek to kill me, because my word hath not free course in you. 38. I speak the things which I have seen with my Father: and ye also do the things which ye heard from your father. 39. They answered and said unto him, Our father is Abraham. Jesus saith unto them, If ye were Abraham's children, ye would do the works of Abraham. 40. But now ye seek to kill me, a man that hath told you the truth, which I heard from God: this did not Abraham. 41. Ye do the works of your father. They said unto him, We were not born of fornication; we have one Father, even God. 42. Jesus said unto them, If God were your Father, ye would love me: for I came forth and am come from God; for neither have I come of myself, but he sent me. 43. Why do ye not understand my speech? Even because ye cannot hear my word. 44. Ye are of your father the devil, and the lusts of your father it is your will to do. He was a murderer from the beginning, and stood not in the truth, because there is no truth in him. When he speaketh a lie, he speaketh of his own: for he is a liar, and the father thereof. 45. But because I say the truth, ye believe me not.*

## ABRAHAM AND JESUS: THE BLASPHEMY OF THE JEWS CONTRASTED WITH THE RECOGNITION OF JESUS BY THE PATRIARCH ABRAHAM

*46. Which of you convicteth me of sin? If I say truth, why do ye not believe me? 47. He that is of God heareth the words of God: for this cause ye hear them not, because ye are not of God. 48. The Jews answered and said unto him, Say we not well that thou art a Samaritan, and hast a devil? 49. Jesus answered, I have not a devil; but I honour my Father, and ye dishonour me. 50. But I seek not mine own glory; there is one that seeketh and judgeth. 51. Verily, verily, I say unto you, If a man keep my word, he shall never see death. 52. The Jews said unto him, Now we know that thou hast a devil. Abraham is dead, and the prophets; and thou sayest, If a man keep my word, he shall never taste of death. 53. Art thou greater than our father Abraham, which is dead? and the prophets are dead: whom makest thou thyself? 54. Jesus answered, If I glorify myself, my glory is nothing: it is my Father that glorifieth me; of whom ye say, that he is your God; 55. and ye have not known him: but I know him; and if I should say, I know him not, I shall be like unto you, a liar: but I know him, and keep his word. 56. Your father Abraham rejoiced to see my day; and he saw it, and was glad. 57. The Jews therefore said unto him, Thou art not yet fifty years old, and hast thou seen Abraham? 58. Jesus said unto them, Verily, verily, I say unto you,*

*Before Abraham was, I am.* 59. *They took up stones therefore to cast at him: but Jesus hid himself, and went out of the temple.*

### THE WITNESS OF JESUS AND THE WITNESS OF THE FATHER

viii. 12–20. The discourse opens with the majestic witness which Jesus bears to Himself—*I am the Light of the World* (cf. iv. 26, vi. 35, 48, viii. 23, ix. 5, x. 7, 9, xi. 25, xiii. 19, xiv. 6, xv. 1, xviii. 5, 6, 8; contrast i. 20, iii. 28). The metaphor of the water of life which flows from Jesus and which satisfies the thirst of all true believers (vii. 37, 38) is displaced by the metaphor of the light of life by which the light of the sun is eclipsed and the darkness of sin dispersed, so that those who follow Jesus (i. 37, xii. 26, xxi. 22) walk no longer in darkness, but are filled with the knowledge of God (i. 4–9, iii. 19, ix. 4, 5, xii. 35, 36, 46; 1 John i. 5, 6, ii. 9–11). The believer in Jesus *shall have* in himself the light of life, as he has been promised the water of life (iv. 14, vii. 38) and the bread of life (vi. 51–8). He becomes one of the sons of light (xii. 36), and walks in the Way, which is Jesus (xiv. 6). Modern commentators have endeavoured to provide a non-scriptural background to the words *I am the light of the world*. They suggest that it was provoked by the ceremony of lighting the great candelabra in the Court of the Women on the first night of the Feast of Tabernacles (see Strack-Billerbeck, vol. II, pp. 806, 807), or by some similar ceremony in connection with the Feast of Dedication (*J.T.S.* ii, p. 138; where, however, the theory is dismissed); or that the author of the gospel was moved to introduce it by the desire to attach to Jesus an honourable phrase familiar to the worshippers of Oriental deities (see Bauer). Interesting though such parallels may be, and important as they are for the student of comparative religion the use of the metaphor of light in the earlier Christian writings (Matt. ·iv. 14 sqq., v. 14–16; Luke ii. 32; Acts xiii. 47; Eph. v. 8; Phil. ii. 15; Col. i. 12, 13, cf. 1 Pet. ii. 9) and in the Old Testament (Exod. x ¡ii. 21, 22; Ps. xxvii. 1; Isa. ix. 1, xlii. 6, xlix. 9, lx. 1, 19; Mal. iv. 2 ) is wholly sufficient to account for the manner and form in which it is employed in the Johannine writings. It is, moreover, significant that in Isa. xliii. 8–13 not only is the importance of witnessing associated with the divine *I am*, but also the whole is directed towards the removal of the blindness of the people and for the salvation of the nations. Nor do the words *I am the light of the world* say more than is implied in the words of Jesus in the Sermon on the Mount, *Ye are the light of the world* (Matt. v. 14), since the light which the disciples furnish to the world depends upon their relation to Jesus, the Messiah (for 'Light' as a name of the Messiah in the sayings of the Rabbis see Strack-Billerbeck on Matt. i. 21, p. 67).

The metaphor of light is not directly maintained in the discourse occasioned by the saying of Jesus; its exposition is deferred until the record of the healing of the blind man (ch. ix), which forms a commentary in action upon the words *I am the light of the world* (ix. 5, cf. xii. 35, 36, 46). The Pharisees, who are now present in person (contrast vii. 32, 45), raise the general question of the validity of the witness which Jesus bears to Himself (v. 18, 31, vii. 18, 28, viii. 54); they do not demand the elucidation of the particular content of that witness. His witness, they maintain, proceeds from egotism, and, for this reason, bears the marks of evident falsity. Jesus categorically denies the truth of this judgement. The witness of Jesus, that is of the Christ, the Son of God, is inevitably a witness to Himself which can, as yet at least, be corroborated by no human witness. He is a solitary witness among men, since He alone knows whence He comes and whither He goes (cf. iii. 13, vi. 33, 38, vii. 27–9, 33, viii. 21–3, xiii. 3, xvi. 28. For Greek and Oriental parallels see Bauer). His witness to Himself is therefore not only inevitable, but also true and valid. The judgement which the Pharisees make upon His witness is therefore a judgement *according to the flesh*, that is, it is a merely human judgement, and lacks the necessary spiritual insight which will belong to His true disciples (vi. 63, vii. 24, xiv. 26, xv. 26, xvi. 13, cf. 1 Cor. i. 26, 2 Cor. v. 16).

The word *judgement* is a Johannine key word capable of subtle distinctions of meaning. In the parallel passage v. 30 sqq. it is practically synonymous with *witness*. But it is a witness grounded upon evidence; hence it becomes also synonymous with *knowledge*. Finally, it means *condemnation* (compare the various suggestions latent in the Greek word translated *convict* in xvi. 8). The argument has hitherto been moving in terms of witnessing and of insight into truth, and the conclusion is reached that the judgement of the Pharisees is a judgement according to the flesh. The reader expects the further statement that the knowledge or judgement of Jesus is a true judgement, according to the will of God (cf. 2 Cor. v. 16). Instead, the third meaning of the word is suddenly thrust into the foreground, and the paradox is uttered *I judge no man* (v. 15, cf. viii. 11, Matt. vii. 1). The mission of the Son of God is a mission, not of condemnation, but of salvation (iii. 17, xii. 47, xx. 31). And yet, since the rejection of Jesus involves present (iii. 18) and ultimate (xii. 48) condemnation, the work of salvation is inevitably also a work of condemnation; and if He condemns, His condemnation is true and genuine; there is no escape from it. This truth is expressed in a typically Johannine contradiction—*I judge no man* (v. 15)—*For neither doth the Father judge any man, but he hath given all judgement unto the Son* (v. 22, cf. v. 27). The judgement of the Pharisees is therefore a false opinion; the judgement of Jesus is a sovereign decision, a divine decree, pronounced in strict accordance with the will of God.

The paradox occasioned by the use of the verb *to judge* is, however, but an aside, and the author returns at once to his main theme, the witness of Jesus to Himself, leaving in their obscurity the subtle meanings associated with the idea of judgement. The witness of Jesus is not a solitary witness. He is never alone, for His Father is not only *with Him* (xvi. 32), but *in Him* (xiv. 10, 11, xvii. 21–3). Consequently, the witness of Jesus is a double witness, His own witness and the witness of the Father who sent Him (v. 37, xii. 49). This double witness amply fulfils the demands of the Jewish Law. For, if in a criminal investigation a matter be established at the mouth of two human witnesses (Deut. xix. 15, cf. Deut. xvii. 6; Num. xxxv. 30; Matt. xviii. 16; 2 Cor. xiii. 1; 1 Tim. v. 19), it follows *a fortiori* that, in an investigation concerning the action of God for the salvation of His people, the matter is finally established by the combined witness of the Father and the Son. The passage from Deuteronomy is freely cited, *The witness of two men* being substituted for *At the mouth of two witnesses*, in order to emphasize the argument from the less to the greater—*If we receive the witness of men, the witness of God is greater* (1 John v. 9). The author does not here define the nature of the witness of the Father to Jesus. The readers of the Gospel know how wide a ground is covered by that witness. The witness of John was grounded upon a divine revelation (i. 32–4, iii. 26–36); the miracles and the Old Testament scriptures are the witness of the Father to the Son (v. 36–9); but, since the Father abides in the Son, the witness of the Father is present in all that the Son says and does (xiv. 10, 11). In the First Epistle the whole Christian experience of salvation unto eternal life is stated to be the witness of God to His Son. The believer *hath the witness in Him* (1 John v. 10–12).

The argument from the validity of the evidence of two independent human witnesses to the greater validity of that single witness which proceeds from the essential union of the Father and the Son is beyond the comprehension of the Pharisees. They demand the concrete visibility of the Father of Jesus. The question *Where is thy Father?* is a supreme formulation of Jewish misunderstanding and unbelief. On the one hand, it is the counterpart of Philip's demand, *Shew us the Father* (xiv. 8), and is a demand doubly blasphemous, since it presumes an ignorance of the invisibility of God (v. 37; 1 John iv. 12) and an ignorance of the Son, who is the visible and only way to the knowledge of God and to the reality of His presence among men (xiv. 6, 9). The question therefore implies primarily a misunderstanding concerning Jesus. The conditional clause *If ye knew me, ye would know my Father also* is an unfulfilled condition in present time. If the Pharisees were in possession of knowledge concerning Jesus, they would now possess knowledge of the Father (xvi. 3, cf. xii. 44, 45). On the other hand if the question *Where is thy Father?* be set on the background of the comment in *v.* 27, *They perceived not that he spake to them of the Father*, the blasphemy of the Pharisees is of a different nature. They are ignorant of the true paternity of Jesus, and demand either the presence of Joseph (i. 46, vi. 42), or, referring to the supposed illegitimacy of

Jesus (viii. 41; Matt. i. 19), they cynically demand the presence of His
unknown father. Cyril of Alexandria, admirably perceiving the different applications of the question of the Pharisees, notes the ignorance
of God presumed in the question, and continues his comment thus, 'But
it is likely that the words of the Jews had some other deep meaning.
For since they thought that the Holy Virgin had committed adultery
before marriage, they therefore rail most bitterly against Christ as not
even knowing from whom He is. . . . They indeed suppose Jesus to be
either of Joseph or of fornication.'

The first section of the discourse concludes with a reference to the
locality where it was spoken (cf. vi. 59) and to the continuance of the
murderous intention of the Jewish authorities, which they are as yet
unable to carry out (v. 18, vii. 19, 25, 32, 44, viii. 44, 59, x. 39, xviii.
12–14). The words of Jesus were spoken in or near the Treasury. If the
Greek preposition *in* be taken literally it conveys the impression that
Jesus spoke in the actual headquarters of the Jewish authorities, since
the Treasury, the Hall where the Temple treasure was kept, was situated near the Hall in which the Sanhedrin met, and was not generally
accessible (Strack-Billerbeck on Mark xii. 41). If, however, the preposition means no more than *near*, it may be a reminiscence of Mark xii.
41, *over against the treasury* (cf. Luke xxi. 1), and the discourse is spoken
in the Court of the Women near the place where the thirteen chests
were set to receive the offerings of the people.

### THE DESTINY OF UNBELIEF

*vv.* 21–30. The words of Jesus recorded in vii. 33, 34 (see COMMEN-
TARY, cf. xiii. 33) are repeated with alterations which express more
clearly the tension occasioned by the presence of Jesus in the midst of
the Jews. There is no escape from the necessity of death in sin except
by faith in Jesus; consequently, His imminent removal strictly limits
the opportunity of their salvation, and renders the witness which He
bears to Himself pregnant with judgement. The purpose of His witness
is to evoke faith; its rejection involves ultimate condemnation.

The judgement which threatens the Jews (cf. Luke xix. 41–4) is
emphasized by the substitution of *And shall die in your sin* (cf. Deut.
xxiv. 16; Ezek. iii. 19, xviii. 24–8; Prov. xxiv. 9–12) for *And shall not find
me* (vii. 34), so that the whole Saying runs: *I go away, and ye shall seek me
—and shall die in your sin; whither I go ye cannot come.* The inadequacy of
the Jewish interpretation of the saying is correspondingly intensified,
and caricatures a truth more fundamental than the mission to the Gentiles. For whereas, formerly (vii. 35), the Jews had explained the imminent inaccessibility of Jesus by the supposition of His undertaking
a mission to the Greeks, they now imagine His removal from their reach
to be occasioned by self-inflicted death. And since, as Josephus writes,

a suicide migrates into the gloom of Hades (*B.J.* iii. 375), it is manifestly impossible for them to follow Him thither. This alternative interpretation of the words of Jesus is also a prophetic caricature of the truth. The Christian mission to the world depends upon the sacrificial and voluntary death of Jesus (x. 18), and His true disciples, dying to this world (xii. 25), will alone be able to follow Him and to be where He is (xii. 26, xiii. 36–xiv. 3). And yet, paradoxically, the circumstances of the death of Jesus are not those of suicide. His death is murder, effected maliciously by the Jews. Jesus no more kills Himself than He makes Himself equal with God (v. 18).

The misunderstanding, by which the sin of the Jews is exposed, proceeds from an already existing deep-seated corruption. In the contrast between Jesus and the Jews two antagonistic realities are directly opposed the one to the other. It is an ultimate contrast embodied in flesh and blood, which provokes for its expression a series of terse descriptive phrases, Hebraic in their strict parallelism, and running to a final and precise climax. They judge according to the flesh (*v.* 15); He judges according to the will of God (v. 30). They are from below; He is from above: they are from this world; He is not from this world; He has descended from heaven (iii. 13, 31, xviii. 36): they are of their father, the Devil; He is the Son of God (viii. 41–4): their father was a murderer from the beginning (viii. 44) and they are his murderous servants; His Father so loved the world that He sent His only begotten Son that the world might be saved by Him and have eternal life (iii. 16, 17). Moreover, this contrast between Jesus and the Jews is expanded into a permanent opposition between His disciples and the world, which is summed up in the distinction between that which is born of flesh and that which is born of Spirit (iii. 6, xvii. 14, 18; 1 John iv. 17, cf. Rom. viii. 9). In the perspective of the Johannine narrative this double opposition becomes one majestic whole in which the Truth is revealed—in which God manifests Himself as Love (1 John iv. 7 sqq.).

And yet, the procession of the Jews along the road of sin which leads to death is imposed upon them by no categorical necessity. They are riveted to the world by unbelief; but the opportunity of their removal from this slavery is provided by the presence of Jesus in their midst and by the public and insistent witness which He bears to Himself— *Except ye believe that I am, ye shall die in your sins* (i. 12, iii. 15, 18, vi. 40, xx. 31). It may be doubted whether the author intended any particular significance to be attached to his alteration of the singular *sin* (*v.* 21) into the plural *sins* (*v.* 24). (See, however, Plummer and Westcott.) The absolute claim of Jesus is denoted by the majestic *I am*: majestic, and numinous, because of its Old Testament background (Exod. iii. 14; Deut. xxxii. 39; Isa. xliii. 10). No predicate is expressed or provided by the context (cf. *vv.* 28, 58, iv. 26, ix. 9, xiii. 19, xviii. 5, 6, 8). The Jews demand that the omission be corrected and that a definite predicate be provided for the *I am*. The question *who art thou?* (cf. i. 19), has now become presumptuous because, in so far as it is capable of an answer, the answer has been given publicly and continuously from the beginning of His ministry. Jesus can initiate no new teaching about Himself. The issue is now not the necessity of removing a justifiable ignorance of His claim, but the necessity of even clearer teaching concerning their condition; and this inevitably means their further condemnation: *I have many things to speak and to judge concerning you.*

[In the above comment *v.* 25 has been taken to mean (*I am*) *that which I have spoken unto you from the beginning* (cf. R.V.); but the Greek is extremely obscure, and no certain interpretation of its meaning is possible. The translators of the early Latin and Syriac Versions give a merely literal rendering of the Greek without, apparently, being able to extract from it any precise meaning. Since, however, the Latin word for *beginning* is both nominative and accusative, the Latin version, aided by Rev. xxi. 6, could be taken to mean *I am the Beginning*. The Latin Fathers, depending upon the Vulgate, tend to take it thus. In the Clementine Vulgate the ruling Latin exegesis reacted back upon the text, which emerged as *I who am speaking unto you am the Beginning*. The true text of the Vulgate is restored by Wordsworth and White. Saint Augustine, aware that in the Greek the word *beginning* is firmly in the accusative, suggested that some such word as *I declare* must be understood, and translated the opening words of the sentence *I declare that I am the Beginning* (see Lagrange). In commenting upon the Greek text, the Latin tradition of exegesis must be wholly disregarded, since it almost completely ignores the Greek. The Greek text is, however, patient of various interpretations. There is a Greek idiom which permits the words *the beginning* to be translated *absolutely, altogether, at all*. The sentence may then be translated either *I am essentially* (or *primarily*) *that which I am telling you*, or, as a threat to break off the discourse (cf. Mark ix. 19) *How is it that I even speak unto you at all?* The Greek Fathers, Chrysostom, Cyril, Theodore of Mopsuestia, Euthymius, favour the latter meaning, and those modern commentators who regard classical erudition as an adequate handmaid to Johannine exegesis are inclined to adopt one or other of the interpretations which rest upon the Greek idiom (Lagrange, Westcott, Bernard, Bauer, R.V. mg.). It may, however, be doubted whether the author of the gospel could permit the word *beginning*, which is to him so important a word, to disappear so completely or whether so delicate a Greek idiom was natural to him. If the phrase *the beginning*, which is in the accusative case, be compared with the usage in the LXX, the meaning *at the beginning* is sufficiently justified (Gen. xli. 21, xliii. 19; Dan. ix. 21, cf. viii. 1 Theodotion.) It then becomes a variant for other phrases in the Johannine writings meaning *at* or *from the beginning* (i. 1, vi. 64, viii. 44, xv. 27, xvi. 4; 1 John i. 1, ii. 7, iii. 8, etc.). The author uses the word *beginning* to express a series of overlapping suggestions. It means the Creation (i. 1, viii. 44; 1 John i. 1, iii. 8), the opening period of the public ministry of Jesus (ii. 11, vi. 64, xv. 27, xvi. 4), the whole earthly ministry of Jesus contrasted with the later work of His disciples (1 John ii. 7), and the Apostolic Age contrasted with the Christians of the second generation (1 John ii. 13, 14, 24, iii. 11; 2 John 5, 6). But in any given passage it is often difficult to be certain which of these meanings is uppermost in the author's mind. The whole sentence is therefore capable of translation either *at the beginning I am what I even now tell you* or *I am what I have even told you at* (or *from*) *the beginning*. (The perfect, *I have told you*, is the best way of expressing in English the meaning of the idiomatic Greek present, *I am telling you*.) Both meanings are admirably Johannine (xii. 50, xvi. 4). The explanation of the difficult present tense may well be that the double meaning attaching to the word *beginning*—The Creation and the Opening of the ministry of Jesus—has complicated the grammar (cf. vii. 37, 38), and that both meanings overlap in the sentence as it stands. Jesus was at the Creation what He had publicly claimed to be since the beginning of His ministry.]

Though there can how be no modification of, or addition to, the witness which Jesus has borne to Himself, and though the purpose of the discourse is the condemnation of the sin of the Jews, yet, since their sin is consummated in His rejection, the full significance of His presence in their midst is at once more solemnly affirmed. The judgement pronounced upon the Jews is therefore inevitably a final answer to their question *Who art thou?* The great Johannine series of statements—The Father sent Him, the Father is with Him, the Father is in Him, He and the Father are one—underlie the solemn affirmation here made to the Jews; but only the simpler statements are actually expressed. He is the Emissary of His Father, and He gives no other teaching than that which He has heard from His Father; and more than this, the Father who sent Him is now with Him, so that He is never alone, and no action or word of His is removed from the context of this relationship. In the appearance of Jesus all that is pleasing to God stands concretely in the midst of the Jews and for this reason His teaching is directed beyond the Jews to the world. In the concrete relation of Jesus to the Father the truth of God is therefore manifested to the Jews and to the world. The misunderstanding of the Jews is, however, complete. They did not recognize that He was speaking of His relation to God, supposing Him to be speaking of a relationship to some one who did not happen to be present, rather than of His union with Him whom no man hath seen at any time (i. 18, v. 37, vi. 46; 1 John iv. 12, 20).

This overwhelming picture of the ignorance of the Jews is relieved by the reference to the many Jews who *believed on him* (how inadequate their belief was is exposed in the continuation of the discourse, *vv.* 31 sqq.), and by the solemn declaration that when they lift up the Son of man they will penetrate the mystery of His Person and recognize who He is. Since the action of lifting up is an action of the Jews, the reference is clearly to the crucifixion (cf. iii. 14, 15). It is, therefore, difficult to suppose that the author is referring to a general conversion of the Jews under the pressure of the despair occasioned by the destruction of Jerusalem (Chrysostom, Westcott, Lagrange). The pressure is rather occasioned by the witness which the Christians bore to the efficacy of the Cross, and the thought here is of those Jews who were converted by the fact of the crucifixion and by its proclamation in the life of the Church (xii. 24; 1 John i. 7; Gal. iii. 1–4).

### JESUS, THE SON OF GOD, LIBERATES MEN FROM THE SLAVERY OF SIN

*vv.* 31–6. The theme of Christian freedom from the slavery of sin, which is now introduced, overlaps with the Pauline doctrine of the *glorious liberty of the children of God* from sin and from corruption (Rom. vi. viii. 1–4, 21; Gal. iv. 21–v. 1). The origin of the Johannine, as of the Pauline, teaching lies in the traditional record of the sayings and actions of Jesus, interpreted by the light of the Church's experience of righteousness by faith in Jesus. In the synoptic gospels Jesus, as the Christ, the Son of man, exercises His power on earth to remit sins (Mark ii. 1–12, cf. Matt. xxvi. 28), and to call men to effective repentance (Mark ii. 17). The word *remit* in the Greek suggests not only forgiveness, but also freedom from captivity or slavery (Luke iv. 18, cf. Isa. lviii. 6, lxi. 1). The miracles of healing are therefore signs of that deeper messianic cure which the Lord expects will be operative in His disciples who stand within the Kingdom of God. Their righteousness must exceed the righteousness of the scribes and Pharisees, and they must be perfect even as their Father which is in heaven is perfect (Matt. v. 20, 48); they are the true sons of God, and *the sons are free* (Matt. xvii. 24–6).

The Johannine teaching concerning liberty is set on the contrasted background of the slavery of the unbelieving Jews. The Jews, because of their refusal to believe in Jesus, the Son of God, remain outside the sphere of the righteousness of God, in spite of their descent from Abraham. This contrast of Jew with Christian has its counterpart in the teaching of Saint Paul (Rom. iv. 1–17; Gal. iii. 4–14); but the origin of this radical criticism of the Jews is to be found in the teaching of Jesus Himself. In the Gospels of Mark and Luke the narrative of the mission of Jesus is prefaced by the denial by John the Baptist of the validity of mere physical descent from Abraham (Matt. iii. 9; Luke iii. 8); but the judgement uttered by Jesus is even more terrible. The rejection of Jesus by the Jews is the rejection of the Messiah, and because of their unbelief He pronounces them to be under the Judgement of

God (Matt. xi. 20–4, xii. 34, 38–42). It is not therefore beyond the horizon of the synoptic gospels when the scribes and Pharisees are named 'Children of hell' (Matt. xxiii. 15), or when those who oppose the work of Jesus are compared to tares sown by an enemy in a field of wheat, or when the good seed is interpreted of the *Sons of the kingdom* and the tares of the *Sons of the evil one*, whilst *the Enemy* is frankly identified with *the Devil* (Matt. xiii. 24–30, 36–43). No doubt the directness and precision of the language used by the author of the Fourth Gospel is occasioned by the long history of Jewish opposition to the Christians; but the judgement pronounced upon the Jews is not more severe in the Fourth Gospel than is involved in the Sayings of Jesus in the synoptic gospels. It is the certainty of the author's interpretation of the earlier tradition that enables him to use language at once simple and yet allusive. The allusions in the discourse, which the commentator has to detect, are limited to the Old Testament Scriptures, to the tradition of the teaching of Jesus, and to the Johannine cycle of teaching. The commentator is not at liberty to introduce allusions to the Stoic doctrine of the freedom of the wise man or to the Philonic adaptation of Stoic doctrine for the interpretation of the Old Testament (see Bauer on viii. 32, 34).

The discourse concerning Christian liberty and Jewish slavery is addressed to those Jews who had believed as a result of the teaching of Jesus (*v.* 30). They correspond with the Jews who believed when they saw His miracles, and to whom Jesus did not trust Himself (ii. 23, 24, cf. vii. 31, xi. 45, xii. 11, 42, 43). The purpose of the discourse is to expose this false belief and to reveal its compatibility with murderous action. The episode concludes with the note that they *took up stones to cast at him* (*v.* 59). The believing Jews do not therefore foreshadow those who would, after the crucifixion, perceive the truth (*v.* 28); they anticipate rather, as Judas did, those false Christians who hated their Christian brothers (1 John iii. 15) and left the fellowship and returned to the world, because they did not believe that *Jesus Christ is come in the flesh* (vi. 60–6; 1 John ii. 19, iv. 1–3; 2 John 7). The mark of the true disciples of Jesus is that they abide permanently in His word. The Christians abide in the teaching of Jesus as His teaching abides in them (*v.* 38, xv. 7; 2 John 9, cf. 1 John ii. 6, 24, 27). This constant penetration of the Christians by the teaching of Jesus is highly significant. It leads to a clear and active perception of the truth which is productive of complete freedom from sin. And yet it would be to misunderstand the Johannine doctrine here if it were supposed that the teaching or the truth or the freedom from sin could be detached from the figure of flesh and blood which was Jesus. He is the truth (xiv. 6), and He is the liberator from sin (*v.* 36; 1 John iii. 6), because He did indeed overcome the World (xvi. 33; 1 John ii. 12–14, iii. 8, v. 4, 5). There can therefore be no abiding in His teaching apart from an abiding in Him, nor can

His teaching abide in men unless He abides in them (vi. 56, xv. 4-7). Jesus is the Word of God.

The Jews misunderstand the meaning of the word 'Freedom'; and their misunderstanding sets in motion the discourse in which they are completely exposed. Since the servants of God can be slaves of no man (Lev. xxv. 42), freedom was for the Jew a present reality, not a future hope. Josephus cites the teaching of Judas the Galilean that the Jews can rightly call no man lord, since God is their only Ruler and Lord, and regards this inviolable attachment to liberty as the cause of revolt from the authority of Rome (Joseph. *Ant.* xviii. 23-5, cf. *B.J.* vii. 323-5). It is not political freedom, however, that is at issue between the Jews and the Christians. The issue is between that liberty of service to God which the Jews claimed because they were the physical descendants of Abraham, and the liberty which belonged to the Christians who had passed from sin to righteousness, from slavery to freedom, because they had been born of God by faith in Jesus (1 John iii. 9, v. 1, cf. Rom. vi. 12-22, viii. 1-4). In this context, both for Jew and for Christian, political liberty was trivial; and the Jews could rightly say that they were never in bondage to any man, as Cyril of Alexandria well commented: 'Joseph was sold to be a bond slave, yet he was free, all radiant in the nobility of his soul.' There is, however, a freedom—the only true freedom—which remains unknown to the descendants of Abraham, the freedom from the tyranny of sin. To this freedom the whole teaching and life of Jesus pointed as His gospel—for the Jews. The author of the Fourth Gospel crystallizes this into a great *Logion*, and does so consciously by introducing it with the words *Verily, verily. Jesus answered them, Verily, verily, I say unto you, Every one that committeth (doeth) sin is the bondservant (slave) of sin.* Codex Bezae, the Verona fragment of the Old Latin Version, and the Sinaitic Syriac, supported by some Patristic evidence, have the Saying in a more poignant form which may be original. They omit the final *of sin*, so that the saying runs: *Everyone that doeth sin is a slave.* With these words, the conclusion of the discourse (*v.* 44) is already suggested subtly, since the opening words of the Saying have another Johannine conclusion, *He that doeth sin is—of the devil* (1 John iii. 8).

This confidence of the Jews in their physical descent from Abraham (Gen. xvii. 16, xxii. 17; Ps. cv. 6; Isa. xli. 8; Luke i. 55) is abruptly undermined (cf. Matt. iii. 9; Luke xvi. 19-31; Gal. iii. 7). The popular argument of the Jews was that the righteousness of Abraham was of sufficient merit for the justification of his physical children, so that Justin Martyr concluded from the argument of Trypho that his doctrine meant that 'the eternal kingdom will be given to those who are of the seed of Abraham according to the flesh, even though they be sinners and unbelievers and disobedient to God' (*Dial. c. Tryph.* cxl., cf. Strack-Billerbeck on Matt. iii. 9). Against this confidence the New

Testament is one long protest which is here sharply formulated by the author of the Fourth Gospel. Freedom was not possessed by the Jews. It had to be created for them and offered to them. *Ye shall be free.* This true freedom was wrought out in their midst and offered to them; but they rejected it: *How sayest thou, ye shall be made free?*

The distinction between the true and false disciples of Jesus is therefore marked by contrasted behaviour. The slave does not remain in his master's house permanently; but the son does. [The omission of the words *The Son abideth for ever* in some few manuscripts, headed by Codex Sinaiticus, is presumably due to homœoteleuton.] So it is with the household of God (Heb. iii. 2–6). Those who have been genuinely set free by the Son of God remain in the fellowship of the sons of God; the false believers, who are still slaves, mark their slavery by leaving the fellowship and returning to the world outside (vi. 60–6; 1 John ii. 19, iv. 1–3), and cannot again be received (2 John 9, 10). So here the Jews who had believed, when confronted with a clear statement of Christian truth, sink back into the crowd of unbelieving Jews, from whom they are indistinguishable. For Saint Paul the exclusion of Hagar and Ishmael from the house of Abraham is typical of this destiny of slavery (Gal. iv. 30). But for the author of the Fourth Gospel the whole conception and reality of sonship springs from the sonship of Jesus. He is the Son of God who abides in the house of God for ever (xii. 34, cf. Heb. iii. 5, 6). All that the Christians are, they are because of His creative activity (cf. Gal. iv. 31, v. 1), and only those whom He has liberated are, in any genuine sense of the word, free.

### JESUS PRONOUNCES THE UNBELIEVING JEWS TO BE THE SONS OF THE DEVIL, WHO IS THE ANTI-CHRIST

*vv.* 37–45. The intention of the Jews to put Jesus to death (v. 18, vii. 1, 25, cf. Mark iii. 6) is now emphasized in order to expose the behaviour of the physical descendants of Abraham. To the author of the Fourth Gospel the compatibility of murderous intention with a profession of faith is, in the story of the events which led to the crucifixion, the historical archetype of the behaviour of those false Christians of his own day who hated their brethren, and whom he names *murderers*. *Whosoever hateth his brother is a murderer: and ye know that no murderer hath eternal life abiding in him* (1 John iii. 15). . . . *In this the children of God are manifest, and the children of the devil: whosoever doeth not righteousness is not of God, neither he that loveth not his brother* (1 John iii. 10). The hatred which led to the murder of Jesus, and the later hatred of apostate Christians for their brethren, are powerful signs of the continued energy of the Devil who originally inspired the murder of Abel by his brother Cain (1 John iii. 12). The whole passage 1 John iii. 4–17 forms the best introduction to the interpretation of this corresponding passage in the gospel, cf. INTRODUCTION, pp. 49, 50.

The physical descent of the Jews from Abraham is not denied. They are his seed. But true sonship consists in conformity of the action of sons to that of their father. The murderous designs of the Jews against the Son of God deprive them of all genuine relationship with Abraham. There was none like Abraham in glory; *who kept the law of the Most High, And was taken into covenant with him: In his flesh he established the covenant; And when he was proved, he was found faithful* (Ecclus. xliv. 19 sqq.). The actions of the Patriarch proceeded from his faith and knowledge. With his physical descendants, it is, however, completely otherwise. The Word of Jesus, which is the Word of God, makes no pervading and penetrating progress in them, and they are consequently preoccupied in planning His murder. The Greek word translated R.V. *hath not free course* and A.V. and R.V. mg. *hath no place* expresses motion, as in Wisd. vii. 23, 24 (cf. 2 Pet. iii. 9 and the famous saying of Heracleitus as cited by Socrates (Plato, *Cratylus* 402 A) 'Everything moves and nothing abides', see Bauer). The Jews who had believed do not allow the creative activity of the Word of Jesus to move them, and they are consequently in no better position than the Jews in whom the Word found no place of entry. The action of both is identical; they move towards murder. Their refusal to hear the Word of Jesus is the rejection of the Word of God (Deut. xviii. 18), because Jesus speaks only what He has seen when He was with the Father (v. 19 sqq.). The reference is not here to a continuous vision of the Father; but to the pre-existence of the Son with the Father, which gives supreme authority to the teaching and action of Jesus (i. 1, 18, iii. 31–5, vi. 46).

The clear statement of the complete obedience of Jesus to the Father —*I speak the things which I have seen with the Father*—enables the author of the gospel to suggest somewhat enigmatically the diabolical paternity of the Jews (cf. *v.* 34). The Jews proceed with a parallel but contrasted obedience—*Ye then also do what ye heard from the (your) Father.* The words, however, could also be translated *Do ye also then what ye heard from the Father.* [In the majority of witnesses (including Codices Sinaiticus, Bezae, the Koridethi Codex and the Sinaitic Syriac) the real meaning of the saying is brought out by the addition of *My* and *your* to the word Father. Jesus speaks what He has seen with *His* Father; the Jews do what they heard from *their* father. It can hardly be doubted that this represents an editorial gloss which, whilst bringing out the meaning, deprives the words of their delicate obscurity.] The complete distinction of behaviour between Jesus and the Jews, since, whilst Jesus is the giver of Eternal Life (*v.* 51), the Jews are filled with murderous designs, involves a distinction of paternity. The Jews, perceiving the direction in which the discourse is moving, vehemently assert that they are not only of the seed of Abraham (*v.* 36) but are his true children (*v.* 39).

Jesus answers that their actions declare their spiritual illegitimacy. There is no advantage in vaunting descent from one whose actions men do not intend to imitate. *If they were the children of Abraham, they would now be doing what Abraham did.* [There is an obscurity here similar to the obscurity in *v.* 38. For the variant readings see Bernard and Lagrange. The sentence can be translated with Lagrange: *If ye are children of Abraham, do what he did.* But the connection with *v.* 40 seems to demand not an imperative but an unfulfilled condition in present time, cf. v. 19.] It was the distinction of Abraham to have received the emissaries of God with faith and with obedience (Gen. xviii. 2 sqq., cf. Gen. xv. 1 sqq.). His physical descendants, however, reject Him whom God has sent, and plan His murder. Grammatically the use of the word *man* in *v.* 40 is simply equivalent to an indefinite article (see Bauer). Its use here has therefore no dogmatic implications.

The pedigree of the Jews is invalid. They are physically descended from one father and imitate the works of another. The Jews correctly perceive that this double paternity is, in fact, an accusation of spiritual illegitimacy, and they deny it with what is apparently a malicious reference to the supposed physical illegitimacy of Jesus (Origen *In Evan. Ioan.* ed. Brooke, vol. II, p. 57, and *Contra Celsum* i. 28, Cyril of Alexandria on *v.* 39, *Acts of Pilate* ii. 4). Modern commentators on the whole deny this reference (see, however, Calmes); some, because they treat the discourse as a faithful record of an episode in the life of Jesus, in which case a reference to a controversy which presumes knowledge of the Virgin Birth and of its explanation by the Jews would be an anachronism (Lagrange, Plummer); others because they are persuaded that the author has no knowledge of controversies concerning the irregularity of the birth of Jesus, and would not therefore introduce an illusion to such controversies in composing the discourses (Holtzmann, Bauer). This is, however, not the only passage in which the author introduces an allusion to a peculiarity concerning the birth of Jesus (see notes on i. 13, 14, vii. 27, 28, viii. 19 and DETACHED NOTE 2, p. 163).

The Jews answer the charge of spiritual illegitimacy by making explicit what is spiritually involved in their descent from Abraham. They belong to the congregation of God, into which no bastard can enter (Deut. xxiii. 2). God alone is their true Father, the ultimate cause of their existence, and they are His sons (Exod. iv. 22; Deut. xxxii. 6; Isa. lxiii. 16, lxiv, 8; Mal. ii. 10). Their divine sonship is a solid concrete reality, not a future hope. The language in which this confidence is expressed—*We were not born of fornication*—is an almost verbal contradiction of the passage in Hosea where the people of Israel are named *the children of whoredom* because of their idolatrous unbelief and where it is promised that in the future they would be called *The sons of the living God* (Hos. i. 9–ii. 4). The Lord's answer to this vigorous claim to divine sonship is inevitable. If they were indeed the sons of God, they would at once receive the Son of God with brotherly love. This is the supreme Johannine test of truth: *Every spirit which confesseth not Jesus is not of God* (1 John iv. 3), *Whosoever believeth that Jesus is the Christ is born of God: and everyone that loveth him that begat loveth him also that is begotten of him* (1 John v. 1): *If a man say, I love God, and hateth his brother, he is a liar* (1 John iv. 20). Jesus came forth from God and stands concretely in the midst of the Jews; this is the meaning of the Greek word translated *am come* (R.V. cf. 1 John v. 20) and it corresponds with the Johannine emphasis that Jesus came *in the flesh* (i. 14; 1 John iv. 2; 2 John 7). He is the Apostle of God, and His mission is intelligible only when it is recognized that the initiative rests with God. The mission of Jesus is not self-appointed (v. 19 sqq. and *passim* in the Fourth Gospel). The failure of the Jews to perceive the meaning of His spoken word (*speech*) can be explained only by their inability to hear the Word of God which is made manifest in the teaching (*word*) of Jesus (cf. 1 Cor. ii. 14).

The discourse now reaches its carefully prepared climax. What has been latent since *v.* 34 is at last spoken openly. The behaviour of the Jews in the presence of the mission of the Son of God, their rejection of His teaching and their determination to put Him to death, is capable of but one explanation. *Ye are of your father the devil.* So far from being born of God, they are like Cain the children of the Evil One (1 John iii. 12; Jude 11), and are the willing agents in the accomplishment of his lustful desires (1 John ii. 16). Bauer cites the description of the Jews in the Mandæan *Ginza* (xii. 5 Lidzbarski, p. 276) 'They sow wickedness and reap a harvest of lies. Their heart is full of darkness. . . . They are the poison of those who murder the sons of men. . . . They stand without the Kusta (i.e. the Truth) . . . and kill the sons of men'. The Devil is the Anti-Christ (xiii. 2, 27). Jesus declares the Truth and gives Life to men (*vv.* 45, 51); the Devil is the Father of Lies (Rev. xii. 9, xx. 2, 3) and the Slayer of men. The behaviour of the Jews is thus traced to its only adequate source.

The Johannine description of the Devil is in general sufficiently plain, but obscure in certain details. He is described as a murderer *from the beginning*. It is attractive, in view of 1 John iii. 12, where the Devil is said to have instigated the murder of Abel, to interpret *from the beginning* in the light of Gen. iv. 1–15. But, since murder and deception are here closely associated, and death and sin are overlapping words (viii. 21, 24, cf. Rom. v. 12, vii. 11), a more natural meaning is given to *from the beginning* if it be referred to the story of the Fall. The Devil deceived Eve and *by the deceit of the Devil death entered into the world* (Wisd. ii. 23, 24, summarizing Gen. ii. 17, iii. 19).

The English Versions leave open a possible reference to the Fall of the Devil (A.V. *Abode not in the truth*, R.V. *stood not*). This reference is wholly absent in the Greek. The verb is either an imperfect or a perfect with the force of a present (R.V. mg. *standeth*) according to the reading adopted. The imperfect form is probably the original, and the meaning is that in the whole course of human history the Devil remains outside the sphere of truth, *because there is no truth in him*. Falsehood proceeds from the essence of his being (Matt. xii. 34, 35). No speculation about the Fall of the Devil can be supported from this passage.

The description of the Devil's falsehood concludes with the words *For he is a liar, and the father thereof*. That is, he is the father of lies or of liars. But the Greek sentence, if it stood alone, would be translated most naturally, *For his father also is a liar*. Westcott was so persuaded of the correctness of this translation that he proposed a change of subject in the preceding clause, *Whenever a man speaketh a lie, he speaketh of his own, for his father also is a liar* (cf. R.V. mg.). The change of subject is so harsh that the suggestion of Westcott has been generally discarded (Bernard). Wellhausen followed many early Patristic writers in identifying the murderer (*v.* 44a) with Cain (Aphraates, Ambrosiaster, Cyril), and then claimed that *v.* 44 originally began *Ye are of your father Cain* and ended *For his father* (i.e. the Devil) *is also a liar*. The suggestion that the passage as it stands at present is the result of radical editing is, however, at best precarious and seems unnecessary. Augustine, Epiphanius, and Cyril were forced to dismiss the Gnostic interpretation of the passage as referring to the Demiurge who was the father of the Devil and the grandfather of the Jews. This is wholly beyond the horizon of the Fourth Gospel, and Cyril's judgement is here final: 'No one will shew us such a reading in the holy and divine Scriptures'. We are therefore thrown back upon the usual translation of the sentence, which is demanded by its context *For he* (the Devil) *is a liar and the father thereof*.

### ABRAHAM AND JESUS: THE BLASPHEMY OF THE JEWS CONTRASTED WITH THE RECOGNITION OF JESUS BY THE PATRIARCH ABRAHAM

*vv.* 46–59. The theme of the relation between Abraham and the Jews being exhausted by the judgement that they are the children of the Devil, it remains to define the relation between Abraham and Jesus, to include the Patriarch among those who bore witness to the Messiah, and to contrast his faith with the unbelief of the Jews. Jesus stands in the midst of the Jews as the concrete and realized righteousness of God. In Him righteousness and truth meet together for the salvation of men, as murder and falsehood are united in the Devil for their destruction. And yet righteousness and truth, sin and falsehood, are not parallel and independent realities. Righteousness has its origin in truth, and sin is generated from falsehood. Jesus confidently challenges the Jews to discover in Him any moral blemish (vii. 18, xiv. 30, xviii. 38, cf. 1 Pet. i. 19, ii. 22. The word translated A.V. *convince*, R.V. *convict*, means primarily *examine* and so *expose*, see note on xvi. 8). Their inability to expose sin in Him ought consequently to compel them to recognize the truth of His claim to be the Son of God, *Why do ye not believe me?* The formal expression of the sinlessness of Jesus in the Fourth Gospel reflects the confidence which the Christians have by experience learned to place in Him (1 John i. 7, ii. 2, iii. 5, 6). Christian piety at no point founders on the rock of its origin in the life of Jesus. But competence to recognize the truth underlying this moral perfection depends upon spiritual rebirth and upon incorporation into the spiritual community which bears witness to Jesus and guards the record of His life and teaching. *He that is of God* (i.e. *born of God*, i. 13; 1 John iii. 9, 10, iv. 4–7, v. 18, 19, cf. Matt. i. 20) *heareth the words of God* (i.e. recognizes in the words of Jesus the truth of God: cf. 1 John iv. 6). The absence of spiritual generation from God explains the inability of the Jews to believe in Jesus (cf. *vv.* 42–4).

Confronted by the challenge of righteousness which they are unable to answer, the Jews display their helplessness by denouncing Jesus as a Samaritan who is subject to demoniac possession. The accusation of demoniac possession belongs to the earlier tradition (Mark iii. 22–30; Matt. xii. 24–37; Luke xi. 15–26, cf. Matt. ix. 34, xi. 18, 19); the words *Say we not well that thou art a Samaritan?* are, however, peculiar to the Fourth Gospel, and require explanation. Bauer suggests that the connection between Samaria and demoniac possession may be explained as an allusion to the messianic claims of the Samaritan prophets Dositheus and Simon Magus (Bauer, and see also his detached note on i. 34). But allusions to later Palestinian history do not seem characteristic of the author of the Fourth Gospel. Most commentators are satisfied with a reference to the heresy or apostasy of the Samaritans and to their hatred of the Jews. So far as they go these suggestions are, no doubt, intended by the author of the gospel (iv. 9). The question is, however, whether, in a discourse revolving round the theme of legitimate and illegitimate generation, the reference to the Samaritans should not be explained in this context. The Samaritans were the product of irregular unions between Israelite women and the Gentile immigrants (a natural deduction from 2 Kings xvii. 24 sqq., see Strack-Billerbeck I, 539, note 1), and their inexact Judaism is the consequence of their origin. If this be the allusion here, *v.* 46 refers back to *v.* 41, and the irregularity of the birth of Jesus is contrasted with the legitimacy of the Jews, who were not *born of fornication* (see note on iv. 17 sqq.). He is by birth a stranger to the congregation of Israel. Jesus answers only the accusation of demoniac possession. With his usual subtlety the author of the Gospel refuses to do more than suggest controversies concerning the birth of Jesus (see DETACHED NOTE 2, p. 163).

The accusation of demoniac possession is simply denied, and the Jews are pronounced to be under the imminent judgement of God, *There is one that seeketh and judgeth.* By the dishonour they do the Son, whose life is the glorification of God, His Father (xvii. 4), the Jews dishonour God (1 Cor. xii. 3). It does not, however, belong to the work of the Son to protect His honour (v. 41, 45, vii. 18), since the Father Himself is the avenger and protector of the glory of His Son (xvi. 11; 1 Pet. ii. 23). He it is that *seeketh and judgeth*. Bauer takes both words in a legal sense and translates *investigates and judges*, but in his dictionary he is able to advance only non-biblical evidence for the translation *investigates* (Preuschen-Bauer, *Wörtenbuch zu den Schriften des Neuen Testaments*, p. 529, cf. Lagrange). Most commentators supply the object *my honour* to the verb *seeketh* (Plummer, Bernard), and this is obviously intended by the author (vii. 18). But the word carries with it a further allusion, when it is placed in its common Johannine context. The Jews suppose that they are protecting the honour of God by seeking to put Jesus to death (v. 18, vii. 1, 19, viii. 37, 40, xviii. 4 sqq.). They sought Jesus, they judged Him, and finally they put Him to death. The ultimate truth is, however, precisely opposite. It is God who is *seeking* (*requiring*, cf. Philo's comment on Gen. xlii. 22 cited by Westcott, He that requireth is not man but God, or the Word, or the Divine Law: *de Jos.* 174) and *judging* those who reject His Son (xii. 47, 48). They and not Jesus, are under sentence of death (viii. 21, 24). The emphatic Saying introduced by *Verily verily*, rounds off the judgement of God by setting the Christians who keep the word of Jesus (viii. 31, 32, xiv. 15, 21, 23, 24, xv. 20, xvii. 6) firmly within the sphere of eternal life. *Verily, verily, I say unto you, If a man keep my saying, he shall never see death* (v. 24, vi. 51, xi. 25, 26; 1 John iii. 14. The phrase *see death* (cf. Luke ii. 26; Acts ii. 27, 31, xiii. 35; Heb. xi. 5) in *v.* 52 is strengthened into *taste of death*, cf. Luke ix. 27; Mark ix. 1; Heb. ii. 9). The contrast between Jesus and the Devil, and between the Christians and the unbelieving Jews, is now complete. The work of Jesus provides the opportunity of eternal life (vi. 51), the action of the Devil ensures certain and permanent death.

The Jews are now persuaded that what they had before voiced as an opinion (*v.* 48) is an entirely correct judgement: *Now we know that thou hast a devil* (contrast vi. 69). Being capable only of physical perception they suppose His reference to eternal life to mean that those who believe in Him will enjoy in His company permanent existence in this world. Such a hope is manifestly ridiculous, since Abraham and the prophets, the supreme believers in God, went to corruption like other men in spite of their faith (Zech. i. 5, 6). Surely Jesus is not greater than their father Abraham and greater also than the prophets? Whom does He make Himself (v. 18, x. 33, xix. 7, 12)? The Jews ask the question with intentional insult; the Samaritan woman had asked a similar question with critical doubt (cf. Chrysostom).

The answer to Jewish misunderstanding concerning eternal life lies in the resurrection of Jesus from the dead and in the eternal life which is given to those who believe on Him. This eternal life is compatible not only with physical death (xi. 25), but even with violent death at the hands of the enemies of the Truth. There is here no question of self-glorification, since the resurrection of Jesus, which is His glorification and the vindication of His work, is the action of God Himself, His effective ratification of the obedience of His Son (xiii. 31, 32, xvii. 1–5, cf. vii. 39, xii. 16, 23, 24, xvi. 14). It is wholly sufficient that the glorification of Jesus rests in the safe hands of Him whom the Jews name their Father, and of whom they are wholly ignorant. The glorification of Jesus depends, however, not upon an arbitrary action of God; it is the Divine recognition of the unswerving obedience of the incarnate Son of God. Jesus in His life consistently translated His original knowledge of God into action: *I know him, and keep his word.* Christian confidence in the future likewise depends upon a present knowledge of God and a present obedience to His commands (1 John ii. 3–6, 20–9). If this knowledge be challenged, the challenge must be met openly, for silence with regard to it is equivalent to a lie.

Of His resurrection Jesus speaks in the presence of the Jews with marked reserve and does nothing to correct their misunderstanding concerning eternal life. He speaks clearly and openly, however, of their misunderstanding concerning His relation to Abraham. Abraham fore-saw the Advent of the Son of God; he recognized it, and rejoiced over it. Bauer supports the prevalent modern Roman Catholic exegesis of this passage (Schanz, Calmes, Belser, see also Maldonatus and Plummer) in reversing the Patristic interpretation (Augustine, Chrysostom, Cyril); he regards the vision of Abraham as comparable to the vision of Moses and Elijah at the Transfiguration. Abraham, living in Paradise (Luke xvi. 22–31, cf. Mark xii. 26), rejoices in his ability to watch the work of Jesus. But the point here is not that Abraham is alive and that he bears a mystical witness to Jesus. The theme of eternal life is let fall; the verbs *rejoiced, saw, was glad,* are firmly in the past tense; the verses which follow are meaningless unless an event is referred to which lies not only in the past, but in the distant past; and finally, grammatically, the phrase *to see my day* does not mean *that he should see my day* (R.V. mg.) or *in hope of seeing my day*: it explains the ground of Abraham's joy (Bernard). He rejoiced, in that he saw. The reference is therefore to some witness of Abraham suggested in the Old Testament Scriptures. He foresaw the Advent of Jesus just as the Prophet Isaiah spake of Him *because (when A.V.) he saw his glory* (xii. 41). These men saw the promises and *greeted them from afar* (Heb. xi. 13). This is the Patristic interpretation of the passage, and it is difficult to deny that it is correct. It remains then to endeavour to locate the passage in the Old Testament narrative upon which this appeal to the foresight and joy of Abraham is grounded. According to later Rabbinic tradition God revealed to Abraham the distant future when He established the Covenant (Gen. xv. 9 sqq.). Some Rabbis interpreted the Hebrew phrase *gone into days* (Gen. xxiv. 1, A.V. mg: translated A.V. and R.V. *well stricken in age*) of a vision of Abraham through the curtain which separates the present from the future. For example, Rabbi Eleazar (A.D. 270) said: 'He (Abraham) gained insight into this world and into the future world. Therefore it is said *he was gone into the days*, that is, in an absolute sense into all the days there are' (Strack-Billerbeck). The emphasis, however, here laid on Abraham's joy suggests that the reference may be to the laughter of Abraham (Gen. xvii. 17), interpreted not as scorn, but as joyful recognition (Holtzmann, *Jubilees* xvi. 19, cf. Philo, *De Mutat. Nomin.*, 131), or to the birth of Isaac (laughter), the type of the Messiah (Lagrange, Loisy). The precise reference, however, eludes the commentator, and the joy of Abraham may have as vague an Old Testament background as the joy of Adam, in the saying of the Rabbi Simeon ben Lakish (*c.* A.D. 250): 'It (Gen. v. 1) teaches that God shewed Adam each generation and its learned men. . . . When He reached Akiba, Adam rejoiced over Akiba's knowledge of the Torah and grieved over his death' (cited by Strack-Billerbeck, vol. II, p. 345). The general meaning is given in the Epistle of Barnabas, 'Abraham first gave the Jews circumcision, then in spirit looked forward to Jesus' (ix. 7).

In the perspective of the Johannine writings the claim is not only that Abraham bore witness to Jesus, but that the Son of God, being in the Beginning the Word of God, saw Abraham and marked his faith. The Jews therefore rightly transpose the words of Jesus, and answer with the question *Hast thou seen Abraham?* The variant reading *Has Abraham seen thee?* (Codex Sinaiticus, and the Sinaitic Syriac and Sahidic Versions) is almost certainly a correction of the original reading (see, however, Bernard). The Jews knowing that they are separated from Abraham by many centuries and, supposing Jesus to be merely their contemporary, dismiss as ridiculous a relationship between the Patriarch and a man not yet fifty years old. It seems scarcely justifiable to combine the forty-six years in ii. 20 with the fifty years here and to deduce that the author of the gospel intended to suggest the precise age of Jesus at the time of the ministry (contrast Luke iii. 23). Fifty years is a round number marking the end of the active period of a man's life (Num. iv. 3, 39, viii. 24, 25). It should, however, be noted that Irenæus quotes the Presbyters of Asia Minor, who, he says, derived their information from John, the disciple of the Lord, as stating that Jesus was just under fifty years old at the time of the ministry *Adv. Haer.* ii. 22, 5. The variant reading *forty* for *fifty*, commented upon by Chrysostom, is no doubt a correction introduced into the text in order to avoid a seeming contradiction of Luke iii. 23.

The question of the Jews, *Hast thou seen Abraham?* and their judgement that the claims of Jesus proceed from arrogant self-glorification,

*Whom makest thou thyself?* (*v.* 53, cf. x. 33), evoke the saying which finally concludes the discourse: *Verily, verily, I say unto you, Before Abraham was* (i.e. *was born* R.V. mg., *came into being,* cf. Gal. iv. 4 in the Greek), *I am*. The contrast is between an existence initiated by birth and an absolute existence (i. 1–3, viii. 28, xiii. 19; for the form of the sentence cf. Ps. xc. 2 LXX). The Son of God is not merely antecedent in time to Abraham; if so, the Saying would have been *Before Abraham came into being, I was.* The Being of the Son is continuous, irrespective of all time (Chrysostom). As Cyril of Alexandria comments, 'He therefore is not rivalling Abraham's times, nor does He affirm that He is some little precedent to his times; but since He is above all time and o'erpasseth the number of every age, He says that He is before Abraham'. The story of the life and death and resurrection of Jesus is then not the story of the supposed ascent of a man to the throne of God (x. 33); still less is it the record of intolerable human arrogance. The story of the life and death of Jesus is the story of the descent of the Word of God; and His resurrection is not an ascent to the Father, but a return thither.

The blasphemy of the Jews is now translated from words into action (x. 31, 36–9); *They took up stones therefore to cast at him*, intending to inflict the proper punishment for blasphemy against God (Lev. xxiv. 16, cf. Josephus *Ant.* xvii. 213–17; *B.J.* ii. 224, 225). They are, however, powerless to anticipate the Hour of the death of Jesus (vii. 30, 44, viii. 20); and consequently, He passed out of the Temple without their being able to perceive His method of escape (x. 39, xii. 36, cf. Luke iv. 30, which in some manuscripts is added to the text here). Their blindness suggests the theme for the narrative of the miracle which follows, where the blindness of the Jews is contrasted with the sight of the man who believed that Jesus is the Son of God (ix. 35–41).

# THE HEALING OF
# THE MAN BORN BLIND

## IX

THE healing of blind men forms an important element in the synoptic tradition. Particular instances are recorded; of the healing of a blind beggar (Mark x. 46–52; Matt. xx. 29–34; Luke xviii. 35–43); of healing with spittle and laying on of hands (Mark viii. 22–6, cf. vii. 32, 33), and by touching the eyes (Matt. ix. 27–34); of the blasphemy of the Pharisees the immediate cause of which was the healing of a blind and dumb demoniac (Matt. xii. 22–37). The general references to the healing of the blind show that the writers of the gospels regarded such miracles as important, not merely because they occurred frequently, but because, for those who possessed sufficient insight to recognize in them the fulfilment of Old Testament prophecy, they were manifestations of the advent of the Messiah (Isa. xxix. 18, xxxv. 5, xlii. 6, 7, lxi. 1 LXX; Luke iv. 18, 19, vii. 21; Matt. xi. 5, xv. 31). In Isa. xxxii. 3 sqq. clarity of vision is one of the characteristics of the Messianic age; but in this passage sight is understood to be the possession of the knowledge of God. The prophetic emphasis on sight as contrasted with blindness is dependent upon that imagery in which the knowledge of God and righteousness of the heart is light, and ignorance and sin darkness (cf. Isa. lx. 1 sqq. *Arise, shine; for thy light is come*). It seems, therefore almost impossible to draw a clear distinction between physical and moral sight in Isaiah's imagery (so Westcott), for the former is but the latter given vivid and concrete expression. The references to the healing of the blind in the synoptic gospels are also governed by this symbolism. The phraseology is carefully chosen in order to recall the language of the prophets, and in certain cases the context in which an account of the healing of a blind man is introduced has quite peculiar significance. For example, Mark, after emphasizing the blindness and ignorance of the disciples, and before recording Saint Peter's recognition of Jesus as the Christ, inserts the narrative of the healing of a blind man (Mark viii. 17 sqq.). In the gospels miracles of the healing of the blind seem never to be recorded merely as acts of physical healing, but as actions that reveal the Messiahship of Jesus and the illumination of those who believe in Him and follow Him.

Since conversion, freedom from sin, and baptism were interdependent experiences within primitive Christianity, the prophetic imagery
of passing from darkness to light or from blindness to sight was from
very early days interpreted as symbolic of conversion and baptism
(Acts xxvi. 16–18; 2 Cor. iv. 6; Eph. i. 18, v. 7–14; Heb. vi. 1–6;
1 Pet. ii. 9). In one of the early second-century frescoes in the catacombs the healing of a blind man is portrayed among other symbols
of baptism, such as the salvation of Noah and the miracle of Moses'
striking the rock (Wilpert, pl. 68, 3). When Tertullian opened his tract
on baptism with the words, 'Happy is the sacrament of our water, in
that, by washing away the sins of our early blindness, we are set free
unto eternal life' (*De Bapt.* i), he used language which presented no
difficulty to his readers. We ought not, therefore, to be surprised if the
author of the Fourth Gospel is found to stand completely within the
tradition of Christian symbolism, and to have given that tradition such
classic expression as to ensure its further development.

ix. 1. *And as he passed by, he saw a man blind from his birth.* 2. *And his
disciples asked him, saying, Rabbi, who did sin, this man, or his parents, that
he should be born blind?* 3. *Jesus answered, Neither did this man sin, nor his
parents: but that the works of God should be made manifest in him.* 4. *We must
work the works of him that sent me, while it is day: the night cometh, when
no man can work.* 5. *When I am in the world, I am the light of the world.*
6. *When he had thus spoken, he spat on the ground, and made clay of the spittle,
and anointed his eyes with the clay,* 7. *and said unto him, Go, wash in the pool
of Siloam (which is by interpretation, Sent). He went away therefore, and washed,
and came seeing.* 8. *The neighbours therefore, and they which saw him aforetime,
that he was a beggar, said, Is not this he that sat and begged?* 9. *Others said, It
is he: others said, No, but he is like him. He said, I am he.* 10. *They said
therefore unto him, How then were thine eyes opened?* 11. *He answered, The
man that is called Jesus made clay, and anointed mine eyes, and said unto me,
Go to Siloam, and wash: so I went away and washed, and I received sight.*
12. *And they said unto him, Where is he? He saith, I know not.*

13. *They bring to the Pharisees him that aforetime was blind.* 14. *Now it
was the sabbath on the day when Jesus made the clay, and opened his eyes.*
15. *Again therefore the Pharisees also asked him how he received his sight. And
he said unto them, He put clay upon mine eyes, and I washed, and do see.* 16. *Some
therefore of the Pharisees said, This man is not from God, because he keepeth not
the sabbath. But others said, How can a man that is a sinner do such signs?
And there was a division among them.* 17. *They say therefore unto the blind man
again, What sayest thou of him, in that he opened thine eyes? And he said, He is
a prophet.* 18. *The Jews therefore did not believe concerning him, that he had
been blind, and had received his sight, until they called the parents of him that
had received his sight,* 19. *and asked them, saying, Is this your son, who ye say*

*was born blind? how then doth he now see?* 20. *His parents answered and said, We know that this is our son, and that he was born blind:* 21. *but how he now seeth, we know not; or who opened his eyes, we know not: ask him; he is of age; he shall speak for himself.* 22. *These things said his parents, because they feared the Jews: for the Jews had agreed already, that if any man should confess him to be Christ, he should be put out of the synagogue.* 23. *Therefore said his parents, He is of age; ask him.* 24. *So they called a second time the man that was blind, and said unto him, Give glory to God: we know that this man is a sinner.* 25. *He therefore answered, Whether he be a sinner, I know not: one thing I know, that, whereas I was blind, now I see.* 26. *They said therefore unto him, What did he to thee? how opened he thine eyes?* 27. *He answered them, I told you even now, and ye did not hear: wherefore would ye hear it again? would ye also become his disciples?* 28. *And they reviled him, and said, Thou art his disciple; but we are disciples of Moses.* 29. *We know that God hath spoken unto Moses: but as for this man, we know not whence he is.* 30. *The man answered and said unto them, Why, herein is the marvel, that ye know not whence he is, and yet he opened mine eyes.* 31. *We know that God heareth not sinners: but if any man be a worshipper of God, and do his will, him he heareth.* 32. *Since the world began it was never heard that any one opened the eyes of a man born blind.* 33. *If this man were not from God, he could do nothing.* 34. *They answered and said unto him, Thou wast altogether born in sins, and dost thou teach us? And they cast him out.*

35. *Jesus heard that they had cast him out; and finding him, he said, Dost thou believe on the Son of God?* 36. *He answered and said, And who is he, Lord, that I may believe on him?* 37. *Jesus said unto him, Thou hast both seen him, and he it is that speaketh with thee.* 38. *And he said, Lord, I believe. And he worshipped him.* 39. *And Jesus said, For judgement came I into this world, that they which see not may see; and that they which see may become blind.* 40. *Those of the Pharisees which were with him heard these things, and said unto him, Are we also blind?* 41. *Jesus said unto them, If ye were blind, ye would have no sin: but now ye say, We see: your sin remaineth.*

ix. 1. *Passed by:* that is along one of the roads leading from the Temple (cf. Matt. ix. 27). No break in the narrative is indicated. The miracle, therefore, takes place in the vicinity of the Temple on the last day of the feast of Tabernacles.

*Blind from his birth:* The man had never seen (cf. Acts iii. 2, xiv. 8). To become a Christian is not to recover what has been lost, but to receive a wholly new illumination (cf. *v.* 34).

*v.* 2. The popular assumption that sin is the real cause of any calamity that may befall a nation or an individual, an assumption which lay behind the development of the detailed regulations governing the Jewish law of sacrifice and which set the problem dealt with by the author of the Book of Job, leads the disciples to ask the question (Gen. iii. 14-16; 1 Cor. xi. 30). The answer gives the key to the interpretation of the miracle.

The actual form of the question presents a difficulty. If the cause of the man's blindness was his own sin, then he must have sinned, either whilst still in his mother's womb, or in some previous existence, punishment being deferred. Both these speculations are found in Jewish literature. Bauer, commenting on this passage, quotes the answer given by a Rabbi to one of his pupils, who had asked him whether evil first laid hold of a man after birth, or whilst he was being formed in the womb. The answer given was 'From the time of his formation'. References to the belief in the pre-existence of souls in later Judaism occur in Wisd. viii. 19, 20, where the good soul receives an undefiled body (cf. *Secrets of Enoch* xxiii. 4, 5, xxx. 16, ed. Charles note; Josephus *B.J.* ii. 154–8).

Frequent mention is made in the Old Testament of the punishment of children for the sins of their parents (Exod. xx. 5, xxxiv. 7; Num. xiv. 18; Deut. v. 9; Jer. xxxi. 29, 30; Ezek. xviii. 2; Tob. iii. 3, 4).

*v.* 3 (cf. xi. 4). The attempt to attribute a special calamity to some peculiar sinfulness is not merely inappropriate and useless speculation, but leads to a false interpretation of the miracles of Jesus and to a quite unjustifiable sense of security in those who suffer no extraordinary punishment (Luke xiii. 1–5). The blind man represents fallen humanity languishing in the darkness of ignorance and sin without hope of salvation (Loisy). To regard his recovery as the result of a merciful action towards one who has been peculiarly sinful, or who has been especially harshly punished for the sins of his parents, is to misunderstand the representative significance of the miracle. The healing of the blind man is the visible manifestation of the power of God available for men through Him who had been sent 'on purpose to enlighten the world, which lay buried in the darkness of ignorance and sin' (Quesnel).

*v.* 4. The easier reading—*I must work the works of him that sent me*—has considerable support in the manuscripts and versions, but the more difficult reading (*we*) is probably correct. The writer, by using the first person plural, associates the Apostles with the work of the Christ; for they, by the power of the spirit and as witnesses of what they had seen, became Sons of light for the illumination of the world (xii. 36; Matt. v. 14; Mark iv. 21; for the interchangeable use of *I* and *we* cf. iii. 11, ix. 31 and the INTRODUCTION, pp. 86–95).

Day—night: cf. xi. 9, 10. The day is for work, the night for rest. The salvation of men is effected by the incarnate Christ, who, having completed His redemptive and creative work, passes to His rest (xix. 30). There may be here an allusion to the days of the first creation and to the divine rest which the Sabbath commemorated (Gen. ii. 2, 3). The Apostles were chosen to continue the work of the incarnate Christ, *as my Father hath sent me, even so send I you* (xx. 21); and, when their work is done, they are promised resting places in heaven, that where He is they may be also (xiv. 2, 3). The night also suggests the Passion of the

Christ and the persecution or martyrdom of the Apostles. 'Dark, the privation of light, is the hue of death, and, by similitude, of calamity and evil'. Since, however, the Passion was the road to peace, the elemental imagery of night and day is capable of both interpretations.

*v.* 5. The repetition of the claim which was the starting point of the discourse in Chapter viii firmly connects the miracle with the discourse, and is intended to ensure the correct interpretation of the miracle as a representative and symbolical action (i. 4, 8, 9, iii. 19, viii. 12, xii. 35).

*v.* 6. The eyes, which are to see the Christ (*v.* 37) are made whole, or perhaps created, from the dust of the ground and the spittle of the Lord, and by the washing in the water of *Siloam*, that is, of *him who has been sent*. The Emperor Vespasian is said to have healed a blind man with his spittle (Tacitus, *Hist.* iv. 81; cf. also COMMENTARY on *v.* 32). For the healing power of spittle cf. Klostermann's note on Mark vii. 33; Doughty, *Wanderings in Arabia*, vol. I, pp. 148, 194.

The anointing of the eyes with spittle and the making of clay were expressly forbidden on the Sabbath, healing being permitted only when life was actually in danger (see Lightfoot, *Horae Hebraicae*, Schanz, p. 369, note 2). The readers of the gospel are presumably expected to recognize in the procedure adopted the authoritative abrogation of Jewish tradition by the Christ for the salvation of the world (*vv.* 14, 16). Irenæus (*Adv. Haer.* v. 15. 2), followed by other fathers (see Cramer's *Catena*), finding in the action an allusion to Gen. ii. 7, argues against the Gnostics that He who once created men again manifested His creative power: 'Now the work of God is the fashioning of men. For as the Scripture says, He made man by a kind of process: *and the Lord took clay from the earth and formed men*. Wherefore the Lord also spat on the ground and made clay and smeared it upon the eyes, pointing out the original fashioning of men, how it was effected, and manifesting the hand of God to those who can understand by what hand the man was fashioned out of the dust. For that which the artificer—the Word—had omitted to form in the womb (i.e. the man's eyes) He then supplied in public, that the works of God might be manifested in Him'. Chrysostom interprets the action as the manifestation of the hidden glory of the 'Architect of the Creation' (on John ix. 3). Quesnel comments: 'He who made man out of earth cures him with earth.' Clay is used instead of dust by the author of the Book of Job in phrases reminiscent of Gen. ii. 7, iii. 19 (Job iv. 19, x. 9, xxxiii. 6, xxxviii. 14, LXX).

*v.* 7. *Siloam*, cf. Neh. iii. 15. For the situation of the pool see Hastings' *Dict. of the Bible*, article 'Siloam'. The interest of the author is centred upon the significance of the name. *Siloam* means literally a discharge (of waters), but is interpreted here as a perfect participle passive: *he who has been sent*. And therefore, since Jesus is so frequently described as *He whom the Father has sent* that the phrase has almost become a title

(iii. 17, iv. 34, v. 24, 30, 37, vi. 29, 38, 39, 44, 57, vii. 16, 18, 28, 29, 33, viii. 16, 18, 26, 29, 42, ix. 4, xvii. 3, &c., cf. *Epistola Apostolorum, passim,* cf. INTRODUCTION, pp. 92, 93), in the mind of the author the waters of Siloam disappear in the living water of the Christ; in fact in Christian baptism and in that purification and illumination which formed both the starting point and the permanent background of primitive Christian experience. The comments of the Fathers cannot be dismissed so easily as has been done by modern commentators. 'Man, . . . having fallen into transgression, needed the laver of regeneration' (Irenæus, *Adv. Haer.* v. 15. 3). 'As then Christ was the spiritual rock, so also was He the spiritual Siloam' (Chrysostom, *Hom. in Ioan.* ix. 6, 7). 'It is not sufficient for the catechumens to hear that the Word was made flesh; let them haste unto the laver, if they seek light' (Saint Augustine, *In Ioan. Ev. Tract.* ix. 1). Saint Ambrose connects the reading of this chapter with the instruction of the catechumens preparing for baptism (*De Sacramentis* iii. 2, 11. For the use of this chapter in the early lectionaries see DETACHED NOTE 6, p. 363).

It is possible that the identification of Siloam with the Christ and the emphasis throughout the narrative on His rejection by the Jews may have been influenced by the messianic interpretation of Gen. xlix. 10: *The sceptre shall not depart from Judah until Shiloh come;* and by Isa. viii. 6, *This people hath refused the waters of Shiloah* (LXX *Siloam*) *that go softly* (Westcott. Abbott-Schmiedel. *Encycl. Bibl.* II, 1803. For general parallel cf. 2 Kings v. 10).

*v.* 8. The man is referred to as a public beggar, presumably at one of the gates of the Temple (cf. Acts iii. 3; Mark x. 46).

*v.* 9. The author establishes the reality of the miracle and draws attention to the division in the crowd (*v.* 16, cf. vii. 43), and to the hostility of the Pharisees (*vv.* 13–34). 'A sinner whose heart God has enlightened and changed by his grace, is not easily known again. He is no longer the same man' (Quesnel).

*v.* 11. The Greek word translated *received sight* belongs to the terminology of the narratives of the healing of the blind (Mark x. 51, 52; Matt. xx. 34; Luke xviii. 42, 43; Mark viii. 24 sqq.). The word means either, to see again, to recover sight, or, to look up. The second meaning is never altogether lost, for the blind men both recover their sight and look up at Jesus and follow Him. The word can, therefore, be used here, in spite of its unsuitability in the case of a man born blind, because it suggests the climax of the narrative, where the man sees the Christ and believes in Him (*vv.* 37, 38).

*v.* 12. The Christ is recognized, first, as the man that is called Jesus, of whose whereabouts the blind man is ignorant (*vv.* 11, 12); then, as a prophet, because He has performed a miracle (*vv.* 17, 25), and as *sent from God* because the miracle is without parallel since the world began *vv.* 30, 32, 33); and, finally, as the Son of man (the Christ) and the Lord, to whom worship must be given (*vv.* 35 sqq.). The man, as he passes thus from blindness to complete illumination and consequently to adoration, is contrasted step by step with the Pharisees and with the Jews, who, regarding the Christ as a man and a sinner, and denying the miracle (*vv.* 16, 18, 24), are shown to be ignorant (*v.* 29), and blasphemous (*v.* 34), and are finally formally declared blind and in sin (*vv.* 39–41).

. *v.* 16. The apostasy of the Pharisees and of the Jews is, however, not universal. There were many Christians who had been Jews, and some who had been Pharisees. The author carefully notes the division among the Pharisees because he regards the Jewish religion as having been weakened to such an extent by the schism caused by the increase in the number of converts to Christianity that the High Priests and the Pharisees complain that their religion is threatened with destruction (see note on xi. 48, cf. vii. 43, x. 19, 42).

*v.* 17, cf. iii. 2, iv. 19, vi. 14. In the Old Testament a miracle is regarded as one of the signs that a prophet or a messenger of God has appeared, the true prophet being attested by the miracles He works. The test by miracles is, however, not a certain test, since they may be performed by false prophets in order to lead men into idolatry (Exod. iv. 1–17; Deut. xxxiv. 10–12; 2 Kings ii–vi; Deut. xiii. 1–5, cf. Matt. xii. 38–40; Mark iii. 22; vi. 14, 15. For the importance of miracles as a test of peculiar sanctity see *Catholic Encyclopædia*, art. 'Beatification and Canonization'; Klein, *The Religion of Islam*, pp. 75 sq.).

*vv.* 18–21. The identity of the man is established by an appeal to his parents, the reality of his cure by his own declaration. 'A father is always ready to receive all the honour and advantage he can from the talents of an understanding son, whom the world applauds: but he is the first who draws back, when the use of those talents is likely to bring him into any trouble from the great' (Quesnel).

*v.* 22. *He should be put out of the synagogue.* That is, excluded from the fellowship of Israel (xii. 42, xvi. 2). The Acts of the Apostles and the Pauline Epistles do not suggest that the Christians were formally excommunicated from Judaism. Taken as a whole the earlier Christian literature refers to persecution of the Christians by the Jews, but excommunication would seem to be excluded, and the prophecies of the Lord recorded in the synoptic gospels are prophecies of persecution, not of excommunication (Luke vi. 22, cf. Matt. v. 11, xxiv. 9). From this passage it must, however, be understood that, when the Fourth Gospel was written, the breach between Judaism and Christianity was complete, and conversion to Christianity involved formal excommunication from Jewish worship. (For Jewish excommunication see Schürer, *The Jewish People in the Time of Jesus Christ*, II, ii. 60–2.)

*v.* 24. Give glory to God, cf. Joshua vii. 19. The man is solemnly put on oath to declare the truth and to own that he is guilty of deception.

But the words call to mind the gratitude which the enlightened Christian owes to God (Acts xii. 23; Rom. iv. 20; Rev. xix. 7).

*vv.* 27, 28. The blind man is identified with the disciples of Jesus and contrasted with the unbelieving Jews. 'To abandon Moses for Jesus would be in their eyes the worst of apostasies' (Loisy).

*v.* 29. *We know not whence he is.* The importance of the phrase and the implications suggested by its use here are presumed to be familiar to the readers of the gospel. The questions at issue between the Jews and the Christians concerned the origin of Jesus, His home and parentage, and the authority upon which His mission was based. The Jews asserted that His home was the unclean district of Galilee (vii. 27 sqq., 41, 52), that His parentage was obscure, with the suggestion that He was born out of wedlock (viii. 41), and that He was, therefore, a man and a sinner, possessing no divine authority. He was not the Christ, not even a prophet. The Christians met this attack by asserting the counter-claim that He came from heaven (iii. 13, 31, vi. 33), that God was His Father, and that He was the only begotten Son of God sent by the Father for the salvation of the world. His authority was the authority of God. This was the openly expressed claim of the Lord Himself (viii. 14, cf. iii. 13 sqq., vi. 38, 41, 51, viii. 21–5, xvi. 28), accepted by the Apostles, who were enabled to see His glory and to know Him, and through Him to see and to know the Father (i. 14, vi. 40, xii. 45, xiv. 6, 19, xvi. 27, xvii. 7, 8, 25), accepted also by those who believed through their preaching (xvii. 18, 20). The proud insight of the Jews was, in fact, blindness, for not only were they unable to see the Christ, but they could not even see the meaning of the law given by Moses, which was accepted by them as authoritative (v. 45 sqq.). Their ignorance of the origin of Jesus, here openly expressed, and their rejection of Him is, therefore, the rejection of God. They are completely blind (vii. 29, viii. 18, cf. xiv. 17).

*v.* 31. *Worshipper of God . . . do his will.* The phrases, used almost as titles, are descriptive of the Christians (iv. 20–4, 34, v. 30, vi. 38–40, vii. 17; 1 John ii. 17, cf. Mark iii. 35; Matt. vii. 21; Eph. vi. 6). The Christ was pre-eminently *he who did the will of the Father*; those who believe in Him are they who *do the will of God*, and, therefore, the true worshippers of God in contrast to the Jews. (For the use in the Papyri of the Greek word translated *worshipper of God* see Moulton-Milligan *Vocabulary of the Greek Testament* under θεοσεβής. The interpretation of the use of the first person plural 'we know' rather than 'I know' or 'ye know' is dependent upon the recognition of the Christian claims suggested by these titles.)

*We know,* cf. 1 John v. 15. We Christians. For the author of the gospel the use of the first person plural does not imply that all men alike know (Westcott), nor merely that we Jews know, but that Christians more than all others know (see INTRODUCTION, pp. 86–95). The man voices a conviction of primitive Christianity, based upon experience and upon the promise of the Lord. Christian prayer is effective because the Christians are the true worshippers of God, and because they do His will. The meaning of the Saying cannot be interpreted adequately from Old Testament parallel passages (Job xxvii. 8, 9, xxxv. 12, 13; Ps. lxvi. 17-20, cix. 7; Prov. xv. 29; Isa. i. 15), still less from similar beliefs referred to by Homer, Plato, Iamblichus, Philostratus, Plautus (Bauer): the exegesis is conditioned by the words of Jesus and by Christian piety (Mark vi. 23, 24; Matt. vii. 7 sqq., ix. 29; Phil. iv. 6, 7; James v. 13 sqq., and especially the Johannine writings xi. 22, 41, 42, xiv. 13, 14, xv. 7, 16, xvi. 23-6; 1 John iii. 21, 22, v. 14-16). The argument is, therefore: since Christian prayer is effective prayer, because the Christians are the holy ones of God, how much more must Jesus be holy in whose name the Christians pray, and by whom miracles without parallel were worked since the world began. The Jewish statement that He is a sinner is, therefore, absurd and blasphemous.

*vv.* 32, 33. Cases of the recovery of sight under the stimulus of intense religious faith were not unknown in the Roman Empire. A votive tablet from the temple of Aesculapius in Rome bears the following inscription: 'The God commanded Valerius Aper, a blind soldier, to come and receive the blood of a white cock, to mix it with honey and eyesalve, and to anoint his eyes for a period of three days. He received his sight, and came and gave thanks publicly to the God' (Dittenberger *Syll.* 1173, 15 sqq. quoted by Bauer). Except in the Book of Tobit vii. 7, xi. 7-13, xiv. 1 (2), the Old Testament contains no record of the healing of a blind man. Here, it is not merely the healing of a blind man that is held to be of such unique significance, but the healing of a man born blind. The unique miracle bears witness to the unique power of him who had performed the miracle. If once it be assumed that a miracle proclaims the presence of a prophet, a miracle without parallel since the world began proclaims the presence of the Christ. The conclusion of the argument, however, is suppressed; the author is content with the vague phrase, He is *from God*, reserving till *v.* 38 the record of the man's complete faith. Christian insight into truth is based primarily upon the vision of the Christ (Gal. iii. 1), rather than upon a logical deduction from a miracle, however unique.

*v.* 34. The true interpretation of the miracle is given unconsciously by the Jews themselves (cf. xi. 50). He who was altogether born in sins, that is to say, blind in Judaism, has been saved from sin and blindness by the Saviour, the Light of the world. He must of necessity, therefore, teach the Jews, in spite of their proud claim to be taught of God and in need of no instruction (Rom. ii. 17-25).

The sentence of excommunication involved, for those who enforced it, condemnation (*v.* 39), for the blind man, entrance into a new life, as the verses which follow make clear. The Greek word translated in this verse *cast out* is in x. 4 translated *put forth*. A Jew converted to Christianity is cast out of Judaism by the Jews, but put forth by the Christ, the Good Shepherd, whom he then follows. 'As long as they expected that he would deny the Christ they deemed him trustworthy. But when he spoke the truth unabashed, then, when they ought to have admired, they condemned him' (Chrysostom).

*v.* 35. 'The Jews cast him out of the Temple, the Lord of the Temple found him' (Chrysostom).

*Found.* The Greek word need not imply search (Matt. xviii. 28, xxvii. 32; Acts xiii. 6); but, since in the Fourth Gospel the word is only used either of an action of the Christ which is a definite and conscious fulfilment of Old Testament prophecy (xii. 14), or of a meeting which issues in discipleship (i. 41, 43, 45, v. 14), it is never descriptive of a merely fortuitous meeting. (For the contrary opinion see Loisy, Bauer.)

[*Son of God.* The manuscript evidence suggests that the reading *Son of man* represents the original text. *Son of man* is found in the Greek Codices, Sinaiticus, Vaticanus, Bezae, and in the Sinaitic Syriac and Egyptian Sahidic Versions. The Latin Versions, however, support the reading *Son of God.* When the original significance of the title *Son of man* was forgotten, and it was used to express the human nature of the Christ as distinct from His divine nature, the substitution of the title *Son of God* in such a passage as this, which clearly refers to the supernatural and incarnate Christ, is easy to understand. The substitution of *Son of man* for *Son of God* would, on the other hand, be difficult to explain.]

*v.* 36. The meaning of the question must be interpreted from iv. 24–6. The man is ignorant neither of the existence of the Christ nor of his future advent (as Bauer interprets the passage). He understands the significance of the title *Son of man*, but he does not know that the Messiah has come, nor, if He has come, does he know who He is. He admits, at the word of Jesus, that there is a Messiah, and asks only to know Him that he may believe on Him.

*vv.* 37, 38. Jesus reveals Himself as the Christ. To see Him and recognize Him is perfect sight and enlightenment, is, in fact, the vision of God: *He that hath seen me hath seen the Father* (xiv. 9).

*He worshipped him.* Not, as in Ruth ii. 10; 1 Sam. xx. 41, the respectful salaam due to a superior from an inferior, but the attitude of worship and adoration due from men to God. Christian adoration of the Christ, the intuitive and impulsive expression of insight and faith, is the true and spiritual worship of God (xii. 44, 45), by which Jewish worship in the Temple and all other worship is superseded (iv. 20–4, xii. 20, 21).

The blind man, who has passed from Judaism to Christianity, passes out of the story as the typical believer, the worshipper of God in Spirit and in Truth. This is the climax of the narrative and the purpose for which it was told.

*v.* 39. The concluding verses refer back to *v.* 3, and the symbolical character of the narrative is again emphasized. The Advent of the Christ and of Christianity imply the divine condemnation of Judaism, the destruction of the darkness of the world and the escape of the enlightened believers from the judgement of God. The commentators give the contrasted phrases more definite content than they in point of fact allow. Thus Loisy says that the blind who see are the Gentile Christians, and that those who see and become blind are the Jews. Schanz applies the first clause to those who know and feel their blindness and ignorance of the truth; Weiss to the poor who know not of the Law, in contrast to the Pharisees. The author of the gospel, however, sums up the significance of the miracle in a saying, reminiscent of Matt. xi. 25, xiii. 13–17; Mark iv. 11, 12, in which the contrast between Christianity and the World is stated in general terms. The converted Christians, whether born Jews or Gentiles, have passed from darkness to light; the unconverted World, whether Jewish or Gentile, with all its proud authority and wisdom (1 Cor. i. 18–25), is condemned to darkness and ignorance by the advent of the Christ and by the effectual mission of His disciples. A similar oxymoron occurs in xi. 25, 26, where the paradox is in part suppressed—*He that believeth on me, though he die, yet shall he live: and whosoever liveth and believeth on me shall never die.* The believers who have passed from death to life are by implication contrasted with the unbelievers who, though apparently alive, are in reality dead.

*vv.* 40, 41. *The Pharisees which were with him.* Not the Pharisees who believed on Him, but those whose presence was necessary that they might hear their sentence of condemnation. The introduction of a representative group of Pharisees at this point rounds off the narrative. The sin of the Pharisees is set off against the faith of the man born blind, and the unbelieving and arrogant Jews are placed solidly within the sphere of darkness. This leads to a further distinction between blindness that is accompanied by the claim to sight and that is characteristic of the Pharisees, and blindness accompanied by no such claim. The former is reckoned as sin, the latter, though real blindness, is not so reckoned. The conditional sentence grammatically expresses an unfulfilled condition in present time; *If ye were blind* (which ye claim not to be), *ye would not now be in sin* (which ye are). The Pharisees thus pass out of the story blind, but claiming authority to teach the world and therefore abiding in sin. *If therefore the light that is in thee be darkness, how great is the darkness* (Matt. vi. 23).

### THE NARRATIVE COMPARED WITH v. 1–18

Taken as a whole the narrative recalls the account of the healing of the lame man. The two accounts are closely parallel in structure, the miracle on the sabbath day, investigation by the Jews, meeting of Jesus with the healed man; and in detail, the two pools Bethesda, Siloam v. 2, ix. 7; the man lame for thirty-eight years, the man born blind v. 5, ix. 1; the proclamation of Jesus as the Son of God (Son of man) v. 18, ix. 35–8; the ignorance concerning who Jesus is v. 12, 13, ix. 25, 29; the reference to him as *the man* v. 12, ix. 11, 16. Blindness and lameness are connected in the mind of the author. Blind and lame wait at the pool of Bethesda, hoping to be healed. The similarity of the narratives arises in the natural connection between blindness and lameness and between sight and the power to walk which is expressed in the saying: *I am the Light of the world. He that* followeth *me shall not* walk *in darkness, but shall have the light of life* (viii. 12, cf. Eph. v. 8; Rev. xxi. 24). The miracles of the healing of the lame man and of the blind man supplement one another in proving the truth of this claim. The converted Christians walk freely and see clearly, for they walk according to the commandments of the Lord (2 John 6; Heb. xii. 12, 13), and know the Truth (2 John 1).

The narrative of the healing of the blind man is constructed out of materials drawn from various sources, and has a far more complicated background than is generally recognized. It cannot be explained as a reminiscence of ancient history committed to writing lest the memory fail and the details be lost; nor is it an ancient Christian tradition, which, in the course of time, has grown under the influence of the popular tendency to heighten what is miraculous and to insert imaginary conversations in order to fill out the story; nor is it the product of imaginary and fantastic symbolism, in which the idea of Jesus as the Light of the world was embodied in the picture of a blind man receiving his sight at the command of the Lord; nor is it the fruit of the meditation of some quiet mystic upon an incident in the life of Jesus preserved in his memory or presented to him by the tradition of the Church.

The background of the narrative is Christianity at the close of the first or the beginning of the second century, engaged in a fierce battle with Judaism, felt on both sides to be a battle to the death. For the Jews the issue at stake was the defence of their religion, for the Christians the salvation of the world. The Jews were the guardians of a piety indissolubly bound up with national customs sanctioned by the authority of Moses, the Prophet; the Christians of a piety under the influence of which a new religious tradition had been creatively evolved out of the materials of Judaism by the authority of Jesus, the Christ, the Son of God, the Saviour of the world.

The intensity of the struggle between the two religions was, however, due, not so much to theological friction, as to the success of the Christian mission, which led to the passing over from Judaism to Christianity of an ever-increasing stream of converts, who were denounced by the Jews as apostates, but welcomed by the Christians as men who had passed from darkness to light and from death to life. It was not unnatural that the Jews endeavoured to prevent this constant leakage, both by the threat of excommunication and by the denial of the truth of the beliefs upon which Christian piety was based.

Behind the controversy with the Jews lay the intensity of the moral and spiritual experience of conversion to Christianity, apart from which the controversy is hardly intelligible. To the reality of this experience the authors of the extant primitive Christian documents again and again refer; presumably they did but write what the Christians were in the habit of saying. The Christian missionaries were evangelists, who were driven into controversy, and the argument they made use of primarily was the argument from experience. They had been reborn, had passed from death to life, from darkness to light; the power of sin had been broken; they stood within the peace of God, they walked in the law of God; they were free men, they knew the Truth. This overwhelming experience had come to them by faith in Jesus as the Christ, the Son of God, and by baptism into His Name. The promises of the Old Testament had been literally fulfilled, for the Messiah had come. The experience of conversion and of the life which followed conversion gave reality to their Christology and controlled their interpretation of the Old Testament. The Jews were therefore forced, not only to deny that Jesus was the Christ who had been sent from heaven and to protest against the Christian exegesis of the Old Testament, but also to deny the experience of conversion, which was felt by the Christians to be miraculous.

The opposition of the Jews to Christianity had its counterpart in the opposition of the Jews to Jesus. In broad outlines his life was reflected in the history of the community of his disciples. The controversy with the Jews was both the expression of this, and the proof that those who believed in Him were indeed inspired by His Spirit. The miracles He had once worked were repeated in the miracles of conversion. Blind men saw the truth, lame men were set free to walk in the commandments of God, and the dead were raised to a new life. Thus by a natural and unconscious symbolism the traditional narratives of His miraculous actions were related in such a way as to identify the converts with those who had originally been healed, and the later opponents of Christianity, with the original opponents of Jesus. The earlier narratives tended to become more and more clearly symbolical of the later experiences of the Christians, the original history providing the framework within which reference was made to contemporary history, and the materials out of which narratives and discourses could be constructed.

The story of the blind man is not, therefore, the outcome of a desire to give concrete embodiment to the idea of Jesus as the Light of the world, but is, rather, the result of a very complicated and complete fusion into one narrative of the experience of conversion to Christianity, of the controversy with the Jews which was caused by the success of the Christian mission, and of the traditional accounts of the healing of blind men by Jesus.

# THE USE OF THE FOURTH, FIFTH, AND NINTH CHAPTERS OF SAINT JOHN'S GOSPEL IN THE EARLY LECTIONARIES

The study of the lectionary systems of the early Church is still in its infancy. Such evidence as we have, however, points to a rather surprising agreement in the liturgical use of the sections in the Fourth Gospel commonly called Of the Samaritan Woman, Of the Paralytic, Of the Blind Man.

The two treatises attributed to Saint Ambrose, *De Mysteriis* and *De Sacramentis*, contain references to a lectionary system. The treatises belong to the end of the fourth or the beginning of the fifth centuries and consist of a series of addresses given during Easter week to those who had been baptized on the previous Easter Eve. The author of the tract *De Sacramentis* assumes that the narrative of the healing of the paralytic had been read on Easter Tuesday, for he says in his address given on Easter Wednesday; 'What was read yesterday? An angel, it says, went down at a certain season into the pool, and so often as the angel descended, the water was troubled: and whosoever descended was made whole of every disease whatsoever he had, which signifies a figure of our Lord Jesus Christ who was to come' (*De Sacr.* ii. 2, 3, cf. *De Myst.* iv. 22). At some time also during their preparation the catechumens had heard the narrative of the healing of the blind man: 'Thou hast to come to the altar, whither thou hast not come before; thou hast to see the things which thou didst not see before, that is, the mystery which thou hast read in the Gospel; if, however, thou hast not read it, thou hast certainly heard it. A blind man presented himself to the Saviour to be healed, And he . . . brought back the light of the eyes by a command, yet, in the book of the Gospel which is entitled "according to John" . . . he wished to prefigure this mystery (that is, baptism) in that miracle . . . Whatever he (John) spoke is a mystery' (*De Sacr.* iii. 2, 11). From these casual references it may be deduced that John v was read in Easter week and that ch. ix had been read some time during Lent, these chapters being specially chosen because the miracles of the healing of the paralytic and of the blind man were interpreted as baptismal miracles. This conclusion is supported by the evidence of the *Manuale Ambrosianum*, which contains the cycle of lessons used in the church of Milan in the eleventh century.[1] The relevant Johannine lessons in the *Manuale* are:

| | |
|---|---|
| 1st Sunday in Lent | St. John iv. The Sunday of the Samaritan Woman. |
| 3rd Sunday in Lent | St. John ix. The Sunday of the Blind Man. |
| Easter Vigil | St. John iii. Mass for the newly baptized. |
| Tuesday in Easter Week | St. John v. Mass for the newly baptized. |
| Thursday and Friday in Easter Week | St. John vi. Mass for the newly baptized. |

From a comparison of the liturgical notes in eleven Greek manuscripts of the New Testament Scrivener was able to draw up a complete lectionary for the year (Scrivener, *Introduction to the Criticism of the New Testament*, fourth edition, vol. I, Appendix to ch. iii). Since the manuscripts were written during the eighth or ninth centuries it must be assumed that by the ninth century, and probably very much earlier, the Greek Church possessed a uniform lectionary. According to this system Saint John's Gospel was read continuously on the weekdays from the Wednesday after Easter until the vigil of Whitsunday: chs. i. 1–17, iv. 5–42, v. 1–15, ix. 1–38, and the narrative of the Passion were, however, omitted. The reason for this dislocation is quite clear. i. 1–17 had been read on Easter Sunday, and the narrative of the Passion on the Thursday in Holy Week. The other three passages, being apparently regarded as of especial importance, were transferred to the third, fourth, and fifth Sundays after Easter, which were called the Sundays of the Paralytic, of the Samaritan Woman, of the Blind Man. The transference was presumably conditioned by the desire to mark these Sundays as commemorative of the miracle of baptism.

In the year 1923 Burkitt communicated to the British Academy a translation of a sixth-century Syriac manuscript, consisting of an Index to the lessons proper for the festivals of the whole year and other occasions. Since the Index claims to be based on 'Laws and enactments made by Constantine and Theodosius and Leo, believing Emperors', Burkitt dated the table of lessons shortly after the death of the Emperor Leo (A.D. 474). A comparison of this manuscript with the lectionary notes in the Syriac biblical manuscripts of the sixth and seventh centuries provides evidence of the liturgical reading of the Bible in the churches of the Euphrates valley in the sixth century (F. C. Burkitt,

[1] For a general discussion of the evidence of the Ambrosian Treatises and of the *Manuale* cf. Thompson and Srawley, *St. Ambrose 'On the Mysteries' and the Treatise On the Sacraments*, Introduction, pp. xxvii. sqq., and the *Manuale Ambrosianum*, edited by Magistretti, vol. II, pp. 134, 151, 218, 221, 223.

*The Early Syriac Lectionary System*). During Lent the Gospel lessons were chosen mainly from Saint John's Gospel. The narrative of the healing of the lame man was read on the Saturday in the middle week of the Fast, the following note being added in the Index: 'Now on the Saturday of the first and of the middle week there is a commemoration of all our Fathers the Bishops, and of all those who have been baptized in Christ our Lord'. The same passage formed also the special gospel in the baptismal office. The narrative of the healing of the blind man was read on the Mid-Lent Sunday. In the lectionary system St. John v. and ix were, therefore, closely related passages. If we may assume that Mid-Lent was an important stage in the preparation of the catechumens for baptism, the choice of the Saturday for the commemoration of all the baptized and of the lessons on the Saturday and on the Sunday is adequately explained. Further evidence is supplied by Dr. Anton Baumstark in his book: *Festbrevier und Kirchenjahr der Syrischen Jakobiten*, pp. 216–30, 256. In the Jacobite Church St. John v. 1–18 was read on the third Sunday in Lent and ix. 1–41 on the fifth Sunday, the Sundays being called 'Of the Lame Man' and 'Of the Blind Man'. iv. 13–24 was used as the Gospel lesson at the service of the Bending of the Knee on Whitsunday.

There is, therefore, a fairly general agreement about the importance of these three sections of Saint John's Gospel in the lectionaries of the early Church and about their liturgical use. This agreement points to a traditional usage reaching back behind the fourth century. Since the Woman of Samaria, the Paralytic, and the Blind Man appear in the second century frescoes in the catacombs at Rome as baptismal symbols, the liturgical baptismal use of these chapters may perhaps have its roots in the second century.

# THE PARABLE OF THE SHEEP,
# THE SHEPHERD,
# AND THE BRIGANDS

## X. 1–21

THE contrast between the Pharisees who are blind (ix. 39–41) and the blind man who sees (ix. 36–8), between the rulers of the Jews who persecuted the blind man (ix. 22, 34) and Jesus who healed him, provides the context in which the Parable of the Sheep, the Shepherd, and the Brigands is recorded; and further, the general significance of the miracle is exposed in the Parable and in its interpretation. The words *verily*, *verily* in the gospel mark the movement of an argument (v. 19, 24, 25, vi. 26, 32, 47, 53, viii. 34, 51, 58, xii. 24, &c.). They are not used to introduce a wholly new episode. The interpretation of the parable concludes with a reference to the miracle and to the division which it occasioned among the Jews (x. 19–21, cf. ix. 16). The blind man—who obeys the command of Jesus, is put forth from the synagogue of the Jews and recognizes and believes in Jesus as Lord and Son of man—reappears in the description of the sheep who hear the voice of the shepherd, are put forth from the various folds in which they have awaited His call (x. 4, 16) and form a new flock secure in the care of the One Good Shepherd. Similarly, the Pharisees, who strove energetically to disturb the relation between the blind man and Jesus, reappear in the company of thieves and robbers and hirelings who either have no care for the sheep or attempt to steal and murder and destroy them. Moreover, the relation between blindness and inability to understand the teaching and parables of Jesus (ix. 40, 41, x. 6) is an important theme in the synoptic tradition (Matt. xv. 14–16, xxiii. 16–19, 24–6; Mark iv. 10–12, cf. Mark vii. 17, 18), so that, for those familiar with the earlier tradition, the transition between the conclusion of ch. ix and the record of the parable at the beginning of ch. x would occasion no surprise. The two chapters therefore stand in the closest possible relationship, and the Evangelist presupposes the ability of his readers to recognize it.

The biblical literature is everywhere concerned to direct attention to the true authority under which the people of God must live, and to expose those who presume to exercise a false and tyrannical rule over them.

*They have set up kings, and not by me;*
*They have made princes, and I knew it not.*

(Hos. viii. 4, cf. Isa. xxxi; Luke xxii. 25 sqq.)

Prominent also is the use of the metaphor of sheep and shepherds to express this profound critical teaching. The long passage in which the prophet Ezekiel, on the background of the picture of David, the true Shepherd, denounces the shepherds who feed themselves and do not feed the people of God, but rule over them with force and cruelty, kill the fatlings and permit the sheep to wander uncared for through all the mountains and upon every high hill, is classical (Ezek. xxxiv). And it is classical, because the metaphor, which lies deep in the Old Testament literature, is expanded by the prophet and handled with exemplary clarity and firmness. Israel is God's flock (Ps. xxiii, lxxiv. 1, lxxviii. 52, 71, lxxix. 13, lxxx. 1, xcv. 7, c. 3; Isa. xl. 11; Jer. xxiii. 1–4), which though in the hands of false shepherds (Jer. ii. 8, R.V. mg., x. 21, xii. 10; Zech. xi. 3–9, 15–17, cf. 2 Esdras v. 18), shall assuredly be saved by David, the servant of God, the true shepherd of Israel or by a branch from the stem of David (Jer. xxiii. 1–8; Ezek. xxxiv. 22 sqq., cf. 1 Enoch xxxv–xc; Ps. of Solomon xvii. 40 sqq.), as in time past they had been led by the great king (Ps. lxxviii. 70–2) and by the hand of Moses and Aaron (Ps. lxxvii. 20). So shall they be *no more a prey to the heathen, neither shall the beast of the earth devour them; but they shall dwell securely, and none shall make them afraid* (Ezek. xxxiv. 28).

In the New Testament this rich and impressive metaphorical lanage comes to rest with its application to Jesus as the true Shepherd of the people of God (Mark vi. 34, xiv. 27; Luke xii. 32, xv. 3–7; Matt. ix. 35, 36, xv. 24, xviii. 12 sqq., xxvi. 31; Heb. xiii. 20; 1 Pet. ii. 25, v. 4, cf. Rev. xii. 5, xix. 15 in the Greek), and to His disciples as the shepherds who exercise authority in His name (Matt. x. 6; Acts xx. 28; Eph. iv. 11; 1 Pet. v. 2, 3, cf. Rev. ii. 27). The activity of the false shepherds reaches its climax both in the opposition of the Jewish authorities to Jesus, and in those false prophets and powerful men who, having broken into the Church, usurp the authority of the true pastors of the sheep (Matt. vii. 15, 16; Acts xx. 29, 30). This Christian background of language and metaphor, which itself presumes the Old Testament background, is wholly sufficient to account for the form and content of the parable in the Fourth Gospel. It should, however, be noticed that, important as is the Old Testament background of the parable of the Shepherd and the sheep, it fails to give adequate expression to the supreme truth of the Christian revelation. Consequently, in Mark xiv. 27, 28, the description of the destruction of the false shepherd in Zech. xiii. 7 sqq. is transformed into a prophecy of the death and resurrection of Jesus, and in the Fourth Gospel the whole parabolic heritage is focused upon the picture of the Good Shepherd who lays down His life for the sheep that He may take it again (*vv.* 15–18). The parable is completed only when it has borne witness to the death and resurrection of Jesus. In similar fashion the significance of the Feeding of the Five Thousand is not exhausted until the bread is expounded as the flesh which Jesus will give for the life of the world, and the feeding which provides life is declared to be the eating of His body and the drinking of His blood (vi. 51 sqq.). The background of the parable is, then, the Old Testament heritage of metaphor as that heritage has been transformed by Christian truth; and the readers of the Gospel are presumed to be familar with the language. Some commentators (e.g. Bauer) have endeavoured to disturb this precise heritage by placing the parable upon the background of general Hellenistic and Oriental mysticism. The picture of a shepherd and his sheep not unnaturally provides, throughout the history of mystical religion, a means of expressing the relationship between the unseen God and His faithful worshippers; thus in Egyptian religion Anubis was the Shepherd God, Attys in Phrygia, Tammuz and Marduk in Persia and Babylonia. Philo describes the Word of God as the Shepherd of souls (*De Agric.* 26–9, 39–44) and in the Hermetic Literature *Nous* is the Pastor of mankind (Reitzenstein, *Poimandres*, pp. 115, 116). To place the parable in the Fourth Gospel upon the background of such general mysticism is to obscure the delicate allusions to the Old Testament, and to destroy that vigorous sense for history which it is the main purpose of the Evangelist to expose as the ground of Christian truth. Moreover, the commentator has not only to explain the significance of the metaphor of the shepherd and the sheep, but also to interpret the thieves and robbers and hirelings who occupy so prominent a place both in the parable and in its interpretation.

In the immediate literary context the Pharisees are, as had been noted above, the blasphemous opponents of Jesus, and the reader is intended to recognize them again in the thieves and robbers of the parable. This is, of course, quite essential to the author of the Gospel, for the opposition of the Jews to Jesus was a supreme blasphemy. But blasphemy is not for him exhausted in a single historical occurrence. In the perspective of the Fourth Gospel it is repeated in the opposition of the Jews to the Church, and, what is perhaps more important to him, in the appearance within the Church of those anti-Christs who deny the authority of the historical Jesus, who *is come in the flesh* (vi. 60, 66; 1 John ii. 18 sqq., iv. 1 sqq.; 2 John 7), and who, like Diotrephes, love to have the pre-eminence (3 John 9). Barabbas, whom the Jews preferred to Jesus, was appropriately enough a robber (xviii. 40); and Judas, the disciple who *went out* (xiii. 30, cf. vi. 66; 1 John ii. 19, iv. 1) into the night and betrayed his Master, was equally appropriately a thief (xii. 6). But more is involved even than this, for there is no point in human history which lies beyond the horizon of the thieves and robbers of the parable. Wherever men have claimed to announce the gift of life, or shall claim to announce it, apart from faith in Jesus, they proclaim themselves as thieves and robbers, and their activity has been, and is, and will be, a destructive activity (*vv.* 8–10).

[In *v.* 6, the Evangelist defines the form of teaching which Jesus had used by the Greek word παροιμία. In xvi. 29, where the same word is used, it is presumed that Jesus had normally employed such a method of teaching, but that in the Upper Room the disciples suppose Him to be speaking at last *openly* and not enigmatically, and that, consequently, they are able to perceive His meaning (xvi. 30). Here the same contrast between clear and enigmatic teaching is assumed, since the Jews (? the Pharisees) are said not to have understood *what things they were which he spake unto them*. The Evangelist presumes that his readers are familiar with that form of the teaching of Jesus which was named by the earlier Evangelists teaching in parables. It is therefore at first sight strange that he should have substituted here the word παροιμία for παραβολή, and that he should nowhere have used the latter word. In the New Testament the word παροιμία is used outside the Fourth Gospel only in 2 Pet. ii. 22, where it introduces a quotation from the Book of Proverbs. This, however, causes no surprise, since in the LXX the word is used in the opening verse of the Book of Proverbs (cf. Prov. xxv. 1). The translation of the word here by *proverb* (R.V. mg.) is, however, inadequate, since the Evangelist can hardly be thought to be referring merely to a terse and wise utterance. The solution of the problem seems to lie in another meaning of the word, which is found in the Greek versions of the Old Testament. In the LXX translation, the Hebrew word *Mashal* is translated normally by παραβολή, but its translation by παροιμία in the Book of Proverbs and the use of παροιμία in the Book of Ecclesiasticus (xxxix. 3, xlvii. 17) show that the Hebrew word could be reproduced by either of the Greek words. The later Jewish translators, moreover, at times substituted παροιμία for the LXX παραβολή, precisely as the author of the Fourth Gospel has done. Thus in Ps. lxxviii. 2, Symmachus substitutes διὰ παροιμίας for the LXX ἐν παραβολαῖς (see Hatch, *Essays in Biblical Greek*, pp. 64 sqq.). But these words are therefore used to reproduce the two meanings of the Hebrew *Mashal* (a) a proverb, (b) a symbolical saying requiring interpretation. But it is the second of these meanings that is important for New Testament exegesis, whether we are concerned with the word παραβολή in the synoptic gospels or with the word παροιμία in the Fourth Gospel. The biblical writers are not really concerned to draw nice distinctions between metaphors and parables and proverbs and allegories, as were the Greek writers on the art of rhetoric. They were concerned to assert that human language can and does reveal the secrets of the Lord to those possessed of the Wisdom of the Lord, and that only those who possess the Wisdom of the Lord can penetrate His secrets. Thus even the proverbs of Solomon were not thought of as utterances of worldly wisdom, but as utterances of the Wisdom of God which Solomon had been enabled to hear and proclaim. The author of the Epistle of Barnabas has well understood this: 'Blessed be our Lord, brethren, who hath put into us wisdom and understanding of his secrets; for what the prophet says is a parable of the Lord. Who will understand it but he who is wise and knowing, and who loves his Lord?' (Barn. vi. 10). The statement in some modern commentaries (e.g. Loisy, pp. 75, 87, sqq., 608) that the author of the Fourth Gospel has substituted allegories for the simpler parabolic teaching in the earlier tradition is in the end irrelevant, because the whole teaching and action of Jesus is recorded both in the earlier tradition and in the Fourth Gospel as the Revelation of God in human speech and action. The word παραβολή in the synoptic gospels calls attention to this revelation, just as the word παροιμία does in the Fourth Gospel; and understanding of it does not depend upon an increase of human intelligence, but upon love of the Lord and the possession of His Spirit. The modern attempt to draw a nice distinction between parable and allegory hardly therefore assists the interpretation of the gospels. The author of the Fourth Gospel adds an interpretation to the parable of the Good Shepherd, just as previously he had added an interpretation to the miracle of the Feeding of the Five Thousand. But it is a paradoxical procedure, because, humanly speaking, in both cases the interpretation is more difficult than the parable or the miracle; but in the perspective of the Fourth Gospel the whole—parable, miracle and interpretation —moves on one plane, a plane in which God reveals Himself to men through the words and actions of Jesus. Consequently, when the disciples (xvi. 29–30) suppose that the Lord has moved from parabolic to open speech, they misunderstand Him utterly (xvi. 32), since throughout His ministry the Lord had spoken and acted openly to those who believed and in parables to those who did not believe. The distinction lies in His hearers, and not in the various methods of teaching which He adopted.]

## THE PARABLE

x. 1. *Verily, verily, I say unto you, He that entereth not by the door into the fold of the sheep, but climbeth up some other way, the same is a thief and a robber. 2. But he that entereth in by the door is the shepherd of the sheep. 3. To him the porter openeth; and the sheep hear his voice: and he calleth his own sheep by name, and leadeth them out. 4. When he hath put forth all his own, he goeth before them, and the sheep follow him: for they know his voice. 5. And a stranger will they not follow, but will flee from him: for they know not the voice of strangers. 6. This parable spake Jesus unto them: but they understood not what things they were which he spake unto them.*

## THE INTERPRETATION OF THE PARABLE
### JESUS, THE DOOR OF THE SHEEP-FOLD AND THE GOOD SHEPHERD OF THE SHEEP

7. *Jesus therefore said unto them again, Verily, verily, I say unto you, I am the door of the sheep. 8. All that came before me are thieves and robbers: but the sheep did not hear them. 9. I am the door: by me if any many enter in, he shall be saved, and shall go in and go out, and shall find pasture. 10. The thief cometh not, but that he may steal, and kill, and destroy: I came that they may have life, and may have it abundantly. 11. I am the good shepherd: the good shepherd layeth down his life for the sheep. 12. He that is a hireling, and not a shepherd, whose own the sheep are not, beholdeth the wolf coming, and leaveth the sheep, and fleeth, and the wolf snatcheth them, and scattereth them: 13. he fleeth because he is a hireling, and careth not for the sheep. 14. I am the good shepherd; and I know mine own, and mine own know me, 15. even as the Father knoweth me, and I know the Father; and I lay down my life for the sheep. 16. And other sheep I have, which are not of this fold: them also I must bring, and they shall hear my voice; and they shall become one flock, one shepherd. 17. Therefore doth the Father love me, because I lay down my life, that I may take it again. 18. No one taketh it away from me, but I lay it down of myself. I have power to lay it down, and I have power to take it again. This commandment received I from my Father.*

### THE BLASPHEMY OF THE JEWS

19. *There arose a division again among the Jews because of these words. 20. And many of them said, He hath a devil, and is mad; why hear ye him? 21. Others said, These are not the sayings of one possessed with a devil. Can a devil open the eyes of the blind?*

### THE PARABLE

x. 1–6. The Parable of the Sheep, the Shepherd and the Brigands, unlike the Parable of the Vine, the Husbandman and the Branches (xv. 1 sqq.), moves smoothly to its conclusion without the intrusion of any interpretation into the actual framework of the Parable. And yet, so transparent is the narrative, that the attentive reader, familiar with the Johannine movement of thought and expression, can hardly fail to weave the interpretation into the Parable as the Evangelist has himself done in the parallel passage in ch. xv—*Every branch that beareth fruit, he cleanseth it, that it may bear more fruit. Already ye are clean because of the word which I have spoken unto you* (xv. 2, 3).

The courtyard adjoining a house (xviii. 15) serves as the fold for the sheep belonging to the owner of the house. Access to the house, and, consequently to the sheep, is provided by a single door in the wall of the courtyard, over which a door-keeper keeps permanent watch (xviii.

17; Mark xiii. 34). The situation is such that the behaviour of those who purpose to do harm to the sheep is sharply distinguished from the behaviour of those responsible for their care. A shepherd enters by the door with the porter's full permission; thieves and robbers[1] must start their nefarious proceedings from some other place and can approach the sheep only by climbing over the wall. And, moreover, the behaviour of the sheep betrays equally clearly the proximity of the shepherd or of those who purpose their destruction. The sound of the shepherd's voice is well known to them; individually they recognize their names as he calls them one by one, and they follow him willingly as he leads them out through the door, for they are his sheep. The approach of a stranger causes consternation among the sheep. His voice is strange to them, nor is he able in friendly fashion to pronounce their names. The terror he occasions makes it impossible for them to follow him, and so they have no alternative but flight.

And yet, this analysis of the contents of the Parable hardly does justice to the point upon which the emphasis is most firmly laid. The shepherd is not *a* figure in the Parable, he is *the* figure; and it is upon the description of his behaviour that the narrative lingers, in order that the attention of the readers may be concentrated there. Not only are the sheep his own sheep, not only has he full authority to approach them, not only does he call his sheep by name, not only do they hear his voice; but he leads them out, and, when he has put forth all his sheep, he goes before them, and the sheep follow him. It is by the description of the shepherd that the reader is intended to recognize the significance of the Parable, quite apart from the interpretation which follows. Each phrase echoes a main theme of the Fourth Gospel. There is but one Saviour, who comes *to his own* (i. 11), and calls men to *follow* Him (i. 43, viii. 12, xxi. 19–22). The call is given individually and by name (xi. 43, xii. 17); the believers hear His voice (v. 25, xviii. 37, cf. iii. 29); and the consequence of obedience to the call is that men no longer walk in darkness, but possess the light of Life (viii. 12), and pass from death to life (v. 24, 25). In the perspective of the gospel, however, this true discipleship depends upon a final action of the Christ, in which His work was completed. Having by His death finished the work of the Father (v. 36, xix. 30), He precedes His faithful disciples to His Father's house, whither He goes to prepare a place for them (xiv. 2), in order that where He is, they also may be with Him (xiv. 3, xvii. 24).

When the profound significance of the language in which the Parable is recorded is recognized, it is perhaps possible to give a judgement upon two difficulties of detail. The phrase *his own sheep* in *v.* 3 and the absence of the definite article in *v.* 2 (R.V. mg. *a shepherd*) are taken by

---

[1] Obad. 5. The Greek word translated *robber* corresponds, however, more nearly with the English word *brigand*; xviii. 40, cf. Jer. vii. 11; Hos. vi. 9; Matt. xxvi. 55; Mark xv. 27; Luke x. 30.

some commentators to imply that the courtyard contains more than one flock (e.g. Plummer), and that the Shepherd is concerned to gather together only those sheep which belong to Him. A plurality of shepherds seems, however, foreign both to the Parable and to its significance. The sheep belong—all of them—to the one shepherd (vi. 68). They may, however, pass under the control of false shepherds, who, in fact, are not shepherds at all, but thieves and robbers (*v.* 8). The other difficulty concerns the precise significance of the Greek word translated *put forth* in *v.* 4 (cf. v. 7). Though the word, which means literally *cast forth,* need not suggest the employment of physical force (Matt. xii. 35, xiii. 52; Luke x. 35; James ii. 25; see Moulton-Milligan, *Vocab.*), it is not simply equivalent to *lead forth.* The helplessness of the sheep (v. 7) is contrasted with the free action of the shepherd, for their freedom depends upon his action, and they are thus constrained to freedom. This suggestion of constraint (ix. 34, 35) is admirably adapted to the expression of the relation of the believing Christian to the Christ: *I, if I be lifted up from the earth, will draw all men unto myself.* For the use of the word to express a divine constraint which in no way excludes willing surrender, cf. Luke x. 2.

### THE INTERPRETATION OF THE PARABLE
### JESUS, THE DOOR OF THE SHEEP-FOLD AND THE
### GOOD SHEPHERD OF THE SHEEP

*vv.* 7, 8. The emphasis upon the behaviour and work of the shepherd in the narrative of the Parable prepares the way for the concentration of the interpretation upon the pregnant Sayings, *I am the door of the sheep—I am the good shepherd,* each being repeated twice (*vv.* 7, 9, 11, 14). 'When He bringeth us to the Father He calleth Himself a "Door", when He taketh care of us, a "Shepherd"' (Chrysostom). The Sahidic Version simplifies the interpretation by substituting 'the Shepherd' for 'the Door', and thus removing the Saying *I am the Door.* This, however, is almost certainly a correction, though it is accepted as original by Wellhausen, Heitmüller, Moffatt, and some other modern commentators. Jesus is the Door (see note on xix. 29), as He is the Way (xiv. 6); and He is the only Door through which men can pass to the Father— *No one cometh unto the Father, but through me* (xiv. 6 R.V. mg.), and through which Christian Pastors can have access to the Believers and perform their ministry (xxi. 15 sqq.). Faith in Jesus, the Christ, who is come *in the flesh* (1 John iv. 2, 3) controls the whole life of the Church, and love of Him must control the work of the ministry as it controls the behaviour of all the faithful. To deny the historical revelation of God in Jesus is to deny the Truth and to destroy the Church. Hence, the Evangelist delays his description of the Good Shepherd by pausing to interpret the opening words of the Parable—*He that entereth not by the door . . . is a thief and a robber.* Jesus is the *Door of the sheep,* meaning that He is the

Door through which the sheep pass and the Door through which alone men can rightly approach the sheep. He is the Sheep Gate (*v.* 2). The metaphor of the Door or Gate applied to Jesus is fairly common in primitive Christian literature (Ignatius *Philad.* ix. 1; Clement 1 *Cor.* xlviii; Hermas *Sim.* ix. 12; Hegesippus cited by Eusebius, *Hist. Eccl.*, ii. 23. 8; Hippolytus, *Ref.* v. 8. 21; *Acts of John* xcv, cf. Ps. cxviii. 19, 20; Rev. iii. 8: see Bernard).

The vigorous and exclusive insistence that Jesus is the only Door and the only Shepherd—*all that came before me are thieves and robbers*—has caused great difficulty to commentators. Gnostic writers used the words to justify their antagonism to the Jewish Law and the Prophets and this usage may explain the emergence in the early Church of variant readings which relieved the tension of their possible application to the Prophets of the Old Testament. *Before me* is omitted by Codex Sinaiticus, and by some other uncial and cursive Greek manuscripts, by most of the Old Latin manuscripts, by the Vulgate, by the Sinaitic Syriac Codex and by the Peshitto, by the Egyptian Sahidic Version, and by Cyril of Alexandria and Augustine. Lagrange regards the words as an addition. *All* is omitted by Codex Bezae. The very difficulty of *all* and *before me*, however, makes the longer reading more probably original, and in any case demands explanation. Modern, as well as ancient, commentators, while retaining the longer reading, have, nevertheless, in various ways limited the application of the words. They are directed, according to Origen (*c. Celsum* vii. 9), against contemporary prophets (cf. Joseph. *Ant.* xx. 185–7); according to Chrysostom and Wellhausen, against false Messiahs: 'He referreth to those who had been before and to those who should be after Him, anti-Christ and false Christs, Judas and Theudas, and whatever others there have been of the same kind' (Chrys. on x. 1); according to Wetter, against Hellenistic cults of the sons of God (*Der Sohn Gottes*, p. 164); according to others, against the Jewish authorities in general or particularly against those who provoked the revolution against Rome in A.D. 70, and themselves escaped from the catastrophe (Schanz, quoted by Loisy, p. 614). But any such limitation is foreign to the Evangelist. His horizon is nowhere limited, *all—before me—are*. Every claim in the past or in the present to give life except through Jesus is destructive of life; all who make the claim have been and are thieves and robbers, whom the true servants of God have never followed. In this all-embracing condemnation the Hebrew Patriarchs, Moses, and the Prophets of Israel are, of course, not included. Their inclusion would contradict the whole tenor of the Fourth Gospel (e.g. iv. 22, v. 45–7, vi. 45, vii. 19, viii. 56, xii. 38–41) and of every other New Testament document: and moreover, it would mean that the Old Testament Scriptures were in themselves life-giving or claimed to be so. But this is precisely what the Evangelist will not allow. The Jews search the Scriptures because they suppose wrongly that in them they have eternal life—*and these are they which bear witness of me; and ye will not come to me, that ye may have life* (v. 39, 40). The great men of the Old Testament are contrasted with Jesus on the one hand and with the thieves and robbers on the other hand, not because, as Holtzmann writes (p. 197, cf. his *Neu-testamentlichen Theologie*, II, p. 356), 'the Old Testament is less an historical episode than a collection of types and oracles: its prophets did not belong to genuine history, but, like Abraham (viii. 56) and Isaiah (xii. 38–41), exist beyond the sphere of time', but because the Old Testament is a prophetic book, containing the record of a prophetic history, which is fulfilled in the redemptive history, namely, the coming of Jesus, His death and resurrection, and because both the Old Testament prophets and Jesus, in Whom their prophecy is fulfilled, are contrasted with every other claim to give life and salvation to men. The same movement of thought occurs in the Epistle of Ignatius to the Philadelphians (ch. ix): 'He is the door of the Father, through which enter Abraham and Isaac and Jacob and the Prophets and the Apostles and the Church. All these things are joined in the unity of God. . . . For the beloved prophets had a message pointing to Him, but the Gospel is the perfection of incorruption'. Earlier in the Epistle (ch. vi) Ignatius had written of non-Christian Jews and Gentiles. 'Both of them, unless they speak of Jesus Christ, are to me tombstones and sepulchres of the dead, on which have been engraved only the names of men', and he had previously exhorted the Christians to 'follow as sheep where the Shepherd is' (ch. ii).

*vv.* 9–11. Salvation is by faith in Jesus, and only by faith in Him —*By me if any man enter in, he shall be saved* (iii. 17, 18, iv. 42, v. 34, xii. 44–7, cf. Rom. i. 16, 17). The salvation is described in language applicable both to the sheep and to those responsible for their care. The security and freedom of the whole Christian community is conditioned by the all-embracing *through Jesus*. Through Him, both sheep and shepherds *shall go in and go out, and shall find pasture*. The phrases that describe the security and freedom of the faithful Christians are Old Testament phrases (Num. xxvii. 17; Deut. xxviii. 6; 1 Sam. xxix. 6; 2 Sam. iii. 25; 1 Kings iii. 7; 2 Chron. i. 10; Ps. cxxi. 8; Jer. xxxvii. 4; 1 Chron. iv. 40, cf. Ezek. xxxiv. 13); and the verbs are in the future, not the present, tense, because in the perspective of the narrative, this salvation must await the completion of the work of the Christ.

The Evangelist now reaches the supreme Christian truth; and the whole parabolic language is wrested to make it clear. The theme is Life, and Life through the voluntary Death of Jesus. To mark the contrast it is now no longer merely a question of thieves and robbers, but of thieves who come to *steal and kill and destroy*, and not merely of the shepherd, but of the Good Shepherd, who *layeth down his life for the sheep. I came that they may have life, and may have it abundantly*. The adjective *good* is reserved until this moment in the interpretation of the Parable, not because in the idealistic thought of the Greeks it marked the supreme combination of beauty, truth, and goodness, nor because the Shepherd is one 'who tends his flock perfectly without any failure of foresight or tenderness, of courage or unselfishness', but because the Evangelist now introduces the supreme Christian truth that the whole life of the Christian community depends upon the Death of Jesus. It is His willingness to lay down His life on behalf of the sheep that marks Him as the good Shepherd (xi. 50). The aorist *I came* contrasts the 'single unparalleled fact' (Westcott) of the life and death of Jesus with the general and universal presence of the powers of destruction—the thief *cometh*. Through the life and death of Jesus Christians not only have life, but have it abundantly. This does not mean that they have life more richly than other people. Their life is different in kind; and it is abundant, because it is life according to the will of God; and, being the consequence of His action, it is measureless and unlimited (iii. 16, 34, cf. Ps. xxiii. 1; Matt. xxv. 29; Luke vi. 38; Rom. v. 15; 2 Cor. i. 5).

The phrase *lay down his life* is characteristically Johannine. It denotes the voluntary death of Jesus (xv. 13; 1 John iii. 16) and that martyrdom which is conditioned by faith in Him (xiii. 37, 38). The application of the complementary phrase *take it again* (*vv.* 17, 18) to the Resurrection is important for the exegesis of the Washing of the Feet (see note on xiii. 4–12). Whether or no the words *lay down his life* echo the Marcan *give his life* (Mark x. 45; Matt. xx. 28), the meaning is the same. It is not surprising that the two passages should have been assimilated in some manuscripts. Codices Sinaiticus and Bezae have *give his life* here and in *v.* 15; the Washington Codex joins them in *v.* 15. The Rabbinic parallels cited by Strack-Billerbeck suggest that the two verbs *lay down* and *give* may reproduce the two Hebrew verbs *masar* and *nathan* used to express surrender of life for the sanctification of the Divine Name.

*vv.* 12–15. The picture of Jesus as the Good Shepherd who lays down His life for the sheep and of those good shepherds who, by faith in Him, are also willing to lay down their lives for their brethren causes an extension of the metaphor to meet the precise situation that occasioned the writing of the Fourth Gospel. The Christian community is threatened, not only by hostile attacks from outside, but by the desertion of men who have been responsible for its care. These are the *many antichrists* and false prophets. *They went out from us, but they were not of us* (1 John ii. 18, 19, cf. iv. 1), and their desertion was occasioned by their lack of any true relationship with Jesus. They deny that *Jesus is the Christ* (1 John ii. 22) and they do not confess that *Jesus Christ is come in the flesh* (1 John iv. 3). The attention of the reader is called to this dangerous situation by a change in the details of the parable. For the thieves and robbers who violently break into the fold from outside is substituted the hireling who, having no intimate relation with the sheep—*whose own the sheep are not*—when he *beholdeth the wolf coming,* deserts the sheep, because he is merely a hireling and *careth not for the sheep*. So Judas had fled not merely because he was a thief, but because he had no care for the poor (xii. 6, contrast xviii. 8). Deserted by faithless prophets the Christians fall a pray to the wolves. Some are seized and the rest are scattered. The flock of God must be entrusted to no such faithless hirelings. For the duty of the shepherd compare the picture of David, the true shepherd, who protected his sheep from wild beasts and the people of Israel from Goliath and the armies of the Philistines (1 Sam. xvii. 34-6, cf. also Isa. xxxi. 4; Amos iii. 12). In the earlier tradition also the disciples of Jesus are compared to sheep threatened by wolves and false prophets (Matt. vii. 15, x. 16; Luke x. 3, xii. 32, cf. Acts xx. 29). The whole background of the Parable of the Good Shepherd is not unlike the background of the Parable of the Good Samaritan (Luke x. 25-36), where the love of God towards the man who has fallen a victim to the brigands (the word is identical in both parables) is displayed not by the leaders of Judaism (the Priest and the Levite), but by the Good Samaritan. It is difficult to interpret the Lucan parable as merely an exhortation to human kindness, because of the passage which immediately precedes it (Luke x. 21-4).

But the Christians are not deserted, for they live under the care of the Good Shepherd, and their security rests ultimately not upon their knowledge of Jesus or His knowledge of them, but upon the relation between Jesus and the Father (cf. xiv. 20, xv. 10, xvii. 8, 9, 18-23), and upon the death of Jesus in which His knowledge of the Father was realized in concrete obedience to His will (xii. 32). The Christians are therefore the flock of God, and are secure under His protection, through their knowledge of Him by faith in His Son. (For similar mutual knowledge cf. Matt. xi. 27; Luke x. 22; 1 Cor. xiii. 12; Gal. iv. 9.) Bauer comments: 'This interchange of knowledge brings us within the sphere of Hellenistic mysticism', and he quotes Reitzenstein *Poimandres*, pp. 20, 21, 245, to establish this relationship: 'I know thee, Hermes, who thou art and whence thou art. I know thee and thy barbarous names. I know thee, Hermes, and thou me—I am thou and thou art I.' It is strange that Bauer should not perceive that the Johannine passage moves in an exactly contrary direction. The passage he selects to illustrate mysticism moves to the identification of the subject with the object of knowledge, and there lies the climax—'I am thou and thou art I'. The Johannine passage moves from knowledge to actual obedience, and there lies the climax—*and I lay down my life for the sheep*. The truth is that the Fourth Gospel, and indeed the whole biblical literature, delivers men from all such mysticism.

*v.* 16. Since the Christians are the flock of God, and since they have been brought into being by the knowledge of God, which is in Jesus and by His actual obedience to the will of God, it is impossible that the people of God should be subject to any limitation. *He is the pro-*

*pitiation for our sins; and not for ours only, but also for the whole world* (1 John ii. 2). The believers cannot be confined to those who have come out of Judaism—*of* (lit. *out of*) *this fold. Other sheep I have . . . them also must I bring, and they shall hear my voice.* Here is opened up the vast panorama of the mission to the Gentiles, to which the Evangelist returns at the conclusion of the gospel under the imagery of *fish* and *sheep* and *lambs* (xxi. 1–17, see COMMENTARY). The mission is the mission of Jesus. They are His sheep, led by Him from wheresoever they may hitherto have been confined: confined, if the contrast be between the fold of Judaism and other folds; scattered (xi. 52), if the contrast be between the fold of Judaism and the Gentiles who have no fold at all. The whole company of the faithful, whatever may have been their original condition, shall form one flock, because all are under the care of one shepherd. There is no other bond of union—*they shall become one flock, one shepherd.* The verbs here are in the future tense, not merely because from the standpoint of the narrative the mission to the world lies in the future, but because Jesus must first accomplish the will of the Father. The mission to the world depends upon the death of the Christ; and it is precisely the thought of the death of the Good Shepherd that evokes at this point the thought of the mission—*I, if I be lifted up, will draw all men unto myself. But this he said, signifying by what manner of death he should die* (cf. iii. 14, 15, xi. 51, 52 and the sequence xii. 20, 24, 32, 25, 33). Wellhausen's suggestion, followed by Loisy in the second edition of his Commentary (p. 325), that the reference to *the other sheep* (*v.* 16) is an interpolation, because it breaks the rhythm, proceeds from a failure to recognize how firmly the Evangelist has grasped and expounded the nature of the Gospel. If there be a break in the rhythm of the passage, it marks a necessity of exposition rather than the hand of an interpolator.

The sense for the totality of Christ's flock does not, as Bauer says, reflect a sense for unity 'beginning at the time when the Evangelist is writing'; nor can it be said, with Holtzmann, that it is 'obvious that such an outlook was impossible for the Jesus of history'. No doubt the language here is Johannine, and no doubt also the Christians at the time when the Evangelist was writing were conscious of a sense of unity; but it was a demand inherent in Christian faith, rather than the result of an evolution in Primitive Christian history. The picture of the one shepherd and the one flock already stood in the prophecies of Ezekiel (xxxiv. 20–4, xxxvii. 21–4), and the refusal to limit the sphere of the call of God was characteristic of certain passages in Old Testament prophecy (Isa. xlii. 6, xlix. 6, lii. 15, lvi. 8; Mic. iv. 2), but even more characteristic of the words of Jesus in the earlier tradition (Matt. viii. 11, xiii. 37, 38, xxii. 8–14, xxviii. 19, cf. Mark xiii. 9, 10; Luke xiii. 29). Even when a severe limitation is recorded (e.g. Matt. x. 6, xv. 24), the author of the first Gospel does not mean his readers to think of the ministry of Jesus as ultimately limited to Jews; he means precisely what

the author of the Fourth Gospel means when he insists that the mission
to the world is, of divine necessity, subsequent to the limited mission
in Palestine and to the Death accomplished within that limitation
(Mark x. 45; Matt. xx. 28). For Universalism and Particularism in the
teaching of the Rabbis see Strack-Billerbeck.

[A certain disturbance in the understanding of *v.* 16 was caused by
the translation in the Vulgate of the Greek word meaning a *flock* by
the Latin word meaning a *fold*. Hence Wyclif, the Great Bible, and the
A.V. have *one fold, one shepherd*. But Tyndale, Coverdale, and the Gen-
evan Versions translate correctly *one flock, one shepherd*, and the R.V. has
quite firmly *one flock* with no alternative in the margin. It should be
noted (see Bernard) that all the surviving manuscripts of the Old Latin
Versions, except Codex Sangallensis, have the Latin word *grex* (flock),
not *ovile* (fold).]

*vv.* 17, 18. The whole discourse comes to rest with the clear pronouncement in *vv.* 17, 18 of the Death and Resurrection of Jesus
—*I lay down my life, that I may take it again* (cf. xiii. 4, 12). Both
form a single Divine command, and, consequently, a single Divine
necessity—*This commandment received I from my Father* (iv. 34, v. 30,
36, vi. 38). The love of the Father for the Son is set in the context
neither of the original creation nor of a relationship which existed before
the world was made, but of the love of the Father for the world of men
and women. For men and women, although created by Him, have fallen
out of the sphere of His active love, and are in need of salvation (iii.
16, 17). The love of the Father is directed towards the Son, because by
Him, by His voluntary death, the obedience upon which the salvation
of men depends has been accomplished. The Resurrection is the inevitable consequence of the obedience of Jesus, and human salvation
depends upon the Resurrection of Jesus only because it points back to
His obedience—*Therefore doth the Father love me, because I lay down my
life, that I may take it again*. This direction of emphasis is of supreme
importance to the Evangelist, because there is no question here of the
metaphor of the Good Shepherd dissolving in some mystical guidance
of the souls of men by the Divine Logos or Spirit (cf. 1 Cor. i. 23, 24;
Phil. ii. 5–8). The concrete community of Christians in the world has
been brought into being by a concrete historical act of obedience, and
the whole life of the Church must be controlled by faith in Jesus. In
Him the love of God and the faith of men meet, and they meet in the
death of Jesus, because there the will of God was finally accomplished:
accomplished, because His death was neither the result of the man-
œuvres of the Jews nor of some impetuous or capricious decision of
Jesus to surrender Himself to His enemies. It was the climax of a Divine
necessity, and His whole life and ministry moved steadily towards it—
*No one taketh it away from me, but I lay it down of myself*. The Good Shepherd is not the kind of shepherd that is willing or ready to lay down his

life for the sheep, but Jesus, the Master, who had actually done so. This is the main theme of the Fourth Gospel, and the Evangelist here rests upon the earlier tradition, where the truth is summed up in the words *The Son of man must suffer* (lit. *it is necessary that*, Mark viii. 31, cf. Matt. xvi. 21; Luke ix. 22; Matt. xxvi. 54; Luke xiii. 33, xvii. 25, xxiv. 7, 26, 44). The synoptic tradition also treats the death of Jesus as a Divine necessity laid upon Him as the Christ of God. [Codices Vaticanus and Sinaiticus have *no one took it away*. The aorist represents a correct appreciation that the discourse, in fact, looks back upon the Death and interprets it; but in the perspective of the actual narrative the Death still lies in the future, and therefore the reading *taketh it away* is probably to be preferred. Lagrange, however, takes the aorist as referring to previous attempts upon the life of Jesus, and considers it should be preferred.]

The Resurrection is here and in ii. 19 thought of as an action of Jesus Himself—*that I may take it again*—*I have power to take it again*. Elsewhere throughout the New Testament the Resurrection of Jesus is always referred to as an act of God. Jesus was raised from the dead by the Father (e.g. Acts ii. 24; Rom. 1. 4). The contradiction is, however, more apparent than real. The Evangelist can use language that seems to attribute independent action to Jesus, only because there was nowhere in His words or actions any independence whatever—*I can do nothing of myself* (v. 30). The Resurrection is here included in this absolute dependence upon the authority of the Father. Elsewhere the Evangelist uses the passive *was raised from the dead* (ii. 22, xxi. 14).

### THE BLASPHEMY OF THE JEWS

*vv.* 19–21. Having reached the climax of Christian truth in the reference to the Death and Resurrection of Jesus and in the thought of the believer, who should be brought from all quarters and be united in the one flock under the one Good Shepherd, the Evangelist brings his readers abruptly back to the original history and to the unbelief of the Jews. Words which, according to the will of God, declare the possibility of union among men by offering them life and ultimate salvation, are, in fact, provocative of division (cf. vii. 43, ix. 16; Matt. x. 34–6), and are rejected as proceeding from that madness which marks the active presence of a destructive and evil power—*He hath a devil and is mad* (cf. vii. 20, viii. 48; Wisd. v. 4; Mark iii. 21, 22, cf. Matt. xii. 29, ix. 34; Luke vii. 33, xi. 15; Acts xxvi. 24; 1 Cor. iv. 10). And even those who object that madness can hardly be an adequate explanation of so manifestly a good action as the restoration of sight to a blind man, fail to perceive that the actions of Jesus are misunderstood if they be regarded in isolation. They are manifestations of the presence in their midst of the Christ Who is the Saviour of the world. There is here no question

of a division between the Jews who believed and those who did not.
The division is between two kinds of misunderstanding, the one more
brutal than the other. No doubt, however, the author of the gospel sees
in this division an anticipation of the distinction between faith and unbelief (cf. iii. 2, ix. 16, x. 41, 42).

In the earlier tradition the controversy concerning the madness of
Jesus and His possession by an evil spirit is occasioned by the miracles of
casting out devils (Mark iii. 21 sqq.; Matt. xii. 22 sqq.; Luke xi. 14
sqq.). In the Fourth Gospel the accusations remain, but the miracles
that occasioned them are wholly deleted from the narrative.

# THE DEDICATION OF THE TEMPLE
# AND THE SANCTIFICATION OF
# JESUS AS THE SON OF GOD

## x. 22–42

At first sight the controversy with the Jews, at the Feast of the Dedication, concerning the authority of Jesus appears to be a new episode, separated from what precedes not only by subject matter, but also by an interval of time, since the Feast of Dedication was celebrated some two months after the Feast of Tabernacles, which had formed the background of chs. vii–x. 21. But a comparison of x. 33 with v. 18, 19 and viii. 12–14 shows that the nature of the authority of Jesus is the main theme of the Evangelist. Inevitably the words and actions of Jesus raise this issue. Faith or unbelief spring from man's judgements concerning His authority. By their attitude to His authority men are finally divided. If His authority be self-appointed He is guilty of blasphemy—if, however, the authority by which He acts and speaks be the authority of God, His divine Sonship adequately expresses the nature of His authority, and it is necessary that men should believe in Him. Every word and action of Jesus which is recorded in the Fourth Gospel therefore contains this challenge to faith, and is ultimately a challenge to faith in God. Consequently, as in ch. v the miracle of the healing of the impotent man at the pool of Bethesda on the sabbath day led inevitably to the accusation of blasphemy, and as the claim to be the Light of the World occasioned a similar outburst among the Jews (viii. 12, 13, 52, 59), so here they perceive clearly that the same issue is raised by the words *I am the Good Shepherd*, and by the significance that is attached to them in x. 17, 18 with their solemn conclusion *This commandment received I from my Father*. The controversy with which ch. x ends is therefore no new episode but serves to bring out clearly what is involved in the application of the metaphor of the shepherd and His flock to Jesus and His faithful disciples, just as the discourse in ch. v brought out clearly what was involved in the miracle of the healing of the impotent man. Nor is the interval of time at all obvious to the reader of the gospel, whose attention is rightly fixed upon the exposition of Christian truth which it contains. No doubt a Jewish reader would perceive the break in the same fashion as it is perceived by a modern

382

scholar who has access to learned works upon the ancient customs of the Jewish people. But the author of the gospel is writing in Greek for the benefit of Christian readers, and he is interested only in fostering their perception of the nature of the Truth in which they have believed and their knowledge of the ground of its authority. Hence he links the two sections of his narrative quite simply with the words *and it was the feast of the dedication* or, according to other manuscripts (see note below), *at that time was the feast*. Whether these words are merely a literary connection or whether they betray the use by the author of material which was originally disconnected, it is impossible for the modern commentator to discover. Not only is there no change of subject matter and no perceptible interval of time, but the actual phraseology picks up and continues the language of x. 1–21. The phrases *Ye are not of my sheep—My sheep hear my voice—I know them and they follow me—I give unto them eternal life; and they shall never perish* (*vv.* 26–8), the use of the same Greek word (translated *snatch*) in *vv.* 28, 29 as had been used of the wolf in *v.* 12, and the absence of any suggestion that the Jews who question Jesus in *v.* 24 are to be distinguished from those who had heard the parable of the Good Shepherd and its interpretation which had been the occasion of so serious a disagreement (*v.* 19), emphasize the continuity of the whole. More subtle is the connection in the Greek, obscured in the English Versions, between the phrases *lay down my life, take it again, taketh it away from me* (*vv.* 15–18) and the form of the question in *v.* 24 which, in order to preserve the sequence of thought, must surely be translated *How long dost thou continue to take away our life?* rather than *How long dost thou hold us in suspense?* The Jews perceive clearly that the conclusion of the application of the parable of the Good Shepherd links the death of Jesus with the emergence of the new people of God, and they see also that this involves the destruction of Judaism as an independent political and religious organism (cf. xi. 47–54). To the Evangelist Judaism is fulfilled and superseded, to the Jewish opponents of Jesus it is destroyed, its life is taken away—unless indeed Jesus be veritably the Christ of God. Hence the question *If thou art the Christ, tell us plainly* (*v.* 24) forms the logical conclusion of the parable of the Good Shepherd, since it raises in an acute form the supreme issue of the relation of Jesus to the Father, and the demand that Jesus should speak *plainly* presumes a contrast with the previous use of parabolic language (*v.* 6).

But since the Fourth Gospel is one literary whole which moves steadily to its conclusion, the controversy with the Jews recorded in x. 22–42 not only forms the conclusion of the parable of the Good Shepherd, but also prepares the way for the record of the miracle of the Raising of Lazarus. The words *My sheep hear my voice, and I know them, and they follow me: and I give unto them eternal life* (*vv.* 27, 28) look backwards to the parable and forwards to the miracle. Moreover, the hostile actions of the Jews (*vv.* 31, 39) both preserve the connection with the preceding narrative (v. 18, vii. 25, 44, viii. 59) and lead up to the final decision of the council to put Him to death, which is the direct consequence of the miracle of the Raising of Lazarus (xi. 47-54).

### THE FEAST OF THE DEDICATION

x. 22. *And it was the feast of the dedication at Jerusalem: it was winter;* 23. *and Jesus was walking in the temple in Solomon's porch.* 24. *The Jews therefore came round about him, and said unto him, How long dost thou hold us in suspense? If thou art the Christ, tell us plainly.* 25. *Jesus answered them, I told you, and ye believe not: the works that I do in my Father's name, these bear witness of me.* 26. *But ye believe not, because ye are not of my sheep.* 27. *My sheep hear my voice, and I know them, and they follow me:* 28. *and I give unto them eternal life; and they shall never perish, and no one shall snatch them out of my hand.* 29. *My Father, which hath given them unto me, is greater than all; and no one is able to snatch them out of the Father's hand.*

### THE SANCTIFICATION OF JESUS, THE SON OF GOD

30. *I and the Father are one.* 31. *The Jews took up stones again to stone him.* 32. *Jesus answered them, Many good works have I shewed you from the Father; for which of those works do ye stone me?* 33. *The Jews answered him, For a good work we stone thee not, but for blasphemy; and because that thou, being a man, makest thyself God.* 34. *Jesus answered them, Is it not written in your law, I said, Ye are gods?* 35. *If he called them gods, unto whom the word of God came (and the scripture cannot be broken),* 36. *say ye of him, whom the Father sanctified and sent into the world, Thou blasphemest; because I said, I am the Son of God?* 37. *If I do not the works of my Father, believe me not.* 38. *But if I do them, though ye believe not me, believe the works: that ye may know and understand that the Father is in me, and I in the Father.* 39. *They sought again to take him: and he went forth out of their land.*

### JESUS AND JOHN

40. *And he went away again beyond Jordan into the place where John was at the first baptizing; and there he abode.* 41. *And many came unto him; and they said, John indeed did no sign: but all things whatsoever John spake of this man were true.* 42. *And many believed on him there.*

### THE FEAST OF THE DEDICATION

x. 22, 23. The Feast was celebrated throughout Palestine for eight days, beginning on the 25th of the month Kislev (December). On that day 168 B.C. Antiochus Epiphanes had desecrated the Temple and erected within it an altar to Zeus. Three years later on the same day Judas Maccabæus had restored, purified, and rededicated the Temple; and from that time the Jews kept the day in order that they might by invigorated by the memory of their last great national deliverance. The Feast was named in the Hebrew *Chanukkah*, and the Evangelist renders it into Greek by the word which in different forms had been used in the LXX to describe the dedication of the altar in the original tabernacle (Num. vii. 10, 11), of the Temple of Solomon (1 Kings viii. 63; 2 Chron. vii. 5), and of the new Temple which was built after the return from the Babylonian captivity (Ezra vi. 16). The Feast therefore called to mind the whole dignity of Hebrew worship in the commemoration of a particular episode in Jewish history (1 Macc. iv. 34-59; 2 Macc. i-ii. 18, x. 1-8; Josephus *Ant.* xii. 316-25). Like the Feast of Tabernacles its most characteristic ritual was centred upon the kindling of lights; hence, according to Josephus, it was named the 'Feast of Lights', and the references to it in the later Rabbinic literature are almost wholly concerned with the significance of this ritual (see Strack-Billerbeck). The close ceremonial similarity of the two feasts is carefully noted in 2 Macc. i. 9, x. 6 sqq. The author of the Fourth Gospel has already associated the words *I am the light of the world* with the Feast of Tabernacles (vii. 2, viii. 12, ix. 5); he now links the Sanctification of Jesus (*v.* 36) to the Feast of the Dedication. Both Jewish feasts are thus fulfilled in the ministry of Jesus, as the Passover is fulfilled in His Passion and Death. Moreover, the steady movement of the narrative towards the Death is emphasized by the sequence of the Feasts in the Jewish year which is carefully preserved in the gospel—*Tabernacles* (vii. 2, the month Tishri, September–October), *Dedication* (x. 22, Kislev, November–December), *Passover* (xi. 55, Nisan, March–April).

[There is some textual difficulty concerning the original particle used by the author to connect *vv.* 21 and 22. Codex Vaticanus, the Washington Codex and three other Greek manuscripts, supported by the Egyptian and Armenian Versions, read *At that time was the feast* (R.V. mg.); Codices Sinaiticus, Alexandrinus, Bezae, Koridethianus and the generally accepted textual tradition have the normal Johannine narrative particle *but* or *now* (A.V., R.V. *and it was the feast*). There is some manuscript support for both particles and for no particle at all. The uncertainty of the textual tradition is difficult to explain. Since, in any case, the particles are connecting particles which do not mark a break in the narrative (see, however, Bernard), the variant readings woudl not be of great importance for English readers, had not Westcott, adopting *at that time* as the original reading, insisted upon the close connection of chs. ix and x and, proposing a break at the conclusion of ch. viii, attached chs. vii and viii to the Feast of Tabernacles and chs. ix and x to the Feast of Dedication (Westcott on ix. 1 and additional note on x. 22. See also *J.T.S.*, October 1900, pp. 137 sqq.).]

N

The author emphasizes the importance of the occasion by prefacing the narrative with precise details of place and time. *It was winter* and Jesus was *walking* (cf. vii. 1; Mark xi. 27) *in the temple in Solomon's porch. And the Jews came round about him.* These details may do no more than fill in quite naturally the details of the scene. Since it was winter, Jesus, owing to the inclemency of the weather, entered within the Temple precincts and took up His position under the cover of the eastern portico which was thought to have survived from the glories of Solomon's Temple (Acts iii. 11, v. 12; Josephus *Ant.* xv. 398–402, xx. 221; *B.J.* v. 185; Strack-Billerbeck on Acts iii. 11). And the Jews, in order the more easily to ask their question and hear His answer, press around Him. But it is doubtful whether the author intends his readers so to understand what he has written. The narrative marks rather the extreme tension of the situation. Jesus, the fulfilment of the hope of Judaism, stands in the most sacred place of the Jewish religion, compassed about by its leaders, who are intent on His destruction (Ps. xxii. 12, 16, cix. 3, cf. cxviii. 10–12.). It was indeed *winter*, as it was *night* when Judas left the company of Jesus in order to betray Him (xiii. 30). In the mind of the author the external and internal situation correspond and overlap so completely that the attentive reader perceives the latter in the description of the former.

*v.* 24. The Jews then propound their question. *If thou art the Christ, tell us plainly.* In the immediate Johannine context the Jews request plain speech in contrast to the parabolic language which Jesus had used in the preceding passage (x. 6). In the larger context of the gospel as a whole the Jews demand a simple explanation of the entire behaviour of Jesus (xvi. 25, 29), just as the High Priest in the earlier tradition had finally demanded in almost identical language whether He was the Christ or no (Matt. xxvi. 63; Luke xxii. 66, cf. Mark xiv. 61). They perceive, as the high priests and scribes and elders had perceived at the conclusion of the parable of the Wicked Husbandmen, which was also spoken when Jesus was *walking in the temple* (Mark xi. 27), *that he had spoken the parable against them* (Mark xii. 12). According to the English Versions (A.V., R.V.) the Jews ask the question because they are puzzled and their minds are disturbed. *How long dost thou make us to doubt?* (A.V.)*: How long dost thou hold us in suspense?* (R.V.). The Greek can, of course, mean this; and it is accepted as correct by most commentators. The souls of the Jews are excited (Àlford) and nationalistic hopes are running high. But the author of the gospel had already used the same Greek words in the immediately preceding passage, where they mean *take away* (or *destroy*) *life* (x. 18). The natural meaning of the words repeated here is therefore, *How long dost thou continue to take away our life?* The paradox is identical with the paradox of the parable of the Wicked Husbandmen. The ministry and death of Jesus involve the destruction of Judaism, in order that the Scriptures may be fulfilled.

The Jews understand the peril without perceiving that it is necessary in order that they may fulfil their true destiny. Jesus is taking away their life. It is this sense of peril that forces the question of the Messiahship which alone could justify His behaviour, and which later compels Caiaphas formally to propose His Death that *the whole nation perish not* (xi. 50).

*vv.* 25–8. Jesus answers the question with the same reserved attitude to the word Christ which marks His answer in the Matthæan-Lucan version of the Passion narrative (Matt. xxvi. 64; Luke xxii. 67 sqq., contrast Mark xiv. 61), in the Q narrative of the answer to the question of John (Matt. xi. 4–6; Luke vii. 22, 23), and which marks also the words which follow the Marcan narrative of the confession of Peter (*Son of man* is substituted for Peter's *Christ*, Mark viii. 30, 31). This reserve, which is as characteristic of the Fourth Gospel as it is of the synoptic gospels (only in iv. 26 does Jesus openly name Himself Christ), does not, of course, mean in any New Testament document that Jesus is not the Christ, the fulfilment of the hope of Israel; it is occasioned only by the impossibility of setting the Messiahship of Jesus in the context of contemporary Jewish messianic ideas. The Messiahship of Jesus is throughout the Fourth Gospel interpreted in terms of Sonship. Jesus is the Son of God sent into the world as the Son of man. Only thus can His Messiahship be understood; and moreover understanding involves faith, since knowledge is the product of faith. Hence though nowhere in the Fourth Gospel does Jesus tell the Jews openly that He is the Christ (see, however, iv. 25, 26), His whole teaching and action presumed it, declared it, interpreted it, and demanded that they should accept and believe it. *I told you, and ye believe not.* Both His teaching and His works converge upon, and bear witness to, His Sonship and, consequently, upon His Messiahship—*the works that I do in my Father's name, these bear witness of me* (cf. v. 36). The conclusion is inevitable. Since there is no weakness or obscurity in the ministry of Jesus, there can be but one explanation of the misunderstanding and unbelief of the Jews— *ye are not of my sheep* (cf. vi. 44). As Chrysostom comments: 'If ye follow me not, it is not because I am not a shepherd, but because ye are not my sheep'. The Jews, as the Evangelist had stated elsewhere (viii. 23), are *of this world.* This is no formal doctrine of predestination; it describes a general behaviour with which the behaviour of the true disciples of Jesus is contrasted. His disciples, like the sheep of the parable, hear His voice, follow Him, and will never perish, that is, they will survive the final judgement. This ultimate security is not, however, the reward of human achievement: it is the gift of Jesus who knows His faithful disciples and gives them now and at once that life which belongs to the age which is to be, and which, consequently, will enable them to pass unscathed through the final judgement of God (v. 24–9, vi. 35, 39, 40, 54, viii. 51, 52, xi. 26. The whole is summed up in the story of the

Raising of Lazarus, ch. xi). Their behaviour and their security proceed from their faith in Jesus (1 John iv. 14–17), and no one, neither their human enemies who are *of this world* nor their supreme enemy who is the *prince of this world* (xii. 31, xiv. 30, xvi. 11), *shall snatch them out of His hand* (cf. Matt. xviii. 14).

The ultimate and eschatological security which is here pronounced is, in the context of the Old Testament Scriptures, a security that can belong only to those who are under the protection of God Himself: *I, even I, am the Lord; and beside me there is no saviour . . . and there is none that can deliver out of my hand: I will work, and who shall let it?* (Isa. xliii. 11–13)—*The Lord is my shepherd: therefore can I lack nothing . . . yea, though I walk through the valley of the shadow of death, I will fear no evil* (Ps. xxiii. 1–4)—*The souls of the righteous are in the hand of God, and there shall no torment touch them* (Wisd. iii. 1, cf. Isa. xlix. 2, li. 16). There can, of course, be no deflecting of this solid Old Testament truth; and consequently the words of Jesus move to their inevitable conclusion. Those who believe in Jesus are under the protection of God Himself; *no one is able to snatch them out of my Father's hand*. Those who are under the protection of, in the hand of, Jesus are under the protection of, in the hand of, the Father, because they have been given to Jesus by the Father. The complete supremacy of God is therefore secured by the relation of Jesus to the Father.

[The words in which this supremacy is expressed present considerable difficulty to the commentator because of the existence of an extremely complicated series of variant readings. The simplest alternatives are provided by the reading which is found in the majority of the Greek manuscripts and the variant which occurs in Codex Vaticanus. The majority of the Greek manuscripts read *My Father, which hath given them unto me, is greater than all* (the object to the verb *given* is, however, not supplied in the Greek, and is supplied in the English versions by the addition of *them* in italics). This reading is also supported by the sinaitic Syriac, by the Peshitto, and by Basil, Chrysostom, and Cyril of Alexandria. Codex Vaticanus has an object to the verb: *That which the Father hath given me is greater than all*, and this agrees with vi. 39 and xvii. 2 (cf. the neuter in Matt. xii. 6). The alternative reading is, however, not unlike xiv. 28. Neither can therefore be pronounced un-Johannine. A further complication is introduced by combinations of both readings in very ancient manuscripts. Thus Codices Alexandrinus, Koridethianus and Bezae have *My Father which hath given them to me is a greater power* (neuter) *than all*, whilst Codex Sinaiticus and two other Greek manuscripts have a combination which seems to defy translation. Between the variants it seems impossible to decide which is the original reading. Bernard, and Loisy (in the first edition but not in the second) accept the reading of the majority of the manuscripts; Burney, and Torrey (*Harvard Theol. Rev.*, October 1923), suppose that the neuters represent a mistranslation of an original Aramaic source, in which the indeclinable relative was, in fact, masculine. Westcott accepts the reading of Codex Vaticanus, but is unwilling to discard the reading of Codex Alexandrinus altogether (see his Commentary on x. 29 and Additional Note). The general meaning of all the readings is, however, the same. The Father is the only source of the ultimate security of the believers in Jesus. They belong to Jesus because they have been given to Him by the Father.]

### THE SANCTIFICATION OF JESUS, THE SON OF GOD

*vv.* 30, 31. It is, however, not sufficient that the Christian challenge to the Jews, or indeed to the world, should be presented merely in the form of a delicate argument concerning the security of the disciples of Jesus. It must be stated precisely, in order to force the issue of faith or unbelief. The division among men must not be between those who suppose Jesus to be mad and those who accept His ability to do genuine miracles (x. 19–21), but between those who, clearly perceiving the nature of His claim to authority either reject it as the supreme blasphemy and proceed actively against Him, or accept it as the truth and proceed to faith and active discipleship. The Evangelist therefore forces the issue with the clearest possible precision and describes in vigorous language the consequent behaviour of the Jews. *I and the Father are one. The Jews took up stones again to stone him. . . . For a good work we stone thee not, but for blasphemy; and because that thou, being a man, makest thyself God.* The situation here described is not unique in the Fourth Gospel, for it is anticipated in the Prologue (i. 11), is repeated with some variation in v. 17, 18, and vi. 40–3, 51, 52, 60, 66, vii. 29, 30, viii. 58, 59, and reaches its climax in the narrative of the crucifixion. But it is more than this. Everywhere in his gospel the Evangelist is concerned to expose the tension between Jesus and the Jews, because that same tension is repeated in the relation between the Church and the World (xvii. 14–18; 1 John iii. 1, 13), since the faithful disciples of Jesus share in His union with the Father: *and the glory which thou hast given me I have given unto them; that they may be one, even as we are one* (xvii. 22).

The author of the gospel does not define the precise nature of the union between the Father and the Son. The unity is neither merely a moral unity or agreement of character, since the Jews would not presumably have treated as blasphemy the idea that a man could regulate his words and actions according to the will of God; nor is the unity a metaphysical unity which carries with it a necessary agreement of character, for the Evangelist is describing the union of the flesh and blood of Jesus of Nazareth with the Father and the word 'metaphysical' introduces a philosophical conception foreign to the gospel; nor is the union one which can be explained in terms of mysticism, as though it were constituted by the 'real presence of the Spirit' in Jesus (Loisy); nor is it really legitimate for the commentator to regard the unity as explained when the neuter *one* is interpreted as one substance, and the plural *are* of two Persons of the Trinity. No doubt, this passage was rightly regarded by the Fathers as of supreme importance when they had to meet Christian philosophies which undermined the authority of Jesus. No doubt also the Evangelist used language which to some extent controlled the course of later controversy. But he used the language because the material behind him demanded, not an explanation of the union between Jesus and the Father, but a clear statement that Jesus is the object of Faith and the organ of revelation and salvation, and that the honour which is paid to Him is honour paid to the Father. *He that hath seen me hath seen the Father* (xiv. 9, cf. v. 22). Nor is it in the least satisfactory to suggest with Bauer and Holtzmann that the author of the Fourth Gospel has with some facility transferred to Jesus the language of contemporary mythology or of Stoic speculation. The background of the Johannine language and thought lies in the earlier tradition of the ministry of Jesus and, as the author carefully points out, in the Old Testament.

*vv.* 32, 33. The episode does not end, as did viii. 58, 59, with the formulation of the claim of Jesus and with the record of the active procedure of the Jews against Him for blasphemy (Lev. xxiv. 16; 1 Kings xxi. 10). The second attempt to stone Him (cf. viii. 59) is interrupted first by an appeal to the works of Jesus and then by an appeal to the Old Testament. The movement of the narrative is occasioned less by the desire of explaining the union between Jesus and the Father, than of showing that the action of the Jews is open to grave objection even apart from the ultimate criticism that proceeds from faith.

Jesus appeals to the goodness of His many charitable works (cf. viii. 46), works which are in manifest agreement with the will of God, and which in fact display the active love of the Father, and He asks whether such works justify the stoning of Him, through whose instrumentality they were done, as though the works were blasphemous—*for which of those works do ye stone me?* The author of the gospel has made a selection of such works, and has carefully narrated them (ii. 1–11, iv. 46–v. 9, vi. 1–21, ix, xi), but he presumes that there had been many others with which his readers were no doubt familiar (ii. 18, xxi. 25) and, moreover, he has also carefully recorded that many of the Jews themselves had recognized the goodness of these works and had stated that they provided no ground for proceeding against Jesus (vi. 14, vii. 31, 51, ix. 25, x. 21, xi. 45, xii. 11). Here, however, the Jews show greater perception. They perceive that these works are not isolated works of charity, but bear witness to and proceed from a claim which they regard as blasphemous; they perceive that the works are signs. *For a good work we stone thee not, but for blasphemy; and because that thou, being*

*a man, makest thyself God* (cf. v. 18). The same opposition to the faith of
the Christians reappears in the later Rabbinic literature. For example,
the Saying of Rabbi Abbahu (*c*. A.D. 300): 'If a man say to thee "I am
God", he is a liar; "I am the Son of man" (i.e. the Messiah), he will
afterwards regret it; "I ascend into heaven", he may say it, but he will
not accomplish it.' Compare also the same Rabbi's comment on Exod.
xx. 2: 'A king of flesh and blood is able to exercise his regal authority
whilst possessing a father or a brother or a son. With God, however,
as He Himself says (Isa. xliv. 6), it is otherwise. "I am the first",
therefore, I have no father; "I am the last", therefore I have no brother;
"beside me there is no God", therefore I have no son' (see Strack-
Billerbeck).

*vv.* 34–6. Jesus then appeals to the Old Testament in order to show
that the application of the Divine Name to men need not be blasphemous—*Is it not written in your law, I said, Ye are gods?* The citation is from
Ps. lxxxii. 6. The 'Law' therefore here, as in xii. 34, xv. 25, Rom. iii.
19; 1 Cor. xiv. 21, and in the Rabbinic literature (see Strack-Billerbeck)
embraces the whole *corpus* of Old Testament Scriptures. It is *your*
(omitted in Codices Sinaiticus Bezae, Koridethianus, in some manuscripts of the Old Latin Version, and in the Sinaitic Syriac) *law*, not
because the author of the gospel regards the Old Testament as belonging to the Jews and not to the Christians; but because the argument
consists in an appeal to its plain meaning which the Jews are bound to
accept, rather than to its deeper meaning according to which the Old
Testament betrays its incompleteness and demands its own fulfilment
(cf. viii. 17, xv. 25). The Jews therefore cannot escape from a particular
passage written in their own Scriptures, according to which the rulers
of the people of God are named *gods*. The passage, moreover, cannot be
deprived of its authority, because in it is recorded the word of God
Himself—*I said, Ye are Gods*—*If he called them gods unto whom the word of
God came (and the scripture cannot be broken), say ye.* . . . Though the argument rests upon a single Old Testament passage, and in the Fourth
Gospel, *the scripture* in the singular means a particular passage (vii. 38,
42, xiii. 18, xvii. 12, xix. 24, 28, 36, the plural *scriptures*, v. 39, denotes
the whole Old Testament), yet the reference of the words in the Psalm
to those *unto whom the word of God came* demands a wider application
than merely to Jewish or Hebrew magistrates or rulers or judges. In
the mind of the author of the gospel the reference is to all the inspired
men of the Old Testament, including the prophets, and prepares the
way for the contrast between those to whom the word of God came and
Jesus, who is veritably the Son of God. Nor is Ps. lxxxii. 6 an entirely
isolated passage. Bauer cites Exod. vii. 1, xxii. 28; Deut. i. 17, xix. 17,
and in the Greek Versions of the Old Testament by Aquila and Symmachus, Exod. xxi. 6 is translated: *His master shall bring him unto the
gods* for *unto the judges* (A.V., R.V. mg.). There follows an *a fortiori*

argument (cf. vii. 23). *If he called them gods, unto whom the word of God came (and the scripture cannot be broken),* (cf. v. 18, vii. 23; Matt. v. 19) *say ye of him, whom the Father sanctified and sent into the world, Thou blasphemest; because I said, I am the Son of God?* The same movement from the less, that is, from men who receive the word of God, which is the theme of the Old Testament, to the greater, that is, to Him who is the Son of God, which is the theme of the New Testament, is paralleled in the movement of Peter's confession of faith (vi. 68, 69): *Lord, to whom shall we go? thou hast the words of eternal life. And we have believed and know that thou art the Holy One of God* (v.l. *Christ, the Son of the living God*). The Evangelist has so phrased the contrast that the readers of the gospel recognize the distinction between those *unto whom the word of God came* and the Son of God sanctified and sent into the world, a delicate reference to the Prologue, according to which Jesus is Himself the Word become Flesh (i. 1, 14). The author is satisfied with this delicate suggestion, because, whereas Jesus as the Son of God is completely justified in the earlier tradition, Jesus as the incarnate Word, though rightly included in the preface to a narrative of His Ministry, cannot, without hopeless anachronism, be included in the record itself.

The unique mission of Jesus, the Son of God, is most significantly described as the result of the veritable sanctification by the Father. In Jesus the divine work of consecration, dedication, and sanctification reaches its climax and is fulfilled. Appropriately enough these words are spoken at the Feast of Dedication, because the mission of Jesus is the fulfilment of Judaism, and its feasts anticipate their own fulfilment. According to the will of the Father, Jesus dedicates Himself to voluntary death, which is His final sanctification (xvii. 19), and as a result of His consecration there emerges in the world the mission of His disciples, who are themselves indeed consecrated to the service of God (xvii. 17–19). Thus Judaism is fulfilled in the Church, and the Church owes its origin and its life to the mission and consecration of Jesus (ii. 18–21, iv. 21–4; Heb. x. 19–25).

The author does not use the same Greek word for the dedication or consecration of the Temple (x. 22) as he uses for the consecration of Jesus and His disciples (cf. xvii. 17–19). This is not because there is in his mind no connection between the two, but because the first marks the consecration of things, the second of human flesh and blood. In the Old Testament a single Hebrew word is used both for the dedication of things and for the consecration or sanctification of men and women. In the LXX translation the Greek word for *dedication* is confined to things, the word *sanctification* is used when men and women are the objects of divine consecration. Thus Moses (Ecclus. xlv. 4), Jeremiah (Jer. i. 5; Ecclus. xlix. 7), Israel (2 Macc. i. 25) are consecrated to the Service of God. In the LXX, however, the word is also used of things (Lev. xvi. 4).

*vv.* 37–9. The words of Jesus in which His claim is expressed: *I and the Father are one* (*v.* 30)—*I am the Son of God* (*v.* 36)—*The Father is in me, and I in the Father* (*v.* 38) are not isolated or irrelevant opinions of a man concerning himself, for the works of Jesus correspond with, and bear witness to, the truth of His teaching concerning His relation to the Father (v. 17, 36, ix. 3, 4, x. 25, xiv. 10, 11). Were there a discrepancy between action and teaching, the discrepancy would invalidate the teaching: *If I do not the works of the Father, believe me not.* Rightly understood the works of Jesus are sufficient for faith, even apart from His teaching: *But if I do them* (i.e. the works of my Father), *though ye believe not me* (i.e. my teaching), *believe the works: that ye may know and understand that the Father is in me, and I in the Father.* The ministry of Jesus is one coherent whole; but the whole is contained in each part. This is of great importance for the author of the gospel, since it enables him to perceive the entire validity of that Christian faith which is not, and indeed cannot be, evoked by the actual sight of the miracles of Jesus or of His actions in the flesh: *Thomas answered and said unto him, My Lord and my God. Jesus saith unto him, Because thou hast seen me, thou hast believed: blessed are they that have not seen, and yet have believed* (xx. 28, 29).

The Jews, however, are thrown back upon their actual observation of the works of Jesus, in order that they may, through a single act of perception (*know*, aorist), pass on to a state of permanent understanding (*understand*, present). The delicate distinction in the Greek between the aorist and the present tenses is destroyed in Codices Sinaiticus and Alexandrinus, in a few other Greek uncial manuscripts, and in the Vulgate, by the substitution of *believe* for *understand*. Perception and understanding come to rest in the recognition that Jesus is the organ for the operation of the Father. In Jesus the Father works, and He works by His knowledge of the Father's will: *The Father is in me, and I in the Father* (xiv. 10, 11, xvii. 21; 1 John iii. 24, iv. 15, cf. Ignatius *Magn.* vii. 1). There is no contrariety between the words and the works of Jesus, such as the Jews suppose; 'when the works cry aloud, they seek words, and when the words teach, then they betake themselves to works (vi. 30), ever setting themselves to the contrary' (Chrysostom). For the Jews the works of Jesus were a sufficient ground of faith, and by implication the Christians who possess the words of Jesus have also a sufficient ground of faith, and they ought not to desire miracles in order that the teaching may be provided with a further guarantee of its truth.

But the Jews are not persuaded to faith. On the contrary *they sought again to take him: and he went forth out of their hand.* This fresh attempt upon His life is ineffectual (vii. 30, 32, 44, viii. 59, cf. Luke iv. 30). If the sheep of Jesus cannot be snatched out of His hand, how much less can the enemy have power over the Shepherd of the sheep, until the time should come for Him to deliver Himself into their hand and to lay down His life (x. 17, 18, xviii. 4 sqq.). But the time is not yet (vii. 30).

### JESUS AND JOHN

*vv.* 40–2. The episode concludes, not with the record of a flight of Jesus from His enemies in Jerusalem (Wellhausen, Luke xiii. 31 sqq.; Mark vi. 14–16, where Wellhausen supposes a flight from Herod to have been suppressed!), not even with a retirement to Peræa (Mark x. 1; Matt. xix. 1), but with an emphatic re-statement of the relation between the ministry of John and the ministry of Jesus. Having accomplished His work in Jerusalem, Jesus returns to the place where John had first (i. 28 contrasted with iii. 23) exercised his ministry, and had uttered his prophecy concerning Him. And those who came to Jesus in that locality perceived the truth of what John had said, *and many believed on him there—and they said, John indeed did no sign: but all things whatsoever John spake of this man were true.* The topographical note—*and he went away again beyond Jordan into the place where John was at the first baptizing; and there he abode*—is of the utmost importance, for it calls to mind the great witness of John to Jesus (i. 8), contrasts the unbelief of the Jews in Jerusalem with the faith that emerges outside Judæa where that witness is recognized and serves as an introduction to the record of the events leading directly to the death of Jesus, in which the words of John are finally fulfilled: *Behold, the Lamb of God, which taketh away the sin of the world!* (i. 29, 36).

A ministry of Jesus *on the borders of Judæa and beyond Jordan* immediately before the Passion belongs to the earlier tradition (Mark x. 1; Matt. xix. 1); and it would seem that the author of the Fourth Gospel presumes his readers to be familiar with it. He is not concerned, however, to record incidents in that ministry, but merely to draw the attention of his readers to the significance of the locality as the place where John had exercised his ministry and uttered his prophecy. The locality therefore is important for Christian faith: *and many believed on him—there;* that is, where witness is borne to the Spirit abiding on Jesus (i. 32) and where remission of sin is declared to be through Him, as the Lamb of God, there faith breaks forth.

# THE DEATH AND RESURRECTION
# OF LAZARUS OF BETHANY

## XI. 1–46

IN the Prologue to the gospel the two themes of Light and Life are closely interwoven: *In him was life; and the life was the light of men* (i. 4). In the course of the narrative, however, they are disentangled; and Jesus stands before the reader of the gospel as the Light of the World (viii. 12, ix. 5) and as the Giver of Life everlasting (v. 21–9, x. 27, 28). Moreover, in order that the Christian religion may not seem to sink into a general symbolical mysticism, the author characteristically presses his doctrine into concrete fact and rivets it into the concrete actions of Jesus of Nazareth (cf. viii. 12 with ch. ix, and v. 24 with ch. xi). As Jesus gave sight to the man who had been born blind (ix), so now He raises from the grave Lazarus who had been four days dead. These miraculous actions are not introduced as proofs of a doctrine or as symbolical illustrations of Christian mysticism; they constitute the revelation of the power of Jesus, and the truth is manifested in His historical action. The supremacy of Christian faith is thus shown to rest upon decisive actions in the human life of Jesus. The purpose of the author is not to record crises in the life of Jesus in order to explain historically why the Jews put Him to death, but to isolate important actions of Jesus and to display them as providing a firm foundation of Christian faith. The disentangling of the themes of Light and Life consequent upon this method of arrangement is, however, more apparent than real, since in the thought of the author there can be no eternal life apart from faith and knowledge and sight. To know Jesus and to recognize Him as the Son of God is to be born of God and to have passed from death to life. The Jews therefore quite rightly regard the power of Jesus to save a man from death as consequent upon His power to open the eyes of the blind (xi. 37).

However, in spite of the author's emphasis on historicity, the narrative of the raising of Lazarus presents the historian with a very delicate problem. The story as it stands is Johannine throughout. It is not only in itself a complete literary unity, but is so closely interwoven into the texture of the whole gospel as to be unintelligible apart from its relation to the whole gospel. Wherever it is possible to check the author's literary method, it is clear that he is working upon traditional material

395

that, in part at least, can be identified in the synoptic gospels. It is therefore unlikely that he has created the whole episode of Lazarus of Bethany in order to present his readers with a concrete illustration of Jesus as the giver of Eternal Life. Nevertheless, the earlier tradition, so far as it is accessible, contains little that can be regarded as sufficient to provide the rough material for the Johannine story of the raising of Lazarus.

Miracles of raising the dead are recorded or assumed in synoptic tradition. The raising of the daughter of Jairus (Mark v. 22–43 and parallels) and of the widow's son at Nain (Luke vii. 11–17) illustrate the Q Saying *Tell John what things ye have seen and heard; how that the blind see, the lame walk, the lepers are cleansed, the deaf hear, the dead are raised, to the poor the gospel is preached* (Luke vii. 22; Matt. xi. 4, 5). The Old Testament (1 Kings xvii; 2 Kings iv) and the Acts of the Apostles (ix. 36–42) contain somewhat similar miracles. The miracle of the raising of Lazarus is, however, more remarkable than any of these. Here is no young girl or youth who has just died. Lazarus is apparently a full-grown man who has been four days in the grave, and his body would, in the eastern heat, be already in process of corruption (xi. 39). The miracle is, moreover, not introduced into the narrative casually, but is recorded as the supreme climax of the manifestation of the power of Jesus to the Jews.

Martha and Mary are familiar to readers of Saint Luke's Gospel, and (Luke x. 38–42) to some extent the Lucan description of the two sisters is reflected in the Johannine narrative. The Greek words for *village—seated—at His feet—was serving* are common to both (Luke x. 38–40; John xi. 1, 20, 32, xii. 2). In both Jesus is a guest in their house (Luke x. 38; John xii. 2). A further link with the earlier tradition is established by the identification of Mary with the nameless woman who anointed Jesus in the house of Simon the Leper at Bethany (xi. 2, xii. 1–8; Mark xiv. 3–9; Matt. xxvi. 6–13, cf. Luke vii. 36 sqq.). Lazarus, however, is wholly absent from the earlier tradition as we know it. He appears only as a character in the Lucan parable of Dives and Lazarus (Luke xvi. 19–31). This, it is true, is a resurrection parable, and it concludes with the request of Dives that Lazarus might return from the dead and 'testify' to his brothers. To which Abraham replies: *If they hear not Moses and the prophets, neither will they be persuaded, though one rose from the dead* (Luke xvi. 31, cf. John v. 46). Loisy and Holtzmann think that this scattered Lucan material is sufficient to account for the Johannine narrative. In mystical contemplation of the gospel the author saw Lazarus raised from the dead. By a powerful inspiration, and not by conscious literary creation, fragments which lie scattered in the earlier tradition break forth spontaneously into one whole under the influence of symbolical perception of religious truth (Loisy). This may be a satisfactory explanation of the Johannine narrative, but it presupposes that the author had access only to the synoptic tradition as we know it. The truth is, however, that we cannot safely impose so severe a limitation upon the rough material with which the author was working, and have therefore to rest content with the interpretation of the narrative as it stands. It must be remembered that it is possible that the Lucan parable may have been evoked by some historical event that provided the author of the Fourth Gospel with the material out of which he constructed his narrative.

### THE DEATH OF LAZARUS

xi. 1. *Now a certain man was sick, Lazarus of Bethany, of the village of Mary and her sister Martha. 2. And it was that Mary which anointed the Lord with ointment, and wiped his feet with her hair, whose brother Lazarus was sick. 3. The sisters therefore sent unto him, saying, Lord, behold, he whom thou lovest is sick. 4. But when Jesus heard it, he said, This sickness is not unto death, but for the glory of God, that the Son of God may be glorified thereby. 5. Now Jesus loved Martha, and her sister, and Lazarus. 6. When therefore he heard that he was sick, he abode at that time two days in the place where he was. 7. Then after this he saith to the disciples, Let us go into Judæa again. 8. The disciples say unto him, Rabbi, the Jews were but now seeking to stone thee; and goest thou thither again? 9. Jesus answered, Are there not twelve hours in the day? If a man walk in the day, he stumbleth not, because he seeth the light of this world. 10. But if a man walk in the night, he stumbleth, because the light is not in him. 11. These things spake he: and after this he saith unto them, Our friend Lazarus is fallen asleep; but I go, that I may awake him out of sleep. 12. The disciples therefore said unto him, Lord, if he is fallen asleep, he will recover. 13. Now Jesus had spoken of his death: but they thought that he spake of taking rest in sleep. 14. Then Jesus therefore said unto them plainly, Lazarus is dead. 15. And I am glad for your sakes that I was not there, to the intent ye may believe; nevertheless let us go unto him. 16. Thomas therefore, who is called Didymus, said unto his fellow-disciples, Let us also go, that we may die with him.*

17. *So when Jesus came, he found that he had been in the tomb four days already.*

### JESUS AND MARTHA

18. *Now Bethany was nigh unto Jerusalem, about fifteen furlongs off; 19. and many of the Jews had come to Martha and Mary, to console them concerning their brother. 20. Martha therefore, when she heard that Jesus was coming, went and met him: but Mary still sat in the house. 21. Martha therefore said unto Jesus, Lord, if thou hadst been here, my brother had not died. 22. And even now I know that, whatsoever thou shalt ask of God, God will give thee. 23. Jesus saith unto her, Thy brother shall rise again. 24. Martha saith unto him, I know that he shall rise again in the resurrection at the last day. 25. Jesus said unto her, I am the resurrection, and the life: he that believeth on me, though he die, yet shall he live:*

26. *and whosoever liveth and believeth on me shall never die. Believest thou this?*
27. *She saith unto him, Yea, Lord: I have believed that thou art the Christ, the Son of God, even he that cometh into the world.*

### JESUS AND MARY

28. *And when she had said this, she went away, and called Mary her sister secretly, saying, The Master is here, and calleth thee.* 29. *And she, when she heard it, arose quickly, and went unto him.* 30. *(Now Jesus was not yet come into the village, but was still in the place where Martha met him.)* 31. *The Jews then which were with her in the house, and were comforting her, when they saw Mary, that she rose up quickly and went out, followed her, supposing that she was going unto the tomb to weep there.* 32. *Mary therefore, when she came where Jesus was, and saw him, fell down at his feet, saying unto him, Lord, if thou hadst been here, my brother had not died.*

### JESUS AND THE JEWS

33. *When Jesus therefore saw her weeping, and the Jews also weeping which came with her, he groaned in the spirit, and was troubled,* 34. *and said, Where have ye laid him? They say unto him, Lord, come and see.* 35. *Jesus wept.* 36. *The Jews therefore said, Behold how he loved him!* 37. *But some of them said, Could not this man, which opened the eyes of him that was blind, have caused that this man also should not die?* 38. *Jesus therefore again groaning in himself cometh to the tomb. Now it was a cave, and a stone lay against it.*

### THE MIRACLE

39. *Jesus saith, Take ye away the stone. Martha, the sister of him that was dead, saith unto him, Lord, by this time he stinketh: for he hath been dead four days.* 40. *Jesus saith unto her, Said I not unto thee, that, if thou believedst, thou shouldest see the glory of God?* 41. *So they took away the stone. And Jesus lifted up his eyes, and said, Father, I thank thee that thou heardest me.* 42. *And I knew that thou hearest me always: but because of the multitude which standeth around I said it, that they may believe that thou didst send me.* 43. *And when he had thus spoken, he cried with a loud voice, Lazarus, come forth.* 44. *He that was dead came forth, bound hand and foot with grave-clothes: and his face was bound about with a napkin. Jesus saith unto them, Loose him, and let him go.*

45. *Many therefore of the Jews, which came to Mary and beheld that which he did, believed on him.* 46. *But some of them went away to the Pharisees, and told them the things which Jesus had done.*

### THE DEATH OF LAZARUS

xi. 1–4. In characteristically Johannine fashion the details which pre-

pare the scene for the narrative of the miracle are introduced in two
awkward and ill-formulated sentences (cf. vi. 22, 23. In the Sinaitic
Syriac the awkwardness is removed: *Now it came to pass that Lazarus of
Bethany was sick. He was the brother*, &c.). There is no reason to suspect
than an editor has inserted the detailed information concerning the
family at Bethany (Bernard, Wellhausen, Loisy, second edition, E.
Schwartz). The author states first the fact of chief importance, *Now a
certain man was sick*. The man was, in fact, the brother of Mary and
Martha (Luke x. 38–42), and his name was Lazarus, an abbreviation of
Eleazar, meaning the man whose *help is God* (cf. Luke xvi. 20; Josephus
*B.J.* v. 576). Mary is identified with the nameless woman who anointed
the Lord in the house of Simon the leper at Bethany (Mark xiv. 3–9;
Matt. xxvi. 6–13); the author records the incident later, substituting
Lazarus for Simon (xii. 1–9). The effect of this identification is to enable
the author also to identify the village where Mary and Martha lived as
Bethany. In Luke x. 38 it is simply *a certain village*. It is strange that the
words selected here and in xii. 3 to describe the anointing (*wiped, feet,
hair*) occur in the Lucan narrative of the anointing by the harlot (Luke
vii. 36 sqq.) and not in the Marcan–Matthæan narrative. It should also
be noted that the grief of the sinner (Luke vii. 38) and of Mary in the
Johannine narrative (xi. 33) is expressed by the same Greek word. This
does not, however, necessarily imply that the author intends to identify
Mary also with the Lucan sinner, still less with Mary of Magdala. For
a note on the Renaissance controversy concerning the 'Three Maries' in
which John Fisher, Bishop of Rochester, vigorously engaged, see Calmes,
pp. 339, 340. For Patristic identifications, see Bernard, vol. II, p. 412.

Jesus is still in retirement at the other Bethany beyond Jordan (x. 40,
i. 28) when He receives a message from the sisters informing Him of
their brother's illness. The address *Lord* and the description of Lazarus
as *he whom thou lovest* (cf. *vv.* 5, 11) mark the family as believing disciples
of Jesus. The sisters state their need; but, like the Mother of Jesus in
ii. 3, they make no definite request. The words of Jesus declare by means
of a paradox the significance of the narrative which follows, and provide
both comfort for the sisters and a lesson to the disciples. The sickness of
Lazarus is for the glory of God and for the glorification of the Son of
God (ix. 3, xiii. 31), and is *not unto death* (1 John v. 16, 17). The words
*not unto death* mean to the hearers that the malady is temporary, but to
Jesus they mean that the death of Lazarus is but a temporary death
(cf. Mark v. 39, *The damsel is not dead, but sleepeth*). He knew that Lazarus
would die, or rather perhaps was already dead. He also knew what He
would do (vi. 6). The death of Lazarus therefore provides the opportunity for a miracle in which the glory of God may be manifested by the
action of His Son (x. 30).

*vv.* 5–10. After the receipt of the message Jesus remained where He
was for two whole days, and *then after that* (the words emphasize the

provocative delay) He proposed a journey into Judæa (vii. 9, 10; Mark x. 32). The disciples, who have no thought of Lazarus, since his recovery was assured by the statement that his sickness was not unto death, protest against a return to so dangerous a place. They remind Jesus that He had only just (cf. vii. 10) escaped from death at the hands of the Jews (x. 31, 40) and that they were still searching for Him to stone Him for blasphemy. Such fears, however, have no weight with Him whose divine mission is to die in Jerusalem for the salvation of the world; and Jesus answers in words which were obscure to the disciples but not to the readers of the gospel, who have read ix. 4, 5. As men journey securely during the twelve hours of the day when the sun shines (for the division of the period of sunshine into twelve hours see Strack–Billerbeck), but stumble during the night when the light is removed, so the work of the Son of God must be accomplished in the allotted time. The hour of darkness when He will be handed over to the powers of evil is not yet come (vii. 8, 33, xiii. 30, xvii. 1, cf. Luke xxii. 53). He must therefore continue openly and freely to do the will of the Father (ix. 4). Apollinaris well comments (cited by Bauer), 'The Lord teaches that He would suffer nothing at the hands of the Jews until the time of the Passion.' This is the primary meaning of the parable. But the natural run of the parable is broken by a secondary application.

The light of the sun is described as the *light of this world*, suggesting another light more powerful than the light of the sun; and, instead of writing, *the light is not in it*, that is, *in the night* (the reading in Codex Bezae), the author wrote, *is not in him*. The crossing thought here is that which was more clearly expressed in ix. 5. Jesus is the true Light of the World (viii. 12), and movement in His company is movement in the Light and possession of the Light (xii. 46). If a man walk apart from Him, he stumbles as in the night, because he has no light abiding in him (1 John ii. 10, 11, cf. Matt. vi. 23; Luke xi. 35, see, however, Lagrange). Whilst Jesus is in the world (ix. 5), the disciples must follow Him, even though He advances towards danger and death.

*vv.* 11–17. The purpose of the journey is then precisely stated: *Our friend Lazarus is fallen asleep; but I go, that I may awake him out of sleep.* In the context of the Johannine narrative as a whole the journey to Judæa is undertaken not merely to raise Lazarus from the dead, but because the Hour of the Passion is at hand. In the author's thought, however, these two aims are not so distinct as appears at first sight, since the record of the death and resurrection of Lazarus for the glory of God and for the glorification of His Son is enclosed by references to the death and resurrection of Jesus for the salvation of the world (x. 17, 18, xi. 50–2), which is the greater glory of God and the greater glorification of His Son (xvii. 1). Accordingly the Johannine record of the death and resurrection of Lazarus for the glory of God forms a significant introduction to the narrative of the Passion and Resurrection of Jesus.

The disciples misunderstand the meaning of the words *has fallen asleep* (iv. 33, xiv. 5, 8, 22), and suppose that a journey to awaken a sick man from the sleep that ensures his recovery is entirely unnecessary. And yet the Greek words in which they express their misunderstanding are capable of suggesting the truth that the death of a Christian is a sleep which leads to final salvation: *If he is fallen asleep* (i.e. has died), *he shall be saved* (cf. the Christian word *cemetery*, *place of sleeping*. For misunderstanding containing unintentional truth, cf. vii. 35, xi. 50).

The Greek word translated *has fallen asleep*, from which the word *cemetery* is derived, is frequently used in the New Testament as a euphemism for death (Matt. xxvii. 52; Acts vii. 60, xiii. 36; 1 Cor. vii. 39, xi. 30, xv. 6, 18, 20, 51; 1 Thess. iv. 13–15, cf. Job iii. 13, xiv. 12). Jesus then plainly tells the disciples that Lazarus is dead, and that his death is the joyful occasion of their faith. The disciples are to see Lazarus raised from the dead, and Jesus rejoices that He was not there, because, as Origen comments, 'If He had been there, Lazarus would not have died (cf. *vv.* 21, 32), for it is impossible for anyone to die in the presence of Jesus'. The narrative presses on with the words *Let us go unto him*, that is, not to comfort his sisters, but to Lazarus 'as to a living person' (Cyril). Thomas (known among the Greek Christians as *Didymus*, a twin, which is the meaning of the Aramaic name *Thomas*, cf. xx. 24, xxi. 2) with a more desperate misunderstanding heroically persuades the disciples to advance with Jesus towards the certainty of death (cf. Mark xiv. 31).

On their arrival at Bethany the words of Jesus are shown to be entirely justified. Not only is Lazarus dead, but he has been four days in the tomb.

### JESUS AND MARTHA

*vv.* 18, 19. The proximity of Bethany to Jerusalem enabled the friends of Martha and Mary to perform a recognized Jewish work of mercy without difficulty, by visiting the bereaved sisters (Strack–Billerbeck *Excursus*, vol. IV, pt. 1, pp. 573 sqq.). The presence of the Jews from Jerusalem is important in the narrative not, however, because of their kindness to the sisters, but in order to emphasize the publicity of the miracle and to set it within the context of the work of Jesus in Jerusalem. The Jews who had heard His teaching and who had been witnesses of the controversy concerning the healing of the man born blind are now to witness the climax of the philanthropy of Jesus, 'It is not among possibilities that the illumination which proceeds from Jesus should be shrouded from the Jews without having fully reached its fitting measure of philanthropy' (Cyril on *v.* 9).

*vv.* 20–7. When the news of the arrival of Jesus reaches Martha, she acts with the vigour which marks her character in the Lucan gospel (x. 38). She goes at once to meet Him, while Mary remains seated in the house. Martha's first words express a combination of faith in the power of Jesus with disappointment that it had not been exercised. The presence of Jesus would have saved her brother from death (contrast iv. 46 sqq.). And yet, in spite of his death, she has confidence in the efficacy of the prayer of Jesus, without venturing to give definite expression to her hope. She seems to regard Him as a virtuous man powerful in prayer (ix. 31). The words of Jesus concentrate attention upon the certainty of resurrection which annihilates grief. *Thy brother shall rise again.* In the presence of Jesus resurrection is a present imminent reality. Martha, however, understands resurrection as an event deferred to the distant future. As a Jewess she knows only of a resurrection at the last day (Luke xiv. 14, xx. 35, cf. Isa. xxvi. 19). Jesus then openly declares the truth. *I am the resurrection, and the life* (*and the life* is omitted from the Chester-Beatty papyrus, from the Sinaitic Syriac, from two manuscripts of the Old Latin Version and by Origen and Cyprian). What to the Jews is a future hope, is to the Christians a present reality. *As the Father hath life in himself, even so gave he to the Son also to have life in himself* (v. 26). Faith in Jesus overcomes death. There is no limitation to the power of Christian faith (iii. 15). Every believer is removed from the possibility of death, and he shall live, though he die (vi. 44–58, viii. 51). Two thoughts here cross each other. First the general Christian truth, according to which physical death is trivial and irrelevant. Jesus is the Resurrection, because He is the Life. Through faith in Jesus Christians possess eternal life. Secondly, in the context of the narrative Lazarus will be brought back to life, though he is dead. In the words of Jesus the emphasis, however, lies wholly upon the first. The raising of Lazarus can be rightly understood only in relation to the general Christian truth concerning Life and Resurrection; it is not an isolated miracle incapable of spiritual repetition in the experience of the Church. The significance of the miracle is therefore detached from the miracle itself, because it is imperative that Martha, and also the readers of the gospel, should first be grounded in the truth. Without faith no man can see the glory of God (*v.* 40). Miracles remain mere miracles apart from the wisdom of faith which provides knowledge of their spiritual meaning (vi. 26, 27). Martha, having heard the truth, declares her faith with complete formal correctness. *I have believed that thou art the Christ, the Son of God, even he that cometh into the world* (cf. i. 49, iv. 42, vi. 69). The sequel, however, shows (*vv.* 39–41) that she does not recognize the immediate implication of her faith.

### JESUS AND MARY

*vv.* 28–32. Martha returns at once to the house in Bethany, and privately, perhaps because of the known hostility of the Jews to Jesus, informs Mary of the presence of the Master (i. 39, xiii. 13, 14, xx. 16, cf. Mark xiv. 14) and of His desire to see her. The author has not

recorded any such expressed desire, but the reader familiar with the
Lucan story (Luke x. 38–42) would regard such a desire as inevitable.
The Jews, who have not heard what Martha said, see Mary rise quickly
and leave the house, and they follow her, supposing that she intends
to visit the tomb and mourn there (Wisd. xix. 3). But Mary goes straight
to Jesus, and, since He has remained where Martha had met Him, she
finds Him at once, and repeats Martha's words with a more intense
accompanying action. *She fell down at his feet.* Whether this is merely a
typical Johannine intensification of repetition, or whether the author
intends a reference to Mary's position in the Lucan account (Luke x.
39), it is impossible to determine. Now, however, she hears no words of
teaching. The Lord moves at once to raise Lazarus from the dead in
the presence of the sisters and of the Jews.

## JESUS AND THE JEWS

*vv.* 33–8. There precedes the narrative of the miracle a scene of
overwhelming grief in which Jesus Himself is engulfed. Indeed, his
grief is described in language far more intense than that which depicts
the grief of Mary and of the Jews. They *weep* (*wail*, R.V. mg.). He
*groaned in the spirit* (repeated in *v.* 38), *was troubled* (A.V. mg. and R.V.
mg. *troubled himself*), *wept* (the aorist means *burst into tears*). The passionate expression of the grief of Jesus is, as the author expressly states,
caused by the sight of the grief of Mary and of the Jews: *When Jesus
therefore saw her weeping, and the Jews also weeping which came with her, he
groaned in the spirit.* The Jews voice the natural explanation of the emotion of Jesus: *Behold how he loved him!* The second outburst of the grief of
Jesus (*v.* 38) is apparently caused by the protest of the Jews that One
who had been able to open the eyes of the blind man ought to have been
able to prevent the death of His friend.

The care with which the author of the gospel has emphasized the
intense emotion of Jesus, not only by his choice of very emphatic words,
but also by the juxtaposition of the grief of Jesus and the manifestation
of His power in raising Lazarus from the dead, requires explanation;
unless indeed the explanation of the Jews be considered adequate, which
in the Fourth Gospel is surely impossible. From the earliest days of
Patristic exegesis until modern times the interpretation of this passage
has been diverse and to some extent uncertain. Lagrange adopts an
interpretation which goes far back in the history of Johannine exegesis.
He writes, 'He manifests His humanity', and explains the second outburst of grief, 'Jesus loved Lazarus and experienced a more intense
feeling of compassion when he drew near to the place where he lay'.
Bernard agrees with Lagrange. Interpreting the word translated *he
groaned* Bernard writes: 'It represents the inarticulate sounds which
escape men when they are physically overwhelmed by a great wave of

emotion. And Jesus, the Perfect Man, experienced this as He experienced all else that is human and not sinful.' With this may be compared the comment of Pseudo-Hippolytus, 'He would teach us sympathy and human love for our neighbours.' Westcott saw in this intensity of human sympathy the cause of the power of Jesus to raise Lazarus from the dead and to work other miracles. According to other commentators it is the concrete fact of death that moved Jesus to tears: 'Seeing man made in the image of God marred by corruption—not Lazarus only but all humanity.' Chrysostom, and recently Tillmann, regarding the horror of death as the cause of the grief of Jesus, compare this passage with the disturbance of Jesus in the garden of Gethsemane; and, since the episode of Gethsemane is omitted in the Fourth Gospel, Chrysostom comments 'John made up here what he omitted there', and translates *groaned in the spirit* by *groaned at his spirit*, with the result that he extracts from the passage the record of a discipline by Jesus of His human emotions, 'He restrained His trouble'—*he rebuked his feeling* (cf. also Origen and Cyril). Since in Christian thought death and sin are inseparable, many commentators have seen in the grief of Jesus at the death of Lazarus an all-embracing sorrow over human sin which is the cause of suffering and death (Schanz, Zahn, Loisy). A somewhat different emphasis is introduced into the interpretation of the passage by the recognition that the word translated *groaned* denotes in the Greek anger rather than sorrow (R.V. mg. *was moved with indignation in the spirit*). The grief of Jesus proceeds then from anger, and the question concerns the cause of the anger of Jesus. Here the commentators part company. For some it is anger at the hypocritical lamentation of the Jews compared with the genuine grief of Mary (Plummer); for others it is irritation at a too vivid emotion arising within Himself (Origen, Chrysostom, Cyril); for others it is anger at the triumph of sin and death (Schanz, Zahn); for others it is indignation at the unbelief of the Jews (Loisy, Bauer). Bauer thinks that in the earlier form of the narrative the grief of Jesus was the sorrow of sympathy with the mourners, but that the author has turned the sympathy of Jesus into indignation at the unbelief of His enemies.

The interpretation of the passage depends upon four fixed points which must not be obscured by dogmatic or sentimental considerations. First, the passage occurs in a particular context. The death of Lazarus has been declared necessary for the glory of God and for the glorification of His Son, and Jesus, in order that He may not, by His presence, prevent Lazarus from dying, refuses to journey to Bethany until Lazarus is quite certainly dead. Moreover Jesus approaches the grave as the Lord of Life. He is the Resurrection and the Life. Secondly, whatever the word translated *groaned in the spirit* might mean in certain contexts (see Lagrange), in biblical Greek (Dan. xi. 30, LXX; Lam. ii. 6; Mark i. 43, xiv. 5; Matt. ix. 30, cf. Ps. vii. 12 in the version of Aquila, and Isa. xvii. 13 in the version of Symmachus) it expresses anger and indignation.

Thirdly, the indignant disturbance of the spirit of Jesus is occasioned by the behaviour of the company surrounding Him, first by the weeping of Mary and of the Jews, then by the hardly veiled scepticism of a section of the Jews (*v.* 37). The disturbance of spirit here is precisely similar to that at the betrayal by Judas (xiii. 21). Fourthly, the natural meaning of the Jewish explanation of the grief of Jesus, *See how he loved him*, must in the intention of the author be a wholly inadequate explanation, though, in a manner in which they do not perceive, the words of the Jews may contain a significant Christian truth. All these considerations rule out the explanation that the angry grief of Jesus is occasioned by the emotion of normal human sympathy with the bereaved and with their friends. The Jews suppose that Jesus is advancing to the tomb to share their grief and the grief of the sisters. In fact the Lord of Life advances to raise Lazarus from the dead and to manifest the triviality of physical death in the presence of the Son of God, who is the Resurrection and the Life. It is the unbelief of the Jews and the half-belief of Martha (*v.* 39) and Mary that in the context of the Johannine narrative cause Jesus to burst angrily into tears. The whole situation is comparable to that other occasion when it is recorded in the gospels that Jesus wept: *And when he drew nigh, he saw the city and wept over it, saying, If thou hadst known in this day, even thou, the things which belong unto peace! but now they are hid from thine eyes* (Luke xix. 41). The author of the gospel shows no tendency to remove from Jesus passionate emotion; it is, however, his intention to concentrate that emotion upon the sight of human unbelief and upon that grim reality of the death of Jesus which is the act of the love of God for the salvation of men (xii. 22 sqq., cf. Heb. v. 7). The emphatic Johannine description of the grief of Jesus does not spring from a desire to contrast His behaviour with that of the poise and balance of the ideal Stoic good man (Holtzmann), but from the intense Christian sense of the depths of suffering which it was necessary for the Son of God to endure in order to effect human salvation. In the grief and suffering of Jesus the love of God is manifested. In this sense the explanation of the Jews is a correct explanation. *See how he loved him* (iii. 16, xiii. 1).

## THE MIRACLE

*vv.* 39-46. Jesus stands before the tomb which contains the corpse, and takes complete control of the situation. The author gives no indication whether he thinks of the tomb as horizontal or vertical; whether, that is, it is hewn in a rock or dug in the ground. The removal of the stone is commanded. Martha protests, fearful lest offence may be given to the bystanders, since the third day has passed, and the body of Lazarus will have gone to permanent corruption (see DETACHED NOTE 4, pp. 199, 200). Jesus at once silences her expression of unbelief. The wonder of the miracle lies, as Theodore of Mopsuestia well noted, precisely in the raising of one who is dead beyond possibility of recovery. Martha is reminded that the believer is to see the glory of God (*vv.* 4, 23–5, cf. ii. 11, v. 26).

Jesus then lifted up His eyes (xvii. 1), and publicly gives thanks to His Father. The action and the words declare the impending miracle to be the action of God, and declare also the union of Father and Son. The expression of thanks presumes Jesus to have prayed. But the prayer of Jesus is distinguished from normal human prayer and even from the intense prayer of the prophet Elijah on a somewhat similar occasion (1 Kings xvii. 20–2). His life is a life of complete obedience to the will of God, and His prayer therefore admits of no uncertainty of answer, *I knew that thou hearest me always*. Consequently, the public expression of thanks does not represent surprise, but is uttered in order that the crowd may recognize the union of the Father and the Son, and may believe in the Divine mission of Jesus (xii. 28–30). Many modern commentators, failing to recognize the Johannine distinction between prayer which is so completely in accord with the will of God that its answer is inevitable and prayer which is not thus conditioned, have concluded from this passage that the Johannine Christ is incapable of prayer. Thus Holtzmann comments 'He prays only by accommodation' whatever precisely that may mean (cf. also Loisy). Bauer writes 'The question where or when Jesus had uttered a prayer is irrelevant, since the Johannine Christ is incapable of genuine prayer', and suggests that the original form of the story related the dependence of the works of Jesus upon Prayer, but that the author of the gospel has removed this element in the original tradition. Bernard obscures the point of the whole passage by adopting a very weakly attested reading which substitutes *because of the multitude . . . I do it* for *because of the multitude . . . I said it*, thus referring the words to the miracle and not to the public expression of gratitude. Even Chrysostom commented 'What could be a greater sign of weakness, if He needed prayer?' and answers his question 'Why did he assume the form of prayer?' by saying 'For the sake of the weak and grosser sort'. For the author of the gospel, however, the contrast is not between real and unreal prayer, but between prayer which is heard because it is in accord with the will of God, and prayer which possesses no such certainty of answer. And the certainty of answer is not only characteristic of the prayer of Jesus (xiv. 16, xvii. 9, 15, 20, 21), but of the prayer of His true disciples in His name (xiv. 13, 14, xv. 7, 16, xvi. 23, 24, 26; 1 John iii. 22, v. 14, 15). Nor is this certainty of Christian prayer merely a Johannine conception; it belongs also to the words of Jesus in the synoptic tradition. It is the privilege of the children of the Messianic order that their prayers are heard (Matt. vi. 6–9, vii. 7–11, xxi. 22; Mark xi. 24; Luke xi. 9–13).

Having thus publicly manifested the obedience of the Son to the Father, Jesus with a loud voice called Lazarus by name and bade him come forth from the grave. As the sheep hear the voice of the Good Shepherd when He calls them by name and leads them out of the cramped sheepfold (x. 3), so Lazarus is immediately drawn forth from the grave by the word of Jesus. It seems as though the author, as Basil suggested (*Corderii Catena*, p. 295), intends to record a miracle within a miracle. Lazarus does not walk out of the grave; he is rather drawn out tightly bandaged (for the Greek word cf. Prov. vii. 16) hand and foot (cf. xix. 40), with his face covered with a cloth (xx. 7, cf. Luke xix. 20; Acts xix. 12). Only when he has been drawn out of the tomb does Jesus command him to be loosed, in order that he may walk freely and of his own initiative. And yet the attention of the reader is not meant to rest upon a miracle once wrought by Jesus. The form of the record of the raising of Lazarus suggests the freedom that results from the mighty act of God by which the Christians have passed from death to life.

The narrative concludes with no further information concerning Lazarus. The author baldly records a division (vii. 43, ix. 16, x. 19–21) among the Jews who had witnessed the miracle. Some believed (ii. 23, iv. 39, viii. 30), others reported the matter to the Pharisees.

# THE DESPERATE COUNSEL
# OF CAIAPHAS AND THE
# CONFIDENT DEVOTION OF MARY

## XI. 47–XII. 11

IF the Fourth Gospel be regarded as a carefully written historical narrative of the sequence of events which led to the crucifixion, the raising of Lazarus must be held to have been the most significant single cause of the crystallizing of the opposition of the Jewish authorities (v. 18, vii. 1, 19, 25, 32, 45, viii. 40, 59, x. 31, xi. 8, 16) into a formal decision to put Jesus to death. But this would be, almost certainly, a misunderstanding of the author's purpose and of the method according to which he constructed his gospel. Having completed the narrative in which the nature of the ministry of Jesus has been finally declared in terms of death and life, he attaches as a pendant to the narrative two contrasted acts—a supreme act of ignorant unbelief and a supreme act of intelligent faith. The Jewish authorities decree the death of Jesus in order to retain their own authority; Mary sees in His imminent death an opportunity of pouring out her substance in His honour. The order of events in the earlier tradition is rearranged to serve the author's purpose. Not only does he attach the council to the miracle of the raising of Lazarus, but he also inverts the entry into Jerusalem and the anointing at Bethany (contrast Mark xi. 1–10, xiv. 3–9). In the perspective of the Fourth Gospel the record of the death and resurrection of Lazarus merges into the record of the death and resurrection of Jesus, since historically the Passion crowned by the Resurrection is the true ground of that eternal life which belongs to the Christians by faith in Jesus. The concrete figure, Lazarus, therefore stands as a visible sign that incites both to passionate faith and to passionate unbelief (xi. 45, 46, xii. 1, 2, 9–11, 17).

### THE HIGH PRIEST BEARS PROPHETIC WITNESS TO THE
### TRUTH, AND THE JEWISH AUTHORITIES DECREE
### THE DEATH OF JESUS

xi. 47. *The chief priests therefore and the Pharisees gathered a council, and said, What do we? for this man doeth many signs.* 48. *If we let him thus alone, all men will believe on him: and the Romans will come and take away both our place and our nation. 49. But a certain one of them, Caiaphas, being high priest that year, said unto them, Ye know nothing at all, 50. nor do ye take account that it is expedient for you that one man should die for the people, and that the whole nation perish not. 51. Now this he said not of himself: but being high priest that year, he prophesied that Jesus should die for the nation; 52. and not for the nation only, but that he might also gather together into one the children of God that are scattered abroad. 53. So from that day forth they took counsel that they might put him to death.*

*54. Jesus therefore walked no more openly among the Jews, but departed thence into the country near to the wilderness, into a city called Ephraim; and there he tarried with the disciples. 55. Now the passover of the Jews was at hand: and many went up to Jerusalem out of the country before the passover, to purify themselves. 56. They sought therefore for Jesus, and spake one with another, as they stood in the temple, What think ye? That he will not come to the feast? 57. Now the chief priests and the Pharisees had given commandment, that, if any man knew where he was, he should shew it, that they might take him.*

### MARY ANOINTS JESUS EXTRAVAGANTLY FOR HIS BURIAL

*xii. 1. Jesus therefore six days before the passover came to Bethany, where Lazarus was, whom Jesus raised from the dead. 2. So they made him a supper there: and Martha served; but Lazarus was one of them that sat at meat with him. 3. Mary therefore took a pound of ointment of spikenard, very precious, and anointed the feet of Jesus, and wiped his feet with her hair: and the house was filled with the odour of the ointment. 4. But Judas Iscariot, one of his disciples, which should betray him, saith, 5. Why was not this ointment sold for three hundred pence, and given to the poor? 6. Now this he said, not because he cared for the poor; but because he was a thief, and having the bag took away what was put therein. 7. Jesus therefore said, Suffer her to keep it against the day of my burying. 8. For the poor ye have always with you; but me ye have not always.*

*9. The common people therefore of the Jews learned that he was there: and they came, not for Jesus' sake only, but that they might see Lazarus also, whom he had raised from the dead. 10. But the chief priests took counsel that they might put Lazarus also to death; 11. because that by reason of him many of the Jews went away, and believed on Jesus.*

### THE HIGH PRIEST BEARS PROPHETIC WITNESS TO THE TRUTH, AND THE JEWISH AUTHORITIES DECREE THE DEATH OF JESUS

xi. 47–57. The Jewish authorities perceive that the resurrection of Lazarus raises the whole question of the miraculous activity of Jesus (ii. 23, v. 17, x. 41) and their own helpless inaction. He acts powerfully and they do nothing at all. At a council consisting of the more important members of the Sanhedrin (vii. 32) the marked contrast is honestly, though despondently, stated. Convinced that His power proceeds from an illegitimate assumption of divine authority (v. 18, viii. 13), they assume that powerful arrogance of this kind must have political results (xviii. 33–5, xix. 12, 16) and they are uncertain whether, so long as He remains at liberty, they have sufficient power to control the crowds. The author of the gospel has recorded significant movements of the crowds towards Jesus as a result of His miracles (ii. 23, vi. 22–6, vii. 31, x. 21, 41, 42, xi. 45), and on one occasion an attempt had actually been made to declare Him the messianic King (vi. 15). The fears of the authorities were, moreover, abundantly justified by the tumultuous welcome of the Messiah which took place a few days later (xii. 9–19, especially 13). The result of such an uncontrolled messianic explosion in the capital seemed to them inevitable. The Romans would regard it as a revolution and would deprive them of their authority, as a penalty for their incapacity. This would mean the end of the Temple as the centre of the worship of the true God and of the Jewish people as a particular and independent race. Its position in the sentence makes the *our* so emphatic that the sentence may justifiably be translated *The Romans will come and take away from us both the place and the nation.* What is at stake is the position of the Jewish authorities (cf. Mark xii. 1–12). In the thought of the author, *They loved the glory of men more than the glory of God* (xii. 43). *Place* may mean the city of Jerusalem, but almost certainly it here denotes the Temple (iv. 20; Matt. xxiv. 15; Acts vi. 13, 14, vii. 7, xxi. 28, cf. 2 Macc. v. 19). The author gives no indication that he intends his readers to see in these words an unconscious prophecy of the destruction of Jerusalem by the Romans in A.D. 70; not, presumably, because he is ignorant of that event, but because for him the end of the old Judaism was occasioned, not by the action of the Romans, but by its fulfilment in the death and resurrection of Jesus and by the emergence of the new children of God (ii. 19–22).

The uncertainty of the council when confronted by so dangerous and difficult a situation is relieved by the courage and wisdom of one of its members. Caiaphas, the High Priest, alone possesses sufficient political sagacity to handle the matter. Whatever Jesus may be is now irrelevant. The time for discussing the ground of His authority has passed. He brutally brushes discussion aside—*Ye know nothing at all*—and, agreeing that it is their authority that is at stake—*It is expedient for you*—he pronounces with prophetic authority, since he was high priest *that year*, that one man must die, in order that the people of God may live, and in order that the whole race be not destroyed. Every word the High Priest spoke, was, as the author points out, verbally inspired. Caiaphas was an ignorant man moved by prophetic inspiration. He did not speak *of himself* (cf. Matt. xvi. 17): *but being high priest that year, he prophesied.* In the Christian Church the Jews who have believed—*the people* in the first part of the prophecy of Caiaphas—and the believing Gentiles—*the whole nation* in the second part of the prophecy of Caiaphas—have been united into one family. This expanded operation of the power of God depends, however, wholly upon the death of Jesus, by which He draws all men unto Himself, and becomes the effective Saviour of the World (iii. 14–17, xii. 32; 1 John ii. 2). The language here echoes the distinction in ch. x between the sheep who have been called out of Judaism (x. 1–15) and the *other sheep* who have not come out of *this fold*, the whole, however, forming *one flock* under the *one shepherd who layeth down his life for the sheep* (x. 11, 16). The phrase *the children of God that are scattered abroad*, which in a Jewish context would denote the dispersion of the Jews among the Gentiles, is here transferred to describe the Gentiles beyond the borders of Israel who await their liberation and are destined to believe through the preaching of the disciples of Jesus (i. 13, vii. 35, xvii. 20, 21; 1 John iii. 1, 10, cf. Eph. ii. 15; *Did.* ix. 4). 'The Christ collected us all together again and brought us through faith into one fold, the Church' (Cyril). 'The dweller in Rome deemeth the Indians a member of himself' (Chrysostom).

The phrase *being high priest that year* has caused the commentators considerable inconvenience. Its natural meaning would be that the office of High Priest was held annually, which was not the case. It was a position held for life, although, during the Roman occupation, High Priests were frequently deposed by the Romans. Valerius Gratus had deposed successively Annas, Ismael, Eleazar, and Simon. Caiaphas (Matt. xxvi. 3, 57; Luke iii. 2. He is not named by Mark), in fact held office for eighteen years (A.D. 18–36, when he was deposed by Vitellius, see Josephus *Ant.* xviii. 34, 35, 95). Many Patristic commentators understood the phrase to imply an annual office, without concerning themselves with the historical inaccuracy involved (Chrysostom, Theodore of Mopsuestia, Isho'dad, Augustine). Jerome misquoted Josephus, and thus secured authority for a single year when Caiaphas was High Priest (Jerome on Matt. xxvi. 57, see Lagrange on John xi. 49). Bauer, recognizing that Jewish archpriests held office annually in Asia Minor, imagines that the author transferred to Palestine an Asiatic custom. But it may be questioned whether the author intended to convey to his readers so trivial a piece of information as that the Jewish High Priest held office annually. He repeats the phrase solemnly three times (xi. 49, 51, xviii. 13). It can hardly be doubted that what he wishes to emphasize is that the office of Caiaphas coincided with the year of the salvation of the world, and that this coincidence evoked a prophetic utterance from the High Priest of that year under the constraining power of God Himself. In the year in which the 'economy of salvation' (Origen) was completed the High Priest of Judaism temporarily recovered his power of prophecy, and unconsciously bore His authoritative witness to the nature of the truth by which Judaism was fulfilled and superseded (cf. the witness of Pilate, xix. 20–2). For the High Priest as the organ of divination cf. Exod. xxviii. 30; Lev. viii. 8; Num. xxvii. 21; Josephus *Ant.* vi. 115; *B.J.* i. 68, iii. 352–4. For a similar priestly outburst of Christian prophecy cf. Luke i. 67, and for the association of prophecy and priesthood see Philo, *De special. Leg.* IV. 192. It is presumed in Ezra ii. 63; Neh. vii. 65 (cf. Hos. iii. 4) that the High Priestly power of divination was lost during the Captivity. In the later Rabbinic literature unintentional prophecy provoked a number of sayings of the Jewish Fathers. For example, Eleazar (A.D. 270), speaking in the name of Rabbi Jose ben Zimia (*c.* A.D. 220), said: 'No prophets who have uttered prophecies have known what they prophesied. Only Moses and Elijah knew.' Again he said: 'Samuel, the Master of the Prophets, did not know what he prophesied' (Strack–Billerbeck on John xi. 51, cf. 2 Pet. i. 20, 21).

It is difficult to bring out in English the subtle distinction which the author of the gospel discovers in the two Greek words used by Caiaphas to describe the Jews, translated in the English versions *people* and *nation*. The former word emphasizes that they stand in a peculiar relation to God as His people (Matt. ii. 6, citing Mic. v. 2, and Luke, Acts *passim*), the latter that they are a race united by a common descent. In his interpretation of the prophecy of Caiaphas the author avoids repeating the word which implies that the Jews are the people of God, and substitutes *nation* for *people*.

When Caiaphas has uttered his authoritative decision, there is no more to be said. The members of the council, unable to detach the prophecy from its setting in the intelligence of the High Priests, ratify his decision, and decree the death of Jesus (Matt. xxvi. 3–5). The Hour of the death of the Son of God is now imminent. But since the time of the Passover of the Jews had as yet not actually come, though it was *at hand*, Jesus secretly retired with His disciples into temporary safety to a city, called Ephraim, in the country and near the desert. The position of Ephraim cannot be determined with any confidence. A city of that name is mentioned in connection with Bethel in 2 Chron. xiii. 19 (cf. Josephus *B.J.* iv. 551; 2 Sam. xiii. 23; 1 Macc. xi. 34, and Eusebius *Onomasticon*). Codex Bezae has a geographical addition: *To the country Sapfurim near the desert, to a city called Ephraim.* But this does not help to identify Ephraim, since Sapfurim is even more unintelligible. Modern geographical uncertainty provides no ground for supposing the author of the gospel to have had no accurate knowledge of Palestinian topography. Loisy helplessly supposes the name to contain some allegorizing symbolism, but is unable to suggest what it may have been (p. 668).

Meanwhile, the preparations for the feast are already in progress. The pilgrims have arrived and the time of their purification for the feast has come (contrast xiii. 1–17, xvii. 17–19; but cf. Gen. xxxv. 2; Exod. xix. 10–15; Num. ix. 13; 2 Chron. xxx. 1–3, 17, 18). The crowds of

pilgrim Jews are, however, less anxious concerning their own purification than to stand about in the Temple and express their curiosity
whether Jesus will appear at the feast or not (cf. vii. 11). The question
engages their attention all the more since the authorities have made
public their desire to know where He is, and have issued instructions
that any one who knows His place of retreat should at once make it
known, in order that He may be arrested.

### MARY ANOINTS JESUS EXTRAVAGANTLY FOR HIS BURIAL

xii. 1–6. Six days before the Passover Jesus returns to Bethany from
His seclusion, and the author at once narrates the action of Mary in
marked contrast with that of the Jewish authorities. The form of the
narrative presents the commentator with a nice critical problem. In
the main the Marcan narrative (Mark xiv. 3–9) forms the basis of the
Johannine narrative. The general situation is identical, and there are
striking verbal reminiscences (e.g. *ointment of spikenard*. John xii. 5 and
8 are almost verbally identical with Mark xiv. 5 and 7. In the Saying
of Jesus the words *let her alone* and *burial* are common to both). And yet,
as in the narrative of the Feeding of the Five Thousand, there are certain slight approximations to the Matthæan version of Mark (Matt. xxvi.
6–13). *Very precious* is added to *ointment of spikenard* (cf. Matt. xxvi. 7);
Matt. xxvi. 11 is identical with John xii. 8; in both the Marcan *whenso-
ever ye will ye can do them good* is omitted. In Mark the protest against the
extravagance is not definitely a protest made by the disciples. Matthew
adds: *When the disciples saw it, they had indignation, saying.* John writes:
*Judas Iscariot, one of his disciples . . . saith.* In the reference to the meeting
of the Sanhedrin which immediately precedes the anointing at Bethany
(Mark xiv. 1, 2; Matt. xxvi. 3), Matthew alone mentions Caiaphas by
name. And yet, in spite of the clear Marcan-Matthæan background of
the Johannine narrative, it is disturbed not only by typically Johannine
alterations such as the identification of the unnamed woman with
Mary of Bethany, the introduction of Lazarus and the consequent
omission of any mention of Simon the Leper (Mark xiv. 3), the concentration upon Judas, who is roundly declared to have been a thief (cf.
vi. 70, 71), the replacing of Mark xiv. 9, *wheresoever the gospel shall be
preached throughout the whole world, that also which this woman hath done shall
be spoken of for a memorial of her,* by xii. 3, *and the house was filled with the
odour of the ointment,* and the emphatic statement that Mary *consciously*
acted in anticipation of the death of Jesus (see below). The Marcan-
Matthæan background is also disturbed by definite verbal reminiscences
of the Lucan account of the anointing of Jesus by the unnamed harlot
(Luke vii. 36–50; in the Lucan gospel this takes the place of the later
anointing, which Luke wholly omitted). In the Lucan-Johannine version all reference to the anointing of the head of Jesus is definitely sup-

pressed. His feet, twice emphatically mentioned, by both Luke and John, are anointed and wiped with the woman's hair (cf. xi. 2, xii. 3). In Luke, but not in John, the woman, who is a penitent sinner, weeps and dries her tears with her hair. It should also be noted that *Martha served* is also Lucan (Luke x. 40).

The problem to be explained is, Why do Luke and John carefully refuse to state that the woman anointed the head of Jesus—Luke by a radical alteration of the Marcan source, John by much less drastic treatment? In the Marcan-Matthæan version the whole point lies in the acceptance by Jesus of a significant regal and messianic act, the anointing of the head (Ps. xxiii. 5, cf. Bacon, *Beginnings of Gospel Story*, p. 199; *Fourth Gospel in Research and Debate*, p. 427, note), and in the fact that He, and not the woman, refers it to His death. This dangerous expression of messianic devotion has been removed by the two later writers. Luke avoids the regal reference by making the act one of penitence; John concentrates the devotion of the woman, not on the Messiah as King, which would merely make Mary's action an anticipation of the enthusiasm of the crowds (xii. 12–19), but upon Jesus as the Messiah about to die (xii. 32, 33).

A critical comparison of the four narratives of the anointing places the commentator in a position from which an interpretation of the Johannine version becomes possible. The incident takes place on the arrival of Jesus at Bethany six days before the Passover (contrast Mark xiv. 1). Since the Thursday following was the day before the Passover (xiii. 1), the author presumably intends the reader to understand that the arrival of Jesus took place on the Sabbath. At Bethany He is publicly entertained; Martha served and Lazarus was one of the guests. The author carefully avoids stating that the meal took place in the house of Lazarus and his sisters (he simply writes: *they made him a supper there*: however, in the Sinaitic Syriac Version Lazarus is definitely stated to have been the host), presumably because he knew that the meal had been prepared in the house of Simon the Leper (Mark xiv. 3; Matt. xxvi. 6. Simon, a Pharisee, Luke vii. 36, 40). There is no reason to suppose with Loisy that Lazarus *who had died* (added to *v.* 1 in Codices Alexandrinus, Bezae, &c.) has taken the place of the Leper as the 'figure of redeemed humanity' (Loisy, pp. 671, 672, cf. also O. Holtzmann, p. 10).

During the meal Mary took a pound (the exact amount is a Johannine addition) of precious ointment (for the description of the ointment see Swete on Mark xiv. 3), and, anointing His feet, wiped them with her hair. So extravagant was her generosity that the house was permeated by the odour of the ointment. A comparison with the Marcan-Matthæan narrative shows that this statement replaces the words of Jesus: *Wheresoever the gospel shall be preached throughout the whole world, that also which this woman hath done shall be spoken of for a memorial of her.* The action of Mary is of universal significance, and its odour permeates the Church and reaches the extremities of the world (cf. Origen, Cyril, Augustine, cf. also 2 Cor. ii. 15; Ignatius, *Eph.* xvii). Bernard denies any symbolism here. Compare, however, the Rabbinic saying: 'Good ointment reaches from the innermost chamber to the hall: a good man moves from one end of the world to the other' (Strack-Billerbeck, cited also by Westcott). Loisy presses the symbolism too hard when he writes: 'Mary, the Church of the Gentiles, poured out at the feet of Jesus the odour of the gospel which fills the whole universe'.

Judas, a disciple and the betrayer of his Master, with hypocritically pious impiety protests in the interests of the poor against such wasteful extravagance. Why, he asks, was not the ointment sold for 300 *denarii* (say £25), and the money given to the poor. Before recording the Lord's answer to the question of Judas the author interpolates the explanation of his generous philanthropy. Judas was a thief, and he misused his privilege of carrying the common box, by 'lifting' the money placed in it. The Greek word translated *bag* (A.V., R.V.) is used in the New Testament only here and in xiii. 29. In the LXX (2 Chron. xxiv. 8, 10 sqq.) it is used for a chest for offerings of money. In the Rabbinic literature the Greek word is found transliterated into Hebrew, and means a box used for the preservation of something valuable (e.g. the Torah when the owner was travelling: a coffin containing a corpse). Originally the word meant a case containing the reeds of wind instruments. The right translation here is a *box* (R.V. mg.). The Greek word translated *bare* (A.V.), *took away* (R.V.), *carried* (R.V. mg.), has a double meaning. It means normally simply to *carry* (x. 31, xvi. 12, xix. 17), but it can also mean *carry off* (xx. 15). In Josephus *Ant.* viii. 258, &c., and frequently in the papyri the word means *rob* or *pilfer* (Moulton-Milligan). The word therefore corresponds exactly to the English word *lift* with its double meaning. Judas carried the money-box and 'lifted' what was put into it.

*vv.* 7, 8. The Saying of Jesus presents very great grammatical difficulties in the Greek. But, before these are considered, it must be remembered that the words are an answer to a definite question of Judas, and that in the context of the Fourth Gospel the action of Mary stands in direct opposition to the action of the Jewish authorities. Therefore the words of Jesus must explain why Mary had not given the money to the poor, but had expended it in order to honour Jesus. The reading in the majority of Greek manuscripts, headed by Codex Alexandrinus, presents no difficulty. *Let her alone: against the day of my burying hath she kept this* (i.e. the ointment). This is the translation in A.V. In other words, Mary must not be disturbed. She has preserved the ointment, and not given its money equivalent to the poor, because she has reserved it for the care of the body of Jesus. The hour of His death has now come, and she has poured it over Him in anticipation of His burial. This translation, however, rests upon a Greek text that is almost certainly a simplification of the original text preserved in Codices Vaticanus, Sinaiticus, Bezae, Koridethianus, &c. The original reading is grammatically difficult. It may be translated: *Let her alone, in order that she may keep it*, &c.; or *Suffer her to keep it*, &c. (R.V.). In both of these translations Mary is to be permitted to reserve something for future use. Many modern commentators (Holtzmann, Bernard) suppose that the remainder of the ointment is intended, and Mary is to be allowed to keep it for the embalming of Jesus (xix. 40). But in the context this is really intolerable. Thus interpreted the words of Jesus do not answer Judas's question, and it is clear that Mary has poured out all the ointment. In the Marcan narrative the woman *brake the cruse* (see Lagrange). In the Johannine narrative the odour of the ointment fills the house; there is no reserve in the action of Mary. Loisy characteristically escapes the difficulty by supposing a miracle. The ointment is inexhaustible, and remains for later use. But of this there is no hint in the text. The grammatical structure of the sentence must therefore be examined again. Though it is true that *suffer her to* may translate the Greek, it may equally well be an independent statement; and indeed this is demanded by the Marcan background and by the Johannine context. *Let her be*, i.e. *Do not disturb her*. Then follows an explanatory clause, introduced by what in classical Greek would be a final particle, but in Hellenistic Greek, and most characteristically in the Fourth Gospel (e.g. vi. 29, xv. 13, see Preuschen-Bauer, *Wörterbuch*, § 589; Robertson, *Grammar of the Greek N.T.*, p. 992), simply introduces an epexegetical statement, which in classical Greek would be expressed by an articular infinitive. This gives an entirely adequate meaning here. It explains why Mary did not give the money to the poor. *It was that she might keep it for my burial* (cf. R.V. mg.). The simplification in the *Textus Receptus* has adequately preserved, as Lagrange insists, the meaning of the original reading, and has merely removed its grammatical obscurity. In other words, then, in the Johannine narrative, Mary consciously recognized the necessity of the death of Jesus, and also, recognizing that the Hour had come, anticipated His burial by an act of intelligent devotion. In Christian piety generosity to the poor springs from the recognition of the love of God manifested in the Passion and Death of Jesus, His Son; and thus the command in Deut. xv. 11 is capable of Christian fulfilment. From Codex Bezae and the Sinaitic Syriac *v.* 8 is omitted. Perhaps the verse was added by assimilation to the Matthæan narrative. But the manuscript evidence is not sufficient to justify this conclusion.

The author adds to the narrative a note emphasizing the publicity of the presence of Jesus in Bethany, and by implication also the publicity of Mary's significant act of devotion. The great crowd of Jews journeyed to Bethany not only to see Jesus, but also to see Lazarus, both of whom are under sentence of death. It was because of Lazarus, the author notes, that many of the Jews withdrew (i.e. from their obedience to the Jewish authorities, cf. vi. 67) and began to believe on Jesus. Loisy thinks that the mention of the sentence against Lazarus reflects 'the mortal hatred of Judaism for the growing Church and the method by which an attempt was made to check the defection of the Jews'.

# THE FINAL COMING TO JERUSALEM

XII. 12–50

### JESUS ENTERS JERUSALEM AND IS WELCOMED AS THE MESSIANIC KING

xii. 12. On the morrow a great multitude that had come to the feast, when they heard that Jesus was coming to Jerusalem, 13. took the branches of the palm trees, and went forth to meet him, and cried out, Hosanna: Blessed is he that cometh in the name of the Lord, even the King of Israel. 14. And Jesus, having found a young ass, sat thereon; as it is written, 15. Fear not, daughter of Zion: behold, thy King cometh, sitting on an ass's colt. 16. These things understood not his disciples at the first: but when Jesus was glorified, then remembered they that these things were written of him, and that they had done these things unto him. 17. The multitude therefore that was with him when he called Lazarus out of the tomb, and raised him from the dead, bare witness. 18. For this cause also the multitude went and met him, for that they heard that he had done this sign. 19. The Pharisees therefore said among themselves, Behold how ye prevail nothing: lo, the world is gone after him.

### JESUS ADDRESSES THE CROWD, AND IN THE PRESENCE OF HIS DISCIPLES AND OF CERTAIN GREEKS, EXPOSES THE SCANDAL OF THE CROSS

20. Now there were certain Greeks among those that went up to worship at the feast: 21. these therefore came to Philip, which was of Bethsaida of Galilee, and asked him, saying, Sir, we would see Jesus. 22. Philip cometh and telleth Andrew: Andrew cometh, and Philip, and they tell Jesus. 23. And Jesus answereth them, saying, The hour is come, that the Son of man should be glorified. 24. Verily, verily, I say unto you, Except a grain of wheat fall into the earth and die, it abideth by itself alone; but if it die, it beareth much fruit. 25. He that loveth his life loseth it; and he that hateth his life in this world shall keep it unto life eternal. 26. If any man serve me, let him follow me; and where I am, there shall also my servant be: if any man serve me, him will the Father honour. 27. Now is my soul troubled; and what shall I say? Father, save me from this hour. But for this cause came I unto this hour. 28. Father, glorify thy name. There came therefore a voice out of heaven, saying, I have both glorified it, and will glorify it again. 29. The multitude therefore, that stood by, and heard it, said that it had thundered: others said, An angel hath spoken to him. 30. Jesus answered and said, This voice hath not come for my sake, but for your sakes.

31. *Now is the judgement of this world: now shall the prince of this world be cast out.* 32. *And I, if I be lifted up from the earth, will draw all men unto myself.* 33. *But this he said, signifying by what manner of death he should die.* 34. *The multitude therefore answered him, We have heard out of the law that the Christ abideth for ever: and how sayest thou, The Son of man must be lifted up? who is this Son of man?* 35. *Jesus therefore said unto them, Yet a little while is the light among you. Walk while ye have the light, that darkness overtake you not: and he that walketh in the darkness knoweth not whither he goeth.* 36. *While ye have the light, believe on the light, that ye may become sons of light.*

*These things spake Jesus, and he departed and hid himself from them.*

## THE AUTHOR OF THE GOSPEL DECLARES THE REJECTION OF JESUS BY THE JEWS TO HAVE BEEN THE FULFILMENT OF PROPHECY AND THE DENIAL OF THE WORD OF GOD

37. *But though he had done so many signs before them, yet they believed not on him:* 38. *that the word of Isaiah the prophet might be fulfilled, which he spake,*

> *Lord, who hath believed our report?*
> *And to whom hath the arm of the Lord been revealed?*

39. *For this cause they could not believe, for that Isaiah said again,*
40. *He hath blinded their eyes, and he hardened their hearts;*

> *Lest they should see with their eyes, and perceive with their heart,*
> *And should turn,*
> *And I should heal them.*

41. *These things said Isaiah, because he saw his glory; and he spake of him.* 42. *Nevertheless, even of the rulers many believed on him; but because of the Pharisees they did not confess it, lest they should be put out of the synagogue:* 43. *for they loved the glory of men more than the glory of God.*

44. *And Jesus cried and said, He that believeth on me, believeth not on me, but on him that sent me.* 45. *And he that beholdeth me beholdeth him that sent me.* 46. *I am come a light into the world, that whosoever believeth on me may not abide in the darkness.* 47. *And if any man hear my sayings, and keep them not, I judge him not: for I came not to judge the world, but to save the world.* 48. *He that rejecteth me, and receiveth not my sayings, hath one that judgeth him: the word that I spake, the same shall judge him in the last day.* 49. *For I spake not from myself; but the Father which sent me, he hath given me a commandment, what I should say, and what I should speak.* 50. *And I know that his commandment is life eternal: the things therefore which I speak, even as the Father hath said unto me, so I speak.*

## JESUS ENTERS JERUSALEM AND IS WELCOMED AS THE MESSIANIC KING

xii. 12–19. On the next day (Sunday, if the chronological note in *v.* 1 means that Jesus had arrived in Bethany on the Saturday), the fears of the Jewish authorities are wholly justified. The great crowds of pilgrims, instead of preparing themselves quietly for the Passover (xi. 55), hearing that Jesus is on His way from Bethany and is about to enter the city, procure branches of palms, the symbol of regal triumph, and go forth to meet Him. Their cry of welcome is suited to their action, for they wrest the words of Ps. cxviii. 25, 26, from their merely liturgical setting, and apply them to a living historical person, to Jesus, the Messiah, on His entry into the Holy City: *Hosanna: Blessed is the King of Israel, that cometh in the name of the Lord.* The tumultuous welcome of the pilgrim crowd is, moreover, reinforced by the witness which the crowd of Jerusalem Jews bore who had been with Him when He *called Lazarus out of the tomb, and raised him from the dead.* The passionate messianic greeting is thus justified by the knowledge that the Messiah had already wrought a mighty and miraculous sign. The Pharisees (cf. Matt. xxi. 15; Luke xix. 39, 48) at once recognize that their plans have miscarried. The matter has gone beyond their control, and they can no longer hope to procure His death. Their words are both judgement on what is happening and a prophecy of what is to come: *Lo, the world is gone after him* (xii. 32).

Into the midst of the records of this messianic welcome the author thrusts upon the attention of his readers a single significant action of Jesus Himself. He procured an ass (in the Greek a diminutive, a young ass), and entered Jerusalem riding upon it. The action is a challenge to the crowd, for while it focuses their attention upon a regal advent of the Messiah, this regal advent is not for war, but in peace and in humility. The whole passage in Zech. ix. 9, 10, of which the action of Jesus is a conscious fulfilment, runs: *Rejoice greatly, O daughter of Zion; shout, O daughter of Jerusalem: behold, thy king cometh unto thee: he is just, and having salvation; lowly, and riding upon an ass, even upon a colt the foal of an ass. And I will cut off the chariot from Ephraim, and the horse from Jerusalem, and the battle bow shall be cut off; and he shall speak peace unto the nations: and his dominion shall be from sea to sea: and from the River to the ends of the earth.* The author does not draw out the implications of the action of Jesus, because the discourse which follows (*vv.* 23–36) makes sufficiently clear the distinction between the Messiahship of Jesus and the royal messiah whom the Jews supposed they were welcoming into the city. He is content merely to note that the disciples did not understand until later after the glorification of Jesus, either the significance of His action or the precise nature of the misunderstanding of the crowd. Presumably the disciples simply joined ignorantly in the tumult of the welcome. 'The Evangelist', writes Saint Cyril of Alexandria, 'does not blush to mention the ignorance of the disciples and again their knowledge, since his object was to take no heed of respect for men, but to plead for the glory of the Spirit'.

The Johannine narrative depends upon the Marcan narrative (Mark xi. 1–10). However, in addition to what is peculiarly Johannine, it contains certain approximations to the Lucan and Matthæan versions (Luke xix. 28–38; Matt. xxi. 1–9). In the welcome of the crowds, Luke inserts the word *King* (Luke xix. 38; Mark *Kingdom*; John *King of Israel*, cf. i. 49); and he, like John, also states that the intensity of the welcome was, in part at least, grounded upon the knowledge of the miraculous power of Jesus (Luke xix. 37, cf. Matt. xxi. 15). Matthew, like John, but unlike Mark and Luke, draws out the reference to the prophecy in Zechariah, and to this end records that the ass was accompanied by her foal (Matt. xxi. 2–5). Purely Johannine are the dating of the incident on the Sunday preceding the Passover (this is, however, seemingly implied in the Marcan chronology of the Holy Week of the Passion, but is obscured both by Matthew and Luke), the palms, the reference to the raising of Lazarus, the despairing comment of the Pharisees, the reserving of the intelligence of the disciples until after the crucifixion and resurrection of Jesus (cf. ii. 22, vii. 39, xx. 9), the suppressing of all reference to the mission of the disciples to procure the ass (the use of the word *found* in xii. 14, cf. Mark xi. 4; Luke xix. 32, seems to indicate the author's knowledge of the earlier narrative), and the emphasis laid upon the spontaneous action of the crowds in Jerusalem who *went forth* to meet Him. In the synoptic narratives it is the multitude entering the city with Jesus (Luke, *The whole multitude of the disciples*) that utters the messianic cry. The action of Jesus in procuring the ass precedes the entry into the city and occasions the cry of welcome. In the Johannine version this is reversed. The cry of welcome is the cause of the significant action of Jesus.

The Johannine word for *palms* occurs here only in the New Testament; but it is used in 1 Macc. xiii. 51 and in Symmachus' version of Song of Sol. vii. 8. The awkward Greek phrase translated *branches of the palm trees* occurs in the Testament of Naphtali (ch. v), where it is said that 'since Levi was like the sun, a man gave him twelve branches of palm-trees', i.e. as a sign that he would be the chief of all the tribes of Israel. The point here is that palms adorn the triumph of kings (Rev. vii. 9, where Charles cites 1 Macc. xiii. 51; 2 Macc. x. 7; Tertullian *Scorp.* 12). Psalm cxviii, containing the words *Hosanna; Blessed be he that cometh* (cf. xi. 27; Matt. xi. 3) *in the name of the Lord* (*vv.* 25, 26), was used for the ritual blessing by the priests of the pilgrims entering Jerusalem, especially at the Feast of Tabernacles, but also at other festivals (Strack-Billerbeck on Mark xi. 9).

The word *Hosanna* is untranslateable into Greek, as the Septuagint translator recognized by paraphrasing it with *Save now* (Luke characteristically omits the word); and into Latin, as Saint Augustine recognized: 'For in some languages there are words that cannot be translated into the idiom of another language. And this happens chiefly in the case of interjections, which are words that express an emotion of the mind rather than any part of a thought we have in our mind. And the two given above are said to be of this kind, *Racha* expressing the cry of an angry man, *Hosanna* that of a joyful man' (Augustine, *De Doct. Christ.* xi. 16). The importance of the occurrence of the word in the narrative of the Triumphal Entry is therefore not its accurate translation, but its marking of the fulfilment of an Old Testament citation and of a ritual practice among the Jews. The reference in *v.* 15 to Zech. ix. 9 is clear, but the Evangelist does not cite it verbally. He abbreviates it, substituting *Fear not, daughter of Zion* (cf. Isa. xliv. 2 and Zeph. iii. 16) for *Rejoice greatly, O daughter of Zion*. Some manuscripts (including Codex Bezae, and supported by the Latin and the Sinaitic Syriac Versions) read *the whole world* for *the world* in *v.* 19. This undoubtedly brings out the author's meaning (1 John v. 19, cf. Luke xix. 48). In the sayings of the Rabbis the Hebrew word for *the world* means *everybody*, and often has the adjective *whole* added to it (Strack-Billerbeck).

The Johannine version of the Entry into Jerusalem is occasioned by its position in the structure of the Fourth Gospel. The whole incident illustrates the complete misunderstanding of the crowds who believed on Jesus. The Jewish authorities decree His death, the crowds welcome Him as the messianic King. The incident therefore forms a fitting conclusion to that great section of the gospel which describes the unbelief of the Jews. It is the weaving of the incident into the structure of the gospel that occasions the deviations from the synoptic narratives. The palms emphasize the regal nature of the welcome, the reference to the raising of Lazarus and the despair of the Pharisees link the narrative to what has immediately preceded it, the reserving of the intelligence of the disciples rests upon the Johannine teaching about the Spirit, which was not yet given (vii. 39, cf. xiv. 25, 26, xv. 26, xvi. 13, 14). But more important still, the action of Jesus in procuring an ass and riding on it into Jerusalem is not the occasion of the tumultuous welcome. The action of Jesus is occasioned by the nature of the welcome, and is a protest against it, explained in the discourse that follows (xii. 23–36). Loisy, wholly misunderstanding the character of the Johannine narrative, here imagines that the two crowds which welcome Jesus symbolically represent converts from Palestinian Judaism and converts from Judaism dispersed among the Gentiles (p. 681). In fact, the crowds illustrate the words in the Prologue: *He came unto his own, and his own received him not* (i. 11). The ecclesiastical Palm Sunday Festival is grounded upon the Johannine version of the entry into Jerusalem: in the light of Christian faith the misunderstanding of the crowds is redressed, and the Church welcomes the Christ advancing to die for the salvation of the world.

JESUS ADDRESSES THE CROWD, AND IN THE PRESENCE
OF HIS DISCIPLES AND OF CERTAIN GREEKS, EXPOSES
THE SCANDAL OF THE CROSS

*vv.* 20–6. The dangerous messianic tumult, pregnant with revolution, is checked by the intervention neither of the Roman soldiery nor of the Jewish authorities. It is checked and ended by the action of Jesus Himself. The occasion of the discourse is the nature of the welcome given to Him by the crowd. Before recording the discourse of Jesus, the author of the gospel, however, first increases the significance of the crowd and ratifies the judgement of the Pharisees—*The world is gone after him* (*v.* 19)—by stating that it included certain Greeks who had come to Jerusalem to be present at the Passover festival, but who now desired to see Jesus (cf. Luke xix. 3; Mark vii. 26). These men were not Hellenistic Jews, named in Acts Hellenists (Acts vi. 1, ix. 29); they were Gentiles of Greek birth, attracted to the worship of Israel (cf. Luke vii. 2–10), and described as 'God-fearers' (Acts x. 2, 22, 35, xiii. 16, 26, cf. Acts xiii. 43, xvii. 4). Being foreigners they were admitted to the outer court of the Temple, but were not permitted to be present at the Passover sacrifices (Josephus, *B.J.* vi. 422–6, cf. Strack-Billerbeck) The Greeks appropriately selected Philip (i. 43, 44) as the mediator of their request, since, as the author carefully notes, he was from Bethsaida, which was situated in Galilee—*of the Gentiles* (Isa. ix. 1, cited in Matt. iv. 15. It may be doubted whether Bethsaida was strictly in Galilee: see, however, Bernard). Philip tells Andrew, who was also of Bethsaida (i. 44); and the two Apostles (vi. 5–9), who alone possessed Greek names, and who may have been connected in the author's mind with the mission to Asia Minor (see Loisy, pp. 28–31), inform Jesus of the desire of the Gentiles.

The presence of the Greeks and their desire to see Jesus, which anticipate the mission to the world (vii. 35), the gathering together of the scattered children of God (xi. 52), and the coming of the sheep from another fold (x. 16), provide the immediate occasion of the discourse which follows. *And Jesus answered them* (i.e. the disciples), *saying, The hour is come* (xiii. 1, xvii. 1, cf. Mark xiv. 41), *that the Son of man should be glorified.* The discourse is not, however, addressed to the Greeks: indeed He made no movement towards them, since their coming to Him must be deferred until after His Crucifixion and Resurrection (xii. 24, 32, 33, cf. iii. 14, vi. 53). The discourse is addressed to the disciples in the presence of the crowd (*vv.* 29, 34). The tension is, however, increased by the presence of the Greeks, as Saint Cyril of Alexandria perceived: 'Seeing therefore that the Gentiles are hastening in eager desire to see Him and to turn towards Him, on this account He says: *The hour is come.*' The approach of the Gentiles marks the glorification of Jesus;

but His death must precede, and is indeed itself the glorification upon which the further glory of Jesus depends (vii. 39, xiii. 31, 32, cf. xi. 4, 16). The economy of salvation is like the story of a grain of wheat. There is no fruit apart from death and burial (1 Cor. xv. 36, 37). If it be not buried in the ground, it remains what it is, just a single isolated, unproductive grain of wheat (vi. 15, 35, 51). Death is the only means whereby it can be multiplied and produce much fruit (xv. 8). The law of nature is the law of the Word of God (cf. Mark iv. 3–9, &c., cf. Clement 1 *Cor.* xxvii). The reference here is not, as Holtzmann suggested, to the mysteries of Demeter. The true disciples of the Son of God do not cling to life with passionate affection—this is unproductive and permanent death; rather, they hate life in this world, and, by the paradox of the law of God, they preserve it for ever. Service unto death is the only guarantee of eternal life. Christian service is to follow as the original disciples followed Him (i. 37–44, viii. 12, x. 4, 5, 27, xiii. 36, 37, xxi. 19–22, cf. Mark i. 18, &c.) and the reward is to be with Him in heaven (xiv. 3, xvii. 24). To serve Jesus, that is to live according to the sequence obedience-death-life, is to live the life which is honoured by the Father. In these two verses (*vv.* 25, 26), the author reproduces and, to some extent (see Lagrange), clarifies for his readers the teaching of Jesus scattered about in all the various strata of the synoptic tradition —in Mark (Mark viii. 35–8, ix. 35, x. 42–5); in Q (Matt. x. 39; Luke xvii. 33); in Special Matthew (Matt. xxv. 31–46); in Special Luke (Luke xiv. 25–35, containing the word *hate*; xvii. 7–10, xxii. 24–34).

But the parable of the grain of wheat is not applied primarily to the lives of the disciples of Jesus, as though their fruitful obedience to the will of God was to burst forth independently on its own. They are the fruit of the isolated (xvi. 32) obedience and death of Jesus; and their fruitfulness springs from His death, and is joined organically to it. Thus the parable has its primary reference to His death on the Cross, which is the necessary prelude to the mission to the world: *I, if I be lifted up from the earth, will draw* (cf. vi. 44) *all men unto myself. But this he said, signifying* (cf. xviii. 32, xxi. 19) *by what manner of death he should die* (iii. 14–17, viii. 28). The universality of the significance of the death of Jesus (xi. 51, 52) is the answer to the request of the Greeks to see or come to know Him, and explains why He can as yet enter into no direct relation with them. They will believe on Him through the preaching of His disciples (xvii. 20).

*vv.* 27–36. The obedience of Jesus and of His disciples unto death is no easy and passionless obedience to the will of God (xvi. 1, 2). Consequently, the natural movement of the discourse is interrupted by the Johannine reference to the Agony of Jesus, recorded in greater detail by the earlier evangelists in their narratives of what took place in the Garden of Gethsemane immediately before the Arrest (Mark xiv. 34–6 and parallels). *Now is my soul troubled.* These words (cf. xi. 33–8, xiii. 21) do not merely echo Mark xiv. 33. They refer even more directly to the agony of the servant of God described in Ps. xlii. 5, 6, lv. 4, 5 (LXX, cf. Lam. ii. 11). And yet, precisely in the overcoming of this trembling in the presence of death is set the obedience of the Son to the will of the Father. This obedience is the glorification of the Father's name, and constitutes the foundation of the Christian religion (Heb. v. 7–10). The thought that the necessity of obedience unto death might be removed or the prayer for its removal—since it is uncertain whether the Greek should be translated as a double interrogative: *What shall I say? Father, save me from this hour?* (R.V. mg.); or as a prayer: *Father, save me from this hour* (A.V., R.V.)—is crushed, almost before it is uttered, into an act of complete surrender: *Father, glorify thy name.* The surrender of the Son of God is based upon the clear recognition that the hour of His death is imposed upon Him by divine necessity and that precisely in His obedience the purpose of His coming into the world is fulfilled (xix. 30): *For this cause came I unto this hour.* The obedience of Jesus is marked at once by its public ratification in the presence of the crowd. *There came therefore a voice out of heaven, saying, I have both glorified it, and will glorify it again.* This external divine witness to the glory of God manifested in the whole concrete appearance of Jesus of Nazareth was was not for the encouragement of Jesus (cf. xi. 41, 42). He needed no external sign to ratify His union with the Father. He is in the Father and the Father in Him (x. 38, xiv. 10, xvii. 21, cf. x. 30) and He hath the witness in Himself (cf. 1 John v. 10). The voice from heaven was the Father's public witness to the crowd of His acceptance of the obedience of the Son (1 John v. 9), just as at the Transfiguration the voice from heaven came for the sake of the disciples and not for the encouragement of Jesus: *This is my beloved Son: hear ye him* (Mark ix. 7; Matt. xvii. 5, 6; Luke ix. 31 definitely relates the Transfiguration to the death of Jesus). Matthew's editing of the Marcan narrative of the Baptism of Jesus emphasizes in precisely similar fashion the significance of the voice from heaven (Mark i. 11, cf. Matt. iii. 17), and Luke shows a similar desire by adding that the Holy Ghost descended upon him *in a bodily form,* as *a dove* (Luke iii. 22).

The concrete obedience of the Son is not only ratified in public by the Father Himself; it explains the universal significance of the Death of Jesus, and marks the moment of the dethronement of the Devil from his tyranny over men. In the light of the victory of Jesus over the disobedience of the world enslaved in the power of the Devil (xiv. 30, xvi. 11), the world itself is set under the judgement of God (iii. 18, 19, v. 22, 24, 30, xvi. 8–11): *Now is the judgement of this world: now shall the prince of this world be cast out. And I, if I be lifted up from the earth, will draw all men unto myself.* That is, the obedience of Jesus and His victory over the world (xvi. 33) will expand in the obedience and victory of His disciples (1 John ii. 13, 14, v. 4, 5; Rev. ii. 7, 11, 17, 26, &c.), who will come to Him not only from the Jews, but from the Gentiles also. Herein is the manifestation of the dethronement of the Devil. In the thought of the author of the Fourth Gospel the death of Jesus has therefore no magical setting. Its efficacy depends upon His obedience to the will of God wrought out in flesh and blood, and upon the obedience of His disciples wrought out likewise in flesh and blood through union with Him (Rev. xii. 11), since perfect love casteth out fear (1 John iv. 18).

For the Devil as the Prince of this World cf. Matt. iv. 8, 9; Luke iv. 6; 2 Cor. iv. 4; Eph. ii. 2, vi. 12; Ignatius *Eph.* xvii, xix. The Midrash on Exod. xxiv. 7 runs: 'God called to Satan, Although I have made thee Ruler of the World (*Cosmocrator*) over mankind, yet thou hast nothing to do with this nation (Israel), for they are my children' (Strack-Billerbeck): for the dethronement of the Devil (*cast down* in the Sinaitic Syriac and Old Latin Versions, and in Chrysostom) cf. Luke x. 18 (cf. also Matt. xii. 28; Luke xi. 20), 1 Cor. ii. 6; Col. ii. 14, 15, contrasted with the elevation of the Christ (Rev. xii. 7-12, xx. 1-6).

Some modern commentators, misunderstanding the significance of this passage, as they had misunderstood xi. 41, 42, regard it as a Johannine method of escaping from the record of the Agony in the Garden of Gethsemane. Thus Loisy (p. 689): 'The Johannine Christ could not pray as the synoptic Christ could. Since His divine will was that of the Father, He could no more submit to the Agony of Gethsemane than to the temptation by the Devil in the desert. He was above human conditions.' Bauer comments: 'The spoken words of Jesus are no genuine prayer, as the immediate discarding of the thought and the *Not for my sake*, which follows in *v.* 30, prove.' Holtzmann is satisfied with noting that the words of Jesus are a 'reflection in the form of a prayer'.

The crowd hears the sound of the voice from heaven, but does not understand its meaning. Some judge it to be the sound of thunder (Exod. ix. 23 sqq.; Job xxxvii. 4, 5; Ps. xxix. 3-9; Jer. x. 13), others suppose an angel to have spoken to Jesus (Gen. xxii. 11; Luke xxii. 43; 1 Cor. xiii. 1). No one perceives that it is the voice of God (Acts xi. 7; Rev. x. 4) and that He has spoken to them words of supreme importance. The people do, however, understand the meaning of the words of Jesus. At least, they now understand His removal to be imminent, and they perceive that He has shattered their hopes that He would act as the Messiah. He had said that the Son of man would be lifted up from the earth (iii. 14, viii. 28); but the Law (i.e. the Scriptures, cf. x. 34) promised them a Messiah who would abide for ever. Who then is this Son of man? It seems almost as if they rightly understood the words *lifted up* to mean *die*. The scandal of the Cross is meaningless to them (1 Cor. i. 18-25; Gal. v. 11) and the paradox, The Christ must suffer (cf. Mark viii. 31), puts an end to their welcome of Jesus as the Messiah of the Jews. They had welcomed in Him the permanent and glorious messianic king; He declares the necessity of His imminent death and removal. To their question, *Who is this Son of man?* that is, *Who is this Messiah?*—for in this passage the Jews rightly understand the phrase *Son of man* to be equivalent to the Messiah (see, however, Bernard)—Jesus gives them no answer than can satisfy them. He repeats language He had used before (vii. 33, viii. 12, ix. 4, 5, cf. i. 4, iii. 19–21). The Light is but temporarily in their midst. It is the hour of their judgement. The issue is clear. They must either believe in Him, walk in the Light, and thus themselves become sons of light (i. 12; Luke xvi. 8; 1 Thess. v. 5; Eph. v. 8), or the darkness will overtake them (i. 5, cf. vi. 17), and they will know not whither they go, as they pass to their inevitable destruction (viii. 21, ix. 4, xi. 9, 10; 1 John ii. 11). This is the last appeal to the Jews in the Johannine narrative. The public ministry of Jesus is ended, and the separation between the Messiah and His own people (i. 11) is complete. Henceforward He speaks only to His disciples and to Pilate. The darkness has descended upon them.

The opinion of the Jews that according to the Scriptures the dominion of the Messiah would *abide for ever* is here seemingly grounded upon Dan. vii. 13, 14, since the Messiah is named *Son of man*. For the permanence of the reign of the Messiah see also Ps. cx. 4; Is. ix. 6. In the immediately pre-Christian Jewish literature the messianic age was regarded as the end of history, and consequently as eternal. *The glory of the Messiah will never fail* (1 Enoch xli. 1, cf. xlix. 1, lxii. 14). *The Messiah will possess the sceptre over the whole world for ever and ever* (Sib. Or. iii. 49, 50, cf. Pss. Sol. xvii. 4). In later Rabbinic thought the messianic age was regarded as limited in time and as a definite epoch (see Strack-Billerbeck).

THE AUTHOR OF THE GOSPEL DECLARES THE REJECTION OF JESUS BY THE JEWS TO HAVE BEEN THE FULFILMENT OF PROPHECY AND THE DENIAL OF THE WORD OF GOD

*vv.* 37–43. Before proceeding to the record of the final teaching delivered by Jesus to His disciples, the author rounds off the story of His public ministry by a comment of his own upon the unbelief of the Jews—and yet, it is not a comment of his own, since he does but expand the Lord's own explanation of Jewish unbelief recorded in the earlier tradition (Mark iv. 12; Matt. xiii. 14, 15; Luke viii. 10) and made use of by the Apostles in their defence of the Gospel (Acts xxviii. 26, 27, cf. Rom. x. 16). To this explanation the author adds a concise statement by Jesus Himself concerning the ultimate significance of His teaching and the ultimate destiny of those who reject it.

Having publicly declared the necessity of the death of the Messiah and of His own imminent removal from this world (*vv.* 24–36), Jesus departed and was hidden from the Jews. And so, the author comments, in spite of the number of miraculous signs He had wrought in their midst and before their very eyes, yet they did not believe in Him. Though he has himself elected to record only a few miraculous actions of Jesus, the reference here is not merely to the significance of the miracles (signs), but to their number (vii. 31, xi. 47). The A.V. R.V. translation *so many* rather than *so great* is justified by vi. 9, xxi. 11. The reader is supposed to be familiar with the earlier tradition (xx. 30). The fact of the unbelief of the Jews is, however, only superficially a scandal to Christian faith (cf. Rom. ix–xi). Rightly understood in the light of the Old Testament Scriptures it is the ground of the manifestation of the inevitable judgement of God upon unbelief. The unbelief of the Jews is not a problem; it is the precise fulfilment of prophecy (cf. Isa. xlii. 19–25; Jer. v. 21–9; Ezek. xii. 2–16). The prophet Isaiah saw the Lord (Isa. vi. 1–3). To the Evangelist this vision of the prophet was not a naked vision of God (i. 18), but a vision of the future glory of Jesus the Messiah (cf. viii. 56) and of His earthly mission to His own people. The words which the prophet spoke concerning the unbelief of the people of God therefore refer to the mission of Jesus, for *He spake of him*. In the light of this vision of the Christ (some manuscripts, including Codex Bezae, read *when he saw* for *because he saw*) two passages are selected as of supreme significance. The Evangelist selects first the words which introduce the prophecy of the despised and rejected slave of God: *Lord, who hath believed our report? and to whom hath the arm of the Lord been revealed?* (Isa. liii. 1). He cites the passage verbally from the LXX version (cf. Rom. x. 16. The Hebrew does not contain the address *Lord*), understanding by *our report* (lit. *that which they heard from us*) the teaching which the Jews heard from Jesus and which Jesus received from His Father (*v.* 49), and by *the arm of the Lord* the mighty actions (Luke i. 51; Acts xiii. 17) of Jesus which were the works of His Father (v. 19–21). No doubt in the perspective of the author's thought *our report* alludes also to the transmission of the teaching of Jesus through the preaching of His disciples (xvii. 20), and *the arm of the Lord* refers also to the mighty works wrought through His Apostles (xiv. 12); but the reference to the ministry of Jesus is primary. Neither the truth which Jesus proclaimed nor the miracles which He wrought moved the Jews to faith. The Evangelist then introduces a second passage from the prophecies of Isaiah, not merely to reinforce the first and to show that the unbelief of the Jews should occasion no surprise, but in order to emphasize its divine inevitability. *For this cause they could not believe, for that Isaiah said again.* The passage now cited (Isa. vi. 9, 10) occurs in the actual context of Isaiah's vision and gains its peculiar significance from this context. The prophecy of the unbelief of the Jews is the direct consequence of the prophet's vision of the Christ, and the words in which it is foretold are spoken to the Prophet by the Christ Himself. The words of the prophecy agree verbally neither with the original Hebrew nor with the LXX version (cited in Matt. xiii. 15 and in Acts xxviii. 26, 27). But it is the LXX version that seems to form the background of the Johannine citation, since the words *and I should heal them* belong to the LXX and not to the Hebrew text. The alterations are best explained by the intention of the writer of the gospel to emphasize the judgement as the action of God (cf. Isa. xliv. 18). Consequently he writes *He hath blinded their eyes* for *their eyes they have closed* (LXX), and *He hardened their heart* for *the heart of this people was hardened* (LXX). Moreover, the reference to the hearing of the people in the Hebrew and in the LXX is omitted, because the thought of the author is concentrated here upon the miracles of Jesus wrought before the eyes of the Jews rather than upon His teaching. The meaning of the prophecy is then that the Christ revealed to the prophet that God would blind the eyes of the Jews lest they should perceive the significance of His miracles, and He (the Christ) would then of necessity heal them, and consequently obscure the judgement of God upon unbelief.

The passage therefore reads like the crudest possible statement of a naked doctrine of predestination. And yet it can be confidently stated that this is not the intention of the author. Nowhere in the Johannine writings does the problem of the relation between the will of God and human freedom appear above the horizon, and it is therefore important for their interpretation to avoid the temptation of reading them in the light of later controversies. The Johannine language inevitably causes a controversy concerning predestination, but there is no evidence whatever that the controversy gave rise to the Johannine language. Throughout his gospel the author insists that, though the life and death of Jesus in the flesh was for the salvation of the world, this very fact involved the ultimate judgement of God upon those who rejected Him. It is the clear recognition of the alternative of judgement or salvation that provides the acute tension which runs through his narrative from beginning to end. The Jews did reject Jesus, and consequently they remain dead in their sins (viii. 21, 24) and under the judgement of God (v. 48). The Jews are manifestly culpable, since the Evangelist has recorded the mission of Jesus in such a manner as to exclude the thought that it was impossible for them to recognize Him as the Son of God. The purpose of his final summary of the public ministry of Jesus is not to deny the whole tenor of his narrative, but to point out that the rejection of the Messiah by His own people ought not to surprise those familiar with the Old Testament Scriptures. He therefore sees in the foresight of the prophet Isaiah the foresight of God Himself; and, in accordance with the natural instinct of those who are filled with the sense of the power of God (vi. 44), teaching concerning divine foresight passes over into the expression of the inevitability of that which is foreseen. Hence he ends his summary with a glaring paradox: *For this cause they could not believe. . . . Nevertheless even of the rulers many believed on him.* That is, in addition to many of the common people, many of the Jewish authorities also believed (iii. 1, vii. 47–50, xix. 38, 39). It is true that these Jewish believers did not, for fear of excommunication from Judaism (ix. 22), openly confess Him. Their action was no doubt timid and unsatisfactory. They preferred the glory of men to the glory of God. But was it more reprehensible than the behaviour of the disciples who scattered to their own homes and left Jesus to die alone, without any human companions (xvi. 32)? These timid believers did, in fact, later become the nucleus of the new Israel of God. The truth then lies precisely in the paradox: *They could not believe—Nevertheless many believed.* And this is no naked doctrine of predestination. If therefore, this passage be set in the context of later controversies, the commentator is compelled to gloss the words *they could not* by *they would not*, as Chrysostom did; but something is lost by such a simplification. The Evangelist is, however, not satisfied merely to declare the unbelief of the Jews to have been the fulfilment of prophecy. More important is it to define precisely the nature of that unbelief, and to explain why the unbelieving Jews stand under the judgement of God (Matt. xxiii. 37–9; Luke xiii. 34, 35). Accordingly he adds what is, in form, a new discourse of Jesus Himself, but, in fact, a summary of the main points in the teaching of Jesus already related and about to be related. The verses thus contain no new teaching: *v.* 44, cf. iii. 15, 16, v. 36–8, 46, vi. 29, 35, 40, vii. 38, viii. 19, 24, 42, 45, 46, xiii. 20; *v.* 45, cf. i. 18, vi. 40, viii. 19, 42, x. 30, 38, xiv. 7, 9; *v.* 46, cf. i. 4, 5, viii. 12, ix. 5, xii. 35, 36; *v.* 47, cf. iii. 17, v. 24, viii. 15, 31; *v.* 48, cf. iii. 18, v. 45, viii. 40; *vv.* 49, 50, cf. v. 30, vi. 38, vii. 16, 17, viii. 28, 38, x. 18, xiv. 10.

*vv.* 44–50. The meaning of the teaching of Jesus is unmistakable. He did not merely speak; He *cried* (i. 15, vii. 28, 37) in language which was clear and precise. Unlike the Jews, He loved the glory of God, rather than the glory of men. Christian faith is not a cult of Jesus; it is faith in God (xiii. 20; Matt. x. 40; Luke ix. 48; 1 Thess. i. 9). Faith therefore does not rest in Jesus, but in the Father who sent Him and commissioned Him. There cannot, moreover, be two objects of faith or of sight. To see Jesus is to see the Father, since He is in the Father and the Father in Him. It is this faith and this sight alone that are entirely effective for human salvation, since by them the believer is removed from the sphere of darkness. Jesus came into the world as the Light of the world, in order that all who believe in Him should not abide in darkness. The Truth which He was is therefore the ground of life; and it is necessary not merely to hear the words of Jesus, but to guard them and abide in them (cf. Matt. vii. 26; Luke vi. 46, 47). Those who do not guard the words of Jesus as the active rule of life stand under the judgement of God. It was no part of the mission of Jesus to decree their judgement. He came to save the world, not to judge it (cf. Luke ix. 56 A.V.). Yet the judgement of God is implicit in the advent of Jesus, the Saviour of the world; inasmuch as he who rejects Jesus and does not accept His teaching, has *Him that judgeth him*. He stands under the judgement of God. At the last day the criterion of the final judgement is precise; it is the teaching of Jesus, which is the word of God. The Son of God did not originate His teaching (cf. Deut. xviii. 18). He proclaimed the word of God as the commandment of His Father, who sent Him and gave Him what he should say and utter. This commandment of God received and delivered by Jesus is eternal life (vi. 63; 1 John ii. 25). Consequently, its rejection (Luke x. 16, cf. 1 Thess. iv. 8) is the complete and final avoidance of life (cf. Luke ix. 23–5). *The things therefore which I speak, even as the Father hath said unto me, so I speak.*

Thus the author does not conclude his narrative of the rejection of Jesus by the Jews with a mere statement that it was the fulfilment of prophecy. He ends by declaring, as authoritatively as he can, what that rejection was. It was the denial of God. For this reason the Jews must bear all the consequences of that denial. The rearrangement of the text which Bernard suggested (commentary, and introduction, p. xxv) without any manuscript support whatever, and by which *vv.* 44–50 are transposed so as to follow *v.* 36a, is consequently not only unnecessary, but almost intolerable.

# THE EVE OF THE CRUCIFIXION

ON THE EVE OF THE CRUCIFIXION
JESUS REVEALS THE TRUTH TO HIS DISCIPLES

THE reader of the gospel is abruptly translated into the room where Jesus for the last time partook of a meal with His disciples. According to the earlier tradition this was marked by peculiarly solemn and obscure words and actions of Jesus. These words and actions related the meal to His death, so that the sharing in the bread and wine placed the disciples within the new order to be inaugurated by the death of the Messiah (Mark xiv. 22–5; Matt. xxvi. 26–9; Luke xxii. 15–20). In the Marcan narrative the events leading up to the assembling of the disciples in the Upper Room are carefully recorded, and both Matthew and Luke depend here upon Mark. But the account of what took place in the Upper Room is described with such reserve in Mark and Matthew as to be almost unintelligible. Jesus first refers to the Betrayer in their midst, but does not unmask him, and then acts and speaks with even greater obscurity. Luke, aware of the importance of the scene, and aware also of its obscurity, records first the solemn action of Jesus, then the reference to the Betrayal, and then adds what is almost a discourse of Jesus (Luke xxii. 24–38), opening with the paradox of that authority which consists in service: *I am in the midst of you as he that serveth* (Luke xxii. 27). Luke has set this teaching, not, as Mark did (Mark x. 41–5), in relation to a prophecy of the death of the Messiah (Mark x. 38, 39, 45), but in the context of the Passion itself. The words are therefore explanatory, not only of the death of Jesus, but also, to some extent, of the meaning of the words and actions of Jesus in the Upper Room as recorded in the Marcan narrative.

The Johannine narrative is wholly controlled by the need of that interpretation of which Luke had already been conscious. How great that need was is made clear by the fact that the author of the Fourth Gospel twice, in ch. vi as well as in chs. xiii–xvii, undertakes the authoritative interpretation of the words spoken in the Upper Room. The readers of the gospel are presumed to be familiar with the earlier tradition. Consequently, the author omits to record the events which led to the assembling of the disciples in the Upper Room. He substitutes for these events a brief theological introduction to the Passion of Jesus (xiii. 1–3). Similarly, he omits the repetition of the Marcan narrative of what Jesus had said and done in the Upper Room. He passes at once to the interpretation of these words and actions, since their understanding is not merely the understanding of an isolated Saying or action of Jesus; it is the understanding of the truth which is the Christian Religion. The Johannine authoritative revelation of the truth contained in the earlier narrative of what Jesus had said and done during the night in which He was betrayed (1 Cor. xi. 23) consists of a significant action of Jesus—He washed the feet of His disciples (xiii. 4–11)—followed by explanatory words (xiii. 12–20) that to some extent overlap with the Lucan sayings (Luke xxii. 24 sqq.) of the record of the final departure of the false disciple from the company of Jesus and of His faithful disciples (xiii. 21–30); of a long discourse (xiii. 31–xvi. 33), broken into two parts by the words *Arise, let us go hence* (xiv. 31, cf. Mark xiv. 42), in which the nature of the new order consequent upon the glorification of Jesus is made manifest to His disciples; and lastly, the whole substance of the teaching is gathered up in the prayer in which Jesus, confident of His imminent glorification, offers Himself to the Father, and intercedes for His disciples who remain in the world and for those who will believe through their teaching (xvii).

# THE EVE OF THE CRUCIFIXION

## I

## THE SIGNIFICANT ACTION OF JESUS AND THE TREACHEROUS DEPARTURE OF JUDAS

### XIII. 1-30

#### THE THEOLOGICAL INTRODUCTION TO THE NARRATIVE OF THE PASSION

xiii. 1. *Now before the feast of the passover, Jesus knowing that his hour was come that he should depart out of this world unto the Father, having loved his own which were in the world, he loved them unto the end. 2. And during supper, the devil having already put into the heart of Judas Iscariot, Simon's son, to betray him, 3. Jesus, knowing that the Father had given all things into his hands, and that he came forth from God, and goeth unto God,*

#### JESUS WASHES HIS DISCIPLES' FEET

*4. riseth from supper, and layeth aside his garments; and he took a towel, and girded himself. 5. Then he poureth water into the bason, and began to wash the disciples' feet, and to wipe them with the towel wherewith he was girded. 6. So he cometh to Simon Peter. He saith unto him, Lord, dost thou wash my feet? 7. Jesus answered and said unto him, What I do thou knowest not now; but thou shalt understand hereafter. 8. Peter saith unto him, Thou shalt never wash my feet. Jesus answered him, If I wash thee not, thou hast no part with me. 9. Simon Peter saith unto him, Lord, not my feet only, but also my hands and my head. 10. Jesus saith to him, He that is bathed needeth not save to wash his feet, but is clean every whit: and ye are clean, but not all. 11. For he knew him that should betray him; therefore said he, Ye are not all clean.*

#### THE NATURE OF TRUE DISCIPLESHIP OF JESUS

*12. So when he had washed their feet, and taken his garments, and sat down again, he said unto them, Know ye what I have done to you? 13. Ye call me, Master, and, Lord: and ye say well; for so I am. 14. If I then, the Lord and the Master, have washed your feet, ye also ought to wash one another's feet. 15. For I have given you an example, that ye also should do as I have done to you. 16.*

434

*Verily, verily, I say unto you, A servant is not greater than his lord; neither one that is sent greater than he that sent him.* 17. *If ye know these things, blessed are ye if ye do them.* 18. *I speak not of you all: I know whom I have chosen: but that the scripture may be fulfilled, He that eateth my bread lifted up his heel against me.* 19. *From henceforth I tell you before it come to pass, that, when it is come to pass, ye may believe that I am he.* 20. *Verily, verily, I say unto you, He that receiveth whomsoever I send receiveth me; and he that receiveth me receiveth him that sent me.*

## THE JUDGEMENT OF JUDAS

21. *When Jesus had thus said, he was troubled in the spirit, and testified, and said, Verily, verily, I say unto you, that one of you shall betray me.* 22. *The disciples looked one on another, doubting of whom he spake.* 23. *There was at the table reclining in Jesus' bosom one of his disciples, whom Jesus loved.* 24. *Simon Peter therefore beckoneth to him, and saith unto him, Tell us who it is of whom he speaketh.* 25. *He leaning back, as he was, on Jesus' breast saith unto him, Lord, who is it?* 26. *Jesus therefore answereth, He it is, for whom I shall dip the sop, and give it him. So when he had dipped the sop, he taketh and giveth it to Judas, the son of Simon Iscariot.* 27. *And after the sop, then entered Satan into him. Jesus therefore saith unto him, That thou doest, do quickly.* 28. *Now no man at the table knew for what intent he spake this unto him.* 29. *For some thought, because Judas had the bag, that Jesus said unto him, Buy what things we have need of for the feast; or, that he should give something to the poor.* 30; *He then having received the sop went out straightway: and it was night.*

## THEOLOGICAL INTRODUCTION TO THE NARRATIVE OF THE PASSION

xiii. 1–3. The hour of the death of the Messiah has come (cf. xii. 23. Luke xxii. 14, contrast ii. 4, vii. 6), and Judas has accepted the diabolical suggestion that he should betray Him (cf. xiii. 27). Jesus, however, knew, not only that the Passover Festival would be inaugurated by His death, and that one of His chosen disciples would betray Him (vi. 64, 70, 71, xiii. 11, 18, 19), but also what the significance of His death must be. Consequently, during the final meal (some manuscripts followed by A.V. read *and supper being ended*; but see *vv.* 12, 26) and *before the feast of the passover,* since, in the Johannine chronology, the Last Supper was not the Jewish Passover (xviii. 29), Jesus initiated His disciples into the significance of His death.

The author of the gospel summarizes the significance of the Hour of the death of Jesus in four phrases which are to be interpreted in the following chapters, and emphatically states the foreknowledge of Jesus. Jesus knew *that he should depart out of this world unto the Father, that the Father had given all things into his hands, and that he came forth from God, and goeth unto God.* Consequently, *having loved his own which were in the world, he loved them unto the end.* The death of Jesus is therefore the return of the emissary of God to His Father in heaven, and the Father has placed in His hands the whole efficacy of salvation (iii. 34, 35). But the death of Jesus is not merely the return to the Father. It is in itself an end, since it is the final and complete act of the love of the Son of God for those whom He had gathered out of the world—for His own disciples. That is to say, the ministry of the love of God finds its complete expression in the death of His Son for the salvation of the world (iii. 14–16, xix. 30). *He loved them unto the end* is not a mere chronological statement, *He loved them at the end* (Luke xviii. 5; Creed, in his commentary upon Saint Luke's Gospel, translates: *Lest her visits end in causing me great trouble*); nor does it mean *He loved them to the end* (Mark xiii. 13, cf. Ps. ix. 18, LXX version), that is, always, to the end of His earthly life; it means, He loved them completely and finally, to the uttermost, unto death (Ps. lxxiv. 1, LXX version; 1 Thess. ii. 16, cf. Phil. ii. 8).

## JESUS WASHES HIS DISCIPLES' FEET

*vv.* 4–11. In interpreting the *Pedilavium* the modern commentator has a somewhat complicated heritage. Most commentators begin by seeing in it a lesson in humility (*v.* 15), as though the Lord intends to reinforce an ethical truth by a concrete example. Some commentators (Chrysostom, Tillmann, Lagrange) not only begin, but end here. It is a lesson in condescension. Others, and pre-eminently Loisy, treat the narrative as primarily sacramental and symbolical; that is, it rests upon the Christian sacraments of Baptism and the Eucharist, and interprets them.

Thus Loisy, commenting on *v.* 9, writes 'The assertion of the Saviour refers to the Christian mysteries, Baptism and the Eucharist, and proclaims the necessity of both by relating them to the single symbol of the living water, to the single idea of salvation procured by the death and resurrection of Jesus', and again, 'Without the humiliation of the death of the Messiah there are no sacraments, and without the sacraments there is no union of the Christian with his Saviour.' Bauer (p. 167), following Loisy, writes, 'The deeper meaning of this episode concerns the two Christian Mysteries, Baptism, which effects a general cleansing of the unbeliever, and the Lord's Supper, which repeatedly cleanses the Christians, whose feet are ever soiled by contact with this finite world.' Against all this symbolism Lagrange vigorously protests. Now, it cannot be doubted that the author of the Fourth Gospel is writing for Christians who have been cleansed by Baptism and who share in the Christian Eucharist. The discourse to Nicodemus (iii. 1 sqq.), and the discourse which follows the Feeding of the Five Thousand (vi. 22 sqq.), are otherwise hardly intelligible. But the two sacraments are not detached in the thought of the author in such a manner as to justify the language of Loisy and Bauer. For him the whole life of the Christian *Ecclesia* depends upon the manifestation of the love of God in the death of the Messiah, and it is his aim to hold his readers firmly to that truth. Purification from sin, and the mutual affection which binds together the faithful Christians, are grounded upon the historical fact of the complete obedience of Jesus to the will of His Father and of His humiliation unto death. Baptism and the Eucharist are, of course, illuminated by the clarity of the author's perception of the historical foundation of Christian faith, and he is fully aware that this is so. But he is not preoccupied with two sacraments, as Loisy seems to be; he is preoccupied with the Jesus of History, with His life, death, and resurrection, and he is confident that this preoccupation ensures the spiritual and true understanding of the nature of the Church. The new order or covenant, which is the manifestation of the love of God in human life, is historically conditioned by the humiliation of Jesus unto death. This is the meaning of the Lord's words in the earlier tradition—the Covenant in His blood (Mark xiv. 24, and parallels)—and it is their significance which is drawn out in the *Pedilavium*. Consequently, the washing of the disciples' feet rests upon and interprets the death of the Lord, and is not a detached action containing in itself a merely ethical lesson. Not only is such ethical teaching beyond the horizon of the Fourth Gospel, but the context of the incident and the manner of its narration alike forbid it to be thus interpreted.

The Hour of the death of the Messiah has come (*v.* 1); Judas is about to betray Jesus (*vv.* 2, 11, 18, 27, 30); the faithful disciples are to remain in the world, but Peter will lay down his life (*vv.* 36–8); and Jesus, *having loved his own which were in the world, . . . loved them to the uttermost* (*v.* 1, R.V. mg.). This is the context in which the *Pedilavium* is recorded.

Jesus *riseth from supper, and layeth aside his garments; and he took a towel, and girded himself.* In the Greek the words *layeth aside his garments* and the corresponding words in *v.* 12 *had taken his garments*, are strikingly significant, since the verbs *lay aside* and *take* have been previously used with reference to the death and resurrection of Jesus. *Therefore doth the Father love me, because I lay down my life, that I may take it again* (x. 17, 18, cf. x. 11, 15, xiii. 37, 38, xv. 13; 1 John iii. 16). The girding with the towel marks the action of a slave; compare the Midrash on Abraham's dismissal of Hagar (Gen. xxi. 14), 'Abraham dismissed her with a bill of divorcement and took a cloth and girded it about her loins, that men might know her to be a slave' (Strack-Billerbeck). The Lord, having thus removed His clothes and assumed the vesture of a slave, undertakes the action of a slave. He poured water into a basin, and began to wash the disciples' feet and wipe them with the towel. To wash the feet of their masters belonged to the duties of slaves (1 Sam. xxv. 41). According to Rabbinic teaching, slaves of Jewish birth were not bound to perform this menial action, though wives were expected to wash the feet of their husbands (Strack-Billerbeck, and Excursus on *Das Altjüdische Sklavenwesen*, I, 3, d, and II, 1, d, vol. IV, pp. 712, 717 seq.).

There is no indication in the text of any particular order of Apostolic precedence. Jesus *began to wash* (probably here a genuine usage of the verb *begin*, unlike its pleonastic use in the synoptic gospels, e.g. Mark ii. 23, see *J.T.S.* 1924, pp. 390 sqq.) the feet of His disciples, and, in the course of so doing, He came to Simon Peter. Chrysostom supposed that Judas was first washed, Origen that Peter came last because he was least in need of cleansing, Augustine, that the action began with Peter, the chief of the Apostles (see Lagrange). Peter vigorously and emphatically protests, the pronouns in the Greek being emphatic, *Lord, dost* thou *wash* my *feet?* The contrast is not between the humiliation of Jesus and the pride of Peter, for there is no pride in Peter's words. The contrast is between the knowledge of Jesus which is the ground of His action, and the ignorance of Peter, who does not as yet perceive that the humiliation of the Messiah is the effective cause of Christian salvation (cf. Mark viii. 32 sqq.). The answer of Jesus draws out this contrast: *What I do thou knowest not now; but thou shalt understand hereafter.* As Origen well perceived, these words mark the mysterious nature of the action of Jesus. It is no mere action of humility, such as would have been the case if Jesus had undertaken to perform a normal act of feet-washing before a meal (Luke vii. 44, cf. Gen. xviii. 4, 5, xxiv. 32, 33). The meal has already been begun, if not concluded, when Jesus rises to perform an act so impressive and symbolical that the disciples can understand its meaning only in the light of later events. For the present, implicit obedience alone is demanded of them. In the perspective of the Johannine thought the words, *thou shalt understand hereafter*, do not refer primarily to the explanation given in *vv.* 12–17, which is itself only a partial revelation, but to the spiritual understanding granted to the disciples after the Resurrection through the gift of the Spirit of Truth (ii. 22, vii. 39, xii. 16, xiv. 25, 26, xv. 26, xvi. 13, xx. 9). Peter persists in his active ignorance and asserts his determination never to be thus cleansed. Jesus then declares that his refusal (there is no reference now to the feet only, *if I wash thee not*) excludes him from the society of his Master. There is no place in the society of Christians for those who have not been purified by Jesus Himself. For the phrase *thou hast no part with me* meaning *thou hast no place with me*, cf. Matt. xxiv. 51; Luke xii. 46; 2 Cor. vi. 14–16; Ps. l. 18, R.V. mg.; 1 Kings xii. 16. Peter, then, as though union with Jesus depended on the physical extent of the symbolical act, offers every available part of his body to be washed. The answer of Jesus is exceedingly difficult to interpret, partly because the text is uncertain, and partly because, whatever text be adopted, the meaning is obscure. Codex Sinaiticus, and the original text of the Vulgate, according to Wordsworth and White, supported by Tertullian, Optatus, Augustine (*Ep.* xliv. 10, but not in his commentary) and above all by Origen, omit the words *save* and *his feet*, so that the text runs: *He that is bathed needeth not to wash, but is clean every whit.* The rest of the manuscript evidence supports the longer reading, *He that is bathed needeth not save to wash his feet, but is clean every whit*, with minor variations. Before pausing to consider these two readings, it must be pointed out that the point of the saying lies in the change of verb, *bathe* instead of *wash*. In the Greek *He who has been bathed* means *He who has taken a complete bath*. The significance of the variant reading is then clear. Either, He who has been completely bathed needs no further washing, but is wholly clean, or, He who has taken a complete bath afterwards only needs to wash from his feet the comparatively trivial dirt gathered in the course of the day. Now, the long reading seems unintelligible in the context of the narrative, unless, with Lagrange, the meaning is taken to be that Peter in fact needs no cleansing, but only an illustration of humility. As Bernard writes, 'It is not a symbol of cleansing, but an illustration of the dignity of service, even menial service; and therefore the washing was of the *feet*, rather than of the hands or the head.' But the words *If I wash thee not, thou hast no part with me* (v. 8) seem to make it impossible to remove the idea of the cleansing of the disciples from the very centre of the meaning of the incident. Or alternatively, if the longer reading be regarded as the original, the reference might be to the need of comparatively trivial washing, represented here by the washing of the feet only, after the complete purging of baptism (Holtzmann, pp. 237, 238). But the action of Jesus here is not even comparatively trivial. It is a symbol of complete cleansing, and it rests upon and interprets the efficacy of the death of Jesus. The commentator is thus driven back upon the shorter reading. Jesus humiliates Himself to wash the feet of the disciples, and thus symbolically declares their complete purification through the humiliation of the death of the Messiah. The faithful Christian is *cleansed by the blood of Jesus* (1 John i. 7, cf. Rom. vi. 1-3; 1 Cor. x. 16). When therefore Peter mistakes the symbol for the reality, and requires further physical washing, Jesus pronounces the adequacy of the symbolical act by declaring it to be a complete bath, and that no further washing of hands and head is necessary. When the relation between the washing of the feet and the death of the Christ is recognized, the *Pedilavium* is a complete bath. It may therefore be suggested that the addition of *save his feet* to the text became necessary only when the original meaning of the narrative was misunderstood (see, however, Bernard).

The disciples are clean through their submission to an action of Jesus which relies for its efficacy upon its relation to the death of Jesus. But they are not all clean. For it is impossible that he who procured the death of Jesus by betraying Him should partake of its spiritual benefits. *Therefore said he, Ye are not all clean* (vi. 64, 70, 71, xvii. 12).

### THE NATURE OF TRUE DISCIPLESHIP OF JESUS

*vv.* 12-20. The humiliation of Jesus is but temporary. Having washed the disciples' feet, He resumed His garments (see above, *v.* 4), and sat down again to teach His disciples as their Master and Lord. The short discourse that follows does not completely elucidate the significance of the action of Jesus. Its full meaning can be understood only after His Death and Resurrection, when the disciples will have received the Spirit of Truth (*v.* 7). Nevertheless, the plain meaning of the action is open to their immediate understanding. The Lord therefore asks whether they have understood what He has done to them, and answers the question Himself. They recognize in Him their Master (i. 38, iii. 2, xi. 8, 28, xx. 16, cf. Mt. xxiii. 7 sqq.) and Lord (vi. 68, xiii. 6, 9, 25, 36, 37, xiv. 5, 8, 22, xx. 28, xxi. 7, 15–17, 20, 21), and address Him, not by name, but with the titles with which Jewish disciples were wont to address their teachers. The Rabbis forbade that teachers should be addressed by name (Strack-Billerbeck). Jesus accepts this respect as rightly due to Him. But His disciples must learn the nature of Christian authority, since they will have to exercise authority. As the slave is not greater than his master, so an Apostle of Jesus is not greater than He from whom he received his commission. The behaviour of the disciples of Jesus must be conditioned by His behaviour (Matt. x. 24; Luke vi. 40). His action in washing their feet expresses the very essence of Christian authority. It consists in mutual humility, and of this authority exercised in humility the washing of the feet of the disciples was a concrete illustration. They also must likewise wash one another's feet. (1 Tim. v. 10.) (For the imitation of the humility of Jesus, cf. Rom. xv. 1–5; 1 Cor. x. 33, xi. 1; Phil. ii. 5–8.; 1 Thess. i. 2–7; Eph. v. 1, 2.) That is to say, their authority is exercised in complete humility and must be thus exercised, since final blessedness does not depend upon knowledge of the truth, but upon doing the truth. *If ye know these things, blessed are ye if ye do them.* The Evangelist thus introduces, on the basis of the Washing of the Feet of the Disciples, the theme of mutual love which is the essence of the life of the Church. He does not, however, at once draw out what is implied in this definition of the life of the Church, nor indeed, what is implied in the Washing of the Feet. In the following chapters obedience to the new commandment—*A new commandment I give unto you, that ye love one another* (*v.* 34, cf. xv. 12; 1 John ii. 7–11, iv. 21; 2 John 4–6)—is shown to depend upon the efficacy of the love of Jesus unto death—*as I have loved you* (xv. 12, 13)—and to imply a love unto death for His sake (*vv.* 37, 38; 1 John iii. 16), exercised in the context of the mission to a hostile world (xv. 16–19). And further, this exercise of love does not depend merely upon the effective example of the love of Jesus, but upon His conquest over the world (xvi. 33), and upon the purification that results from the victory which was His death —*For their sakes I sanctify myself, that they may be sanctified in truth* (xvii. 19). Therefore it is in the end the love of God manifested in the whole concrete appearance of His Son in flesh and blood, and pre-eminently and finally in His death, that evokes and makes possible the mutual love of His faithful disciples—*Beloved, let us love one another: for love is of God; Herein was the love of God manifested in us, that God sent His only begotten Son into the world, that we might live through him. Herein is love, not that we loved God, but that he loved us, and sent his Son to be the propitiation for our sins. Beloved, if God so loved us, we also ought to love one another* (1 John iv. 7–11).

The full exposition of the meaning of the *Pedilavium* is, however, still disturbed by the presence of the traitor in the midst of the faithful disciples, just as, in the perspective of the thought of the Evangelist, the exposition of the truth is disturbed by the presence of false disciples within the Christian Fellowship. Until Judas has gone forth, it is impossible for the final discourse of Jesus to move freely (*v.* 31). The exhortation to mutual love is not applicable to all—*I speak not of you all.* The presence of Judas, who is removed from the sphere of effective love by becoming the instrument of the murderous hatred of the Devil (*vv.* 2, 27, viii. 44; 1 John iii. 10–12), provides, however, no ground for lack of confidence in Jesus as though, in calling him to be a disciple, Jesus was, as it were, the unwilling patron of sin. The betrayal of the Messiah by a disciple lay within the horizon of Old Testament prophecy (Ps. xli. 9); moreover, Jesus not only selected him with full knowledge of his destiny (*v.* 11. cf. vi. 64, 70, 71, xvii. 12), but now, before its actual occurrence, declares the fact of His betrayal by a disciple (Isa. xli. 26, xlii. 9, xlviii. 5, 6). The defection of Judas, and consequently of apostate Christians (1 John ii. 19, iv. 1; 2 John 7), is no sign of weakness in Jesus. It rather corroborates and establishes His witness to Himself, which is summed up in the pregnant words *I am* (viii. 24, 28, 58; Isa. xliii. 10, cf. Ezek. xxiv. 24), and provides paradoxically a significant ground of faith (xiv. 29, xvi. 4). The citation from Ps. xli. 9 is introduced with the words, *that the scripture may be fulfilled* (xvii. 12, xix. 24, 28, 36; Mark xiv. 49, cf. Mark xii. 10), and is abbreviated. The words *mine own familiar friend, whom I trusted* are omitted as inapplicable, since Jesus did not trust Judas. Nor does the Johannine form of the citation agree verbally with the LXX version. The singular *bread* is substituted for the plural *breads* perhaps because, in the thought of the author, the particular reference is to Mark xiv. 22; and the strong word *munch* (cf. vi. 54–8) is substituted for the normal word *eat.* The variant reading *eateth his bread with me* (Codices Sinaiticus, Bezae, &c., R.V. mg.) for *eateth my bread* is presumably a correction due to assimilation to Mark xiv. 18; Luke xxii. 21. The metaphor of lifting the heel is that of the sudden kick of a horse.

The short discourse, which has been interrupted by the reference to Judas, is then solemnly (*Verily, verily,* cf. i. 51, v. 19, vi. 53, &c.) concluded with a Saying which is closely paralleled in Mark ix. 37; Matt. x. 40; Luke ix. 48 (cf. Ignatius *Eph.* vi). The disciples must exercise their authority in mutual service. The extent of authority thus exercised is now declared. They are the emissaries of God. Whosoever receives the emissaries of Jesus, receives Jesus Himself, and whosoever receives Jesus, receives the Father who sent Him (cf. Matt. xxv. 31 sqq.). The thought is more clearly expressed in *v.* 35—*By this shall all men know that ye are my disciples, if ye have love one to another.* There seems no reason to suppose, with Lagrange, that *v.* 20 introduces a new discourse which was interrupted by the emotion of Jesus (*v.* 21).

### THE JUDGEMENT OF JUDAS

*vv.* 21–30. The Johannine version of the witness which Jesus bore to His betrayal by one of the disciples (Mark xiv. 18–21; Matt. xxvi. 21–5; Luke xxii. 21–3) is marked by the emergence of the Beloved Disciple for the first time as a distinct figure. In the Marcan-Matthæan narrative the incident occurred before Jesus took the Bread and the Cup, and all the disciples question Him *Is it I?* In the abbreviated Lucan narrative the order of the incidents is reversed, and the disciples question one another. Since the Johannine narrative presumes the words concerning the Bread and the Wine to have been already spoken (see pp. 506, 507), the order here agrees with the Lucan order.

Jesus, deeply disturbed both at the presence of absolute unbelief in the midst of His disciples (cf. xi. 33, xii. 27) and because of His clear knowledge of the destiny of Judas (vi. 70), now bears solemn and unmistakable witness to His betrayal by one of the disciples (*v.* 18), in order that His foreknowledge may provide a sure ground of faith in Him: *Now I tell you before it come, that, when it is come to pass, ye may believe that I am* (*v.* 19 R.V. mg.). Except for the reduplicated *Verily*, the words *Verily, verily, I say unto you, that one of you shall betray me* are identical with the opening Saying in the Matthæan narrative (Matt. xxvi. 21, cf. Mark xiv. 18). The disciples, being ignorant of the precise reference of the words (*they were grieved*, Mark, Matthew), merely look at one another, wholly at a loss. Peter and the Beloved Disciple alone act. Peter beckons to the disciple whom Jesus loved and who was lying in His bosom, and bids him make known the identity of the betrayer. The Beloved Disciple, however, has no independent knowledge. But, because of his position, he is able to question the Lord discreetly, and to receive privately and at once the answer that is both a saying and an action. The phrase *lying in the bosom of Jesus*, strengthened, as Cyril noted in *v.* 25 into *lying on the breast* and repeated in its strengthened form in xxi. 20, may only denote the position of the disciple at the Supper. He occupied the position on the right of Jesus. Reclining on his left arm with his head close to his Master's breast, he was consequently able to hold easy and quiet conversation with Him. The reclining position at meals is presumed in Luke vii. 38. In view of i. 18, however, the language suggests more than this. As Jesus is in the bosom of the

Father, so the Beloved Disciple lies in the bosom of the Son; thus the concrete position of the disciple marks the verity that the true disciples are in Jesus as Jesus is in the Father (xiv. 20, xv. 4, 5, xvii. 21–3). This perfect relationship was in the thought of the author of the gospel anticipated historically in the relation between the Beloved Disciple and His Master.

To the Beloved Disciple Jesus unmasks the betrayer. He will dip a morsel of bread or meat (either meaning of the Greek word is possible) in the dish, and will present it to the disciple who is to betray Him. He takes the morsel, dips it, and hands it to Judas, the son of Simon Iscariot. The moment of his exposure is also the moment when Satan finally takes possession of him wholly (viii. 44, xiii. 2; Luke xxii. 3). The narrative does not suggest, as Loisy and Bauer maintain, some mysterious Eucharistic condemnation (1 Cor. xi. 29); nor does the author mean the reader to understand that by giving Judas the sop, He handed him over to Satan (1 Cor. v. 5; 1 Tim. i. 19, 20). Cyril's comment is surely right: 'Let no one suppose that the sop was to the traitor the cause of his being possessed by Satan.' His exposure in the presence of the disciples by the Lord Himself provides the opportunity for his complete surrender to the promptings of the Devil. The judgement of Judas is set in the words which follow. The Lord commands him to proceed with his work as quickly as possible. Then he went forth *immediately* into the darkness. Having surrendered himself to the Prince of this world, Judas is banished from the light, and passes out into the darkness under the judgement of God (iii. 19, ix. 4, xi. 10, cf. Luke xxii. 53).

The disciples fail to understand (xi. 12, xiv. 8) the terrible significance of the command, *That thou doest, do more quickly*; even the Beloved Disciple, who knows the identity of the traitor, does not grasp the imminence of the betrayal. They suppose the urgency of the departure of Judas to be occasioned by some lack of preparation for the Feast, or by the need of some exercise of charity in view of its proximity: and think that, as the treasurer of the society (xii. 6), he was instructed to make good the deficiency or perform the required act of mercy.

DETACHED NOTE 7

# THE LITURGICAL USE OF THE *PEDILAVIUM* OR THE WASHING OF THE FEET

According to an ancient custom Catholic monarchs washed the feet of twelve poor men on Maundy Thursday as a sign of humility. Queen

Elizabeth performed the ceremony, after the yeomen of the laundry had first washed the feet of the paupers with warm water and sweet herbs. The custom fell into disuse in England with the accession to the throne of William and Mary. On the Continent, however, until 1914, the King and Queen of Bavaria and the Emperor and Empress of Austria knelt before twelve carefully chosen poor men and washed their feet, sending them away with gifts of money, food, and clothes.

There are indications in the ancient liturgies of the Church and in the writings of the Fathers that the *Pedilavium* once formed an integral part of the baptismal office. Saint Ambrose reminds the newly baptized of the Gospel lesson which had been read at the washing of their feet, when they had 'gone up from the Font' (*De Myst.* vi. 31, 32). The author of the closely related treatise *De Sacr.* (iii. 1. 4, 5) adds that 'the high priest was girt up (for though the presbyters also carried it out, yet the ministry is begun by the high priest) the high priest was girt up and washed thy feet'. He also states that the Church in Rome did not have this custom, and suggests that this was 'on account of the numbers'. Presumably the ceremony took too much time.

From certain early sacramentaries it is clear that the rite was practised in Gaul and Ireland. In the Stowe Missal the *Pedilavium* follows immediately the giving of the white robe (chrisom), and precedes the Communion of the newly baptized (Warren, *Liturgy and Ritual of the Celtic Church*, pp. 217, 218). The Bobbio Missal has the washing of the feet at the same place: 'I wash thy feet as our Lord Jesus Christ did to his disciples. Thus do thou to guests and to strangers. Our Lord Jesus Christ wiped the feet of his disciples with the towel wherewith he was girded. As I do to thee, do thou to strangers, to guests, and to the poor.' In the *Missale Gothicum* the *Pedilavium* follows the anointing with the Chrism, and precedes the vesting with the Chrisom: 'I wash thy feet as our Lord Jesus Christ did to his disciples. Thus do thou to guests and to strangers that thou mayest have eternal life.' (Henry Bradshaw Society's publications: *The Bobbio Missal*, 251, 252; *Missale Gothicum*, 262.) In Spain the rite must have existed in the third century, since it was abolished by the forty-eighth canon of the Council of Elvira, A.D. 305: 'Nor are the feet of the baptized to be washed by the priests or by any of the clergy.'

The relation between the *Pedilavium* and the sacrament of baptism itself presented a doctrinal difficulty. Was it a sacrament, or not? If it was a sacrament, how was it to be distinguished from baptism? The author of the treatise *De Sacramentis* tells us that some asserted it to be 'not a work of sanctification but an act of humility' and that it ought to be performed 'not at baptism, not at the regeneration; but only as we should wash the feet of a guest'. He does not, however, agree with this interpretation: 'Learn', he says, 'how it is a sacrament and a means of sanctification', and he has an explanation of his own. In baptism all guilt is washed away, but since Adam was tripped up by the Devil, and since even baptized Christians may similarly be caused to stumble, 'at that point where the serpent made his treacherous attack a stronger reinforcement may be applied that he may not be able to trip thee up afterwards' (*De Sacr.* iii. i. 7). Saint Ambrose also finds himself in some difficulty, and is forced to distinguish between personal and hereditary sin: 'His (Peter's) foot is washed that hereditary sins may be removed, for our own sins are removed by baptism' (*De Myst.* vi. 32). Saint Augustine, on the other hand, held that the *Pedilavium* was not an element in the sacrament of Baptism, but merely a lesson in humility. He mentions the fact that some churches would never admit the custom at all, lest it should seem to belong to the sacrament of baptism, and that other churches had abrogated the custom where it had been received (*Ep.* lv. (*ad Januar.*) 33; see Bingham, *Antiquities*, pp. 561, 562; Thompson and Srawley, *Saint Ambrose 'On the Mysteries' and the Treatise On the Sacraments* xv, xvii, xxiv, xxviii, 58, 98, 99).

With the spread of the Roman liturgy the custom of the washing of the feet at baptism disappeared in the West. A faint memory of the ancient use survived in the reading of St. John xiii. 1–16 at the Mass of the newly baptized in the Ambrosian liturgy at Milan (Magistretti, *Rituale Ambrosianum*, vol. II, p. 225). Perhaps the doctrinal problem was too great to admit of its being retained. Warren suggests that Saint Augustine's demand that the Celtic bishops should conform to the Roman method of administering the sacrament of baptism was, in point of fact, a demand for the abolition of the *Pedilavium*. The use of the *Pedilavium* in the Maundy Thursday liturgy was, however, open to no such objection and the Eastern Church possesses a dramatic ceremony, the origins of which reach back probably at least to the fifth century. The Greek liturgy of the Divine and Sacred Basin was edited with a Latin translation by Goar in his Εὐχολόγιον (Paris 1647, pp. 745 sqq., cf. Nilles, *Kalendarium Manuale*, vol. II, pp. 219 sqq. For a description of the present-day ceremony in Jerusalem, see *The Times*, 17 March 1924, 'Eastern Ceremonies in Jerusalem', by H. C. Luke). The Archbishop, Bishop, or Chief Priest, gorgeously vested, enters the church through the great gates of the sanctuary, accompanied by twelve priest and the reader of the Gospel (the Evangelist). One of the priests takes the part of a doorkeeper to represent Judas, another of a steward to rep sent Saint Peter. When the choir has sung the introits and appropri collects have been read, the celebrant, who represents the Christ, moves his vestments and, girding himself with a towel, pours wa into a basin and advances to Judas, who rudely pushes forward feet to be washed and kissed, thereby indicating his hardness of he When the feet of the other disciples have been washed, the celebr comes last to Simon Peter, who with tears withdraws his feet and sh with his hand, his expression, and his whole body, his reluctance to

thus washed. The dialogue in St. John xiii is recited, ending with th
washing of Peter's feet. At the words *Now ye are clean, but not all*, th
celebrant turns to Judas and points his finger at him. The celebran
then returns to his throne, removes the towel, and is vested. This ritua
drama does not commemorate merely an isolated incident in the lif
of the Christ, nor is it merely an exhortation to humility. It forms par
of the commemoration of the Passion: and the liturgy is dominated by
the thought of the Incarnation, the Death, and the Resurrection of th
Son of God. This is what lies behind the peculiar significance that wa
attached to the removal and taking again of the vestments. For Christia
humility is dependent upon the humiliation and the glorification of th
Christ.

Nor is the idea of sanctification wholly eliminated by the emphasis
on humility. The Euchologion contains a prayer for those who came to
the *Pedilavium*. This prayer is a prayer of penitence: *O Lord Jesus
Christ Our Governor, Father of pity . . . who didst free us from the chains of sin,
and dost call us to penitence . . . We, therefore, humble and unworthy sinners,
pray that at this hour and on the holy and saving day of the Passion we may fulfil
thy will to the praise and honour*, &c. In the third canon of the seventeenth
Council of Toledo (A.D. 694), the non-observance of the practice of the
washing of the feet on the Thursday in Holy Week was censured, and a
strict performance of the ceremony was enforced both as an example of
humility and as an act of preparation for the Supper of the Lord, with
which the ceremony was closely associated. Disobedient priests were
ordered to be excluded from Communion for two months. Further,
since the penitents were publicly reconciled at the Paschal season, the
liturgy of the *Pedilavium* had special reference to the remission of sin
after baptism. There is some evidence to show that the reconciliation
of penitents took place on Maundy Thursday (Duchesne, *Christian
Worship*, p. 437).

The *Pedilavium* was, therefore, originally both an example of Christian humility and a means of post-baptismal sanctification. The two
elements were so closely interwoven that the one was never entirely
dissociated from the other. But both Christian humility and Christian
sanctification were conditioned, primarily not by the washing of the
disciples' feet by the Christ, but by the humiliation of the Son of God
in the Incarnation and in the Passion; so that the *Pedilavium* was in
point of fact a parable of the humiliation of the Son of God and of the
effects of that humiliation.

The liturgical use of John xiii. 1–16 thus formed an admirably
correct commentary on the passage itself.

# THE EVE OF THE CRUCIFIXION

## II
## THE FIRST DISCOURSE

XIII. 31–XIV. 31

### THE NEW COMMANDMENT

xiii. 31. *When therefore he was gone out, Jesus saith, Now is the Son of man glorified, and God is glorified in him;* 32. *and God shall glorify him in himself, and straightway shall he glorify him.* 33. *Little children, yet a little while I am with you. Ye shall seek me: and as I said unto the Jews, Whither I go, ye cannot come; so now I say unto you.* 34. *A new commandment I give unto you, that ye love one another; even as I have loved you, that ye also love one another.* 35. *By this shall all men know that ye are my disciples, if ye have love one to another.*

### THE PROPHECY OF PETER'S DENIAL

36. *Simon Peter saith unto him, Lord, whither goest thou? Jesus answered, Whither I go, thou canst not follow me now; but thou shalt follow afterwards.* 37. *Peter saith unto him, Lord, why cannot I follow thee even now? I will lay down my life for thee.* 38. *Jesus answereth, Wilt thou lay down thy life for me? Verily, verily, I say unto thee, The cock shall not crow, till thou hast denied me thrice.*

### THE DESTINY OF THE DISCIPLES OF JESUS

xiv. 1. *Let not your heart be troubled: ye believe in God, believe also in me.* 2. *In my Father's house are many mansions; if it were not so, I would have told you; for I go to prepare a place for you.* 3. *And if I go and prepare a place for you, I come again, and will receive you unto myself; that where I am, there ye may be also.*

### THE WAY TO THE FATHER

4. *And whither I go, ye know the way.* 5. *Thomas saith unto him, Lord, we know not whither thou goest; how know we the way?* 6. *Jesus saith unto him, I am the way, and the truth, and the life: no one cometh unto the Father, but by me.* 7. *If ye had known me, ye would have known my Father also: from henceforth ye know him, and have seen him.* 8. *Philip saith unto him, Lord, shew us the Father, and it sufficeth us.* 9. *Jesus saith unto him, Have I been so long*

*time with you, and dost thou not know me, Philip? he that hath seen me hath seen the Father; how sayest thou, Shew us the Father? 10. Believest thou not that I am in the Father, and the Father in me? the words that I say unto you I speak not from myself: but the Father abiding in me doeth his works. 11. Believe me that I am in the Father, and the Father in me: or else believe me for the very works' sake.*

## FAITH EFFECTIVE—PRAYER EFFECTIVE

*12. Verily, verily, I say unto you, He that believeth on me, the works that I do shall he do also; and greater works than these shall he do; because I go unto the Father. 13. And whatsoever ye shall ask in my name, that will I do, that the Father may be glorified in the Son. 14. If ye shall ask me anything in my name, that will I do.*

## THE MISSION OF THE SPIRIT OF TRUTH

*15. If ye love me, ye will keep my commandments. 16. And I will pray the Father, and he shall give you another Comforter, that he may be with you for ever, 17. even the Spirit of truth: whom the world cannot receive; for it beholdeth him not, neither knoweth him: ye know him; for he abideth with you, and shall be in you.*

## THE ADVENT OF THE SON

*18. I will not leave you desolate: I come unto you. 19. Yet a little while, and the world beholdeth me no more; but ye behold me: because I live, ye shall live also. 20. In that day ye shall know that I am in my Father, and ye in me, and I in you. 21. He that hath my commandments, and keepeth them, he it is that loveth me: and he that loveth me shall be loved of my Father, and I will love him, and will manifest myself unto him. 22. Judas (not Iscariot) saith unto him, Lord, what is come to pass that thou wilt manifest thyself unto us, and not unto the world? 23. Jesus answered and said unto him, If a man love me, he will keep my word: and my Father will love him, and we will come unto him, and make our abode with him. 24. He that loveth me not keepeth not my words: and the word which ye hear is not mine, but the Father's who sent me.*

## THE TEACHING OF THE HOLY SPIRIT
## AND THE VALEDICTORY PEACE OF CHRIST

*25. These things have I spoken unto you, while yet abiding with you. 26. But the Comforter, even the Holy Spirit, whom the Father will send in my name, he shall teach you all things, and bring to your remembrance all that I said unto you. 27. Peace I leave with you; my peace I give unto you: not as the world giveth, give I unto you. Let not your heart be troubled, neither let it be fearful. 28. Ye heard how I said to you, I go away, and I come unto you. If ye loved me, ye would have rejoiced, because I go unto the Father: for the Father is greater than I. 29. And now I have told you before it come to pass, that, when it is come to pass, ye may believe.* 30. *I will no more speak much with you, for the prince of the world cometh: and he hath nothing in me;* 31. *but that the world may know that I love the Father, and as the Father gave me commandment, even so I do. Arise, let us go hence.*

## THE NEW COMMANDMENT[1]

xiii. 31–3. Judas having departed and in so doing set in motion the events leading immediately to the Death of Jesus, the glorification of the Son of man is once again (xii. 23) declared as a present fact. The 'hour' to which the whole ministry has been looking forward (ii. 4, vii. 30, viii. 20) has come (xvii. 1). *Now* the eschatological present which, with the presence of Jesus, has always tended to usurp the eschatological future (iv. 23, v. 25) enters more explicitly into its own. But it does so only because, in the sequence of history, the moment of the Death of Jesus has *now* been reached. Just as, in the earlier discourses, the theme *Jesus Himself*, Jesus in the flesh as the Revelation of God, has been followed and qualified by the theme *The Death of the Son of man and the love of God*, lest the glory of the Son of man should be thought to be an earthly glory and the Revelation of the glory of God should be misconstrued and obscured (cf. pp. 218, 219 and the sequences iii. 11–13, 14–17; vi. 29–50, 51–9), so *now* the qualifying context of the Passion and Death makes possible direct speech about the glory of the Son of man (cf. xii. 23–8). For the glory of the Son of man is the glory of the Father. This has been shown already by the double, interchangeable attribution of the *glory* manifest in the signs of Jesus (ii. 11, xi. 4, 40). It is to be further emphasized in the interdependent definitions of the great Prayer of Consecration, *I have glorified thee on the earth, having accomplished the work which thou hast given me to do . . . and all things that are mine are thine, and thine are mine: and I am glorified in them* (xvii. 4, 10). Yet, although the words and actions of Jesus have already manifested the glory of God and the glory of the Son of man, human apprehension of this glory has hitherto had to wait upon *the hour* that was *not yet*. Accordingly the hour when the work of the Son of man is consummated (cf. xix. 30) has already been referred to as the hour when Jesus shall be glorified (vii. 39, xii. 16), because as a result of His glorification, still future in relation to the events of the ministry, the true understanding of what Jesus says and does will be bestowed upon His disciples. This glorification of the Son (xvii. 1) is to be glorification with the glory which He had with the Father before the world was (xvii. 5). But it does not consist simply in a return to the Father whence He came: the hour is not the hour of glorification merely because it is the hour of departure (xiii. 1). The Father who has been glorified on earth in the life of the Son is to be particularly and supremely glorified

[1] This and the following sections (xiii. 31–8) have been supplied by the editor on the basis of a few preliminary notes by the author.

in His death (xii. 27, 28, xvii. 1). It is this, and not any assurance of future vindication or reward, that makes the Death no scandal but the supreme manifestation of glory, and the purposeful departure of the traitor—*That thou doest, do quickly* (*v.* 27)—the occasion of triumphant assurance of immediate glorification: *God shall glorify him in himself, and straightway shall he glorify him.* Consequently in this context of His death Jesus will *now* be able to speak of the giving of the glory which the Father has given Him to those whom He has been given by the Father, and to those who believe through their word (xvii. 6, 20, 22, 24), because the hour of death is the hour of the assurance of fruitfulness (xii. 23, 24).

[The glorification of the Son of man is therefore past, present and future: any logical distinction between these tenses breaks down, since the significance of the Death and of the Coming of the Spirit to the believers, events in time as they are, cannot be limited to their event. Consequently the variant reading of the *Textus Receptus* in *v.* 32, which is supported by a corrector of Codex Sinaiticus, in some manuscripts of the Old Latin and Egyptian Versions, and by Origen, misses the point in an attempt to achieve a logical sequence—*Now is the Son of man glorified, and God is glorified in him. If God be glorified in him, God shall glorify him in himself.* . . .]

*v.* 33. But the glorification of the Son of man involves separation from His disciples. Employing the same mode of address *Little children,* as that by which the writer of the First Epistle addresses his readers (1 John ii. 1, 12, 28, iii. 18, iv. 4, v. 21, cf. Gal. iv. 19, John xxi. 5, 1 John ii. 13, 18, iii. 7), since the Christians are not only reborn in Him but are taught by Him, Jesus goes on to speak at once of the other immediate effect of the action of Judas and consciously refers to His words to the Jews at the Feast of Tabernacles (vii. 33, 34, 36). But whereas the Jews can never go where Jesus goes, because they do not believe, the disciples receive no such warning of final exclusion. There is here no parallel to the words *shall not find me,* although the disciples, like the Jews, *shall seek* (viii. 21). For the moment, however, attention is concentrated, not on the future comforting (xvi. 17) and eventual glorification (xvii. 24) of the disciples, but on the *going away* of Jesus. This also has been spoken of in anticipation (viii. 21, 22). Indeed, although the Jews could not apprehend His destination, the readers of the Gospel know well that Jesus is to go away, whence He came, to Him that sent Him (vii. 33, viii. 14, xiii. 3). The disciples are to be amply assured of this (xiv. 4, xvi. 5, 10, 17). Here is no aimless, blind, haphazard departure, no 'going' like the going of those who walk in darkness (xii. 35, cf. 1 John ii. 11). On the contrary it is the deliberate inauguration of the way that is to be followed by the children of light (cf. xiv. 2, 4, 6). Thus, it would seem, does the Fourth Evangelist draw out the meaning of the Saying which in Saint Mark's gospel follows the questions about the betrayer and the significant reference to Psalm xlix. 9: *The Son of man indeed goeth, even as it is written of him* (Mark xiv. 21).

*vv*. 34, 35. The disciples cannot follow Jesus because they are not yet to die. For them there is still a 'not yet' comparable to that which until now has conditioned the words and actions of Jesus. In this situation, therefore, Jesus gives the disciples *a new commandment,* which He will presently re-affirm as summing up all His commandments and interpret as to be modelled upon His keeping of His Father's commandments (xv. 10–12). They are to love one another as He has loved them. This commandment is, indeed, old (Lev. xix. 18; Matt. xix. 19, xxii. 39; cf. 1 John iii. 7, ii. 23, 2 John 4, 5), but it is also new, for whereas the Old Testament demanded that men should love their neighbours as themselves, the New Law is that they should love the brethen better than themselves (Matt. v. 43–8, xxii. 39, 40, xxv. 34–46; Rom. xii. 9, 10, xiii. 8–10; Gal. v. 13, 14; Jas. ii. 8), and die for their friends (xv. 13). The new commandment of love is given *now*, not simply because with the departure of Judas murder has broken out in the heart of the fellow-ship (cf. 1 John iii. 15), and not simply because the event of the Death of Jesus is the necessary context for defining the love that is to be modelled upon the love of God (iii. 16, 1 John iii. 16). *By this*—the phrase is instrumental—*shall all men know that ye are my disciples.* The love between Christians is itself to testify to the fact that they have been called into being by Him whose disciples they are, and so to the fact that He Himself has been sent by the Father (xvii. 21, 23, cf. 26; 1 John iv. 12). Now that the departure of Jesus, the Revelation of the Father, is imminent, the only manner in which His disciples may continue His witness must be declared. The supplementation of the old command-ment to love the neighbour by the new commandment to *love one another* is therefore no retrograde and narrow exclusivism. The love of the brethren is to bear witness to the love of God for the world and so to offer eternal life to *all men* (cf. 1 John i. 3)

## THE PROPHECY OF PETER'S DENIAL

*vv*. 36–8. The Epistles of Saint John show how appropriately the new commandment is set in the situation brought about by the departure of Judas, since their predominant, paradoxical theme is the necessity of that love of the brethren apart from which there is no true knowledge of God, and the prevalence of apostasy, denial and hatred among those who think they know God. The recognition of this terrible paradox leaves no room for complacency. *If we say that we have no sin, we deceive ourselves, and the truth is not in us* (1 John i. 8). But *there is a sin not unto death* (1 John v. 17). It is possible that an analogous, two-fold motive— the desire to insist that he *that thinketh he standeth* should *take heed lest he fall*, and, at the same time, to recognize that *while we were yet sinners,*

*Christ died for us*, may explain why the prophecy of Peter's Denial is set immediately after the story of the apostasy of Judas. As in vi. 66–71, the pressing home of the fact of apostasy into the very heart of the body of disciples, humiliating as it is, is yet not utterly without promise. A similar transition of thought may perhaps have determined the position of the same prophecy in Saint Luke's gospel (Luke xxii. 31–4), where it follows closely upon the announcement of the betrayal (Luke xxii. 21–3), whereas in the other synoptic gospels (Mark xiv. 26–31, Matt. xxvi. 30–5) it takes place on the road to Gethsemane.

The prophecy of Peter's Denial is occasioned by Peter's question, *Lord, whither goest thou?* cf. xiii. 6, xiv. 5, 22). An indirect answer foretells Peter's martyrdom (cf. xxi. 18, 19; Rev. xiv. 4). The 'following' to which the disciples have been called (i. 43, x. 27, xii. 26; cf. Mark ii. 14, x. 21), which has already in some sense become a fact in the literal following of Jesus (i. 37, 40, cf. xxi. 20)—a theme well established in the synoptic tradition (Mark i. 18, ii. 14; cf. Mark vi. 1)—is here boldly redefined in the light of the approaching Death of Jesus (cf. Mark viii. 34). Peter does not understand what is required: *Lord, why cannot I follow thee even now? I will lay down my life for thee* (cf. Mark. xiv. 31). He proposes to do for his Master what the Good Shepherd does for His sheep (x. 11, 15, 17; cf. xv. 13). The laying down of life after the fashion of Jesus cannot be achieved by an act of self-immolation, but only when the appointed *hour* is come. This is so even in the case of Jesus Himself (xii. 27, xiii. 1). Some speech of Peter such as is preserved in Mark—*If I must die with thee, I will not deny thee*—seems to have been recast by the Fourth Evangelist so as to bring out a double significance: its eventual truth as well as its present falsehood (cf. xi. 50). The time will come *hereafter*, when another shall gird him and carry him where he would not, and Peter will glorify God by his death (xxi. 18, 19). But in his own strength and his own time he cannot do what he now impetuously promises. *Jesus answereth, Wilt thou lay down thy life for my sake? Verily, verily, I say unto thee, The cock shall not crow, till thou hast denied me thrice.* Here the words of the Greek approximate more closely to the Lucan than to the Matthæan and Marcan accounts.

### THE DESTINY OF THE DISCIPLES OF JESUS

xiv. 1–3. In these verses the declaration *If any man serve me, let him follow me; and where I am, there shall also my servant be* (xii. 26, cf. xvii. 24) is expanded. The imminent death and departure of the Lord (xiii. 33, 36), and the sure martyrdom of at least one of His disciples (xiii. 37, 38) must cause the faithful neither disturbance nor alarm. If they remain confident in their belief in the Father and the Son, their final destiny is assured. The home of God (Matt. v. 34, vi. 1), the eternal antitype of the transitory temple in Jerusalem (ii. 16, Westcott) and of the abiding of the Father and the Son in the believer (xiv. 23, xvii. 21), is capacious and many-roomed. There the disciples, reunited with the Lord, will abide for ever. Had God surrounded Himself with celestial beings only, and closed the door of heaven to His faithful servants on earth, the Lord, who descended thence to reveal the things which are in heaven (iii. 11–13), would have exposed indeed a grim divine sporting with the lives of men. But it is not so: and, moreover, His departure is necessary that He, the divine forerunner (Heb. vi. 20), may prepare for His disciples their heavenly habitations. He will Himself return to remove them from the world, that they may abide with Him in the Fellowship of the Father. Provided with such a definition of heaven, and secure in their final destiny, the faithful disciples can support the departure of the Lord, and undertake the service of God.

It may be, however, that the allusion here is less to sayings of Jesus previously recorded in the gospel than to the Marcan narrative of the command to prepare the Passover (Mark xiv. 12–16). According to the earlier tradition two disciples, named Peter and John in Luke xxii. 8, *went forth* and *made ready a guest-chamber* or *lodging place*, which is also described as a *large upper room*, in which Jesus intended to meet His disciples. The disciples did not *know* the way and they were told to follow—the unknown owner of the house. In fact they found everything already *prepared* as Jesus *had said unto them*. On this familiar but unrelated background the opening words of John xiv are most easily intelligible. The scene in the upper room foreshadows a more secure and permanent refuge possessed of infinitely larger accommodation and far more adequately prepared, for it is the home of God, in which the Son of God Himself will prepare a place for the residence of His faithful disciples. *In my Father's house are many mansions; if it were not so, I would have told you; for I go to prepare a place for you. . . . that where I am, there ye may be also. And whither I go, ye know the way.* The disciples are then instructed to follow Him who is *the way and the truth and the life* (cf. xiii. 36). Thus 'the familiar words of the "Fourteenth of John" turn the disciples' recent errand with the surrounding experience of the whole passing day into a closely pursued parable of the impending and eternal future' (cf. H. M. Foston, *The Evening of the Last Supper*, pp. 39–44).

*Ye believe in God, believe also in me*, A.V., R.V. This translation, supported by the Vulgate, and by some commentators ancient and modern (Lagrange), suits neither the grammar, since the accompanying verbs are imperatives, nor the sense, since belief in Christ is to the Evangelist less a belief to be added to belief in God than the ground of all true faith in Him. It is preferable therefore with R.V. mg. and most modern commentators (Westcott, Bauer, &c.) to preserve the double imperative: *Believe in God, believe also in me.*

Confident belief in God and in His Son is thus set in opposition to that disturbance of mind which proceeds from unbelief, but not to such disturbance as is caused by the contemplation of the unbelief of others, or even by the divinely ordered consequences of such unbelief, both of which the Evangelist attributes to the Lord (xi. 33, xii. 27, xiii. 21).

*Mansions.* The word, which is used in the New Testament only here and in *v.* 23, is a substantive formed from the significant Johannine verb *abide* (cf. 2 Cor. v. 1). *For I go to prepare.* The clause may be causal, depending upon the imperatives in *v.* 1. *Be not troubled, but believe . . . because I go . . .* or it may continue the Lord's words *and I tell you that I go . . .* ; or it may be taken closely with the words immediately preceding as a direct statement or as a question, *I would have told you that I go . . .* (Spitta), *Would I have told you that I go?* (Heitmüller, Bauer). The latter, in either form, is most improbable since (*a*) the disciples are at once told that the Lord is going to prepare a place for them, (*b*) the Evangelist had not previously recorded any such statement. Between the first two it is impossible to decide, and the sense is identical: the mansions of God have a real existence in heaven. If it were not so, the Lord would have told His disciples since the work of salvation would then indeed be to no purpose—and moreover, His departure is necessary for the preparation of these mansions. Burney treats the clause as a translation into Greek of an Aramaic relative clause, *I who go to prepare . . .* , by which the sense is unaltered. Loisy suggests that the words are a spiritual interpretation of Mark xiv. 28, *I will go before you into Galilee.*

*I come again.* The words may refer to the death of each Christian believer (2 Cor. v. 8; Phil. i. 23), but they recall the eschatology of xxi. 22, 23; 1 John ii. 28; Matt. xvi. 28; 1 Thess. iv. 16, 17. The thought of the final advent of the Lord and the eschatological reunion of the disciples with Him does not exhaust the conception of His coming, since the eschatological coming is anticipated in the appearances of the risen Lord (xx. 19, 24, 26, xxi. 13), in the present reality of the fellowship of the disciples with the Father and the Son (*v.* 23; 1 John i. 3), in the advent of the Paraclete (*v.* 18), and in the Eucharist of which the Walking on the Sea is the type (vi. 19–21, 33, 51).

### THE WAY TO THE FATHER

*vv.* 4–11. The Lord attributes to His disciples the knowledge both of the destination to which He is proceeding, and of the way by which they also must follow Him thither. But so important is it that all Christians should perceive the goal of human life and the road by which it is attained, that the discourse passes into a dialogue, less in order to record a conversation, than to extract a precise statement of that faith by which alone men can have access to the Father. Thomas, the type of those who demand 'tangible proofs and precise definitions' (xi. 16, xx. 24, xxi. 2; Loisy, p. 745), and understanding no more than Peter (xiii. 36) the true nature of discipleship, declares that they all are ignorant of the destination, and can therefore have no knowledge of the way thither. The Lord, instead of answering directly the double question of Thomas, develops His own previous words. Assuming the end of human life to be union with God, now accomplished by His own return to the bosom of the Father (i. 18, iii. 13), it is more necessary that He should clearly state the nature of the road by which His disciples can follow in His footsteps. The road to God is knowledge of the Truth, and regeneration, enlightenment and the possession of Life. Truth and Life are no ideal abstractions. They are present concretely in the incarnate Son of God, who is both the Truth and the Life. He gives the Life which He is (xi. 25, 43, 44), He reveals the Truth which He is, He offers the Light which He is (i. 9, viii. 12, ix. 7), just as He speaks the Word and provides the Bread which He is (i. 1, viii. 43, vi. 27, 35, 63). Consequently He is the Way, as He is the Door (x. 7, 9). No man can attain the Father except by perceiving the Truth and participating in the Life which is revealed to men in His Son. Thus, while being the guide, He does not guide to what is beyond Himself. Knowledge of the Son is the knowledge of God, and moreover, knowledge is also vision. In these verses, then, faith, knowledge, and sight are held in complete equilibrium; focused on one point, they serve one purpose; directed towards the Son, they effect union with the Father. Philip correctly perceives that the revelation of God is the desirable content of all religion, and is alone entirely sufficient. He requests a theophany such as was given to Moses (Exod. xxiv. 9–11, xxxiii. 18, cf. Isa. vi. 1, xl. 5), and therefore fails to perceive that his prayer has long been answered, and that the complete revelation of God is present for his eyes to behold and his hands to handle (i. 17, 18; 1 John i. 1, 2). This failure in insight is complete misunderstanding of the meaning of companionship with Jesus. Life with Him is the vision of God and inability to recognize this is both ignorance of Jesus and ignorance of God. Jesus is the Truth and the Life, not merely because He has been sent by God (xi. 42), but because God is in Him, and He in God (xvii. 23); and His words and acts are the words and acts of God (xii. 44–50). The Father and the Son are one (x. 30). Since belief in the concrete appearance of God in His incarnate Son is the Christian Faith, the words *I am in the Father, and the Father in me* are repeated, and the belief not of Philip only, but of all the disciples is demanded (*Believe ye*, v. 11 substitute for *Believest thou*, v. 10). And moreover, so important is this faith, that, if the direct perception of the truth be not yet attained, the evidence afforded by the miraculous works of the Christ must be recognized as having provided sufficient ground for belief. The words show forth the abiding of the Son in the Father, the works expose the Father abiding in the Son (x. 37, 38, cf. iii. 2, v. 17 sqq., 36  viii. 19, 26–9, xii. 49).

Bauer and other commentators suppose that the Evangelist is here making use of language and ideas current in Hellenistic syncretism or

Oriental mythology. It is true that parallel conceptions underlie the Gnostic speculations of the heavenly journey of the soul under the guidance of Hermes or of some other divine helper; and that in a papyrus preserved in the British Museum Isis declares 'I am the Truth'; and that the Mandæan writings contain references to the Way, the Truth and the Life. Such similarities are exceedingly interesting to the student of comparative religion. But the theory that the Evangelist is consciously 'simplifying the mysticism of his age' (Loisy), or that he is consciously transferring to Jesus terminology elsewhere applied to Hermes or Isis or other divinities (Bauer) is entirely unnecessary. Christian background is wholly sufficient to explain his language. That access to God is by Christ only was the innermost kernel of the Gospel in the Pauline Epistles and in the Christian writings which depend upon them (Rom. v. 2; Eph. ii. 13, 18, iii. 12; 1 Pet. ii. 5, iii. 18, Heb. vii. 25. x. 19–21), and was involved in the claim of Jesus to be the Messiah. That Christianity was commonly designated the Way is proved from the use of the title in Acts (Acts ix. 2, xix. 9, 23, xxii. 4, xxiv. 14, 22); that it was regarded as Life and Truth needs no proof. The fourth Evangelist inherits the whole wealth of primitive Christian traditional language; and his contribution to the development of Christian theology is to have simplified the tradition by discarding much that was purely Jewish, and by causing all that remained to converge upon the Christ, and upon Him alone (see DETACHED NOTE 1, pp. 161–3).

[*v. 4.* The reading *Whither I go ye know, and the way ye know*, A.V. and R.V. mg., supported by the great majority of the Greek manuscripts, including Codices Alexandrinus and Bezae, and by the Syriac and Latin Versions, is probably a correction of the original text preserved in Codices Sinaiticus and Vaticanus, and by some other important Greek manuscripts, by one manuscript of the Old Latin Version, and by the Egyptian Versions, *Whither I go, ye know the way*, R.V. The correction eases the grammar, and explains the double question of Thomas.

*v. 7.* There are two possible readings. Codex Vaticanus and a few other Greek manuscripts have an unfulfilled condition in present time, reading *If ye were knowing me* (which they do not), *ye would also now have knowledge of my Father.* Codices Sinaiticus and Bezae, the Washington Codex, and the Old Latin Versions, however, preserve a different reading, *If ye know me* (which in fact they do), *ye will know my Father also.* The second reading is admirably appropriate (cf. *v.* 20), since it expresses the confidence of the Lord in His disciples (*v.* 4), and prepares the way for the immediate resolution of the future into a present *henceforth* (that is *even now* xiii. 19) *ye both know and see Him.* The first reading may perhaps be explained by assimilation to viii. 19.]

FAITH EFFECTIVE—PRAYER EFFECTIVE

*vv.* 12–14. The Lord continues the consolation of His disciples. They are set apart for the service of God, and to continue the work of the incarnate Son. The separation which disturbs them is the effective cause of their being endowed with powers greater even than those of the Lord Himself when He was with them on earth. Faith is no detached perception or achievement, nor are the works of the Christ peculiar and inimitable. Belief in the Son is miraculously effective; and the acts of His disciples will be greater than His. The Evangelist has not in mind here such miracles as were foretold in Mark xvi. 18, or recorded in Acts v. 15, xix. 12. The contrast is rather between the few disciples of Jesus and the vast number of those converted by the preaching of His apostles; between the mission of Jesus to the Jews and the mission of His disciples to the world. The diffusion of Christianity in the world (iv. 35–8), symbolized by the 153 fishes (xxi. 1–14), the conversion of the Greeks, whom the Lord refused even to see (xii. 20 sqq.), the union of both Jews and Greeks in one Church (x. 16, xi. 52), these are the *greater* works, these converts are the *much* fruit (xv. 8, cf. xv. 2), and for them *many* mansions must be prepared in heaven (*v.* 2). And yet, this extension of the work of the incarnate Son by His disciples is not wrought independently by men. The life of the Church is the divinely intended accomplishment of the Gospel, and its growth and extension beyond the narrow limits of Judaism are the consequence of the exaltation of the Son to the bosom of the Father. The life and death of the Christ do not result in the emerging in human history of a race of supermen whose works are their own glorification. These miraculous acts are wrought by faith in Jesus and by prayer in His name. They are in fact His acts (x. 16, xxi. 6), the signs of His Ascension, and of the glory of the Father.

The efficacy of Christian prayer is also a consolation. The Death and Resurrection and Ascension of the incarnate Son of God provide His disciples with the right to address their petitions boldly and directly to the Father Himself. *In that day ye shall ask me nothing. Verily, verily, I say unto you, If ye shall ask anything of the Father, he will give it you in my name* (xvi. 23 sqq., cf. xv. 16). Such prayer, since it is offered by the servants of the Christ, and according to His will (1 John v. 14–16), is inevitably effective. Petitions so addressed to the Father will be answered by the Son, who will have resumed His position as the instrument in heaven of the actions of God (i. 3). And yet, prayer addressed to the Son is not excluded, *If ye shall ask me anything in my name, that will I do.*

*v.* 13. *In my name*, cf. xvi. 23–6. No doubt prayer in the name of Jesus means primarily the powerful invocation of His name (Acts iii. 6, v. 40, x. 43; Col. iii. 17, see Heitmüller, *Im Namen Jesu, passim*). But the synonymous phrase *according to his will* (1 John v. 14) shows that the idea expressed here is that the prayers of the disciples will be heard because the faithful petitioners belong to Christ (Mark ix. 41), and, being united with Him, offer only such prayers as are agreeable to Him, the formal mention of His name proceeding from a real correspondence with Him. The whole Johannine conception of prayer to the Father in the name of Jesus is well illustrated in the Roman Mass, where the Lord's Prayer concludes the Canon, and is recited audibly. Elsewhere, in all the Roman liturgical offices, the Lord's Prayer is said *secreto*.

[*v.* 14. The verse is omitted by the original text of Codex Alexandrinus, in some other Greek manuscripts, in one manuscript of the Old Latin Version, and in the Sinaitic Syriac. In the early manuscripts which contain the verse there is considerable textual confusion. The first hand in Codex Alexandrinus, Codex Bezae, and other Greek manuscripts, some manuscripts of the Old Latin Version, and the Egyptian Versions read *If ye ask in my name, I will do it;* but Codices Sinaiticus, Vaticanus, and other Greek manuscripts, supported by the Vulgate, read *If ye ask me in my name, I will do it.* Some commentators treat the last reading as an addition introduced later to justify prayer addressed to Jesus (see Bauer); but the textual tradition is easier to explain if this reading be genuine; the omission of the whole verse, or the omission of *me*, being two different attempts to avoid the contradiction with xvi. 23.]

### THE MISSION OF THE SPIRIT OF TRUTH

*vv.* 15–17. The attachment of the disciples to Jesus, which is the ground of their effective prayers, is no mere passionate emotion of the heart. It is a love whose reality is exposed by keeping His commandments (1 John ii. 3–5, iii. 23 sqq., v. 2–4). Secure in faith, and dedicated to the mission, they will remain united to one another by mutual charity (xiii. 34), and detached from the world; victorious over its enticements (1 John ii. 14–17); in it, but not of it (xvii. 14–17). The commandments of the Lord are His, because they are the fulfilment of the Law (viii. 31). Since such obedience is no human achievement, to the effective petitions of the disciples will be added the even more effective petition of the Son; in answer to which the Father will send the Spirit of Truth (xvi. 13; 1 John ii. 27, v. 6, 7) to remain with the faithful Christians until the end of the world. The Lord Himself is their first and supreme Paraclete, Helper or Guardian (xvii. 12; 1 John ii. 1); the Spirit of Truth is *another Paraclete* (xiv. 16, 26, xv. 26, xvi. 7), whom they recognize, because He abides with them, and shall be in them (i. 33). The possession of the Spirit effects a complete separation between the Church and the World. The World, being under the rule of the Spirit of deceit (1 John iv. 6), neither perceives nor recognizes the Spirit of truth, and is therefore unable to receive Him (1 Cor. ii. 8–14).

## THE ADVENT OF THE SON

*vv.* 18–24. The greatest consolation has hitherto remained inspoken. Neither the promise of the heavenly habitations and of the final coming of Jesus, nor the power of the mission and the efficacy of prayer, nor the possession of the Spirit, are in themselves sufficient to dispel the disturbance of mind caused by the thought of the absence of the Lord. The disciples still remain orphans, separated from their guardian and the author of their life. The climax of their consolation is attained only with the words *I am coming to you* (xvi. 22). This advent of the Christ is not an interpretation of the coming of the Spirit, as many commentators ancient and modern have supposed: 'He promises that He will come Himself, showing that the Spirit is not something other than what He is Himself' (Cyril of Alexandria, cf. Plummer, Calmes, Bauer, cites 2 Cor. iii. 17, and identifies the Spirit and the Son). It is, rather, a distinct appearance, and the primary reference is to the Resurrection appearances. For the disciples the absence of the Lord extends only for the short period of the entombment (xvi. 16–22); for the unbelievers He disappears for ever (vii. 33–6). On that day—the day of the Resurrection—He will come to His disciples (xx. 19, 26, cf. xxi. 4), and they will see Him, and, because He lives, they will live also (xx. 22, 31); and moreover, initiated into the real significance of His glorification, they will perceive the union of the Father and the Son (*vv.* 10, 11, cf. x. 38), and the union of the Son with those who believe on Him. The reference to the Resurrection appearances conditions the language of the passage, but does not exhaust its meaning. The Resurrection inaugurates a new era; and the day of the Resurrection is extended in the experience of all who love the Lord, and whose love is exposed in the possession and performance of His commands. Such love directed towards the Son calls forth the love of both Father and Son, and their love is exposed by the gift of a spiritual vision of the Christ to the believer, *I will manifest myself unto him.*

The vision of the glorified Christ, whether at the Resurrection, or in the life of the Church, and in the experience of the faithful, is confined to those who believe. Outside the Church, the family of God united by mutual love, there is no salvation. Elsewhere the Evangelist seems to refer directly to a special coming of the Lord in Baptism and in the Eucharist, by water and blood, to which the Spirit bears witness. The world neither perceives the risen Christ, nor participates in that vision which is granted to those who believe and love and obey Him, and which is a veritable coming of the Lord. Judas, not of course Iscariot, who had gone out into the darkness, but that other Judas, voices the disappointment, almost horror, occasioned by so grave a seeming limitation of the power of God, and so serious an apparent failure to fulfil His promises (Acts i. 6; Ps. ii. 8, cf. Origen, *Contra Celsum*, ii. 63 sqq.; Macarius Magnes, *Apocriticus*, ii. 14). Will He not discover Himself in public to the world as risen and glorified? (vii. 3, 4). The Lord contemplates no public discovery of power, but only a domestic visitation of love (Bernard), and answers the question of Judas by stating the inflexible law of conversion (Wisd. i. 2). There is neither external nor spiritual manifestations of the risen Christ to the world (Acts x. 40, 41). Only where the love of the Son is born, and in those who love the brethren and are detached from the world, can the Father and the Son reside. The World is simply those who do not love the Son (xv. 18); He comes to His own, and only those who are His receive Him (i. 11, 14). Since the teaching of Jesus is the Word of God (vii. 16, 17, viii. 26, xii. 49), this stern exclusiveness is also the Word of God.

With the use of the same word *mansion* to describe the co-habitation of the Father and the Son in the believer which he had used earlier (*v.* 2) to describe their heavenly habitations, the implication involved in the coming of the Son is drawn out to the full: *We will come unto him, and make our abode* (lit. *mansion*) *with him* (1 John iv. 15; 2 John 9; Gal. ii. 20; Eph. i. 3, iii. 17). The sanctuary and home of God, which is in heaven, and was but incompletely revealed in the temple at Jerusalem, will descend upon each Christian believer. Thus the promises in the Old Testament are completely fulfilled: *Let them make me a sanctuary; that I may dwell among them* (Exod. xxv. 8, xxix. 45; Lev. xxvi. 11, 12; Ezek. xxxvii. 26, 27; Zech. ii. 10). The promise of the habitation of God in the believers is, however, enclosed by a double demand for love and obedience, since there is no spiritual union with Him which is not also a moral union. (For the teaching of Philo concerning the habitation of the Logos in the human soul, see Lagrange, pp. 389, 390.)

*v.* 20. *In that day*, cf. xvi. 23, 26. The phrase is eschatological (e.g. Mark xiii. 32), and some commentators take it in that sense here (Zahn); but the verses which follow make this almost impossible. The words refer first to the Resurrection, then to the new era which it inaugurates (Loisy). The Evangelist sees the eschatological hope fulfilled, at least in part, in the life of the Church.

*v.* 21. *Manifest*. The Greek word, which is not elsewhere the word for *manifest*, means in Acts *to disclose a secret* (Acts xxiii. 22), or *to make known* what would otherwise remain unknown (Acts xxiv. 1, xxv. 15). In Matt. xxvii. 53, it refers to appearances of the dead, and in Heb. ix. 24 to the appearance of Christ before God at His Ascension. The word may therefore be suggested to the Evangelist by the Resurrection appearances, and means an appearance in 'clear, conspicuous form' (Westcott, cf. Wisd. i. 2, LXX).

*v.* 22. *Judas*, cf. Luke vi. 16; Acts i. 6. The Syriac Sinaitic Version reads *Thomas*, the Curetonian *Judas Thomas*, the Egyptian Sahidic

*Judas the Canaanite.* For the possible identification of Judas and Thomas, see Calmes, p. 333, note.

## THE TEACHING OF THE HOLY SPIRIT
## AND THE VALEDICTORY PEACE OF CHRIST

*vv.* 25–31. The complete consolation is to be found in the words of Jesus. The Paraclete, who is the Holy Spirit, will remind the believers of the Lord's teaching (ii. 22, xii. 16, xiii. 7): and yet His work is more than a reminiscence of the *ipsissima verba* of the Son of God: it is a living representation of all that He had once spoken to His disciples, a creative exposition of the Gospel. There is therefore no opposition between *these things* which the Lord had spoken whilst remaining with them and *all things* which the Spirit will teach, as though the teaching of Jesus were fragmentary and incomplete. Jesus is the Truth, and the Spirit will both call to mind and expound all that He had taught. The Paraclete will be sent by the Father in the name of the Son. The Son was sent by the Father to declare His words (*v.* 24, cf. i. 18, v. 43, x. 25, xvii. 14, 17); the Spirit will be sent by the Father to declare the words of the Son both to the believers and to the world (xvi. 7 sqq.).

There is therefore no room for distress or cowardly fear. The new order is simply the peace of God in the world, though not proceeding from it. It is the peace of Christ, manifested in His opposition to the world, and sharply distinguished from that peace which is customarily desired in oft-repeated salutations and farewells (1 Sam. i. 17) and which consists merely in the cessation of strife (Matt. x. 34; Luke xii. 51), or in that false security which cries *Peace, peace; when there is no peace* (Jer. vi. 14). The peace of Christ is manifested in unbroken union with the Father, maintained in continuous strife with the world, in persecution, in humiliation, and in death for the glory of God. Such is the peace which Jesus leaves with His disciples, and offers to them as His supreme gift (xx. 19, cf. Mark v. 34; Luke vii. 50; Num. vi. 26; Isa. liv. 13, lvii. 19; Ezek. xxxvii. 26), the peace which Philo said was 'the greatest good, which no man is able to provide' (*De Vit. Moys.* I. 304, quoted by Westcott). The effectual benediction of peace depends, however, upon the return of Jesus to the Father and upon His risen and glorified appearance to His disciples; His departure is therefore a ground of rejoicing rather than sorrow. Were they filled with genuine love they would have rejoiced on His behalf because He is released from further humiliation and re-established in His original glory, and on their own behalf because the work of the Son in opening the way to the Father, who is greater than He, is now to be completed (xix. 30). *He that believeth on me, the works that I do shall he do also; and greater works than these shall he do; because I go unto the Father (v.* 12). Christian faith is thus shown to be grounded upon the express words of Jesus: it is not primarily a deduction from the work of the Spirit or from Christian experience (xiii. 19, xvi. 4).

The betrayer, the emissary of Satan (vi. 70, xiii. 2, 27), is at hand, and the sacrifice of the Lamb is imminent. Little more can be said. The death of Christ, which is apparently the victory of the Prince of this world, is in fact its precise opposite (xii. 31, xvi. 33, xix. 30). The Crucifixion is the public exposition to the world of the completed love and obedience of the Son to the Father; complete, not only because He did not waver in the presence of death, but because the Devil discovered in Him no sin (viii. 46; 1 John iii. 3–5; 1 Pet. ii. 22), and therefore could present no claim against Him which would place Him within his power.

The reference to the approach of Judas and the phrase *Arise, let us go hence* echo Mark xiv. 42 (Matt. xxvi. 46), *Arise, let us be going: behold, he that betrayeth me is at hand.* The well-known words in the older narrative of the Passion provide the author with a formal conclusion to the first section of the discourse in the upper room; they imply no change of scene. The Lord does not leave the house until the conclusion of the sacrificial Eucharistic prayer (xviii. 1). The discourse continues without interruption, and the themes are taken up again and developed more fully.

*v.* 26. *The Holy Spirit. The Spirit* (vii. 39, xix, 30, see notes), *Holy Spirit* (i. 33, xx. 22). The full description including the adjective and the definite article occurs only here in the Fourth Gospel.

*v.* 27. *Neither let it be fearful.* The Greek verb, which is not used elsewhere in the New Testament, is naturally though not exclusively used to denote that fear which is provoked by the imminence of war (Deut. i. 21, xxxi. 6, 8; Josh. i. 9; 2 Macc. xv. 8, cf. the use of the adjective in Rev. xxi. 8). The suggestion would be admirably appropriate here, since the peace of Christ implies war with the world.

*v.* 28. *The Father is greater than I.* The Arians detached these words from their context, and then found in them the New Testament counterpart to the LXX translation of Prov. viii. 22, *The Lord created me,* thus securing scriptural support for their doctrine of the inferiority of the Son. The Father alone is without beginning and eternal; the Son is a creature, the product of a definite act of the will of the Father. The inferiority of the Son therefore consists in the fact that He was created, the superior greatness of the Father lies in the fact that He was the Creator. Ever since Arius thus expounded the passage, Christian commentators have been unable to interpret it without betraying the marks of the controversy which followed. Two interpretations control the exegesis. The orthodox Fathers of the fourth century (Athanasius, Basil, Gregory of Nazianzus, Chrysostom) carefully rephrased the pre-Arian language, since it was capable of an interpretation which asserted a veritable inferiority of the Son in such a manner as to endanger His equality with the Father: 'For we who say that the visible world is under the government of Him who created the world, do thereby declare that the Son is not mightier than the Father, but inferior to Him. And this belief we ground on the saying of Jesus Himself *the Father who sent me is greater than I*' (Origen, *Contra Celsum*, viii. 15); 'The Father is not the same as the Son, since they differ one from the other in the mode of their being. The Father is the whole substance, the Son is an outflow and portion of the whole' (Tertullian, *Adversus Praxean*, ix). The fourth-century Fathers denied a veritable inferiority, since the Son received from the Father His identical nature, and the superior greatness of the Father consists solely in the fact that the Father gives and the Son receives: 'If any one say that the Father is greater in so far as He is the cause, we will not contradict this. But this, however, does not make the Son to be of a different essence' (Chrysostom). The second line of exegesis, noticed by the earlier Fathers but treated by them as inadequate, is formulated in the Athanasian creed, 'Equal to the Father, as touching His Godhead: and inferior to the Father, as touching His Manhood.' This interpretation in a fully developed form goes back to Augustine and especially to Cyril of Alexandria, who in his commentary limited the inferiority of the Son solely to the incarnation. The assumption of humanity by the Son renders Him, as man, inferior to the Father who remained in His unapproachable glory. 'As He still wore the guise of a servant, and the time had not yet come that He should be reinstated, He calls God the Father greater. . . . The Father then is greater since the Son was still a servant and in the world. . . . Speaking of His divine glory in contrast with His place as a servant and His position of subjection, we say that the Son was inferior to the Father in so far as He was human; but that He was reinstated into His equality with the Father after His sojourn here, not endowed with any new, or adventitious, or unaccustomed glory, but rather restored to that state in which He was at the beginning with the Father' (Cyril of Alexandria). This interpretation has dominated Western exegesis; 'Of this (dust and ashes) the very body of Christ is composed, and it was in clothing Himself therewith that He became less than the Father' (Quesnel).

In any summary of the use made by the Fathers of the Saying recorded in the Fourth Gospel it must be remembered that they were defending Christian worship of Jesus against a theology which made such worship idolatry. 'My good sir, if He be not really God, we shall worship the creature in preference to the Creator, and not we only who inhabit this earthly sphere, but also the multitude of heavenly angels' (Cyril of Alexandria). They were therefore compelled to detach the Saying and then to discuss it in the light of the controversy. When, however, the Saying is returned to its context it is clear that the Fathers were completely in the right as against Arius; the passage implies nothing about the creation of the Son, and no exegesis is justifiable which puts Him into the category of creatures. On the other hand the rigid theologizing of the Fathers does not lead to an altogether satisfying interpretation, since the author of the Fourth Gospel is less concerned with the relation between the Father and the Son, than with the relation between the Father and Son and the disciples. The Gospel is the Gospel of salvation. Throughout his work the writer is careful to emphasize that Christianity is not an independent cult of Jesus, but the revelation of the Father and the worship of God. The Christ humiliated, crucified, and glorified is the Way to the Father and the Truth; through faith in Him the believer has access to the Father, *He that hath seen me hath seen the Father* (xiv. 9). *I and the Father are one* (x. 30). Since the Father is the ultimate goal, He is greater than the Son. But a further meaning underlies the words *The Father is greater than I.* In the Fourth Gospel the phrase *greater than* means *of greater power and authority than* (iv. 12, viii. 53, x. 29, xiii. 16; 1 John iii. 20), and this meaning must be relevant here. The humiliation of the Son involved in some real sense a separation from the Father; His glorification and return to the Father restores to Him a position from which He can communicate to His disciples greater power, *Greater works than these shall he do* (the believer); *because I go unto the Father* (xiv. 12). It is the certainty of union with the Father through faith in the Son, and the promise of the greater power which is to be theirs because of the death and resurrection of Jesus, that renders the saying a consolation to the disciples. No further speculation moves the mind of the author. The Fourth Gospel is not the beginning of the application of Greek philosophy to the varieties of the Christian Faith; it is rather a living and Christian exegesis of the words of Jesus preserved in the early tradition of the Church, an exegesis which the writer claims to be inspired by the possession of the Holy Spirit of God (cf. 1 John ii. 20, 27). For the Patristic exegesis of the passage see Cornelius a Lapide, and Westcott's detached note at the conclusion of his commentary on ch. xiv.

*v.* 30. *He hath nothing in me.* The phrase is Hebraic, and means *He has no claim against me* (see Strack-Billerbeck).

*v.* 31. *Arise, let us go hence.* Commentators who refuse to regard these words as an echo of Mark xiv. 42, marking a formal pause in the discourse rather than a change of scene, suggest various explanations. Those who think that xviii. 1 must originally have followed xiv. 31 are compelled either to insert chs. xv–xvii after xiii. 31a (Spitta) or to treat them as a later interpolation (Wellhausen, ed. Meyer). Since, in the second edition of his Commentary, he has swung over to the opinion that the Fourth Gospel has been drastically edited by a later hand, Loisy must now be associated with Wellhausen. Bacon and Wendt refuse to remove ch. xvii, but imagine that chs. xv and xvi must be inserted somewhere before ch. xiv. No theory of rearrangement or interpolation satisfactorily solves the problem. Chs. xv and xvi continue and develop the themes outlined in ch. xiv, and there is not the slightest suggestion of a difference of authorship. Moreover, xv. 26 and xvi. 7 appear to presume the previous mention of the Paraclete in xiv. 16, 17. Ch. xvii manifestly concludes the discourse and is an even more significant introduction to the Passion than xiv. 30, 31. Other commentators are of the opinion that xviii. 1 means that the city, not the house, was then left, whereas xiv. 31 means that the house was left. Chs. xv–xvii may therefore have been spoken, or intended to have been spoken, either in the streets of the city, or, as Westcott supposed, in the court of the Temple. But the streets are a hardly suitable locality, especially for the prayer which concludes the discourse, and Westcott's theory ultimately rests solely on the rather fantastic supposition that the imager of the vine was called forth by the sight of the golden vine upon the gates of the Temple (see his notes on xv. 1, 2, xvii. 3). It is, however, far more natural to think that the imagery is Eucharistic, *I am the vine* being the counterpart of *I am the bread*. No more precise occasion is required to explain the language. Lagrange has an explanation of his own. As far as historical reminiscence is concerned ch. xvii follows ch. xiv. The author of the gospel, however, introduced at the conclusion of ch. xiv material which belonged in the main to an earlier period. xv. 1–17 belongs to the period of the call of the disciples; xv. 18–xvi. 4 originally formed part of the eschatological speech recorded in Mark xiii: xvi. 5–33 returns to the Upper Room. It is exceedingly difficult to take seriously so complicated a theory even when it is put forward by such an eminent scholar. Finally, the ancient explanation of Cyril of Alexandria should not be forgotten. The words are a spiritualized version of Mark xiv. 42 and mean 'Arise, let us remove from death unto life, and from corruption unto incorruption'. For a general discussion of the problem see Bauer's detached note.

DETACHED NOTE 8 (by the Editor)

# THE MEANING OF *ΠΑΡΑΚΛΗΤΟΣ*

(It is clear that the author intended to include in this Commentary a Detached Note upon the meaning of παράκλητος. That Note was never written, and it is not now proposed to reconstruct it from the few indications of the author's intention. For the benefit of readers it does, however, seem necessary to show briefly why the translation of παράκλητος is by no means a simple matter. Fuller treatment will be found in *Encyclopædia Biblica*, 3567 sqq. (Jülicher); Hastings's *Dictionary of the Bible*, III, 665 sqq.; Field, *Notes*, pp. 102, 103; Lagrange, pp. 381 sqq.; Bauer, pp. 177 sqq.; Sasse in *Zeitschrift für die neutestamentliche Wissenschaft*, xxiv, 1925, 260–77; Windisch in *Festgabe für Adolf Jülicher*, pp. 110–37; and in the Lexicons.)

1. παράκλητος is found five times in the New Testament; four times in the Fourth Gospel (xiv. 16, 26, xv. 26, xvi. 7) and once in the First Epistle of St. John (1 John ii. 1).

2. It is a noun derived from the verb παρακαλέω and passive in form. Its etymological meaning is therefore *one called to the side of*.

3. It is so used, though very rarely, in Classical Greek, with the particular meaning of *an advocate* (cf. *advocatus*) in a Law Court. It therefore tends to acquire the secondary, active meaning of one who intercedes for him whom he is called to help.

4. The word does not occur in the LXX.

5. Philo uses παράκλητος in the primarily *passive* sense of *advocate*, *intercessor*, or *helper*, though without the particular judicial setting of a Law Court.

6. The word was transliterated into Hebrew and Aramaic by the Rabbinical writers as pĕraklît, and used in much the same way. The most relevant example is *Aboth* iv. 11: 'R. Eliezer b. Jacob says: He that performs one precept gets for himself one advocate (פְּרַקְלִיט) but he that commits one transgression gets for himself one accuser. Repentance and good works are as a shield against retribution.'

7. A similar use of παράκλητος, as meaning an advocate, is found in early Christian writings, and in the Papyri.

The translation of παράκλητος by *advocatus* in all the Latin Versions of 1 John ii. 1 therefore seems justified, and indeed makes very good sense: *If any man sin, we have an advocate with the Father, Jesus Christ the righteous.* . . . Moreover the application of the same epithet to the Holy Spirit, in the sense of one called to the side of the Christians to intercede for them, is paralleled in the argument of Rom. viii. 26–34. Nevertheless, although some manuscripts of the Old Latin Versions do boldly translate παράκλητος by *advocatus* in one or more of the passages in the Fourth Gospel, in the others they take refuge in the transliterations *paracletus* or *paraclitus*, as does the Vulgate in all four passages, and the Syriac, Ethiopic and other Versions.

In his English Version, however, Wyclif translated the word in the gospel by *comforter* (i.e. *strengthener*), and in so doing revived a rendering *consolator* found in Hilary, Jerome and Orosius, and anticipated in Greek by Gregory of Nyssa, Cyril of Jerusalem and Origen (Westcott). This rendering does, of course, fit gratefully into the context. The three chapters in which the word παράκλητος is found are revolving round the theme of Jesus' departure, and His assurance that He will not leave His disciples *desolate* (*bereft*, xiv. 18). Sorrow has filled their hearts at the news of His impending departure (xvi. 6): it is therefore fitting that this *other* (xiv. 16) *paraclete*, who is to abide with them for ever, should be understood as His agent actively assuaging the sorrow of the disciples by supplying what Jesus Himself had supplied.

Such an exegesis is no doubt encouraged by the modern significance attached to the idea of comforting, and as a result of a faulty understanding of such passages as xiv. 18. But it is made particularly attractive for three reasons.

1. In Biblical Greek, and occasionally, though rarely, in Classical authors, the verb παρακαλέω has the particular force of *to console, strengthen by consolation, comfort*, and the noun παράκλησις that of *consolation, comfort, solace*.

2. In the LXX both noun and verb had been used in contexts expressing the *consolation* of Israel by God, both in the present and in the messianic age to come (cf. Ps. lxxi. 21, cxxxv. 14; Isa. xl. 1, 2, lxi. 2. &c.: Ps. xciv. 19; Isa. lvii. 18, lxvi. 11, &c.), and so lay ready to the hand of New Testament writers seeking to affirm the coming of the messianic age and the active consolation of God (Matt. v. 4, 2 Cor. i. 3, 4, 6, vii. 6; Luke ii. 25, Rom. xv. 5).

3. An active noun formed from παρακαλέω, παρακαλήτω, existed and was used in the LXX of Job xvi. 2 for Job's comforters, but the later Jewish translators of the Old Testament, Aquila and Theodotion, used παράκλητος in this connection. Aquila and Theodotion may have been influenced 'by the associations which had gathered round παράκλητος in the second century' (Westcott): their procedure is none the less a somewhat disturbing reminder that the movement in the meaning of a word does not always continue to be controlled by its etymological structure.

Two possible courses therefore seem to lie open to the translator wishing to proceed upon secure linguistic grounds, and unwilling to shirk his duty, whether by transliterating παράκλητος, or by paraphrasing it exclusively in terms of its context. Either he may conclude, with Westcott, that the strict etymological meaning is unescapable, and that in the gospel, as in the First Epistle, 'the sense of advocate, counsel, one who pleads, convinces, convicts, in a great controversy, who strengthens on the one hand and defends on the other, meeting formidable attacks, is alone adequate'. He will then have the general support of Lagrange, who, however, tries to avoid the professional connotation of *avocat* by adopting Loisy's word *défenseur*, and of Bauer, who employs *Helfer*. Or he may conceivably be justified in making the most of the very scanty evidence of Aquila, Theodotion, and the patristic exegetes listed above, and conclude that παράκλητος is best Englished *comforter*, provided that the word be kept rigorously to its root meaning of strengthener, and set against the background of the mercy of God.

It is, however, not only inevitable but right that interpretation should take full account of the contexts. Windisch, for instance, finds that by its use παράκλητος combines three distinct meanings. The Paraclete is (1) a vindicating and punishing witness; (2) one who assists and supports; (3) a counsellor and tutor. 'In short, in the Paraclete in John is fused the figure of a prophet bearing witness, bestowing counsel, teaching and disclosing the future' (*Festgabe für Adolf Jülicher*, p. 127).

This paraphrase would be more convincing were it made clear that in all four contexts in the Fourth Gospel the work of the Paraclete is specifically related, not only to the Christ—who prays the Father to give the Paraclete to His disciples (xiv. 16), in whose name the Paraclete will be sent by the Father (xiv. 26), who indeed will Himself send the Paraclete from the Father (xv. 26), when, and only when, He Himself has gone away (xvi. 7)—but also to the life in the flesh of Jesus who is the Revelation of God. The Paraclete is the Spirit of Truth, which is, in the Fourth Gospel, no abstract or moral quality, but the Revelation in history of the ultimate truth of God. The Spirit of Truth is given to those who keep the commandments of Jesus (xiv. 16). *He shall teach you all things, and bring to your remembrance all that I said unto you* (xiv. 26). The Spirit of Truth will bear witness of Jesus, as also will the disciples who have been with Jesus from the beginning (xv. 26, 27, cf. i. 14). He will accordingly guide the disciples into all truth, *for he shall not speak from himself; but what things soever he shall hear, these shall he speak: and he shall declare unto you the things that are to come.* (See the COMMENTARY, pp. 576–9.) Even the revelation of all Truth is focused upon Jesus. *He shall glorify me: for he shall take of mine, and shall declare it unto you. All things whatsoever the Father hath are mine: therefore said I, that he taketh of mine and shall declare it unto you* (xvi. 13–15). Finally, the Paraclete cannot be received by the world, *for it beholdeth him not, neither knoweth him* (xiv. 17): indeed, *He will convict the world in respect of sin, and of righteousness, and of judgement*—three acts themselves related to Jesus (see the COMMENTARY) since sin springs immediately and fundamentally from the rejection of Jesus, which rejection is the rejection of God; and righteousness is the Righteousness of Jesus vindicated and ratified by the Father in His Resurrection and Ascension, which righteousness is the Righteousness of God; and judgement is the judgement of the Prince of this world effected by the victory of Jesus (xvi. 33) and of those who believe in his name, which judgement is the Judgement of God. Seen in their full context, set side by side and in relation to the whole gospel, the four occasions on which παράκλητος is used in the gospel give no foundation for the supposition, which Windisch in effect countenances, that the Paraclete is a Christ-Spirit prophetically leading and guiding the Christian fellowship, and freely authoritative apart from the event of the Life and Death of Jesus. Against this supposition, not only the Johannine, but all Apostolic writings, vigorously protest.

Two final considerations may now serve to show that a rigorous distinction between the 'active' and 'passive' forces of παράκλητος and between the meanings *comforter* and *advocate*, are to some extent artificial and unilluminating. In the first place, the business of *comforting* so frequently referred to in the Old Testament, involved, when practised with due responsibility, the exposition of the misfortune experienced so as to set it in the full context of the wisdom and purpose of God. It is this that Job's comforters attempt, inadequately and unsuccessfully, to do. Similarly Ben Sirach expounds Isaiah xl. 1 as comfort of them that mourned in Sion because Isaiah, *by an excellent spirit, shewed the things that should be to the end of time, and the hidden things or ever they came* (Ecclus. xlviii. 24, 25). It is not wholly irrelevant that Pallis wishes to translate παρακλήσεως in Rom. xv. 4 *instruction* (*To the Romans*, p. 153) and παρακαλῶν in Luke iii. 18 *instructing* (*Notes on St. Luke and the Acts*, p. 9). It may be doubted whether παράκλητος can be translated primarily *comforter*, and whether the messianic background of παρακαλέω and παράκλησις can be regarded as primarily responsible for the choice of the word. None the less, in the perspective of the gospel the Spirit can rightly be called the *Comforter* because He shows to the believers the truth of the ultimate victorious glory of the Son and of the Father, and so strengthens them against the insidious spectacle of the world in which they are still persecuted and troubled, within as well as without. So the chaotic world, in the insight of the Spirit, itself illuminates more fully the basis of their faith.

In the second place: Lagrange dislikes the specifically legal associations of *advocatus*. It would indeed be grotesquely inadequate to picture the Paraclete as simply a counsel pleading with God for the Christians on the grounds that they believe. But the Fourth Gospel is from beginning to end concerned with judgement, the Judgement of God, which is inevitably exerted upon men wherever Jesus speaks or His Word is preached (cf. iii. 17–21, ix. 39, xii. 31, &c.). The difference between light and darkness, between knowledge and blindness, between faith and unbelief, is no unimportant, secondary, ephemeral matter, but a difference whose consequences are final. God sent His Son into the world through love for the world, but the rejection of God's love in the Jesus of history brings man under judgement. Consequently the Spirit of Truth, just because He reveals God's love and assures men of it, Himself exposes the blindness and darkness of the world. The consolation of the disciples is consolation in the midst of condemnation, and if *Comforter* secures recognition of God's boundless mercy, *Advocate* secures recognition of the sternness of the issue.

In conclusion: Jesus, the emissary of God tabernacling in the midst of His disciples, speaks of *another* (xiv. 16) who will be sent to them to take His place by their side. It is perhaps for this reason that the noun παράκλητος was chosen, since it has the natural, obvious meaning of 'one called to the side of' somebody for their benefit. But any noun, however passive in form, that is used to describe any part of the work or purpose of God, must inevitably acquire active significance in the process, and both translations, *advocate* as well as *comforter*, do in fact recognize that more than the mere passive form of the word has conditioned its use. What is perhaps more important than the actual choice of this translation or of that, is that the word chosen should not be such as to appear to limit the active functions of the Spirit of Truth, whether towards the disciples or towards the world, or to obscure the fact that these functions are complementary and issue directly from the nature of God's act of Revelation in Christ, whose Word is a two-edged sword.

# THE EVE OF THE CRUCIFIXION

## III

## THE SECOND DISCOURSE

XV. 1–XVI. 33

The background is still the Last Supper, the distribution of the Bread and the Wine, the traditional words which accompanied the distribution, and the apostasy of Judas. The whole scene is an epitome of the Christian religion; and the author draws out its significance, aided, it can hardly be doubted, by authoritative interpretations of Christian worship delivered by prophets and teachers during the course of the Eucharist. The significance of the Bread is passed over, since it has been fully expounded in ch. vi. The thought of the disciples drinking the Wine, and of their consequent union with the Father and the Son, *He that eateth my flesh and drinketh my blood abideth in me, and I in him* (vi. 56), calls forth the metaphor of the vine and its branches: *Abide in me, and I in you. As the branch cannot bear fruit of itself, except it abide in the vine; so neither can ye, except ye abide in me* (xv. 4). As Jesus is the Bread of God (vi. 33), so He is the Vine of God. As the Father gives the faithful disciples the true Bread from heaven which is His Son whom He hath sealed as His own (vi. 27, 32), so the Father is the Husbandman to whom the true Vine belongs. As the disciples must live by eating the Son of God (vi. 57) so the branches can live only as they remain organically united with the vine. The apostasy of the Jews, of Judas and of the unbelieving disciples, which is emphasized in vi. 41, 52, 60, 66, 70, 71, here reappears under the figure of the useless branches contrasted with those which bear much fruit (cf. vi. 68). The close similarity between chs. vi and xv can be adequately explained only if it be recognized that both rest ultimately upon the double foundation of the tradition of the words and actions of Jesus at the Last Supper and the teaching associated with the Eucharist at the time when the gospel was composed.

### THE HUSBANDMAN, THE VINE AND ITS BRANCHES

xv. 1. *I am the true vine, and my Father is the husbandman. 2. Every branch in me that beareth not fruit, he taketh it away: and every branch that beareth fruit, he cleanseth it, that it may bear more fruit. 3. Already ye are clean because of the word which I have spoken unto you. 4. Abide in me, and I in you. As the branch cannot bear fruit of itself, except it abide in the vine; so neither can ye, except ye abide in me.* 5. *I am the vine, ye are the branches: He that abideth in me, and I in him, the same beareth much fruit: for apart from me ye can do nothing.* 6. *If a man abide not in me, he is cast forth as a branch, and is withered; and they gather them, and cast them into the fire, and they are burned.* 7. *If ye abide in me, and my words abide in you, ask whatsoever ye will, and it shall be done unto you.* 8. *Herein is my Father glorified, that ye bear much fruit; and so shall ye be my disciples.*

### THE EXPOSITION OF THE MYSTERY OF THE DEATH OF JESUS
### THE MANIFESTATION OF LOVE AND THE DUTY OF OBEDIENCE

9. *Even as the Father hath loved me, I also have loved you: abide ye in my love.* 10. *If ye keep my commandments, ye shall abide in my love; even as I have kept my Father's commandments, and abide in his love.* 11. *These things have I spoken unto you, that my joy may be in you, and that your joy may be fulfilled.* 12. *This is my commandment, that ye love one another, even as I have loved you.* 13. *Greater love hath no man than this, that a man lay down his life for his friends.* 14. *Ye are my friends, if ye do the things which I command you.* 15. *No longer do I call you servants; for the servant knoweth not what his lord doeth: but I have called you friends; for all things that I heard from my Father I have made known unto you.* 16. *Ye did not choose me, but I chose you, and appointed you, that ye should go and bear fruit, and that your fruit should abide: that whatsoever ye shall ask of the Father in my name, he may give it you.* 17. *These things I command you, that ye may love one another.*

### THE *VIA CRUCIS* AND THE HATRED OF THE WORLD

18. *If the world hateth you, ye know that it hath hated me before it hated you.* 19. *If ye were of the world, the world would love its own: but because ye are not of the world, but I chose you out of the world, therefore the world hateth you.* 20. *Remember the word that I said unto you, A servant is not greater than his lord. If they persecuted me, they will also persecute you; if they kept my word, they will keep yours also.* 21. *But all these things will they do unto you for my name's sake, because they know not him that sent me.* 22. *If I had not come and spoken unto them, they had not had sin: but now they have no excuse for their sin.* 23. *He that hateth me hateth my Father also.* 24. *If I had not done among them the works which none other did, they had not had sin: but now have they both seen and hated both me and my Father.* 25. *But this cometh to pass, that the word may be fulfilled that is written in their law, They hated me without a cause.*

### THE WITNESS OF THE DISCIPLES; BEING THE TESTIMONY OF JESUS,
### DECLARED AND INTERPRETED BY THE PARACLETE

26. *But when the Comforter is come, whom I will send unto you from the*

*Father, even the Spirit of truth, which proceedeth from the Father, he shall bear witness of me:* 27. *and ye also bear witness, because ye have been with me from the beginning.*

xvi. 1. *These things have I spoken unto you, that ye should not be made to stumble.* 2. *They shall put you out of the synagogues: yea, the hour cometh, that whosoever killeth you shall think that he offereth service unto God.* 3. *And these things will they do, because they have not known the Father, nor me.* 4. *But these things have I spoken unto you, that when their hour is come, ye may remember them, how that I told you. And these things I said not unto you from the beginning, because I was with you.* 5. *But now I go unto him that sent me; and none of you asketh me, Whither goest thou?* 6. *But because I have spoken these things unto you, sorrow hath filled your heart.* 7. *Nevertheless I tell you the truth; It is expedient for you that I go away: for if I go not away, the Comforter will not come unto you; but if I go, I will send him unto you.* 8. *And he, when he is come, will convict the world in respect of sin, and of righteousness, and of judgement:* 9. *of sin, because they believe not on me;* 10. *of righteousness, because I go to the Father, and ye behold me no more;* 11. *of judgement, because the prince of this world hath been judged.* 12. *I have yet many things to say unto you, but ye cannot bear them now.* 13. *Howbeit when he, the Spirit of truth, is come, he shall guide you into all the truth: for he shall not speak from himself, but what things soever he shall hear, these shall he speak: and he shall declare unto you the things that are to come.* 14. *He shall glorify me: for he shall take of mine, and shall declare it unto you.* 15. *All things whatsoever the Father hath are mine: therefore said I, that he taketh of mine, and shall declare it unto you.*

### THE NATURE AND SIGNIFICANCE OF THE THINGS
### THAT ARE TO COME

16. *A little while, and ye behold me no more; and again a little while, and ye shall see me.* 17. *Some of his disciples therefore said one to another, What is this that he saith unto us, A little while, and ye behold me not; and again a little while, and ye shall see me: and, Because I go to the Father?* 18. *They said therefore, What is this that he saith, A little while? We know not what he saith.* 19. *Jesus perceived that they were desirous to ask him, and he said unto them, Do ye inquire among yourselves concerning this, that I said, A little while, and ye behold me not, and again a little while, and ye shall see me?* 20. *Verily, verily, I say unto you, that ye shall weep and lament, but the world shall rejoice: ye shall be sorrowful, but your sorrow shall be turned into joy.* 21. *A woman when she is in travail hath sorrow, because her hour is come: but when she is delivered of the child, she remembereth no more the anguish, for the joy that a man is born into the world.* 22. *And ye therefore now have sorrow: but I will see you again, and your hearts shall rejoice, and your joy no one taketh away from you.* 23. *And in that day ye shall ask me nothing. Verily, verily, I say unto you, If ye shall ask anything of the Father, he will give it you in my name.* 24. *Hitherto have ye asked nothing in my name: ask, and ye shall receive, that your joy may be fulfilled.*

473

## CHRISTIAN KNOWLEDGE AND PRAYER
## THE MISUNDERSTANDING OF THE DISCIPLES

25. *These things have I spoken unto you in proverbs: the hour cometh, when I shall no more speak unto you in proverbs, but shall tell you plainly of the Father.* 26. *In that day ye shall ask in my name: and I say not unto you, that I will pray the Father for you;* 27. *for the Father himself loveth you, because ye have loved me, and have believed that I came forth from the Father.* 28. *I came out from the Father, and am come into the world: again, I leave the world, and go unto the Father.* 29. *His disciples say, Lo, now speakest thou plainly, and speakest no proverb.* 30. *Now know we that thou knowest all things, and needest not that any man should ask thee: by this we believe that thou camest forth from God.* 31. *Jesus answereth them, Do ye now believe?* 32. *Behold, the hour cometh, yea, is come, that ye shall be scattered, every man to his own, and shall leave me alone: and yet I am not alone, because the Father is with me.* 33. *These things have I spoken unto you, that in me ye may have peace. In the world ye have tribulation: but be of good cheer; I have overcome the world.*

### THE HUSBANDMAN, THE VINE AND ITS BRANCHES

xv. 1, 2. *The true vine* (cf. Ecclus. xxiv. 17–19; *Didache*, ix. 2). Although the immediate background is the tradition of the Last Supper and in particular the words concerning the Cup, including the promise to the disciples that they would drink of the fruit of the vine in the Kingdom (Matt. xxvi. 27–9), the Johannine interpretation of the scene is constructed upon the great Old Testament passages in which Israel is described as a *noble vine* planted by God (Jer. ii. 21, LXX *fruit-bearing and altogether true*), *fruitful and full of branches* (Ezek. xix. 10–14, cf. Ezek. xv. 1–6, xvii. 5–10) which *sent out her branches into the sea, and her shoots into the River* (Ps. lxxx. 8–19, cf. Isa. xxvii. 2–6). Since these passages almost invariably conclude with a description of the corruption of the vine, the metaphorical language is, with some adjustment, capable of application to the fate of Judas and of those who have gone out into the world and separated themselves from the Christian fellowship. The faithless Israel was compared with the *branch* which is *burned with fire* (Ps. lxxx. 16), and to the vine which is *given to the fire for fuel* (Ezek. xv. 6), whose *strong rods were broken off and withered; the fire consumed them* (Ezek. xix. 12.) In the Syriac Apocalypse of Baruch (2 Bar. xxxvi–xxxix) the vine which *opened its mouth and spake* and destroyed the Cedar, the prince of iniquities, is the Messiah. The use of a vine as a metaphor for Israel is frequent in the Rabbinic literature, for example 'as the vine is the least of all trees, and yet is the master of all, so the people of Israel appear insignificant in this world, but in the future (i.e. in the Messianic Age) their sovereignty will extend from one end of the world to the other' (quoted by Strack-Billerbeck on John xv. 1). The phrase *the fruit of the vine* (Mark xiv. 25 and parallels) echoes the Jewish grace over wine (see J. Lightfoot, *Horae Hebraicae*, Matt. xxvi. 26). The Old Testament imagery of the vine of God, set for the salvation of men, but liable to destruction if proved faithless, underlies the Johannine interpretation of the Last Supper. But the imagery is radically transformed. Jesus, the Son of God, is the incorruptible vine, His faithful disciples are the living and fruit-bearing branches, Judas and all other apostates are branches, broken off, withered, and fit only as fuel for the fire. *I am the true vine* is therefore not an illustration of the assimilation of Christian language to the formulæ of Oriental mysticism (Bauer); it is, rather, a formal denial of Jewish claims and the fulfilment of prophecy. Jesus, not Israel, is the vine of God; the disciples, not the Jews, are the branches of the vine. The synagogue is superseded by the Christian *Ecclesia*, and the true and genuine vine is contrasted with all that is counterfeit, false and inadequate for salvation. Saint Paul had made use of the metaphor of the Church as the Body of Christ and of the Christians as limbs of His Body to express the same truth (1 Cor. xii. 12 sqq.; Col. i. 18, ii. 19, cf. 1 Cor. x. 17).

*The husbandman* (cf. Isa. v. 1). The superseding of Judaism and the fulfilment of prophecy by the emerging of the Christian *Ecclesia* is an act of God. In the recent history of the Church He is neither idle nor inert. The vine is God's vine, for Jesus is the Son of God. The Father is therefore the owner of the vine and the prime agent in the care of the branches and the production of the fruit. His action is revealed in the moral purification of the true disciples who abide in His Son, and in the removal of the false disciples, who in actual fact leave the Christian Fellowship and return to the World as Judas had done (xiii. 30, cf. 1 John ii. 19, iv. 1).

*Taketh away—cleanseth.* There is in the Greek a play upon words which it is difficult to render into English. The Father *cleareth away* the unprofitable branches, and *cleanseth* those that bear fruit. He *lightens* the vine of its useless branches, and *enlightens* the true branches. The latter rendering, of course, only calls attention to the play upon words, it does not reproduce their literal meaning.

*vv.* 3–5. There is a double element in the purification of the disciples: the initial purgation occasioned by the Word of Jesus (vi. 63, cf. Eph. v. 26), and its conservation through the maintaining of a permanent union with Him, which is effected by the abiding of His Words in them (*v.* 7). In the Upper Room the initial purification had been declared and symbolized (xiii. 1–11, see COMMENTARY). The retention of this cleansing is their task in the future. Hence the urgent demand *abide in me* and the categorical assertion *Apart from me ye can do nothing*. As the Son can do nothing apart from the Father (v. 19), so the disciples can do nothing apart from the Son. The imperative *abide in me* is therefore immediately followed by the statement *and I in you*. This does not mean that if they abide in Him, He will abide with them, but rather because He abides in them, they are enabled to fulfil His command.

*Beareth much fruit*. The result of the divine cleansing of the disciples is their capacity to bear much fruit. Those who have believed in Jesus through the apostolic preaching are the fruit of the vine and its branches (xvii. 20), hence the addition *go and bear fruit* (v. 16), that is, *go out into the world* (xvii. 18, cf. Matt. xxviii. 19, 20). The narrative of the miraculous draught of fishes is the fulfilment of this command. The seven disciples *go a fishing* (xxi. 3). So long as they acted on their own initiative *they took nothing*, but under the direction of the Lord and in His presence they enclosed a multitude of fishes (xxi. 6): *Apart from me ye can do nothing*.

*v. 6*. The language belongs to the earlier tradition (Matt. v. 13, xiii. 30, 40–2, xv. 13, xviii. 8, 9, and elsewhere). Compare also Rom. xi. 22. *Behold then the goodness and the severity of God: toward them that fell, severity; but toward thee, God's goodness, if thou continue in his goodness: otherwise thou also shalt be cut off*. Here, however, the attention of the readers is directed less towards a future punishment than to the immediate result of an interior secession from the Christ (vi. 66, xiii. 30; 1 John ii. 19, iv. 1). The faithless disciple is at once *cast out* and *withers away*. The reverse side of the truth is stated in vi. 37: *Him that cometh to me I will in no wise cast out*.

*v. 7*. The phrase *abide in me* is expanded and defined as the abiding of the words of the Lord in the disciple. His words are redemptive acts of the Father (xiv. 10). They are spirit and life (vi. 63). The action of the Spirit ensures both their memory and their living interpretation (xiv. 26). Effective Christian prayer and the avoidance of disordered petitions are conditioned by the perception of the meaning of the Lord's teaching (xiv. 13 echoing Mark xi. 24).

*v. 8*. The active dependence of the disciples upon the Son is the glorification of the Father. The Father is glorified in the Son (xiv. 13), and in the good works of the disciples, that is in their effective missionary work, which is the evident proof of true discipleship (xiii. 35, xiv. 12, cf. Matt. v. 13, vii. 16–20). The sense is not altered if the reading *That ye may bear much fruit and become my disciples* is preferred (Codices Vaticanus and Bezae, and a few other authorities).

### THE EXPOSITION OF THE MYSTERY OF THE DEATH OF JESUS
### THE MANIFESTATION OF LOVE AND THE DUTY OF OBEDIENCE

*vv. 9–17*. The relation between the Father and the Son is the type and original of the relation between the Son and His disciples. His love for them can therefore be comprehended only when it is compared with the love of the Father for the Son. *Even as the Father have loved me, I also have loved you*. The aorist (*loved* rather than *hath loved*) is used in both clauses. It does not denote the secret and eternal love of the Father for the Son, but that love which, exposed in the life and work and death of the Son, is directed towards men, and is laid as it were in the bosom of the disciples (xvii. 26): *God so loved the world that he gave his only begotten Son, that whosoever believeth on him should not perish, but have eternal life* (iii. 16). The Son 'is not loved apart and for his own sake only, but that he may join us unto the Father with himself' (Calvin). And to this love is annexed obedience—indissolubly; for the fidelity of love is proved and shown forth in obedience. The Father loved the Son and gave Him definite commandments (iii. 35, cf. v. 20), and the Son showed forth His love by absolute obedience. *To abide in His love* and *to keep His commandments* are therefore but two modes of saying the same thing. In the same way the Son loved His disciples and gave them commandments, and their love for Him must likewise be exhibited in obedience to these commandments (xiv. 15); thus only can they abide in His love (xiv. 15, 21; 1 John iv. 16).

The abiding of the Son in the love of the Father perfected in submission to death at the Father's command (iv. 34, x. 17, 18, xix. 30, cf. Phil. ii. 8) is the joy and happiness of Jesus. It is therefore not by chance that this joy is first declared openly to His disciples on the eve of the Crucifixion. The joy of the Son in dying for the salvation of men, foreshadowed in the joy of the Baptist (iii. 29), who proclaimed Him to be the *Lamb of God which taketh away the sin of the world* (i. 29, 36), reveals the purpose of His mission. In so far as the disciples abide in His love and obey His commandments they too share in His joy (xiv. 20–4, xvii. 13; 1 John i. 4; 2 John 12), as they share in His peace (xiv. 27, xx. 21). The delightful divine merriness of the Christians, which originates in the Son and is deposited in His disciples (xvii. 3), is matured and perfected as they love one another, undergo persecution, and readily lay down their lives for the brethren (1 John iii. 16). *Walk in love, even as Christ also loved you, and gave himself up for us, an offering and a sacrifice to God for an odour of a sweet smell* (Eph. v. 2). This hierarchy of love and reciprocal charity is the life of the Church. The commandments of Jesus are therefore summed up in one commandment: *Love one another* (1 John iii. 23, iv. 21), as the commandments of the Father were comprehended in the one supreme demand that the Son should *lay down His life* (x. 17, 18). The commandment that the disciples should *love one another* is *a new commandment* (xiii. 34, 35). *New*, not so much because love is the fulfilment of the Law (Gal. v. 14), but rather because effective obedience to it depends upon the perception of the love of God manifested in the life and death of His Son. *Herein is love, not that we loved God, but that he loved us, and sent his Son to be the propitiation for our sins* (1 John iv. 7–11). Voluntary death is the supreme expression of love, and Jesus died for His friends. His action was, however, not an illustration of that human love which reaches to sacrifice of life, but the love of God mani-

477

fested to men in the obedience of His Son. Christian charity is thus shown to proceed from the recognition of the love of God in the death of His Son: and for this reason it is a new charity in obedience to a new commandment.

Thus the disciples are initiated into the mystery of the life and death of Jesus, and into the fellowship of His sufferings and of His love. This initiation is the dividing line between slavery and friendship. Hitherto He had named them servants (xiii. 16, cf. xii. 26); now, when they are consciously enrolled in His service, He names them friends, because to them He has disclosed His purpose. The phrase *the friends of Jesus* (cf. Luke xii. 4) echoes the Old Testament description of Abraham as *the friend of God* (Isa. xli. 8; 2 Chron. xx. 7; James ii. 23, cf. Wisd. vii. 27), from whom He did not hide the things which He was about to do (Gen. xviii. 17). Similarly, the making known of the love of God in the death of His Son removes the ignorance of the disciples and casts out fear. As *there is no fear in love*, so there can be no slavery (1 John iv. 18). It must not therefore be supposed that the meaning of the life and death of Jesus was laid bare to the world, and that only some few chose to accept Him. The truth is precisely the reverse (xiv. 22). The initiative belonged to and remained with the Son. He selected the few, and initiated them into the mystery of His death, in order that they might go forth, and declare the truth to the world (vi. 70; Luke vi. 13). The appointment of the chosen disciples to lead the mission to the world is the direct outcome of the death of the Christ. It is just possible that this is most delicately expressed by the writer's choice of the same Greek word for the *appointing* of the disciples as he had used in *v.* 13 for the *laying down* of the life of the Son. The allusion is preserved in the Vulgate translation. The Lord *divested* Himself of life that He might *invest* them with the apostolate to the world. He *set aside* His life and *set* them to their work. In this sense the work of the disciples was greater than that of the Lord (xiv. 12). His work was confined, theirs is world-wide. Their apostolic activity will consist in bearing fruit, 'catching fish' (xxi. 1 sqq.), making converts. And their converts will be capable of persistence. Those who believe through the apostolic preaching will *abide*. They are counted among the true disciples of Jesus, and will abide in the love of the Son, preserved under the care of His apostles (xxi. 15 sqq.), and purged of their sins by their powerful prayers (1 John v. 14–17); and finally, they will be raised up at the last day, for the fruit is gathered *unto life eternal* (iv. 36). The appointment of the disciples to the mission is also their appointment to a direct relation with the Father in prayer. Both appointments are interdependent, for just as the fruit can be secured and garnered only by the effective prayers of the faithful disciples, so prayer for the extension of the Church is the one petition proper to Christians. The command that the disciples should love one another is then solemnly repeated, for as the branches cannot bear fruit apart from the vine, so neither can one branch bear fruit without the assistance of the others. The evangelical labourers must be filled with that mutual charity which the author symbolizes in another place, when he tells that the six disciples accompanied Peter in his fishing: *We also come with thee* (xxi. 3). There can be no isolated apostolic fishing.

The redemptive importance of the death of the Son underlies the whole passage. It contains a further expansion of the saying *The bread which I will give is my flesh, for the life of the world* (vi. 51). The phrase *lay down his life* recalls the death of the Good Shepherd in accordance with the divine command (x. 14–18); it recalls also the *laying aside* of the garments (xiii. 4), symbolical of the humiliation of the Son which is the necessary condition of the cleansing of His disciples (1 John i. 7). The description of the mission to the world under the imagery of *bearing fruit* must be interpreted in close connection with xii. 20–4, where it is clearly implied that the mission to the Greeks is deferred until the death of the Christ is accomplished, since the grain of wheat remains alone until it does; but *If it die, it beareth much fruit.*

In these verses all this is presupposed. The emphasis is laid not upon the fact of the death, but upon the initiation of the disciples into its significance as the certain pledge of the love of God. The disciples become the friends of the Son because He reveals to them the meaning of what He is doing and its final purpose. Here again the background of the whole passage is the tradition of the Last Supper. The words and actions of the Lord in the Upper Room declared to His disciples the redemptive significance of His death. The new covenant is to be established through the outpouring of His Blood. By drinking the fruit of the vine, which is His Blood, the disciples are initiated into the new order, and must take up their cross and follow Him (Matt. xxvi. 26 sqq. and parallels). The author of the Fourth Gospel, however, does not merely interpret this ancient tradition and draw out its meaning: he is concerned to interpret it, because, through the interpretation of the Lord's words and actions, he is also interpreting the Eucharist. For the Eucharist is the exposition of the significance of the death of the Son of God, not to the world, but to the faithful Christians there gathered together (cf. 1 Cor. xi. 26). And as insight into the nature of the Christian religion enlightens the Eucharist, so the reverse is true; insight into the significance of the Eucharist and of the actions of the Lord in the Upper Room carries with it insight into the nature of the Christian religion.

### THE *VIA CRUCIS* AND THE HATRED OF THE WORLD

*vv.* 18–25. If then Charity be the mark of the Church, the World is disclosed by its hatred of this Charity. For the World is perceived in its ability to hate (1 John iii. 11–15). The implacable hatred of the World for the friends of Jesus is the sign of the verity of that friendship.

The initiation of the disciples into the mystery of the death of Christ therefore involves also their recognition of the powerful hatred of the World which caused His death. Both the love of God and the hatred of the World are subjects for revelation. Accordingly it is better perhaps to follow the Vulgate translation of *v.* 18, *If the world hateth you, know* (imperative) *that it hath hated me before it hated you* (R.V. mg.), rather than the R.V. *ye know* (indicative). The friendship of Jesus carries with it a corresponding enmity of the World. The separation of the disciples from the World renders them objects of its hatred. As their Master is not *of the world* (viii. 23), so His chosen disciples likewise are not of it, though they remain in it. Had they remained *of the world* it would be impossible for the World to hate them, as it was impossible for the World to hate the unbelieving brethren of Jesus (vii. 5-7). To be a Christian and at the same time to be *of the world* and loved by it is a paradox and a contradiction, since, as the Lord bore witness against it *that its works are evil* (vii. 7), so the disciples must perpetuate His teaching and share in its hatred. They are therefore reminded of the saying in xiii. 16 *A servant is not greater than his lord*, where it was applied to the necessity of mutual charity among the disciples and to the humility of their mutual love. Here its meaning is extended to cover also their humiliation in persecution. Its reference is precisely parallel to Matt. x. 24, 25. *A disciple is not above his master, nor a servant above his lord. It is enough for the disciple that he be as his master, and the servant as his lord. If they have called the master of the house Beelzebub, how much more shall they call them of his household! Fear them not therefore.* For the prophecies of persecution in the earlier tradition compare also Matt. v. 10-12, 44, x. 16-23, xxiii. 34; Mark xiii. 9-13; Luke ix. 23, 24, xiv. 27, and, of course, by implication the words at the Last Supper. The attitude of the World to Jesus conditions its attitude to His disciples. Those who persecuted Him will likewise persecute those who speak in His name, and those who kept His word will likewise observe the teaching of His disciples. In view of the fixity of the meaning, in the Johannine writings, of the Greek word translated *keep* or *observe* (viii. 51-5, xiv. 15, 21-4, xvii. 6; 1 John ii. 3-5, iii. 22, 24, v. 3), it is improbable that it should be here taken to mean *spy upon* (Bengel, and Loisy in the first edition of his commentary: in the second edition this decision is reversed).

It is necessary for the disciples to perceive precisely what is involved in the rejection of Jesus and in their persecution. It is sin, grounded upon ignorance of the Father. The hatred of the World is in fact enmity against God (1 John ii. 23). The advent of the Son was not a bare coming, not a bodily presence only. It was a coming joined with words and works. The Son was sent by the Father for the salvation of the world (iii. 17), and the words which He spake and the works which He accomplished are the words and works of the Father (v. 36, 37, xiv. 10, 11). Hatred of the Son is therefore hatred of the Father. The rejection of

Jesus is sin, distinguished from all other sin. It is inexcusable, for the World is held responsible to discern the truth when the truth is thus presented to it (ix. 41, cf. Deut. xviii. 18, 19). The apostasy of the World is the fulfilment of the prophecy in the Law *They hate me without a cause* (Ps. xxxv. 19, lxix. 4, cf. cix. 3, cxix. 161). The citation is taken from the Psalms and the writer includes it in the Law (cf. xii. 37–40). 'For all the doctrine of the prophets was nothing else but an appurtenance of the Law' (Calvin). The writer, moreover, names the Law *your Law* (viii. 17, x. 34), not so much that he may dissociate himself from it, as so many modern commentators maintain (see Bauer, detached note on i. 19), but rather in order to rivet upon the Jews those scriptures in which they boast themselves so proudly, and then to prove those same scriptures prophetic of their apostasy.

## THE WITNESS OF THE DISCIPLES; BEING THE TESTIMONY OF JESUS, DECLARED AND INTERPRETED BY THE PARACLETE

*vv.* 26, 27. Since the hatred of the World is provoked by the teaching of the disciples, it is of prime importance that they should be clearly instructed concerning the nature and authority of their teaching. They are set in the world as witnesses of Jesus, their ability to bear witness being grounded upon their intimate companionship with Him *from the beginning* (i. 14, vi. 64, 70; 1 John i. 1–4), that is, from their election at the outset of His messianic activity. The original purpose of their election was *that they might be with him* (Mark iii. 14). Saint Luke had defined the period of this companionship as *From the baptism of John unto the day that he was received up* (Acts i. 21, 22, cf. Luke i. 2). The authority of this witness to the World does not, however, rest solely upon the memory of their companionship with Jesus. The Son will send to them from the Father the Paraclete, who is the Spirit of truth. Jesus is the Truth; and the Spirit will bear witness to Jesus by giving the disciples understanding of the words which He spoke and the works which He wrought (xiv. 16, 26). He is able to do this because He proceeds from the Father. Nothing is said or implied here concerning the eternal relations of the Father and the Son and the Spirit. The words refer only to the mission of the Spirit for the enlightenment of the disciples, and consequently for the salvation of men. Nor is the work of the Spirit for one moment thought of as independent of the disciples of Jesus. The Spirit is sent to them. *He abideth with you, and shall be in you* (xiv. 17). When therefore the author proceeds, with an imperative which is also a present indicative (cf. xiv. 1, xv. 18), *And bear ye also witness* (R.V. mg.): *And ye also bear witness* (R.V.), he must not be understood to add an additional witness to the witness of the Spirit (Acts v. 32, xv. 28). The Greek words mean *and, moreover, it is ye who must and do bear witness*. The witness is the witness of the disciples who have been with Jesus from the beginning and in whom the Spirit of truth resides. The passage is parallel to 3 John 12, where the argument seems to be: Demetrius is a good man, all men agree in this; and the Truth bears witness to him, that is, *we also bear witness*, we who have seen (1 John i. 1–4) and have received the Spirit (1 John iv. 13, 14), *and thou knowest that our witness is true*. The witness of the disciples of Jesus is the witness of the Truth. The work of the Spirit is thus trebly circumscribed. His witness is the witness of the Father to the Son through the disciples. The truth is Jesus, and the Spirit can only disclose that truth. His witness can therefore be neither false nor independent. With the promulgation of this truth to the World the disciples are entrusted. They are the instruments of the operation of the Spirit, and He works in them. The purpose of the writer is, however, not so much to limit the activity of the Spirit of God as to enhance and declare the authority of the Church (Rom. viii. 16, 17; Acts i. 8). Of the Church, because in the perspective of the gospel the phrase *Because ye have been with me from the beginning* is not limited to the original disciples. *The beginning* means also in the Johannine writings conversion (1 John ii. 13, 14, 24; 2 John 6). All who have remained faithful since their conversion are also the chosen instruments of the Spirit. The authority of the disciples of Jesus is therefore the authority of Father, Son, and Holy Spirit, and their teaching is invested with this authority. It is possible that the Saying preserved in the earlier tradition (Mark xiii. 11; Matt. x. 19, 20; Luke xii. 11, 12) underlies the Johannine exposition of the operation of the Spirit.

xvi. 1–4. This clear exposition of the authority of the Apostles was necessary lest they should stumble in the presence of the enmity of the World or revolt at the obscurity and roughness of the Lord's words (vi. 61, 64, 70). *These things have I spoken unto you that ye should not be made to stumble* (Mark iv. 17, xiv. 27, 29; Matt. xi. 6, xv. 12; Luke vii. 23, cf. 1 John ii. 10). The hostility of the world can now be delineated more sharply than in the previous verses (xv. 20 sqq.). The possibility, nay even probability, of death (1 John iii. 12), which was then only suggested (see, however, xiii. 38), is now openly announced. The Jews will excommunicate the disciples from the company of Israel and from the ancient worship of God (ix. 22, xii. 42, cf. Luke vi. 22), and the generality of men will suppose that in putting them to death they are rendering to God a signal act of devotion, as it had been supposed that the death of Jesus was for the safety of the people of God (xi. 50). The reference is primarily to the murderous hatred of the Jews (Acts xxiii. 12, xxvi. 9 sqq., &c., cf. *Mart. of Polycarp*, xiii. 1). Lagrange compares Justin *Dial.*, chs. xcv, cx, cxxxi, cxxxiii). Strack-Billerbeck calls attention to the right of the zealous Jew to kill a man caught in a blasphemous act, which is allowed in the Mishnah, and stated to be a *Halakal of Moses of Sinai*, that is, an ancient Halakic tradition, cf. the Midrash to

Num. xxv. 13 'Every man who pours out the blood of the godless is as one who offers a sacrifice' (Strack-Billerbeck). Such an act of devotion, however, when directed against the disciples of Jesus, is revolt against God, grounded upon ignorance both of the Father and of the Son (xv. 21; Luke xxiii. 34; Acts iii. 17; Rom. x. 2). This is said, not to mitigate the offence, but to expose the ground of the hatred of the world. To be thrust out from the synagogue does not signify alienation from the people of God, indeed the disciples need have no horror of becoming 'strangers from the congregation out of which Christ is banished' (Calvin). The phrase *the hour cometh*, which is used elsewhere of the hour of the crucifixion (xii. 23, xiii. 1, xvi. 32), is here extended to include the hour of the corresponding humiliation of the disciples. This solemn initiation of the disciples into the sufferings of Jesus, of which they are reminded at each subsequent Eucharist, was deferred until the end of His ministry, because His bodily presence was until then their sufficient safeguard, and because the time of their humiliation was not yet. Now, however, when He is to be separated from them, He foretells their persecution, in order that the memory of His words may provide an additional protection (xiii. 19, xiv. 29, cf. Luke xxiv. 44). In the synoptic tradition the prophecies of persecution belong on the whole to the later period (Mark xiii. 9; Matt. v. 11, x. 17, xxiv. 9; Luke xii. 11, xxi. 12). But it is not these sayings that the author has chiefly in mind here. The reference is primarily to the words and actions of the Lord at the Last Supper, when the disciples were bidden to share in the Lord's broken Body and drink His Blood.

*vv.* 5, 6. In spite of the dangers which threaten the disciples of Jesus, there must be no sense of bereavement among them occasioned by His removal from their company. The contrast between the ancient time, when He was bodily present with them, and their subsequent bereavement, causes the writer again to reverse the human judgement upon this distinction. The desire for the continuance of the ancient days of bodily companionship is a false desire, presupposing ignorance of the purpose of the death of Jesus, and the goal of His journey. Grief at His departure remains only when the disciples fail to persist in asking the question *Domine, quo vadis?* (xiii. 36, cf. xiv. 5, xvi. 17). The answer to this proper question concerning the purpose and goal of the Lord's journey destroys grief, even though they cannot follow Him yet. The *Via Crucis* is the way to the Father, the necessary prelude to their mission of salvation to the World, the beginning of an even greater work entrusted to His disciples. The Son journeys to become their Paraclete with the Father (1 John ii. 1), to inaugurate the apostolic mission to the world, to send them another Paraclete who abides with them (xiv. 16, 17), and to deposit His joy in them (xiv. 28, xv. 11). There can be no mission of the Spirit that proceeds from the Father, until the Son has accomplished the command of the Father, and has returned to His side (vii. 39, xix. 30). 'My stay will deprive you of Him. My absence will procure you Him' (Bishop Andrewes, quoted by Swete).

*vv.* 7–11. If then the authority of the disciples is grounded upon the authority of the Father and of the Son and of the Spirit of Truth, and if they are set in the world and not removed from it, the nature of the mission invested with such high authority must be set forth in order that they may undertake the mission of salvation joyfully and without any sense of bereavement. The operation of the Spirit of Truth in the disciples of Jesus is defined as an effective exposition of the World, concerning Sin, Righteousness, and Judgement. These are the themes of the apostolic preaching (Acts xxiv. 25)—old themes, set and developed in a new tonality, because the witness of the Spirit and of the disciples is focused upon Jesus, and the nature of Sin, of Righteousness, and of Judgement is exposed in relation to Him, and thereby shown to be present, concrete realities. *And he, when he is come, will convict the world.* The Greek word translated *convict* (R.V.), *reprove* (A.V.), *rebuke* (Tyndale, Cranmer), *argue* (Rheims Version, reproducing the Vulgate), means literally to *put to the test, set forth, unmask, bring to light* (1 Cor. xiv. 24; Eph. v. 11), so that a judgement may be possible concerning what is true or false, good or bad, hence to *convince, convict, judge* (iii. 20, viii. 46. See Moulton-Milligan, *Vocabulary*; Preuschen-Bauer, *Wörterbuch*). The word is almost exactly equivalent to the English *expose*, which has precisely the same double meaning, *display to the public gaze, expound, explain, unmask, show up, hold up to reprobation* (*N.E.D.*). The operation of the Spirit in exposing Sin and Righteousness and Judgement is concisely illustrated in 1 Cor. xiv. 24–6, *If all prophesy, and there come in one unbelieving or unlearned, he is reproved* (R.V. mg. *convicted*, literally *exposed*) *by all, he is judged by all; the secrets of his heart are made manifest; and so he will fall down on his face and worship God, declaring that God is among you indeed.*

*Of sin, because they believe not on me.* It is preferable to preserve the translation *because* rather than *in that*, since it is not the unbelief of the world which is exposed, but the fact that sin is caused by unbelief (Loisy). That sin is the inevitable result of unbelief in Jesus is a truth consistently set forth in the Johannine writings, and the first Epistle was written primarily in order to assert it. Belief in Jesus is the mainspring of charity and of righteousness. They are rooted and grounded in faith in Jesus as the Christ, the Son of God who came in flesh. Remove this faith, and hatred and immorality appear as the concrete signs of its removal. If this is true of those who have once been Christians, how much more must it be true of the World which rejects the Son of God and persecutes the Church (iii. 19–21, vii. 7, viii. 47, ix. 41, xv. 22, 23; 1 John iii. 2–5, 8–11, 23, 24, iv. 2–21, v. 5, 18–20; 2 John 6–9). In rejecting Jesus the world deprives itself of the hope of virtue. This is the witness of the Spirit to the world through the disciples, who have been cleansed and purified by the faith which they are commissioned to publish abroad.

*Of righteousness, because I go to the Father, and ye behold me no more.* Jesus is the *Righteous One* (1 John ii. 1), no sin can be discovered in Him (viii. 46, xiv. 30). But His righteousness is not authenticated by human perception only; it is vindicated and ratified by the Father in His Resurrection and Ascension (Acts iii. 14, 15). The return to the Father is God's imprimatur upon the righteousness manifested in the life and death of His Son, and His very invisibility to His disciples still resident amidst the sin of the World is a sure sign that His righteousness is the righteousness of God. But the righteousness of God is not only manifested in Jesus, but is made available for men through His departure from the world. As sin is grounded upon unbelief, so faith is productive of righteousness and virtue. *Everyone who doeth righteousness hath been born of him* (1 John ii. 29, iii. 7). *He rose again for our justification* (Rom. iv. 25; 1 Pet. iii. 18-22). The truth concerning righteousness is therefore made known in the paradox of His departure.

*Of judgement, because the prince of this world hath been judged.* The victory of Jesus over the World (xvi. 33), and the derived victory of His faithful disciples (1 John ii. 13, 14), involve the judgement of the Prince of this World who opposed the Son of God and procured His death by empowering Judas to be the instrument of his murderous activity (viii. 44, xiii. 27, cf. xix. 11; 1 John iii. 12; 1 Cor. ii. 8). Though it is still true that the whole world lies in the power of the Evil One (1 John v. 19), yet he is fallen from power, and the World has been judged by a righteous decree of the Father (xii. 31, cf. Eph. ii. 2-10, vi. 12) following the manifestation of the Son of God who came to *destroy the works of the devil* (1 John iii. 8). Swete compares the conclusion of Saint Mark's Gospel according to the Washington manuscript, and to some manuscripts known to Jerome, *Christ said to them, the limit of the years of Satan's rule hath been reached and passed* (cf. also Ignatius, *Trall.* iv. 2). The dethronement of the devil must be exposed to the World and become the theme of the apostolic preaching.

*vv.* 12-15. This concise and pregnant definition of the apostolic gospel is capable of vast expansion and application. Not that the definition is incomplete, for, as the Samaritan woman had correctly judged, *when he* (Messiah) *is come, he will declare unto us all things* (iv. 25). But further insight is necessary to bring out its full meaning. This is precisely the work of the Spirit. *He shall guide you into all the truth*, that is, not into further new truth, but into the whole truth concerning that which was concretely and concisely set forth by the Son of God. The Greek word translated *guide* recalls the story in the LXX of God's leading His children in the desert and the language of the Psalms *Guide me in thy truth* (Num. xxiv. 8; Deut. i. 33; Ps. xxv. 5, 9, cxliii. 10; Is. lxiii. 14; Wisd. ix. 11, x. 17; see Swete). There is therefore no necessity to

introduce further references to the use of the word in the language of
the mystery religions (Bauer). But the old language is given a new and
more precise direction. Jesus is the Way in which the disciples must be
led by the Spirit, and He is also the Truth to which they must be guided.
The author is therefore concerned to impress upon his readers the
danger of false conceptions of the work of the Spirit. Inspiration does
not detach men from the Truth which is in Jesus, and set them free to
wander into new realms of truth apart from the sanctuary of God
(Ignatius, *Eph.* v. 2, *Trall.* vii. 2). With such private and secret revelations and inspirations the author is perfectly familiar, and he knows the
pride and hatred and immorality which they occasion (1 John ii. 18
sqq., iv. 1 sqq.; 2 John 7 sqq.; 3 John 9–11). The power of the Spirit
does not consist in secret and mystical revelations, but in the external
preaching of the Gospel, which makes men revolt from the World and
attaches them to the Church; and His action does not consist in delivering new truths to the disciples, but in providing a larger, deeper, and
more perfect understanding of the teaching which Jesus had given them
(xiv. 26, xv. 15, see Loisy) 'So soon as the Spirit is plucked away from
the word of Christ the gate is open unto all manner of dotings and
seducings' (Calvin). The author of the gospel therefore proceeds *What
things soever he shall hear, these shall he speak. . . . He shall glorify me.* The
sole work of the Spirit is the glorification of the Son, which is the glorification of the Father (xi. 4, xii. 23, xiii. 31, 32). As the teaching of the
Son was derived from the Father (vii. 16, 17, viii. 26, 40, xii. 49, 50), so
the Spirit will declare only what He shall hear, the identity of the teaching of the Son and of the Spirit being guaranteed by an identity of
origin. [There are three variant readings, to two of which the manuscript
witnesses are impressive: the future *shall hear*, which is found in Codices
Vaticanus, Bezae, the Koridethi Codex, and other Greek manuscripts,
and is well supported by the Versions; and the present *hears*, which is
found in Codices Sinaiticus and Regius, the best minuscule, three manuscripts of the Old Latin, and one manuscript of the Vulgate. Lagrange
suggests that the reading *hears* may reflect the developed doctrine of the
Spirit, according to which the future would obscure the eternal relation
of the Spirit to the Father.]

*He shall declare unto you the things that are to come.* Most modern commentators take this to mean that the Spirit will enable the disciples to foretell the future. The Christian prophet in the Book of Revelation in the
power of the Spirit undoubtedly claimed to foretell the events of the
End. *For the testimony of Jesus is the spirit of prophecy. And I saw the heaven
opened* (Rev. xix. 10 sqq.). *Come up hither and I will shew thee the things
which must come to pass hereafter. Straightway I was in the Spirit* (Rev. iv.
1 sqq., cf. i. 19, ii. 7, 11, 17, 29, iii. 6, 13, 22, xiv. 13). The reference
here may therefore be to the apocalyptic aspect of primitive Christian
prophecy (Bauer). But it is exceedingly doubtful whether this is in

fact intended by the author. He presumes that his readers are thinking of the words of the Lord before the crucifixion, and *the things that are to come* are not the end, but the new order which results from the departure of Jesus. 'Some do restrain this unto the spirit of prophecy, but in my judgement he meaneth rather the estate of his spiritual kingdom which should come, such as the Apostles saw shortly after his resurrection' (Calvin). This is the constant meaning in the Fourth Gospel of that which is *coming*. *The hour cometh, and now is, when the true worshippers shall worship the Father in spirit and in truth* (iv. 23, cf. the new purification, ii. 4, the new passing from death to life, v. 25). *He shall glorify me* defines the future announcement by the Spirit. The Spirit will announce (iv. 25; 1 John i. 5) and declare the mystery of the Church, which is the mystery of Christ (Col. iii. 11).

### THE NATURE AND SIGNIFICANCE OF THE THINGS THAT ARE TO COME

*vv.* 16–24. The interpretation of the *things that are to come* (*v.* 13), of the events which were imminent rather than of the End, is strongly supported, if not rendered absolutely necessary, by these verses. The Lord partially discloses His death and resurrection, the resurrection appearances and His ascension, the joy of the disciples and the fulfilment of that joy in the new economy of prayer. What the Spirit will fully declare He outlines in prophetic language that still preserves its parabolic form. The obscurity and the scandal of the Christian belief consist in the belief, not in a general restoration of all things at the End, but in that restoration which is accomplished in the death and resurrection of the Lord. This is acutely perceived by those disciples who fixed upon the phrase *a little while* (cf. xiv. 18, 19) as unintelligible.[1] The Lord perceives their questioning (ii. 25, vi. 61), but does not clearly enlighten them concerning His death and resurrection. He recalls the classical passages in the Old Testament in which the joy of the age of the messianic action of God, contrasted with the sorrow of the time preceding it, is compared with the sorrow and joy of childbirth (Isa. xxi. 3; Jer. xiii. 21, xxii. 23; Mic. iv. 9, 10). The important passages are, however, Isa. xxvi. 17 sqq., lxvi. 7–14; Hos. xiii. 13–15; for not only is the imminence of the deliverance compared with the birth of a child, but direct reference is made to the resurrection of the dead: *Thy dead shall live . . . awake and sing ye that dwell in the dust. . . . Come my people, enter thou into thy chambers, and shut thy doors about thee: hide thyself for a little moment, until the indignation be overpast* (Isa. xxvi. 19, 20; see the LXX version,

---

[1] This is so even if the phrase be glossed with the words *Because I go to the Father* (from *vv.* 5. 10): words which, according to the overwhelming evidence of the manuscripts, must, with R.V. against A.V., be omitted from *v.* 16.

which contains the actual Greek word *a little while* and an almost Johannine description of the resurrection of the dead); *I will ransom them from the power of the grave; I will redeem them from death: O death, where are thy plagues? O grave, where is thy destruction?* (Hos. xiii. 14); *Who hath heard such a thing? who hath seen such things? Shall a land be born in one day? shall a nation be brought forth at once? for as soon as Zion travailed she brought forth her children. . . . As one whom his mother comforteth, so will I comfort you; and ye shall be comforted in Jerusalem. And ye shall see it, and your heart shall rejoice* (Isa. lxvi. 8, 13, 14). The last passage contains not only the identical 'scandal' that the redemption should occur *at once, in a little while,* but the LXX version contains words virtually reproduced in the Fourth Gospel, *ye shall see, and your heart shall rejoice.* The parable of the joy of the woman in childbirth is therefore no mere general comparison, it is Old Testament messianic resurrection imagery. It is not irrelevant to suggest that the writer may have preserved the true originals of the belief of the primitive Church and of the Lord Himself, that the Christ must suffer death and rise again *according to the scriptures* or *in order that the scriptures might be fulfilled.*

The paradox of sorrow and joy (Matt. v. 4) will be wrought out in the experience of the disciples and in the revised experience of the world through the events which are to occur in *a little while.* What is to cause the disciples acute pain (Luke xxiv. 17; Mark xvi. 10; *Gospel of Peter* xi. 59) will become the ground of their fulfilled joy; what gives pleasure to the world will effect its grief-laden destruction. The reverse side of the paradox is, it is true, not at once fully expressed, and its expression is reserved until *v.* 33 *I have overcome the world.* Since it is the sorrow and joy of the disciples that are here primarily emphasized, it seems illegitimate exegesis to press a further significance upon the woman who gives birth to the son, and, with Loisy, under the influence of Rev. xii to allegorize her as the 'faithful synagogue' which gives painful birth to the Messiah, or as that faithful humanity which is the mother of the elect (cf. Westcott's citation from Rupert of Deutz), though it must be owned that the Johannine expression *born into the world* does suggest i. 9 (see note), iii. 17, xvi. 28, & c.

Great as the joy of the disciples will be when they see the Lord, their joy is not thereby fulfilled. It will be fulfilled only in that intimate fellowship with the Father (1 John i. 4) which is to be effected by the death and resurrection of Jesus. The significance of the death and resurrection is therefore adequately interpreted by the words *I go to the Father* (xiv. 28, xvi. 10), and the fulfilled joy of the disciples consists in the termination of the era of their anxious questioning and in the advent of a wholly new and effective economy of prayer—prayer to the Father in the name of Jesus. *In that day ye shall ask me nothing* (R.V. mg. *ask me no question*). The Greek word (ἐρωτάω) translated *ask* is as obscure as its Latin (cf. Augustine) and English equivalents. It may mean *question* or *petition*. In the Fourth Gospel it is used in both senses *question* (i. 19, 21, xvi. 19, 30, &c.), *petition* (xiv. 16, xvii. 9, 15, 20, &c.). The context must therefore determine what is its meaning here. There can indeed be no real doubt that *question* is demanded by the context. The disciples have continually questioned the Lord (xiii. 24, 25, 37, xiv. 5, 8, 22, xvi. 17, 18), but they have not addressed prayers to him; and further the words *verily, verily,* which introduce the following clause, habitually introduce a new thought, they do not merely recapitulate what has already been said. Here then the meaning is that the future joy of the disciples will be a joy in knowledge (vi. 45, xiv. 20); they will no longer busily question the Lord. The second meaning of the word does, however, suggest what follows. *Verily, verily, I say unto you, If ye shall ask anything of the Father, he will give it you in my name.* (Matt. vii. 7, xviii. 19; Luke xi. 13). The manuscripts show some variations in the text. The majority of Greek manuscripts, including Codices Bezae and Alexandrinus, and the Latin and Syriac Versions have *If ye shall ask anything of the Father in my name, he will give it you,* as in *v.* 26, cf. xiv. 13, xv. 16. In any case, both readings preserve the author's meaning. The new economy of prayer is prayer in the name of Jesus and it is effective because of what He has done. 'The name of Christ is both the passport by which the disciples may claim access into the audience chamber of God, and the medium through which the Divine answer comes' (Swete). The nature of Christian knowledge and prayer is further defined in the succeeding verses.

It should be noted that chs. xx and xxi are so phrased as to fulfil this prophecy. Mary's grief is turned into joy at the sight of Jesus, but her joy cannot be fulfilled until the risen Lord is ascended to the Father (xx. 11–18). *The disciples rejoiced when they saw the Lord,* but their true peace and effective work depends upon the gift of the Holy Spirit (xx. 20). It is expressly stated in xxi. 12 that the disciples did not *inquire of him* (cf. xvi. 23), for they knew *that it was the Lord.* Peter does, it is true, question Jesus, and is severely rebuked (xxi. 21, 22).

### CHRISTIAN KNOWLEDGE AND PRAYER
#### THE MISUNDERSTANDING OF THE DISCIPLES

*vv.* 25–33. The author of the gospel is fully aware that the Lord had taught His disciples by parables and by hard sayings. The Greek words translated *parable* and *proverb* reproduce the LXX translations of the single Hebrew word *mashal*, which means simply a hard, enigmatic, obscure, saying. 'Dark speeches or notable sayings, which the Greeks call *apophthegmata*, which have for the most part some doubtful or obscure thing in them' (Calvin). No subtle distinction between parable and allegory is suggested. The Lord's teaching was characterized by this obscurity throughout; not merely the so-called *parables* but the 'sayings of the ministry in general' (Swete). In this obscurity the messianic prophecy of Isaiah is fulfilled: *Here a little and there a little ... With stammering lips and with another tongue will he speak unto this people.* (Isa. xxviii. 10, 11, R.V. mg.). The author is, however, also aware that in the power of the Spirit the Church has been enabled to understand the Lord's teaching and to interpret it correctly (Matt. xiii. 11 and parallels). Consequently, though he introduces into his narrative parabolic similes in order to preserve the atmosphere of enigma characteristic of the earlier tradition (iii. 8, x. 6, xi. 13, xvi. 21), and though he speaks even less clearly of the death and resurrection than the earlier evangelists had done (Mark viii. 31, &c.), yet he knows the interpretation and allows it to control his narrative. It is therefore only with an effort that he attempts to recapture a past history that has been superseded by incorporating the ancient obscurity into his narrative. In the words *I shall no more speak unto you in proverbs, but shall tell you plainly of the Father* the distinction between the original teaching of Jesus and the teaching of the Church is justified and explained. The return of Jesus to the Father inaugurated a new era, in which the Lord speaks to His disciples no longer obscurely but clearly and openly; it is presumed that the readers of the gospel understand that He speaks to them through the Spirit which they have received (Matt. xxviii. 19, 20). Here is the Christian knowledge of God, a knowledge gained through the spiritual interpretation of the teaching of Jesus. The hour—*the hour cometh*—which separates the era of ignorance from the era of knowledge is the hour of the death and resurrection of Jesus (ii. 4, iv. 23, v. 25, 28, xii. 23, 27, xvii. 1, cf. Mark xiv. 41). The new era is, however, characterized, not only by knowledge, but by fellowship with the Father in prayer, *In that day ye shall ask in my name*, and by the initiative of the love of the Father, which responds not to an interpolated petition of the Son, but to the love and faith of the disciples. There is no parallel here to the passage of Philo (*De Migr. Abr.* 174, 175) where, commenting on Exod. xxiii. 20, 21, he says that the perfect soul has no need of the assistance of the divine *Logos* (Bauer). The meaning is precisely opposite. The new economy of knowledge and prayer is *in the name of Jesus* (Eph. ii. 8), and it depends upon the disciples' love for Him and faith in Him: *Because ye have loved me and have believed that I came forth from the Father* (*from God* according to several Greek manuscripts, including Codex Alexandrinus and the original reading of Codex Sinaiticus, and the Latin and Sinaitic Syriac Versions, cf. viii. 42, xiii. 3, xvi. 30). Compare the parallel distinction of the prophetic revelation of God to Aaron and Miriam in visions and dreams and in dark speeches, and His revelation to His servant Moses *from mouth to mouth, even manifestly*, because *He is faithful in all my house* (Num. xii. 6 sqq.). The contradiction with xiv. 13, 14 (cf. 1 John ii. 1), which has caused such difficulty to commentators both ancient and modern, is superficial rather than real. The point here is not that the disciples must not petition Jesus or that He will have no part in answering their petitions, but that they need no mediated or interpolated prayer to mitigate the anger of God, *For the Father himself loveth you*. Saint Augustine has penetrated the meaning of the passage when he comments, 'The Son asketh not the Father, but Father and Son alike listen to those who ask.' Nor must 1 John ii. 1 be so interpreted as to destroy this conception of the love of God. Jesus is the Paraclete who is with the Father, not an advocate with the Father, as though the Father were to the Christians a judge who must be persuaded to mercy and love by the Son. The believers 'have the heart of God' (Calvin), and prayer to Christ which proceeds upon the assumption that He is distinct from the Father and more open to the prayers of men is forbidden both here and in xiv. 14, where the union of the Father and the Son provides the basis of prayer to Christ and of His answer to prayer.

The belief which conditions Christian knowledge and the new economy of prayer is now clearly stated. Christian faith is two-fold, paradoxical, and historical. The two clauses are separated by the word translated *again*, but it marks a contrast (1 John ii. 8; Matt. iv. 7), and should be rendered *but now*. He who left the Father and entered the world is He who left the world and returned to the Father. In thus stating the paradox of the humiliation and glorification of the Christ the Gospel is formulated and declared. The disciples frowardly imagine that they have already perceived the meaning of this definition of faith in Jesus. So far as it goes their faith is sincere and formally correct (xvii. 8), but it is none the less inadequate, since they repeat but a part of the Lord's words, and immature, since their conduct will fail to correspond with their belief. Like Nathanael and the woman of Samaria (i. 47 sqq., iv. 19, 29) the disciples propose to base their belief in the divine origin of Jesus upon His discernment and omniscience which render their questions unnecessary (ii. 25). The awkward *that anyone should ask thee* must therefore not be corrected in favour of the easier *that thou shouldest ask any man* (Sinaitic Syriac). Their faith must rest securely on greater things than these (i. 51), and so the Lord roughly shatters their confident faith and understanding (cf. vi. 69, 70, xiii. 38) by foretelling their faithless flight and desertion (Mark xiv. 50; Matt. xxvi. 56; *Gospel of Peter* xi. 59), and their scattered return to the homes which they had formerly abandoned at His call. The Christ must suffer alone; *I have trodden the winepress alone; and of the peoples there was no man with me* (Isa. lxiii. 3). Alone the grain of wheat must fall into the earth and die, that it may bear much fruit (cf. xii. 24). But this is no cry for human assistance or friendship, for *the Father is with Him* (viii. 29). He does not depend upon the support of men, and there is no desertion by God. Holtzmann and other commentators find in these words a correction or gloss upon the words in the older tradition *My God, my God, why hast thou forsaken me?* (Mark xv. 34; Matt. xxvii. 46). But this saying is a citation from Ps. xxii, and the whole meaning of the Psalm is that God does not desert His suffering servants. The Johannine saying does not gloss or correct the earlier tradition; it presumes and interprets it, and, it may be added, interprets it correctly.

The sentence which concludes the discourses in the Upper Room sums up this meaning. The flight and desertion of the disciples is but an episode, due to the immaturity of their faith. The tribulation which caused their flight will remain, but in Jesus they will find peace in adversity (xiv. 27, xx. 19, 26). The words which the Lord had spoken will become the ground of that confidence which will be theirs when they remember them and perceive their meaning (xvi. 4). Finally the paradox is uttered. The Christ in His humiliation, desertion, and death, has conquered the world (xii. 31, xiii. 31; Rev. iii. 21, v. 5). The author rivets the attention of his readers upon the victory of the Christ, because their victory is thereby declared and made possible (1 John ii. 12-15, iv. 4, v. 4, 5; Rev. xii. 11). The victory of Jesus inaugurates the victorious mission of His disciples in the tribulation of the world: *Thanks be to God, which giveth us the victory through Jesus Christ* (1 Cor. xv. 57).

The final section of the discourse is as closely linked to the earlier narrative of the words and actions of the Lord in the Upper Room narrated in Mark xiv. 17-31 as were the earlier sections. This is because the author is interpreting the earlier tradition. Just as he had preserved the break in the Marcan narrative (xiv. 31, cf. Mark xiv. 26, 42), so here the use of the Greek words translated *made to stumble* (xvi. 1) and *scattered* (xvi. 32), and the context in which they occur, call to mind the Marcan citation of Zech. xiii. 7 (Mark xiv. 27). Further, the words *the hour cometh, yea, is come* (xvi. 32) echo the Marcan words *to-day in this night* (Mark xiv. 30). The prophecies of the new order which is to be brought into being by the death and resurrection of Jesus, and of the necessity of the future suffering of the disciples, expand and explain the words concerning the (new) covenant and the partaking of the bread and wine which is the Body and Blood of the Lord. They too must take up their cross and follow Him (Mark xiv. 22-5). The truth is that the discourse always tends to return to its origin in the earlier tradition, and any new material that is incorporated also rests upon Sayings of Jesus preserved in the synoptic record. The definition, for example, of the new economy of knowledge and prayer rests upon Mark iv. 11 and parallels, and upon Matt. vii. 7, xviii. 19; Luke xi. 13. To such an extent is the earlier tradition presupposed that the fulfilment of the prophecy of the desertion and flight of the disciples is found in Mark xiv. 50 *And they all left him and fled* (cf. Matt. xxvi. 56), but not in the Johannine narrative of the Passion. Here the desertion is definitely obscured. They are allowed to depart at the direct command of the Lord (xviii. 8, 9), two of the disciples follow Him to the court of the High Priest (xviii. 15), the Beloved Disciple, so far from returning *to his own home* (xvi. 32) stands by the cross, watches the end, and then departs with the mother of the Lord *unto his own home*, presumably in accordance with the will of Jesus (xix. 27, 35), and all the disciples remain in Jerusalem (xx. 3, 19, 26). Ch. xxi does, it is true, presuppose that the disciples had returned to Galilee to their fishing. It is, however, possible that the author has in mind the flight of the disciples to Galilee rather than the flight at the arrest, and that the opening of ch. xxi is the fulfilment of the prophecy recorded here and in Mark xiv. 27. It should be noted that the *Gospel of Peter* records a flight into Galilee and the return of the Apostles to their former occupation: 'But we, the twelve disciples of the Lord, were weeping and mourning. And each one, grieving at what had occurred, returned to his home. But I, Simon Peter, and Andrew my brother, took nets and returned to the sea (Galilee), and there was with us Levi, the son of Alphæus, whom the Lord . . .'. The manuscript breaks off at this point; but it can hardly be doubted that originally it contained an account of an appearance by the lake. If the fourth Evangelist also is referring to a general flight into Galilee, presumed in ch. xxi, the introduction of xix. 26, 27 may be intended to exonerate the Beloved Disciple from this general act of faithless cowardice. Moreover, the question arises whether this tradition of a flight into Galilee may not have been originally recorded in the lost end of Mark (see note on pp. 663 sq.).

# THE EVE OF THE CRUCIFIXION

## IV

## THE CONSECRATION PRAYER

### XVII

#### THE CONSECRATION OF JESUS
#### TO DEATH AND OF HIS DISCIPLES TO THE MISSION—
#### AD GLORIAM DEI

In the earlier tradition the lonely prayers of Jesus are handled with great reserve (Mark i. 35, vi. 46, xiv. 32–42, and parallels, Luke iii. 21, v. 16, ix. 18, xi. 1, cf. Matt. xi. 25 sqq., Luke x. 21 sqq.), and the author of the Fourth Gospel has hitherto only on two occasions recorded anything which could be described as prayer (xi. 41, 42, xii. 27, 28), and these are of the nature of ejaculations. Here, however, is set forth a collected, sustained address to the Father in the presence of the disciples (cf. Bernard). According to a venerable tradition, originating, it would seem, with David Chytræus, who died in 1600 and is described by Lagrange as 'one of the last of the Fathers of Lutheranism', most commentators entitle this extended prayer of the Lord the High-priestly Prayer—*Precatio Summi Sacerdotis*. The matter of the title is, however, to be found in the Patristic commentaries; Cyril of Alexandria, for example, writes, 'Since He is the High Priest of our souls. . . He most fittingly makes His prayer on our behalf. . . . Then also, since He is an High Priest, in so much as He is Man, and, at the same time, brought Himself a blameless sacrifice to God the Father. . . . He moulds the prayer for blessing towards us, as Mediator and High Priest.' And yet, it may be that Westcott's heading 'The Consecration Prayer' even more appropriately summarizes its content and efficacy, because it preserves the reference to a particular historical occasion, which is certainly intended by the author of the Gospel. *These things spake Jesus; and lifting up his eyes to heaven, he said, Father. . . .* The prayer is the solemn consecration of Himself in the presence of His disciples as their effective sacrifice; it is His prayer for glorification in and through His death; it is His irrevocable dedication of His disciples to their mission in the world, and His prayer that both they and those who believe through their teaching may be consecrated to the service of God; and finally, it concludes with the prayer that the Church thus consecrated may at

494

the End behold the glory of the Son and dwell in the perfect love of
the Father and the Son. The address *Father—Holy Father—Righteous*
(Just) *Father* marks the movement of prayer from the death of the Christ
to the glorification of the Church. No doubt, in the author's perspective,
the prayer may appear as the perpetual prayer of the ascended Christ,
or as the model prayer of the Church, but the origin and prime significance of the prayer lie in the historic situation in the Upper Room,
and its content in the words and actions of the Lord in the Upper Room,
interpreted and reproduced in the teaching and worship of the Church,
the whole being given literary form by the author of the gospel. The
prayer cannot therefore be understood as the free invention of the
Evangelist, or as the particular Eucharistic prayer of a Christian
prophet (Loisy, second edition, p. 441), nor is it adequately explained
as composed under the influence of Oriental mystery religions, or as
resulting from an experience similar or identical with that which gave
birth to the effusions of the mysteries (Bauer, detached note on xvii.
26). It is, as Quesnel well comments, 'the order obeyed by the Church
in her liturgy that the readings and expounding of the words of Christ
and His Apostles should precede the prayer of consecration', and it may
be that the structure of chs. xiii–xvii corresponds with the structure of
Christian worship at the time when the gospel was written, in which the
scene in the Upper Room was reproduced and creatively interpreted
by spiritual teaching (chs. xiv–xvi), and finally summed up in a comprehensive Eucharistic prayer (ch. xvii, cf. *Didache* ix, x, see Loisy). If
this be so, the author does intend to describe that perfect conjunction
of teaching, exhortation, and prayer, and that model worship in which
the Lord Himself is the teacher and in which the Lord Himself provides the Eucharistic prayer. But it would be a grave misunderstanding
of his purpose to explain this as merely a mystical idealizing of Christian
worship. In these chapters he returns to the origin of the Church and
of its worship, to the death and resurrection of Jesus, and more precisely
to the tradition of what He said and did in the night in which He was
betrayed. These are what require interpretation, and the author is
confident that the Church in the power of the Spirit possesses their true
interpretation. The Lord had then, in the presence of His disciples,
consecrated Himself to death as the effective sacrifice upon which their
sanctification was to depend, and He had solemnly dedicated them to
the mission which was to be the effective result of His death and resurrection. The Church must therefore in its teaching and worship preserve and reproduce this double consecration, for upon it the hope of
ultimate glory rests. In thus preserving and reproducing the original
consecration it is not only free to interpret the original scene, but compelled to do so by the possession of the Spirit of Truth. Even if it could
be proved that the author of the gospel, or the primitive Church, used
the language of the mysteries for its interpretation, it would be an ir-

relevant discovery since the *hard saying* is not the Johannine, but the Marcan language, *This is my blood of the covenant—Take ye; this is my body—I will no more drink of the fruit of the vine, until that day when I drink it new in the Kingdom of God.*

## THE COMPLETED WORK OF THE SON

xvii. 1. *These things spake Jesus; and lifting up his eyes to heaven, he said, Father, the hour is come; glorify thy Son, that the Son may glorify thee:* 2. *even as thou gavest him authority over all flesh, that whatsoever thou hast given him, to them he should give eternal life.* 3. *And this is life eternal, that they should know thee the only true God, and him whom thou didst send, even Jesus Christ.* 4. *I glorified thee on the earth, having accomplished the work which thou hast given me to do.* 5. *And now, O Father, glorify thou me with thine own self with the glory which I had with thee before the world was.* 6. *I manifested thy name unto the men whom thou gavest me out of the world: thine they were, and thou gavest them to me; and they have kept thy word.* 7. *Now they know that all things whatsoever thou hast given me are from thee:* 8. *for the words which thou gavest me I have given unto them; and they received them, and knew of a truth that I came forth from thee, and they believed that thou didst send me.*

## THE LORD PRAYS FOR HIS DISCIPLES

9. *I pray for them: I pray not for the world, but for those whom thou hast given me; for they are thine:* 10. *and all things that are mine are thine, and thine are mine: and I am glorified in them.* 11. *And I am no more in the world, and these are in the world, and I come to thee. Holy Father, keep them in thy name which thou hast given me, that they may be one, even as we are.* 12. *While I was with them, I kept them in thy name which thou hast given me: and I guarded them, and not one of them perished, but the son of perdition; that the scripture might be fulfilled.* 13. *But now I come to thee; and these things I speak in the world, that they may have my joy fulfilled in themselves.* 14. *I have given them thy word; and the world hated them, because they are not of the world, even as I am not of the world.* 15. *I pray not that thou shouldest take them from the world, but that thou shouldest keep them from the evil one.* 16. *They are not of the world, even as I am not of the world.* 17. *Sanctify them in the truth: thy word is truth.* 18. *As thou didst send me into the world, even so sent I them into the world.*

## JESUS DEDICATES HIMSELF AS AN EFFECTIVE SACRIFICE

19. *And for their sakes I sanctify myself, that they themselves also may be sanctified in truth.*

## THE PRAYER FOR THE CHURCH

20. *Neither for these only do I pray, but for them also that believe on me through their word;* 21. *that they may all be one; even as thou, Father, art in*

*me, and I in thee, that they also may be in us: that the world may believe that
thou didst send me.* 22. *And the glory which thou hast given me I have given unto
them; that they may be one, even as we are one;* 23. *I in them, and thou in me,
that they may be perfected into one; that the world may know that thou didst send
me, and lovedst them, even as thou lovedst me.* 24. *Father, that which thou hast
given me, I will that, where I am, they also may be with me; that they may behold
my glory, which thou hast given me: for thou lovedst me before the foundation of
the world.* 25. *O righteous Father, the world knew thee not, but I knew thee; and
these knew that thou didst send me;* 26. *and I made known unto them thy name,
and will make it known; that the love wherewith thou lovedst me may be in
them, and I in them.*

### THE COMPLETED WORK OF THE SON

xvii. 1. *The hour* (xii. 23, 27, xiii. 1, xvi. 32, &c.) has now arrived in
which the work of the Christ must be completed by the voluntary sacrifice of His life for the salvation of the world and by His consequent
glorification (xii. 23, xiii. 31, cf. Phil. ii. 6–11). The time which was
hitherto *not yet* (ii. 4, vii. 6, 8, 30, viii. 20) is now fulfilled. He has
handed over to His disciples teaching concerning His relation to the
Father, concerning His death and resurrection, concerning the new
order of knowledge and prayer in His name, and concerning their
mission in a hostile world. The whole truth is now theirs, and its meaning
will also be theirs in a little while by the power of the Spirit which is
to be given to them. But, 'since doctrine waxeth cold unless it be made
effectual by God' (Calvin), it now remains only for Him to consecrate
Himself in their presence as their sacrifice, to commit them into the
hands of His Father for their present and future welfare, and to enter
Himself upon the *Via Crucis*, which is also the *Via Gloriosa*. The transition from teaching to consecration and confident prayer is marked
by the eyes turned upward (xi. 41, cf. Mark vi. 41, vii. 34; Acts vii.
55, contrast Luke xviii. 13) and by the repeated address *Father, Holy
Father, Righteous Father* (*vv.* 1, 5, 11, 21, 24, 25, cf. xii. 27, 28; Matt. xi.
25; Luke x. 21). Loisy is persuaded that not only the address *Father*
echoes the Lord's Prayer in its Lucan form (Luke xi. 2, cf. Matt. vi. 9),
but that the author 'seems almost to have intended to paraphrase them
[the clauses of the Lord's Prayer] one after another, interpreting them
according to his mystical theology' (second edition, p. 451).

*v. 2. Glorify thy Son, that the Son may glorify thee. . . . Glorify thou me with
thine own self* (lit. *by thy side,* i.e. in heaven contrasted with *on the earth,
v. 4*) *with the glory which I had with thee before the world was.* The glorification of the Son is not to be understood as the reward of virtue. The glorification of the Son is for the glorification of the Father, and the glorification of the Father is the salvation of men (vii. 39, viii. 54, ix. 3, xi. 4,
xii. 16, 23, 28, xiii. 31, 32, xiv. 13, xv. 8, xvi. 14, cf. Phil. ii. 11). For this

reason universal authority was committed unto Jesus, *authority over all flesh*, and for this reason also He must be exalted. The expression *all flesh* is a Hebraism denoting 'mankind in their weakness and transitoriness, as contrasted with the majesty of God' (Westcott); but here it gains an added significance from the words of the Prologue, *The Word became flesh* (i. 14), since it was precisely because the Son of God *became flesh* that He received *authority over all flesh*, in order that he might *give eternal life—to whatsoever thou hast given him*. The faithful disciples are the gift of God to the incarnate Son, and they alone recognized the authority of Jesus. In the contrast between *all flesh* and *whatsoever thou hast given* is expressed the inevitable tragedy of the mercy of God; it is offered to all, but received by the few, and those the elect. The Christ was given power over all in order that He might give eternal life to the elect (Holtzmann). The grammatically awkward neuter *that which thou hast given him* (*me, vv.* 11, 24, cf. vi. 39) subsequently resolved into the masculine plural *to them* (cf. *v.* 9), seems to reproduce a descriptive title of the disciples of Jesus and of the faithful Christians. They were the 'Gift of God', Nathans, Theodores, Deodati, dedicated to God and given by Him to Christ for His glory and to the world for its salvation. Those manuscripts therefore in which the neuter singular is changed into the masculine plural represent glosses upon the original text.

*v.* 3. There is then but one road to eternal life—the knowledge of the Father of Jesus as *the only true God* and the recognition of Jesus Christ as Him whom the Father sent (aorist, cf. vi. 29, xv. 12) into the world for its salvation. The name *Jesus Christ*, which is used in the gospel only here and in i. 17, but frequently in the first Epistle (1 John i. 3, &c.), suggests that the whole sentence is an epitome of Christian faith (cf. 1 Thess. i. 9, 10; Rom. xvi. 26, 27; 1 Tim. vi. 13–16; Rev. xv. 4) as similar words are of Mohammedan belief. This knowledge of the Father and of the Son is no double knowledge (vii. 28), any more than the *fellowship with the Father, and with his Son Jesus Christ* (1 John i. 3) is a double fellowship. It is one faith in God and one knowledge of Him, by which the knowledge of God in the Old Testament (Deut. vi. 4) is fulfilled, and which is set against the ignorance of Jew (viii. 55) and Gentile alike. Faith in Jesus Christ as The Apostle of the Father—*him whom thou didst send*—is the ground of the Christian knowledge of God, and this true and full knowledge of God is the ground of eternal life, or, as Cyril of Alexandria says, it is the 'Mother and nurse of eternal life', because it is the foundation of the vital communion between God and the believers in Christ by charity (Loisy). It would therefore be an entire misunderstanding of the passage were it supposed that Christian faith, knowing God, afterwards descended to Christ (cf. Calvin).

*vv.* 4–8. The work of Jesus *on the earth* had been *perfected* (v. 36, xix. 30, cf. Luke xiii. 32; Heb. ii. 10, v. 9, vii. 28) precisely because He had manifested this faith, which is both the glory and the name of God, to those especial men who had been called out of the world by the Father and dedicated to the Son as the instruments of His extended mission to the world. The incarnate Son of God has, therefore, completed His work by bringing into concrete existence in the world the messianic congregation of the faithful disciples. Thus the work of Jesus is not defined as a general proclamation of the Fatherhood of God and the Brotherhood of men, but rather as the creation of the Church, the *Ecclesia* of God, consisting of men of flesh and blood extracted from the world to which they had hitherto belonged—by the power of God. The repeated insistence upon the faithful disciples of Jesus as the gift of God (vi. 37, 44, x. 29) implies no technical doctrine of predestination; it is simply the clear recognition that the faith of the original disciples, and, in the perspective of the gospel, veritable entrance into the fellowship of the Church by faith, were and are no human achievement, but an act of God, whose glory is the glory of God. Upon the fidelity of the original disciples of Jesus the salvation of the scattered children of God in the world was to depend; but their fidelity was assured, because they were the true disciples; they belonged to the Father and were given to the Son; they were the faithful guardians of the Word of the Father, which they had received in the Words of the Son—*they have kept thy word*; and finally they recognized the nature of all that the Father had given to the Son, namely, that all, both the words and the works of Jesus, were in very truth the words and works of God. Immature as their faith may have been before the advent of the Spirit, yet they knew assuredly that Jesus came forth from God (xvi. 30) and they believed in Him as The Apostle whom God had sent. Knowledge and faith are therefore closely interwoven, since knowledge is appropriated by faith, and also supports it (vi. 69).

The annunciation of the name of God to the original disciples was, then, the perfected work of the incarnate Son of God *on the earth*: the extension of this work in the world could, however, be inaugurated only by the glorification of the Son by the Father's side with the glory which He had with the Father before the world was, for upon this exaltation the efficacy of the Church's work depends. *I glorified thee on the earth. . . . And now, O Father, glorify thou me with thine own self with the glory which I had with thee before the world was.* Loisy has summed up the distinction between the work of the Christ on earth and in heaven admirably: 'The glory of the Father, which is the salvation of all the children of God, could not be fully realized by the Son under the conditions of his earthly activity, because that was an external existence subject to all the limitations of human action. When, however, the action of Christ, wholly spiritualized in the divine glory, should become spiritual and universal, instead of being limited to a useless preaching to the Jews, then the Son would be able to exercise the full powers given him for the benefit of humanity' (Loisy, second edition, pp. 441, 442). *Verily, verily, I say unto you, He that believeth on me, the works that I do shall he do also; and greater works than these shall he do; because I go unto the Father* (xiv. 12).

## THE LORD PRAYS FOR HIS DISCIPLES

*vv.* 9–14. The prayer, though strictly limited to prayer for the disciples (Jer. vii. 16, xi. 14, xiv. 11, cf. 1 John v. 16), is, however, an oblique prayer for the world (see *vv.* 21, 23), since the salvation of the world or, at any rate, of the scattered children of God in the world, depends upon the fidelity of the disciples of Jesus. The Son therefore at His departure solemnly commits them into the care of the Father to whom they rightfully belong. But this surrender does not mean that in passing under the direct care of the Father they are removed from the care of the Son, for three reasons. First, all that belongs to the Father belongs equally to the Son, for the property of the one is the property of the other; secondly, because their glory, that is, their effective mission in the world, is not only for the glory of the Father, but also for the glory of the Son, who is therefore vitally concerned with their work; and thirdly, because, though He departs from the world and they remain in it, yet, in going to the Father, He attains an even closer and more effective union with them.

The nature of the petition is denoted by the address *Holy Father*. The holiness of God marks His separation from the unbelief and wickedness of the world, which lies in the power of the Devil (1 John v. 19). It is precisely this holiness that marks the true disciples of Jesus, who are in the world but not of it, and which provides the ground of their unity. Hitherto their unity and their distinction from the world had been preserved by the bodily presence of Jesus on earth. 'He brooded them under his wings as a hen doth her chickens; but now, when he departeth he prayeth his Father to cover them with his safeguard' (Calvin). Now their holiness must proceed from the holiness of the Father, and their unity must reflect the unity of the Father and the Son, and can therefore be of no human conspiring or contriving. *Holy Father, keep them in thy name which thou hast given me, that they may be one, even as we are.* The power of God towards unity and the limit of this power have been revealed by the Son: *I kept them in thy name which thou hast given me: and I guarded them.* The antecedent of the relative clause *which thou hast given me* (*vv.* 11, 12) must, according to the grammatical structure of the sentences be *thy name*. Jesus prays for the fidelity of His disciples to the manifestation of God (the Name of God) which He had revealed to them, and to which they had been kept faithful whilst He remained with them (cf. *vv.* 4, 8). But in the whole context (see *vv.* 2, 6, 9, 24, cf. vi. 39) the phrase *which thou hast given me* must be taken as descriptive also of the disciples, who were the gift of God to the Son. The reading therefore *whom thou hast given me* (Vulgate, supported by one of the correctors of

Codex Bezae and by other manuscripts), though certainly not the original reading, yet brings out a meaning latent in the text.

No one of the men who had been given to the Son by the Father had been lost (Isa. xxxiv. 16, LXX), save Judas, the son of loss (cf. 2 Thess. ii. 3; Matt. xxiii. 15), who went out from the fellowship of the Lord and His disciples (xiii. 30), and perished. But his perdition was caused by no lack of vigilance of Jesus. Judas belonged to the power of evil, as the Scriptures had foretold (xiii. 18; Ps. xli. 8, cf. Acts i. 16–20; Ps. cix. 8), and he went out into the world to his own place (Acts i. 25).

The apostasy of Judas and its interpretation is not mentioned here in an irrelevant parenthesis. Both the gospel and the first epistle were written at a time when men who had shared in the fellowship of the Church had apostasized and returned to the world (vi. 66; 1 John ii. 18–26, iv. 1–3, cf. 2 John 7). The case of Judas is therefore typical, and the faithful Christians needed the encouragement of these words lest they should suppose that the blame of apostasy lay at their doors, and in order that their joy might be retained. The fall of Judas did not darken the joy of the Lord, and His joy must be fulfilled in His disciples in spite of the apostasy of those who *went out from us, but they were not of us; for if they had been of us, they would have continued with us: but they went out, that they might be made manifest how that they all are not of us* (1 John ii. 19). The joy of Jesus must, however, be fully reproduced in His disciples, not only in spite of Christian apostasy, but also in spite of the wider and far more general hostility of the world. They succeed to His position in the world, which still remains the theatre of the work of God for the salvation of men. As His joy was to do the work of His Father in the world, so His joy will be fulfilled in them (xv. 11) when the mission for the glory of the Father and the Son is committed into their hands. And they are fully armed for conflict with the world; for not only is Jesus with the Father as the guarantee of their victory (xvi. 33), but they possess the word of God delivered to them by the Son. Thus armed they stand distinct from the world (xv. 18, 19) and pursued with inevitable hatred because of this distinction. It is their glory to reproduce the persecuted holiness of Jesus. He was not of this world (viii. 23); He bore witness to the world of the evil of its works (vii. 7, cf. iii. 19); and they hated Him (vii. 7, xv. 18–25).

*vv.* 15–18. Being thus set for the salvation of the scattered children of God, no prayer for the removal of the disciples from the world is possible; it would obstruct the purpose of God (xiii. 1). Jesus therefore solemnly dedicates His disciples to the mission. As the Father consecrated the Son and sent Him into the world (x. 36, cf. iv. 38, xx. 21), so now the Son sends His disciples into the world and prays that they also may be consecrated by the Father. And, since divine consecration must of necessity involve personal moral holiness, He prays that they may not be contaminated by the world, and that they may be preserved from the power of the Evil One (R.V.). A comparison with 1 John ii. 13, 14, iii. 12, v. 18, 19, and with xiii. 27 seems to demand the masculine rather than the neuter *evil* or *the evil* (A.V., see, however, Lagrange on xvii. 15).

The power of the Devil begins where the sovereignty of the word of God ends. Consequently, holiness can belong only to those who possess the Truth of God. Possessing the words of Jesus, the disciples possess the words of God, and, possessing the words of God, they possess the Truth which sanctifies (xv. 3, cf. Eph. v. 26). *Thy word is truth* echoes Ps. cxix. 142 (LXX). The words of Jesus are the fulfilment of the Law (i. 17), and by keeping His words the disciples actually possess that holiness which was demanded by God in the Old Testament Scriptures. In the Rabbinic literature it is axiomatic that sanctification is attained by keeping the commandments of the Law: 'He who sanctified us through His commandment, and commanded us to dwell in tabernacles' or 'Has given us the commandment of circumcision' (see Strack-Biller-beck).

#### JESUS DEDICATES HIMSELF AS AN EFFECTIVE SACRIFICE

*v.* 19. The holiness of the disciples of Jesus does not, however, rest primarily upon their fidelity to His teaching, even though His words are the words of the Father. The efficacy of His teaching is grounded upon the efficacy of His death as a sacrifice offered on behalf of His disciples, that is, for their sanctification—*The blood of Jesus his Son cleanseth us from all sin* (1 John i. 7, ii. 2, iv. 10, and in the gospel, cf. the COMMENTARY on xiii. 1–15 and on xix. 34). But even here there is no separation between Word and Work. The Death of Jesus was much more than a mere event carrying with it a mysterious redemptive significance for the world and capable of theological interpretation. It is an effective sacrifice because Jesus by His word made it to be so, and it is an effective sacrifice for His disciples only, because the consecrating word was spoken in their presence only and on their behalf only. The Death of Jesus is effective for the world only in so far as it believes in Him, and receives and accepts His consecrating word, since it is this consecrating word, not the murderous activity of the Jews, that makes His death an effective and redemptive act. This was the significance of the Lord's words and actions in the Upper Room, and it is here plainly and formally declared in words of similar significance.

This exegesis depends upon purely philological considerations. The Greek word ἁγιάζειν is of far greater significance than is suggested by its English translation *sanctify*. Neither the editors of the ninth edition of Liddell and Scott's *Greek-English Lexicon* nor Moulton and Milligan in the *Vocabulary of the Greek Testament illustrated from the Papyri and other Non-literary Sources* are able to furnish evidence for the use of the word outside the Scriptures and apart from authors dependent upon the

Old or New Testaments. Bauer does, it is true, cite its use in three
Gnostic texts (Preuschen-Bauer, *Wörterbuch*), but the passages cited are
precisely those in which a biblical influence may be detected (see especially *Hermetica*, i. 32). The word is a biblical variant to the cognate
ἁγίζειν, which means *to make sacred*, especially by burning a sacrifice
(see Liddell and Scott, ninth edition). Recent investigation therefore
entirely supports Cremer's judgement that the word is 'peculiar to biblical Greek' (*Biblico-Theological Lexicon of New Testament Greek*, English
translation, fourth edition, 1895, p. 53). Its use in the LXX, where it
translates the Hebrew *Kadash*, therefore provides the background for
its use in the New Testament.

In the LXX the verb ἁγιάζειν means, quite generally, to set apart
and dedicate a person or thing for the service of God, and, more precisely, to dedicate as a sacrifice. For example, in Jer. i. 5; Ecclus. xlv. 4,
xlix. 7; 2 Macc. i. 25, 26, it denotes the setting apart and consecration
of Jeremiah, of Moses, and of the Chosen People for the particular service of God: *For they entreated him* (Jeremiah) *evil; And yet he was sanctified in the womb to be a prophet, to root out, and to afflict, and to destroy; and in
like manner to build and to plant* (Ecclus. xlix. 7). In Exod. xiii. 2, xxviii.
41, xxix. 1, 21, 37, xl. 9; Lev. xvi. 4; Deut. xv. 19, the word is sacrificial.
It denotes the consecration of Aaron and his sons to the office of priesthood, the consecration of the altar of sacrifice, of the furniture of the
tabernacle, of Aaron's sacrificial vestment worn by the High Priest
on the Day of Atonement, the setting apart of all the first-born, both
of man and of beast, and the sacrifice of *all the firstling males that are
born of thy herd and of thy flock* (Deut. xv. 19). In the two commands
*thou shalt sanctify unto the Lord thy God* (Deut. xv. 19) and *thou shalt not
sacrifice it unto the Lord thy God* (Deut. xv. 21) the words *sanctify* and *sacrifice* are entirely synonymous. In the passage in which the word *sanctify*
is used for the sacrifice of animals the previous perfection of the animal
sacrificed is also expressly demanded. No firstling of the flock which has
any blemish whatever may be sanctified or sacrificed (Deut. xv. 21).
It must therefore be concluded that the word has a double meaning.
It may denote the consecration of a prophet to the service of God, and
so imply that he is thereby both separated and made righteous; but it
may also denote the dedication to sacrifice of what is already without
blemish. In both cases the dedication is irrevocable, for *it is a snare to a
man hastily to sanctify anything that is his, for after he has made his vow repentance comes* (Prov. xx. 25).

Now it is precisely this double meaning of the word and this Old
Testament background that are, perhaps inevitably, obscured in the
English versions. *For their sakes I sanctify myself, that they themselves also
may be sanctified in truth* does not mean that Jesus achieved righteousness
or exercised a strict moral self-control in order that His disciples might
be granted a similar righteousness; still less does it mean that Jesus

made Himself righteous in order that His disciples might possess an example for their active imitation. It means that the Son of God consecrated His blameless life as an effective sacrifice on behalf of His disciples in order that they might be set forth in the world as the concrete righteousness of God (xvi. 7, cf. 2 Cor. v. 21), sanctified by Christ Jesus (1 Cor. i. 2, vi. 11; Heb. x. 10, 29, xiii. 12), and dedicated to the service of God, even to death for His glory. The consecration of the disciples therefore depends upon the consecration of the Son of God. But the similarity of consecration rests upon a great dissimilarity: they are consecrated, He consecrated Himself; and His consecration must precede theirs. And they are sanctified *in truth*, that is *veritably* (1 John iii. 18; 2 John 1, 4; 3 John 1, 4), not because their holiness is capable of accurate measurement; but because it proceeds from the sacrifice of the Son of God, and is for this reason contrasted with all that was prophetically and typically dedicated in the Old Testament, and with all that was falsely dedicated in pagan worship (iv. 23, 24). The last four verses of the first epistle contain an entirely adequate delineation of this veritable consecration and they conclude with the inevitable deduction—*My little children, guard yourselves from idols* (1 John v. 21). The comment of Saint Chrysostom would therefore seem to be admirably correct: 'What', he writes, 'is *I sanctify myself*'? and he answers '*I offer to thee a sacrifice . . .* for whereas of old the sanctification was typically by sheep, yet now it is no longer typical, but by the Truth itself' (cf. Cyril of Alexandria). And yet it must not for one moment be supposed that the Old Testament provides the immediate background of xvii. 19, or that the author of the gospel is here interpreting the significance of the death of Jesus independently in terms of Old Testament sacrifice. He is interpreting Mark xiv. 22–5. It should in this connection be noted that the Old Testament provides no authority for the words *I sanctify myself*, nor can Strack-Billerbeck cite any parallel use of the word from the Rabbinic literature. They can only quote the saying *If a man sanctifies himself a little, God will sanctify him much*, which is obviously irrelevant. As in ch. vi the immediate background is still the tradition of the words and actions of Jesus in the Upper Room, according to which He consecrated Himself to death in the presence of His disciples declaring that the (new) covenant would be effectively inaugurated by His Blood, and according to which He also consecrated His disciples to His service by demanding that they should eat His Body and drink His Blood. This evangelical background is almost verbally preserved in the two clauses, *The bread which I will give is my flesh, for the life of the world* (vi. 51) and *Except ye eat the flesh of the Son of man and drink his blood, ye have not life in yourselves* (vi. 53). Here the same evangelical background is equally present to the mind of the author, and *for their sakes I sanctify myself, that they themselves also may be sanctified in truth* is explanatory of the earlier tradition.

### THE PRAYER FOR THE CHURCH

*vv.* 20–6. Since the words of Jesus and His sacrifice are of universal validity through the preaching of the disciples, the Lord extends His prayer to embrace the whole body of the faithful. With the dedication of the original disciples to the service of God the thought of their mission to the world comes once more into the foreground, and is formulated as prayer to the Father for those who believe through their word. The Church, which is the concrete body of those who believe in Jesus as The Apostle of God, is the witness of God to the world and His call to repentance and faith. The Church is the call of God to the world, because it is the manifestation of the love and glory of God in the world. What the incarnate Son of God had once been to the Jews, the Church is now to the world—the incarnate charity and glory of God: *The glory which thou hast given me I have given unto them* (i. 14) . . . *that the world may know that thou . . . lovedst them, even as thou lovedst me* (v. 20). But the power of the Church to declare the word and manifest the glory and love of God depends upon its union with the Father and the Son (xiv. 23), as the authority of Jesus depends upon His union with the Father (x. 38, xiv. 10, 11). Since the perfection of charity is the consummation of unity, fellowship with the Father and the Son is perfected in the fellowship of all believers. *By this shall all men know that ye are my disciples, if ye have love one to another* (xiii. 35). Upon this perfection of charity the efficacy of the Church's mission to the world rests. For this reason the prayer for the unity of the Church is the prayer for its perfection on earth, and in it all other subjects of prayer are included. But, as Loisy well says, Christian unity is not merely a unity of purpose and a unity of means employed to effect this purpose, it is, rather, a vital organic union, not only similar to, but veritably identical with, the union of the Father and the incarnate Son, *that they may be one, even as we are one; I in them and thou in me.* This peace of the Church does most surely draw to God His scattered children, for it is the concrete expression of His love. It must not therefore be supposed that the unity of the Church is to be attained by a long history of human endeavour. The believers are wrought into one concrete organic union of charity by an act of God, since to *perfect* is an almost technical term for a mighty act of the Father or the Son (iv. 34, v. 36, xvii. 4, xix. 30; 1 John ii. 5, iv. 12, 17, 18). In this sense the Lord prays *that they may be perfected into one*. Nor must it be supposed that this exaltation of the Church results simply in the substitution of the Church for the Christ as the object of belief. Faith remains faith in Jesus as The Apostle of God, and belief in Him means obedience to His commands, so that, when all is said, the purpose of the glory and unity of the Church is that the world may believe in Jesus, *that the world may know that thou didst send me*, since everything depends upon this faith and knowledge. Therefore obedience, not ecstasy or an esoteric mysticism, and apostolate, not prophecy, are the ground of the Church's authority. Here is the root distinction between the Fourth Gospel and all Gnosticism and Philonism and Neo-Platonism (see Bauer).

The prayer now proceeds from the thought of the *Ecclesia Militans* to that of the *Ecclesia Glorificata*, from faith to hope (cf. Rom. viii. 17). The language in which the glory of the Church Militant is expressed is capable of expressing also the final realization of its destiny. Though the original disciples saw the glory of the incarnate Christ (i. 14), and though those who believe through their word receive the glory which the Father gave to His incarnate Son (xvii. 22), yet there is a greater glory of the Son and a greater love of the Father to the Son—that glory and that love which existed before the foundation of the world. To this ineffable glory and to this ineffable love the Son returns when He has been removed from the turmoil of the world. The prayer of Jesus therefore concludes with the confident eschatological hope (1 John iii. 3) that faith may be transformed into sight, that the faithful Christians may be with Him, and that they may behold His glory and share in His love (cf. Luke xxii. 28–30). From the eschatological point of view the vision of the glory of Christ on earth is, as Calvin wrote 'But as a small glimmering of light doth come through chinks unto a man that is shut up in darkness' (1 Cor. xiii. 12; 1 John iii. 2).

There are therefore three epochs in the history of the Church, the time of the manifestation of the glory of God to the original disciples, *I have made known unto them thy name*, the time of the manifestation of the name of God to the Church and through the Church to the world, *I will make it known*, and the final and eternal manifestation of the love of God, *that the love with which thou lovedst me may be in them, and I in them*. The last verses of the prayer concern the eschatological hope of the Church, not of the individual believers. Nothing is said of the death of each disciple, as though that were his removal to be with Jesus. Wellhausen's comment is irrelevant: 'It is difficult to think that the whole Church will be united with Jesus through His Parousia, the thought is rather that each individual will be joined to Jesus at his death.' What Wellhausen finds 'difficult to think' is precisely what the author of the gospel records. The words *I will that, where I am, they also may be with me* must be interpreted in connection with xiv. 3. *I come again, and will receive you unto myself; that where I am, there ye may be also* (cf. 1 John iii. 2. *If he shall be manifested*).

The conclusion of the prayer is therefore pure eschatology, the prayer that the *Ecclesia Militans* may become the *Ecclesia Glorificata*, and that the *Theologia Crucis* may be transformed into the *Theologia Gloriae*. The vision of the full splendour of the Son is a matter of confident hope and prayer grounded upon the justice and righteousness of God. In the concluding section of the prayer God is therefore addressed as *Righteous Father*. The apotheosis of the Church has as its reverse the judgement of the unbelieving world; but the judgement of the world can form no direct subject of the Lord's prayer, the Son was not sent *to condemn the world, but that the world through him might be saved* (iii. 17). The destiny of the unbelieving world is therefore suggested, but left to the justice of the Father, God; *O righteous Father, the world knew thee not, but I knew thee; and these knew that thou didst send me.* Those who have known the Father through the revelation of the Son will finally share in the perfect love of the Father and the Son; but, since the world cannot receive, nor behold, nor know, the Spirit of Truth (xiv. 17), neither can it share in the love of the Father and the Son.

Again, it should be noted that the eschatological conclusion to the Prayer of Consecration is paralleled in the earlier tradition, for the record of the words of Jesus in the Upper Room concludes with the saying *Verily I say unto you, I will no more drink of the fruit of the vine, until that day when I drink it new in the kingdom of God* (Mark xiv. 25); Matthew's interpretative gloss *new with you* (Matt. xxvi. 29) almost certainly gives the correct meaning of the Saying (cf. Luke xxii. 29, 30).

# THE NARRATIVE OF THE PASSION

## XVIII, XIX

## I

## THE ARREST

### XVIII. 1–11

*xviii. 1. When Jesus had spoken these words, he went forth with his disciples over the brook Kidron, where was a garden, into the which he entered, himself and his disciples. 2. Now Judas also, which betrayed him, knew the place: for Jesus oft-times resorted thither with his disciples. 3. Judas then, having received the band of soldiers, and officers from the chief priests and the Pharisees, cometh thither with lanterns and torches and weapons. 4. Jesus therefore, knowing all the things that were coming upon him, went forth, and saith unto them, Whom seek ye? 5. They answered him, Jesus of Nazareth. Jesus saith unto them, I am he. And Judas also, which betrayed him, was standing with them. 6. When therefore he said unto them, I am he, they went backward, and fell to the ground. 7. Again therefore he asked them, Whom seek ye? And they said, Jesus of Nazareth. 8. Jesus answered, I told you that I am he: if therefore ye seek me, let these go their way: 9. that the word might be fulfilled which he spake, Of those whom thou hast given me I lost not one. 10. Simon Peter therefore having a sword drew it, and struck the high priest's servant, and cut off his right ear. Now the servant's name was Malchus. 11. Jesus therefore said unto Peter, Put up the sword into the sheath: the cup which the Father hath given me, shall I not drink it?*

xviii. 1. *Went forth*, cf. xiii. 31, Mark xiv. 26 and parallels. That is *from the house*, in spite of xiv. 31, unless the author means *from the city* (Bauer). *The brook Kidron*. Johannine only. The phrase is biblical (1 Kings ii. 37; 2 Kings xxiii. 6, 12, cf. Josephus *Ant.* vii. 17, &c.). The Greek word translated *brook*, here only in the New Testament, means a *winter torrent* (R.V. mg.), in Arabic a *Wadi*. *Kidron* is treated as an indeclinable proper noun, being a transliteration into Greek of a Hebrew word meaning *black*, in Codex Alexandrinus, the Old Latin, Vulgate, and Sinaitic Syriac Versions, &c., cf. 1 Kings ii. 37; in the third hand of Codex Sinaiticus, in the Codex Vaticanus, &c., Origen, Chrysostom, cf. LXX, 2 Sam. xv. 23, 1 Kings xv. 13, it is treated as a genitive plural *of the cedars*; and in the first hand of Codex Sinaiticus, and Codex Bezae, as a genitive singular, *of the cedar*.

The author, though familiar with the Prayer in Gethsemane (*v.* 11, xii. 27), omits both it and the falling asleep of the disciples. He states simply that the place was a garden. The garden is important to him, for he carefully records that not only the arrest took place there, but also the Resurrection, and that it was *in the place where He was crucified* (xix. 41, xx. 15, see *J.T.S.* April 1920, pp. 214 sqq.). The comments of the Fathers may have elucidated the symbolism correctly. The Passion and Resurrection which effected the salvation of the world are contrasted with the Fall in the *garden* of Eden.

*v.* 2. Since His death is a free offering, Jesus seeks no secrecy. He proceeds to the place where He and His disciples were accustomed to meet.

*v.* 3. The soldiery, guided by Judas, the embodiment of Satan (xiii. 27), are composed not only of the servants of the Jewish authorities (cf. vii. 32, 45; Acts v. 26), as in the Marcan-Matthæan narrative (Mark xiv. 43; Matt. xxvi. 47), but also of a Roman battalion (cohort, 600 men) under the command of its chiliarch (*v.* 12). The force was quartered in the tower of Antonia overlooking the Temple, and was responsible for the peace of the city. Lagrange and others quote Polyb. xi. 23. 1 to prove that the *band* was only a third of a cohort (a maniple); but the normal use of the word and the presence of the chiliarch himself suggest that the whole cohort is intended by the author (see Grimm-Thayer, *Lexicon,* and Westcott). In the synoptic narrative the Roman soldiery do not play their part until after the appeal to Pilate (Mark xv. 16; Matt. xxvii. 27), and they are under the command of a centurion (Mark xv. 39; Matt. xxvii. 54). In the Johannine account the forces of darkness, the Roman and Jewish authorities, and the apostate disciple are arrayed against the Christ from the beginning.

*vv.* 4–9. This heterogeneous force united in opposition to Jesus is unable to recognize, still less to grasp, Him who is the Light of the World, though they are provided with lights (a Johannine addition) and weapons. The circumstances of the arrest form an unconscious comment on i. 5. Loisy thinks the scene is coloured by the circumstances of later persecutions. For the Rabbinic association of torches and lamps, see Strack-Billerbeck. They are referred to in Dionys. Hal. *Ant.* xi. 40. 2 as the normal equipment of a Roman military unit.

*v.* 5. Jesus informs the soldiery of His identity in the mysterious and majestic utterance *I am* (see note on vi. 20, cf. viii. 24).

*v.* 6. The utterance is not only majestic, but effective (see note on vi. 63). The instruments of evil fall prostrate before their true commander (Isa. xi. 4). In the former parallel passages (vii. 44, viii. 59, x. 39) Jesus had removed Himself from those who were ordered to seize Him. Now, however, the Hour has come and He surrenders Himself into their hands, after ensuring the freedom of the disciples as the Good Shepherd (cf. x. 11, 12). The writer omits all reference to the pre-arranged sign of the kiss of Judas.

*v.* 9. The action of Jesus is a symbolical fulfilment of xvii. 12, and it may be added, of xi. 51. The physical safety of the disciples is a figure of their moral and spiritual salvation.

*v.* 10. In the earlier tradition (Mark xiv. 47; Matt. xxvi. 51 sqq.; Luke xxii. 50, 51) neither the disciple nor the servant is named. John agrees with Luke in the addition that the *right* ear was struck off, but he does not record that the ear was healed.

*v.* 11. The command to put up the sword (cf. Matt. xxvi. 52) depends upon Jer. xlvii. 6; Ezek. xxi. 30. The saying concerning the cup is reminiscent of the prayer in Gethsemane (Mark xiv. 36 and parallels). Jesus of fixed purpose surrenders Himself to the soldiery; He is not arrested by them. John makes no reference to the prayer by which this fixity of purpose was achieved.

# THE NARRATIVE OF THE PASSION

## II

## THE EXAMINATION BEFORE ANNAS
## AND PETER'S DENIAL

### XVIII. 12–27

xviii. 12. *So the band and the chief captain, and the officers of the Jews, seized Jesus and bound him,* 13. *and led him to Annas first; for he was father in law to Caiaphas, which was high priest that year.* 14. *Now Caiaphas was he which gave counsel to the Jews, that it was expedient that one man should die for the people.*

15. *And Simon Peter followed Jesus, and so did another disciple. Now that disciple was known unto the high priest, and entered in with Jesus into the court of the high priest;* 16. *but Peter was standing at the door without. So the other disciple, which was known unto the high priest, went out and spake unto her that kept the door, and brought in Peter.* 17. *The maid therefore that kept the door saith unto Peter, Art thou also one of this man's disciples? He saith, I am not.* 18. *Now the servants and the officers were standing there, having made a fire of coals; for it was cold; and they were warming themselves: and Peter also was with them, standing and warming himself.*

19. *The high priest therefore asked Jesus of his disciples, and of his teaching.* 20. *Jesus answered him, I have spoken openly to the world; I ever taught in synagogues, and in the temple, where all the Jews come together; and in secret spake I nothing.* 21. *Why askest thou me? ask them that have heard me, what I spake unto them: behold, these know the things which I said.* 22. *And when he had said this, one of the officers standing by struck Jesus with his hand, saying, Answerest thou the high priest so?* 23. *Jesus answered him, If I have spoken evil, bear witness of the evil: but if well, why smitest thou me?* 24. *Annas therefore sent him bound unto Caiaphas the high priest.*

25. *Now Simon Peter was standing and warming himself. They said therefore unto him, Art thou also one of his disciples? He denied, and said, I am not.* 26. *One of the servants of the high priest, being a kinsman of him whose ear Peter cut off, saith, Did not I see thee in the garden with him?* 27. *Peter therefore denied again: and straightway the cock crew.*

The record of an examination before Annas and the obscure reference to further examination before Caiaphas (*v.* 24) present considerable difficulties, since the synoptic narrative records only one Jewish trial, which Matthew explicitly states to have been before Caiaphas. Exegetical and textual tradition from time to time betrays the desire to harmonize the Johannine and the synoptic narratives by altering the order of the verses. The Sinaitic Syriac has the following order: *vv.* 12, 13, 24, 14, 15, 19–23, 16–18, 25–7, which has the effect of restoring the scene of Peter's denial to the court of the High Priest Caiaphas; this has been accepted by some modern commentators as the original text (see Bauer, p. 207). One Greek manuscript (225) secures the same result more simply by inserting *v.* 24 after 13a, so that *vv.* 19–23 apply to a trial before Caiaphas, not before Annas (cf. Cyril of Alexandria, Theodore of Mopsuestia, Luther, Beza, Lagrange, Calmes). If it be assumed that the received order is incorrect, it is difficult, if not impossible, to explain how it came into being. If, on the other hand, the received order is the original order, the variations can be easily explained as due to attempts to harmonize the Fourth Gospel with the synoptic tradition. The real problem is therefore to explain the introduction of the examination before Annas.

The plural, *high priests*, belongs to the synoptic tradition. Mark leaves them unnamed; Matthew names only Caiaphas; Luke, however, gives their names as Annas and Caiaphas (Luke iii. 2; Acts iv. 6), and he names them in this order. There is, moreover, a discrepancy between Luke and Matthew-Mark as to the time of the trial. According to the former the trial took place in the early morning before the whole *assembly of the elders, chief priests and scribes* (Luke xxii. 66–71); according to the latter during the night (Mark xiv. 55 sqq.; Matt. xxvi. 59 sqq.). In the morning it remained only to send the prisoner formally to Pilate. The structure of the Johannine narrative is most easily explained as a harmony of this double tradition. The author therefore records two trials, one before Annas during the night, one before Caiaphas in the early morning. The trial before Annas is constructed from material appearing in other contexts in the synoptic gospels. The Saying of the Lord (*vv.* 20, 21) occurs in the account of the arrest (Mark xiv. 49 and parallels), the striking in the face takes place during the trial before Caiaphas (Matt. xxvi. 67, 68, and parallels). The introduction of the trial before Annas carries with it the transference of the scene of Peter's denial to the court of Annas, so that Peter's movements after the arrest become continuous. This literary process of harmonization may be paralleled in the account of the Resurrection appearances, where the Lucan tradition of appearances in Jerusalem is harmonized with the Matthæan, and presumably Marcan, tradition of appearances in Galilee.

xviii. 12. *Chiliarch.* The commander of a cohort, cf. Acts xxi. 31 sqq.; Num. xxxi. 14 sqq.; 1 Sam. xviii. 13. The title is used also of civilian officials.

*v.* 13. *First.* Because the examination before Annas precedes the examination before Caiaphas.

*Annas.* Josephus mentions the monument of Annas the high priest as a well-known site on the high ground west of Jerusalem (*B.J.* v. 506). Annas had been high priest from A.D. 6 to 15, when he was deposed by Valerius Gratus, the predecessor of Pilate. He was succeeded in his office by his five sons, Eleazar A.D. 16–17, Jonathan A.D. 36–7, Theophilus A.D. 37–41, Matthias A.D. 41–4 (?), Annas the younger about A.D. 62, but his dates are uncertain. During the intervening period A.D. 18–36 the office was held by Joseph, commonly named Caiaphas. If, as the author of the Fourth Gospel alone records, he was son-in-law to Annas, the office of high priest was for a long period monopolized by one family, and Annas himself, so long as he lived, presumably held a patriarchal position. The references in the later Rabbinic writings and in Josephus declare the priestly aristocracy to have had a reputation for intrigue, bribery, and love of money (Strack-Billerbeck; Josephus, *Ant.* xx. 179–81, 205–7; Hastings, *Dict. Bib.* under *Annas*; Schürer, *Hist. of Jew. People*, E.T., Div. II, vol. I, pp. 182 sqq.).

*v.* 14. Refers back to xi. 49 sqq., see note.

*vv.* 15–17. *Another disciple.* Presumably the Beloved Disciple. The friendship of the other disciple with the high priest enables Peter to enter the court, and the scene is set for his denial. The author thus explains the presence of Peter in the inner court (Mark xiv. 54). He is questioned first by the doorkeeper as he enters, not as in the synoptic narrative by a maid whilst he warms himself at the fire (Mark xiv. 66, 67 and parallels). The suggestion in Mark xiv. 68, 69 is, however, that she was the doorkeeper.

*This man* expresses scorn, not pity.

*v.* 18. The Greek word, meaning the glowing embers of a charcoal fire, is used in the New Testament only here and in xxi. 9. It is a correct literary Greek word (see Liddell and Scott, ninth edition. Cf. also Ecclus. xi. 32; 4 Macc. ix. 20). Peter and the servants stand, they do not sit as in Mark xiv. 54 and parallels.

*vv.* 19 sq. The two sections of the narrative of Peter's denial, which in Matthew-Mark enclose the story of the examination before the chief priests and the whole Sanhedrin, here enclose the examination by Annas alone. No more than an allusion is made to a trial before Caiaphas (*vv.* 24, 28). In the examination before Annas the author only records words of Jesus which fulfil Isa. xlv. 19 and xlviii. 6, and the act of cruelty which fulfils Isa. l. 6.

*vv.* 20, 21. The words of Jesus are a Johannine expansion of the synoptic Saying at the arrest (Mark xiv. 49 and parallels). In Luke xxii. 52 it is addressed to the chief priests, and therefore suggests the trial as a more appropriate occasion. For the Johannine phraseology cf. vi. 59, vii. 4, 12, 14, 26, x. 23, xi. 54, xii. 19. Throughout the Fourth Gospel the scene of our Lord's public preaching is normally the Temple; the discourse in ch. vi is given in the synagogue at Capernaum.

*Ask them that have heard me.* The questions of the high priest concerning the disciples of Jesus and His teaching, and our Lord's answer were pertinent and appropriate at the time when the gospel was written. The author insists that the teaching of Jesus must be known through attention to His disciples, who by the guidance of the Spirit preserve and interpret His words (cf. ii. 22, xiv. 25, xvi. 4 sqq.). A true judgement of the world upon the Christ depends upon the fidelity of His disciples. 'He gave them no secret maxims, no private doctrines, which he designed should be concealed', still less did He incite them to political revolution.

*v.* 22. Cf. Acts xxiii. 2 sqq. The answer of the Lord is treated by one of the servants as derogatory to the dignity of the high priest and an offence against the Law (Exod. xxii. 28).

*Struck with his hand* (R.V.), *with the palm of his hand* (A.V.) *with a rod* (A.V. and R.V. margin). Cf. xix. 3; Mark xiv. 65 and parallels. The Greek word means literally a blow with a staff, but it was commonly used for a blow with the hand in the face or on the cheeks, and was so understood in the Sinaitic Syriac Version. *He struck Jesus on the cheeks* (cf. Matt. v. 39). If this be the correct translation, the action of the servant fulfils Isa. l. 6 and suggests the sufferings of the servant, who is the Lamb of God.

*vv.* 23, 24. The answer of the Lord shows the action of the servant to have been unjustifiable, and Annas, reduced to silence and unable to continue the examination, hands over the prisoner to Caiaphas.

*vv.* 25–7. In spite of *v.* 24 the scene is still the court of the house of Annas, and the narrative returns to Peter and picks up *v.* 18. The narrative fulfils xiii. 38. A question of the bystanders mentioned in *v.* 18 leads to the second denial. With the third denial a climax is reached, since the question which occasions it proceeds from the identification of Peter as the disciple who had struck off Malchus' ear by one who both was present in the garden and was a relative of Malchus. Peter's falsity and infidelity are thus apparent to all. Three questions calling out three denials are common to all the evangelists. Luke gains his climax by recording questions first by a woman, then by two men, the second of whom after an hour's interval recognizes Peter's Galilean accent or appearance, and by the poignant reference to the look of Jesus (Luke xxii. 56–62). In the Marcan-Matthæan narrative (Mark xiv. 54, 66–72; Matt. xxvi, 58, 69–75) the first two questions are asked by a servant girl (Mark), or by two different girls (Matthew), and the third by the male bystanders; the climax is achieved less by the certain identification of Peter as a Galilean than by the passionate blasphemy of his last denial: *He began to curse, and to swear, I know not the man* (Mark, *this man of whom ye speak*).

# THE NARRATIVE OF THE PASSION

## III

## JESUS AND PILATE

### XVIII. 28–XIX. 16a

THE FINAL AND FORMAL APOSTASY OF THE JEWS
(cf. Mark xv. 1–19; Matt. xxvii. 11–30; Luke xxiii. 1–25)

The author of the Fourth Gospel passes quickly over the examination before the Jewish authorities. The examination before Annas is 'broken off almost before it has begun', and only a passing reference is made to the examination before Caiaphas. The writer presses on to describe the scenes in which the sovereignty of this world and the sovereignty which is not of this world are compared concretely in the contrast between Pilate and Jesus, and the scenes in which the apostasy of the Jews is finally exposed. He presumes that his readers are familiar with the older tradition in which the trial before Caiaphas was narrated at length. Luke had already betrayed a similar tendency. He curtailed drastically the record of the trial before the Sanhedrin (Luke xxii. 66–71), in order that he might depict Jesus standing before Pilate, the Governor, and Herod, the King; in fulfilment of Ps. ii. 2. *The kings of the earth stand up, and the rulers take counsel together: against the Lord and against his anointed* (cf. Acts iv. 26; Mark xiii. 9).

In the Johannine narrative there emerges, however, not merely the contrast between Pilate and Jesus, but also the contrast between Pilate and the Jews. Pilate represents the world in need of salvation, and half conscious of this need. The Jews on the other hand are simply apostate, their apostasy being more and more clearly revealed, until it reaches its consummation in the declaration—*We have no king but Cæsar*. Throughout the narrative also there runs the conviction of the author that, whereas the Jews were the instruments of the Prince of the darkness of this world, Pilate was the unconscious agent in the divine purpose of God for the salvation of the world, and that his authority over Jesus was therefore given him from above. This conviction is due in part, no doubt, to the desire to remove the blame for the crucifixion as far as possible from the imperial authorities and to fix it firmly upon the Jewish authorities, but much more to the perception that Jesus must have been lifted up in His death in order that He might draw all men unto Him.

This involved death by crucifixion, and not by stoning. Pilate alone was able to order that Jesus should be crucified, and thus fulfil the purpose of God and the prophecy of the Lord.

### THE JEWS LEAD JESUS BEFORE PILATE

xviii. 28. *They lead Jesus therefore from Caiaphas into the palace: and it was early; and they themselves entered not into the palace, that they might not be defiled, but might eat the passover.* 29. *Pilate therefore went out unto them, and saith, What accusation bring ye against this man?* 30. *They answered and said unto him, If this man were not an evil-doer, we should not have delivered him up unto thee.* 31. *Pilate therefore said unto them, Take him yourselves, and judge him according to your law. The Jews said unto him, It is not lawful for us to put any man to death:* 32. *that the word of Jesus might be fulfilled, which he spake, signifying by what manner of death he should die.*

### THE FIRST CONVERSATION WITH PILATE

33. *Pilate therefore entered again into the palace, and called Jesus, and said unto him, Art thou the King of the Jews?* 34. *Jesus answered, Sayest thou this of thyself, or did others tell it thee concerning me?* 35. *Pilate answered, Am I a Jew? Thine own nation and the chief priests delivered thee unto me: what hast thou done?* 36. *Jesus answered, My kingdom is not of this world: if my kingdom were of this world, then would my servants fight, that I should not be delivered to the Jews: but now is my kingdom not from hence.* 37. *Pilate therefore said unto him, Art thou a king then? Jesus answered, Thou sayest that I am a king. To this end have I been born, and to this end am I come into the world, that I should bear witness unto the truth. Every one that is of the truth heareth my voice.* 38a. *Pilate saith unto him, What is truth?*

### JESUS AND BARABBAS

38b. *And when he had said this, he went out again unto the Jews, and saith unto them, I find no crime in him.* 39. *But ye have a custom, that I should release unto you one at the passover: will ye therefore that I release unto you the King of the Jews?* 40. *They cried out therefore again, saying, Not this man, but Barabbas. Now Barabbas was a robber.*

### THE MOCKERY OF THE KING OF THE JEWS
### AND THE FLAGELLATION

xix. 1. *Then Pilate therefore took Jesus, and scourged him.* 2. *And the soldiers plaited a crown of thorns, and put it on his head, and arrayed him in a purple garment;* 3. *and they came unto him, and said, Hail, King of the Jews! and they struck him with their hands.*

## ECCE HOMO

4. *And Pilate went out again, and saith unto them, Behold, I bring him out to you, that ye may know that I find no crime in him.* 5. *Jesus therefore came out, wearing the crown of thorns and the purple garment. And Pilate saith unto them, Behold, the man!* 6. *When therefore the chief priests and the officers saw him, they cried out, saying, Crucify him, crucify him. Pilate saith unto them, Take him yourselves, and crucify him: for I find no crime in him.* 7. *The Jews answered him, We have a law, and by that law he ought to die, because he made himself the Son of God.*

## PILATE AND THE SON OF GOD

8. *When Pilate therefore heard this saying, he was the more afraid;* 9. *and he entered into the palace again, and saith unto Jesus, Whence art thou? But Jesus gave him no answer.* 10. *Pilate therefore saith unto him, Speakest thou not unto me? knowest thou not that I have power to release thee, and have power to crucify thee?* 11. *Jesus answered him, Thou wouldest have no power against me, except it were given thee from above: therefore he that delivered me unto thee hath greater sin.*

### THE FORMAL BLASPHEMY OF THE JEWS
### AND THE SURRENDER OF PILATE

12. *Upon this Pilate sought to release him; but the Jews cried out, saying, If thou release this man, thou art not Cæsar's friend: every one that maketh himself a king speaketh against Cæsar.* 13. *When Pilate therefore heard these words, he brought Jesus out, and sat down on the judgement-seat at a place called The Pavement, but in Hebrew, Gabbatha.* 14. *Now it was the Preparation of the passover: it was about the sixth hour. And he saith unto the Jews, Behold, your King!* 15. *They therefore cried out, Away with him, away with him, crucify him. Pilate saith unto them, Shall I crucify your King? The chief priests answered, We have no king but Cæsar.* 16a. *Then therefore he delivered him unto them to be crucified.*

### THE JEWS LEAD JESUS BEFORE PILATE

xviii. 28. *Prætorium* (R.V. mg.); *palace* (R.V.); *hall of judgement* (A.V.); *Pilate's house* (A.V. mg.). The Latin word *praetorium* in its Greek form in the papyri frequently denotes the seat of the civil government and also the official residence of the governor (cf. Matt. xxvii. 27; Mark xv. 16; Acts xxiii. 35, see Moulton-Milligan, *Vocabulary*). Pilate occupied Herod's palace in Jerusalem.

*Eat the passover.* The corresponding phrases *prepare the passover, slay the passover* (Mark xiv. 12–16 and parallels; 1 Cor. v. 7) show that *eat the passover* must mean *eat the passover lamb* (see Strack-Billerbeck, op. cit., vol. II, pp. 837 sqq.). The Jews have not yet eaten the passover (cf. xiii. 1, 29, xix. 14), and are therefore careful lest they be polluted by entering the house of a Gentile. They who pretend to so great devotion are in fact guilty of gross superstition, for the execution of the Messiah becomes the preparation for their solemn festival. In order to avoid a contradiction with the synoptic gospels, in which the crucifixion takes place on the day after the Passover, some commentators (e.g. Zahn) suppose *eat the passover* to be a vague phrase meaning 'keep the seven days' Passover festival'. The Sinaitic Syriac Version gives this theory some support, since it translates *passover* by *unleavened bread* throughout the Fourth Gospel. But this seems to be either a peculiarity of translation or a definite attempt to bring the Fourth Gospel into harmony with the synoptic tradition (see Lagrange).

*vv.* 29–32. The Jews conduct the prisoner to Pilate in order that he may pronounce and carry out the sentence of death by crucifixion, this being the normal Roman capital punishment for sedition (Hastings, *Dict. of the Bible* under 'Cross'). Pilate demands to know the nature of the accusation brought against the prisoner. On being told that He is an evil-doer, Pilate authorizes the Jews to proceed according to their Law. This may mean merely that he supposes that the case does not involve capital punishment, and therefore lies within the competence of the Jews. But more probably *according to your law* is meant to imply that Pilate definitely authorizes the Jews to sentence the prisoner and to inflict punishment by stoning, this being the legal penalty for blasphemy, breaking the Sabbath, and other offences against the Jewish Law (Exod. xxxi. 14, xxxv. 2; Lev. xxiv. 10–23; Deut. xiii. 5–10; John viii. 5–7, x. 31; Luke xx. 6; Acts vii. 58, xiv. 5). This is, however, not at all what the Jews intend. The prisoner must be crucified, not stoned (xix. 6). That is, He must die in public as guilty of sedition, not of blasphemy; and Pilate alone can effect this. They therefore reply *It is not lawful for us to put any man to death*. The interpretation of these words is exceedingly difficult. Origen connects the saying with xi. 55. The Jews have come to Jerusalem in order to purify themselves before the Passover. They cannot therefore put any man to death (*In Ioan.* ed. Brooke II. 145, cf. also Cyril). But *v.* 32 shows that the issue is not the power of capital punishment, but the nature of the punishment—stoning or crucifixion. This distinction is of vital importance for the author of the gospel (Chrysostom). In the synoptic gospels the phrase *it is lawful* refers to what is illegal according to the Law of God revealed in the Old Testament, and never has any other reference. In the only other passage where it occurs in the Fourth Gospel it has the same reference (v. 10). If it be legitimate to find in the phrase *put to death* a subtle reference to shedding blood as distinct from stoning, the latter being to the Jews as far removed from killing as burning a heretic was for the officers of the Inquisition, then the meaning of the passage is

simple and straightforward. In answer to Pilate the Jews state that their
Law does not permit them to shed blood, and therefore they cannot
crucify the prisoner (cf. xix. 6, 7). To the author of the gospel the discussion between Pilate and the Jews has a far deeper significance. It is
of little importance to him whether the formal accusation be blasphemy or sedition; both are equally false. It is, however, vital to him
that the blood of Jesus should be poured out for the salvation of the
world (xix. 34, cf. vi. 53–6; 1 John i. 7, v. 6–8), and that He shall be
lifted up that He may draw all men unto Him (iii. 14, 15, xii. 32, 33).
Crucifixion, therefore, not stoning, fulfils the divine plan of salvation
and the prophecies of the Lord (Mark x. 34; Matt. xx. 19; Luke xviii.
33). In an earlier passage (x. 31–9, cf. xi. 8) he had carefully recorded
how Jesus escaped from stoning by the Jews. Pilate must therefore
execute the sentence, since to him had been entrusted the power of
crucifixion, and the Jews, in insisting upon the crucifixion, are moved
by a divine necessity of which they are totally unconscious. The whole
narrative leads up to the pregnant conclusion of the trial before Pilate:
*Then therefore he delivered him unto them—to be crucified* (xix. 16).

If this interpretation be not accepted, and *It is not lawful for us to put
any man to death* be taken to mean that, since Palestine had come directly
under the authority of Rome, capital punishment was no longer within
the competence of the Jews, then the usual exegesis holds good. Pilate
does not regard the case as sufficiently serious to involve the death
penalty; the Jews, however, are determined that the prisoner must die,
and that since they are incompetent to impose any death sentence, Pilate
must be compelled to deal with the case himself. In this case *v.* 32 is
somewhat irrelevant, unless the author intends to suggest that Jewish
incompetence has a divine significance. Moreover, if this interpretation
be correct, a further historical problem becomes pressing. There is no
doubt that after A.D. 70 the Jews possessed no legal power of life and
death, but the extent of this legal competence before the destruction of
Jerusalem is exceedingly obscure. The problem has been discussed at
great length by Jean Juster (*Les Juifs dans l'Empire Romain*, vol. II, pp.
127–52, see especially pp. 133–8. The author provides an exhaustive
bibliography). Juster reaches the conclusion that the Sanhedrin was
competent in strictly religious cases to pronounce sentence, including
the death sentence, and to execute the sentence; and he maintains that
no documentary evidence justifies any other conclusion. He grudgingly
admits the possibility that sentences passed by the Sanhedrin may have
required confirmation by the governor, but apart from the gospels he
can discover no evidence which suggests that this was so. The same
opinion is more guardedly stated by Strack-Billerbeck (vol. I, p. 1026).
Schürer, on the other hand, definitely commits himself to the statement
that in fact no right of pronouncing sentences of life or death 'could
be said to have belonged to the Jews ever since Judæa came under

procurators at all' (*Hist. of Jew. People*, E.T., Div. II, vol. I, p. 188 n., cf. Mommsen, *Röm. Strafrecht*, p. 240, and *Z.N.T.W.* 1902, p. 199, and Lagrange).

### THE FIRST CONVERSATION WITH PILATE

*vv.* 33–38*a*. Pilate then takes the matter into his own hands, and proceeds to conduct the inquiry on the supposition that he has to deal with a case of sedition. The refusal of the Jews to enter the palace enables the author to record two conversations between Jesus and Pilate alone (*vv.* 33–8, xix. 9–12), and provides two scenes—the inside and the outside of the palace—in which the drama moves alternately. Pilate is also thereby enabled to present Jesus publicly to the Jews, first as *the man* and then as *your king*.

In the synoptic gospels the trial before Pilate takes place in the presence of the Jews, who make the deposition against Jesus (Mark xv. 2 sqq. and parallels). Pilate's question to Jesus *Art thou the King of the Jews?* and his answer *Thou sayest* are verbally the same as in the synoptic gospels, but they are expanded, so that the whole passage in the Fourth Gospel becomes a Johannine explanatory paraphrase. The synoptic record of the vehement accusation of the Jews is inevitably omitted, because they are not present. The Matthæan-Marcan statement that Jesus made no answer to this accusation is omitted, but an echo of it appears in xix. 9 in a different context. It should be noted that Luke likewise omits the reference to the silence of Jesus, not, however because he knows of conversations between Jesus and Pilate, but simply because he is about to record the silence before Herod (Luke xxiii. 9).

In answer to Pilate's question *Art thou the king of the Jews?* Jesus asks whether the question proceeds from a spontaneous recognition that he is in the presence of royalty (i. 49, xii. 13), or whether it is an echo of the Jewish accusation (Luke xxiii. 2). Pilate disclaims the first and avows the second, asking what Jesus had done to justify the accusation. Jesus then states quite clearly that a kingdom and sovereign authority and power are His by right, but that the source of His authority is not *of this world*. He does not say that this world is not the sphere of His authority, but that His authority is not of human origin. The other-worldly nature of His authority is, moreover, patent from the fact that no military forces operate on His behalf. No soldiers are present to prevent the King of the Jews from falling into their hands. The action of Peter is therefore again disavowed. And yet neither here nor in xix. 9 does Jesus openly say that He is the Son of God, who has come from heaven for the salvation of the world. Pilate, however, concludes that Jesus is a king, *So then thou art a king*. Jesus reminds him that he first introduced the title. But, rightly understood, the title is correct. The nature of His sovereignty corresponds with the nature of His mission. He is the king of

Truth, and He manifests His royal power not by force, but by the witness He bears to the Truth (iii. 32, v. 33, cf. 3 John 3). For this He was born, and for this He entered the world. His loyal subjects are therefore not those who fight, but those who, being of the Truth, obey their King. The language echoes the Prologue (i. 9, 18), and the readers of the gospel know that His birth was the incarnation of the Son of God, and that the Truth which is manifested in Him is the knowledge of God, and that those who believe in Him are born of God and have seen His glory. All this is, however, beyond Pilate's comprehension; and when he asks *What is truth?* there is nothing more to be said. Yet Pilate is neither indifferent nor sceptical, but simply incapable of apprehending since he is not of the Truth. *If ye will not believe, neither shall ye understand* (Isa. vii. 9 LXX). He is, however, convinced that there is no question here of a sovereignty which incites political revolution. Mr. Gardner-Smith (*Saint John and the Synoptic Gospels*, pp. 62, 63) tentatively suggest that the words translated *Art thou a king then?* should be understood, not as a question, but as a declaration whose force is affirmative—*So you are a king!* The author, unlike the synoptists, is not concerned to show that Pilate attached no serious importance to the charge brought against Jesus. Rather, he desires to convey the impression that Pilate does vaguely, albeit quite inadequately, recognize the kingship of Jesus (cf. *v.* 39, xix. 15, 19–22).

In this passage the author outlines the necessary limitations of the defence of the Christian religion before unbelieving officials of the Roman Empire, and provides the Christians of his day with the classical explanation of the distinction between the Empire and the Church. Roman officials are normally incapable of perceiving the Truth, and Christians must be content to make it quite plain that they are not seditious. This is no hopeless task, since it was the blasphemous activity of the Jews, not the convictions of Pilate, which led him to the decision that Jesus should be crucified.

### JESUS AND BARABBAS

*vv.* 38b–40. Pilate openly declares his opinion that the prisoner is innocent of any crime and proposes, if the Jews approve, to exercise his privilege of releasing a prisoner at the Passover by setting Jesus free. The Jewish rulers, however, receive spontaneous and emphatic support from the crowd in demanding the release of the lawless brigand Barabbas (Mark xv. 7; Luke xxiii. 25) and the execution of the ruler of the kingdom of God, whom they have ostensibly charged with sedition.

That Pilate regarded Jesus as innocent is involved in the Matthæan-Marcan narrative (Matt. xxvii. 18, 19, 23 sqq.; Mark xv. 10, 14, 15), but the Johannine sequence of events approximates closely to the Lucan tradition where Pilate's formal declaration of the innocence of the prisoner is conjoined with the proposal to scourge Him and let Him go (Luke xxiii. 4, 13 sqq., 22, cf. however, Mark xv. 14, 15). The repeated cries of the crowd are recorded in the synoptic narratives (Mark xv. 11, 13, 14 and parallels); in the Johannine narrative they are presumed, but not recorded: *They cried out therefore again, saying*— There is no known reference, apart from the evangelical tradition, either to the custom of setting free a prisoner at the Passover season, or to Barabbas. Barabbas, however, was a common Jewish name (Strack-Billerbeck, vol. I, p. 1031).

## THE MOCKERY OF THE KING OF THE JEWS
## AND THE FLAGELLATION

xix. 1–3. Pilate endeavours to satisfy the Jews without violating his conscience (Lagrange), and fulfils the prophecy of Jesus: *The Son of Man shall be delivered unto the chief priests and the scribes; and they shall condemn him to death, and shall deliver him unto the Gentiles: and they shall mock him, and shall spit upon him, and shall scourge him, and shall kill him* (Mark x. 33, 34 and parallels). The spitting is omitted. The author uses the word for scourging which occurs in this prophecy, whereas the other evangelists make use of synonyms. Luke suggests the scourging, but does not record it (Luke xxiii. 16, 22), having already described the mockery by Herod (Luke xxiii. 11). The Johannine narrative is an abbreviation of the Matthæan-Marcan description (Matt. xxvii. 27–31; Mark xv. 16–20), where, however, the scourging is simply the normal preliminary to crucifixion, not, as here, an element in the conflict between Pilate and the Jews (cf. Luke xxiii. 16).

Pilate and his soldiers proceed in their blasphemous ignorance. The soldiers jest with the Jewish king. Jesus, robed in purple and wearing the crown of thorns, is honoured in mockery with royal pomp, and Christian worship is poignantly caricatured. Sir James Frazer, following certain notable students of comparative religion, has suggested that the mockery is a reminiscence of the ritual of human sacrifice in Western Asia (*Golden Bough*, vol. III, second edition, pp. 186–98. For other literature see Klostermann, *Marcus-evangelium*, 1926, p. 180). But there is no reason to suppose such a theory to be more than one of those ingenious fancies which from time to time encroach upon the interpretation of the New Testament from other spheres. The learned scholar has now, however, removed the passage from the original text, but preserved it as an appendix to the *Scapegoat* (pp. 412 sqq.) with the note 'The hypothesis which it sets forth has not been confirmed by subsequent research, and is admittedly in a high degree speculative and uncertain.'

## ECCE HOMO

*vv.* 4–7. The episode, which has no parallel in the synoptic gospels, takes place outside the palace. Pilate presents Jesus, the Son of God, to the crowd with the words *Behold, the man*, in order that he may release the prisoner after satisfying the Jews by an exhibition of public mockery. To the readers of the gospel *Behold, the man* (cf. Luke xxiii. 4, 6, 14) stands in sharp contrast with the truth *Behold, the Lamb of God* (i. 29, 36) or with, *Behold, your God* (Isa. xl. 9), and even with Pilate's own words, *Behold, your King* (*v.* 14). There is no reason to suppose that the writer intends his readers to understand that Pilate wished to appeal to the pity of the crowd. Pilate continues the mockery of the soldiers, and exposes his own ignorance. The Evangelist uses Pilate's words to prepare for the second interview between Pilate and Jesus the subject of which is the nature and origin of the mysterious prisoner whom Pilate had so glibly named *the man*. The Jews, possessing deeper perceptions than Pilate of the issues involved, demand the crucifixion of Jesus, and in answer to Pilate's petulant permission to them to crucify the prisoner themselves, since he can discover no crime in him, they reveal what is really at stake. *He made himself the Son of God* (cf. v. 18, x. 33). He is therefore guilty of blasphemy, and, according to Jewish Law, He must die (Lev. xxiv. 16; Mark xiv. 64). Moved by a power of which they are the instruments, they insist that he must die by crucifixion, and not by stoning, which is the legal punishment for blasphemy. Since, however, they are not permitted by their Law to inflict crucifixion, and since Pilate cannot permit what the Law does not expressly allow, they persist in their demand that Pilate must order and execute the death of the prisoner. The argument is exactly parallel to xviii. 31, 32. It should be noted that both Pilate and the Jews are unconscious witnesses to Christian truth. Pilate proclaims the sinlessness of Jesus, and the Jews declare His death to be the fulfilment of the Law (cf. xi. 50, 51).

## PILATE AND THE SON OF GOD

*vv.* 8–11. The limited humanitarianism of Pilate is shaken by the new accusation, which, instead of furthering the purpose of the Jews, makes Pilate afraid. What if the prisoner be more than a man? He therefore retires again with Jesus within the palace, and asks the pertinent question *Whence art thou?* The question is familiar to the readers of the gospel, and presumes *from heaven* or *of God*, not *of Galilee*, to be the correct answer (vii. 27, 28, viii. 14 sqq., ix. 29 sqq.). Luke records a similar question, and the information which Pilate receives that Jesus is of Galilean origin leads in the Lucan narrative to the examination before Herod (Luke xxiii. 5–7).

Since Pilate had already shown himself incapable of perceiving truth, and since he had no apprehension of the kingdom which is not of this world, it was impossible that any answer could be given to his question (Mark xv. 5; Matt. xxvii. 12–14, cf. Luke xxiii. 9). Pilate therefore proceeds to assert his authority to set Jesus free or to crucify Him as he wills. Jesus at once denies that he possesses any such independent authority. The power to lay down His life and to take it again belongs to the Son of God according to the commandment of the Father (x. 17, 18). Pilate's competence to order the crucifixion of the Son of God is derived from God Himself. It is not stated here, as Bauer maintains, that all human authority has its source and limitation in the divine will, but simply that the power of handing Jesus over to be crucified is given to Pilate from above. The whole action of the Passion is the necessary consequence of human sin, but the greater sin attaches to the Jews who delivered Jesus into Pilate's hands, and especially to the apostate disciple who betrayed Him (xiii. 2, 11, 21, xviii. 2, 5). This murderous activity, however, has its ultimate source in the homicidal energy of the Devil, who is the prince of this world (viii. 44, xii. 31, xiii. 2, 27).

### THE FORMAL BLASPHEMY OF THE JEWS AND THE SURRENDER OF PILATE

*vv.* 12–16*a*. Pilate is again unintelligently, perhaps superstitiously, impressed, and determines to release the prisoner. For the third time he declares Jesus to be innocent (xviii. 38, xix. 6, 12, cf. Luke xxiii. 4, 14, 16). But the Jews, by recalling the dangerous title *King*, make it impossible for a servant of the Emperor to maintain his office and set Jesus free. The prisoner has made Himself a king, and set Himself in opposition to the Emperor. He is therefore guilty of sedition, and, if Pilate passes over so heinous an offence, he also is guilty of sedition. The friend of Cæsar cannot also be the friend of Jesus (xv. 14. For the title *Friend of Cæsar* see Bauer).

The sentence of death is now inevitable, and the author solemnly records the place and the hour. Pilate brings Jesus forth to hear the sentence, and takes his seat on the throne of judgement. Loisy translates the passage *Pilate set Him* [*Jesus*] *on the judgement seat*, and finds in the enthronement of Jesus the climax of Pilate's prophetic mockery of the King of the Jews. But, though the translation is grammatically possible (Acts ii. 30; 1 Cor. vi. 4; Eph. i. 20) and the symbolism may be suggested in the Greek, it is an unnecessary subtlety, since the verb is in the New Testament normally intransitive (cf. Acts xii. 21, xxv. 6, 17, see Lagrange). The name of the place is recorded both in Greek and in Hebrew, to denote the universal significance of Pilate's action (cf. *vv.* 17, 20); λιθόστρωτον, the Pavement or Mosaic (literally a place spread with stones; the word is used to describe the Court of the Temple, 2 Chron. vii. 3; Josephus, *B.J.* v. 192, vi. 85, 189; *Letter of Aristeas*, lxxxviii): *Gabbatha*, the Heights or the Ridge (literally, an elevation, but the derivation of the word is obscure, see Bauer). The place-names are not recorded elsewhere. The hour of the double sacrifice is drawing near. It is midday. The Passover lambs are being prepared for sacrifice, and the Lamb of God is likewise sentenced to death. Hence the hour 'marks the end of Judaism' (Lagrange). In Mark xv. 25 the crucifixion takes place at the third hour (9.0 a.m.), and the variant reading *third* in some later manuscripts of the Fourth Gospel represents an early attempt to harmonize the two narratives (for the traditional explanations of the divergence in the tradition see Cornelius a Lapide and Calmes).

Before Pilate hands Jesus over to be crucified the author records the complete and formal apostasy of the Jews. The governor now presents the prisoner to the Jews not as *the man*, but as *your King*. The crowd again repeats the cry *crucify him*. Pilate asks them finally whether they intend him to crucify their king, and the chief priests answer in the name of the apostate people of God *We have no king but Cæsar*. The rejection of Jesus by the Jews has now reached its inevitable conclusion. They have denied the sovereignty of God, and abdicated their right to be His chosen people. By undertaking the execution of the Messiah in defence of the majesty of Cæsar the mystery of iniquity is consummated, and the blasphemy of the Jews is complete. Having played their part, except for passing references in *vv.* 21, 31, xx. 19. the Jews disappear from the narrative.

# THE NARRATIVE OF THE PASSION

## IV

## THE CRUCIFIXION

### XIX. 16B–42

#### GOLGOTHA

xix. 16b. *They took Jesus therefore:* 17. *and he went out, bearing the cross for himself, unto the place called The place of a skull, which is called in Hebrew Golgotha:* 18. *where they crucified him, and with him two others, on either side one, and Jesus in the midst.* 19. *And Pilate wrote a title also, and put it on the cross. And there was written,* JESUS OF NAZARETH, THE KING OF THE JEWS. 20. *This title therefore read many of the Jews: for the place where Jesus was crucified was nigh to the city: and it was written in Hebrew, and in Latin, and in Greek.* 21. *The chief priests of the Jews therefore said to Pilate, Write not, The King of the Jews; but, that he said, I am King of the Jews.* 22. *Pilate answered, What I have written I have written.*

#### THE SEAMLESS ROBE

23. *The soldiers therefore, when they had crucified Jesus, took his garments, and made four parts, to every soldier a part; and also the coat: now the coat was without seam, woven from the top throughout.* 24. *They said therefore one to another, Let us not rend it, but cast lots for it, whose it shall be: that the scripture might be fulfilled, which saith,*

> *They parted my garments among them,*
> *And upon my vesture did they cast lots.*

*These things therefore the soldiers did.*

#### THE BELOVED DISCIPLE AND MARY,
#### THE MOTHER OF THE LORD

25. *But there were standing by the cross of Jesus his mother, and his mother's sister, Mary the wife of Clopas, and Mary Magdalene.* 26. *When Jesus therefore saw his mother, and the disciple standing by, whom he loved, he saith unto his mother, Woman, behold, thy son!* 27. *Then saith he to the disciple, Behold, thy mother! And from that hour the disciple took her unto his own home.*

CHRISTUS MORTUUS EST; EMITTIT SPIRITUM SANCTUM
ET VIVIFICANTEM

28. *After this Jesus, knowing that all things are now finished, that the scripture might be accomplished, saith, I thirst.* 29. *There was set there a vessel full of vinegar: so they put a sponge full of the vinegar upon hyssop, and brought it to his mouth.* 30. *When Jesus therefore had received the vinegar, he said, It is finished: and he bowed his head, and gave up his spirit.*

CRURIFRAGIUM—THE EFFUSION OF THE BLOOD
AND THE WATER

31. *The Jews therefore, because it was the Preparation, that the bodies should not remain on the cross upon the sabbath (for the day of that sabbath was a high day), asked of Pilate that their legs might be broken, and that they might be taken away.* 32. *The soldiers therefore came, and brake the legs of the first, and of the other which was crucified with him:* 33. *but when they came to Jesus, and saw that he was dead already, they brake not his legs:* 34. *howbeit one of the soldiers with a spear pierced his side, and straightway there came out blood and water.* 35. *And he that hath seen hath borne witness, and his witness is true: and he knoweth that he saith true, that ye also may believe.* 36. *For these things came to pass, that the scripture might be fulfilled, A bone of him shall not be broken.* 37. *And again another scripture saith, They shall look on him whom they pierced.*

THE INTERMENT

38. *And after these things Joseph of Arimathæa, being a disciple of Jesus, but secretly for fear of the Jews, asked of Pilate that he might take away the body of Jesus: and Pilate gave him leave. He came therefore, and took away his body.* 39. *And there came also Nicodemus, he who at the first came to him by night, bringing a mixture of myrrh and aloes, about a hundred pound weight.* 40. *So they took the body of Jesus, and bound it in linen cloths with the spices, as the custom of the Jews is to bury.* 41. *Now in the place where he was crucified there was a garden; and in the garden a new tomb wherein was never man yet laid.* 42. *There then because of the Jews' Preparation (for the tomb was nigh at hand) they laid Jesus.*

GOLGOTHA
(Mark xv. 21–7; Matt. xxvii. 32–8; Luke xxiii. 26–38)

xix. 16b–22. As Isaac bore the wood for the burnt offering, so Jesus, the victim of God and the prisoner of men, was led forth from the city, bearing His cross, to a place elevated in the form of a skull, and named ὁ κρανίου τόπος or *Golgotha*. On this eminence outside the city, but in close proximity to it (Num. xv. 36; Heb. xiii. 12), the Messiah of the Jews and the Saviour of the world was crucified between two nameless malefactors. And yet His royal dignity was attested by the central position of His cross, and published by the superscription, set by the Roman governor above His head, *Jesus of Nazareth, the King of the Jews*. The elevation of Jesus had the result which He Himself foretold (iii. 14, 15, viii. 28, xii. 32). Many Jews were drawn out of the city to read His title and behold their King; and moreover, since He died not for the Jewish nation alone, *but that he might also gather together into one the children of God that are scattered abroad* (xi. 52), the trilingual title summons the Gentiles to knowledge of Him. Thus did Pilate *tell it out among the heathen that the Lord is King* (Ps. xcvi. 10). The Jews, fully aware of the danger of this undesirable publicity, request him to modify the text of the inscription, so as to make it plain to all that the sovereignty of their victim existed only in the fantasy of His own imagination. Pilate abruptly refused to change the truth into a lie. No reference is made to Simon of Cyrene, who, according to the synoptic narrative, bore the cross (Mark xv. 21; Matt. xxvii. 32). Luke adds that he bore it *after Jesus* (Luke xxiii. 26, in fulfilment of Luke ix. 23, xiv. 27). The author of the Fourth Gospel, however, carefully emphasizes that Jesus bore the cross Himself; perhaps in order to declare that He offered Himself as the sacrifice without human assistance; perhaps in order to give greater precision to the Lord's saying—*If any man would come after me, let him deny himself, and take up his cross, and follow me* (Mark viii. 34 and parallels, cf. xxi. 19). Basilides, in the interests of Docetic Christology, maintained that Simon of Cyrene died instead of Jesus (Irenæus, *Haer.* i. 24. 4). For the Mohammedan version of the legend see Plummer on Luke xxiii. 6). It is just possible that undesirable stories were gathering round Simon when the Gospel was written, and that for this reason the author omits all reference to him. Origen says that Jesus first carried the Cross, then Simon. This is the usual means of harmonizing the Johannine with the synoptic narratives. It was customary for a prisoner to be compelled to carry his cross to the place of crucifixion (Strack-Billerbeck, vol. I, p. 587).

*Golgotha*. Greek *Kranion* (Judges ix. 53, 54; 2 Kings ix. 35), Latin *Calvaria*. Literally a *skull*, therefore a hill or mound shaped like a skull. According to early Christian tradition it was the site of the burial of Adam's skull. Jerome notes that the legend was 'a popular interpretation—but not true' (see Swete on Mark xv. 22).

*Title*. For the custom see Swete and Klostermann on Mark xv. 26. Bauer refers to the title erected by the Roman soldiery over the tomb of Gordian, 'in Greek, Latin, Persian, Jewish, and Egyptian writing, in order that it might be read by all'.

*Of Nazareth*, cf. Luke xxiii. 6.

## THE SEAMLESS ROBE
### (Mark xv. 24; Matt. xxvii. 35; Luke xxiii. 34)

*vv.* 23, 24. The quaternion of soldiers (cf. Acts xii. 4) to whom the details of the crucifixion were entrusted fulfil precisely Ps. xxii. 18, where a contrast is implied in the LXX version between the plural *clothes* and the singular *vesture.* The soldiers strip their victim, dividing the garments into four parts, one for each man. Since, however, the under-robe, which immediately covered the Lord's body, could not be torn without injury, being woven throughout from top to bottom without seam, they decide to cast lots whose it should be. The addition of the words *These things the soldiers did* implies that their action was especially significant. The exact fulfilment of the prophecy may sufficiently account for the significance of the incident to the author, but more seems to be suggested. The synoptic narratives record the division of the garments and the casting of lots, but make no explicit reference either to the seamless robe or to the Psalm.

The Greek word translated *Let us not rend* suggests not only the tearing of garments (Isa. xxxvii. 1), but also the division of the people of God into factions (vii. 43, ix. 16, x. 19, cf. 1 Kings xi. 29 sqq.; 1 Cor. i. 10, xi. 18, xii. 25). The indivisible robe, which is closely associated with the body of the Lord, may therefore symbolize the unity of the believers who are joined to the Lord and feed upon His Body, in contrast to the division of the Jews, who are torn into factions because of Him (x. 16, xvii. 11, 20 sqq. contrasted with vii. 43, ix. 16, x. 19). The seamless robe of the High Priest (Josephus *Ant.* iii. 161, based on Exod. xxxi. 10; Lev. xxi. 10), which Philo interpreted as the cohesion of the world by the powers of the Logos (see Bauer) may be suggested here. The ancient and modern interpretation of the robe as the Church may therefore rightly penetrate the author's meaning (see Cyrpian *De Unitate Ecclesiæ,* ch. vii. Loisy, Calmes, and others). If this be so, the soldiers fulfil an Old Testament prophecy and at the same time proclaim the indivisibility of the Church. Cyril of Alexandria regarded such symbolism as speculations 'which do no damage to the elements of the faith, but are rather fertile of profit' (cf. Lagrange).

## THE BELOVED DISCIPLE AND MARY,
### THE MOTHER OF THE LORD
### (Mark xv. 40, 41; Matt. xxvii. 55, 56; Luke xxiii. 49)

*vv.* 25-7. The names of the women who stood near the cross (not *afar off,* as in the synoptic narratives) are carefully recorded. 'The weaker sex then appeared the more manly, so entirely henceforth were all things transformed' (Chrysostom). In the Lucan account, however, *all his acquaintance* (masculine), *and the women, stood afar off seeing these things:* an echo of Ps. xxxviii. 11, lxxxviii. 8. The number of the women is obscure. Tradition has taken from this passage the three Marys beneath the cross, but more probably the author intends four women, the faithful counterpart of the four unbelieving soldiers—Mary and her sister (? Salome, Mark xv. 40; Matt. xxvii. 56, the mother of the sons of Zebedee, see Lagrange, Westcott); Mary, the wife of Clopas (Luke xxiv. 18; ? Alphæus; Mark iii. 18, cf. xv. 40; according to Hegesippus Clopas was the brother of Joseph, see Euseb. *Hist. Eccl.* iii. 11. 2), and Mary Magdalene. But the attention of the reader is directed towards the Beloved Disciple, and the Mother of Jesus, neither of whom is referred to in the synoptic narratives in this context.

At the time of the Lord's death a new family is brought into being. If the unity of the Church is symbolized by the seamless robe, the peculiar nature of that unity is indicated here. The Church proceeds from the sacrifice of the Son of God, and the union of the Beloved Disciple and the Mother of the Lord prefigures and foreshadows the charity of the *Ecclesia* of God. Mary, the Mother of the Lord, becomes the mother of the faithful (cf. Rev. xii. 5 sqq., see *J.T.S.* April 1920, pp. 210 sqq.), and the Beloved Disiciple here seems to denote the ideal Christian convert. Loisy thinks that Mary symbolizes faithful Judaism in so far as it gave birth to the Christ and to the Apostolic Church, and that the Beloved Disciple represents the Gentile Christians, the sons of the Jewish Christian community. But this is unnatural symbolism, since there is no indication that the author of the Fourth Gospel regarded Judaism, faithful or unfaithful, as the mother of the Lord, nor that he could have thought of Jewish Christianity as the parent of the gentile converts—both were *born of God.* There is no suggestion in the text that the Beloved Disciple at once led the Mother of the Lord to his own home, and then returned to see the water and the blood pour from His pierced side (*vv.* 33–5). *From that hour* means from the hour of the completed sacrifice of the Christ (ii. 4, vii. 30, viii. 20, xii. 23, 27, xiii. 1, xvi. 2, 4, 32, xvii. 1). It is recorded in Acts xii. 12 that the house of Mary, the mother of John (whose surname was Mark), was the meeting place of the primitive church in Jerusalem (see Wellhausen). It is possible that the author intends a contrast between the Beloved Disciple, who went *to his own home* with the Mother of the Lord in obedience to a direct command, and the other disciples who were scattered in flight *to their own homes* (xvi. 32, see note).

#### CHRISTUS MORTUUS EST; EMITTIT SPIRITUM SANCTUM ET VIVIFICANTEM

*vv.* 28–30. Save for the actual death of the Lamb and His return to the glory of the Father, the whole design of God for the salvation of men is now accomplished in the perfect obedience of the Son (iv. 34, v. 36,

xvii. 4). The death of Jesus is the completion of the Scriptures. Having accomplished the will of God the Christ longs for His return to the Father. The words *I thirst* and the action of the soldiers echo a series of passages in the Psalms. *My soul is athirst for God, yea, even for the living God* (Ps. xlii. 2); *My soul thirsteth for thee, my flesh also longeth after thee: in a barren and dry land where no water is* (Ps. lxiii. 1); *They gave me gall to eat: and when I was thirsty they gave me vinegar to drink* (Ps. lxix. 21). The soldiers, misunderstanding the meaning of the word, find a fresh opportunity of cruelty, and offer their victim vinegar to drink in order to aggravate the thirst: as Chrysostom comments, 'they become more savage and increased their wrong'. The reed of the Marcan-Matthæan narrative, upon which the sponge of vinegar was set, is here changed to a twig of hyssop. Twigs of hyssop were used for sprinkling in Hebrew ritual cleansing (Lev. xiv. 4, 6; Num. xix. 18; Ps. li. 7). More important, however, is the use of hyssop for sprinkling the doors of the Jewish homes during the Passover season in memory of Exod. xii. 22. Since Jesus is, in the Fourth Gospel, both the Lamb of God and the Door (x. 7), the action of the soldiers is appropriately significant and is of value in reminding the reader that the Jewish Passover is fulfilled in the sacrifice of the true Paschal Lamb (cf. *vv.* 33, 36).

An old emendation of the text has recently been revived (Field, *Notes on the Translation of the New Testament*, p. 107, Lagrange) by which *hyssos* (a javelin) is substituted for *hyssopos*. This would make excellent sense; the soldier raised the sponge of vinegar to Jesus upon his javelin. But the manuscript evidence for this emendation is slight (one eleventh century cursive, 476; see Bernard). It is possible that the word *hyssos* suggested hyssop to the author and enabled him by a slight alteration to secure his allusion to the Passover.

*It is finished* (literally, *it has been completed*) announces the victory of the victim. The Christ has accomplished His mission, and the salvation of the world is attained. The word sums up the messianic interpretation of Ps. xxii applied to Jesus. The Psalm begins *My God, my God, why hast thou forsaken me?* and, after describing the sufferings of the man of God, breaks out into an almost eschatological cry of victory:

*When he called unto him he heard him. . . . All the ends of the world shall remember themselves, and be turned unto the Lord: and all the kindreds of the nations shall worship before him. . . . They shall come, and the heavens shall declare his righteousness: unto a people that shall be born, whom the Lord hath made.* The Matthæan-Marcan word, *My God, my God, why hast thou forsaken me*, and the Johannine, *It is finished*, have therefore the same significance; the former cites the first words of the Psalm, and in so doing involves the whole; the latter sums up its meaning, and is less open to misunderstanding. The Johannine word is not the substitution of a cry of victory for a cry of despair (Loisy and others). For the Rabbinic interpretations of Ps. xxii see Strack-Billerbeck.

*He bowed his head, and gave up his spirit* (literally, *He handed over the spirit*). Mark has, *Jesus uttered a loud voice, and gave up the ghost*; Matthew *Jesus cried again with a loud voice, and yielded up his spirit;* Luke records the words of the cry echoing Ps. xxxi. 5: *Father, into thy hands I commend my spirit; and having said this, he gave up the ghost.* The Johannine record may be so phrased as to describe the voluntary death of the Christ, and may have no further significance. But it is very strange language. If it be assumed that the author intends his readers to suppose that the Beloved Disciple and Mary the Mother of Jesus remain standing beneath the cross, the words *He bowed his head* suggest that He bowed His head towards them, and the words *He handed over the Spirit* are also directed to the faithful believers who stand below. This is no fantastic exegesis, since *vv.* 28–30 record the solemn fulfilment of vii. 37–9. The thirst of the believers is assuaged by the rivers of living water which flow from the belly of the Lord, the author having already noted that this referred to the giving of the Spirit. The outpouring of the Spirit here recorded must be understood in close connection with the outpouring of the water and the blood (*v.* 34). The similar association of Spirit and Water and Blood in 1 John v. 8, *There are three who bear witness, the Spirit, and the water, and the blood: and the three agree in one*, seems to make this interpretation not only possible, but necessary.

### *CRURIFRAGIUM*—THE EFFUSION OF THE BLOOD AND THE WATER

*vv.* 31–7. The whole passage is without parallel in the synoptic gospels. Luke seems to have no knowledge of the pierced side (Luke xxiv. 39 contrasted with John xx. 25, 27). The Jews, still busying themselves about the scrupulous fulfilment of the Law, approach Pilate with a second request (*v.* 21). According to the Law *If a man have committed a sin worthy of death, and he be put to death, and thou hang him on a tree; his body shall not remain all night upon the tree, but thou shalt surely bury him the same day; for he that is hanged is accursed of God; that thou defile not thy land which the Lord thy God giveth thee for an inheritance* (Deut. xxi. 22, 23, cf. Josephus, *B.J.* iv. 137). In this case it was especially important that the Law should be accurately fulfilled, not only because the Jews had expressly come up to Jerusalem *in order to purify themselves* (xi. 55), but because this particular night was the beginning both of the Sabbath and of the first and great day of the Passover Festival (Mark xv. 42; Luke xxiii. 54). They therefore demanded that the legs of the criminals should be broken as soon as possible in order to hasten their death, and the corpses forthwith removed from sight. The Roman custom was to leave the corpses for the vultures to devour (for the association of crucifixion and *Crurifragium* see Bauer). Pilate presumably grants the Jewish request, though this is not recorded. The soldiers immediately proceed to break the legs of the two malefactors; but when they come to Jesus they find Him already dead. He had offered Himself a willing victim, and His death coincided with the killing of the Passover Lamb (Plummer). In unconscious fulfilment of prophecy, and, as the Fathers' comment, in order that the Lord's risen body may not be damaged or incomplete (see Cornelius a Lapide), the soldiers therefore abstain from breaking the legs of the Lamb of God—*They shall leave none of it until the morning, nor break a bone thereof* (Num. ix. 12, cf. Ps. xxxiv. 19, 20); *neither shall ye break a bone thereof* (Exod. xii. 46). One of them, however, also in unconscious fulfilment of prophecy, and in order that the redemptive efficacy of the Lord's death may be visible to all who can perceive its meaning, pierces the side of the Christ with a lance, *and straightway there came out blood and water—and I will pour upon the house of David, and upon the inhabitants of Jerusalem, the spirit of grace and of supplication; and they shall look unto me whom they have pierced* (Zech. xii. 10); *Out of his belly shall flow rivers of living water. But this spake he of the Spirit, which they that believed on him were to receive* (vii. 38, 39). The new covenant by which the old is fulfilled is thus inaugurated. The author of the Epistle to the Hebrews reminds his readers that the first covenant was inaugurated with blood and water and hyssop (Heb. ix. 19).

The witness of the mysterious disciple, who must be the Beloved Disciple of *vv.* 26, 27, is then solemnly recorded, and the truth of his witness is attested by the Lord Himself: *He knoweth that he saith true* (see note below). The Beloved Disciple does not merely bear witness against the Docetists to the evident proof of the actual death of Christ, nor merely to the miraculous occurrence which followed His death, but rather to the significance of that occurrence. He perceived that purification (water) and new life (blood) flow from the completed sacrifice of the Lamb of God, and he bears witness to the truth and efficacy of the Gospel, in order that those who read his gospel may believe that Jesus is the Saviour of the world, and that they are cleansed and enlivened by His Blood (1 John i. 7). And since, moreover, the benefits of the Sacrifice on Calvary are appropriated by the faithful Christian when he is reborn from above of water and the Spirit (iii. 3–5), and when he drinks the blood of the Son of man (vi. 53–6), the death of the Christ and the effusion of the Spirit (*v.* 30) and of the blood and the water, are declared to be the true institution of Christian Baptism and of the Eucharist. The sacraments are not to the author of the gospel two independent rites, but means by which each faithful Christian is enabled to stand on Calvary with the Beloved Disciple and receive that purification and new life which is the life of the Spirit. The whole passage (*vv.* 30–7) must therefore be taken into account in commenting upon 1 John v. 8. *There are three who bear witness, the Spirit, and the water, and the blood: and the three agree in one.*

If the Beloved Disciple is intended to be John the Apostle, further insight into the careful literary structure of the Fourth Gospel is here provided. The two great Johns bear solemn witness to the effective sacrifice of the Lamb of God, the one at the beginning of the narrative, the other at its conclusion; and for this reason the witness of the Beloved Disciple is reserved until the Passion. The Baptist cries *Behold, the Lamb of God, which taketh away the sin of the world* (i. 29, 36); the Apostle sees the concrete fulfilment of the prophecy, and bears witness to its truth. The medieval illuminators who depicted the two Johns standing by the Cross and bearing witness to its significance may therefore preserve a subtle penetration of the intention of the author of the Fourth Gospel (cf. the historiated initial to Saint John's Gospel in manuscript 120 in the Library of Pembroke College, Cambridge).

Since the emission of the Blood and the Water from the side of the crucified Son of God is the visible expression of the essential Christian truth, it is not surprising that Christian commentators have found it patient of many various precise explanations, and have supposed the mixed chalice to represent its significance symbolically in the celebration of the Liturgy of the Church. In addition to the normal interpretations of the blood and the water as symbols of the efficacy of the Lord's death and of the sacraments, the Fathers find in them references to the reality of the human body of Jesus, or to His humanity and His divinity, or to Baptism (water) and Martyrdom (blood), or to the Church proceeding from the side of the second Adam, as Eve did from the side of the first Adam. Of the traditional interpretations the following citations may be taken as typical. 'He poured out from his side the two cleansing elements, Water and Blood, Word and Spirit' (Apollinaris). 'Who was unlike other dead men; but even in death manifested signs of life in the water and the blood, and was, so to speak, a *new* dead man' (Origen, *Contra Celsum*, ii. 69; Origen is arguing that the details of the Passion served the purposes of the whole economy of salvation). 'This was in order that the opened side might grant an inlet to the cleansing, which had hitherto been closed, so that when the blood and the water flowed like a spring, those who dwell in the country of the captivity might be delivered by the blood, and those who had the stripes of their sins might be washed in the water' (Macarius Magnes, *Apocriticus* ii. 19, E.T. by T. W. Crafer). 'Not without purpose or by chance, did those founts come forth, but because by means of these two the Church consisteth. And the initiated know it, being by water regenerate, and nourished by the blood and the flesh. Hence the Mysteries take their beginning; that when thou approachest that awful Chalice, thou mayest so approach, as drinking from that very side' (Chrysostom). 'God presenting us thereby with a type, as it were, and foreshadowing of the mystery of the Eucharist and Holy Baptism. For Holy Baptism is of Christ and Christ's institution; and the power of the mystery of the Eucharist grew up for us out of His Holy Flesh' (Cyril of Alexandria).

'Martyrdom will be another baptism. For "I have withal", saith He, "another baptism" (Luke xii. 50). Whence, too, it was there flowed out from the wound in the Lord's side water and blood, the materials of either baptism' (Tertullian, *De Modestia*, xxii).

'He makes blood and water gush forth, fashioning anew two baptisms; the one of blood, which is the baptism of martyrdom, the other of water, which is the baptism of regeneration' (Euthymius Zigabenus).

'For when at the beginning of the human race woman was formed from the side of Adam (the man) by the withdrawal of a rib, it was fitting that even then in that occurrence Christ and the Church should be foretold. Now that sleep of Adam (the man) was the death of Christ, whose side was pierced with a lance while He hung lifeless upon the Cross. And thence flowed forth blood and water, in which we perceive the Sacraments, by which the Church is built up' (Augustine, *De Civ. Dei*, xxii. 17).

'The woman, who was formed from the side, led the way to sin; but Jesus who came to bestow the grace of Pardon on men and women alike, was pierced in the side for women, that He might undo the sin' Cyril of Jerusalem, *Catecheses*, xiii. 21).

'Let the Armenians be put to shame, who do not mix water with wine in the Mysteries. For they do not appear to believe that water was emitted from the side of Christ which is the greater miracle—but blood alone' (Theophylact). On the patristic interpretation of xix. 34 see Cornelius a Lapide, and Westcott's additional note to ch. xix.

*He knoweth that he saith true.* Since in the Greek the 'He' of *He knoweth* is the emphatic demonstrative pronoun, which in iii. 28, 30, vii. 11, ix. 28; 1 John ii. 6, iii. 3, 5, 7, 16, refers to the Lord; and since the similarly constructed phrases in xxi. 24 and 3 John 12 introduce an additional witness, it seems almost necessary to regard this phrase as the attestation of the witness of the Beloved Disciple by the Lord Himself, so as to fulfil the Old Testament Canon of Evidence referred to in viii. 13–18 (cf. v. 31). If this passage and xxi. 24 *We know that his witness is true* be taken together the general meaning is that the witness of the whole apostolic body converges upon and supports the witness of the Beloved Disciple, which is, moreover, continuously attested by the Christ Himself (see note on xxi. 24).

*They shall look on him whom they pierced.* The passage in Zech. xii. 10 describes the eschatological mourning of the people of God for a crime which they have committed against God, *They shall look unto me whom they have pierced.* The intensity of their grief is likened to the mourning over an only and first-begotten son. The crude anthropomorphism implied in the piercing of God caused the LXX translator to substitute *danced in triumph* or *insulted* for *pierced*, presuming the verb *rakad* in place of *dakar* in the original Hebrew, so that the passage in the LXX runs *They shall look upon me instead of insulting me* (see Strack-Billerbeck).

The messianic application of the prophecy both here and in Rev. i. 7 preserves the meaning of the Hebrew original (cf. Theodotion, Aquila, Symmachus, Justin, *Apol.* i. 52, *Dial.* 14, 32, 64, 118). The author of the book of Revelation and Justin Martyr perceive the fulfilment of the prophecy in the advent of the Christ in judgement (cf. Matt. xxiv. 30), but the author of the Fourth Gospel sees the anticipation of the eschatological scene in the concrete situation in which the soldiers and the crowd beheld the pierced side of the crucified Christ. The Vulgate, two manuscripts of the Old Latin version, and the Philoxenian and Harklean Syriac Versions have *opened* for *pierced*, *One of the soldiers with a spear opened his side*. This may be merely a mistranslation of the Greek, but more likely the mistranslation was facilitated by the desire to suggest that the soldier opened the Lord's side in order that the Blood and the Water might flow forth, rather than in order to ensure the death of Jesus. 'He did not say *pierced through* or wounded, but *opened*, in order that the gate of life might be stretched wide, whence the sacraments of the Church, without which there is no entrance into the true life, might have their origin' (Augustine, cf. Leo *Ep.* xxviii, *ad Flav.* § 5).

### THE INTERMENT
(Mark xv. 42–7; Matt. xxvii. 57–61; Luke xxiii. 50–6)

*vv.* 38–42. Pilate receives yet another deputation. The first request of the Jews he had roundly refused (*v.* 22); to the second he made no recorded reply (*v.* 31); but he immediately gives his approval to the proposal of the two secret disciples of Jesus that they might be permitted to remove the body, and give it such burial as would accord with the manners of the Jews and the dignity of the Saviour. Joseph of Arimathæa, one of the timorous believers referred to in xii. 42, 43, in striking contrast to the cruelly utilitarian proposal of the Jews (*v.* 31), reverently removed the body, and Nicodemus, *the teacher of Israel*, to whom the Lord had delivered the teaching concerning that new birth which is from above (iii. 1 sqq.), provided, as a mark of his respect, a royal gift of an immense quantity of myrrh and aloes (2 Chron. xvi. 14, cf. Ps. xlv. 8). The gift of one hundred pounds of spices suggests the sweet-smelling odour, which went forth into the world from the sacrifice of the Son of God (xii. 3; 2 Cor. ii. 14–16; Eph. v. 2). Together, the two eminent men bandaged the body in linen cloths, and covered it with the mixture of myrrh and aloes, and laid it in a new tomb hitherto unused. Thus the two timorous believers are publicly and courageously drawn to the Christ after His exaltation upon the Cross (xii. 32). The tomb was in close proximity to Golgotha, so that the interment was completed before the beginning of the Festal Sabbath (Luke xxiii. 54), and, moreover, the garden, in which afterwards Mary first saw the risen Lord, enclosed the place of burial. So the Christ was buried in the place where He was crucified, and was embalmed, as Lazarus had been, according to the Jewish custom, which was unlike the Egyptian in that it involved no mutilation of the body. The divine purpose moves towards its complete fulfilment, since the site of the Crucifixion was also the site of the Resurrection, and the body was prepared for its rising again, and the resting place of the Lord was glorious (Isa. xi. 10).

The narrative is constructed within the same framework as the synoptic narratives. The request of Joseph, Pilate's permission, the deposition, the covering of the body, the careful reference to the time of day (which in Matthew-Mark introduce the record, but in Luke as in John conclude it), are common to all four evangelists. But Nicodemus, the anointing of the body, the linen cloths as opposed to the single sheet, the garden, the proximity of the tomb to Golgotha, are all Johannine additions. The significant details concerning the tomb itself echo the Lucan and Matthæan descriptions:

*Laid him in a tomb which had been hewn out of a rock* (Mark); *Laid him in his own new tomb, which he had hewn out in the rock* (Matthew); *Laid him in a tomb that was hewn in stone, where never man had yet lain* (Luke); *In the garden a new tomb wherein was never man yet laid* (John). The presence of the women who watched is omitted in the Fourth Gospel, but xx. 1 presumes that at least Mary Magdalene had knowledge of what had been done.

*A mixture of myrrh and aloes, about a hundred pound weight.* The Codex Alexandrinus and the Codex Vaticanus have *roll* for *mixture*. Lagrange, without any manuscript authority, proposes that the immensity of the gift is due to a scribal error in copying the numeral. A late rabbinic tradition records that when the proselyte Onkelos burnt eighty pounds of spices at the death of Gamaliel the elder, and was asked why he had done so, he replied, citing Jeremiah xxxiv. 4: 'Thou shalt die in peace; and with the burnings of thy fathers (the former kings) which were before thee. Is not R. Gamaliel far better than a hundred kings?' (Strack-Billerbeck).

*As the custom of the Jews is to bury.* The Egyptian method of embalming involved the removal of the brain and the bowels (Holtzmann).

# THE RESURRECTION APPEARANCES

## I

## IN JERUSALEM

### XX

#### THE EMPTY TOMB

XX. 1. *Now on the first day of the week cometh Mary Magdalene early, while it was yet dark, unto the tomb, and seeth the stone taken away from the tomb. 2. She runneth therefore, and cometh to Simon Peter, and to the other disciple, whom Jesus loved, and saith unto them, They have taken away the Lord out of the tomb, and we know not where they have laid him. 3. Peter therefore went forth, and the other disciple, and they went toward the tomb. 4. And they ran both together: and the other disciple outran Peter, and came first to the tomb; 5. and stooping and looking in, he seeth the linen cloths lying; yet entered he not in. 6. Simon Peter therefore also cometh, following him, and entered into the tomb; and he beholdeth the linen cloths lying, 7. and the napkin, that was upon his head, not lying with the linen cloths, but rolled up in a place by itself. 8. Then entered in therefore the other disciple also, which came first to the tomb, and he saw, and believed. 9. For as yet they knew not the scripture, that he must rise again from the dead. 10. So the disciples went away again unto their own home.*

#### THE APPEARANCE TO MARY MAGDALENE
#### AND THE GOSPEL OF THE NEW ORDER

11. *But Mary was standing without at the tomb weeping: so, as she wept, she stooped and looked into the tomb; 12. and she beholdeth two angels in white sitting, one at the head, and one at the feet, where the body of Jesus had lain. 13. And they say unto her, Woman, why weepest thou? She saith unto them, Because they have taken away my Lord, and I know not where they have laid him. 14. When she had thus said, she turned herself back, and beholdeth Jesus standing, and knew not that it was Jesus. 15. Jesus saith unto her, Woman, why weepest thou? whom seekest thou? She, supposing him to be the gardener, saith unto him, Sir, if thou hast borne him hence, tell me where thou hast laid him, and I will take him away. 16. Jesus saith unto her, Mary. She turneth herself, and saith unto him in Hebrew, Rabboni; which is to say, Master. 17. Jesus saith to her, Touch me not; for I am not yet ascended unto the Father:*

*but go unto my brethren, and say to them, I ascend unto my Father and your Father, and my God and your God.* 18. *Mary Magdalene cometh and telleth the disciples, I have seen the Lord; and how that he had said these things unto her.*

## THE GIFT OF THE HOLY SPIRIT
## AND THE UNBELIEF OF THOMAS

19. *When therefore it was evening, on that day, the first day of the week, and when the doors were shut where the disciples were, for fear of the Jews, Jesus came and stood in the midst, and saith unto them, Peace be unto you.* 20. *And when he had said this, he showed unto them his hands and his side. The disciples therefore were glad, when they saw the Lord.* 21. *Jesus therefore said to them again, Peace be unto you: as the Father hath sent me, even so send I you.* 22. *And when he had said this, he breathed on them, and saith unto them, Receive ye the Holy Ghost:* 23. *whose soever sins ye forgive, they are forgiven unto them; whose soever sins ye retain, they are retained.*

24. *But Thomas, one of the twelve, called Didymus, was not with them when Jesus came.* 25. *The other disciples therefore said unto him, We have seen the Lord. But he said unto them, Except I shall see in his hands the print of the nails, and put my finger into the print of the nails, and put my hand into his side, I will not believe.*

## THE CONFESSION OF THOMAS AND THE FAITH OF
## THE CHRISTIANS

26. *And after eight days again his disciples were within, and Thomas with them. Jesus cometh, the doors being shut, and stood in the midst, and said, Peace be unto you.* 27. *Then saith he to Thomas, Reach hither thy finger, and see my hands; and reach hither thy hand, and put it into my side: and be not faithless, but believing.* 28. *Thomas answered and said unto him, My Lord and my God.* 29. *Jesus saith unto him, Because thou hast seen me, thou hast believed: blessed are they that have not seen, and yet have believed.*

30. *Many other signs therefore did Jesus in the presence of the disciples, which are not written in this book:* 31. *but these are written, that ye may believe that Jesus is the Christ, the Son of God; and that believing ye may have life in his name.*

## THE EMPTY TOMB
### (Mark xvi. 1–8; Matt. xxviii. 1–8; Luke xxiv. 1–11)

xx. 1–10. The great day of the Jewish Feast is passed over in grim silence; the festival has no importance. In the early morning of the following day, the first day of the week and the third day after the sacrifice of the true Lamb of God, Mary Magdalene arrived at the tomb, and discovered the stone moved from its place. Concluding from the removal of the stone that the body of the Lord had also been removed, she ran at once to tell first Peter and then the Beloved Disciple, who had been scattered each to his own dwelling, as Jesus had foretold (xvi. 32). *They have taken away the Lord out of the sepulchre, and we know not where they have laid him.* These words assume other women to have accompanied Mary to the tomb, as is narrated in the synoptic gospels. As soon as the two disciples hear what Mary has to say, they both run to the sepulchre. The Beloved Disciple, being the first to arrive, is content to bend down and look into the tomb. He sees only the linen cloths which had enveloped the body lying deprived of their use. When Peter reaches the tomb, he enters. He too sees the linen cloths, but in addition he beholds the napkin which had covered the Lord's head lying apart and folded (xi. 44). Whatever had been accomplished within the tomb had been done in calm and orderly fashion. Yet, no more than Mary Magdalene, did he perceive the significance of the empty tomb (cf. Luke xxiv. 12); he merely verified in greater detail what she had said. The Beloved Disciple then entered, saw, and believed. From *vv.* 25, 27, 29 it is clear that *believed* means belief in the Resurrection of the Lord. It was not Peter, but the other disciple, who first reached the tomb, and first understood the meaning of the empty tomb and of the position of the cloths and the napkin. He was the first to believe that the Lord had left the grave clothes behind as a sign that He had burst asunder the bonds of death, and was risen. And further, he was the first of the long line of blessed disciples who believed without having actually seen the risen Lord (*v.* 29). The pre-eminence of the faith of the Beloved Disciple is the climax of the narrative. His faith was not derived from ancient prophetic texts; the fact of the empty tomb illuminated the sense of scripture (Ps. xvi. 10, cf. Luke xxiv. 25–7; Acts ii. 24–7, xiii. 35; see Westcott) and of the obscure words of the Lord (ii. 19–22, x. 18, xvi. 16 sqq.). Having concluded their examination of the tomb the two disciples returned each to his own dwelling.

The fact of the empty tomb is of great importance to the author of the Fourth Gospel. He presumes that his readers are familiar with the earlier tradition in which it was recorded that the women saw Joseph lay the body in the tomb and secure the entrance with a stone (Mark xv. 46, 47; Matt. xxvii. 60, 61; Luke xxiii. 55), and that they returned early on the Sunday morning to anoint the body and found the stone rolled away, and the tomb empty. The earlier narrative is drastically abbreviated, the plural *we know* (*v.* 2), however, betrays the writer's knowledge of the presence of the other women. His narrative is so constructed in order that the weight of the evidence for the empty tomb may rest upon the accurate testimony of the two chief disciples, rather than upon the witness of the women; and that the Jewish accusation that the body had been stolen (Matt. xxvii. 64, xxviii. 12–15) may be completely disproved: 'For neither, if any person had removed the body, would they before doing so have stripped it; nor, if any had stolen it, would they have taken the trouble to remove the napkin, and roll it up, and lay it in a place by itself' (Chrysostom, cf. Severus in Corderius's *Catena*, quoted by Bauer). He emphasizes the unpreparedness of the disciples. They do not expect the Resurrection. They run to the tomb, having in their minds neither the Old Testament prophecies nor the words of the Lord. The Beloved Disciple believed that the Lord had risen because the tomb was miraculously empty.

That some of the disciples, as well as the women, visited the tomb is not merely a Johannine tradition. In the conversation on the road to Emmaus occur the words *And certain of them which were with us went to the sepulchre, and found it even so as the women had said: but him they saw not* (Luke xxiv. 24). The *Textus Receptus* of Saint Luke's Gospel also contains the record of Peter's visit to the tomb: *Then arose Peter, and ran unto the sepulchre; and stooping down, he beheld the linen clothes laid by themselves, and departed, wondering in himself at that which was come to pass* (Luke xxiv. 12). Since, however, this verse is omitted by Codex Bezae, and by four manuscripts of the Old Latin Version, and perhaps by the Old Syriac Version, Westcott and Hort regard it as a 'Western non-interpolation', and therefore unauthentic. Most critics explain its presence in all the other manuscripts as due to an early interpolation from the Fourth Gospel. But this is exceedingly difficult. Why should no reference be made to the Beloved Disciple if the verse be a summary of the narrative in the Fourth Gospel? It may be that the verse is authentic, and that Luke xxiv. 24 refers back to xxiv. 12. If so, the author of the Fourth Gospel expands the brief note in the Lucan narrative, preserving its phraseology, and adding that the Beloved Disciple was also present, and believed, whereas Peter merely wondered at that which was come to pass (see Lagrange).

The author of the gospel seems to attach some significance to the fact that the Beloved Disciple outran Peter, but that Peter first entered the tomb. The usual explanations are most unsatisfactory. John ran faster because he was the younger man (Lagrange), and unmarried (Isho'dad); he did not at once enter the tomb because he was afraid (Holtzmann), or in deference to Peter, the chief of the Apostles (Cornelius a Lapide, Lagrange, Heiler). Love discovers truth 'but before it pretends to penetrate into it, and to adhere thereto, it waits till the authorities of the Church examine it, and the pastors approve of it' (Quesnel). 'Peter enters before him, because Peter represents Primitive Christianity, Jewish Christianity; whereas the disciple represents more recent Christianity, contemporaneous with the author, Hellenistic Christianity' (Loisy). Perhaps the reader is intended to detect the love of the Beloved Disciple in the speed with which he reached the tomb; and his entrance is delayed in order that his faith may form the climax of the narrative.

THE APPEARANCE TO MARY MAGDALENE
AND THE GOSPEL OF THE NEW ORDER

*vv.* 11-18. The Lord appeared first neither to the Beloved Disciple, who already believed, nor to Peter (Luke xxiv. 34), but to the woman who had stood by the Cross and discovered the empty tomb, and who announced her discovery to the two disciples. Mary Magdalene had returned to the sepulchre, and remained there weeping. As she bent down to look into it, she saw what the disciples had not seen. Two white-robed angels (Rev. iii. 4, 5, iv. 4) sat marking the place where the body had lain, witnesses to the mystery of the Resurrection. Mary, unconscious of the unsuitability of her tears, answers their natural question *Why weepest thou?* by repeating what she had already told the two disciples. The conversation is, however, interrupted by the presence of a stranger, whom Mary supposes to be the gardener. Perhaps it was he who, disapproving of the presence of a corpse in his garden, had removed the body. She therefore offers to dispose of it, if he will tell her where it is. Receiving no answer she turns again to the sepulchre. Then she hears her own name pronounced, and, turning, recognizes the Lord. The true, life-giving ruler of the Paradise (Garden) of God has called his own sheep by name, and she knows His voice (x. 3, 4). With a solemn confession of faith—*Rabboni, my master*—she throws herself before Him, and clasps His feet. The narrative presupposes some such action (cf. Matt. xxviii. 9, 10), since the Lord bids her cease from touching Him, for He has not yet ascended to the Father, and she too has a duty to perform, as the messenger of the risen and ascending Christ to His brethren (Matt. xxviii. 10; Luke xxiv. 9). The precise content of the message is given to her—The Lord is now ascending to His Father and theirs, to His God and theirs. Mary at once departed, and told the disciples that she had seen the Lord, and handed over His message to them.

The words of Jesus refer back to the teaching given in chs. xiii-xvii (xiii. 1, 3, xiv. 1-4, 28, xvi. 17, 28, xvii. 13, cf. vii. 33), and the difficult *Noli me tangere* must be interpreted by this reference. The problem is to explain why Mary is to cease touching the Lord, because He has *not yet* ascended to the Father. The author did not write *Touch me not for I am ascending to the Father.* Yet most commentators proceed as though he had so written. In chs. xiii-xvii the Lord had taught His disciples that the new order of the Spirit, which was to be a renewed relationship with Himself, would follow His return to the Father (xiv. 12-18, xvi. 5 sqq.). He now declares to Mary, and through her to the disciples, that the time has come for Him to ascend to the Father and therefore for the inauguration of the new order. The command that Mary should cease touching Him refers to the interim period between the Resurrection and the Ascension—and to this period only. So intimate will be the new relationship with Jesus that, though Mary must for the time being cease from touching Him, because He must ascend and she must deliver His message, yet, after the Ascension, both she and the disciples will be concretely united with Him in a manner which can actually be described as 'touching', and of this the eating of the Lord's Body and the drinking of His Blood (vi. 51–8) is the most poignant illustration. The mysterious *not yet*, which runs through the whole gospel (cf. ii. 4, vii. 6, 8, 30, 39, viii. 20) still surrounds the Lord's actions; but it will not be so for long. Mary, by touching Him, did but anticipate a relationship which would be realized almost at once. The message which she had to deliver was therefore that the new order, the order of the powerful action of the Spirit of God, the New Covenant, was now imminent. Within this order the believers, the brethren of the Lord (Matt. xxviii. 10) will be in very truth sons of God. God is the Father both of Jesus and of those who believe in Him, and, moreover, He is both His God and theirs. Yet the distinction between Jesus and His disciples is carefully preserved. He does not say *Our Father and our God*, since what Jesus is by nature, His disciples are by grace (Augustine).

The narrative presupposes the earlier tradition in which the angels (Luke)—a single angel (Matthew, Mark)—appear to the women, and announce the Resurrection. The women are also entrusted with a message to the Apostles (Matthew, Mark; Luke edited the Marcan narrative at this point, in order to avoid the record of appearances in Galilee). Matthew preserves a tradition (Matthew xxviii. 9, 10) that the Lord Himself appeared to the women, as they ran to tell the Apostles. They clasped His feet and worshipped Him; and He bade them tell His *brethren* (cf. John xx. 17) to retire to Galilee, and there they would see Him. In each of the three synoptic gospels Mary Magdalene is the first of the women named. In the Fourth Gospel the emphasis rests entirely upon the appearance of the Lord to Mary and upon the words which He addressed to her. Consequently, the tradition of the conversation with the angels (angel) is abbreviated to such an extent as to become almost unimportant; and for the same reason no mention is made of the other women. The canonical, but unauthentic conclusion to Saint Mark's Gospel records that the Lord appeared first to Mary Magdalene (Mark xvi. 9); but this may be dependent upon the Fourth Gospel. For the failure to recognize the risen Lord, cf. xxi. 4; Mark xvi. 12; Luke xxiv. 16, 37.

*Rabboni*. In the older Jewish literature the word *Rabboni*, as distinct from *Rabbi*, is hardly ever used in reference to men, and never in addressing them. The word is reserved for address to God (Strack-Billerbeck, vol. II, p. 25). Mary's use of it here is therefore probably to be understood as a declaration of faith, parallel to that of Thomas (*v.* 28).

*Touch me not.* The grammar—the verb is a present imperative—and the parallel in Matt. xxviii. 9, 10, show that the command puts an end to an action already in progress. The correct translation is therefore *Cease touching me* (cf. xix. 21; Moulton *Grammar of N.T. Greek,* vol. I, 124 sq.).

*My Father and your Father, and my God and your God.* The ascension is referred to in the opening verses of the Passion narrative as the return to God (xiii. 3, cf. Mark xv. 34; Matt. xxvii. 46; Rev. iii. 2, 12, and according to some manuscripts Rev. ii. 7); more normally it is the return to the Father. Both are combined here, as in Rom. xv. 6; 2 Cor. i. 3, xi. 31; Eph. i. 3 (see Westcott).

### THE GIFT OF THE HOLY SPIRIT
### AND THE UNBELIEF OF THOMAS
### (Luke xxiv. 36–49)

*vv.* 19–25. Late in the evening of the Sunday on which the Lord had risen from the dead the disciples were gathered together secretly behind closed doors for fear of the Jews (vii. 13, xix. 38). None of them had as yet seen the Lord. Such timidity and secrecy cannot long remain, since these are the men who must take up the work of the incarnate Son of God, and proclaim to the world the Gospel of salvation. The Author therefore proceeds at once to record the appearance of the Lord to the disciples, the solemn inauguration of the mission, and the gift of the Spirit by which they are empowered to remit and to retain sins.

The Lord appeared suddenly in their midst (Luke xxiv. 36). The doors, which protect and seclude the disciples from the Jews, can neither exclude the Christ nor prevent Him from discovering His own. Twice He salutes them with the peace which He alone can give (xiv. 27), and the joy of the disciples reflects the peace which they have received (xvi. 20–2). He then displays to them His wounds, less to establish His identity than that their joy might be fulfilled by the sight of the signs of His victory over the world (xvi. 33). Since the conquest of the power of the world by the death and resurrection of the Christ made the Christian mission to the world possible, the exposition of the wounds is at once followed first by the Apostolic commission of the disciples, secondly by their consecration (xvii. 18, 19). They are made Apostles, the Apostles of the Son of God; as the Father has sent the Son, so the Son sends His disciples (Luke xxiv. 47, 48; Acts i. 8; Matt. xxviii. 19, 20; Mark xvi. 15). But in order that they may be adequate for their work, they must be transformed and recreated by the insufflation of the Holy Spirit. As God originally breathed into Adam the breath of life, and he was made a living being, so the Son of God breathed upon His disciples, and they received the Holy Spirit. This is a new creative act of God, a second creation, rather than a repetition of the first creation. Saint Cyril perceived the meaning of the passage when he commented: 'The Christ is the Lamb of consecration, and He consecrates by actual sanctification, making men partakers in His nature, through participation in the Spirit, and in some sort strengthening the nature of man into a power and glory which is superhuman.' Inspired with divine authority, and invested with the power of Father, Son and Holy Spirit, the disciples are enabled to undertake the contest with sin. With the definition of the work of the Spirit as the remission and retention of sins the essential nature of the activity of the Church and of the ministry is also defined. As the Lord washed the feet of His disciples, so must they remit the sins of the faithful; and as the unbelieving Jews and the apostate Judas pass out of the narrative under the darkness of the Judgement of God, so must the disciples declare that both unbelievers and apostates stand under the Judgement of God, and their sins remain. The Apostolic retention of sins is not merely the absence of formal forgiveness, but a positive and effective declaration. The judicial sentence of the Apostles of the Lord, which is in fact the sentence not of men, but of God, is declared to be effectual. Sins so remitted are in very truth remitted, and sins so retained have been in very truth retained. The immediate reference is probably to the remission of sins which accompanied conversion and Baptism, and to the consequent retention of the sins of those who refused to accept the Apostolic preaching. But the reference must not be limited to this. The traditional Catholic exegesis of the passage, emphasized at the Council of Trent, insists on finding here the sanction for the sacrament of Penance. 'If anyone say that these words of the Saviour . . . are not to be understood of the power of remitting and retaining sins in the sacrament of Penance, as the Catholic Church has from the beginning understood, but shall twist their meaning so as to apply them to the authority of preaching the Gospel, and not to the institution of this sacrament, let him be anathema' (Council of Trent, Sess. XIV. Can. 3, see Cornelius a Lapide). If this means no more than that the words contain a reference to the remission and retention of sins committed after conversion, the Catholic exegesis must be upheld, since both the cleaning and the forgiveness of the sins of believer are important elements in the Johannine teaching (xiii. 3–11; 1 John i. 7–9, v. 16, 17), of which the rehabilitation of Peter is the classical illustration (xxi. 15–17). The principle which the evangelist has established is, as Loisy comments, 'susceptible of applications wider and more various than he himself was able to make, or than those to which he bore testimony'.

The controversy whether the commission is given to the Church as a whole or to the apostles is irrelevant. There is no distinction here between the Church and the ministry; both completely overlap. The evangelist records the birth of the Church as the organism of the spirit of God, and the origin of the authority of the ministry. Both are inaugurated together. There are as yet no converts—no fish and no lambs. The Christian community was, at its inception, a community of Apostles.

Neither here nor in ch. xxi. is it stated that the Lord departed from His disciples (Luke xxiv. 51; Acts i. 9–11; Mark xvi. 19). Perhaps this omission is intended. The author wishes his readers to understand that the gift of the Spirit involves the permanent presence of the Lord (xvi. 7, cf. Matt. xxviii. 20). Thomas, one of the disciples of the Lord, was, however, absent when Jesus appeared. When he was told that the others had seen the Lord, he refused to believe without ocular and tangible proof, and stated his unbelief in vigorous, almost brutal, terms. The Apostolic body is therefore incomplete, not merely through the permanent defection of Judas, but also through the temporary unbelief of Thomas *the Twin*, who on two earlier occasions, had misunderstood the meaning of the Lord's words and actions (xi. 16, xiv. 5).

The whole episode is narrated as the fulfilment of teaching previously given to the disciples. Words are now accomplished in deeds. The *coming* of Jesus fulfils xiv. 18, the commission and consecration of the apostles fulfils xvii. 16–19, their joy xvi. 20–2, the gift of peace xiv. 27, and the gift of the Spirit xiv. 16, xvi. 7, 13.

Appearances to the disciples belonged to the earliest Christian tradition (1 Cor. xv. 5–8). The whole episode in the Fourth Gospel is closely and even verbally similar to the Lucan narrative (Luke xxiv. 36–49), where the displaying of the wounds is succeeded by the command that the disciples should proclaim the gospel of repentance and remission of sins to all the Gentiles. The same phrases occur in both narratives. *He stood in their midst* (Luke xxiv. 36); *the joy of the disciples* (Luke xxiv. 41); *remission of sins* (Luke xxiv. 47); the reference to the Spirit (Luke xxiv. 49). And yet there are considerable differences. In the Lucan account all the disciples are bidden *feel* the Lord (cf. 1 John i. 1); the wounds in the feet take the place of the wound in the side, which is Johannine only, and depends upon xix. 34. The Lord solemnly eats in the presence of His disciples. These concrete occurrences are introduced in order to correct their opinion that the Lord is a disembodied spirit. Luke particularly emphasizes the opening of the understanding of the disciples, that they might perceive the fulfilment of Old Testament prophecies. But, most significant of all the differences in the two narratives, Luke postpones the gift of the Spirit until the day of Pentecost (Acts ii). The apparent contradiction with the Lucan record has greatly perplexed the commentators from very early days (Cyril of Alexandria). Luke is content to say that Jesus bade His disciples await in Jerusalem *the promise of my Father*, that is, the *power from on high*, the gift of the Spirit Luke xxiv. 49; Acts i. 8). The fourth Evangelist, however, records the gift of the Spirit on the first Easter Day. Certain commentators have, therefore, endeavoured to detract from the reality of the gift before the

Ascension, maintaining that it was a sign of what was to be, rather than the gift itself (Theodore of Mopsuestia, see also Cornelius a Lapide) or that it was a demonstration that the Spirit proceeds not only from the Father but also from the Son (Augustine, Lagrange), or that it was a very particular power which was given, the authority to remit and retain sins (Lagrange). The first is merely a subterfuge, and was rightly condemned at the Council of Constantinople (*Can.* 22)—the Lord did not give the Spirit in appearance only; the second interpretation is an imposed meaning, not emphasized in the text; the third fails to perceive that the authority to remit and retain sins is not a particular gift, but rather defines the whole work of salvation, and is the characteristic function of the Church in its complete activity. Modern critics imagine that the evangelist has definitely and consciously corrected the earlier tradition, and substituted the resurrection gift for the gift on the day of Pentecost—'the two narratives signify the same thing' (Loisy). Another explanation is, however, possible. The gift of the risen Christ does not completely fulfil the earlier references to the coming of the Spirit. The Evangelist has recorded the teaching of the Lord that the Spirit would be given after His return to the Father, that is, after the Ascension (xiv. 16, 26, xvi. 7, 13). It does not seem necessary to think, with Holtzmann, that, in view of xx. 17, the reader is intended to understand the appearance to the disciples as an appearance of the ascended Lord. There is therefore a distinction between the two gifts of the Spirit. The Resurrection scenes in the Fourth Gospel are all preparatory scenes, preparatory for the mission. What the Lord will do invisibly from heaven He here does visibly on earth. The mission is inaugurated, but not actually begun. The disciples still remain in secret, behind closed doors. The actual beginning of the mission lies outside the scope of the Fourth Gospel. There remains, therefore, room for the Pentecostal outpouring, after which the disciples take up the mission in public in the power of the Spirit descending from Father and Son in heaven.

*v.* 22. *He breathed on them.* The Greek verb echoes Gen. ii. 7 (LXX), where the same word is used. Ezek. xxxvii. 5–10, 14, *Come . . . O breath, and breathe upon these slain, that they may live,* and Wisd. xv. 11, in like manner depend upon the narrative of the creation of Adam. The idea of new birth is also contained in the use of the word in the early baptismal rites (see Bauer).

*v.* 23. *Whose soever sins. . . .* The saying is paralleled in the tradition preserved in Matt. xvi. 19, xviii. 18. In the Matthæan texts the verbs are *bind* and *loose.* These are technical Jewish terms for imposing or relieving the ban of excommunication, or for forbidding or allowing an action as in accordance with, or not in accordance with, the Law (Strack-Billerbeck, vol. I, pp. 738–47). The Greek verbs are simply a literal translation of the Aramaic (cf. Josephus *B.J.* i. 111). In the

Fourth Gospel the technical Jewish terms are avoided, the wider Christian word *remit*, which is limited neither to the relief of a ban of excommunication, nor to a declaration that an action is unlawful, being substituted for the technical Jewish *loose*, and similarly *retain* takes the place of *bind*.

## THE CONFESSION OF THOMAS AND THE FAITH OF
## THE CHRISTIANS

*vv.* 26–9. On the following Sunday the disciples were again gathered together in secret. Their number, however, was complete, for Thomas was with them. Jesus suddenly appeared in their midst, and again saluted them with the salutation of peace. But His appearance is primarily an appearance to Thomas. The exposition of the wounds is here the proof of the Resurrection and of the identity of the risen Lord with the crucified Jesus; and further the repetition of the words of Thomas is the proof of His miraculous knowledge. The Apostle is bidden do as he had desired, behold and touch with his fingers the marks of the nails, and thrust his hand into the side which had been pierced by the soldier's lance. Thomas has not the audacity thus crudely to examine his Lord, but instead, passionately and distinctly confesses the divinity of Jesus, and in so doing gives expression to Christian belief. With the cry *My Lord and my God* Thomas fulfils the Lord's words *That all may honour the Son, even as they honour the Father* (v. 23), and human faith perceives the truth stated in the first verse of the Prologue to the gospel, *and the Word was God*. Such faith is indeed Christian faith, and it is accepted by the Lord; but the means by which it had been attained were not the highest. More blessed are those who did not see, and yet believed. The faith of Thomas, and of all but one of the disciples is contrasted with the faith of the Beloved Disciple, who believed before the appearance of the Lord (xx. 8), and with the faith of those who were to believe the apostolic teaching.

The incredulity of the disciples belongs to the earlier tradition (Luke xxiv. 11, 25, 38, 41, cf. Mark xvi. 11), of some of the disciples (Matt. xxviii. 17). The general statements in the synoptic gospels become in the Fourth Gospel precise and concrete in the person of Thomas, whose unbelief is contrasted with the belief of the other disciples.

*v.* 28. *My Lord and my God*, cf. Hos. ii. 23. The words are addressed to Jesus, and are therefore a statement of faith in Him, not, as Theodore of Mopsuestia maintained, an address of wonder and thanksgiving to the Father, an opinion anathematized at the Council of Constantinople. Since the combination of Lord and God is common in the Old Testament (2 Sam. vii. 28; 1 Kings xviii. 39; Ps. xxx. 2, xxxv. 24, lxxxvi. 15, lxxxviii. 1; Jer. xxxviii. 17), it is unnecessary, with Bauer, to seek further comparisons in the terminology of Cæsar worship. Modern commentators point out that in the New Testament the word *God* with the definite article is reserved for the Father, and that it is anarthrous when applied to Jesus. This distinction is carefully preserved in the Prologue (i. 1, see note). They also insist that this passage is only an apparent exception, since a substantive in the vocative case followed by a possessive pronoun cannot be anarthrous (Bauer, Holtzmann). It may, however, be doubted whether the Evangelist intends this nice grammatical and theological distinction. Thomas honours the Son in the same terms with which the Jews were accustomed to honour the Father. The true exegesis of the passage therefore depends upon the recollection of the words spoken by Jesus in v. 23.

*v.* 29. Cf. the saying of Rabbi Simeon ben Lakish (*c.* A.D. 250): 'A proselyte is more precious before God than those crowds who stood on Mount Sinai. If they had not all seen the thunder, and the flames, and the lightning, and the quaking of the mountain, and had not heard the sound of the trumpet, they would not have submitted themselves to the dominion of God. But the proselyte has seen none of these things; and yet he comes, and surrenders himself to God, and takes upon himself the yoke of His will. Can anyone be more precious than he?' (Strack-Billerbeck, vol. II, p. 586).

*vv.* 30, 31. The four episodes which compose the strictly Resurrection narrative in the Fourth Gospel are divided into two sections, each containing two episodes. The two sections are carefully balanced. The place occupied by Mary Magdalene in the first section is taken by Thomas in the second. Mary weeps at the empty tomb—Thomas doubts the reality of the Resurrection. Mary, who was absent when the two disciples examined the tomb, and when the Beloved Disciple believed in the Resurrection, confesses her faith when the Lord appears to her—Thomas, who was absent when the Lord appeared to the disciples, makes his great confession of faith when the Lord appears to him. In both sections, touching the Lord, or the opportunity of touching Him, is important. And yet each episode possesses an independent significance. Mary's tears are secondary to the faith of the Beloved Disciple, the unbelief of Thomas to the missionary charge given to the disciples; Mary's faith gives place in importance to the messge of the Ascension which she must deliver, and the faith of Thomas to the faith of those who did not see and yet have believed. The narrative is therefore a carefully constructed literary whole. The Evangelist is, however, aware that there were in existence many other traditions of Resurrection appearances of the Lord, which were of great significance for the revelation of the nature of the Christian religion. He has but made a selection, sufficient for his readers to believe sincerely that Jesus is in very truth the Christ, the Son of God, in order that, secure in this belief, they may possess life everlasting (i. 12, vi. 47, xix. 35).

Most commentators, understanding *many other signs* to refer not merely to Resurrection appearances, are of the opinion that *vv.* 30, 31 form the conclusion of the gospel, and that ch. xxi is either an epilogue added by the author himself (Westcott, Plummer), or an appendix added by a later editor, who has imitated the style of the original author (Loisy). But a Christian gospel ends properly, not with the appearance of the risen Lord to His disciples, and their belief in Him, but with a confident statement that this mission to the world, undertaken at His command and under His authority, will be the means by which many are saved. The original ending of Saint Mark's Gospel is lost; but its present ending concludes with a description of the mission: *And they went forth, and preached everywhere, the Lord working with them, and confirming the word by the signs that followed* (Mark xvi. 20). Saint Matthew ends his gospel with the great mission charge, confirmed by the promise: *I am with you alway, even unto the end of the world* (Matt. xxviii. 20). Saint Luke proceeds to add a second volume, describing the progress of Christianity from Jerusalem to Rome, and so concludes his gospel. Nor is it otherwise in the Fourth Gospel. By means of two short scenes its readers are given complete confidence in the catholicity and power of the Church. The capture of the 153 fishes, and the patient apostolic care of the sheep and the lambs, form the climax of the gospel, not the faith of Thomas. Lagrange alone among modern commentatators recognizes that ch. xxi. is not an 'anti-climax'. But he suggests the removal of xx. 30, 31 from their present position, regarding them as the concluding verses of the gospel, which originally followed xxi. 23, and were subsequently displaced by the later addition of xxi. 24, 25. This is, however, unnecessary, since an almost exactly similar passage occurs in 1 John v. 13, but does not end the Epistle.

# THE RESURRECTION APPEARANCES

## II

## BY THE SEA OF TIBERIAS

### XXI

#### THE CAPTURE OF THE 153 FISHES
#### AND THE APOSTOLIC MISSION TO THE WORLD

xxi. 1. *After these things Jesus manifested himself again to the disciples at the sea of Tiberias; and he manifested himself on this wise.* 2. *There were together Simon Peter, and Thomas called Didymus, and Nathanael of Cana in Galilee, and the sons of Zebedee, and two other of his disciples.* 3. *Simon Peter saith unto them, I go a fishing. They say unto him, We also come with thee. They went forth, and entered into the boat; and that night they took nothing.* 4. *But when day was now breaking, Jesus stood on the beach: howbeit the disciples knew not that it was Jesus.* 5. *Jesus therefore saith unto them, Children, have ye aught to eat? They answered him, No.* 6. *And he said unto them, Cast the net on the right side of the boat, and ye shall find. They cast therefore, and now they were not able to draw it for the multitude of fishes.* 7. *That disciple therefore whom Jesus loved saith unto Peter, It is the Lord. So when Simon Peter heard that it was the Lord, he girt his coat about him (for he was naked), and cast himself into the sea.* 8. *But the other disciples came in the little boat (for they were not far from the land, but about two hundred cubits off), dragging the net full of fishes.* 9. *So when they got out upon the land, they see a fire of coals there, and fish laid thereon, and bread.* 10. *Jesus saith unto them, Bring of the fish which ye have now taken.* 11. *Simon Peter therefore went up, and drew the net to land, full of great fishes, a hundred and fifty and three: and for all there were so many, the net was not rent.* 12. *Jesus saith unto them, Come and break your fast. And none of the disciples durst inquire of him, Who art thou? knowing that it was the Lord.* 13. *Jesus cometh, and taketh the bread, and giveth them, and the fish likewise.* 14. *This is now the third time that Jesus was manifested to the disciples, after that he was risen from the dead.*

#### PETER, THE SHEPHERD AND THE MARTYR

15. *So when they had broken their fast, Jesus saith to Simon Peter, Simon, son of John, lovest thou me more than these? He saith unto him, Yea, Lord; thou knowest that I love thee. He saith unto him, Feed my lambs.* 16. *He saith to him again a second time, Simon, son of John, lovest thou me? He saith unto him, Yea, Lord; thou knowest that I love thee. He saith unto him, Tend my*

*sheep.* 17. *He saith unto him the third time, Simon, son of John, lovest thou me? Peter was grieved because he said unto him the third time, Lovest thou me? And he said unto him, Lord, thou knowest all things; thou knowest that I love thee. Jesus saith unto him, Feed my sheep.* 18. *Verily, verily, I say unto thee, When thou was young, thou girdedst thyself, and walkedst whither thou wouldest: but when thou shalt be old, thou shalt stretch forth thy hands, and another shall gird thee, and carry thee whither thou wouldest not.* 19. *Now this he spake, signifying by what manner of death he should glorify God. And when he had spoken this, he saith unto him, Follow me.*

### THE DESTINY OF THE BELOVED DISCIPLE

20. *Peter, turning about, seeth the disciple whom Jesus loved following; which also leaned back on his breast at the supper, and said, Lord, who is he that betrayeth thee?* 21. *Peter therefore seeing him saith to Jesus, Lord, and what shall this man do?* 22. *Jesus saith unto him, If I will that he tarry till I come, what is that to thee? follow thou me.* 23. *This saying therefore went forth among the brethren, that that disciple should not die: yet Jesus said not unto him, that he should not die; but, If I will that he tarry till I come, what is that to thee?*

24. *This is the disciple which beareth witness of these things, and wrote these things: and we know that his witness is true.*
25. *And there are also many other things which Jesus did, the which if they should be written every one, I suppose that even the world itself would not contain the books that should be written.*

### THE CAPTURE OF THE 153 FISHES
### AND THE APOSTOLIC MISSION TO THE WORLD
(Cf. Luke v. 1–11, xxiv. 41, 42; Mark i. 17; Matt. iv. 19, xiii. 47, xiv. 28)

xxi. 1–14. The sea of Tiberias, Galilee of the nations (Isa. ix. 1), is the scene of the last recorded manifestation of Jesus to His disciples. At the suggestion of Simon Peter, he and six of the disciples, Thomas, Nathanael, the sons of Zebedee, and two more, who remain unnamed, *go a fishing. They went forth* together and *entered the ship.* During the night they caught nothing. There is no reason to suppose that the number seven symbolizes a perfect number. It is, rather, a truncated twelve. One has betrayed the Lord to death, all, except the Beloved Disciple (see note on xix. 27) had fled, and now, at the suggestion of Simon, the seven who remain together go back to their fishing. The scene is one of complete apostasy, and is the fulfilment of xvi. 32 (see note). In the early morning Jesus stood unrecognized on the shore, and with some irony, since the negative in the Greek expects the answer 'No', asked them for some fish. With shame the disciples are compelled to own that they have nothing to give Him. He orders them to cast the net on the right side of the ship, and promises them success. Obediently they cast the net, and the result is prodigious. They enclose so many fish that they are unable to drag the net ashore. The Beloved Disciple perceives that it is the Lord, and tells Peter. Peter, covering his nakedness in deference to the presence of the Lord, casts himself into the sea, leaving his companions to drag the net the short hundred yards which separates them from the shore. Those in the ship are the first to reach the land, and they find a meal of bread and fish cooked and ready to eat. The Lord commands them to bring the fish which they have caught and, with the help of Peter, who had now reached the shore, the net is landed, unbroken and full of fish—*one hundred and fifty and three*. All are then invited to share the meal which the Lord had provided, and He *cometh and taketh the bread and* (*having given thanks*, added in Codex Bezae, the Sinaitic Syriac Version, and two manuscripts of the Old Latin Version) *giveth them, and the fish likewise*. The scene is of awful solemnity. None of the disciples durst ask Him who He is, knowing it is the Lord.

At first it would seem that the Evangelist has given his readers a simple record of a miraculous catch of fish. But this is not so. The narrative is bent this way and that under the subtle influence of the symbolism. Why do not the disciples eat the fish they have caught? Why is the strange number of the fish so carefully recorded? Why is eucharistic language used to describe the actions of the Lord at the meal which He has provided? A correct interpretation depends upon a correct interpretation of the significance of the number 153. So long as the accuracy and supposed oddity of the number be explained as preserving the memory of the Evangelist who helped to count the fish (Plummer), no true interpretation of the narrative as a whole is possible.

Now 153 is the sum of the first 17 of the natural numbers: 1, 2, 3, ... 17 = 153, and therefore 153 dots can be arranged in the form of an equilateral triangle (see Fig.) with 17 dots on the base line.

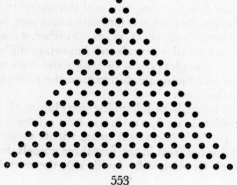

It is therefore a triangular number (cf. Heath, *Greek Mathematics*, p. 76). Moreover, 17, the number of dots in the side of the triangle, is itself a prime number of the form $2^n + 1$, a form of great interest to mathematicians. But the number is not of mathematical interest only. Greek zoologists held that there were 153 different kinds of fishes. Jerome, in his commentary on Ezek. xlvii. 9–12, says 'Writers on the nature and properties of animals, who have learned *Halieutica* in Latin as well as in Greek, among whom is the learned poet Oppianus Cilix, say that there are 153 different kinds of fishes.' The disciples, therefore, make the perfect catch of fish, one of every kind, and fulfil concretely both the prophecy of Ezekiel *And it shall come to pass, that fishers shall stand by it* [the river]: *from En-gedi even unto En-eglaim shall be a place for the spreading of nets; their fish shall be after their kinds, as the fish of the great sea, exceeding many* (Ezek. xlvii. 10), and the parable recorded in Matt. xiii. 47, 48, *The Kingdom of Heaven is like unto a net, that was cast into the sea, and gathered of every kind: which, when it was filled, they drew up on the beach.* Without Jesus, however, the disciples labour to no purpose; alone they can neither catch fish, nor bring them to land, even if they do catch them: *Apart from me ye can do nothing* (xv. 5, cf. Mark xvi. 20). The fish symbolize the converts to the Christian religion, and for this reason the natural imagery breaks down and becomes obscure at the crucial point. The disciples cannot eat the converts. The command *Bring of the fish which ye have caught* remains incomplete because according to the story it should be completed *in order that we may eat some and sell others,* but according to the symbolism it must be completed *in order that they too may share in the meal I have prepared.* The narrative therefore passes over into the record of a miraculous and eucharistic feeding of the multitude, the counterpart of the feeding of the 4,000 (Mark viii. 1–10; Matt. xv. 32–9) in which seven, not twelve, baskets are filled, and therefore seven disciples, not twelve, serve as the Lord's ministers. The purpose and significance of the narrative having been thus exposed, other phrases are seen to contain a double meaning. *I go a fishing* echoes and fulfils the words of the Lord, *I chose you, and appointed you, that ye should go and bear fruit* (xv. 16), and *they went forth* suggests both to the sea of Tiberias, and, what is far more important, into the world. *I sent them into the world* (xvii. 18, cf. xx. 21). Further, a comparison with the parallel Lucan narrative reveals two important differences. In the Lucan account the disciples possess two ships and the net is rent. Here the unbroken net and the single ship express the perfection and unity of the apostles of the Lord.

The language is throughout Johannine (see Plummer). *After this* (v. 1, vi. 1, vii. 1), *manifest* (i. 31, ii, 11, iii. 21, &c.; 1 John i. 2, ii. 19, &c.; Rev. iii. 18, xv. 4), *Again* refers back to xx. 19, 26, *the sea* (vi. 16), *catch* —the Greek word is not used in the first three gospels, but six times in the Fourth Gospel, *the charcoal fire* (xviii. 18), the restraint of the disciples in questioning the Lord (iv. 27, xvi. 23), the failure to recognize the Lord (xx. 14), the eucharistic words (vi. 11). Thomas and Nathanael are especially Johannine characters, Cana is a Johannine place-name (ii. 1, 11, iv. 46). The relation between the Beloved Disciple and Peter recalls xx. 2-8, where the perception of the former and the impetuosity of the latter are emphasized. It is almost impossible, with Loisy, to attribute the subtle similarity of style to conscious imitation. But the narrative, in spite of its Johannine character, rests upon, and seems to presume, scattered traditions preserved in the earlier gospels. In structure it closely resembles the Lucan record of the call of the disciples (Luke v. 1-10), in which Peter and the Sons of Zebedee are mentioned by name. The symbolism of the Apostles as fishers of men goes back to the Lord's words, *I will make you fishers of men* (Mark i. 17; Matt. iv. 19; Luke v. 10). Peter's casting himself into the sea may be compared with the Matthæan addition to the Marcan account of the Walking on the Sea (Matt. xiv. 28-32, cf. Mark vi. 45-52). The Lord's question, *Have ye aught to eat*, and the cooked fish, recall Luke xxiv. 41, 42. With the record of an appearance of the risen Lord in Galilee in addition to the appearances in Jerusalem, the Evangelist harmonizes the Matthæan and the Lucan traditions. Matthew records one appearance only of the risen Lord, and that in Galilee, whereas Luke locates all the appearances in Jerusalem. It seems therefore preferable to regard the narrative in the Fourth Gospel as influenced very subtly by many older traditions, rather than to suppose with Wellhausen and Bauer that the Evangelist has dovetailed together two independent and incompatible narratives *vv.* 1-8, 9-13. It has been suggested that the lost ending of Mark contained not only an appearance in Galilee, but also the record of a miraculous draught of fishes, and that consequently the author of the Fourth Gospel has drawn the episode from Mark. It has also been suggested that the miraculous draught of fishes in Luke v. 1-10 also depends on the lost ending of Mark, and that Luke transferred it to the call of the disciples in order to avoid recording an appearance in Galilee (Rohrbach, *Die Berichte über die Auferstehung*, pp. 42 sqq.; Loisy, pp. 926, 927). These may be mere suppositions. But, if the lost ending of Mark contained not only an account of an appearance in Galilee and of a miraculous draught of fishes, but also of the flight of the disciples, it is possible that some such narrative is the foundation of the episode recorded by the fourth Evangelist.

*v.* 5. *Aught to eat.* The Greek word, which is not used elsewhere in the New Testament, does not mean *something to eat* (cf. Luke xxiv. 41), but a *delicacy* to eat with bread. There is some evidence to show that the word was used especially to denote fish. The Lord's question may therefore be translated simply *Have ye any fish?* (see Moulton-Milligan, *Vocabulary of the Greek Testament*, and Bauer).

*v.* 11. *A hundred and fifty and three.* The Fathers, of course, sought to interpret the number symbolically. Origen, according to Isho'dad, understood it as the Blessed Trinity: fifty multiplied by three, plus three. Cyril of Alexandria, followed by Ammonius (Cramer's *Catena*) and Severus (Corderius' *Catena*), found in the number one hundred heathen, fifty Jews, and the Trinity. Saint Augustine extracted two meanings from the number; first, perceiving the importance of the number 17 (see above), he interpreted 153 as the believers, who, inspired by the sevenfold gift of the Spirit, keep the ten Commandments; secondly, he took the three as the symbol of the Trinity, and the triple fifty as bringing out the idea of unity in the Spirit, who is revealed in a sevenfold operation ($50 = 7 \times 7 + 1$) (see Westcott, additional note to ch. xxi). All these interpretations, however, lack the mathematical discipline necessary to perceive the significance of the number 153. There is no symbolical significance in the number itself: it is important as a number, and must have been recognized as such by educated Greeks, and therefore could be used, by transference, to symbolize a perfect and unique catch of fish.

*v.* 13. *And the fish likewise.* In primitive Christian Eucharistic iconography fish are often substituted for wine. This, and the varying number of the apostles, twelve or seven, is due to the Eucharistic significance inherent in the Feeding of the Five Thousand and of the Four Thousand and also in the Johannine version of the miraculous draught of fishes. There is no evidence that fish ever formed the matter of the Sacrament.

### PETER, THE SHEPHERD AND THE MARTYR

*vv.* 15–19. The Apostolic responsibility is not exhausted by the mission to the unconverted. To care for the converted is also the duty of an Apostle. The scene in which the capture of the fish is recorded is therefore completed by a picture of the Apostolic ministry under the imagery of a Shepherd and a flock of sheep and lambs. The sheep take the place of the fish, because, since fish die when they are caught, they provide no adequate illustration of the life of a Christian after his conversion. Peter is both fisherman and shepherd. But he has thrice denied the Lord. The threefold charge, the reminiscence of Peter's premature boasting (xiii. 37, cf. Mark xiv. 29) contained in the words *Lovest thou me more than these*, and the avoiding of the name Peter (i. 42) recall the proved instability of the Apostle. The solemn institution of Peter as the Shepherd of the sheep is also his own rehabilitation. But his rehabilitation is complete. The Lord, who knows all things (cf. i. 42, ii. 25, xvi. 30), knows the unshakable love which now fills the heart of the Apostle; and Peter's destiny is the complete *imitatio Christi*. As the Father sent the Son to be the good Shepherd of the sheep, and to lay down His life on their behalf (x. 1–18, xii. 24–6), so the Son sends the disciple to be both Shepherd and Martyr. The boisterous and irresponsible freedom of youth is now at an end. He can no longer act as he had just acted when he girded himself, and left the fish half caught, and swam alone to the shore. The service of the Christ, and of His flock, does not admit of such indiscreet independence. The Apostle must look forward to a long period of service, and then, finally, in his old age, his desire to lay down his life will be granted (xiii. 36, 37). He will stretch forth his hands, and his enemies will bind him, and bear him forth to death, for the glory of God (xii. 24–6). It can hardly be doubted that the Evangelist intends his readers to understand that Peter was, like his Master, to suffer death by crucifixion (xii. 33, xviii. 32).

Lagrange entitles the episode 'The Primacy and Martyrdom of Peter', and Calmes sums up its teaching: 'Peter is assimilated to Jesus as supreme pastor of the Church' (p. 474). This is in the strict tradition of Roman Catholic exegesis: 'On His departure into heaven Christ here designates His Vicar upon earth, and creates Peter the Supreme Pontiff, in order that one Church may be governed by one Pastor' (Cornelius a Lapide). But, though this interpretation is supported by Loisy and Bauer, it is open to grave question whether the Evangelist intended so definite a meaning. No doubt he regarded Peter as the leader of the band of Apostles; but he associates the Beloved Disciple in this leadership, and carefully insists that the latter was even more closely united to the Lord. Nor is the uniqueness of Peter in this passage a uniqueness in status in relation to the other apostles; it is rather, as Cyril well perceived, a uniqueness in denying the Lord: 'Why is it that Christ only asks Simon, though the other disciples were present? . . . We reply that . . . Peter's transgression by his thrice-repeated denial was special and peculiar to him. Therefore, as he had received a greater measure of forgiveness than the rest, he is asked to tell Christ whether he loved Him more' (Cyril of Alexandria). It may be added that if Peter had led the flight into Galilee and invited the disciples to return to their fishing he is even more desperately in need of a unique forgiveness. And this is what is here recorded. The whole future destiny of Peter, including the nature of his martyrdom, is the sign of his complete rehabilitation. Apart from the reinstatement of the Apostle, the Lord, in the person of Peter, requires of His disciples nothing but love, and recommends to them nothing but the care of His Sheep. Loisy thinks that the editor of ch. xxi depends upon the lost ending of Mark, not only for the miraculous draught of fishes but also for the investiture of Peter with the primacy over the other apostles, and that Matt. xvi. 18, 19; Luke xxii. 32, and the lost ending of Mark had a common origin (p. 941).

*vv.* 15, 16, 17. *Lovest thou me? Thou knowest that I love thee.* The English versions make no distinction between the two Greek words used in this passage for *love*, though the R.V. calls attention to it in the margin. Westcott and Plummer, however, discover an especial significance in the use the Evangelist has made of the two words. The one, the less exalted word, denotes the warmth of natural affection; the other expresses the higher love, and implies a 'calm discrimination' (see Plummer). Peter thoughout uses the less-exalted word, 'sure of the natural affection which it expresses'. The Lord at first demands the higher love, but when He puts the question the third time, He adopts the word which Peter had used, 'The idea of the loftiest love is given up. It is as if the Lord would test the truth of the feeling which St. Peter claimed' (Westcott). Further examination, however, has made this delicate exegesis almost untenable (see Lagrange, Bauer). Whatever distinction of meaning there may be between the two words considered apart from their use in the Fourth Gospel, in it they are synonymous. The Evangelist uses both words indiscriminately for the love of the Father for the Son (iii. 35, v. 20), for the love of Jesus for Lazarus (xi. 3, 5, 36), and for the Beloved Disciple (xix. 26, xx. 2, xxi. 20). Moreover, the use of synonymous, or almost synonymous, words is characteristic of the passage. Two distinct words are used for *tend* and *know* (vii. 27, viii. 55, xiii. 7, xiv. 7). In all these cases the distinction should not be unduly pressed. The author varies his terms in order to express the perfection of the knowledge of Christ and of the Love and devotion which He demands. Similarly, the variation *sheep—lambs* signifies the Church as one complete organism; it does not indicate a distinction between the ordinary believers and their shepherds, all under the sovereignty of Peter (Cornelius a Lapide, Schanz).

*v.* 19. *Signifying by what manner of death.* The phrase, which in xii. 33, xviii. 32 refers to the crucifixion of the Lord, has almost certainly the same significance here. The lifting up which was characteristic of the earlier references, is here varied by the hands outstretched and then bound, denoting crucifixion (see Field, *Notes*, p. 109). The comment of Tertullian is therefore justified: 'Peter is girded by another when he is bound to the cross' (*Scorp.* 15). The tradition that Peter was crucified head downwards is unsupported here (Theodore of Mopsuestia, Isho'dad).

### THE DESTINY OF THE BELOVED DISCIPLE

*vv.* 20–3. Peter both literally and figuratively sets out to *follow* the Lord (i. 37 sqq., xiii. 36) in answer to a definite command. The Beloved Disciple, needing no command, is also following the Lord. His obedience is assured; it was Peter's love that had been shown to be uncertain. Peter turns round and, seeing the Beloved Disciple, presumes to question the Lord about the destiny of that other who lay on His breast at the supper, and asked Him who it was who should betray Him. The Lord repeats the command that Peter should follow Him without turning back, and answers his question in obscure language (Mark ix. 1; Matt. xvi. 28; Luke ix. 27). In fact the Lord's words are a rebuke to

Peter (xvi. 23), and give him no further information than is involved in the description of the disciple as the disciple *whom Jesus loved*, since *he that keepeth His commandments abideth in Him, and He in him*, just as *he that loveth not abideth in death* (1 John iii. 14, 24). The Greek word translated *tarry* in the A.V. and R.V. is the same significant Johannine word elsewhere translated *abide* (i. 33, &c.). The obscurity of the Lord's words, however, caused misunderstanding among the brethren, and the Evangelist corrects the rumour that the Lord declared the Beloved Disciple to be deathless. And yet in some sense his deathlessness is suggested. Perhaps the opinion may be hazarded that the reader is meant to understand that that perfect discipleship of which the Beloved Disciple is the type and origin will never fail the Church. Modern commentators (e.g. Loisy) usually assume that the death of the apostle must have taken place, and that the author of ch. xxi attempts to justify the Lord's words in the light of his death. But there is no reason to suppose that this is the intention of the author, since the next verse states that the Beloved Disciple wrote the words. This passage must not therefore be used as a starting point from which to argue that the Beloved Disciple cannot have written the gospel because he was dead.

*v.* 24. The conditions of trustworthy evidence laid down in v. 31, 32, viii. 13, 14, are here fulfilled by the introduction of the testimony of others both to the truth of the witness borne by the Beloved Disciple in his oral teaching, and, consequently, to his credibility when he gave that teaching literary expression (cf. xix. 35; 3 John 12). The identification of these additional witnesses depends upon the opinion that is held concerning the relation of ch. xxi in whole or in part, to the rest of the gospel. Those who, with Loisy and Calmes, regard ch. xxi as an appendix added by an editor, suppose that the additional testimony is the testimony of the Church that possessed the gospel, and that the *we* are the elders of that Church, which is presumably Ephesus. Others, with Westcott, who is followed rather uncertainly by Plummer, while maintaining that ch. xxi. 1–23 was written by the author of the gospel, are yet willing to detach *v.* 24 and to treat it as a note added by the Ephesian Elders before the publication of a gospel that would otherwise be anonymous. Neither of these explanations is entirely satisfactory; the first, because ch. xxi is the natural conclusion and climax of the gospel, and the evidence brought forward to justify the introduction of an editor seems entirely inadequate (see below); the second, because, if *vv.* 24, 25 be removed, the gospel has no ending, unless, with Lagrange, it be supposed that xx. 30, 31 originally followed xxi. 23, and was removed to its present position when xxi. 24, 25 were added—a most difficult supposition. To both theories, moreover, the objection seems fatal that the first person plural *we* has a perfectly definite meaning throughout the gospel, which is entirely suitable here. It means the original

apostles of the Lord, of whom the Beloved Disciple was one (i. 14, cf.
1 John i. 1–4, where note especially *and these things we write*; see INTRO-
DUCTION, pp. 93–104). It is therefore possible that the author of the
Muratorian Fragment has very nearly interpreted the verse correctly.
His interpretation was 'The Fourth Gospel is that of John, one of the
disciples. When his fellow disciples and bishops entreated him he said,
"Fast ye now with me for the space of three days, and let us recount to
each other whatever may be revealed to each of us." On the same night
it was revealed to Andrew, one of the apostles, that John should narrate
all things in his own name as they called them to mind. And hence,
although different points are taught us in several books of the gospels,
there is no difference as regards the faith of believers, inasmuch as in
all of them all things are related under one sovereign Spirit which
concern the Lord's nativity, His passion, His resurrection, His conversation with His disciples, and His twofold advent—the first in the humiliation of rejection, which is now past, and the second in the glory of
royal power, which is yet in the future. What marvel is it then that John
brings forward these several things so constantly in his epistles also,
saying in his own person, "What we have seen with our eyes, and heard
with our ears, and our hands have handled, that have we written."
For thus he professes himself to be not only the eye-witness, but also
the hearer; and besides that, the historian of all the wondrous facts
concerning the Lord in their order.' (Translation from *A.N.C.L.*)

Now, of course, this introduces a precision of meaning wholly absent
from the sentence in the gospel which gave rise to his imaginings. While
correctly interpreting the *we*, he has failed to reproduce the obscurity,
the intentional obscurity, perhaps, of the author of the gospel. The
author records the imprimatur of the original disciples to the teaching
of one of their number, whether that teaching was given orally or in
writing. He makes no definite statement that the writing was the gospel
which he has just completed, just as there is no definite statement that
*these things* in 1 John i. 4 necessarily denote the Epistle. Yet the verse
is capable of this interpretation, and it is not surprising that the author
of the Muratorian Fragment and the Church have declared the gospel
to be the work of John, the Apostle and Beloved Disciple of the Lord.
The question of authorship is, however, not so easily disposed of.
Pseudepigraphy, in some form or other, was a recognized literary form
that implied no dishonesty; and here, if we have to deal with pseudepigraphy, it is pseudepigraphy of a very hesitating and peculiar nature.

A protest must be made against Dr. Moffatt's translation of this verse,
and against Mr. Macgregor's deductions from this translation. Dr.
Moffatt translates *This was the disciple who bears testimony to these facts*.
The natural translation is, however, that of the English Versions: *This
is the disciple which testifieth* (beareth witness R.V.) *of these things*. Mr.
Macgregor then proceeds to make use of the doubtful translation to

support the attribution of the statement *His testimony we know is true* (again, Dr. Moffatt's translation), to the 'Redactor and his school speaking for the Church of his day' (Macgregor in Moffatt, *New Testament Commentary, The Gospel of John*, p. 377).

*v.* 25. *I suppose* is clearly the Evangelist. But whether the reader is intended to deduce that this is the Beloved Disciple, or someone who has made use of his oral and written testimony, is left obscure.

The Evangelist concludes his gospel with an apology to his readers for its fragmentary character (cf. xx. 30), and offers his excuse. A complete record of the life of the Lord is impossible: the world could not contain what should be written. Commentators, who feel such an opinion to be an exaggeration, unworthy of the author of the gospel, betray a scepticism entirely foreign to the Evangelist. His conclusion is a most appropriate expression of literary insufficiency, which has contemporary parallels. Rabbi Johanan b. Zakkai (first century A.D.) is reported to have said 'If all heaven were a parchment, and all the trees produced pens, and all the waters were ink, they would not suffice to inscribe the wisdom I have received from my teachers: and yet from the wisdom of the wise I have enjoyed only so much as the water a fly which plunges in the sea can remove' (Strack-Billerbeck, cf. Bauer). It is, of course, possible that this verse is a scribal gloss, which was incorporated into the text of the gospel. But the evidence for this is so slight as to be almost worthless. Origen quotes the verse six times (*In Ioan.*, ed. Brooke, i. 14, 251, 252, ii. 14, 87, 310). All the manuscripts contain it except the Sinaitic Syriac Version, in which it is abridged, and Codex Sinaiticus, in which it is added by the second hand; the second hand is, however, the hand of the original corrector (Westcott and Hort, *Greek Text*, vol. II, pp. 90, 91, reprinted in Westcott, *Saint John*, vol. II, p. 377).

Since the above exegesis of the concluding verses of the gospel depends upon the assumption that ch. xxi is not the work of a later editor, it is necessary to justify this assumption. The arguments for the conclusion that the record of the miraculous draught of fishes is Johannine have already been stated. The same arguments apply to xxi. 15–25. The further definition of the pastoral character of the Apostolic work, and the destiny of the two chief Apostles, form an entirely suitable conclusion to the gospel. The narrative is Johannine in structure, in phraseology, and, most important of all, in the subtle references to passages in the main body of the gospel, the clear recognition of which is necessary for any true exegesis. The rehabilitation of Peter presumes xiii. 36–8 and perhaps xvi. 32, the name Simon, Son of John, echoes i. 42; the martyrdom of the Shepherd recalls x. 1–18, its peculiar nature

xii. 33, xviii. 32, the glory of God, xii. 24–6, xiii. 31, 32, the synonymous words for *know* and *love* are Johannine (see above), so are the phrases *again a second time* (iv. 54), *verily verily* (i. 51, &c.), *by what manner of death* (xii. 33, xviii. 32). The intimacy of the two disciples and their relationship with the Lord (xiii. 6 sqq., 24, xviii. 15, xx. 2, 6), the double meaning of the words *follow* (i. 43, xiii. 36, &c.) and *abide* (i. 33, &c.), the subtle rebuke to Peter for questioning the Lord (xvi. 23), are all characteristically Johannine. *v.* 24 is necessary if the Johannine canon of evidence is to be maintained (v. 31, 32, viii. 13, 14, xix. 35; 3 John 12); *v.* 25 echoes xx. 30; and the alternating *I* and *we* also underlie the First Epistle (1 John i. 1–4, ii. 12 sqq., &c.).

# APPENDIX

# JESUS AND THE WOMAN TAKEN IN ADULTERY

By thirty-four (? 35) votes to seventeen the Council of Trent, on the 1st of April 1546, decided to make no special declaration concerning this passage. It forms an integral part of the Gospel according to Saint John in the Latin Vulgate, and the Council affirmed its canonicity in the general declaration concerning the canonicity of Holy Scripture; that is to say, the four gospels *with all their parts* were to be received as sacred and canonical. The decision was reaffirmed by the Holy Office on the 13th of February 1897, and promulgated by the Pope two days later. Modern Roman Catholic scholars (e.g. Calmes, Lagrange, Tillmann) understand this to mean that, whereas the passage is authentic in the theological and doctrinal sense of the word, its authenticity as part of the original Gospel of Saint John is a matter of free critical investigation. This whole procedure shows that the passage presents considerable difficulty to the commentator, the historian, and the theologian. In fact, the story of the Woman taken in Adultery contains three separate problems: (*a*) Did it form an original part of the Fourth Gospel? (*b*) Does it belong to the authentic tradition concerning Jesus of Nazareth? (*c*) What is the meaning of the story?

To the first question an almost certain answer can be given. The story formed no part of the Fourth Gospel as it was originally planned and written, for the following reasons. In the Greek Codices Sinaiticus and Vaticanus, and in the Washington and Koridethi manuscripts, the text of the Fourth Gospel runs continuously from vii. 52 to viii. 12, without any sign of a break; so also in some important cursive manuscripts. Though both Codex Alexandrinus and the Paris Palimpsest are defective at this point, it is nevertheless clear that neither of them can have contained the passage. No Greek commentator on the gospel before Euthymius Zigabenus (twelfth century) makes any reference to the passage (e.g. Origen, Chrysostom, Cyril, Nonnus); and even Euthymius judges it to be an insertion, since the accurate copies either omitted it or marked it with obelisks. This omission by Patristic commentators is supported by its omission in the Greek *Catenæ* or collections of comments by the Fathers, and by the fact that in the early Lectionaries the passage selected for reading on the Feast of Pentecost runs directly from vii. 52 to viii. 12. The second concerning the Woman taken in Adultery is a separate Lection, and commemorates women saints who had once been wanton sinners: it was presumably added later to the older Greek Lectionary, which did not contain the passage. So in the Eastern Versions of the gospels. The earliest Syriac Versions (the Diatessaron, the Sinaitic and Curetonian Syriac, and the earliest form of the Peshitto) do not contain the passage, and Isho'dad does not mention it in his commentary. It is also absent from the Gothic Version and from the earliest manuscripts of the Egyptian, Armenian and Georgian Versions. It is, moreover, not found in some manuscripts of the old Latin Version. This Western omission is supported by the absence of all reference to it in the writings of Irenæus, Cyprian, and Tertullian, though these Fathers were concerned with the problem which cases of adultery presented to the Church.

Against this negative evidence must be set Codex Bezae, some manuscripts of the Old Latin Version, the Vulgate, and the great mass of the later Greek manuscripts. According to all these the passage belongs to Saint John's Gospel and follows vii. 52. Pacian of Barcelona (fourth century, *Ep. ad Sympronianum*) and Ambrose (*Ep.* xxvi. 2) refer to it as contained in Saint John's Gospel; Augustine comments on the passage in his commentary and deals with it in his tract *De Adult. Conjug.*; Jerome says, apparently with some surprise, that it is found in the Gospel according to John *in many Greek and Latin Codices* (*contra. Pelag.* ii. 17). The passage is also added in the later Coptic and Syriac Versions.

The textual tradition, however, has more to say. It is not merely a matter of deciding whether the passage follows John vii. 52 or belongs nowhere in the text of the gospels, since in the Ferrar group of cursive manuscripts it follows Luke xxi. 38; in the twelfth century Basel Manuscript 1 and in some other cursives it is inserted at the conclusion of the Fourth Gospel, as though it were an appendix not merely to the Fourth Gospel, but to the tradition contained in the four gospels; in one cursive manuscript (225) it follows John vii. 36, and in some Georgian manuscripts it follows John vii. 44.

The manuscript evidence is alone almost conclusive that the passage did not form an original part of the Fourth Gospel. It must, however, have belonged to the ancient tradition of the Church, and was so venerable that a place was required for it in the canonical gospels. The available evidence permits only hazardous suggestions why it should have been inserted in the Fourth Gospel after vii. 52, and why it should have found so secure a resting place there that it was gradually accepted into the received tradition of the text. It may have been used for homiletic purposes to illustrate the words in viii. 15, *Ye judge after the flesh; I judge no man*, and in vii. 24, *Judge not according to appearance, but judge righteous judgement*, and have been attracted into the text of the gospel. This attraction into the text may have been assisted by the similarity of the concluding words, *Go thy way; from henceforth sin no more*, with v. 14.

Or the insertion may have been occasioned by the desire to lighten the long discourse against the Jews (chs. vii, viii) by adding an incident which expressed in action a similar tension between Jesus and the Jews. The precise history of the insertion is, however, wholly uncertain.

The evidence of the tradition of the text is not the only ground for judging the passage to have been inserted into the text. At both ends the junction with what precedes and what follows is so awkward as to make it almost impossible that it could have belonged to the original narrative. Jesus is discoursing to the Jews at the Feast of Tabernacles (vii. 37). viii. 1, however, presumes that the episode of Jesus and the Woman took place at the conclusion of the ministry immediately before the final Passover, when Jesus retired to the mount of Olives and returned each morning to the Temple (Mark xi. 11, 19, xiii. 3; Luke xxi. 37, xxii. 39). viii. 9 leaves Jesus entirely alone. viii. 12, however, presumes the crowd of Jews mentioned in vii. 40, to whom Jesus continues His discourse. Not only are the joins almost intolerably awkward, but if vii. 53–viii. 11 be omitted the narrative runs perfectly smoothly. Moreover, the passage is marked by so large a number of variant readings (Plummer counts eighty variant readings in 183 words) that it would seem to have had a separate and uncertain textual tradition, which would be intelligible if it had had a wandering circulation and only found a disciplined home in the canonical gospels at a fairly late date. Commentators also point out that the style and phraseology bring the passage within the orbit of the synoptic rather than the Johannine tradition. For example, the connecting particle *but* takes the place of the characteristic Johannine *then*, and neither the Mount of Olives nor the scribes are mentioned elsewhere in the gospel. 'It is', writes Loisy, 'as though an old master had strayed into the company of modern paintings'.

Context, a peculiar textual tradition, and to some extent style and subject-matter, combine to support the strong evidence of the earliest Greek manuscripts and of the earliest Versions that the passage did not originally form part of the Fourth Gospel. For these reasons it has seemed preferable, with Westcott and Bernard, to relegate the section to an APPENDIX rather than to disturb the COMMENTARY by retaining it in its canonical position and then commenting upon it as though it did not in fact rightly belong there (Bauer, Calmes, Holtzmann, Lagrange, Loisy, Plummer).

The question now arises whether there are grounds for supposing the episode to belong to the ancient tradition of the Church concerning the history of Jesus of Nazareth. The synoptic character of the narrative has already been noted and attention will be directed again to this feature in the COMMENTARY. Further, the textual tradition which marks it as forming no original part of the Fourth Gospel also insists that it was current at least as early as the third century and that it was by its own inherent authority pressing into the authoritative narrative of the ministry of Jesus. How otherwise could it have been known to Ambrose and Augustine? And why should Jerome have not only inserted it in his Latin Version of the Gospels, but done so because he had already found it in many Greek and Latin Codices? The number of variant readings also has a double significance. If, on the one hand, they indicate the necessity of distinguishing the passage from the rest of the Fourth Gospel, they mark, on the other, its antiquity. But the historian does not depend merely on such indirect evidence. There is positive evidence of the existence of this story in very early days. First, the *Apostolic Constitutions* (ii. 24, about A.D. 400) in the course of warning bishops against too great severity in dealing with sinners, quotes the words of Jesus to the 'woman who had sinned'—*neither do I condemn thee*—in order to sanction leniency of treatment. Now this section of the *Apostolic Constitutions* is taken from the third-century Syriac *Didascalia* and, moreover, there is nothing to show that the author was quoting from the Fourth Gospel. This would seem to constitute positive evidence not only that the story was known in the third century, but that it possessed authority as belonging to the authentic tradition concerning Jesus. Secondly, Eusebius (*H.E.* iii. 39. 16) states that Papias (early second century) refers to a story current in his day concerning a woman who was accused *of many sins* before the Lord, which, he says, is contained in the Gospel according to the Hebrews. Rufinus, in his translation of Eusebius, substitutes *adultery* for *many sins*. In this connection it may perhaps be noted that Codex Bezae and the cursive 1071 have in John viii. 3 *a woman taken in sin* for *a woman taken in adultery*. It therefore appears reasonably certain that Papias was referring to the incident which has now found its home, after much wandering, in the Fourth Gospel. Westcott and Lagrange think that more can be deduced from the statement of Papias than merely that the story was current in very early days. If Papias had knowledge of the teaching of John, then this story may have been part of his reminiscence. It is a Johannine tradition, and this, they think, may account for its later inclusion in the Gospel according to Saint John. The evidence, however, does not appear to justify so detailed an argument.

The external evidence, then, seems to demand that the story was current in very early days, as an authentic episode in the ministry of Jesus, but that it was not contained in any one of the four gospels which came to be regarded as canonical, though it was contained in that literature which lay on the fringe of these gospels. Consequently this episode requires serious attention and a careful commentary, and, to this end, modern sentimentality must be avoided.

vii. 53. *And they went every man unto his own house:* viii. 1. *but Jesus went unto the mount of Olives.* 2. *And early in the morning he came again into*

*the temple, and all the people came unto him; and he sat down, and taught them.*
*3. And the scribes and the Pharisees bring a woman taken in adultery; and having*
*set her in the midst, 4. they say unto him, Master, this woman hath been taken*
*in adultery, in the very act. 5. Now in the law Moses commanded us to stone such:*
*what then sayest thou of her? 6. And this they said, tempting him, that they*
*might have whereof to accuse him. But Jesus stooped down, and with his finger*
*wrote on the ground. 7. But when they continued asking him, he lifted up himself,*
*and said unto them, He that is without sin among you, let him first cast a stone*
*at her. 8. And again he stooped down, and with his finger wrote on the ground.*
*9. And they, when they heard it, went out one by one, beginning from the eldest,*
*even unto the last: and Jesus was left alone, and the woman, where she was, in*
*the midst. 10. And Jesus lifted up himself, and said unto her, Woman, where*
*are they? did no man condemn thee? 11. And she said, No man, Lord. And Jesus*
*said, Neither do I condemn thee: go thy way; from henceforth sin no more.*

vii. 53–viii. 2. The general situation is similar to that described in
the synoptic tradition. During the last days before the Passover at
which Jesus was crucified, He was wont to spend the day in Jerusalem,
and especially in the Temple, and to retire each evening out of the city
to Bethany (Mark xi. 11, 12, 19, 27; Matt. xxi. 17). In both the Marcan
and the Lucan narratives the mount of Olives is especially mentioned
in connection with this accustomed retirement (Mark xiii. 1–3; Luke
xxi. 37, 38, xxii. 39). Early in the morning Jesus took up His position
in the Temple. All the people gathered round Him and, seated (cf. Luke
v. 3), He began to teach them. The Christ of the Fourth Gospel sits
only in iv. 6, being wearied. Elsewhere He stood to teach (vii. 37, x. 23,
24). The Greek of the introduction is phrased in synoptic, not Johannine, language. The Greek word for *early* occurs in Luke xxiv. 1;
Acts v. 21, a different word being used in John xviii. 28, xx. 1; the
synoptic word *people* rather than the normal Johannine *crowd* (some
cursives and three uncial manuscripts have the Johannine word here
—apparently a conscious assimilation to the Johannine style). The whole
sentence *All the people . . . taught them* (omitted however in some cursives)
is almost verbally identical with Mark ii. 13 (cf. Luke xxi. 38). The
mount of Olives does not occur elsewhere in the Fourth Gospel.

*vv.* 3–6. The scene is disturbed by the entrance of *scribes and Pharisees*
—a normal conjunction in the synoptic gospels, specially in Luke
(Mark vii. 5; Matt. v. 20; Luke v. 30, vi. 7, xi. 53, &c.), although
*scribes* are nowhere else mentioned in the Fourth Gospel (some cursives
read *chief priests* for *scribes*, presumably in order to agree with vii. 32).
The scribes and Pharisees demand that Jesus should interrupt His
teaching in order to give His judgement upon a matter of moral de-
linquency. The case is not invented in order to raise a theoretical point
in moral casuistry, for they bring with them a woman whom they have
overtaken and detected in the very act of committing adultery (*in sin*

Codex Bezae and the cursive 1071, cf. Papias in Eusebius *H.E.* iii. 39, 16). They place the woman between Jesus and themselves, and then ask their question (cf. Mark ix. 36; Matt. xviii. 2; Luke vi. 8, ix. 47): *Now in the law Moses commanded us to stone such: what then sayest thou of her?* At first sight it would appear that the scribes and Pharisees are genuinely in difficulties as to what action they ought to take as witnesses of so flagrant a violation of the Law of God. The narrative, however, refuses to permit so generous an interpretation of their action. Their purpose in bringing the woman before Jesus is not to secure His moral guidance, but to place Him in a public dilemma. It is therefore useless to inquire why they had not brought the man also with them, or to suggest either that he had made his escape (Susanna 39) or that they were more lenient to the man than to the woman. The woman is sufficient for their purpose of securing a charge against Jesus: *And this they said, tempting (laying a trap for) him, that they might have whereof to accuse him* (cf. Mark viii. 11, x. 2, xii. 15; Matt. xvi. 1, xix. 3, xxii. 18, 35; Luke xi. 16: the theme is synoptic not Johannine, contrast John vi. 6). Codex Bezae omits these words, but adds *tempting him* after *they say unto him* in *v.* 4.

It is clearly important to understand what is the precise issue raised and why it should be supposed to place Jesus in a dilemma. The story assumes that adultery violates the revealed Law of God. It assumes also that the Jews, living under the Law of God, have the duty of acting as the agents of the punishment or the mercy of God. There is no question here of a merely human morality or of adultery as a threat to the stability of the family and consequently to the State conceived of as a secular authority concerned with the welfare of its citizens. The story is related on the assumption that the righteousness of God must be active in the punishment of sin, and that men are appointed to be the agents of His punishment. It is to this responsive action, authorized by the Law of Moses, that the scribes and Pharisees appeal. *In the law Moses commanded us to stone such.* There is some difficulty here. According to the Law adultery is punishable by death, but only in the case of the adultery of a betrothed virgin is it commanded that both the man and the damsel shall be stoned (Deut. xxii. 23, 24). In other cases the form of death is not specified (Lev. xx. 10; Deut. xxii. 22; Susanna 22, 41, 43, 45). In the Mishnah, however, death by strangulation is commanded in such cases: 'These are they who are to be strangled . . . and he who lives with a married woman' (the adulteress shares the punishment, *Sanhedrin* xi. 1). The legal method of strangulation is laid down in *Sanhedrin* vii. 3: 'The man is to be enclosed in dung up to his knees, and a soft towel set within a rough towel is to be placed round his neck (in order that no mark be made, for the punishment is God's punishment). Then one man draws in one direction and another in the other direction until he be dead.' 'These are they who are to be stoned: . . . he who lies with a betrothed maiden' (*Sanhedrin* vii. 4, see Strack-Biller-beck). Whether the woman here is to be taken as a betrothed maiden is, however, doubtful. The precise regulation concerning strangulation may be later in date, and stoning may have been regarded earlier as the normal punishment for adultery (Ezek. xvi. 38, 40). Since, according to the Law, the witnesses of a transgression of the covenant of God were first responsible for inflicting the penalty of stoning (Deut. xvii. 7, cf. Acts vii. 58), the scribes and Pharisees are not present as judges, but as witnesses of the woman's action and consequently as the agents of the punishment of God. The point at issue is then whether, the case being as clear as it is, they are, or are not, to proceed to the punishment. Why then do they expect their question to place Jesus in a dilemma? Some commentators suppose the dilemma to be that if He recommends mercy He will set Himself in direct opposition to Moses and to the Law of God; if, on the other hand, He demands that the penalty be paid, He would be liable to accusation before the Roman officials for inciting to murder. It is doubtful, however, whether the Roman Government comes within the horizon of the story. It would be more natural to suppose that the scribes and Pharisees, knowing the mercy of Jesus towards sinners, desire to set this mercy in direct opposition to the Law of God, in order that they may accuse Him as a transgressor of the Law.

Jesus refuses to answer their question: *But Jesus stooped down, and with his finger wrote on the ground.* In the *Textus Receptus* there is added *as though he heard them not* (A.V.). The gesture of Jesus means no more than that He will not in their presence give a judgement (Luke xii. 13, 14). Since the Greek word translated *wrote* is used in the LXX for drawing up a register, and even of a list of transgressions (Job xiii. 26), ancient commentators supposed that Jesus wrote a list of the sins of the woman's accusers, and in some manuscripts the words *the sins of each one of them* are added as an object to the verb *wrote* (cf. Jerome *Contra Pelag.* ii. 17, where he quotes Jer. xvii. 17). But in the text the emphasis lies on the gesture of Jesus, not upon what was written on the ground (see, however, Eisler, *Z.N.T.W.* 1923, p. 307).

*vv.* 7–9. The scribes and the Pharisees continue to repeat their question, and their own complete condemnation follows at once: *He that is without sin among you, let him first cast a stone at her.* This does not mean to suggest, as many commentators take it to do, that the woman's accusers were themselves adulterers or at least indulgent to sexual desires. It means what it says. God's action in punishment or mercy can be exercised only through an entirely sinless agent. The scribes and Pharisees are incapable of acting as God's agents, for they are sinners like other men. Jesus does not protest against the rigour of the Law, nor does He remove the problem from a legal sphere and set it in the context of charitable human moral behaviour. Nor does He even raise the question of the capacity of human judges to regulate human society. The only question raised by His answer is the capacity of sinful men to act as the agents of God's dealing with men and women. There is no more to be said. Jesus continues to dissociate Himself from the scribes and Pharisees: *Again he stooped down, and with his finger wrote on the ground*. Not one of them dares to undertake the punishment of the woman, or indeed to utter a sentence of mercy: *And they, when they heard it, went out one by one, beginning from the eldest, even unto the last*. The last four words are omitted in many ancient manuscripts. In their place Codex Bezae and the cursive 1071 read *so that all went away;* and two other manuscripts have simply *all retired*. Some manuscripts have also the addition *being convicted by their own conscience* (A.V.). These variations merely emphasize, in different ways, the point of the story that no single witness is able to hold his ground in face of the words of Jesus, for they all stand under the judgement of God; no single one of them is without sin, and no single one of them is capable of pronouncing the judgement of God.

*And Jesus was left alone*. The word *alone* is omitted by the Ferrar group of manuscripts, but, whether the word is original or not, the whole narrative presses to the point where the woman is confronted only by Jesus. She remains standing *where she was*. She is still *in the midst*, but now between Jesus and the vacuum caused by the defection of human sin.

*vv.* 10, 11. Jesus, the sinless agent of the judgement of God, is alone capable of pronouncing His judgement. Before the judgement concerning the woman is pronounced, the vacuum, which is the judgement of sinners who presume to undertake the judgement of God, is again emphasized by Jesus and recognized by the woman. *And Jesus lifted up himself* (some manuscripts read *looked up*, others add *and saw none but the woman*), *and said unto her, Woman where are they?* (The *Textus Receptus*, supported by the Ferrar group, reads *where are thine accusers?* or *where are those thine accusers?*) *did no man condemn thee? And she said, No man, Lord*.

Then follows the decision of the sinless emissary of God. *And* Jesus said, *Neither do I condemn thee; go thy way: from henceforth sin no more*. There is here no condoning of adultery, for the woman's action is roundly denounced as sinful, here also is no forgiveness of sin, for the woman expresses neither faith nor repentance (contrast Luke vii. 36–50). She is faced by the call of God to righteousness, and sent forth as the object of the mercy of God, who has passed over her sin. Here then the mercy of God and His truth meet. For only in the mouth of the sinless Jesus can the full condemnation of sin, and the full demand for the righteousness of God, march with the authoritative pronouncement of His mercy and charity. In some sections of the Church the supposed leniency of the words *neither do I condemn thee*, which are, however, not lenient at all, must have occasioned scandal (cf. Augustine, *De Adult. Conjug.* ii. 7. 6), since in a tenth-century Armenian manuscript the words of Jesus are altered to *Go in peace, and present the offering for sin, as in their law is written*; and in the Syriac of Barsalibi they are paraphrased *Go thou also now and do this sin no more* (see Bernard).

It is clearly beyond the scope of a critical and historical commentary to draw out the implications of this story for Christian moral theology. That it has implications is directly asserted by the Roman Catholic Church, which retains it in the canonical Scriptures, and as directly elsewhere by its similar retention in the text of the Gospels. This much, however, must be said. The Church cannot deal with sinners except in the name of Jesus Christ, otherwise it comes under the condemnation of the Jews recorded in the story. Theologically the inclusion of the story in the Johannine narrative of the controversy of Jesus with the Jews is wholly relevant. The Johannine theme that Judaism claims, wrongfully, to be an independent religion adequate to give life (v. 39) is the theme of this story also. The contrast between Jesus, against whom no accusation of sin can be levelled (viii. 46), and who is, consequently, the authoritative agent of God for the salvation of men, and the Jews who are yet in their sins, and who are, consequently, unable to act as the agents of God (viii. 21–30), is the contrast emphasized in this story also. The analogy of Loisy, according to which he states that the story appears in the Fourth Gospel like an old master in the midst of a collection of modern paintings, is a true analogy from a purely literary point of view; but it breaks down theologically. For the main theme of the story is the living theme of the whole New Testament, including the Fourth Gospel. The story can therefore remain where it is without breaking the theological sequence of thought by its intrusion; it could be added to give sanction to Saint Paul's words in Rom. ii. 1— *Wherefore thou art without excuse, O man, whosoever thou art that judgest: for wherein thou judgest another, thou condemnest thyself; for thou that judgest dost practise the same things;* or finally, it might be set in the context of the Sermon on the Mount in order to explain the words—*Judge not, that ye be not judged* (Matt. vii. 1).

[In the commentary on *v.* 7 the word ἀναμάρτητος has been taken to mean 'sinless' in an absolute sense. Since some commentators have supposed the implication to be that the scribes and Pharisees were guilty of the same kind of sin as the woman, of lust or sensuality if not actually of adultery, a further examination of the word is necessary.

ἀναμάρτητος is found here only in the New Testament, and is, moreover, not used in the LXX to translate any particular Hebrew word. so that Schlatter gives no parallel in his *Sprache und Heimat*. In Deut, xxix. 18 it occurs in an able, but very free, paraphrase of the Hebrew 'the watered plant with the thirsty', ἵνα μὴ συναπολέσῃ ὁ ἁμαρτωλὸς τὸν ἀναμάρτητον. It occurs also in the relatively cultured Greek of

2 Maccabees. In 2 Macc. viii. 4, Judas Maccabæus 'invoked the Lord . . . to remember the impious massacre of the *innocent* (ἀναμαρτήτων) babes; and in 2 Macc. xii. 42, after recounting the discovery of the amulets of the idols of Jamnia under the shirts of the Jews slain in the battle with Gorgias and his troops, Judas, seeing that these men had been slain because of their hidden idolatry, exhorted the people to keep themselves from sin (ἀναμαρτήτους εἶναι). In Ps. lix. 3, where the LXX has a quite untranslateable rendering of the Hebrew 'not for my transgressions nor for my sin, O Lord', the version of Symmachus has ἐμοῦ τοῦ ἀναιτίου καὶ ἀναμαρτήτου. The word would therefore appear to be used quite generally of innocence and not of any particular sin. So it is in classical Greek. Plato (*Republic* 339b) uses it quite precisely of unerring (Cremer translates 'infallible'): Aristotle uses it (*Politics* 1275b) with πολιτειά of a faultless form of government. In a particular context, of course, it can mean guiltless of a particular offence (cf. Herodotus i. 155, where it is used with a genitive of the offence).

The insertion of the Pericope de Adultera as an introduction to the section of the Fourth Gospel beginning *again Jesus spake unto them saying*: *I am the light of the world*, although no doubt clumsy from the literary point of view, is by no means haphazard or arbitrary. Not merely such words as *I judge no man* (viii. 15), but the fundamental theme (cf. particularly *vv.* 21 and 24), that the Jews claim to act as the agents of God and yet will die in their sins, is illuminated by this story that turns on the word ἀναμάρτητος properly understood. The juxtaposition is therefore theologically intelligent, and Loisy's dictum, that the story has *strayed* into its present position, altogether unsatisfactory.]

# I. INDEX OF OLD TESTAMENT
REFERENCES

# INDEX I

# II. INDEX OF NEW TESTAMENT REFERENCES

# INDEX II

# III. INDEX OF REFERENCES TO JEWISH WRITINGS, AND OF RABBIS CITED BY NAME

## A. APOCRYPHAL, PSEUDEPIGRAPHAL, AND HELLEISTIC JEWISH WRITINGS

### I BARUCH

*iii. 9–iv. 4*, 154
*iii. 12–14*, 143
*iv. 1, 2*, 143, 274
*iv. 3*, 143

### 2 BARUCH

*xxiv. 2*, 317
*xxxvi–xxxix*, 474
*lix. 2*, 143, 155
*lxxviii. 16*, 143, 155

### ECCLESIASTICUS

*i. 1*, 142
*iv. 11*, 155
*xi. 32*, 513
*xv. 3*, 241
*xvi. 21*, 215
*xxiv*, 154
*xxiv. 8*, 148
*xxiv. 9*, 141
*xxiv. 17–19*, 474
*xxxix. 3*, 369
*xliv. 19 sqq.*, 341
*xlv. 4*, 392, 503
*xlvii. 17*, 369
*xlviii. 1*, 272
*xlviii. 10*, 174
*xlviii. 24, 25*, 469
*xlix. 7*, 392, 503 (*bis*)

*l. 25, 26*, 241
*li. 23*, 161

### I ENOCH

*xli. 1*, 427
*xlii*, 155
*xlvi*, 317
*xlviii*, 317
*xlix. 1*, 427
*lxii. 14*, 427
*lxix. 27, 257*, 270
*lxxxv–cx*, 367

### 2 ENOCH

*xxx. 8*, 155
*xxxiii. 3, 4*, 155

### I ESDRAS

*i. 55*, 195
*v. 43*, 195

### 2 ESDRAS (4 EZRA)

*iv. 21*, 216
*v. 9 (10)*, 154
*v. 18*, 367
*vii. 28*, 317
*xiii. 32*, 317

*xiv. 20*, 143
*xiv. 20, 21*, 143, 155
*xiv. 29, 30*, 143

### JOSEPHUS

#### *Antiquitates*

*ii. 257*, 241
*iii. 161*, 529
*iii. 247*, 320
*iv. 123*, 195
*iv. 310*, 146
*vi. 115*, 412
*vii. 83*, 266
*viii. 17*, 508
*viii. 95*, 195
*viii. 100*, 310
*viii. 258*, 415
*ix. 120*, 266
*ix. 288–90*, 241
*ix. 288–91*, 233, 242
*x. 184*, 241
*xi. 165*, 260
*xii. 316–25*, 385
*xiii. 74–9*, 243
*xiii. 256*, 243
*xiii. 293–8*, 228
*xiii. 391*, 187
*xiv. 37*, 210
*xiv. 167*, 325
*xv. 50*, 510
*xv. 289*, 261
*xv. 380*, 195
*xv. 398–402*, 386

# B. RABBINIC WRITINGS

## *C.* RABBIS CITED BY NAME

# IV. INDEX OF REFERENCES TO PATRISTIC AND PAGAN GREEK AND LATIN LITERATURE

(The names of Patristic Commentaries to which general reference is made will be found in Index V)

# V. SELECT INDEX OF
# AUTHORS AND NAMES

Only those books are named in this index which are directly and primarily concerned with the Fourth Gospel.

Where the authors of Commentaries are cited by name in the COMMENTARY, the reference is to their treatment, in the work here named, of the passage of the gospel under discussion.

Particular references to the works of some ancient writers, especially patristic commentators, will be found in Indexes III and IV. These authors are here indicated by an asterisk.